The Editor

J. PAUL HUNTER is Barbara E. and Richard J. Franke Professor Emeritus at the University of Chicago. He is the author of *The Reluctant Pilgrim: Defoe's Emblematic Method and Quest for Form in* Robinson Crusoe; *Occasional Form: Henry Fielding and the Chains of Circumstance*; and *Before Novels: The Cultural Contexts of Eighteenth-Century English Fiction.* He is author of the first nine editions of *The Norton Introduction to Poetry* and the long-time co-editor of *The Norton Introduction to Literature* and *New Worlds of Literature.*

A NORTON CRITICAL EDITION

Mary Shelley

FRANKENSTEIN

THE 1818 TEXT

CONTEXTS

CRITICISM

Second Edition

Edited by

J. PAUL HUNTER

UNIVERSITY OF CHICAGO, EMERITUS

W · W · NORTON & COMPANY · *New York* · *London*

W. W. Norton & Company has been independent since its founding in 1923, when William Warder Norton and Mary D. Herter Norton first published lectures delivered at the People's Institute, the adult education division of New York City's Cooper Union. The firm soon expanded its program beyond the Institute, publishing books by celebrated academics from America and abroad. By mid-century, the two major pillars of Norton's publishing program—trade books and college texts—were firmly established. In the 1950s, the Norton family transferred control of the company to its employees, and today—with a staff of four hundred and a comparable number of trade, college, and professional titles published each year—W. W. Norton & Company stands as the largest and oldest publishing house owned wholly by its employees.

Copyright © 1996, 2012 by W. W. Norton & Company, Inc.

The text of this book is composed in Fairfield Medium
with the display set in Bernhard Modern.
Production Manager: Sean Mintus.
Book design by Antonina Krass.
Composition by Westchester
Manufacturing by Maple-Vail

Library of Congress Cataloging-in-Publication Data

Shelley, Mary Wollstonecraft, 1797–1851.
    Frankenstein : the 1818 text, contexts, criticism / Mary Shelley ;
edited by J. Paul Hunter. — 2nd ed.
        p. cm. — (A Norton critical edition)
    Includes bibliographical references.
    ISBN 978-0-393-92793-1 (pbk.)
    1. Frankenstein, Victor (Fictitious character)—Fiction.
2. Frankenstein's monster (Fictitious character)—Fiction.
3. Scientists—Fiction.   4. Science fiction. gsafd   5. Shelley,
Mary Wollstonecraft, 1797–1851. Frankenstein.   I. Hunter, J. Paul,
date.   II. Title.
    PR5397F7 2012
    823'.7—dc23

                                                            2011047223

W. W. Norton & Company, Inc., 500 Fifth Avenue, New York, NY
10110-0017
wwnorton.com

W. W. Norton & Company Ltd., Castle House, 75/76 Wells Street,
London W1T 3QT

1 2 3 4 5 6 7 8 9 0

Contents

Criticism

Illustrations

Introduction

I

It is almost two hundred years since *Frankenstein* was first published, and it has now become a standard text in the literary canon, one of the world's most popular, widely read, and celebrated novels. It is also one of the most thoroughly studied and analyzed texts, making it ideal for the college or university classroom in which critical reading, cultural analysis, or literary history are at stake. Its history as a text is, however, more complicated than most, in part because its central narrative of creative overreaching and bitter disillusionment in a sense outgrew the novel itself and became a kind of independent trope or "myth" that invaded other art forms—plays, cartoons, advertisements, comic books, conversations, films. Frankenstein (the name) became a kind of all-purpose watchword for creativity gone wrong and monstrosity gone wild. Just about everyone, even people who do not read at all, knows the basic plot situation and its grotesque outcome: an ambitious and talented young scientist seeks and finds the secret of life itself, and he creates from assorted excavated body parts a giant adult being who turns out to be an ugly and savage (although sensitive) monster. And it is perhaps significant that, as often as not, casual observers confuse the creator with the created: in the novel, the scientist is named Frankenstein and his monster is nameless, but in popular lore the creature often takes on the name of the creator, as if there were no differences in the monstrosity of outcomes. In one sense, then, the story of *Frankenstein* now transcends the novel it came from—but only because its origins in the novel itself are so richly suggestive and evocative of larger issues and so resonant about the ambition and fallings-short of the human condition. *Frankenstein* is, in one way of putting it, larger than itself, a text that prompts not just close reading but the pursuit of extended intellectual and cultural implication.

How this novel (and this story) came to be is a complex tale in itself, and it can be very briefly or quite lengthily told: there are many subtleties and ambiguities in the process of its creation. The brief version, incomplete and imperfect but suggestive of both the popular, potboiler appeal and the larger seriousness of major scientific, social, literary, and philosophical issues, involves the occasion and moment of the novel's origin. According to its author and to anecdotes from her companions at the time of initial conception, (see pp. 165–70) it sprang from a proposal to engage in a story-writing contest. The situation was this. The author—later to be known as Mary Shelley but then just eighteen years old, already the mother of two children (one of whom had died in infancy), unmarried and still known by her maiden name, Mary Wollstonecraft Godwin—was traveling in the Swiss alps. Her companions were her lover and soon-to-be husband (the already celebrated poet, Percy Bysshe Shelley, who was still married to someone else), her infant son William, and her troubled and impulsive stepsister, Claire Clairmont. In the late spring of 1816, they settled into a modest house in the mountains near Geneva— and also near the villa where an even more famous (though just as controversial) poet, Lord Byron, had settled more luxuriously with his personal physician and companion, Dr. John William Polidori. The two groups quickly merged and for weeks spent nearly all their waking hours together, often sailing on Lake Geneva (see map, p. 2) by day, and reading and conversing together in the evenings and on days when the weather was unsettled. And it was often unsettled that summer, the coldest and most consistently stormy European summer on record. Later, when annual charts could be compared, 1816 became famous as "the year without a summer." Those conversations were apparently animated and often informed by wide and adventurous reading—of English and ancient classics, of scientific discovery and speculation, of British and European social politics. Byron and Percy Shelley were the acknowledged leaders in the conversations; they were both bold in their ideas and manner, and they were newly friends and getting to know each other's interests and range. Mary—younger, rather quiet, and natively less assertive and argumentative—could nevertheless hold her own on most topics: she was a voracious and retentive reader. The conversations seem to have ranged widely, often guided by individual reading and the kinds of popular topics taken up in current periodicals. We don't know in detail what they talked about day by day; but there are indications that they may have debated the nature and origins of life itself and perhaps discussed the myth of Prometheus in its several forms— years before Percy would interpret it lengthily in *Prometheus Unbound* and some while before it left its imprint as subtitle and suggestive allusion on Mary's first significant work.

On some of those inclement nights, they read German ghost stories. One night in late May or early June, someone (perhaps Byron) suggested that they engage in a ghost-story-writing contest—in competition with the stories they were reading and with each other.

The rules were loose, but the stories were to involve the supernatural in some way. As a contest, it wasn't much of a success. Percy apparently lost interest quickly and Byron not long after, though a fragment of what he wrote became attached later to one of his poems, *Mazeppa*. Polidori seems to have conceived at first a strange Gothic tale that Mary found ludicrous, though his own accounts differ from Mary's (see p. 169 [Polidori] and pp. 165–69 [Mary]), but then, characteristically, he piggybacked on a Byron idea and went on to publish a vampire story under Byron's name. Claire Claremont seems never even to have begun her story. The only significant result was *Frankenstein*, published nineteen months later anonymously, but with broad hints that it might be by Percy Shelley or Byron. Early reviewers *assumed* that it was written by a man.

Besides the competition, conversation, and human stimulation of that summer of origins, there is also a set of creative issues involving place, setting, and tone, a question of the influence of surroundings, location, visual spectacle, and atmosphere. Mary seems to have been acutely responsive to visual stimuli and especially to the influence of scenery, place-sensitivity, climate, nature's moods, and the breathtaking vistas of remote natural scenery that find their way into the brooding landscapes and Gothic tones the novel pursues and projects in its Scots and Arctic scenes as well as its more dominant continental ones. To be sure, Mary meticulously casts these actual settings in historical terms—she is very careful, for example, to project Victor Frankenstein's scientific training at Ingolstadt back into the eighteenth century, repeatedly dating letters "17—" so as to place the action of the novel at a time when that university not only still existed but operated as one of the major European symbols of radical experimental science. (The university was in fact closed by the authorities in 1800 because of its associations with the new science and related radical ideas.) But the larger question of mood and spectacle has less to do with probability and representation than with projecting a sense of wonder and sometimes of impending doom. We now know, thanks to climate scientists of the early twentieth century, what the assembled party shivering in Switzerland could not have then even wildly suspected—that the cold and gloomy summer of 1816 was part of a global phenomenon, the spreading of a cloud of volcanic ash over much of Europe and North America from a volcanic eruption in Indonesia half a year earlier—a phenomenon that meant that significant parts of the earth were deprived of sunshine for very long periods, so that the spectacular, sublime craggy beauties of the lightning-illuminated Alps mixed with invasive mountain gloom and mood-altering spells of hazy light and uncertain perception. Mary chose well the wild and untamed mid-European setting for her tale of discovery and uncertainty, and it was one of those strokes of creative fortune that the Romantic taste for the picturesque, the sublime, the striking, and the haunting led not only to recognizable actual settings but also to projected imaginations in remote, exotic, unexplored northern climes still elusive to all but the most daring explorers. No wonder the nearby Sea of Ice (see the cover reproduction of an 1823–24 painting and Percy Shelley's description on p. 299) became a kind of analogical "source" for the scenes of northern exploration that the narrator Walton experiences at the start and end of the novel.

II

Behind the immediate occasion and stimulation of the circumstances and setting of *Frankenstein*'s origins are many cumulative situations and experiences of Mary's earlier life. Two sets of influences in particular can be isolated as having a notable impact on what and how she wrote. One involves the intensity, complexity, and volatility of family relationships in Mary's own life; the other involves her ambitious, adventurous, and voracious reading. The first suggests much about the human issues and interactions that preoccupy the themes of her novel; the second helps us define and isolate some of the ideas and concepts behind the themes of the novel—themes that include (among others) creativity, ambition, responsibility, duty, family, friendship, authority, education, and social integrity.

Mary had been writing stories and poems since she was a little girl, very much encouraged in her reading and writing by her famous father. Both her father and mother were not only published, popular authors but celebrated controversialists with disciples of their own; both wrote novels (among other things) but were best known for their radical politics and libertine social views, especially on love and marriage. The mother, Mary Wollstonecraft, had been reared in a repressive and abusive family where girls hardly mattered, and she became an articulate and outspoken proto-feminist whose *Thoughts on the Education of Daughters* (1787) and *Vindication of the Rights of Woman* (1792) were both praised and vilified, as was her novel *Mary* (1790). The father, William Godwin, who had grown up in a conservative and devout dissenting household, also rebelled against his upbringing and became a leading radical political theorist, fiery in his rhetoric and widely consulted and deeply involved in arguments in the aftermath of the French Revolution. His *Enquiry Concerning Political Justice* (1793) was a revolutionary bible for some and an incendiary provocation for others, and his novel, *Caleb Williams* (1794), was a kind of fictionalized version of

his philosophy. Godwin and Wollstonecraft were drawn together—
she in her late 30s, he just over 40—by their common views and
very quickly became lovers after meeting in the winter of 1796–97;
the future author of *Frankenstein* was conceived shortly thereafter,
and before she was born they married, much to the consternation
of some of their friends who felt they had compromised their critique of the oppressiveness of legal institutions such as marriage.
But the marriage was short-lived, and the infant Mary was never to
get to know her mother: Mary Wollstonecraft died of childbirth
complications just eleven days after Mary was born.

Godwin was a supportive father and genuinely encouraged Mary's
independence and creativity, but he was feckless in his own emotional and financial affairs—seemingly always out of money and in
serious debt, and pretty much helpless in sorting out personal relationships. Not long after the death of Mary Wollstonecraft he married again and took into his household, with his new wife, her two
illegitimate children, including a three-year-old daughter, Claire
Claremont (who eighteen years later was part of the ghost-story contest in Switzerland). And there was yet another "family" member,
Fanny Imlay, Mary Wollstonecraft's illegitimate daughter from a
previous relationship, who had been taken into the household when
Godwin and Wollstonecraft married. Still further, in 1803 when
Mary was nearly six, an addition of the new Godwin union was
born, a new half brother for Mary, William Godwin Jr. So "family"
here was a kind of loose and uncertain unit. The new Mrs. Godwin
was crude and unpredictable and offered nothing of the intellectual
stimulus of her brief predecessor. Young Mary Wollstonecraft Godwin (she who was to become Mary Shelley) had ideas, ideals, and
aspirations to follow rather than human role models, and her childhood had more clear intellectual directions than emotional ones. If
there was a life lesson to be learned from Mary's growing-up years,
it was about flexibility and pragmatic responses to circumstances
rather than stability and personal security.

And the family she herself began to establish in 1814 with Percy
Shelley reflected and replicated in some ways Mary's own childhood: boldly dedicated to intellectual and emotional exploration and
speculation, somewhat peripatetic and unpredictable, tolerant of
periodic company and lively conversation but fundamentally seden-
tary and reflective. In the man who became her lover when she was
sixteen and her husband at nineteen, she found a fearsome intellect
and creative talent, an adventurous explorer both physically and
mentally, and a firm holder of lofty ideas and attitudes. His temperament was even more complicated than that of either of her parents—
someone who could be an inspiring guide and tutor on matters of
philosophy, history, politics, and aesthetics, but whose human

impulsiveness and volatility helped settle and clarify her own greater solidity and steadier judgment. Mary Shelley in her early adulthood and motherhood did not always project a sense of cuddly maternity, but she was caring and patient in her character and temperament and in some ways was to her husband as much a steady and stable parent and counselor as she was lover and adventurer.

Percy Shelley's direct influence on the writing of *Frankenstein* is palpable but nevertheless debatable in its precise effects and importance. In late manuscript stages he offered alternative wordings and often rewrote lengthy passages or created whole sentences and paragraphs that ended up in the finished novel. (The manuscript of his emendations is preserved in Lord Abinger's collection [now housed at the Bodleian Library, Oxford] and has been meticulously sorted into accessible and readable form by Charles E. Robinson and published by the Bodleian Library in 2008.) Once it was popular to argue that he seriously "improved" the manuscript—his word choices were often more lofty, abstract, and consciously "literary" while Mary's were more simple and direct—, but critical opinion now has shifted toward recognizing Mary's more down-to-earth language and her ability to enrich the directness and texture of the story more simply. Scholarly debates about the nature of Percy's contribution (or diminution) show every sign of continuing briskly, and this kind of textual disagreement about influence at a high scholarly level is part of a larger set of scholarly and critical questions about what Mary did with her heritage from her human guides, especially her parents and Percy Shelley. (For a useful account of Mary's intellectual and emotional debts, see the essay by Chris Baldick p. 173. And for a detailed analysis of the whole Godwin-Shelley nexus, see William St. Clair's excellent biography of the two families, *The Godwins and the Shelleys: The Biography of a Family* [London: Faber, 1989].)

One can see in the text of *Frankenstein* many traces of the political and educational ideas of Percy Shelley as well as of her parents—certainly there is constant parading and questioning of contemporary cultural and educational assumptions and practices. But the utopian optimism that sometimes characterizes their writings seems often in question in Mary's work, and in *Frankenstein* the issue of individual responsibility for one's choices is always in play; guilt plays a lot larger role in Mary's thinking and feeling than it does in her teachers'. A lot of theological and philosophical issues in *Frankenstein* remain ambiguous and uncertain, and if "family" is a helpful guide to the nature and range of many of the issues in the novel, the firm predictable positions of her mother, father, and husband are not necessarily always echoed in Mary's own bold and open explorations of issues about education, power, and the uses of imagination. In her adaptations of inherited Enlightenment ideas, there is more darkness and uncertainty, a lot more for readers to have to sort out for themselves. The many critical disagreements that characterize the essays gathered at the back of this volume suggest that many issues in *Frankenstein* remain unsettled, debatable, or capable of fresh interpretation. *Frankenstein* is the kind of text that opens outward rather than closing in upon itself.

Add one more haunting factor to Mary's experiences of "family": untimely and gruesome death. Not only did her mother die in bearing Mary herself—dramatic enough in itself to emblazon on her consciousness a continuing emotional association of birth and death—but a number of other deaths rudely intruded on Mary's early life before she came to write *Frankenstein*. Her first child, a daughter, was born prematurely in 1815 and died within a few days. (And her second child—an infant when *Frankenstein* was being conceived and written—died at the age of three a year after the novel was published.) Even more hauntingly there were two dramatic suicides in the extended family: Mary's half sister, Fanny Imlay, took her own life in the fall of 1816; and later that winter Percy Shelley's first wife, Harriet, drowned herself in the Serpentine in London; her body was not found for weeks. And then, four years after *Frankenstein* was published, Percy himself drowned in an accident in Italy. It is no wonder that vitality and its opposites preyed on Mary's thinking and that disaster in her novel seems to follow from initiative and creativity.

III

Like her family relationships, Mary's reading is a better guide to her curiosity, topicality, and range of interests than to her own beliefs and considered opinions or to her own comparative writing artistry. In other words, the outreach of her reading tells us a lot about her interests and desires but not necessarily her commitments and conclusions. Obviously, she was guided in her early intellectual and creative choices by her parents' directions (and she found a mostly kindred soul in Percy Shelley); but she did not just read authors and books she agreed with. She was driven at least as much by curiosity about strange and unfamiliar things as by positions, outlooks, or doctrines she found sympathetic. Several of the essays in the appendices to this volume (see especially Richard Holmes, "Mary Shelley and the Power of Contemporary Science" p. 183, and Christa Knellwolf, "Geographic Boundaries and Inner Space," p. 506) trace the reading and thinking that went into *Frankenstein* and show its implications for understanding the completed novel. One of the most important new directions in *Frankenstein* scholarship and criticism has been to search out and clarify the larger intellectual and cultural context of Mary Shelley's reading and bookishness. Much of the best current work on her fiction—and on nineteenth-century literature in general—concentrates on the intellectual history of the period and its social and cultural manifestations—especially on developments in science, technology, and exploration, all matters that she was passionately curious about and that influenced the directions her artistry would take.

About Mary's reading at some points in her life we know a great deal, for she kept a faithful journal and a meticulous list of accomplished and projected reading for most of her life. But the journal for the period around *Frankenstein*'s composition has been lost, and so we are left to infer specific sources of information and inspiration from the text itself. Some of these references and allusions are simple and more or less passing glances outward, more a matter of decoration or ornament than structural beams of support. There are, for example, brief, relevant quotations from contemporary poetry—by Charles Lamb, Samuel Taylor Coleridge, and Percy Shelley himself. All these are appropriately invoked to provide comparisons of atmosphere or tonal support, and they suggest the expansive, resonant practices of reading nineteenth-century novels in a leisurely and outgoing way. Like her contemporaries, Mary engaged in allusive or intertextual practices that invited readers to notice the borrowings and celebrate their own skills of knowing, noticing, and seeing the relevance. Quite a few such passing allusions occur in the course of the book—and they may represent reading done years before as well as reading undertaken during the composition itself. (In this edition, footnotes to the *Frankenstein* text identify several references and allusions that contemporary readers would have readily recognized.)

More significant to the total effect are especially emphatic or insistently repeated thematic underpinnings of the novel. Such for example, are the several quotations from Milton's *Paradise Lost* (see pp. 42, 92, 95, 97, and 146), including the epigraph on the title page (photographically reproduced on p. 3):

> Did I request thee, Maker, from my clay
> To mould me man? Did I solicit thee
> From darkness to promote me?

This is Adam's protest against his lot and the basic "why" question of human existence; it connects the Creature's puzzlement to enduring human questions about basic meanings and origins of life. Similarly, the subtitle on the title page—"The Modern Prometheus" recalls classical (and later) myths of creativity and destruction. Together, the two allusions claim a firm cultural heritage in both the Judeo-

Christian and ancient classical tradition of origins and human purpose—not necessarily claiming a belief system but ensuring that this modern story is positioned in a revered tradition of ideas and questions.

Similarly, in only the second paragraph into the novel, Mary Shelley has Walton's first letter from the beginning of his Arctic excursion speak of his extravagant idealistic expectations for his exploratory quest. He phrases his hopes in mythic, paradisal terms, imagining beyond the bitter cold and ice-locked sea, a vision of perfection:

> There, Margaret, the sun is for ever visible; its broad disk just skirting the horizon, and diffusing a perpetual splendour. There . . . snow and frost are banished, and, sailing over a calm sea, we may be wafted to a land surpassing in wonders and in beauty every region hitherto discovered on the habitable globe. Its productions and features may be without example, as the phenomena of the heavenly bodies undoubtedly are in those undiscovered solitudes. What may not be expected in a country of eternal light? (p. 7).

The reference here is not to a specific text. Mary Shelley is drawing on popular belief or at least desire—pretty much distrusted in her time but still part of the mythic landscape of scientific possibility—that beyond the rigors of exploration and the pursuit of geographical knowledge lay a place with treasures of prelapsarian bliss in a perfect climate and utopian world. The passage thus sets up the comparison between kinds of scientific quests and dreams that later will contextualize Frankenstein's hubris and set up the story-within-a-story, box-within-a box structure of interlocking narratives. Walton's exploration of the unknown is just as wide-eyed, ambitious, and unreliably utopian as is Frankenstein's quest for the secret of life, and through experiments with points of view (with Walton, Frankenstein, and the Creature successively presenting their perspectives), we get both a shifting sense of authority and doubts about the reliability of authority itself.

IV

The text of *Frankenstein* printed here is that of the 1818 first edition, published in London in three volumes by Lackington, Hughes, Harding, Mavor, and Jones. Only glaring typographical errors have been corrected; otherwise the text reproduced here is that read by *Frankenstein*'s first readers, except that explanatory notes have been provided with the needs of modern students in mind. Until the late twentieth century, the tradition had been to use the third-edition text of 1831, which Mary Shelley revised carefully—but from a later perspective when she was considerably older and more detached from the original conception. Scholarship now strongly prefers the first edition; for the issues involved see the essays by M. K. Joseph on p. 170–73 and Anne K. Mellor on pp. 204–11.

A wealth of *Frankenstein*-related documents and interpretive materials are appended to this edition, beginning on p. 165. They are arranged into four sections. The first gathers a series of contemporary texts related to the creation of the novel. Here are passages from the Book of Genesis and Milton's *Paradise Lost* as well as contemporary poems by Percy Shelley, Byron, and Charles Lamb. The second section contains documents and texts related to the circumstances of *Frankenstein*'s creation and revision, including critical accounts of early influences on Mary's thinking. The third section contains responses to *Frankenstein* over the years, including early reviews of the novel and accounts of later adaptations and variations.

Finally, there is an extensive collection of critical materials, suggesting a variety of ways of reading the novel that raise all kinds of critical approaches. As Lawrence Lipking says in one of these essays, *Frankenstein* "furnishes a testing ground for every conceivable mode of interpretation" (p. 416). I have not tried to represent every "school" of criticism in these selections, but I have tried to choose essays that open up a wide range of readings of the novel. Represented quite heavily are the influential essays of the 1970s and 1980s that are largely responsible for the resurgence of *Frankenstein*'s popularity and importance. Later essays suggest a variety of new emphases—especially on the history of science—that have characterized more recent criticism.

In preparing this edition, I have been blessed over time with help and guidance from many colleagues and correspondents. I wish especially to acknowledge the generous sharing of work and knowledge by Sylvia Bowerbank, Marilyn Butler, James Chandler, Lorna Clymer, Morris Eaves, Sandra Gilbert, Susan Gubar, James Heffernan, Jerrold Hogle, Margaret Homans, Larry Lipking, Bette London, Maureen McLane, Anne Mellor, James Rieger, Cynthia Wall, and Elizabeth Young. Many people at W. W. Norton have provided counsel, support, and gentle prodding: I thank John Benedict, Barry Wade, Julia Reidhead, Donald Lamm, Alan Cameron, Carol Hollar-Zwick, Kate Lovelady, Marian Johnson, Rivka Genesen, Pete Simon, and (especially) Carol Bemis. I have also been fortunate to have had research assistants who did much valuable textual, bibliographical, and historical digging: Jayne Greenstein, Willard White, Marianne Eismann, Erica Zeinfeld, Josh Konkol, Annie Kinneburgh, and (especially) Will Pritchard, who provided most of the notes and was more counsel and collaborator than assistant.

J. Paul Hunter
September 2011

The Text of
FRANKENSTEIN

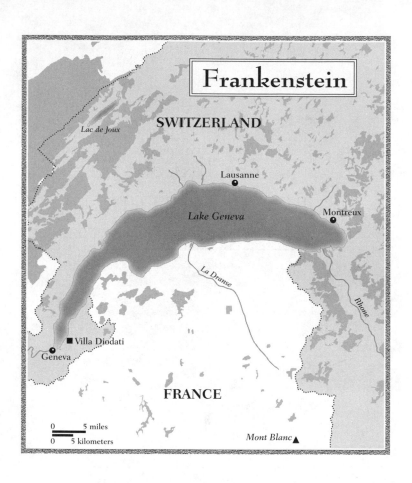

FRANKENSTEIN;

OR,

THE MODERN PROMETHEUS.[1]

IN THREE VOLUMES.

Did I request thee, Maker, from my clay
To mould me man ?   Did I solicit thee
From darkness to promote me ?——
                    PARADISE LOST.[2]

VOL. I.

London :

PRINTED FOR

LACKINGTON, HUGHES, HARDING, MAVOR, & JONES,
FINSBURY SQUARE.

1818.

Courtesy of the Newberry Library.

1. In Greek mythology, the Titan Prometheus created humankind out of mud and water and then stole fire from the gods to give his creation; as punishment, Zeus chained him to a rock where an eagle pecked out his liver. In *Prometheus Unbound* (1820), a poetic drama by Percy Bysshe Shelley, Prometheus is eventually released from captivity.
2. By John Milton (1608–1674). These lines are from book X. 743–45 and are spoken by Adam after the Fall. This epigraph appeared on the title page for each volume.

TO

WILLIAM GODWIN,[3]

AUTHOR OF POLITICAL JUSTICE, CALEB WILLIAMS, &c.

THESE VOLUMES

Are respectfully inscribed

BY

THE AUTHOR.

3. English philosopher and author (1756–1836), husband of Mary Wollstonecraft and father of Mary Shelley; *Enquiry Concerning Political Justice* (1793) was a work of political philosophy, popular in radical circles; *The Adventures of Caleb Williams* (1794) was a novel.

Preface[1]

The event on which this fiction is founded has been supposed, by Dr. Darwin, and some of the physiological writers of Germany,[2] as not of impossible occurrence. I shall not be supposed as according the remotest degree of serious faith to such an imagination; yet, in assuming it as the basis of a work of fancy, I have not considered myself as merely weaving a series of supernatural terrors. The event on which the interest of the story depends is exempt from the disadvantages of a mere tale of spectres or enchantment. It was recommended by the novelty of the situations which it developes; and, however impossible as a physical fact, affords a point of view to the imagination for the delineating of human passions more comprehensive and commanding than any which the ordinary relations of existing events can yield.

I have thus endeavoured to preserve the truth of the elementary principles of human nature, while I have not scrupled to innovate upon their combinations. The *Iliad*, the tragic poetry of Greece—Shakespeare, in the *Tempest* and *Midsummer Night's Dream*,—and most especially Milton, in *Paradise Lost*, conform to this rule; and the most humble novelist, who seeks to confer or receive amusement from his labours, may, without presumption, apply to prose fiction a licence, or rather a rule, from the adoption of which so many exquisite combinations of human feeling have resulted in the highest specimens of poetry.

The circumstance on which my story rests was suggested in casual conversation.[3] It was commenced, partly as a source of amusement, and partly as an expedient for exercising any untried resources of mind. Other motives were mingled with these, as the work proceeded. I am by no means indifferent to the manner in which whatever moral tendencies exist in the sentiments or characters it contains

---

1. Written by Percy Bysshe Shelley; see the 1831 introduction (pp. 165–69, below) for Mary Shelley's account of the genesis of *Frankenstein*.
2. The German physiologists included Blumenbach, Rudolphi, and Tiedemann. Erasmus Darwin (1731–1802), English scientist and poet, proposed early theories of evolution (later developed by his grandson Charles). See the 1831 introduction for Mary Shelley's account of his search for "the principle of life."
3. With Byron and Percy Shelley.

shall affect the reader; yet my chief concern in this respect has been limited to the avoiding the enervating effects of the novels of the present day,[4] and to the exhibition of the amiableness of domestic affection, and the excellence of universal virtue. The opinions which naturally spring from the character and situation of the hero are by no means to be conceived as existing always in my own conviction; nor is any inference justly to be drawn from the following pages as prejudicing any philosophical doctrine of whatever kind.

It is a subject also of additional interest to the author, that this story was begun in the majestic region where the scene is principally laid, and in society which cannot cease to be regretted. I passed the summer of 1816 in the environs of Geneva. The season was cold and rainy, and in the evenings we crowded around a blazing wood fire, and occasionally amused ourselves with some German stories of ghosts, which happened to fall into our hands. These tales excited in us a playful desire of imitation. Two other friends (a tale from the pen of one of whom would be far more acceptable to the public than any thing I can ever hope to produce) and myself agreed to write each a story, founded on some supernatural occurrence.

The weather, however, suddenly became serene; and my two friends left me on a journey among the Alps, and lost, in the magnificent scenes which they present, all memory of their ghostly visions. The following tale is the only one which has been completed.

---

4. Novel-reading was often viewed as both the cause and the result of idleness.

Volume I

Letter I.

To Mrs. Saville, England.

St. Petersburgh,[1] Dec. 11th, 17–.

You will rejoice to hear that no disaster has accompanied the commencement of an enterprise which you have regarded with such evil forebodings. I arrived here yesterday; and my first task is to assure my dear sister of my welfare, and increasing confidence in the success of my undertaking.

I am already far north of London; and as I walk in the streets of Petersburgh, I feel a cold northern breeze play upon my cheeks, which braces my nerves, and fills me with delight. Do you understand this feeling? This breeze, which has travelled from the regions towards which I am advancing, gives me a foretaste of those icy climes. Inspirited by this wind of promise, my day dreams become more fervent and vivid. I try in vain to be persuaded that the pole is the seat of frost and desolation; it ever presents itself to my imagination as the region of beauty and delight. There, Margaret, the sun is for ever visible; its broad disk just skirting the horizon, and diffusing a perpetual splendour. There—for with your leave, my sister, I will put some trust in preceding navigators—there snow and frost are banished; and, sailing over a calm sea, we may be wafted to a land surpassing in wonders and in beauty every region hitherto discovered on the habitable globe. Its productions and features may be without example, as the phænomena of the heavenly bodies undoubtedly are in those undiscovered solitudes. What may not be expected in a country of eternal light? I may there discover the wondrous power which attracts the needle; and may regulate a thousand celestial observations, that require only this voyage to render their seeming eccentricities consistent for ever. I shall satiate my ardent curiosity with the sight of a part of the world never before visited, and may tread a land never before imprinted by the foot of man. These are my enticements, and they are sufficient to conquer all fear of danger

---

1. Russian city at the head of the Gulf of Finland.

7

ιduce me to commence this laborious voyage with
s when he embarks in a little boat with his holiday
.pedition of discovery up his native river. But, sup-
.ese conjectures to be false, you cannot contest the
ε benefit which I shall confer on all mankind to the last
.on, by discovering a passage near the pole to those countries,
to reach which at present so many months are requisite; or by ascertaining the secret of the magnet, which, if at all possible, can only be effected by an undertaking such as mine.[2]

These reflections have dispelled the agitation with which I began my letter, and I feel my heart glow with an enthusiasm[3] which elevates me to heaven; for nothing contributes so much to tranquillize the mind as a steady purpose,—a point on which the soul may fix its intellectual eye. This expedition has been the favourite dream of my early years. I have read with ardour the accounts of the various voyages which have been made in the prospect of arriving at the North Pacific Ocean through the seas which surround the pole. You may remember, that a history of all the voyages made for purposes of discovery composed the whole of our good uncle Thomas's library. My education was neglected, yet I was passionately fond of reading. These volumes were my study day and night, and my familiarity with them increased that regret which I had felt, as a child, on learning that my father's dying injunction had forbidden my uncle to allow me to embark in a sea-faring life.

These visions faded when I perused, for the first time, those poets whose effusions entranced my soul, and lifted it to heaven. I also became a poet, and for one year lived in a Paradise of my own creation; I imagined that I also might obtain a niche in the temple where the names of Homer and Shakespeare are consecrated. You are well acquainted with my failure, and how heavily I bore the disappointment. But just at that time I inherited the fortune of my cousin, and my thoughts were turned into the channel of their earlier bent.

Six years have passed since I resolved on my present undertaking. I can, even now, remember the hour from which I dedicated myself to this great enterprise. I commenced by inuring my body to hardship. I accompanied the whale-fishers on several expeditions to the North Sea; I voluntarily endured cold, famine, thirst, and want of sleep; I often worked harder than the common sailors during the day, and devoted my nights to the study of mathematics, the theory of medicine, and those branches of physical science from which a

2. Voyages of discovery seeking a navigable northwest passage were frequent in Shelley's time, and contemporary periodicals were full of their detailed travel accounts. The old tradition that the lands of "eternal light" might contain a lost paradise was still current, though perhaps more hoped for than believed in.
3. Supernatural inspiration; poetic or prophetic frenzy.

naval adventurer might derive the greatest practical advantage. Twice I actually hired myself as an undermate in a Greenland whaler, and acquitted myself to admiration. I must own I felt a little proud, when my captain offered me the second dignity in the vessel, and entreated me to remain with the greatest earnestness; so valuable did he consider my services.

And now, dear Margaret, do I not deserve to accomplish some great purpose. My life might have been passed in ease and luxury; but I preferred glory to every enticement that wealth placed in my path. Oh, that some encouraging voice would answer in the affirmative! My courage and my resolution is firm; but my hopes fluctuate, and my spirits are often depressed. I am about to proceed on a long and difficult voyage; the emergencies of which will demand all my fortitude: I am required not only to raise the spirits of others, but sometimes to sustain my own, when their's are failing.

This is the most favourable period for travelling in Russia. They fly quickly over the snow in their sledges; the motion is pleasant, and, in my opinion, far more agreeable than that of an English stage-coach. The cold is not excessive, if you are wrapt in furs, a dress which I have already adopted; for there is a great difference between walking the deck and remaining seated motionless for hours, when no exercise prevents the blood from actually freezing in your veins. I have no ambition to lose my life on the post-road between St. Petersburgh and Archangel.[4]

I shall depart for the latter town in a fortnight or three weeks; and my intention is to hire a ship there, which can easily be done by paying the insurance for the owner, and to engage as many sailors as I think necessary among those who are accustomed to the whale-fishing. I do not intend to sail until the month of June: and when shall I return? Ah, dear sister, how can I answer this question? If I succeed, many, many months, perhaps years, will pass before you and I may meet. If I fail, you will see me again soon, or never.

Farewell, my dear, excellent, Margaret. Heaven shower down blessings on you, and save me, that I may again and again testify my gratitude for all your love and kindness.

Your affectionate brother,
R. Walton.

---

4. A port on the northwest coast of Russia. *Post-road*: a road on which the mails were carried, a main road.

Letter II.

To Mrs. Saville, England.

Archangel, 28th March, 17–.

How slowly the time passes here, encompassed as I am by frost and snow; yet a second step is taken towards my enterprise. I have hired a vessel, and am occupied in collecting my sailors; those whom I have already engaged appear to be men on whom I can depend, and are certainly possessed of dauntless courage.

But I have one want which I have never yet been able to satisfy; and the absence of the object of which I now feel as a most severe evil. I have no friend, Margaret: when I am glowing with the enthusiasm of success, there will be none to participate my joy; if I am assailed by disappointment, no one will endeavour to sustain me in dejection. I shall commit my thoughts to paper, it is true; but that is a poor medium for the communication of feeling. I desire the company of a man who could sympathize[1] with me; whose eyes would reply to mine. You may deem me romantic,[2] my dear sister, but I bitterly feel the want of a friend. I have no one near me, gentle yet courageous, possessed of a cultivated as well as of a capacious mind, whose tastes are like my own, to approve or amend my plans. How would such a friend repair the faults of your poor brother! I am too ardent in execution, and too impatient of difficulties. But it is a still greater evil to me that I am self-educated: for the first fourteen years of my life I ran wild on a common, and read nothing but our uncle Thomas's books of voyages. At that age I became acquainted with the celebrated poets of our own country, but it was only when it had ceased to be in my power to derive its most important benefits from such a conviction, that I perceived the necessity of becoming acquainted with more languages than that of my native country. Now I am twenty-eight, and am in reality more illiterate than many school-boys of fifteen. It is true that I have thought more, and that my day dreams are more extended and magnificent; but they want (as the painters call it) *keeping*;[3] and I greatly need a friend who would have sense[4] enough not to despise me as romantic, and affection enough for me to endeavour to regulate my mind.

---

1. Feel correspondingly. Here and elsewhere, Walton employs the vocabulary of "sentiment" popularized by such novels as *The Man of Feeling* (1771) by Henry Mackenzie (1745–1831) and *A Sentimental Journey* (1768) by Laurence Sterne (1713–1768) and parodied in *Sense and Sensibility* (1811) by Jane Austen (1775–1817).
2. Like a character in a romance; also, readily influenced by the imagination.
3. I.e., they lack the proper relation between near and distant objects (as in a picture).
4. Feeling.

Well, these are useless complaints; I shall certainly find no friend on the wide ocean, nor even here in Archangel, among merchants and seamen. Yet some feelings, unallied to the dross of human nature,[5] beat even in these rugged bosoms. My lieutenant, for instance, is a man of wonderful courage and enterprise; he is madly desirous of glory. He is an Englishman, and in the midst of national and professional prejudices, unsoftened by cultivation, retains some of the noblest endowments of humanity. I first became acquainted with him on board a whale vessel: finding that he was unemployed in this city, I easily engaged him to assist in my enterprise.

The master is a person of an excellent disposition, and is remarkable in the ship for his gentleness, and the mildness of his discipline. He is, indeed, of so amiable a nature, that he will not hunt (a favourite, and almost the only amusement here), because he cannot endure to spill blood. He is, moreover, heroically generous. Some years ago he loved a young Russian lady, of moderate fortune; and having amassed a considerable sum in prize-money, the father of the girl consented to the match. He saw his mistress once before the destined ceremony; but she was bathed in tears, and, throwing herself at his feet, entreated him to spare her, confessing at the same time that she loved another, but that he was poor, and that her father would never consent to the union. My generous friend reassured the suppliant, and on being informed of the name of her lover instantly abandoned his pursuit. He had already bought a farm with his money, on which he had designed to pass the remainder of his life; but he bestowed the whole on his rival, together with the remains of his prize-money to purchase stock,[6] and then himself solicited the young woman's father to consent to her marriage with her lover. But the old man decidedly refused, thinking himself bound in honour to my friend; who, when he found the father inexorable, quitted his country, nor returned until he heard that his former mistress was married according to her inclinations. "What a noble fellow!" you will exclaim. He is so; but then he has passed all his life on board a vessel, and has scarcely an idea beyond the rope and the shroud.

But do not suppose that, because I complain a little, or because I can conceive a consolation for my toils which I may never know, that I am wavering in my resolutions. Those are as fixed as fate; and my voyage is only now delayed until the weather shall permit my embarkation. The winter has been dreadfully severe; but the spring promises well, and it is considered as a remarkably early season; so that, perhaps, I may sail sooner than I expected. I shall do nothing rashly;

---

5. I.e., not belonging to the worse part of human nature.
6. Livestock.

you know me sufficiently to confide in my prudence and consider-
ateness whenever the safety of others is committed to my care.

I cannot describe to you my sensations on the near prospect of my
undertaking. It is impossible to communicate to you a conception of
the trembling sensation, half pleasurable and half fearful, with
which I am preparing to depart. I am going to unexplored regions, to
"the land of mist and snow;"[7] but I shall kill no albatross, therefore
do not be alarmed for my safety.

Shall I meet you again, after having traversed immense seas, and
returned by the most southern cape of Africa or America? I dare
not expect such success, yet I cannot bear to look on the reverse
of the picture. Continue to write to me by every opportunity: I may
receive your letters (though the chance is very doubtful) on some
occasions when I need them most to support my spirits. I love you
very tenderly. Remember me with affection, should you never hear
from me again.

Your affectionate brother,
ROBERT WALTON.

Letter III.

To Mrs. Saville, England.

July 7th, 17–.

MY DEAR SISTER,
I write a few lines in haste, to say that I am safe, and well advanced
on my voyage. This letter will reach England by a merchant-man now
on its homeward voyage from Archangel; more fortunate than I, who
may not see my native land, perhaps, for many years. I am, however,
in good spirits: my men are bold, and apparently firm of purpose; nor
do the floating sheets of ice that continually pass us, indicating
the dangers of the region towards which we are advancing, appear
to dismay them. We have already reached a very high latitude; but
it is the height of summer, and although not so warm as in England,
the southern gales, which blow us speedily towards those shores
which I so ardently desire to attain, breathe a degree of renovating
warmth which I had not expected.

No incidents have hitherto befallen us, that would make a figure[1]
in a letter. One or two stiff gales, and the breaking of a mast, are

---

7. Line 403 of "The Rime of the Ancient Mariner" (1798) by Samuel Taylor Coleridge
   (1772–1834); the mariner, by killing an albatross, brings a curse on himself and his ship.
   Mary Shelley recalls having heard Coleridge himself recite the *Rime* when she was nine
   years old.
1. Seem important.

accidents which experienced navigators scarcely remember to record; and I shall be well content, if nothing worse happen to us during our voyage.

Adieu, my dear Margaret. Be assured, that for my own sake, as well as your's, I will not rashly encounter danger. I will be cool, persevering, and prudent.

Remember me to all my English friends.

Most affectionately yours,
R. W.

Letter IV.

To Mrs. Saville, England.

August 5th, 17–.

So strange an accident has happened to us, that I cannot forbear recording it, although it is very probable that you will see me before these papers can come into your possession.

Last Monday (July 31st), we were nearly surrounded by ice, which closed in the ship on all sides, scarcely leaving her the sea room in which she floated. Our situation was somewhat dangerous, especially as we were compassed round by a very thick fog. We accordingly lay to, hoping that some change would take place in the atmosphere and weather.

About two o'clock the mist cleared away, and we beheld, stretched out in every direction, vast and irregular plains of ice, which seemed to have no end. Some of my comrades groaned, and my own mind began to grow watchful with anxious thoughts, when a strange sight suddenly attracted our attention, and diverted our solicitude from our own situation. We perceived a low carriage, fixed on a sledge and drawn by dogs, pass on towards the north, at the distance of half a mile: a being which had the shape of a man, but apparently of gigantic stature, sat in the sledge, and guided the dogs. We watched the rapid progress of the traveller with our telescopes, until he was lost among the distant inequalities[1] of the ice.

This appearance excited our unqualified wonder.[2] We were, as we believed, many hundred miles from any land; but this apparition seemed to denote that it was not, in reality, so distant as we had supposed. Shut in, however, by ice, it was impossible to follow his track, which we had observed with the greatest attention.

---

1. Irregularities; risings and fallings.
2. "Astonishment mingled with perplexity or bewildered curiosity" (*Oxford English Dictionary* [*OED*]).

About two hours after this occurrence, we heard the ground sea;[3] and before night the ice broke, and freed our ship. We, however, lay to until the morning, fearing to encounter in the dark those large loose masses which float about after the breaking up of the ice. I profited of this time to rest for a few hours.

In the morning, however, as soon as it was light, I went upon deck, and found all the sailors busy on one side of the vessel, apparently talking to some one in the sea. It was, in fact, a sledge, like that we had seen before, which had drifted towards us in the night, on a large fragment of ice. Only one dog remained alive; but there was a human being within it, whom the sailors were persuading to enter the vessel. He was not, as the other traveller seemed to be, a savage inhabitant of some undiscovered island, but an European. When I appeared on deck, the master said, "Here is our captain, and he will not allow you to perish on the open sea."

On perceiving me, the stranger addressed me in English, although with a foreign accent. "Before I come on board your vessel," said he, "will you have the kindness to inform me whither you are bound?"

You may conceive my astonishment on hearing such a question addressed to me from a man on the brink of destruction, and to whom I should have supposed that my vessel would have been a resource which he would not have exchanged for the most precious wealth the earth can afford. I replied, however, that we were on a voyage of discovery towards the northern pole.

Upon hearing this he appeared satisfied, and consented to come on board. Good God! Margaret, if you had seen the man who thus capitulated[4] for his safety, your surprise would have been boundless. His limbs were nearly frozen, and his body dreadfully emaciated by fatigue and suffering. I never saw a man in so wretched a condition. We attempted to carry him into the cabin; but as soon as he had quitted the fresh air, he fainted. We accordingly brought him back to the deck, and restored him to animation by rubbing him with brandy, and forcing him to swallow a small quantity. As soon as he shewed signs of life, we wrapped him up in blankets, and placed him near the chimney of the kitchen-stove. By slow degrees he recovered, and ate a little soup, which restored him wonderfully.

Two days passed in this manner before he was able to speak; and I often feared that his sufferings had deprived him of understanding. When he had in some measure recovered, I removed him to my own cabin, and attended on him as much as my duty would permit. I never saw a more interesting creature: his eyes have generally an expression of wildness, and even madness; but there are moments

---

3. Ground swell, deep undulation of the sea.
4. Bargained.

when, if any one performs an act of kindness towards him, or does him any the most trifling service, his whole countenance is lighted up, as it were, with a beam of benevolence and sweetness that I never saw equalled. But he is generally melancholy and despairing; and sometimes he gnashes his teeth, as if impatient of[5] the weight of woes that oppresses him.

When my guest was a little recovered, I had great trouble to keep off the men, who wished to ask him a thousand questions; but I would not allow him to be tormented by their idle curiosity, in a state of body and mind whose restoration evidently depended upon entire repose. Once, however, the lieutenant asked, Why he had come so far upon the ice in so strange a vehicle?

His countenance instantly assumed an aspect of the deepest gloom; and he replied, "To seek one who fled from me."

"And did the man whom you pursued travel in the same fashion?"

"Yes."

"Then I fancy we have seen him; for, the day before we picked you up, we saw some dogs drawing a sledge, with a man in it, across the ice."

This aroused the stranger's attention; and he asked a multitude of questions concerning the route which the dæmon,[6] as he called him, had pursued. Soon after, when he was alone with me, he said, "I have, doubtless, excited your curiosity, as well as that of these good people; but you are too considerate to make inquiries."

"Certainly; it would indeed be very impertinent and inhuman in me to trouble you with any inquisitiveness of mine."

"And yet you rescued me from a strange and perilous situation; you have benevolently restored me to life."

Soon after this he inquired, if I thought that the breaking up of the ice had destroyed the other sledge? I replied, that I could not answer with any degree of certainty; for the ice had not broken until near midnight, and the traveller might have arrived at a place of safety before that time; but of this I could not judge.

From this time the stranger seemed very eager to be upon deck, to watch for the sledge which had before appeared; but I have persuaded him to remain in the cabin, for he is far too weak to sustain the rawness of the atmosphere. But I have promised that some one should watch for him, and give him instant notice if any new object should appear in sight.

Such is my journal of what relates to this strange occurrence up to the present day. The stranger has gradually improved in health,

5. Unable to endure.
6. The OED distinguishes *daemon* (an inferior divinity) from *demon* (an evil spirit), but Mary Shelley does not appear to be making this distinction.

but is very silent, and appears uneasy when any one except myself enters his cabin. Yet his manners are so conciliating and gentle, that the sailors are all interested in him, although they have had very little communication with him. For my own part, I begin to love him as a brother; and his constant and deep grief fills me with sympathy and compassion. He must have been a noble creature in his better days, being even now in wreck so attractive and amiable.

I said in one of my letters, my dear Margaret, that I should find no friend on the wide ocean; yet I have found a man who, before his spirit had been broken by misery, I should have been happy to have possessed as the brother of my heart.

I shall continue my journal concerning the stranger at intervals, should I have any fresh incidents to record.

August 13th, 17–.

My affection for my guest increases every day. He excites at once my admiration[7] and my pity to an astonishing degree. How can I see so noble a creature destroyed by misery without feeling the most poignant grief? He is so gentle, yet so wise; his mind is so cultivated; and when he speaks, although his words are culled with the choicest art, yet they flow with rapidity and unparalleled eloquence.

He is now much recovered from his illness, and is continually on the deck, apparently watching for the sledge that preceded his own. Yet, although unhappy, he is not so utterly occupied by his own misery, but that he interests himself deeply in the employments of others. He has asked me many questions concerning my design; and I have related my little history frankly to him. He appeared pleased with the confidence, and suggested several alterations in my plan, which I shall find exceedingly useful. There is no pedantry in his manner; but all he does appears to spring solely from the interest he instinctively takes in the welfare of those who surround him. He is often overcome by gloom, and then he sits by himself, and tries to overcome all that is sullen or unsocial in his humour.[8] These paroxysms pass from him like a cloud from before the sun, though his dejection never leaves him. I have endeavoured to win his confidence; and I trust that I have succeeded. One day I mentioned to him the desire I had always felt of finding a friend who might sympathize with me, and direct me by his counsel. I said, I did not belong to that class of men who are offended by advice. "I am self-educated, and perhaps I hardly rely sufficiently upon my own powers.[9] I wish there-

---

7. Wonder (or approval).
8. Temperament, constitution.
9. I.e., I rely on my own powers, which are perhaps hardly sufficient.

fore that my companion should be wiser and more experienced than myself, to confirm and support me; nor have I believed it impossible to find a true friend."

"I agree with you," replied the stranger, "in believing that friendship is not only a desirable, but a possible acquisition. I once had a friend, the most noble of human creatures, and am entitled, therefore, to judge respecting friendship. You have hope, and the world before you, and have no cause for despair. But I—I have lost every thing, and cannot begin life anew."

As he said this, his countenance became expressive of a calm settled grief, that touched me to the heart. But he was silent, and presently retired to his cabin.

Even broken in spirit as he is, no one can feel more deeply than he does the beauties of nature. The starry sky, the sea and every sight afforded by these wonderful regions, seems still to have the power of elevating his soul from earth. Such a man has a double existence: he may suffer misery, and be overwhelmed by disappointments; yet when he has retired into himself, he will be like a celestial spirit, that has a halo around him, within whose circle no grief or folly ventures.

Will you laugh at the enthusiasm I express concerning this divine wanderer? If you do, you must have certainly lost that simplicity which was once your characteristic charm. Yet, if you will, smile at the warmth of my expressions, while I find every day new causes for repeating them.

August 19th, 17–.

Yesterday the stranger said to me, "You may easily perceive, Captain Walton, that I have suffered great and unparalleled misfortunes. I had determined, once, that the memory of these evils should die with me; but you have won me to alter my determination. You seek for knowledge and wisdom, as I once did; and I ardently hope that the gratification of your wishes may not be a serpent to sting you, as mine has been. I do not know that the relation of my misfortunes will be useful to you, yet, if you are inclined, listen to my tale. I believe that the strange incidents connected with it will afford a view of nature, which may enlarge your faculties and understanding. You will hear of powers and occurrences, such as you have been accustomed to believe impossible: but I do not doubt that my tale conveys in its series internal evidence of the truth of the events of which it is composed."

You may easily conceive that I was much gratified by the offered communication; yet I could not endure that he should renew his grief by a recital of his misfortunes. I felt the greatest eagerness to hear the promised narrative, partly from curiosity, and partly from a strong desire to ameliorate his fate, if it were in my power. I expressed these feelings in my answer.

"I thank you," he replied, "for your sympathy, but it is useless; my fate is nearly fulfilled. I wait but for one event, and then I shall repose in peace. I understand your feeling," continued he, perceiving that I wished to interrupt him; "but you are mistaken, my friend, if thus you will allow me to name you; nothing can alter my destiny: listen to my history, and you will perceive how irrevocably it is determined."

He then told me, that he would commence his narrative the next day when I should be at leisure. This promise drew from me the warmest thanks. I have resolved every night, when I am not engaged, to record, as nearly as possible in his own words, what he has related during the day. If I should be engaged, I will at least make notes. This manuscript will doubtless afford you the greatest pleasure: but to me, who know him, and who hear it from his own lips, with what interest and sympathy shall I read it in some future day!

Chapter I.

I am by birth a Genevese; and my family is one of the most distinguished of that republic. My ancestors had been for many years counsellors and syndics;[1] and my father had filled several public situations with honour and reputation. He was respected by all who knew him for his integrity and indefatigable attention to public business. He passed his younger days perpetually occupied by the affairs of his country; and it was not until the decline of life that he thought of marrying, and bestowing on the state sons who might carry his virtues and his name down to posterity.

As the circumstances of his marriage illustrate his character, I cannot refrain from relating them. One of his most intimate friends was a merchant, who, from a flourishing state, fell, through numerous mischances, into poverty. This man, whose name was Beaufort, was of a proud and unbending disposition, and could not bear to live in poverty and oblivion in the same country where he had formerly been distinguished for his rank and magnificence. Having paid his debts, therefore, in the most honourable manner, he retreated with his daughter to the town of Lucerne, where he lived unknown and in wretchedness. My father loved Beaufort with the truest friendship, and was deeply grieved by his retreat in these unfortunate circumstances. He grieved also for the loss of his society, and resolved

---

1. Geneva, as a republic, had no monarch but was governed by a legislature; there were four syndics (chief magistrates).

to seek him out and endeavour to persuade him to begin the world again through his credit and assistance.

Beaufort had taken effectual measures to conceal himself; and it was ten months before my father discovered his abode. Overjoyed at this discovery, he hastened to the house, which was situated in a mean street, near the Reuss. But when he entered, misery and despair alone welcomed him. Beaufort had saved but a very small sum of money from the wreck of his fortunes; but it was sufficient to provide him with sustenance for some months, and in the mean time he hoped to procure some respectable employment in a merchant's house. The interval was consequently spent in inaction; his grief only became more deep and rankling, when he had leisure for reflection; and at length it took so fast hold of his mind, that at the end of three months he lay on a bed of sickness, incapable of any exertion.

His daughter attended him with the greatest tenderness; but she saw with despair that their little fund was rapidly decreasing, and that there was no other prospect of support. But Caroline Beaufort possessed a mind of an uncommon mould; and her courage rose to support her in her adversity. She procured plain work; she plaited straw; and by various means contrived to earn a pittance scarcely sufficient to support life.

Several months passed in this manner. Her father grew worse; her time was more entirely occupied in attending him; her means of subsistence decreased; and in the tenth month her father died in her arms, leaving her an orphan and a beggar. This last blow overcame her; and she knelt by Beaufort's coffin, weeping bitterly, when my father entered the chamber. He came like a protecting spirit to the poor girl, who committed herself to his care, and after the interment of his friend he conducted her to Geneva, and placed her under the protection of a relation. Two years after this event Caroline became his wife.

When my father became a husband and a parent, he found his time so occupied by the duties of his new situation, that he relinquished many of his public employments, and devoted himself to the education of his children. Of these I was the eldest, and the destined successor to all his labours and utility. No creature could have more tender parents than mine. My improvement and health were their constant care, especially as I remained for several years their only child. But before I continue my narrative, I must record an incident which took place when I was four years of age.

My father had a sister, whom he tenderly loved, and who had married early in life an Italian gentleman. Soon after her marriage, she had accompanied her husband into her[2] native country, and

2. A slip for "his."

for some years my father had very little communication with her. About the time I mentioned she died; and a few months afterwards he received a letter from her husband, acquainting him with his intention of marrying an Italian lady, and requesting my father to take charge of the infant Elizabeth, the only child of his deceased sister. "It is my wish," he said, "that you should consider her as your own daughter, and educate her thus. Her mother's fortune is secured[3] to her, the documents of which I will commit to your keeping. Reflect upon this proposition; and decide whether you would prefer educating your niece yourself to her being brought up by a stepmother."

My father did not hesitate, and immediately went to Italy that he might accompany the little Elizabeth to her future home. I have often heard my mother say, that she was at that time the most beautiful child she had ever seen, and shewed signs even then of a gentle and affectionate disposition. These indications, and a desire to bind as closely as possible the ties of domestic love, determined my mother to consider Elizabeth as my future wife; a design which she never found reason to repent.

From this time Elizabeth Lavenza became my playfellow, and, as we grew older, my friend. She was docile and good tempered, yet gay and playful as a summer insect. Although she was lively and animated, her feelings were strong and deep, and her disposition uncommonly affectionate. No one could better enjoy liberty, yet no one could submit with more grace than she did to constraint and caprice. Her imagination was luxuriant, yet her capability of application was great. Her person was the image of her mind; her hazel eyes, although as lively as a bird's, possessed an attractive softness. Her figure was light and airy; and, though capable of enduring great fatigue, she appeared the most fragile creature in the world. While I admired her understanding and fancy, I loved to tend on her, as I should on a favourite animal; and I never saw so much grace both of person and mind united to so little pretension.

Every one adored Elizabeth. If the servants had any request to make, it was always through her intercession. We were strangers to any species of disunion and dispute; for although there was a great dissimilitude in our characters, there was an harmony in that very dissimilitude. I was more calm and philosophical than my companion; yet my temper was not so yielding. My application was of longer endurance; but it was not so severe whilst it endured. I delighted in investigating the facts relative to the actual world; she busied herself in following the aërial creations of the poets. The world was to me a secret, which I desired to discover; to her it was a vacancy; which she sought to people with imaginations of her own.

3. Guaranteed.

My brothers were considerably younger than myself; but I had a friend in one of my schoolfellows, who compensated for this deficiency. Henry Clerval was the son of a merchant of Geneva, an intimate friend of my father. He was a boy of singular talent and fancy. I remember, when he was nine years old, he wrote a fairy tale, which was the delight and amazement of all his companions. His favourite study consisted in books of chivalry and romance; and when very young, I can remember, that we used to act plays composed by him out of these favourite books, the principal characters of which were Orlando, Robin Hood, Amadis, and St. George.[4]

No youth could have passed more happily than mine. My parents were indulgent, and my companions amiable. Our studies were never forced; and by some means we always had an end placed in view, which excited us to ardour in the prosecution of them. It was by this method, and not by emulation, that we were urged to application. Elizabeth was not incited to apply herself to drawing, that her companions might not outstrip her; but through the desire of pleasing her aunt, by the representation of some favourite scene done by her own hand. We learned Latin and English, that we might read the writings in those languages; and so far from study being made odious to us through punishment, we loved application, and our amusements would have been the labours of other children. Perhaps we did not read so many books, or learn languages so quickly, as those who are disciplined according to the ordinary methods; but what we learned was impressed the more deeply on our memories.

In this description of our domestic circle I include Henry Clerval; for he was constantly with us. He went to school with me, and generally passed the afternoon at our house; for being an only child, and destitute of companions at home, his father was well pleased that he should find associates at our house; and we were never completely happy when Clerval was absent.

I feel pleasure in dwelling on the recollections of childhood, before misfortune had tainted my mind, and changed its bright visions of extensive usefulness into gloomy and narrow reflections upon self. But, in drawing the picture of my early days, I must not omit to record those events which led, by insensible steps to my after tale of misery: for when I would account to myself for the birth of that passion, which afterwards ruled my destiny, I find it arise, like a mountain river, from ignoble and almost forgotten sources; but, swelling as it proceeded, it became the torrent which, in its course, has swept away all my hopes and joys.

---

4. Robin Hood and St. George are legendary English heroes. *Orlando Furioso* (1532) is a romance epic by Lodovico Ariosto (1474–1535). *Amadis de Gaul* is a Spanish or Portuguese romance of the late 1400s; Robert Southey produced an English version in 1803.

Natural philosophy is the genius[5] that has regulated my fate; I desire therefore, in this narration, to state those facts which led to my predilection for that science. When I was thirteen years of age, we all went on a party of pleasure to the baths near Thonon: the inclemency of the weather obliged us to remain a day confined to the inn. In this house I chanced to find a volume of the works of Cornelius Agrippa.[6] I opened it with apathy; the theory which he attempts to demonstrate, and the wonderful facts which he relates, soon changed this feeling into enthusiasm. A new light seemed to dawn upon my mind; and, bounding with joy, I communicated my discovery to my father. I cannot help remarking here the many opportunities instructors possess of directing the attention of their pupils to useful knowledge, which they utterly neglect. My father looked carelessly at the title-page of my book, and said, "Ah! Cornelius Agrippa! My dear Victor, do not waste your time upon this; it is sad trash."

If, instead of this remark, my father had taken the pains to explain to me, that the principles of Agrippa had been entirely exploded, and that a modern system of science had been introduced, which possessed much greater powers than the ancient, because the powers of the latter were chimerical,[7] while those of the former were real and practical; under such circumstances, I should certainly have thrown Agrippa aside, and, with my imagination warmed as it was, should probably have applied myself to the more rational theory of chemistry which has resulted from modern discoveries. It is even possible, that the train of my ideas would never have received the fatal impulse that led to my ruin. But the cursory glance my father had taken of my volume by no means assured me that he was acquainted with its contents; and I continued to read with the greatest avidity.

When I returned home, my first care was to procure the whole works of this author, and afterwards of Paracelsus and Albertus Magnus.[8] I read and studied the wild fancies of these writers with delight; they appeared to me treasures known to few beside myself; and although I often wished to communicate these secret stores of knowledge to my father, yet his indefinite censure of my favourite Agrippa[9] always withheld me. I disclosed my discoveries to Elizabeth, there-

---

5. Attendant spirit or demon. *Natural philosophy*: the study of nature, i.e., science.
6. Heinrich Cornelius Agrippa (1486–1535), German physician, author of *De Occulta Philosophia* (1531), and reputed magician.
7. Imaginary, fanciful.
8. German philosopher, theologian, and scientist (called "doctor universalis") (c. 1200–1280), who wrote on the natural sciences. *Paracelsus*: Theophrastus Bombastus von Hohenneim (c. 1490–1541), Swiss physician; author of works on chemistry, medicine, and alchemy.
9. More than Paracelsus or Albertus Magnus, Agrippa was concerned with the occult and the supernatural.

fore, under a promise of strict secrecy; but she did not interest herself in the subject, and I was left by her to pursue my studies alone.

It may appear very strange, that a disciple of Albertus Magnus should arise in the eighteenth century; but our family was not scientifical, and I had not attended any of the lectures given at the schools of Geneva. My dreams were therefore undisturbed by reality; and I entered with the greatest diligence into the search of the philosopher's stone and the elixir of life.[1] But the latter obtained my most undivided attention: wealth was an inferior object; but what glory would attend the discovery, if I could banish disease from the human frame, and render man invulnerable to any but a violent death!

Nor were these my only visions. The raising of ghosts or devils was a promise liberally accorded by my favourite authors, the fulfilment of which I most eagerly sought; and if my incantations were always unsuccessful, I attributed the failure rather to my own inexperience and mistake, than to a want of skill or fidelity in my instructors.

The natural phænomena that take place every day before our eyes did not escape my examinations. Distillation, and the wonderful effects of steam, processes of which my favourite authors were utterly ignorant, excited my astonishment; but my utmost wonder was engaged by some experiments on an airpump,[2] which I saw employed by a gentleman whom we were in the habit of visiting.

The ignorance of the early philosophers on these and several other points served to decrease their credit with me: but I could not entirely throw them aside, before some other system should occupy their place in my mind.

When I was about fifteen years old, we had retired to our house near Belrive, when we witnessed a most violent and terrible thunderstorm. It advanced from behind the mountains of Jura; and the thunder burst at once with frightful loudness from various quarters of the heavens. I remained, while the storm lasted, watching its progress with curiosity and delight. As I stood at the door, on a sudden I beheld a stream of fire issue from an old and beautiful oak, which stood about twenty yards from our house; and so soon as the dazzling light vanished, the oak had disappeared, and nothing remained but a blasted stump. When we visited it the next morning, we found the tree shattered in a singular manner. It was not splintered by the shock, but entirely reduced to thin ribbands of wood. I never beheld any thing so utterly destroyed.

---

1. Medieval alchemists sought the philosopher's stone, which would change other metals to gold or silver, and the elixir of life, which would prolong life indefinitely.
2. A machine that creates a vacuum.

The catastrophe of this tree excited my extreme astonishment; and I eagerly inquired of my father the nature and origin of thunder and lightning. He replied, "Electricity;" describing at the same time the various effects of that power. He constructed a small electrical machine, and exhibited a few experiments; he made also a kite, with a wire and string, which drew down that fluid from the clouds.[3]

This last stroke completed the overthrow of Cornelius Agrippa, Albertus Magnus, and Paracelsus, who had so long reigned the lords of my imagination. But by some fatality I did not feel inclined to commence the study of any modern system; and this disinclination was influenced by the following circumstance.

My father expressed a wish that I should attend a course of lectures upon natural philosophy, to which I cheerfully consented. Some accident prevented my attending these lectures until the course was nearly finished. The lecture, being therefore one of the last, was entirely incomprehensible to me. The professor discoursed with the greatest fluency of potassium and boron, of sulphates and oxyds, terms to which I could affix no idea; and I became disgusted with the science of natural philosophy, although I still read Pliny and Buffon[4] with delight, authors, in my estimation, of nearly equal interest and utility.

My occupations at this age were principally the mathematics, and most of the branches of study appertaining to that science. I was busily employed in learning languages; Latin was already familiar to me, and I began to read some of the easiest Greek authors without the help of a lexicon. I also perfectly understood English and German. This is the list of my accomplishments at the age of seventeen and you may conceive that my hours were fully employed in acquiring and maintaining a knowledge of this various literature.

Another task also devolved upon me, when I became the instructor of my brothers. Ernest was six years younger than myself, and was my principal pupil. He had been afflicted with ill health from his infancy, through which Elizabeth and I had been his constant nurses: his disposition was gentle, but he was incapable of any severe application. William, the youngest of our family, was yet an infant, and the most beautiful little fellow in the world, his lively blue eyes, dimpled cheeks, and endearing manners, inspired the tenderest affection.

Such was our domestic circle, from which care and pain seemed for ever banished. My father directed our studies, and my mother

---

3. An allusion to Benjamin Franklin's famous experiment; see his *Experiments and Observations on Electricity* (1751).
4. Georges Louis Leclerc, comte de Buffon (1707–1788), author of the 44-volume *Histoire Naturelle* (pub. 1749–1804). Pliny the Elder (c. 23–79), Roman author of *Historiae Naturalis* (called by the *Encyclopedia Britannica* "a storehouse of ancient errors").

partook of our enjoyments. Neither of us possessed the slightest preeminence over the other; the voice of command was never heard
amongst us; but mutual affection engaged us all to comply with and
obey the slightest desire of each other.

Chapter II.

When I had attained the age of seventeen, my parents resolved that
I should become a student at the university of Ingolstadt.[1] I had
hitherto attended the schools of Geneva; but my father thought
it necessary, for the completion of my education, that I should be
made acquainted with other customs than those of my native country. My departure was therefore fixed at an early date; but, before
the day resolved upon could arrive, the first misfortune of my life
occurred—an omen, as it were, of my future misery.

Elizabeth had caught the scarlet fever; but her illness was not
severe, and she quickly recovered. During her confinement, many
arguments had been urged to persuade my mother to refrain from
attending upon her. She had, at first, yielded to our entreaties; but
when she heard that her favourite was recovering, she could no longer debar herself from her society, and entered her chamber long
before the danger of infection was past. The consequences of this
imprudence were fatal. On the third day my mother sickened; her
fever was very malignant, and the looks of her attendants prognos-
ticated the worst event. On her death-bed the fortitude and benignity of this admirable woman did not desert her. She joined the
hands of Elizabeth and myself: "My children," she said, "my firmest
hopes of future happiness were placed on the prospect of your
union. This expectation will now be the consolation of your father.
Elizabeth, my love, you must supply my place to your younger cousins. Alas! I regret that I am taken from you; and, happy and beloved
as I have been, is it not hard to quit you all? But these are not
thoughts befitting me; I will endeavour to resign myself cheerfully
to death, and will indulge a hope of meeting you in another world."

She died calmly; and her countenance expressed affection even in
death. I need not describe the feelings of those whose dearest ties
are rent by that most irreparable evil, the void that presents itself to
the soul, and the despair that is exhibited on the countenance. It is
so long before the mind can persuade itself that she, whom we saw

1. Founded in 1472, the university in this Bavarian town was important to the Counter-
   reformation and, later, was the birthplace of the Illuminati. This secret society of
   rational freethinkers, holding deistic and republican beliefs, was founded at Ingolstadt
   in 1776 by Professor Adam Weishaupt. The sect was outlawed in 1785, and the university was moved to Landshut in 1800 and then to Munich in 1826.

every day, and whose very existence appeared a part of our own, can have departed for ever—that the brightness of a beloved eye can have been extinguished, and the sound of a voice so familiar, and dear to the ear, can be hushed, never more to be heard. These are the reflections of the first days; but when the lapse of time proves the reality of the evil, then the actual bitterness of grief commences. Yet from whom has not that rude hand rent away some dear connexion; and why should I describe a sorrow which all have felt, and must feel? The time at length arrives, when grief is rather an indulgence than a necessity; and the smile that plays upon the lips, although it may be deemed a sacrilege, is not banished. My mother was dead, but we had still duties which we ought to perform; we must continue our course with the rest, and learn to think ourselves fortunate, whilst one remains whom the spoiler has not seized.

My journey to Ingolstadt, which had been deferred by these events, was now again determined upon. I obtained from my father a respite of some weeks. This period was spent sadly; my mother's death, and my speedy departure, depressed our spirits; but Elizabeth endeavoured to renew the spirit of cheerfulness in our little society. Since the death of her aunt, her mind had acquired new firmness and vigour. She determined to fulfil her duties with the greatest exactness; and she felt that that most imperious[2] duty, of rendering her uncle and cousins happy, had devolved upon her. She consoled me, amused her uncle, instructed my brothers, and I never beheld her so enchanting as at this time, when she was continually endeavouring to contribute to the happiness of others, entirely forgetful of herself.

The day of my departure at length arrived. I had taken leave of all my friends, excepting Clerval, who spent the last evening with us. He bitterly lamented that he was unable to accompany me: but his father could not be persuaded to part with him, intending that he should become a partner with him in business, in compliance with his favourite theory, that learning was superfluous in the commerce of ordinary life. Henry had a refined mind; he had no desire to be idle, and was well pleased to become his father's partner, but he believed that a man might be a very good trader, and yet possess a cultivated understanding.

We sat late, listening to his complaints, and making many little arrangements for the future. The next morning early I departed. Tears gushed from the eyes of Elizabeth; they proceeded partly from sorrow at my departure, and partly because she reflected that the same journey was to have taken place three months before, when a mother's blessing would have accompanied me.

2. Urgent.

I threw myself into the chaise that was to convey me away, and indulged in the most melancholy reflections. I, who had ever been surrounded by amiable companions, continually engaged in endeavouring to bestow mutual pleasure, I was now alone. In the university, whither I was going, I must form my own friends, and be my own protector. My life had hitherto been remarkably secluded and domestic; and this had given me invincible repugnance to new countenances. I loved my brothers, Elizabeth, and Clerval, these were "old familiar faces;"[3] but I believed myself totally unfitted for the company of strangers. Such were my reflections as I commenced my journey; but as I proceeded, my spirits and hopes rose. I ardently desired the acquisition of knowledge. I had often, when at home, thought it hard to remain during my youth cooped up in one place, and had longed to enter the world, and take my station among other human beings. Now my desires were complied with, and it would, indeed, have been folly to repent.

I had sufficient leisure for these and many other reflections during my journey to Ingolstadt, which was long and fatiguing. At length the high white steeple of the town met my eyes. I alighted, and was conducted to my solitary apartment, to spend the evening as I pleased.

The next morning I delivered my letters of introduction, and paid a visit to some of the principal professors, and among others to M. Krempe, professor of natural philosophy. He received me with politeness, and asked me several questions concerning my progress in the different branches of science appertaining to natural philosophy. I mentioned, it is true, with fear and trembling, the only authors I had ever read upon those subjects. The professor stared: "Have you," he said, "really spent your time in studying such nonsense?"

I replied in the affirmative. "Every minute," continued M. Krempe with warmth, "every instant that you have wasted on those books is utterly and entirely lost. You have burdened your memory with exploded systems, and useless names. Good God! in what desert land have you lived, where no one was kind enough to inform you that these fancies, which you have so greedily imbibed, are a thousand years old, and as musty as they are ancient? I little expected in this enlightened and scientific age to find a disciple of Albertus Magnus and Paracelsus. My dear Sir, you must begin your studies entirely anew."

So saying, he stept aside, and wrote down a list of several books treating of natural philosophy, which he desired me to procure, and dismissed me, after mentioning that in the beginning of the following

3. The title of a 1798 poem by the English writer Charles Lamb (1775–1834). See p. 306.

week he intended to commence a course of lectures upon natural philosophy in its general relations, and that M. Waldman, a fellow-professor, would lecture upon chemistry the alternate days that he missed.

I returned home, not disappointed, for I had long considered those authors useless whom the professor had so strongly reprobated; but I did not feel much inclined to study the books which I procured at his recommendation. M. Krempe was a little squat man, with a gruff voice and repulsive countenance; the teacher, therefore, did not pre-possess me in favour of his doctrine. Besides, I had a contempt for the uses of modern natural philosophy. It was very different, when the masters of the science sought immortality and power; such views, although futile, were grand: but now the scene was changed. The ambition of the inquirer seemed to limit itself to the annihilation of those visions on which my interest in science was chiefly founded. I was required to exchange chimeras of boundless grandeur for reali-ties of little worth.

Such were my reflections during the first two or three days spent almost in solitude. But as the ensuing week commenced, I thought of the information which M. Krempe had given me concerning the lectures. And although I could not consent to go and hear that little conceited fellow deliver sentences[4] out of a pulpit, I recollected what he had said of M. Waldman, whom I had never seen, as he had hith-erto been out of town.

Partly from curiosity, and partly, from idleness, I went into the lecturing room, which M. Waldman entered shortly after. This pro-fessor was very unlike his colleague. He appeared about fifty years of age, but with an aspect expressive of the greatest benevolence; a few gray hairs covered his temples, but those at the back of his head were nearly black. His person was short, but remarkably erect; and his voice the sweetest I had ever heard. He began his lecture by a recapitulation of the history of chemistry and the various improve-ments made by different men of learning, pronouncing with fer-vour the names of the most distinguished discoverers. He then took a cursory view of the present state of the science, and explained many of its elementary terms. After having made a few preparatory experiments, he concluded with a panegyric upon modern chemis-try, the terms of which I shall never forget:—

"The ancient teachers of this science," said he, "promised impos-sibilities, and performed nothing. The modern masters promise very little; they know that metals cannot be transmuted, and that the elixir of life is a chimera. But these philosophers, whose hands seem only made to dabble in dirt, and their eyes to pour over the microscope or

4. Pronouncements.

crucible, have indeed performed miracles. They penetrate into the recesses of nature, and shew how she works in her hiding places. They ascend into the heavens; they have discovered how the blood circulates, and the nature of the air we breathe.[5] They have acquired new and almost unlimited powers; they can command the thunders of heaven, mimic the earthquake, and even mock the invisible world with its own shadows."

I departed highly pleased with the professor and his lecture, and paid him a visit the same evening. His manners in private were even more mild and attractive than in public; for there was a certain dignity in his mien during his lecture, which in his own house was replaced by the greatest affability and kindness. He heard with attention my little narration concerning my studies, and smiled at the names of Cornelius Agrippa and Paracelsus, but without the contempt that M. Krempe had exhibited. He said, that "these were men to whose indefatigable zeal modern philosophers were indebted for most of the foundations of their knowledge. They had left to us, as an easier task, to give new names, and arrange in connected classifications, the facts which they in a great degree had been the instruments of bringing to light. The labours of men of genius, however erroneously directed, scarcely ever fail in ultimately turning to the solid advantage of mankind." I listened to his statement, which was delivered without any presumption or affectation; and then added, that his lecture had removed my prejudices against modern chemists; and I, at the same time, requested his advice concerning the books I ought to procure.

"I am happy," said M. Waldman, "to have gained a disciple; and if your application equals your ability, I have no doubt of your success. Chemistry is that branch of natural philosophy in which the greatest improvements have been and may be made; it is on that account that I have made it my peculiar[6] study, but at the same time I have not neglected the other branches of science.[7] A man would make but a very sorry chemist, if he attended to that department of human knowledge alone. If your wish is to become really a man of science, and not merely a petty experimentalist, I should advise you to apply to every branch of natural philosophy, including mathematics."

He then took me into his laboratory, and explained to me the uses of his various machines; instructing me as to what I ought to procure, and promising me the use of his own, when I should have advanced far enough in the science not to derange their mechanism.

5. William Harvey (1578–1657) discovered the circulation of the blood in 1628. Robert Boyle (1627–1691) performed a series of experiments on the properties of air. His *The Sceptical Chymist* (1661) attacked the scientific theories of Aristotle and Paracelsus.
6. Personal, particular.
7. Science was at the time a more general term meaning learning and knowledge.

He also gave me the list of books which I had requested; and I took my leave.

Thus ended a day memorable to me; it decided my future destiny.

Chapter III.

From this day natural philosophy, and particularly chemistry, in the most comprehensive sense of the term, became nearly my sole occupation. I read with ardour those works, so full of genius and discrimination, which modern inquirers have written on these subjects. I attended the lectures, and cultivated the acquaintance, of the men of science of the university; and I found even in M. Krempe a great deal of sound sense and real information, combined, it is true, with a repulsive physiognomy and manners, but not on that account the less valuable. In M. Waldman I found a true friend. His gentleness was never tinged by dogmatism; and his instructions were given with an air of frankness and good nature, that banished every idea of pedantry. It was, perhaps, the amiable character of this man that inclined me more to that branch of natural philosophy which he professed, than an intrinsic love for the science itself. But this state of mind had place only in the first steps towards knowledge: the more fully I entered into the science, the more exclusively I pursued it for its own sake. That application, which at first had been a matter of duty and resolution, now became so ardent and eager, that the stars often disappeared in the light of morning whilst I was yet engaged in my laboratory.

As I applied so closely,[1] it may be easily conceived that I improved rapidly. My ardour was indeed the astonishment of the students; and my proficiency, that of the masters. Professor Krempe often asked me, with a sly smile, how Cornelius Agrippa went on? whilst M. Waldman expressed the most heartfelt exultation in my progress. Two years passed in this manner, during which I paid no visit to Geneva, but was engaged, heart and soul, in the pursuit of some discoveries, which I hoped to make. None but those who have experienced them can conceive of the enticements of science. In other studies you go as far as others have gone before you, and there is nothing more to know; but in a scientific pursuit there is continual food for discovery and wonder. A mind of moderate capacity, which closely pursues one study, must infallibly arrive at great proficiency in that study; and I, who continually sought the attainment of one object of pursuit, and was solely wrapt up in this, improved so rap-

---

1. Worked with such devotion.

idly, that, at the end of two years, I made some discoveries in the improvement of some chemical instruments, which procured me great esteem and admiration at the university. When I had arrived at this point, and had become as well acquainted with the theory and practice of natural philosophy as depended on the lessons of any of the professors at Ingolstadt, my residence there being no longer conducive to my improvements, I thought of returning to my friends and my native town, when an incident happened that protracted my stay.

One of the phænonema which had peculiarly attracted my attention was the structure of the human frame, and, indeed, any animal endued with life. Whence, I often asked myself, did the principle[2] of life proceed? It was a bold question, and one which has ever been considered as a mystery; yet with how many things are we upon the brink of becoming acquainted, if cowardice or carelessness did not restrain our inquiries. I revolved these circumstances in my mind, and determined thenceforth to apply myself more particularly to those branches of natural philosophy which relate to physiology.[3] Unless I had been animated by an almost supernatural enthusiasm, my application to this study would have been irksome, and almost intolerable. To examine the causes of life, we must first have recourse to death. I became acquainted with the science of anatomy: but this was not sufficient; I must also observe the natural decay and corruption of the human body. In my education my father had taken the greatest precautions that my mind should be impressed with no supernatural horrors. I do not ever remember to have trembled at a tale of superstition, or to have feared the apparition of a spirit. Darkness had no effect upon my fancy; and a church-yard was to me merely the receptacle of bodies deprived of life, which, from being the seat of beauty and strength, had become food for the worm. Now I was led to examine the cause and progress of this decay, and forced to spend days and nights in vaults and charnel houses.[4] My attention was fixed upon every object the most insupportable to the delicacy of the human feelings. I saw how the fine form of man was degraded and wasted; I beheld the corruption of death succeed to the blooming cheek of life; I saw how the worm inherited the wonders of the eye and brain. I paused, examining and analysing all the minutiæ of causation, as exemplified in the change from life to death, and death to life, until from the midst of this darkness a sudden light broke in upon me—a light so brilliant and wondrous, yet so simple, that while I became dizzy with the immensity of the prospect which it illustrated, I was surprised that among so many men of genius, who had

---

2. Origin, source.
3. The science of living things.
4. Houses for dead bodies.

directed their inquiries towards the same science, that I alone should be reserved to discover so astonishing a secret.

Remember, I am not recording the vision of a madman. The sun does not more certainly shine in the heavens, than that which I now affirm is true. Some miracle might have produced it, yet the stages of the discovery were distinct and probable. After days and nights of incredible labour and fatigue, I succeeded in discovering the cause of generation and life; nay, more, I became myself capable of bestowing animation upon lifeless matter.

The astonishment which I had at first experienced on this discovery soon gave place to delight and rapture. After so much time spent in painful labour, to arrive at once at the summit of my desires, was the most gratifying consummation of my toils. But this discovery was so great and overwhelming, that all the steps by which I had been progressively led to it were obliterated, and I beheld only the result. What had been the study and desire of the wisest men since the creation of the world, was now within my grasp. Not that, like a magic scene, it all opened upon me at once: the information I had obtained was of a nature rather to direct my endeavours so soon as I should point them towards the object of my search, than to exhibit that object already accomplished. I was like the Arabian who had been buried with the dead, and found a passage to life aided only by one glimmering, and seemingly ineffectual, light.[5]

I see by your eagerness, and the wonder and hope which your eyes express, my friend, that you expect to be informed of the secret with which I am acquainted; that cannot be: listen patiently until the end of my story, and you will easily perceive why I am reserved upon that subject. I will not lead you on, unguarded and ardent as I then was, to your destruction and infallible misery. Learn from me, if not by my precepts, at least by my example, how dangerous is the acquirement of knowledge, and how much happier that man is who believes his native town to be the world, than he who aspires to become greater than his nature will allow.

When I found so astonishing a power placed within my hands, I hesitated a long time concerning the manner in which I should employ it. Although I possessed the capacity of bestowing animation, yet to prepare a frame for the reception of it, with all its intricacies of fibres, muscles, and veins, still remained a work of inconceivable difficulty and labour. I doubted at first whether I should attempt the creation of a being like myself or one of simpler organization; but my imagination was too much exalted by my first success to permit me to

5. Sinbad is buried alive with the corpse of his wife; he perceives and follows a distant light, which turns out to be a small passage through which he escapes (see "Sinbad's Fourth Voyage," *One Thousand Nights and One Night*).

doubt of my ability to give life to an animal as complex and wonderful as man. The materials at present within my command hardly appeared adequate to so arduous an undertaking; but I doubted not that I should ultimately succeed. I prepared myself for a multitude of reverses; my operations might be incessantly baffled, and at last my work be imperfect: yet, when I considered the improvement which every day takes place in science and mechanics, I was encouraged to hope my present attempts would at least lay the foundations of future success. Nor could I consider the magnitude and complexity of my plan as any argument of its impracticability. It was with these feelings that I began the creation of a human being. As the minuteness of the parts formed a great hindrance to my speed, I resolved, contrary to my first intention, to make the being of a gigantic stature; that is to say, about eight feet in height, and proportionably large. After having formed this determination, and having spent some months in successfully collecting and arranging my materials, I began.

No one can conceive the variety of feelings which bore me onwards, like a hurricane, in the first enthusiasm of success. Life and death appeared to me ideal bounds,[6] which I should first break through, and pour a torrent of light into our dark world. A new species would bless me as its creator and source; many happy and excellent natures would owe their being to me. No father could claim the gratitude of his child so completely as I should deserve their's. Pursuing these reflections, I thought, that if I could bestow animation upon lifeless matter, I might in process of time (although I now found it impossible) renew life where death had apparently devoted the body to corruption.

These thoughts supported my spirits, while I pursued my undertaking with unremitting ardour. My cheek had grown pale with study, and my person had become emaciated with confinement. Sometimes, on the very brink of certainty, I failed; yet still I clung to the hope which the next day or the next hour might realize. One secret which I alone possessed was the hope to which I had dedicated myself, and the moon gazed on my midnight labours, while, with unrelaxed and breathless eagerness, I pursued nature to her hiding places. Who shall conceive the horrors of my secret toil, as I dabbled among the unhallowed damps of the grave, or tortured the living animal to animate the lifeless clay? My limbs now tremble, and my eyes swim with the remembrance; but then a resistless, and almost frantic impulse, urged me forward; I seemed to have lost all soul or sensation but for this one pursuit. It was indeed but a passing trance, that only made me feel with renewed acuteness so

6. Imaginary boundaries.

soon as, the unnatural stimulus ceasing to operate, I had returned to my old habits. I collected bones from charnel houses; and disturbed, with profane fingers, the tremendous secrets of the human frame. In a solitary chamber, or rather cell, at the top of the house, and separated from all the other apartments by a gallery and staircase, I kept my workshop of filthy creation; my eyeballs were starting from their sockets in attending to the details of my employment. The dissecting room and the slaughter-house furnished many of my materials; and often did my human nature turn with loathing from my occupation, whilst, still urged on by an eagerness which perpetually increased, I brought my work near to a conclusion.

The summer months passed while I was thus engaged, heart and soul, in one pursuit. It was a most beautiful season; never did the fields bestow a more plentiful harvest, or the vines yield a more luxuriant vintage: but my eyes were insensible to the charms of nature. And the same feelings which made me neglect the scenes around me caused me also to forget those friends who were so many miles absent, and whom I had not seen for so long a time. I knew my silence disquieted them; and I well remembered the words of my father: "I know that while you are pleased with yourself, you will think of us with affection, and we shall hear regularly from you. You must pardon me, if I regard any interruption in your correspondence as a proof that your other duties are equally neglected."

I knew well therefore what would be my father's feelings; but I could not tear my thoughts from my employment, loathsome in itself, but which had taken an irresistible hold of my imagination. I wished, as it were, to procrastinate all that related to my feelings of affection until the great object, which swallowed up every habit of my nature, should be completed.

I then thought that my father would be unjust if he ascribed my neglect to vice, or faultiness on my part; but I am now convinced that he was justified in conceiving that I should not be altogether free from blame. A human being in perfection ought always to preserve a calm and peaceful mind, and never to allow passion or a transitory desire to disturb his tranquillity. I do not think that the pursuit of knowledge is an exception to this rule. If the study to which you apply yourself has a tendency to weaken your affections, and to destroy your taste for those simple pleasures in which no alloy can possibly mix, then that study is certainly unlawful, that is to say, not befitting the human mind. If this rule were always observed; if no man allowed any pursuit whatsoever to interfere with the tranquillity of his domestic affections, Greece had not been enslaved; Cæsar would have spared his country; America would have been discovered more gradually; and the empires of Mexico and Peru had not been destroyed.

But I forget that I am moralizing in the most interesting part of my tale; and your looks remind me to proceed.

My father made no reproach in his letters; and only took notice of my silence by inquiring into my occupations more particularly than before. Winter, spring, and summer, passed away during my labours; but I did not watch the blossom or the expanding leaves—sights which before always yielded me supreme delight, so deeply was I engrossed in my occupation. The leaves of that year had withered before my work drew near to a close; and now every day shewed me more plainly how well I had succeeded. But my enthusiasm was checked by my anxiety, and I appeared rather like one doomed by slavery to toil in the mines, or any other unwholesome trade, than an artist occupied by his favourite employment. Every night I was oppressed by a slow fever, and I became nervous to a most painful degree; a disease that I regretted the more because I had hitherto enjoyed most excellent health, and had always boasted of the firmness of my nerves. But I believed that exercise and amusement would soon drive away such symptoms; and I promised myself both of these, when my creation should be complete.

Chapter IV.

It was on a dreary night of November, that I beheld the accomplishment of my toils. With an anxiety that almost amounted to agony, I collected the instruments of life around me, that I might infuse a spark of being into the lifeless thing that lay at my feet. It was already one in the morning; the rain pattered dismally against the panes, and my candle was nearly burnt out, when, by the glimmer of the half-extinguished light, I saw the dull yellow eye of the creature open; it breathed hard, and a convulsive motion agitated its limbs.

How can I describe my emotions at this catastrophe, or how delineate the wretch whom with such infinite pains and care I had endeavoured to form? His limbs were in proportion, and I had selected his features as beautiful. Beautiful!—Great God! His yellow skin scarcely covered the work of muscles and arteries beneath; his hair was of a lustrous black, and flowing; his teeth of a pearly whiteness; but these luxuriances only formed a more horrid contrast with his watery eyes, that seemed almost of the same colour as the dun white sockets in which they were set, his shrivelled complexion, and straight black lips.

The different accidents of life are not so changeable as the feelings of human nature. I had worked hard for nearly two years, for the sole purpose of infusing life into an inanimate body. For this

I had deprived myself of rest and health. I had desired it with an ardour that far exceeded moderation; but now that I had finished, the beauty of the dream vanished, and breathless horror and disgust filled my heart. Unable to endure the aspect[1] of the being I had created, I rushed out of the room, and continued a long time traversing my bed-chamber, unable to compose my mind to sleep. At length lassitude succeeded to the tumult I had before endured; and I threw myself on the bed in my clothes, endeavouring to seek a few moments of forgetfulness. But it was in vain: I slept indeed, but I was disturbed by the wildest dreams. I thought I saw Elizabeth, in the bloom of health, walking in the streets of Ingolstadt. Delighted and surprised, I embraced her; but as I imprinted the first kiss on her lips, they became livid with the hue of death; her features appeared to change, and I thought that I held the corpse of my dead mother in my arms; a shroud enveloped her form, and I saw the grave-worms crawling in the folds of the flannel. I started from my sleep with horror; a cold dew covered my forehead, my teeth chattered, and every limb became convulsed; when, by the dim and yellow light of the moon, as it forced its way through the window-shutters, I beheld the wretch—the miserable monster whom I had created. He held up the curtain of the bed; and his eyes, if eyes they may be called, were fixed on me. His jaws opened, and he muttered some inarticulate sounds, while a grin wrinkled his cheeks. He might have spoken, but I did not hear; one hand was stretched out, seemingly to detain me, but I escaped, and rushed down stairs. I took refuge in the court-yard belonging to the house which I inhabited; where I remained during the rest of the night, walking up and down in the greatest agitation, listening attentively, catching and fearing each sound as if it were to announce the approach of the demoniacal corpse to which I had so miserably given life.

Oh! no mortal could support the horror of that countenance. A mummy again endued with animation could not be so hideous as that wretch. I had gazed on him while unfinished; he was ugly then; but when those muscles and joints were rendered capable of motion, it became a thing such as even Dante[2] could not have conceived.

I passed the night wretchedly. Sometimes my pulse beat so quickly and hardly, that I felt the palpitation of every artery; at others, I nearly sank to the ground through languor and extreme weakness. Mingled with this horror, I felt the bitterness of disappointment: dreams that had been my food and pleasant rest for so long a space,

---

1. Appearance.
2. Dante Alighieri (1265–1321), Italian poet; *The Inferno*, the first book of his *Divine Comedy*, is a guided tour of Hell.

were now become a hell to me; and the change was so rapid, the overthrow so complete!

Morning, dismal and wet, at length dawned, and discovered to my sleepless and aching eyes the church of Ingolstadt, its white steeple and clock, which indicated the sixth hour. The porter opened the gates of the court, which had that night been my asylum, and I issued into the streets, pacing them with quick steps, as if I sought to avoid the wretch whom I feared every turning of the street would present to my view. I did not dare return to the apartment which I inhabited, but felt impelled to hurry on, although wetted by the rain, which poured from a black and comfortless sky.

I continued walking in this manner for some time, endeavouring, by bodily exercise, to ease the load that weighed upon my mind. I traversed the streets, without any clear conception of where I was, or what I was doing. My heart palpitated in the sickness of fear; and I hurried on with irregular steps, not daring to look about me:

> Like one who, on a lonely road,
>   Doth walk in fear and dread,
> And, having once turn'd round, walks on,
>   And turns no more his head;
> Because he knows a frightful fiend
>   Doth close behind him tread.[3]

Continuing thus, I came at length opposite to the inn at which the various diligences[4] and carriages usually stopped. Here I paused, I knew not why; but I remained some minutes with my eyes fixed on a coach that was coming towards me from the other end of the street. As it drew nearer, I observed that it was the Swiss diligence: it stopped just where I was standing; and, on the door being opened, I perceived Henry Clerval, who, on seeing me, instantly sprung out. "My dear Frankenstein," exclaimed he, "how glad I am to see you! how fortunate that you should be here at the very moment of my alighting!"

Nothing could equal my delight on seeing Clerval; his presence brought back to my thoughts my father, Elizabeth, and all those scenes of home so dear to my recollection. I grasped his hand, and in a moment forgot my horror and misfortune; I felt suddenly, and for the first time during many months calm and serene joy. I welcomed my friend, therefore, in the most cordial manner, and we walked towards my college. Clerval continued talking for some time about our mutual friends, and his own good fortune in being

---

3. Coleridge's "Ancient Mariner" [Mary Shelley's note], lines 446–51. See n. 7, p. 12, above.
4. Public stagecoaches.

permitted to come to Ingolstadt. "You may easily believe," said he, "how great was the difficulty to persuade my father that it was not absolutely necessary for a merchant not to understand any thing except book-keeping; and, indeed, I believe I left him incredulous to the last, for his constant answer to my unwearied entreaties was the same as that of the Dutch schoolmaster in the Vicar of Wakefield: 'I have ten thousand florins a year without Greek, I eat heartily without Greek.'[5] But his affection for me at length overcame his dislike of learning, and he has permitted me to undertake a voyage of discovery to the land of knowledge."

"It gives me the greatest delight to see you; but tell me how you left my father, brothers, and Elizabeth."

"Very well, and very happy, only a little uneasy that they hear from you so seldom. By the bye, I mean to lecture you a little upon their account myself.—But, my dear Frankenstein," continued he, stopping short, and gazing full in my face, "I did not before remark how very ill you appear; so thin and pale; you look as if you had been watching for several nights."

"You have guessed right; I have lately been so deeply engaged in one occupation, that I have not allowed myself sufficient rest, as you see: but I hope, I sincerely hope, that all these employments are now at an end, and that I am at length free."

I trembled excessively; I could not endure to think of, and far less to allude to the occurrences of the preceding night. I walked with a quick pace, and we soon arrived at my college. I then reflected, and the thought made me shiver, that the creature whom I had left in my apartment might still be there, alive, and walking about. I dreaded to behold this monster; but I feared still more that Henry should see him. Entreating him therefore to remain a few minutes at the bottom of the stairs, I darted up towards my own room. My hand was already on the lock of the door before I recollected myself. I then paused; and a cold shivering came over me. I threw the door forcibly open, as children are accustomed to do when they expect a spectre to stand in waiting for them on the other side; but nothing appeared. I stepped fearfully in: the apartment was empty; and my bedroom was also freed from its hideous guest. I could hardly believe that so great a good-fortune could have befallen me; but when I became assured that my enemy had indeed fled, I clapped my hands for joy, and ran down to Clerval.

We ascended into my room, and the servant presently brought breakfast; but I was unable to contain myself. It was not joy only that

5. From chapter 20 of *The Vicar of Wakefield* (1766), a novel by Oliver Goldsmith (1730–1774).

possessed me; I felt my flesh tingle with excess of sensitiveness, and my pulse beat rapidly. I was unable to remain for a single instant in the same place; I jumped over the chairs, clapped my hands, and laughed aloud. Clerval at first attributed my unusual spirits to joy on his arrival; but when he observed me more attentively, he saw a wildness in my eyes for which he could not account; and my loud, unrestrained, heartless laughter, frightened and astonished him.

"My dear Victor," cried he, "what, for God's sake, is the matter? Do not laugh in that manner. How ill you are! What is the cause of all this?"

"Do not ask me," cried I, putting my hands before my eyes, for I thought I saw the dreaded spectre glide into the room; "*he* can tell.—Oh, save me! save me!" I imagined that the monster seized me; I struggled furiously, and fell down in a fit.

Poor Clerval! what must have been his feelings? A meeting, which he anticipated with such joy, so strangely turned to bitterness. But I was not the witness of his grief; for I was lifeless, and did not recover my senses for a long, long time.

This was the commencement of a nervous fever, which confined me for several months. During all that time Henry was my only nurse. I afterwards learned that, knowing my father's advanced age, and unfitness for so long a journey, and how wretched my sickness would make Elizabeth, he spared them this grief by concealing the extent of my disorder. He knew that I could not have a more kind and attentive nurse than himself; and, firm in the hope he felt of my recovery, he did not doubt that, instead of doing harm, he performed the kindest action that he could towards them.

But I was in reality very ill; and surely nothing but the unbounded and unremitting attentions of my friend could have restored me to life. The form of the monster on whom I had bestowed existence was for ever before my eyes, and I raved incessantly concerning him. Doubtless my words surprised Henry: he at first believed them to be the wanderings of my disturbed imagination; but the pertinacity with which I continually recurred to the same subject persuaded him that my disorder indeed owed its origin to some uncommon and terrible event.

By very slow degrees, and with frequent relapses, that alarmed and grieved my friend, I recovered. I remember the first time I became capable of observing outward objects with any kind of pleasure, I perceived that the fallen leaves had disappeared, and that the young buds were shooting forth from the trees that shaded my window. It was a divine spring; and the season contributed greatly to my convalescence. I felt also sentiments of joy and affection revive in my bosom; my gloom disappeared, and in a short time I became as cheerful as before I was attacked by the fatal passion.

"Dearest Clerval," exclaimed I, "how kind, how very good you are to me. This whole winter, instead of being spent in study, as you promised yourself, has been consumed in my sick room. How shall I ever repay you? I feel the greatest remorse for the disappointment of which I have been the occasion; but you will forgive me."

"You will repay me entirely, if you do not discompose yourself, but get well as fast as you can; and since you appear in such good spirits, I may speak to you on one subject, may I not?"

I trembled. One subject! what could it be? Could he allude to an object on whom I dared not even think?

"Compose yourself," said Clerval, who observed my change of colour, "I will not mention it, if it agitates you; but your father and cousin would be very happy if they received a letter from you in your own hand-writing. They hardly know how ill you have been, and are uneasy at your long silence."

"Is that all? my dear Henry. How could you suppose that my first thought would not fly towards those dear, dear friends whom I love, and who are so deserving of my love?"

"If this is your present temper, my friend, you will perhaps be glad to see a letter that has been lying here some days for you: it is from your cousin, I believe."

Chapter V.

Clerval then put the following letter into my hands.

"*To* V. FRANKENSTEIN.

"MY DEAR COUSIN,

"I cannot describe to you the uneasiness we have all felt concerning your health. We cannot help imagining that your friend Clerval conceals the extent of your disorder: for it is now several months since we have seen your hand-writing; and all this time you have been obliged to dictate your letters to Henry. Surely, Victor, you must have been exceedingly ill; and this makes us all very wretched, as much so nearly as after the death of your dear mother. My uncle was almost persuaded that you were indeed dangerously ill, and could hardly be restrained from undertaking a journey to Ingolstadt. Clerval always writes that you are getting better; I eagerly hope that you will confirm this intelligence soon in your own hand-writing; for indeed, indeed, Victor, we are all very miserable on this account. Relieve us from this fear, and we shall be the happiest creatures in the world. Your father's health is now so vigorous, that he appears ten years younger since last winter. Ernest also is so much improved, that you would hardly know him: he is now nearly sixteen, and has lost that sickly appearance which he had some years ago; he is grown quite robust and active.

"My uncle and I conversed a long time last night about what profession Ernest should follow. His constant illness when young has deprived him of the habits of application; and now that he enjoys good health, he is continually in the open air, climbing the hills, or rowing on the lake. I therefore proposed that he should be a farmer; which you know, Cousin, is a favourite scheme of mine. A farmer's is a very healthy happy life; and the least hurtful, or rather the most beneficial profession of any. My uncle had an idea of his being educated as an advocate, that through his interest he might become a judge. But, besides that he is not at all fitted for such an occupation, it is certainly more creditable to cultivate the earth for the sustenance of man, than to be the confidant, and sometimes the accomplice, of his vices; which is the profession of a lawyer. I said, that the employments of a prosperous farmer, if they were not a more honourable, they were at least a happier species of occupation than that of a judge, whose misfortune it was always to meddle with the dark side of human nature. My uncle smiled, and said, that I ought to be an advocate myself, which put an end to the conversation on that subject.

"And now I must tell you a little story that will please, and perhaps amuse you. Do you not remember Justine Moritz? Probably you do not; I will relate her history, therefore, in a few words. Madame Moritz, her mother, was a widow with four children, of whom Justine was the third. This girl had always been the favourite of her father; but, through a strange perversity, her mother could not endure her, and, after the death of M. Moritz, treated her very ill. My aunt observed this; and, when Justine was twelve years of age, prevailed on her mother to allow her to live at her house. The republican institutions of our country have produced simpler and happier manners than those which prevail in the great monarchies that surround it. Hence there is less distinction between the several classes of its inhabitants; and the lower orders being neither so poor nor so despised, their manners are more refined and moral. A servant in Geneva does not mean the same thing as a servant in France and England. Justine, thus received in our family, learned the duties of a servant; a condition which, in our fortunate country, does not include the idea of ignorance, and a sacrifice of the dignity of a human being.

"After what I have said, I dare say you well remember the heroine of my little tale: for Justine was a great favourite of your's; and I recollect you once remarked, that if you were in an ill humour, one glance from Justine could dissipate it, for the same reason that Ariosto gives concerning the beauty of Angelica—she looked so frank-hearted and happy.[1] My aunt conceived a great attachment for her, by which she was induced to give her an education superior to that which she had at first intended. This benefit was fully repaid; Justine was the most grateful little creature in the world: I do not mean that she made any professions,[2] I never heard one pass her lips; but you could see by her eyes that she almost adored her protectress. Although her disposition was gay, and in many respects inconsiderate, yet she paid the greatest attention to every gesture of my aunt. She thought her the model of all excellence, and endeavoured to imitate her phraseology and manners, so that even now she often reminds me of her.

"When my dearest aunt died, every one was too much occupied in their own grief to notice poor Justine, who had attended her during her illness with the most anxious affection. Poor Justine was very ill; but other trials were reserved for her.

"One by one, her brothers and sister died; and her mother, with the exception of her neglected daughter, was left childless. The conscience of the woman was troubled; she began to think that the deaths of her favourites was a judgment from heaven to chastise her partiality. She was a Roman Catholic; and I believe her confessor confirmed the idea which she had conceived. Accordingly, a few months after your departure for Ingoldstadt, Justine was called home by her repentant mother. Poor girl! she wept when she quitted our house: she was much altered since the death of my aunt; grief had given softness and a winning mildness to her manners, which had before been remarkable for vivacity. Nor was her residence at her mother's house of a nature to restore her gaiety. The poor woman was very vacillating in her repentance. She sometimes begged Justine to forgive her unkindness, but much oftener accused her of having caused the deaths of her brothers and sister. Perpetual fretting at length threw Madame Moritz into a decline, which at first increased her irritability, but she is now at peace for ever. She died on the first approach of cold weather, at the beginning of this last winter. Justine has returned to us; and I assure you I love her tenderly. She is very clever and gentle, and extremely pretty; as I mentioned before, her mien and her expressions continually remind me of my dear aunt.

"I must say also a few words to you, my dear cousin, of little darling William. I wish you could see him; he is very tall of his age, with sweet laughing blue eyes, dark eye-lashes, and curling

1. Angelica is the heroine of *Orlando Furioso* (see n. 4, p. 21, above).
2. Declarations, avowals.

hair. When he smiles, two little dimples appear on each cheek, which are rosy with health. He has already had one or two little *wives*, but Louisa Biron is his favourite, a pretty little girl of five years of age.

"Now, dear Victor, I dare say you wish to be indulged in a little gossip concerning the good people of Geneva. The pretty Miss Mansfield has already received the congratulatory visits on her approaching marriage with a young Englishman, John Melbourne, Esq. Her ugly sister, Manon, married M. Duvillard, the rich banker, last autumn. Your favourite schoolfellow, Louis Manoir, has suffered several misfortunes since the departure of Clerval from Geneva. But he has already recovered his spirits, and is reported to be on the point of marrying a very lively pretty French-woman, Madame Tavernier. She is a widow, and much older than Manoir; but she is very much admired, and a favourite with every body.

"I have written myself into good spirits, dear cousin; yet I cannot conclude without again anxiously inquiring concerning your health. Dear Victor, if you are not very ill, write yourself, and make your father and all of us happy; or——I cannot bear to think of the other side of the question; my tears already flow. Adieu, my dearest cousin.

"ELIZABETH LAVENZA.

"Geneva, March 18th, 17——."

"Dear, dear Elizabeth!" I exclaimed when I had read her letter, "I will write instantly, and relieve them from the anxiety they must feel." I wrote, and this exertion greatly fatigued me; but my convalescence had commenced, and proceeded regularly. In another fortnight I was able to leave my chamber.

One of my first duties on my recovery was to introduce Clerval to the several professors of the university. In doing this, I underwent a kind of rough usage, ill befitting the wounds that my mind had sustained. Ever since the fatal night, the end of my labours, and the beginning of my misfortunes, I had conceived a violent antipathy even to the name of natural philosophy. When I was otherwise quite restored to health, the sight of a chemical instrument would renew all the agony of my nervous symptoms. Henry saw this, and had removed all my apparatus from my view. He had also changed my apartment; for he perceived that I had acquired a dislike for the room which had previously been my laboratory. But these cares of Clerval were made of no avail when I visited the professors. M. Waldman inflicted torture when he praised, with kindness and warmth, the astonishing progress I had made in the sciences. He soon perceived that I disliked the subject; but, not guessing the real cause, he attributed my feelings to modesty, and changed the subject from my improvement to the science itself, with a desire, as I evidently saw, of drawing me out. What could I do? He meant to please, and he tormented me. I felt as if he had placed carefully, one by one, in my view those instruments which were to be afterwards used in putting me to a slow and cruel death. I writhed under his words, yet dared not exhibit the pain I felt. Clerval, whose eyes and feelings were always quick in discerning the sensations of others, declined the subject, alleging, in excuse, his total ignorance; and the conversation took a more general turn. I thanked my friend from my heart, but I did not speak. I saw plainly that he was surprised, but he never attempted to draw my secret from me; and although I loved him with a mixture of affection and reverence that knew no bounds, yet I could never persuade myself to confide to him that event which was so often present to my recollection, but which I feared the detail to another would only impress more deeply.

M. Krempe was not equally docile; and in my condition at that time, of almost insupportable sensitiveness, his harsh blunt encomiums gave me even more pain than the benevolent approbation of M. Waldman. "D—n the fellow!" cried he; "why, M. Clerval, I assure you he has outstript us all. Aye, stare if you please; but it is nevertheless true. A youngster who, but a few years ago, believed Cornelius Agrippa as firmly as the gospel, has now set himself at the head of the university; and if he is not soon pulled down,[3] we shall all be out of countenance.—Aye, aye," continued he, observing my face expressive of suffering, "M. Frankenstein is modest; an excellent quality in a young man. Young men should be diffident of themselves, you know, M. Clerval; I was myself when young: but that wears out in a very short time."

M. Krempe had now commenced an eulogy on himself, which happily turned the conversation from a subject that was so annoying to me.

Clerval was no natural philosopher. His imagination was too vivid for the minutiæ of science. Languages were his principal study; and he sought, by acquiring their elements, to open a field for self-instruction on his return to Geneva. Persian, Arabic, and Hebrew, gained his attention, after he had made himself perfectly master of Greek and Latin. For my own part, idleness had ever been irksome to me; and now that I wished to fly from reflection, and hated my former studies, I felt great relief in being the fellow-pupil with my friend, and found not only instruction but consolation in the works of the orientalists. Their melancholy is soothing, and their joy elevating to a degree I never experienced in studying the authors of any other country. When you read their writings, life appears to consist

3. Deposed, dethroned.

in a warm sun and garden of roses,—in the smiles and frowns of a fair enemy, and the fire that consumes your own heart. How different from the manly and heroical poetry of Greece and Rome.

Summer passed away in these occupations, and my return to Geneva was fixed for the latter end of autumn; but being delayed by several accidents, winter and snow arrived, the roads were deemed impassable, and my journey was retarded until the ensuing spring. I felt this delay very bitterly; for I longed to see my native town, and my beloved friends. My return had only been delayed so long from an unwillingness to leave Clerval in a strange place, before he had become acquainted with any of its inhabitants. The winter, however, was spent cheerfully; and although the spring was uncommonly late, when it came, its beauty compensated for its dilatoriness.

The month of May had already commenced, and I expected the letter daily which was to fix the date of my departure, when Henry proposed a pedestrian tour in the environs of Ingoldstadt that I might bid a personal farewell to the country I had so long inhabited. I acceded with pleasure to this proposition: I was fond of exercise, and Clerval had always been my favourite companion in the rambles of this nature that I had taken among the scenes of my native country.

We passed a fortnight in these perambulations: my health and spirits had long been restored, and they gained additional strength from the salubrious air I breathed, the natural incidents of our progress, and the conversation of my friend. Study had before secluded me from the intercourse of my fellow-creatures, and rendered me unsocial; but Clerval called forth the better feelings of my heart; he again taught me to love the aspect of nature, and the cheerful faces of children. Excellent friend! how sincerely did you love me, and endeavour to elevate my mind, until it was on a level with your own. A selfish pursuit had cramped and narrowed me, until your gentleness and affection warmed and opened my senses; I became the same happy creature who, a few years ago, loving and beloved by all, had no sorrow or care. When happy, inanimate nature had the power of bestowing on me the most delightful sensations. A serene sky and verdant fields filled me with ecstacy. The present season was indeed divine; the flowers of spring bloomed in the hedges, while those of summer were already in bud: I was undisturbed by thoughts which during the preceding year had pressed upon me, notwithstanding my endeavours to throw them off, with an invincible burden.

Henry rejoiced in my gaiety, and sincerely sympathized in my feelings: he exerted himself to amuse me, while he expressed the sensations that filled his soul. The resources of his mind on this occasion were truly astonishing: his conversation was full of imagination; and very often, in imitation of the Persian and Arabic writers, he invented

tales of wonderful fancy and passion. At other times he repeated my
favourite poems, or drew me out into arguments, which he supported
with great ingenuity.

We returned to our college on a Sunday afternoon: the peasants
were dancing, and every one we met appeared gay and happy. My
own spirits were high, and I bounded along with feelings of unbri-
dled joy and hilarity.

Chapter VI.

On my return, I found the following letter from my father:—

"*To* V. FRANKENSTEIN.

"MY DEAR VICTOR,

"You have probably waited impatiently for a letter to fix the
date of your return to us; and I was at first tempted to write
only a few lines, merely mentioning the day on which I should
expect you. But that would be a cruel kindness, and I dare not
do it. What would be your surprise, my son, when you expected
a happy and gay welcome, to behold, on the contrary, tears
and wretchedness? And how, Victor, can I relate our misfortune? Absence cannot have rendered you callous to our joys and
griefs; and how shall I inflict pain on an absent child? I wish
to prepare you for the woeful news, but I know it is impossible;
even now your eye skims over the page, to seek the words which
are to convey to you the horrible tidings.

"William is dead!—that sweet child, whose smiles delighted
and warmed my heart, who was so gentle, yet so gay! Victor,
he is murdered!

"I will not attempt to console you; but will simply relate the
circumstances of the transaction.

"Last Thursday (May 7th) I, my niece, and your two brothers,
went to walk in Plainpalais. The evening was warm and serene,
and we prolonged our walk farther than usual. It was already
dusk before we thought of returning; and then we discovered
that William and Ernest, who had gone on before, were not
to be found. We accordingly rested on a seat until they should
return. Presently Ernest came, and inquired if we had seen his
brother: he said, that they had been playing together, that William had run away to hide himself, and that he vainly sought
for him, and afterwards waited for him a long time, but that he
did not return.

"This account rather alarmed us, and we continued to search
for him until night fell, when Elizabeth conjectured that he

might have returned to the house. He was not there. We returned again, with torches; for I could not rest, when I thought that my sweet boy had lost himself, and was exposed to all the damps and dews of night: Elizabeth also suffered extreme anguish. About five in the morning I discovered my lovely boy, whom the night before I had seen blooming and active in health, stretched on the grass livid and motionless: the print of the murderer's finger was on his neck.

"He was conveyed home, and the anguish that was visible in my countenance betrayed the secret to Elizabeth. She was very earnest to see the corpse. At first I attempted to prevent her; but she persisted, and entering the room where it lay, hastily examined the neck of the victim, and clasping her hands exclaimed, 'O God! I have murdered my darling infant!'

"She fainted, and was restored with extreme difficulty. When she again lived, it was only to weep and sigh. She told me, that that same evening William had teazed her to let him wear a very valuable miniature that she possessed of your mother. This picture is gone, and was doubtless the temptation which urged the murderer to the deed. We have no trace of him at present, although our exertions to discover him are unremitted; but they will not restore my beloved William.

"Come, dearest Victor; you alone can console Elizabeth. She weeps continually, and accuses herself unjustly as the cause of his death; her words pierce my heart. We are all unhappy; but will not that be an additional motive for you, my son, to return and be our comforter? Your dear mother! Alas, Victor! I now say, Thank God she did not live to witness the cruel, miserable death of her youngest darling!

"Come, Victor; not brooding thoughts of vengeance against the assassin, but with feelings of peace and gentleness, that will heal, instead of festering the wounds of our minds. Enter the house of mourning, my friend, but with kindness and affection for those who love you, and not with hatred for your enemies.

"Your affectionate and afflicted father,

"ALPHONSE FRANKENSTEIN.

"Geneva, May 12th, 17—."

Clerval, who had watched my countenance as I read this letter, was surprised to observe the despair that succeeded to the joy I at first expressed on receiving news from my friends. I threw the letter on the table, and covered my face with my hands.

"My dear Frankenstein," exclaimed Henry, when he perceived me weep with bitterness, "are you always to be unhappy? My dear friend, what has happened?"

I motioned to him to take up the letter, while I walked up and down the room in the extremest agitation. Tears also gushed from the eyes of Clerval, as he read the account of my misfortune. "I can offer you no consolation, my friend," said he; "your disaster is irreparable. What do you intend to do?" "To go instantly to Geneva: come with me, Henry, to order the horses."

During our walk, Clerval endeavoured to raise my spirits. He did not do this by common topics of consolation, but by exhibiting the truest sympathy. "Poor William!" said he, "that dear child; he now sleeps with his angel mother. His friends mourn and weep, but he is at rest: he does not now feel the murderer's grasp; a sod covers his gentle form, and he knows no pain. He can no longer be a fit subject for pity; the survivors are the greatest sufferers, and for them time is the only consolation. Those maxims of the Stoics,[1] that death was no evil, and that the mind of man ought to be superior to despair on the eternal absence of a beloved object, ought not to be urged. Even Cato[2] wept over the dead body of his brother."

Clerval spoke thus as we hurried through the streets; the words impressed themselves on my mind, and I remembered them afterwards in solitude. But now, as soon as the horses arrived, I hurried into a cabriole,[3] and bade farewell to my friend.

My journey was very melancholy. At first I wished to hurry on, for I longed to console and sympathize with my loved and sorrowing friends; but when I drew near my native town, I slackened my progress. I could hardly sustain the multitude of feelings that crowded into my mind. I passed through scenes familiar to my youth, but which I had not seen for nearly six years. How altered every thing might be during that time? One sudden and desolating change had taken place; but a thousand little circumstances might have by degrees worked other alterations, which, although they were done more tranquilly, might not be the less decisive. Fear overcame me; I dared not advance, dreading a thousand nameless evils that made me tremble, although I was unable to define them.

I remained two days at Lausanne, in this painful state of mind. I contemplated the lake: the waters were placid; all around was calm, and the snowy mountains, "the palaces of nature,"[4] were not

---

1. A philosophical sect in ancient Greece and Rome that emphasized reason and patient endurance.
2. Antagonist of Caesar and notable Stoic (95–46 B.C.).
3. A two-wheeled, horse-drawn carriage.
4. From canto III of Byron's *Childe Harold's Pilgrimage* (1816): "Above me are the Alps, / The palaces of Nature, whose vast walls / Have pinnacled in clouds their snowy scalps, / And throned Eternity in icy halls / Of cold sublimity" (lxii.590–94). See p. 304.

changed. By degrees the calm and heavenly scene restored me, and
I continued my journey towards Geneva.

The road ran by the side of the lake, which became narrower as I
approached my native town. I discovered more distinctly the black
sides of Jura, and the bright summit of Mont Blanc.[5] I wept like
a child: "Dear mountains! my own beautiful lake! how do you welcome your wanderer? Your summits are clear; the sky and lake are
blue and placid. Is this to prognosticate peace, or to mock at my
unhappiness?"

I fear, my friend, that I shall render myself tedious by dwelling on
these preliminary circumstances; but they were days of comparative happiness, and I think of them with pleasure. My country, my
beloved country! who but a native can tell the delight I took in again
beholding thy streams, thy mountains, and, more than all, thy lovely
lake.

Yet, as I drew nearer home, grief and fear again overcame me.
Night also closed around; and when I could hardly see the dark
mountains, I felt still more gloomily. The picture appeared a vast
and dim scene of evil, and I foresaw obscurely that I was destined
to become the most wretched of human beings. Alas! I prophesied
truly, and failed only in one single circumstance, that in all the misery I imagined and dreaded, I did not conceive the hundredth part
of the anguish I was destined to endure.

It was completely dark when I arrived in the environs of Geneva;
the gates of the town were already shut; and I was obliged to pass the
night at Secheron, a village half a league to the east of the city.
The sky was serene; and, as I was unable to rest, I resolved to visit
the spot where my poor William had been murdered. As I could not
pass through the town, I was obliged to cross the lake in a boat to
arrive at Plainpalais. During this short voyage I saw the lightnings
playing on the summit of Mont Blanc in the most beautiful figures.
The storm appeared to approach rapidly; and, on landing, I ascended
a low hill, that I might observe its progress. It advanced; the heavens
were clouded, and I soon felt the rain coming slowly in large drops,
but its violence quickly increased.

I quitted my seat, and walked on, although the darkness and
storm increased every minute, and the thunder burst with a terrific
crash over my head. It was echoed from Salêve, the Juras, and the
Alps of Savoy; vivid flashes of lightning dazzled my eyes, illuminating the lake, making it appear like a vast sheet of fire; then for
an instant every thing seemed of a pitchy darkness, until the eye

---

5. Percy Shelley wrote "Mont Blanc" (subtitled "Lines written in the vale of Chamouni")
in 1816. See p. 295, below.

recovered itself from the preceding flash. The storm, as is often the case in Switzerland, appeared at once in various parts of the heavens. The most violent storm hung exactly north of the town, over that part of the lake which lies between the promontory of Belrive and the village of Copêt. Another storm enlightened Jura with faint flashes; and another darkened and sometimes disclosed the Môle, a peaked mountain to the east of the lake.

While I watched the storm, so beautiful yet terrific,[6] I wandered on with a hasty step. This noble war in the sky elevated my spirits; I clasped my hands and exclaimed aloud, "William, dear angel! this is thy funeral, this thy dirge!" As I said these words, I perceived in the gloom a figure which stole from behind a clump of trees near me; I stood fixed, gazing intently: I could not be mistaken. A flash of lightning illuminated the object, and discovered its shape plainly to me; its gigantic stature, and the deformity of its aspect, more hideous than belongs to humanity, instantly informed me that it was the wretch, the filthy dæmon to whom I had given life. What did he there? Could he be (I shuddered at the conception) the murderer of my brother? No sooner did that idea cross my imagination, than I became convinced of its truth; my teeth chattered, and I was forced to lean against a tree for support. The figure passed me quickly, and I lost it in the gloom. Nothing in human shape could have destroyed that fair child. *He* was the murderer! I could not doubt it. The mere presence of the idea was an irresistible proof of the fact. I thought of pursuing the devil; but it would have been in vain, for another flash discovered him to me hanging among the rocks of the nearly perpendicular ascent of Mont Salêve, a hill that bounds Plainpalais on the south. He soon reached the summit, and disappeared.

I remained motionless. The thunder ceased; but the rain still continued, and the scene was enveloped in an impenetrable darkness. I revolved in my mind the events which I had until now sought to forget: the whole train of my progress towards the creation; the appearance of the work of my own hands alive at my bed side, its departure. Two years had now nearly elapsed since the night on which he first received life; and was this his first crime? Alas! I had turned loose into the world a depraved wretch, whose delight was in carnage and misery; had he not murdered my brother?

No one can conceive the anguish I suffered during the remainder of the night, which I spent, cold and wet, in the open air. But I did not feel the inconvenience of the weather; my imagination was busy in scenes of evil and despair. I considered the being whom I had cast among mankind, and endowed with the will and power to effect

6. Terrifying.

purposes of horror, such as the deed which he had now done, nearly in the light of my own vampire,[7] my own spirit let loose from the grave, and forced to destroy all that was dear to me.

Day dawned; and I directed my steps towards the town. The gates were open; and I hastened to my father's house. My first thought was to discover what I knew of the murderer, and cause instant pursuit to be made. But I paused when I reflected on the story that I had to tell. A being whom I myself had formed, and endued with life, had met me at midnight among the precipices of an inaccessible mountain. I remembered also the nervous fever with which I had been seized just at the time that I dated my creation, and which would give an air of delirium to a tale otherwise so utterly improbable. I well knew that if any other had communicated such a relation to me, I should have looked upon it as the ravings of insanity. Besides, the strange nature of the animal would elude all pursuit, even if I were so far credited as to persuade my relatives to commence it. Besides, of what use would be pursuit? Who could arrest a creature capable of scaling the overhanging sides of Mont Salêve? These reflections determined me, and I resolved to remain silent.

It was about five in the morning when I entered my father's house. I told the servants not to disturb the family, and went into the library to attend their usual hour of rising.

Six years had elapsed, passed as a dream but for one indelible trace, and I stood in the same place where I had last embraced my father before my departure for Ingolstadt. Beloved and respectable parent! He still remained to me. I gazed on the picture of my mother, which stood over the mantlepiece. It was an historical subject, painted at my father's desire, and represented Caroline Beaufort in an agony of despair, kneeling by the coffin of her dead father. Her garb was rustic, and her cheek pale; but there was an air of dignity and beauty, that hardly permitted the sentiment of pity. Below this picture was a miniature of William; and my tears flowed when I looked upon it. While I was thus engaged, Ernest entered; he had heard me arrive, and hastened to welcome me. He expressed a sorrowful delight to see me: "Welcome, my dearest Victor," said he. "Ah! I wish you had come three months ago, and then you would have found us all joyous and delighted. But we are now unhappy; and, I am afraid, tears instead of smiles will be your welcome. Our father looks so sorrowful: this dreadful event seems to have revived in his mind his grief on the death of Mamma. Poor Elizabeth also is quite inconsolable." Ernest began to weep as he said these words.

"Do not," said I, "welcome me thus; try to be more calm, that I may not be absolutely miserable the moment I enter my father's

7. A reanimated corpse.

house after so long an absence. But, tell me, how does my father support his misfortunes? and how is my poor Elizabeth?"

"She indeed requires consolation; she accused herself of having caused the death of my brother, and that made her very wretched. But since the murderer has been discovered—"

"The murderer discovered! Good God! how can that be? who could attempt to pursue him? It is impossible; one might as well try to overtake the winds, or confine a mountain-stream with a straw."

"I do not know what you mean; but we were all very unhappy when she was discovered. No one would believe it at first; and even now Elizabeth will not be convinced, notwithstanding all the evidence. Indeed, who would credit that Justine Moritz, who was so amiable, and fond of all the family, could all at once become so extremely wicked?"

"Justine Moritz! Poor, poor girl, is she the accused? But it is wrongfully; every one knows that; no one believes it, surely, Ernest?"

"No one did at first; but several circumstances came out, that have almost forced conviction upon us: and her own behaviour has been so confused, as to add to the evidence of facts a weight that, I fear, leaves no hope for doubt. But she will be tried to-day, and you will then hear all."

He related that, the morning on which the murder of poor William had been discovered, Justine had been taken ill, and confined to her bed; and, after several days, one of the servants, happening to examine the apparel she had worn on the night of the murder, had discovered in her pocket the picture of my mother, which had been judged to be the temptation of the murderer. The servant instantly shewed it to one of the others, who, without saying a word to any of the family, went to a magistrate; and, upon their deposition, Justine was apprehended. On being charged with the fact, the poor girl confirmed the suspicion in a great measure, by her extreme confusion of manner.

This was a strange tale, but it did not shake my faith; and I replied earnestly, "You are all mistaken; I know the murderer. Justine, poor, good Justine, is innocent."

At that instant my father entered. I saw unhappiness deeply impressed on his countenance, but he endeavoured to welcome me cheerfully; and, after we had exchanged our mournful greeting, would have introduced some other topic than that of our disaster, had not Ernest exclaimed, "Good God, Papa! Victor says that he knows who was the murderer of poor William."

"We do also, unfortunately," replied my father; "for indeed I had rather have been for ever ignorant than have discovered so much depravity and ingratitude in one I valued so highly."

"My dear father, you are mistaken; Justine is innocent."

"If she is, God forbid that she should suffer as guilty. She is to be tried to-day, and I hope, I sincerely hope, that she will be acquitted." This speech calmed me. I was firmly convinced in my own mind that Justine, and indeed every human being, was guiltless of this murder. I had no fear, therefore, that any circumstantial evidence could be brought forward strong enough to convict her; and, in this assurance, I calmed myself, expecting the trial with eagerness, but without prognosticating an evil result.

We were soon joined by Elizabeth. Time had made great alterations in her form since I had last beheld her. Six years before she had been a pretty, good-humoured girl, whom every one loved and caressed. She was now a woman in stature and expression of countenance, which was uncommonly lovely. An open and capacious forehead[8] gave indications of a good understanding, joined to great frankness of disposition. Her eyes were hazel, and expressive of mildness, now through recent affliction allied to sadness. Her hair was of a rich dark auburn, her complexion fair, and her figure slight and graceful. She welcomed me with the greatest affection. "Your arrival, my dear cousin," said she, "fills me with hope. You perhaps will find some means to justify my poor guiltless Justine. Alas! who is safe, if she be convicted of crime? I rely on her innocence as certainly as I do upon my own. Our misfortune is doubly hard to us; we have not only lost that lovely darling boy, but this poor girl, whom I sincerely love, is to be torn away by even a worse fate. If she is condemned, I never shall know joy more. But she will not, I am sure she will not; and then I shall be happy again, even after the sad death of my little William."

"She is innocent, my Elizabeth," said I, "and that shall be proved; fear nothing, but let your spirits be cheered by the assurance of her acquittal."

"How kind you are! every one else believes in her guilt, and that made me wretched; for I knew that it was impossible: and to see every one else prejudiced in so deadly a manner, rendered me hopeless and despairing." She wept.

"Sweet niece," said my father, "dry your tears. If she is, as you believe, innocent, rely on the justice of our judges, and the activity with which I shall prevent the slightest shadow of partiality."

Chapter VII.

We passed a few sad hours, until eleven o'clock, when the trial was to commence. My father and the rest of the family being obliged to

---

8. Physiognomy, or "face-reading," was a traditional way of interpreting physical features as revelations of character or temperament.

attend as witnesses, I accompanied them to the court. During the whole of this wretched mockery of justice, I suffered living torture. It was to be decided, whether the result of my curiosity and lawless devices would cause the death of two of my fellow-beings: one a smiling babe, full of innocence and joy; the other far more dreadfully murdered, with every aggravation of infamy that could make the murder memorable in horror. Justine also was a girl of merit, and possessed qualities which promised to render her life happy: now all was to be obliterated in an ignominious grave; and I the cause! A thousand times rather would I have confessed myself guilty of the crime ascribed to Justine; but I was absent when it was committed, and such a declaration would have been considered as the ravings of a madman, and would not have exculpated her who suffered through me.

The appearance of Justine was calm. She was dressed in mourning; and her countenance, always engaging, was rendered, by the solemnity of her feelings, exquisitely beautiful. Yet she appeared confident in innocence, and did not tremble, although gazed on and execrated by thousands; for all the kindness which her beauty might otherwise have excited, was obliterated in the minds of the spectators by the imagination of the enormity she was supposed to have committed. She was tranquil, yet her tranquillity was evidently constrained; and as her confusion had before been adduced as a proof of her guilt, she worked up her mind to an appearance of courage. When she entered the court, she threw her eyes round it, and quickly discovered where we were seated. A tear seemed to dim her eye when she saw us; but she quickly recovered herself, and a look of sorrowful affection seemed to attest her utter guiltlessness.

The trial began; and after the advocate against her had stated the charge, several witnesses were called. Several strange facts combined against her, which might have staggered any one who had not such proof of her innocence as I had. She had been out the whole of the night on which the murder had been committed, and towards morning had been perceived by a market-woman not far from the spot where the body of the murdered child had been afterwards found. The woman asked her what she did there; but she looked very strangely, and only returned a confused and unintelligible answer. She returned to the house about eight o'clock; and when one inquired where she had passed the night, she replied, that she had been looking for the child, and demanded earnestly, if any thing had been heard concerning him. When shewn the body, she fell into violent hysterics, and kept her bed for several days. The picture was then produced, which the servant had found in her pocket; and when Elizabeth, in a faltering voice, proved that it was the same which, an hour before the child had been missed, she had placed round his neck, a murmur of horror and indignation filled the court.

Justine was called on for her defence. As the trial had proceeded, her countenance had altered. Surprise, horror, and misery, were strongly expressed. Sometimes she struggled with her tears; but when she was desired to plead, she collected her powers, and spoke in an audible although variable voice:—

"God knows," she said, "how entirely I am innocent. But I do not pretend that my protestations should acquit me: I rest my innocence on a plain and simple explanation of the facts which have been adduced against me; and I hope the character I have always borne will incline my judges to a favourable interpretation, where any circumstance appears doubtful or suspicious."

She then related that, by the permission of Elizabeth, she had passed the evening of the night on which the murder had been committed, at the house of an aunt at Chêne, a village situated at about a league from Geneva. On her return, at about nine o'clock, she met a man, who asked her if she had seen any thing of the child who was lost. She was alarmed by this account, and passed several hours in looking for him, when the gates of Geneva were shut, and she was forced to remain several hours of the night in a barn belonging to a cottage, being unwilling to call up the inhabitants, to whom she was well known. Unable to rest or sleep, she quitted her asylum early, that she might again endeavour to find my brother. If she had gone near the spot where his body lay, it was without her knowledge. That she had been bewildered when questioned by the market-woman, was not surprising, since she had passed a sleepless night, and the fate of poor William was yet uncertain. Concerning the picture she could give no account.

"I know," continued the unhappy victim, "how heavily and fatally this one circumstance weighs against me, but I have no power of explaining it; and when I have expressed my utter ignorance, I am only left to conjecture concerning the probabilities by which it might have been placed in my pocket. But here also I am checked. I believe that I have no enemy on earth, and none surely would have been so wicked as to destroy me wantonly. Did the murderer place it there? I know of no opportunity afforded him for so doing; or if I had, why should he have stolen the jewel, to part with it again so soon?

"I commit my cause to the justice of my judges, yet I see no room for hope. I beg permission to have a few witnesses examined concerning my character; and if their testimony shall not overweigh my supposed guilt, I must be condemned, although I would pledge my salvation on my innocence."

Several witnesses were called, who had known her for many years, and they spoke well of her; but fear, and hatred of the crime of which they supposed her guilty, rendered them timorous, and unwilling to come forward. Elizabeth saw even this last resource, her excellent dispositions and irreproachable conduct, about to fail the accused, when, although violently agitated, she desired permission to address the court.

"I am," said she, "the cousin of the unhappy child who was murdered, or rather his sister, for I was educated by and have lived with his parents ever since and even long before his birth. It may therefore be judged indecent in me to come forward on this occasion; but when I see a fellow-creature about to perish through the cowardice of her pretended friends, I wish to be allowed to speak, that I may say what I know of her character. I am well acquainted with the accused. I have lived in the same house with her, at one time for five, and at another for nearly two years. During all that period she appeared to me the most amiable and benevolent of human creatures. She nursed Madame Frankenstein, my aunt, in her last illness with the greatest affection and care; and afterwards attended her own mother during a tedious[1] illness, in a manner that excited the admiration of all who knew her. After which she again lived in my uncle's house, where she was beloved by all the family. She was warmly attached to the child who is now dead, and acted towards him like a most affectionate mother. For my own part, I do not hesitate to say, that, notwithstanding all the evidence produced against her, I believe and rely on her perfect innocence. She had no temptation for such an action: as to the bauble on which the chief proof rests, if she had earnestly desired it, I should have willingly given it to her; so much do I esteem and value her."

Excellent Elizabeth! A murmur of approbation was heard; but it was excited by her generous interference, and not in favour of poor Justine, on whom the public indignation was turned with renewed violence, charging her with the blackest ingratitude. She herself wept as Elizabeth spoke, but she did not answer. My own agitation and anguish was extreme during the whole trial. I believed in her innocence; I knew it. Could the dæmon, who had (I did not for a minute doubt) murdered my brother, also in his hellish sport have betrayed the innocent to death and ignominy. I could not sustain the horror of my situation; and when I perceived that the popular voice, and the countenances of the judges, had already condemned my unhappy victim, I rushed out of the court in agony. The tortures of the accused did not equal mine; she was sustained by innocence,

---

1. Wearisome.

but the fangs of remorse tore my bosom, and would not forego their hold.

I passed a night of unmingled wretchedness. In the morning I went to the court; my lips and throat were parched. I dared not ask the fatal question; but I was known, and the officer guessed the cause of my visit. The ballots[2] had been thrown; they were all black, and Justine was condemned.

I cannot pretend to describe what I then felt. I had before experienced sensations of horror; and I have endeavoured to bestow upon them adequate expressions, but words cannot convey an idea of the heart-sickening despair that I then endured. The person to whom I addressed myself added, that Justine had already confessed her guilt. "That evidence," he observed, "was hardly required in so glaring a case, but I am glad of it; and, indeed, none of our judges like to condemn a criminal upon circumstantial evidence, be it ever so decisive."

When I returned home, Elizabeth eagerly demanded the result.

"My cousin," replied I, "it is decided as you may have expected; all judges had rather that ten innocent should suffer, than that one guilty should escape. But she has confessed."

This was a dire blow to poor Elizabeth, who had relied with firmness upon Justine's innocence. "Alas!" said she, "how shall I ever again believe in human benevolence? Justine, whom I loved and esteemed as my sister, how could she put on those smiles of innocence only to betray; her mild eyes seemed incapable of any severity or ill-humour, and yet she has committed a murder."

Soon after we heard that the poor victim had expressed a wish to see my cousin. My father wished her not to go; but said, that he left it to her own judgment and feelings to decide. "Yes," said Elizabeth, "I will go, although she is guilty; and you, Victor, shall accompany me: I cannot go alone." The idea of this visit was torture to me, yet I could not refuse.

We entered the gloomy prison-chamber, and beheld Justine sitting on some straw at the further end; her hands were manacled, and her head rested on her knees. She rose on seeing us enter; and when we were left alone with her, she threw herself at the feet of Elizabeth, weeping bitterly. My cousin wept also.

"Oh, Justine!" said she, "why did you rob me of my last consolation. I relied on your innocence; and although I was then very wretched, I was not so miserable as I am now."

"And do you also believe that I am so very, very wicked? Do you also join with my enemies to crush me?" Her voice was suffocated with sobs.

2. Small balls used for secret voting.

"Rise, my poor girl," said Elizabeth, "why do you kneel, if you are innocent? I am not one of your enemies; I believed you guiltless, notwithstanding every evidence, until I heard that you had yourself declared your guilt. That report, you say, is false; and be assured, dear Justine, that nothing can shake my confidence in you for a moment, but your own confession."

"I did confess; but I confessed a lie. I confessed, that I might obtain absolution; but now that falsehood lies heavier at my heart than all my other sins. The God of heaven forgive me! Ever since I was condemned, my confessor has besieged me; he threatened and menaced, until I almost began to think that I was the monster that he said I was. He threatened excommunication and hell fire in my last moments, if I continued obdurate. Dear lady, I had none to support me; all looked on me as a wretch doomed to ignominy and perdition. What could I do? In an evil hour I subscribed to a lie; and now only am I truly miserable."

She paused, weeping, and then continued—"I thought with horror, my sweet lady, that you should believe your Justine, whom your blessed aunt had so highly honoured, and whom you loved, was a creature capable of a crime which none but the devil himself could have perpetrated. Dear William! dearest blessed child! I soon shall see you again in heaven, where we shall all be happy; and that consoles me, going as I am to suffer ignominy and death."

"Oh, Justine! forgive me for having for one moment distrusted you. Why did you confess? But do not mourn, my dear girl; I will every where proclaim your innocence, and force belief. Yet you must die; you, my playfellow, my companion, my more than sister. I never can survive so horrible a misfortune."

"Dear, sweet Elizabeth, do not weep. You ought to raise me with thoughts of a better life, and elevate me from the petty cares of this world of injustice and strife. Do not you, excellent friend, drive me to despair."

"I will try to comfort you; but this, I fear, is an evil too deep and poignant to admit of consolation, for there is no hope. Yet heaven bless thee, my dearest Justine, with resignation, and a confidence elevated beyond this world. Oh! how I hate its shews and mockeries! when one creature is murdered, another is immediately deprived of life in a slow torturing manner; then the executioners, their hands yet reeking with the blood of innocence, believe that they have done a great deed. They call this *retribution*. Hateful name! When that word is pronounced, I know greater and more horrid punishments are going to be inflicted than the gloomiest tyrant has ever invented to satiate his utmost revenge. Yet this is not consolation for you, my Justine, unless indeed that you may glory in escaping from so miserable a den. Alas! I would I were in peace with my aunt and my lovely

William, escaped from a world which is hateful to me, and the visages of men which I abhor."

Justine smiled languidly. "This, dear lady, is despair, and not resignation. I must not learn the lesson that you would teach me. Talk of something else, something that will bring peace, and not increase of misery."

During this conversation I had retired to a corner of the prison-room, where I could conceal the horrid anguish that possessed me. Despair! Who dared talk of that? The poor victim, who on the morrow was to pass the dreary boundary between life and death, felt not as I did, such deep and bitter agony. I gnashed my teeth, and ground them together, uttering a groan that came from my inmost soul. Justine started. When she saw who it was, she approached me, and said, "Dear Sir, you are very kind to visit me; you, I hope, do not believe that I am guilty."

I could not answer. "No, Justine," said Elizabeth; "he is more convinced of your innocence than I was; for even when he heard that you had confessed, he did not credit it."

"I truly thank him. In these last moments I feel the sincerest gratitude towards those who think of me with kindness. How sweet is the affection of others to such a wretch as I am! It removes more than half my misfortune; and I feel as if I could die in peace, now that my innocence is acknowledged by you, dear lady, and your cousin."

Thus the poor sufferer tried to comfort others and herself. She indeed gained the resignation she desired. But I, the true murderer, felt the never-dying worm alive in my bosom, which allowed of no hope or consolation. Elizabeth also wept, and was unhappy; but her's also was the misery of innocence, which, like a cloud that passes over the fair moon, for a while hides, but cannot tarnish its brightness. Anguish and despair had penetrated into the core of my heart; I bore a hell within me, which nothing could extinguish. We staid several hours with Justine; and it was with great difficulty that Elizabeth could tear herself away. "I wish," cried she, "that I were to die with you; I cannot live in this world of misery."

Justine assumed an air of cheerfulness, while she with difficulty repressed her bitter tears. She embraced Elizabeth, and said, in a voice of half-suppressed emotion, "Farewell, sweet lady, dearest Elizabeth, my beloved and only friend; may heaven in its bounty bless and preserve you; may this be the last misfortune that you will ever suffer. Live, and be happy, and make others so."

As we returned, Elizabeth said, "You know not, my dear Victor, how much I am relieved, now that I trust in the innocence of this unfortunate girl. I never could again have known peace, if I had been deceived in my reliance on her. For the moment that I did believe her guilty, I felt an anguish that I could not have long sustained. Now my heart is lightened. The innocent suffers; but she whom I thought amiable and good has not betrayed the trust I reposed in her, and I am consoled.

Amiable cousin! such were your thoughts, mild and gentle as your own dear eyes and voice. But I—I was a wretch, and none ever conceived of the misery that I then endured.

END OF VOL. I.

Volume II

Chapter I.

Nothing is more painful to the human mind, than, after the feelings have been worked up by a quick succession of events, the dead calmness of inaction and certainty which follows, and deprives the soul both of hope and fear. Justine died; she rested; and I was alive. The blood flowed freely in my veins, but a weight of despair and remorse pressed on my heart, which nothing could remove. Sleep fled from my eyes; I wandered like an evil spirit, for I had committed deeds of mischief beyond description horrible, and more, much more, (I persuaded myself) was yet behind. Yet my heart overflowed with kindness, and the love of virtue. I had begun life with benevolent intentions, and thirsted for the moment when I should put them in practice, and make myself useful to my fellow-beings. Now all was blasted:[1] instead of that serenity of conscience, which allowed me to look back upon the past with self-satisfaction, and from thence to gather promise of new hopes, I was seized by remorse and the sense of guilt, which hurried me away to a hell of intense tortures, such as no language can describe.

This state of mind preyed upon my health, which had entirely recovered from the first shock it had sustained. I shunned the face of man; all sound of joy or complacency was torture to me; solitude was my only consolation—deep, dark, death-like solitude.

My father observed with pain the alteration perceptible in my disposition and habits, and endeavoured to reason with me on the folly of giving way to immoderate grief. "Do you think, Victor," said he, "that I do not suffer also? No one could love a child more than I loved your brother;" (tears came into his eyes as he spoke); "but is it not a duty to the survivors, that we should refrain from augmenting their unhappiness by an appearance of immoderate grief? It is also a duty owed to yourself; for excessive sorrow prevents improvement or enjoyment, or even the discharge of daily usefulness, without which no man is fit for society."

1. Literally, blown or breathed on by a malignant force, blighted; more generally, cursed or damned.

This advice, although good, was totally inapplicable to my case; I should have been the first to hide my grief, and console my friends, if remorse had not mingled its bitterness with my other sensations. Now I could only answer my father with a look of despair, and endeavour to hide myself from his view.

About this time we retired to our house at Belrive. This change was particularly agreeable to me. The shutting of the gates regularly at ten o'clock, and the impossibility of remaining on the lake after that hour, had rendered our residence within the walls of Geneva very irksome to me. I was now free. Often, after the rest of the family had retired for the night, I took the boat, and passed many hours upon the water. Sometimes, with my sails set, I was carried by the wind; and sometimes, after rowing into the middle of the lake, I left the boat to pursue its own course, and gave way to my own miserable reflections. I was often tempted, when all was at peace around me, and I the only unquiet thing that wandered restless in a scene so beautiful and heavenly, if I except[2] some bat, or the frogs, whose harsh and interrupted croaking was heard only when I approached the shore—often, I say, I was tempted to plunge into the silent lake, that the waters might close over me and my calamities for ever. But I was restrained, when I thought of the heroic and suffering Elizabeth, whom I tenderly loved, and whose existence was bound up in mine. I thought also of my father, and surviving brother: should I by my base desertion leave them exposed and unprotected to the malice of the fiend whom I had let loose among them?

At these moments I wept bitterly, and wished that peace would revisit my mind only that I might afford them consolation and happiness. But that could not be. Remorse extinguished every hope. I had been the author of unalterable evils; and I lived in daily fear, lest the monster whom I had created should perpetrate some new wickedness. I had an obscure feeling that all was not over, and that he would still commit some signal[3] crime, which by its enormity should almost efface the recollection of the past. There was always scope for fear, so long as any thing I loved remained behind. My abhorrence of this fiend cannot be conceived. When I thought of him, I gnashed my teeth, my eyes became inflamed, and I ardently wished to extinguish that life which I had so thoughtlessly bestowed. When I reflected on his crimes and malice, my hatred and revenge burst all bounds of moderation. I would have made a pilgrimage to the highest peak of the Andes, could I, when there, have precipitated him to their base. I wished to see him again, that I might wreak the utmost extent of anger on his head, and avenge the deaths of William and Justine.

2. Leave out, exclude.
3. Remarkable, notable.

Our house was the house of mourning. My father's health was deeply shaken by the horror of the recent events. Elizabeth was sad and desponding; she no longer took delight in her ordinary occupations; all pleasure seemed to her sacrilege toward the dead; eternal woe and tears she then thought was the just tribute she should pay to innocence so blasted and destroyed. She was no longer that happy creature, who in earlier youth wandered with me on the banks of the lake, and talked with ecstacy of our future prospects. She had become grave, and often conversed of the inconstancy of fortune, and the instability of human life.

"When I reflect, my dear cousin," said she, "on the miserable death of Justine Moritz, I no longer see the world and its works as they before appeared to me. Before, I looked upon the accounts of vice and injustice, that I read in books or heard from others, as tales of ancient days, or imaginary evils; at least they were remote, and more familiar to reason than to the imagination; but now misery has come home, and men appear to me as monsters thirsting for each other's blood. Yet I am certainly unjust. Every body believed that poor girl to be guilty; and if she could have committed the crime for which she suffered, assuredly she would have been the most depraved of human creatures. For the sake of a few jewels, to have murdered the son of her benefactor and friend, a child whom she had nursed from its birth, and appeared to love as if it had been her own! I could not consent to the death of any human being; but certainly I should have thought such a creature unfit to remain in the society of men. Yet she was innocent. I know, I feel she was innocent; you are of the same opinion, and that confirms me. Alas! Victor, when falsehood can look so like the truth, who can look so like the truth, who can assure themselves of certain happiness? I feel as if I were walking on the edge of a precipice, towards which thousands are crowding, and endeavouring to plunge me into the abyss. William and Justine were assassinated, and the murderer escapes; he walks about the world free, and perhaps respected. But even if I were condemned to suffer on the scaffold for the same crimes, I would not change places with such a wretch."

I listened to this discourse with the extremest agony. I, not in deed, but in effect, was the true murderer. Elizabeth read my anguish in my countenance, and kindly taking my hand said, "My dearest cousin, you must calm yourself. These events have affected me, God knows how deeply; but I am not so wretched as you are. There is an expression of despair, and sometimes of revenge, in your countenance, that makes me tremble. Be calm, my dear Victor; I would sacrifice my life to your peace. We surely shall be happy: quiet in our native country, and not mingling in the world, what can disturb our tranquillity?"

She shed tears as she said this, distrusting the very solace that she gave; but at the same time she smiled, that she might chase away the fiend that lurked in my heart. My father, who saw in the unhappiness that was painted in my face only an exaggeration of that sorrow which I might naturally feel, thought that an amusement suited to my taste would be the best means of restoring to me my wonted serenity. It was from this cause that he had removed to the country; and, induced by the same motive, he now proposed that we should all make an excursion to the valley of Chamounix. I had been there before, but Elizabeth and Ernest never had; and both had often expressed an earnest desire to see the scenery of this place, which had been described to them as so wonderful and sublime.[4] Accordingly we departed from Geneva on this tour about the middle of the month of August, nearly two months after the death of Justine.

The weather was uncommonly fine; and if mine had been a sorrow to be chased away by any fleeting circumstance, this excursion would certainly have had the effect intended by my father. As it was, I was somewhat interested in the scene; it sometimes lulled, although it could not extinguish my grief. During the first day we travelled in a carriage. In the morning we had seen the mountains at a distance, towards which we gradually advanced. We perceived that the valley through which we wound, and which was formed by the river Arve, whose course we followed, closed in upon us by degrees; and when the sun had set, we beheld immense mountains and precipices overhanging us on every side, and heard the sound of the river raging among rocks, and the dashing of waterfalls around.

The next day we pursued our journey upon mules; and as we ascended still higher, the valley assumed a more magnificent and astonishing character. Ruined castles hanging on the precipices of piny mountains; the impetuous Arve, and cottages every here and there peeping forth from among the trees, formed a scene of singular beauty. But it was augmented and rendered sublime by the mighty Alps, whose white and shining pyramids and domes towered above all, as belonging to another earth, the habitations of another race of beings.

We passed the bridge of Pelissier, where the ravine, which the river forms, opened before us, and we began to ascend the mountain that overhangs it. Soon after we entered the valley of Chamounix. This valley is more wonderful and sublime, but not so beautiful and picturesque[5] as that of Servox, through which we had just passed.

4. "Affecting the mind with a sense of overwhelming grandeur or irresistible power; calculated to inspire awe, deep reverence, or lofty emotion, by reason of its beauty, vastness or grandeur" (OED).
5. "Possessing pleasing and interesting qualities of form and colour (but not implying the highest beauty or sublimity)" (OED).

The high and snowy mountains were its immediate boundaries; but we saw no more ruined castles and fertile fields. Immense glaciers approached the road; we heard the rumbling thunder of the falling avelânche, and marked the smoke of its passage. Mont Blanc, the supreme and magnificent Mont Blanc, raised itself from the surrounding *aiguilles*, and its tremendous *dome*[6] overlooked the valley.

During this journey, I sometimes joined Elizabeth, and exerted myself to point out to her the various beauties of the scene. I often suffered my mule to lag behind, and indulged in the misery of reflection. At other times I spurred on the animal before my companions, that I might forget them, the world, and, more than all, myself. When at a distance, I alighted, and threw myself on the grass, weighed down by horror and despair. At eight in the evening I arrived at Chamounix. My father and Elizabeth were very much fatigued; Ernest, who accompanied us, was delighted, and in high spirits: the only circumstance that detracted from his pleasure was the south wind, and the rain it seemed to promise for the next day.

We retired early to our apartments, but not to sleep; at least I did not. I remained many hours at the window, watching the pallid lightning that played above Mont Blanc, and listening to the rushing of the Arve, which ran below my window.

Chapter II.

The next day, contrary to the prognostications of our guides, was fine, although clouded. We visited the source of the Arveiron, and rode about the valley until evening. These sublime and magnificent scenes afforded me the greatest consolation that I was capable of receiving. They elevated me from all littleness of feeling; and although they did not remove my grief, they subdued and tranquillized it. In some degree, also, they diverted my mind from the thoughts over which it had brooded for the last month. I returned in the evening, fatigued, but less unhappy, and conversed with my family with more cheerfulness than had been my custom for some time. My father was pleased, and Elizabeth overjoyed. "My dear cousin," said she, "you see what happiness you diffuse when you are happy; do not relapse again!"

The following morning the rain poured down in torrents, and thick mists hid the summits of the mountains. I rose early, but felt unusually melancholy. The rain depressed me; my old feelings recurred, and I was miserable. I knew how disappointed my father

---

6. Convex, rounded summit; Mont Blanc's is capped with ice. *Aiguilles*: slender, sharply pointed peaks.

would be at this sudden change, and I wished to avoid him until I had recovered myself so far as to be enabled to conceal those feelings that overpowered me. I knew that they would remain that day at the inn; and as I had ever inured myself to rain, moisture, and cold, I resolved to go alone to the summit of Montanvert. I remembered the effect that the view of the tremendous and ever-moving glacier had produced upon my mind when I first saw it. It had then filled me with a sublime ecstacy that gave wings to the soul, and allowed it to soar from the obscure world to light and joy. The sight of the awful[1] and majestic in nature had indeed always the effect of solemnizing my mind, and causing me to forget the passing cares of life. I determined to go alone, for I was well acquainted with the path, and the presence of another would destroy the solitary grandeur of the scene.

The ascent is precipitous, but the path is cut into continual and short windings, which enable you to surmount the perpendicularity of the mountain. It is a scene terrifically desolate. In a thousand spots the traces of the winter avalanche may be perceived, where trees lie broken and strewed on the ground; some entirely destroyed, others bent, leaning upon the jutting rocks of the mountain, or transversely upon other trees. The path, as you ascend higher, is intersected by ravines of snow, down which stones continually roll from above; one of them is particularly dangerous, as the slightest sound, such as even speaking in a loud voice, produces a concussion[2] of air sufficient to draw destruction upon the head of the speaker. The pines are not tall or luxuriant, but they are sombre, and add an air of severity to the scene. I looked on the valley beneath; vast mists were rising from the rivers which ran through it, and curling in thick wreaths around the opposite mountains, whose summits were hid in the uniform clouds, while rain poured from the dark sky, and added to the melancholy impression I received from the objects around me. Alas! why does man boast of sensibilities superior to those apparent in the brute; it only renders them more necessary[3] beings. If our impulses were confined to hunger, thirst, and desire, we might be nearly free; but now we are moved by every wind that blows, and a chance word or scene that that word may convey to us.

> We rest; a dream has power to poison sleep.
>   We rise; one wand'ring thought pollutes the day.
> We feel, conceive, or reason; laugh, or weep,
>   Embrace fond woe, or cast our cares away;
> It is the same: for, be it joy or sorrow,
>   The path of its departure still is free.

1. Awe-inspiring.
2. Agitation, violent shaking.
3. Dependent, lacking volition.

Man's yesterday may ne'er be like his morrow;
Naught may endure but mutability![4]

It was nearly noon when I arrived at the top of the ascent. For some time I sat upon the rock that overlooks the sea of ice. A mist covered both that and the surrounding mountains. Presently a breeze dissipated the cloud, and I descended upon the glacier. The surface is very uneven, rising like the waves of a troubled sea, descending low, and interspersed by rifts that sink deep. The field of ice is almost a league in width, but I spent nearly two hours in crossing it. The opposite mountain is a bare perpendicular rock. From the side where I now stood Montanvert was exactly opposite, at the distance of a league; and above it rose Mont Blanc, in awful majesty. I remained in a recess of the rock, gazing on this wonderful and stupendous scene. The sea, or rather the vast river of ice, wound among its dependent mountains, whose aërial summits hung over its recesses. Their icy and glittering peaks shone in the sunlight over the clouds. My heart, which was before sorrowful, now swelled with something like joy; I exclaimed—"Wandering spirits, if indeed ye wander, and do not rest in your narrow beds, allow me this faint happiness, or take me, as your companion, away from the joys of life."

As I said this, I suddenly beheld the figure of a man, at some distance, advancing towards me with superhuman speed. He bounded over the crevices in the ice, among which I had walked with caution; his stature also, as he approached, seemed to exceed that of man. I was troubled: a mist came over my eyes, and I felt a faintness seize me; but I was quickly restored by the cold gale of the mountains. I perceived, as the shape came nearer, (sight tremendous and abhorred!) that it was the wretch whom I had created. I trembled with rage and horror, resolving to wait his approach, and then close with him in mortal combat. He approached; his countenance bespoke bitter anguish, combined with disdain and malignity, while its unearthly ugliness rendered it almost too horrible for human eyes. But I scarcely observed this; anger and hatred had at first deprived me of utterance, and I recovered only to overwhelm him with words expressive of furious detestation and contempt.

"Devil!" I exclaimed, "do you dare approach me? and do not you fear the fierce vengeance of my arm wreaked on your miserable head? Begone, vile insect! or rather stay, that I may trample you to dust! and, oh, that I could, with the extinction of your miserable existence, restore those victims whom you have so diabolically murdered!"

"I expected this reception," said the dæmon. "All men hate the wretched; how then must I be hated, who am miserable beyond all

4. These lines are the second half of Percy Shelley's "Mutability" (1816). See p. 300.

living things! Yet you, my creator, detest and spurn me, thy creature, to whom thou art bound by ties only dissoluble by the annihilation of one of us. You purpose to kill me. How dare you sport thus with life? Do your duty towards me, and I will do mine towards you and the rest of mankind. If you will comply with my conditions, I will leave them and you at peace; but if you refuse, I will glut the maw of death, until it be satiated with the blood of your remaining friends."

"Abhorred monster! fiend that thou art! the tortures of hell are too mild a vengeance for thy crimes. Wretched devil! you reproach me with your creation; come on then, that I may extinguish the spark which I so negligently bestowed."

My rage was without bounds; I sprang on him, impelled by all the feelings which can arm one being against the existence of another.

He easily eluded me, and said,

"Be calm! I entreat you to hear me, before you give vent to your hatred on my devoted[5] head. Have I not suffered enough, that you seek to increase my misery? Life, although it may only be an accumulation of anguish, is dear to me, and I will defend it. Remember, thou hast made me more powerful than thyself; my height is superior to thine; my joints more supple. But I will not be tempted to set myself in opposition to thee. I am thy creature,[6] and I will be even mild and docile to my natural lord and king, if thou wilt also perform thy part, the which thou owest me. Oh, Frankenstein, be not equitable to every other, and trample upon me alone, to whom thy justice, and even thy clemency and affection, is most due. Remember, that I am thy creature: I ought to be thy Adam; but I am rather the fallen angel, whom thou drivest from joy for no misdeed. Every where I see bliss, from which I alone am irrevocably excluded. I was benevolent and good; misery made me a fiend. Make me happy, and I shall again be virtuous."

"Begone! I will not hear you. There can be no community between you and me; we are enemies. Begone, or let us try our strength in a fight, in which one must fall."

"How can I move thee? Will no entreaties cause thee to turn a favourable eye upon thy creature, who implores thy goodness and compassion. Believe me, Frankenstein: I was benevolent; my soul glowed with love and humanity: but am I not alone, miserably alone? You, my creator, abhor me; what hope can I gather from your fellow-creatures, who owe me nothing? they spurn and hate me. The desert mountains and dreary glaciers are my refuge. I have wandered here many days; the caves of ice, which I only do not fear, are a dwelling to me, and the only one which man does not grudge. These bleak

---

5. Doomed. "Devoted" has the same meaning throughout the text.
6. Creation.

skies I hail, for they are kinder to me than your fellow-beings. If the multitude of mankind knew of my existence, they would do as you do, and arm themselves for my destruction. Shall I not then hate them who abhor me? I will keep no terms with my enemies. I am miserable, and they shall share my wretchedness. Yet it is in your power to recompense me, and deliver them from an evil which it only remains for you to make so great, that not only you and your family, but thousands of others, shall be swallowed up in the whirl-winds of its rage. Let your compassion be moved, and do not disdain me. Listen to my tale: when you have heard that, abandon or commiserate me, as you shall judge that I deserve. But hear me. The guilty are allowed, by human laws, bloody as they may be, to speak in their own defence before they are condemned. Listen to me, Frankenstein. You accuse me of murder; and yet you would, with a satisfied conscience, destroy your own creature. Oh, praise the eternal justice of man! Yet I ask you not to spare me: listen to me; and then, if you can, and if you will, destroy the work of your hands."

"Why do you call to my remembrance circumstances of which I shudder to reflect, that I have been the miserable origin and author? Cursed be the day, abhorred devil, in which you first saw light! Cursed (although I curse myself) be the hands that formed you! You have made me wretched beyond expression. You have left me no power to consider whether I am just to you, or not. Begone! relieve me from the sight of your detested form."

"Thus I relieve thee, my creator," he said, and placed his hated hands before my eyes, which I flung from me with violence; "thus I take from thee a sight which you abhor. Still thou canst listen to me, and grant me thy compassion. By the virtues that I once possessed, I demand this from you. Hear my tale; it is long and strange, and the temperature of this place is not fitting to your fine[7] sensations; come to the hut upon the mountain. The sun is yet high in the heavens; before it descends to hide itself behind yon snowy precipices, and illuminate another world, you will have heard my story, and can decide. On you it rests, whether I quit for ever the neighbourhood of man, and lead a harmless life, or become the scourge of your fellow-creatures, and the author of your own speedy ruin."

As he said this, he led the way across the ice: I followed. My heart was full, and I did not answer him; but, as I proceeded, I weighed the various arguments that he had used, and determined at least to listen to his tale. I was partly urged by curiosity, and compassion confirmed my resolution. I had hitherto supposed him to be the murderer of my brother, and I eagerly sought a confirmation or denial of this opinion. For the first time, also, I felt what the duties

7. Delicate.

of a creator towards his creature were, and that I ought to render him happy before I complained of his wickedness. These motives urged me to comply with his demand. We crossed the ice, therefore, and ascended the opposite rock. The air was cold, and the rain again began to descend: we entered the hut, the fiend with an air of exultation, I with a heavy heart, and depressed spirits. But I consented to listen; and, seating myself by the fire which my odious companion had lighted, he thus began his tale.

Chapter III.

"It is with considerable difficulty that I remember the original æra of my being: all the events of that period appear confused and indistinct. A strange multiplicity of sensations seized me, and I saw, felt, heard, and smelt, at the same time; and it was, indeed, a long time before I learned to distinguish between the operations of my various senses. By degrees, I remember, a stronger light pressed upon my nerves, so that I was obliged to shut my eyes. Darkness then came over me, and troubled me; but hardly had I felt this, when, by opening my eyes, as I now suppose, the light poured in upon me again. I walked, and, I believe, descended; but I presently found a great alteration in my sensations. Before, dark and opaque bodies had surrounded me, impervious to my touch or sight; but I now found that I could wander on at liberty, with no obstacles which I could not either surmount or avoid. The light became more and more oppressive to me; and, the heat wearying me as I walked, I sought a place where I could receive shade. This was the forest near Ingolstadt; and here I lay by the side of a brook resting from my fatigue, until I felt tormented by hunger and thirst. This roused me from my nearly dormant state, and I ate some berries which I found hanging on the trees, or lying on the ground. I slaked my thirst at the brook; and then lying down, was overcome by sleep.

"It was dark when I awoke; I felt cold also, and half-frightened as it were instinctively, finding myself so desolate. Before I had quitted your apartment, on a sensation of cold, I had covered myself with some clothes; but these were insufficient to secure me from the dews of night. I was a poor, helpless, miserable wretch; I knew, and could distinguish, nothing; but, feeling pain invade me on all sides, I sat down and wept.

"Soon a gentle light stole over the heavens, and gave me a sensation of pleasure. I started up, and beheld a radiant form rise from among the trees. I gazed with a kind of wonder. It moved slowly, but it enlightened my path; and I again went out in search of berries. I was still cold, when under one of the trees I found a huge cloak, with which I covered myself, and sat down upon the ground. No distinct ideas occupied my mind; all was confused. I felt light, and hunger, and thirst, and darkness; innumerable sounds rung in my ears, and on all sides various scents saluted[1] me: the only object that I could distinguish was the bright moon, and I fixed my eyes on that with pleasure.

"Several changes of day and night passed, and the orb of night had greatly lessened when I began to distinguish my sensations from each other. I gradually saw plainly the clear stream that supplied me with drink, and the trees that shaded me with their foliage. I was delighted when I first discovered that a pleasant sound, which often saluted my ears, proceeded from the throats of the little winged animals who had often intercepted the light from my eyes. I began also to observe, with greater accuracy, the forms that surrounded me, and to perceive the boundaries of the radiant roof of light which canopied me. Sometimes I tried to imitate the pleasant songs of the birds, but was unable. Sometimes I wished to express my sensations in my own mode, but the uncouth and inarticulate sounds which broke from me frightened me into silence again.

"The moon had disappeared from the night, and again, with a lessened form, shewed itself, while I still remained in the forest. My sensations had, by this time, become distinct, and my mind received every day additional ideas. My eyes became accustomed to the light, and to perceive objects in their right forms; I distinguished the insect from the herb, and, by degrees, one herb from another. I found that the sparrow uttered none but harsh notes, whilst those of the blackbird and thrush were sweet and enticing.

"One day, when I was oppressed by cold, I found a fire which had been left by some wandering beggars, and was overcome with delight at the warmth I experienced from it. In my joy I thrust my hand into the live embers, but quickly drew it out again with a cry of pain. How strange, I thought, that the same cause should produce such opposite effects! I examined the materials of the fire, and to my joy found it to be composed of wood. I quickly collected some branches; but they were wet, and would not burn. I was pained at this, and sat still watching the operation of the fire. The wet wood which I had placed near the heat dried, and itself became inflamed. I reflected on this; and, by touching the various branches, I discovered the cause, and busied myself in collecting a great quantity of wood, that I might dry it, and have a plentiful supply of fire. When night came on, and brought sleep with it, I was in the greatest fear lest my fire should be extinguished. I covered it carefully with dry wood and

1. Greeted.

leaves, and placed wet branches upon it; and then, spreading my cloak, I lay on the ground, and sunk into sleep.

"It was morning when I awoke, and my first care was to visit the fire. I uncovered it, and a gentle breeze quickly fanned it into a flame. I observed this also, and contrived a fan of branches, which roused the embers when they were nearly extinguished. When night came again, I found, with pleasure, that the fire gave light as well as heat; and that the discovery of this element was useful to me in my food; for I found some of the offals that the travellers had left had been roasted, and tasted much more savoury than the berries I gathered from the trees. I tried, therefore, to dress my food in the same manner, placing it on the live embers. I found that the berries were spoiled by this operation, and the nuts and roots much improved.

"Food, however, became scarce; and I often spent the whole day searching in vain for a few acorns to assuage the pangs of hunger. When I found this, I resolved to quit the place that I had hitherto inhabited, to seek for one where the few wants I experienced would be more easily satisfied. In this emigration, I exceedingly lamented the loss of the fire which I had obtained through accident, and knew not how to reproduce it. I gave several hours to the serious consideration of this difficulty; but I was obliged to relinquish all attempt to supply it; and, wrapping myself up in my cloak, I struck across the wood towards the setting sun. I passed three days in these rambles, and at length discovered the open country. A great fall of snow had taken place the night before, and the fields were of one uniform white; the appearance was disconsolate, and I found my feet chilled by the cold damp substance that covered the ground.

"It was about seven in the morning, and I longed to obtain food and shelter; at length I perceived a small hut, on a rising ground, which had doubtless been built for the convenience of some shepherd. This was a new sight to me; and I examined the structure with great curiosity. Finding the door open, I entered. An old man sat in it, near a fire, over which he was preparing his breakfast. He turned on hearing a noise; and, perceiving me, shrieked loudly, and, quitting the hut, ran across the fields with a speed of which his debilitated form hardly appeared capable. His appearance, different from any I had ever before seen, and his flight, somewhat surprised me. But I was enchanted by the appearance of the hut: here the snow and rain could not penetrate; the ground was dry; and it presented to me then as exquisite and divine a retreat as Pandæmonium appeared to the dæmons of hell after their sufferings in the lake of fire.[2] I greedily devoured the remnants of the shepherd's breakfast, which consisted

---

2. See *Paradise Lost* 1.670ff. for the building of Pandemonium and II.119–69 for the comparison with the lake of fire.

of bread, cheese, milk, and wine; the latter, however, I did not like. [Then] overcome by fatigue, I lay down among some straw, and fell asleep.

"It was noon when I awoke; and, allured by the warmth of the sun, which shone brightly on the white ground, I determined to recommence my travels; and, depositing the remains of the peasant's breakfast in a wallet[3] I found, I proceeded across the fields for several hours, until at sunset I arrived at a village. How miraculous did this appear! the huts, the neater cottages, and stately houses, engaged my admiration by turns. The vegetables in the gardens, the milk and cheese that I saw placed at the windows of some of the cottages, allured my appetite. One of the best of these I entered; but I had hardly placed my foot within the door, before the children shrieked, and one of the women fainted. The whole village was roused; some fled, some attacked me, until, grievously bruised by stones and many other kinds of missile[4] weapons, I escaped to the open country, and fearfully took refuge in a low hovel, quite bare, and making a wretched appearance after the palaces I had beheld in the village. This hovel, however, joined a cottage of a neat and pleasant appearance; but, after my late dearly-bought experience, I dared not enter it. My place of refuge was constructed of wood, but so low, that I could with difficulty sit upright in it. No wood, however, was placed on the earth, which formed the floor, but it was dry; and although the wind entered it by innumerable chinks, I found it an agreeable asylum[5] from the snow and rain.

"Here then I retreated, and lay down, happy to have found a shelter, however miserable, from the inclemency of the season, and still more from the barbarity of man.

"As soon as morning dawned, I crept from my kennel, that I might view the adjacent cottage, and discover if I could remain in the habitation I had found. It was situated against the back of the cottage, and surrounded on the sides which were exposed by a pigstye and a clear pool of water. One part was open, and by that I had crept in; but now I covered every crevice by which I might be perceived with stones and wood, yet in such a manner that I might move them on occasion to pass out: all the light I enjoyed came through the stye, and that was sufficient for me.

"Having thus arranged my dwelling, and carpeted it with clean straw, I retired; for I saw the figure of a man at a distance, and I remembered too well my treatment the night before, to trust myself in his power. I had first, however, provided for my sustenance for

---

3. A beggar's bag.
4. Thrown.
5. "Sanctuary or place of refuge" (OED).

that day, by a loaf of coarse bread, which I purloined, and a cup with which I could drink, more conveniently than from my hand, of the pure water which flowed by my retreat. The floor was a little raised, so that it was kept perfectly dry, and by its vicinity to the chimney of the cottage it was tolerably warm.

"Being thus provided, I resolved to reside in this hovel, until something should occur which might alter my determination. It was indeed a paradise, compared to the bleak forest, my former residence, the raindropping branches, and dank earth. I ate my breakfast with pleasure, and was about to remove a plank to procure myself a little water, when I heard a step, and, looking through a small chink, I beheld a young creature, with a pail on her head, passing before my hovel. The girl was young and of gentle[6] demeanour, unlike what I have since found cottagers and farm-house servants to be. Yet she was meanly dressed, a coarse blue petticoat and a linen jacket being her only garb; her fair hair was plaited, but not adorned; she looked patient, yet sad. I lost sight of her; and in about a quarter of an hour she returned, bearing the pail, which was now partly filled with milk. As she walked along, seemingly incommoded by the burden, a young man met her, whose countenance expressed a deeper despondence. Uttering a few sounds with an air of melancholy, he took the pail from her head, and bore it to the cottage himself. She followed, and they disappeared. Presently I saw the young man again, with some tools in his hand, cross the field behind the cottage; and the girl was also busied, sometimes in the house, and sometimes in the yard.

"On examining my dwelling, I found that one of the windows of the cottage had formerly occupied a part of it, but the panes had been filled up with wood. In one of these was a small and almost imperceptible chink, through which the eye could just penetrate. Through this crevice, a small room was visible, white-washed and clean, but very bare of furniture. In one corner, near a small fire, sat an old man, leaning his head on his hands in a disconsolate attitude. The young girl was occupied in arranging the cottage; but presently she took something out of a drawer, which employed her hands, and she sat down beside the old man, who, taking up an instrument, began to play, and to produce sounds, sweeter than the voice of the thrush or the nightingale. It was a lovely sight, even to me, poor wretch! who had never beheld aught[7] beautiful before. The silver hair and benevolent countenance of the aged cottager, won my reverence; while the gentle manners of the girl enticed my love. He played a sweet mournful air, which I perceived drew tears from the eyes of his amiable companion, of which the old man took no notice,

6. Well-born, or having the character appropriate to one who is well-born.
7. Anything.

until she sobbed audibly; he then pronounced a few sounds, and the fair creature, leaving her work, knelt at his feet. He raised her, and smiled with such kindness and affection, that I felt sensations of a peculiar and overpowering nature: they were a mixture of pain and pleasure, such as I had never before experienced, either from hunger or cold, warmth or food; and I withdrew from the window, unable to bear these emotions.

"Soon after this the young man returned, bearing on his shoulders a load of wood. The girl met him at the door, helped to relieve him of his burden, and, taking some of the fuel into the cottage, placed it on the fire; then she and the youth went apart into a nook of the cottage, and he shewed her a large loaf and a piece of cheese. She seemed pleased; and went into the garden for some roots and plants, which she placed in water, and then upon the fire. She afterwards continued her work, whilst the young man went into the garden, and appeared busily employed in digging and pulling up roots. After he had been employed thus about an hour, the young woman joined him, and they entered the cottage together.

"The old man had, in the mean time, been pensive; but, on the appearance of his companions, he assumed a more cheerful air, and they sat down to eat. The meal was quickly dispatched. The young woman was again occupied in arranging the cottage; the old man walked before the cottage in the sun for a few minutes, leaning on the arm of the youth. Nothing could exceed in beauty the contrast between these two excellent creatures. One was old, with silver hairs and a countenance beaming with benevolence and love: the younger was slight and graceful in his figure, and his features were moulded with the finest symmetry; yet his eyes and attitude expressed the utmost sadness and despondency. The old man returned to the cottage; and the youth, with tools different from those he had used in the morning, directed his steps across the fields.

"Night quickly shut in; but, to my extreme wonder, I found that the cottagers had a means of prolonging light, by the use of tapers, and was delighted to find, that the setting of the sun did not put an end to the pleasure I experienced in watching my human neighbours. In the evening, the young girl and her companion were employed in various occupations which I did not understand; and the old man again took up the instrument, which produced the divine sounds that had enchanted me in the morning. So soon as he had finished, the youth began, not to play, but to utter sounds that were monotonous, and neither resembling the harmony of the old man's instrument or the songs of the birds; I since found that he read aloud, but at that time I knew nothing of the science of words or letters.

"The family, after having been thus occupied for a short time, extinguished their lights, and retired, as I conjectured, to rest.

Chapter IV.

"I lay on my straw, but I could not sleep. I thought of the occurrences of the day. What chiefly struck me was the gentle manners of these people; and I longed to join them, but dared not. I remembered too well the treatment I had suffered the night before from the barbarous villagers, and resolved, whatever course of conduct I might hereafter think it right to pursue, that for the present I would remain quietly in my hovel, watching, and endeavouring to discover the motives which influenced their actions.

"The cottagers arose the next morning before the sun. The young woman arranged the cottage, and prepared the food; and the youth departed after the first meal.

"This day was passed in the same routine as that which preceded it. The young man was constantly employed out of doors, and the girl in various laborious occupations within. The old man, whom I soon perceived to be blind, employed his leisure hours on his instrument, or in contemplation. Nothing could exceed the love and respect which the younger cottagers exhibited towards their venerable companion. They performed towards him every little office of affection and duty with gentleness; and he rewarded them by his benevolent smiles.

"They were not entirely happy. The young man and his companion often went apart, and appeared to weep. I saw no cause for their unhappiness; but I was deeply affected by it. If such lovely creatures were miserable, it was less strange that I, an imperfect and solitary being, should be wretched. Yet why were these gentle beings unhappy? They possessed a delightful house (for such it was in my eyes), and every luxury; they had a fire to warm them when chill, and delicious viands when hungry; they were dressed in excellent clothes; and, still more, they enjoyed one another's company and speech, interchanging each day looks of affection and kindness. What did their tears imply? Did they really express pain? I was at first unable to solve these questions; but perpetual attention, and time, explained to me many appearances which were at first enigmatic.

"A considerable period elapsed before I discovered one of the causes of the uneasiness of this amiable family; it was poverty: and they suffered that evil in a very distressing degree. Their nourishment consisted entirely of the vegetables of their garden, and the milk of one cow, who gave very little during the winter, when its masters could scarcely procure food to support it. They often, I believe, suffered the pangs of hunger very poignantly, especially the two younger cottagers; for several times they placed food before the old man, when they reserved none for themselves.

"This trait of kindness moved me sensibly. I had been accustomed, during the night, to steal a part of their store for my own consumption; but when I found that in doing this I inflicted pain on the cottagers, I abstained, and satisfied myself with berries, nuts, and roots, which I gathered from a neighbouring wood.

"I discovered also another means through which I was enabled to assist their labours. I found that the youth spent a great part of each day in collecting wood for the family fire; and, during the night, I often took his tools, the use of which I quickly discovered, and brought home firing sufficient for the consumption of several days.

"I remember, the first time that I did this, the young woman, when she opened the door in the morning, appeared greatly astonished on seeing a great pile of wood on the outside. She uttered some words in a loud voice, and the youth joined her, who also expressed surprise. I observed, with pleasure, that he did not go to the forest that day, but spent it in repairing the cottage, and cultivating the garden.

"By degrees I made a discovery of still greater moment. I found that these people possessed a method of communicating their experience and feelings to one another by articulate sounds. I perceived that the words they spoke sometimes produced pleasure or pain, smiles or sadness, in the minds and countenances of the hearers. This was indeed a godlike science, and I ardently desired to become acquainted with it. But I was baffled in every attempt I made for this purpose. Their pronunciation was quick; and the words they uttered, not having any apparent connexion with visible objects, I was unable to discover any clue by which I could unravel the mystery of their reference. By great application, however, and after having remained during the space of several revolutions of the moon in my hovel, I discovered the names that were given to some of the most familiar objects of discourse: I learned and applied the words *fire, milk, bread*, and *wood*. I learned also the names of the cottagers themselves. The youth and his companion had each of them several names, but the old man had only one, which was *father*. The girl was called *sister*, or *Agatha*; and the youth *Felix, brother*, or *son*. I cannot describe the delight I felt when I learned the ideas appropriated to each of these sounds, and was able to pronounce them. I distinguished several other words, without being able as yet to understand or apply them; such as *good, dearest, unhappy*.

"I spent the winter in this manner. The gentle manners and beauty of the cottagers greatly endeared them to me: when they were unhappy, I felt depressed; when they rejoiced, I sympathized in their joys. I saw few human beings beside them; and if any other happened to enter the cottage, their harsh manners and rude gait only enhanced to me the superior accomplishments of my friends. The old man,

I could perceive, often endeavoured to encourage his children, as sometimes I found that he called them, to cast off their melancholy. He would talk in a cheerful accent, with an expression of goodness that bestowed pleasure even upon me. Agatha listened with respect, her eyes sometimes filled with tears, which she endeavoured to wipe away unperceived; but I generally found that her countenance and tone were more cheerful after having listened to the exhortations of her father. It was not thus with Felix. He was always the saddest of the groupe; and, even to my unpractised senses, he appeared to have suffered more deeply than his friends. But if his countenance was more sorrowful, his voice was more cheerful than that of his sister, especially when he addressed the old man.

"I could mention innumerable instances, which, although slight, marked the dispositions of these amiable cottagers. In the midst of poverty and want, Felix carried with pleasure to his sister the first little white flower that peeped out from beneath the snowy ground. Early in the morning before she had risen, he cleared away the snow that obstructed her path to the milk-house, drew water from the well, and brought the wood from the outhouse, where, to his perpetual astonishment, he found his store always replenished by an invisible hand. In the day, I believe, he worked sometimes for a neighbouring farmer, because he often went forth, and did not return until dinner, yet brought no wood with him. At other times he worked in the garden; but, as there was little to do in the frosty season, he read to the old man and Agatha.

"This reading had puzzled me extremely at first; but, by degrees, I discovered that he uttered many of the same sounds when he read as when he talked. I conjectured, therefore, that he found on the paper signs for speech which he understood, and I ardently longed to comprehend these also; but how was that possible, when I did not even understand the sounds for which they stood as signs? I improved, however, sensibly in this science, but not sufficiently to follow up any kind of conversation, although I applied my whole mind to the endeavour: for I easily perceived that, although I eagerly longed to discover myself to the cottagers, I ought not to make the attempt until I had first become master of their language; which knowledge might enable me to make them overlook the deformity of my figure; for with this also the contrast perpetually presented to my eyes had made me acquainted.

"I had admired the perfect forms of my cottagers—their grace, beauty, and delicate complexions: but how was I terrified, when I viewed myself in a transparent pool! At first I started back, unable to believe that it was indeed I who was reflected in the mirror; and when I became fully convinced that I was in reality the monster that I am, I was filled with the bitterest sensations of despondence and mortification. Alas! I did not yet entirely know the fatal effects of this miserable deformity.

"As the sun became warmer, and the light of day longer, the snow vanished, and I beheld the bare trees and the black earth. From this time Felix was more employed; and the heart-moving indications of impending famine disappeared. Their food, as I afterwards found, was coarse, but it was wholesome; and they procured a sufficiency of it. Several new kinds of plants sprung up in the garden, which they dressed; and these signs of comfort increased daily as the season advanced.

"The old man, leaning on his son, walked each day at noon, when it did not rain, as I found it was called when the heavens poured forth its waters. This frequently took place; but a high wind quickly dried the earth, and the season became far more pleasant than it had been.

"My mode of life in my hovel was uniform. During the morning I attended the motions of the cottagers; and when they were dispersed in various occupations, I slept: the remainder of the day was spent in observing my friends. When they had retired to rest, if there was any moon, or the night was star-light, I went into the woods, and collected my own food and fuel for the cottage. When I returned, as often as it was necessary, I cleared their path from the snow, and performed those offices that I had seen done by Felix. I afterwards found that these labours, performed by an invisible hand, greatly astonished them; and once or twice I heard them, on these occasions, utter the words *good spirit, wonderful*; but I did not then understand the signification of these terms.

"My thoughts now became more active, and I longed to discover the motives and feelings of these lovely creatures; I was inquisitive to know why Felix appeared so miserable, and Agatha so sad. I thought (foolish wretch!) that it might be in my power to restore happiness to these deserving people. When I slept, or was absent, the forms of the venerable blind father, the gentle Agatha, and the excellent Felix, flitted before me. I looked upon them as superior beings, who would be the arbiters of my future destiny. I formed in my imagination a thousand pictures of presenting myself to them, and their reception of me. I imagined that they would be disgusted, until, by my gentle demeanour and conciliating words, I should first win their favour, and afterwards their love.

"These thoughts exhilarated me, and led me to apply with fresh ardour to the acquiring the art of language. My organs were indeed harsh, but supple; and although my voice was very unlike the soft music of their tones, yet I pronounced such words as I understood with tolerable ease. It was as the ass and the lap-dog;[1] yet surely the gentle ass, whose intentions were affectionate, although his manners were rude, deserved better treatment than blows and execration.

"The pleasant showers and genial warmth of spring greatly altered the aspect of the earth. Men, who before this change seemed to have been hid in caves, dispersed themselves, and were employed in various arts of cultivation. The birds sang in more cheerful notes, and the leaves began to bud forth on the trees. Happy, happy earth! fit habitation for gods, which, so short a time before, was bleak, damp, and unwholesome. My spirits were elevated by the enchanting appearance of nature; the past was blotted from my memory, the present was tranquil, and the future gilded by bright rays of hope, and anticipations of joy.

Chapter V.

"I now hasten to the more moving part of my story. I shall relate events that impressed me with feelings which, from what I was, have made me what I am.

"Spring advanced rapidly; the weather became fine, and the skies cloudless. It surprised me, that what before was desert and gloomy should now bloom with the most beautiful flowers and verdure. My senses were gratified and refreshed by a thousand scents of delight, and a thousand sights of beauty.

"It was on one of these days, when my cottagers periodically rested from labour—the old man played on his guitar, and the children listened to him—I observed that the countenance of Felix was melancholy beyond expression: he sighed frequently; and once his father paused in his music, and I conjectured by his manner that he inquired the cause of his son's sorrow. Felix replied in a cheerful accent, and the old man was recommencing his music, when some one tapped at the door.

"It was a lady on horseback, accompanied by a countryman as a guide. The lady was dressed in a dark suit, and covered with a thick black veil. Agatha asked a question; to which the stranger only replied by pronouncing, in a sweet accent, the name of Felix. Her voice was musical, but unlike that of either of my friends. On hearing this word, Felix came up hastily to the lady; who, when she saw him, threw up her veil, and I beheld a countenance of angelic beauty and expression. Her hair of a shining raven black, and curi-

---

1. The traditional Aesopian fable of the ass and the lapdog was popularized in La Fontaine's *Fables*, Book IV.

ously braided; her eyes were dark, but gentle, although animated; her features of a regular proportion, and her complexion wondrously fair, each cheek tinged with a lovely pink.

"Felix seemed ravished with delight when he saw her, every trait of sorrow vanished from his face, and it instantly expressed a degree of ecstatic joy, of which I could hardly have believed it capable; his eyes sparkled, as his cheek flushed with pleasure; and at that moment I thought him as beautiful as the stranger. She appeared affected by different feelings; wiping a few tears from her lovely eyes, she held out her hand to Felix, who kissed it rapturously, and called her, as well as I could distinguish, his sweet Arabian. She did not appear to understand him, but smiled. He assisted her to dismount, and, dismissing her guide, conducted her into the cottage. Some conversation took place between him and his father; and the young stranger knelt at the old man's feet, and would have kissed his hand, but he raised her, and embraced her affectionately.

"I soon perceived, that although the stranger uttered articulate sounds, and appeared to have a language of her own, she was neither understood by, or herself understood, the cottagers. They made many signs which I did not comprehend; but I saw that her presence diffused gladness through the cottage, dispelling their sorrow as the sun dissipates the morning mists. Felix seemed peculiarly happy, and with smiles of delight welcomed his Arabian. Agatha, the ever-gentle Agatha, kissed the hands of the lovely stranger; and, pointing to her brother, made signs which appeared to me to mean that he had been sorrowful until she came. Some hours passed thus, while they, by their countenances, expressed joy, the cause of which I did not comprehend. Presently I found, by the frequent recurrence of one sound which the stranger repeated after them, that she was endeavouring to learn their language; and the idea instantly occurred to me, that I should make use of the same instructions to the same end. The stranger learned about twenty words at the first lesson, most of them indeed were those which I had before understood, but I profited by the others.

"As night came on, Agatha and the Arabian retired early. When they separated, Felix kissed the hand of the stranger, and said, 'Good night, sweet Safie.' He sat up much longer, conversing with his father; and, by the frequent repetition of her name, I conjectured that their lovely guest was the subject of their conversation. I ardently desired to understand them, and bent every faculty towards that purpose, but found it utterly impossible.

"The next morning Felix went out to his work; and, after the usual occupations of Agatha were finished, the Arabian sat at the feet of the old man, and, taking his guitar, played some airs so entrancingly beautiful, that they at once drew tears of sorrow and delight from my eyes. She sang, and her voice flowed in a rich cadence, swelling or dying away, like a nightingale of the woods.

"When she had finished, she gave the guitar to Agatha, who at first declined it. She played a simple air, and her voice accompanied it in sweet accents, but unlike the wondrous strain of the stranger. The old man appeared enraptured, and said some words, which Agatha endeavoured to explain to Safie, and by which he appeared to wish to express that she bestowed on him the greatest delight by her music."

"The days now passed as peaceably as before, with the sole alteration, that joy had taken place of sadness in the countenances of my friends. Safie was always gay and happy; she and I improved rapidly in the knowledge of language, so that in two months I began to comprehend most of the words uttered by my protectors."

"In the meanwhile also the black ground was covered with herbage, and the green banks interspersed with innumerable flowers, sweet to the scent and the eyes, stars of pale radiance among the moonlight woods; the sun became warmer, the nights clear and balmy; and my nocturnal rambles were an extreme pleasure to me, although they were considerably shortened by the late setting and early rising of the sun; for I never ventured abroad during daylight, fearful of meeting with the same treatment as I had formerly endured in the first village which I entered."

"My days were spent in close attention, that I might more speedily master the language; and I may boast that I improved more rapidly than the Arabian, who understood very little, and conversed in broken accents, whilst I comprehended and could imitate almost every word that was spoken.

"While I improved in speech, I also learned the science of letters, as it was taught to the stranger; and this opened before me a wide field for wonder and delight."

"The book from which Felix instructed Safie was Volney's *Ruins of Empires*.[1] I should not have understood the purport of this book, had not Felix, in reading it, given very minute explanations. He had chosen this work, he said, because the declamatory style was framed in imitation of the eastern authors. Through this work I obtained a cursory knowledge of history, and a view of the several empires at present existing in the world; it gave me an insight into the manners, governments, and religions of the different nations of the earth. I heard of the slothful Asiatics; of the stupendous genius and mental activity of the Grecians; of the wars and wonderful virtue of the early Romans—of their subsequent degeneration—of the decline

1. *Les Ruines, ou Meditations sur les Revolutions des Empires* (1791), by Constantin François Chasseboeuf, comte de Volney (1757–1820).

of that mighty empire; of chivalry, christianity, and kings. I heard of the discovery of the American hemisphere, and wept with Safie over the hapless fate of its original inhabitants.

"These wonderful narrations inspired me with strange feelings. Was man, indeed, at once so powerful, so virtuous, and magnificent, yet so vicious and base? He appeared at one time a mere scion of the evil principle, and at another as all that can be conceived of noble and godlike. To be a great and virtuous man appeared the highest honour that can befall a sensitive being; to be base and vicious, as many on record have been, appeared the lowest degradation, a condition more abject than that of the blind mole or harmless worm. For a long time I could not conceive how one man could go forth to murder his fellow, or even why there were laws and governments; but when I heard details of vice and bloodshed, my wonder ceased, and I turned away with disgust and loathing.

"Every conversation of the cottagers now opened new wonders to me. While I listened to the instructions which Felix bestowed upon the Arabian, the strange system of human society was explained to me. I heard of the division of property, of immense wealth and squalid poverty; of rank, descent, and noble blood.

"The words induced me to turn towards myself. I learned that the possessions most esteemed by your fellow-creatures were, high and unsullied descent[2] united with riches. A man might be respected with only one of these acquisitions; but without either he was considered, except in very rare instances, as a vagabond and a slave, doomed to waste his powers for the profit of the chosen few. And what was I? Of my creation and creator I was absolutely ignorant; but I knew that I possessed no money, no friends, no kind of property. I was, besides, endowed with a figure hideously deformed and loathsome; I was not even of the same nature as man. I was more agile than they, and could subsist upon coarser diet; I bore the extremes of heat and cold with less injury to my frame; my stature far exceeded their's. When I looked around, I saw and heard of none like me. Was I then a monster, a blot upon the earth, from which all men fled, and whom all men disowned?

"I cannot describe to you the agony that these reflections inflicted upon me; I tried to dispel them, but sorrow only increased with knowledge. Oh, that I had for ever remained in my native wood, nor known or felt beyond the sensations of hunger, thirst, and heat!

"Of what a strange nature is knowledge! It clings to the mind, when it has once seized on it, like a lichen on the rock. I wished sometimes to shake off all thought and feeling; but I learned that there was but one means to overcome the sensation of pain, and that

---

2. Lineage, ancestry.

was death—a state which I feared yet did not understand. I admired virtue and good feelings, and loved the gentle manners and amiable qualities of my cottagers; but I was shut out from intercourse with them, except through means which I obtained by stealth, when I was unseen and unknown, and which rather increased than satisfied the desire I had of becoming one among my fellows. The gentle words of Agatha, and the animated smiles of the charming Arabian, were not for me. The mild exhortations of the old man, and the lively conversation of the loved Felix, were not for me. Miserable, unhappy wretch!

"Other lessons were impressed upon me even more deeply. I heard of the difference of sexes; of the birth and growth of children; how the father doated on the smiles of the infant, and the lively sallies of the older child; how all the life and cares of the mother were wrapt up in the precious charge; how the mind of youth expanded and gained knowledge; of brother, sister, and all the various relationships which bind one human being to another in mutual bonds.

"But where were my friends and relations? No father had watched my infant days, no mother had blessed me with smiles and caresses; or if they had, all my past life was now a blot, a blind vacancy in which I distinguished nothing. From my earliest remembrance I had been as I then was in height and proportion. I had never yet seen a being resembling me, or who claimed any intercourse with me. What was I? The question again recurred, to be answered only with groans.

"I will soon explain to what these feelings tended; but allow me now to return to the cottagers, whose story excited in me such various feelings of indignation, delight, and wonder, but which all terminated in additional love and reverence for my protectors (for so I loved, in an innocent, half painful self-deceit, to call them).

Chapter VI.

"Some time elapsed before I learned the history of my friends. It was one which could not fail to impress itself deeply on my mind, unfolding as it did a number of circumstances each interesting and wonderful to one so utterly inexperienced as I was.

"The name of the old man was De Lacey. He was descended from a good family in France, where he had lived for many years in affluence, respected by his superiors, and beloved by his equals. His son was bred in the service of his country; and Agatha had ranked with ladies of the highest distinction. A few months before my arrival, they had lived in a large and luxurious city, called Paris, surrounded by friends, and possessed of every enjoyment which virtue, refinement of intellect, or taste, accompanied by a moderate fortune, could afford.

"The father of Safie had been the cause of their ruin. He was a Turkish merchant, and had inhabited Paris for many years, when, for some reason which I could not learn, he became obnoxious to the government. He was seized and cast into prison the very day that Safie arrived from Constantinople to join him. He was tried, and condemned to death. The injustice of his sentence was very flagrant; all Paris was indignant; and it was judged that his religion and wealth, rather than the crime alleged against him, had been the cause of his condemnation.

"Felix had been present at the trial; his horror and indignation were uncontrollable, when he heard the decision of the court. He made, at that moment, a solemn vow to deliver him, and then looked around for the means. After many fruitless attempts to gain admittance to the prison, he found a strongly grated window in an unguarded part of the building, which lighted the dungeon of the unfortunate Mahometan; who, loaded with chains, waited in despair the execution of the barbarous sentence. Felix visited the grate at night, and made known to the prisoner his intentions in his favour. The Turk, amazed and delighted, endeavoured to kindle the zeal of his deliverer by promises of reward and wealth. Felix rejected his offers with contempt; yet when he saw the lovely Safie, who was allowed to visit her father, and who, by her gestures, expressed her lively gratitude, the youth could not help owning to his own mind, that the captive possessed a treasure which would fully reward his toil and hazard.

"The Turk quickly perceived the impression that his daughter had made on the heart of Felix, and endeavoured to secure him more entirely in his interests by the promise of her hand in marriage, so soon as he should be conveyed to a place of safety. Felix was too delicate[1] to accept this offer; yet he looked forward to the probability of that event as to the consummation of his happiness.

"During the ensuing days, while the preparations were going forward for the escape of the merchant, the zeal of Felix was warmed by several letters that he received from this lovely girl, who found means to express her thoughts in the language of her lover by the aid of an old man, a servant of her father's, who understood French. She thanked him in the most ardent terms for his intended services towards her father; and at the same time she gently deplored her own fate.

---

1. Sensitive to what is proper.

"I have copies of these letters; for I found means, during my residence in the hovel, to procure the implements of writing; and the letters were often in the hands of Felix or Agatha. Before I depart, I will give them to you, they will prove the truth of my tale; but at present, as the sun is already far declined, I shall only have time to repeat the substance of them to you.

"Safie related, that her mother was a Christian Arab, seized and made a slave by the Turks; recommended by her beauty, she had won the heart of the father of Safie, who married her. The young girl spoke in high and enthusiastic terms of her mother, who, born in freedom spurned the bondage to which she was now reduced. She instructed her daughter in the tenets of her religion, and taught her to aspire to higher powers of intellect, and an independence of spirit, forbidden to the female followers of Mahomet. This lady died; but her lessons were indelibly impressed on the mind of Safie, who sickened at the prospect of again returning to Asia, and the being immured within the walls of a haram, allowed only to occupy herself with puerile amusements, ill suited to the temper of her soul, now accustomed to grand ideas and a noble emulation for virtue. The prospect of marrying a Christian, and remaining in a country where women were allowed to take a rank in society, was enchanting to her.

"The day for the execution of the Turk was fixed; but, on the night previous to it, he had quitted prison, and before morning was distant many leagues from Paris. Felix had procured passports in the name of his father, sister, and himself. He had previously communicated his plan to the former, who aided the deceit by quitting his house, under the pretence of a journey, and concealed himself, with his daughter, in an obscure part of Paris.

"Felix conducted the fugitives through France to Lyons, and across Mont Cenis to Leghorn, where the merchant had decided to wait a favourable opportunity of passing into some part of the Turkish dominions.

"Safie resolved to remain with her father until the moment of his departure, before which time the Turk renewed his promise that she should be united to his deliverer; and Felix remained with them in expectation of that event; and in the mean time he enjoyed the society of the Arabian, who exhibited towards him the simplest and tenderest affection. They conversed with one another through the means of an interpreter, and sometimes with the interpretation of looks; and Safie sang to him the divine airs of her native country.

"The Turk allowed this intimacy to take place, and encouraged the hopes of the youthful lovers, while in his heart he had formed far other plans. He loathed the idea that his daughter should be united to a Christian; but he feared the resentment of Felix if he should appear lukewarm; for he knew that he was still in the power of his deliverer, if he should choose to betray him to the Italian state which they inhabited. He revolved a thousand plans by which he should be enabled to prolong the deceit until it might be no longer necessary, and secretly to take his daughter with him when he departed. His plans were greatly facilitated by the news which arrived from Paris.

"The government of France were greatly enraged at the escape of their victim, and spared no pains to detect and punish his deliverer. The plot of Felix was quickly discovered, and De Lacey and Agatha were thrown into prison. The news reached Felix, and roused him from his dream of pleasure. His blind and aged father, and his gentle sister, lay in a noisome dungeon, while he enjoyed the free air, and the society of her whom he loved. This idea was torture to him. He quickly arranged with the Turk, that if the latter should find a favourable opportunity for escape before Felix could return to Italy, Safie should remain as a boarder at a convent at Leghorn; and then, quitting the lovely Arabian, he hastened to Paris, and delivered himself up to the vengeance of the law, hoping to free De Lacey and Agatha by this proceeding.

"He did not succeed. They remained confined for five months before the trial took place; the result of which deprived them of their fortune, and condemned them to a perpetual exile from their native country.

"They found a miserable asylum in the cottage in Germany, where I discovered them. Felix soon learned that the treacherous Turk, for whom he and his family endured such unheard-of oppression, on discovering that his deliverer was thus reduced to poverty and impotence, became a traitor to good feeling and honour, and had quitted Italy with his daughter, insultingly sending Felix a pittance of money to aid him, as he said, in some plan of future maintenance.

"Such were the events that preyed on the heart of Felix, and rendered him, when I first saw him, the most miserable of his family. He could have endured poverty, and when this distress had been the meed of his virtue, he would have gloried in it: but the ingratitude of the Turk, and the loss of his beloved Safie, were misfortunes more bitter and irreparable. The arrival of the Arabian now infused new life into his soul.

"When the news reached Leghorn, that Felix was deprived of his wealth and rank, the merchant commanded his daughter to think no more of her lover, but to prepare to return with him to her native country. The generous nature of Safie was outraged by this command; she attempted to expostulate with her father, but he left her angrily, reiterating his tyrannical mandate.

"A few days after, the Turk entered his daughter's apartment, and told her hastily, that he had reason to believe that his residence at

Leghorn had been divulged, and that he should speedily be delivered up to the French government; he had, consequently, hired a vessel to convey him to Constantinople, for which city he should sail in a few hours. He intended to leave his daughter under the care of a confidential servant, to follow at her leisure with the greater part of his property, which had not yet arrived at Leghorn.

"When alone, Safie resolved in her own mind the plan of conduct that it would become her to pursue in this emergency. A residence in Turkey was abhorrent to her; her religion and feelings were alike adverse to it. By some papers of her father's, which fell into her hands, she heard of the exile of her lover, and learnt the name of the spot where he then resided. She hesitated some time, but at length she formed her determination. Taking with her some jewels that belonged to her, and a small sum of money, she quitted Italy, with an attendant, a native of Leghorn, but who understood the common language of Turkey, and departed for Germany.

"She arrived in safety at a town about twenty leagues from the cottage of De Lacey, when her attendant fell dangerously ill. Safie nursed her with the most devoted affection; but the poor girl died, and the Arabian was left alone, unacquainted with the language of the country, and utterly ignorant of the customs of the world. She fell, however, into good hands. The Italian had mentioned the name of the spot for which they were bound; and, after her death, the woman of the house in which they had lived took care that Safie should arrive in safety at the cottage of her lover.

Chapter VII.

"Such was the history of my beloved cottagers. It impressed me deeply. I learned, from the views of social life which it developed, to admire their virtues, and to deprecate the vices of mankind.

As yet I looked upon crime as a distant evil; benevolence and generosity were ever present before me, inciting within me a desire to become an actor in the busy scene where so many admirable qualities were called forth and displayed. But, in giving an account of the progress of my intellect, I must not omit a circumstance which occurred in the beginning of the month of August of the same year.

"One night, during my accustomed visit to the neighbouring wood, where I collected my own food, and brought home firing for my protectors, I found on the ground a leathern portmanteau, containing several articles of dress and some books. I eagerly seized the prize, and returned with it to my hovel. Fortunately the books were written in the language the elements of which I had acquired at the cottage;[1] they consisted of *Paradise Lost*, a volume of *Plutarch's Lives*, and the *Sorrows of Werter*.[2] The possession of these treasures gave me extreme delight; I now continually studied and exercised my mind upon these histories, whilst my friends were employed in their ordinary occupations.

"I can hardly describe to you the effect of these books. They produced in me an infinity of new images and feelings, that sometimes raised me to ecstacy, but more frequently sunk me into the lowest dejection. In the *Sorrows of Werter*, besides the interest of its simple and affecting story, so many opinions are canvassed, and so many lights thrown upon what had hitherto been to me obscure subjects, that I found in it a never-ending source of speculation and astonishment. The gentle and domestic manners it described, combined with lofty sentiments and feelings, which had for their object something out of self,[3] accorded well with my experience among my protectors, and with the wants which were for ever alive in my own bosom. But I thought Werter himself a more divine being than I had ever beheld or imagined; his character contained no pretension, but it sunk deep. The disquisitions upon death and suicide were calculated to fill me with wonder. I did not pretend to enter into the merits of the case, yet I inclined towards the opinions of the hero, whose extinction I wept, without precisely understanding it.

"As I read, however, I applied much personally to my own feelings and condition. I found myself similar, yet at the same time strangely unlike the beings concerning whom I read, and to whose conversation I was a listener. I sympathized with, and partly understood them, but I was unformed in mind; I was dependent on none, and related to none. 'The path of my departure was free;'[4] and there was none to lament my annihilation. My person was hideous, and my stature gigantic: what did this mean? Who was I? What was I? Whence did I come? What was my destination? These questions continually recurred, but I was unable to solve them.

"The volume of *Plutarch's Lives* which I possessed, contained the histories of the first founders of the ancient republics. This book had a far different effect upon me from the *Sorrows of Werter*. I learned from Werter's imaginations despondency and gloom: but Plutarch taught me high thoughts; he elevated me above the wretched sphere of my own reflections, to admire and love the heroes of past ages.

---

1. I.e., French.
2. *The Sorrows of Young Werther* (1774), by Johann Wolfgang von Goethe (1749–1832), is a novel about a sensitive young artist in love with a woman who is engaged to another. Plutarch (c. 46–119), Greek biographer, author of "parallel lives" of Greek and Roman heroes.
3. Other than self-interest.
4. From Percy Shelley's "Mutability," quoted on pp. 66–67, above.

Many things I read surpassed my understanding and experience. I had a very confused knowledge of kingdoms, wide extents of country, mighty rivers, and boundless seas. But I was perfectly unacquainted with towns, and large assemblages of men. The cottage of my protectors had been the only school in which I had studied human nature; but this book developed new and mightier scenes of action. I read of men concerned in public affairs governing or massacring their species. I felt the greatest ardour for virtue rise within me, and abhorrence for vice, as far as I understood the signification of those terms, relative as they were, as I applied them, to pleasure and pain alone. Induced by these feelings, I was of course led to admire peaceable law-givers, Numa, Solon, and Lycurgus,[5] in preference to Romulus and Theseus.[6] The patriarchal[7] lives of my protectors caused these impressions to take a firm hold on my mind; perhaps, if my first introduction to humanity had been made by a young soldier, burning for glory and slaughter, I should have been imbued with different sensations.

"But *Paradise Lost* excited different and far deeper emotions. I read it, as I had read the other volumes which had fallen into my hands, as a true history. It moved every feeling of wonder and awe, that the picture of an omnipotent God warring with his creatures was capable of exciting. I often referred the several situations, as their similarity struck me, to my own. Like Adam, I was created apparently united by no link to any other being in existence; but his state was far different from mine in every other respect. He had come forth from the hands of God a perfect creature, happy and prosperous, guarded by the especial care of his Creator; he was allowed to converse with, and acquire knowledge from beings of a superior nature: but I was wretched, helpless, and alone. Many times I considered Satan as the fitter emblem of my condition; for often, like him, when I viewed the bliss of my protectors, the bitter gall of envy rose within me.

"Another circumstance strengthened and confirmed these feelings. Soon after my arrival in the hovel, I discovered some papers in the pocket of the dress[8] which I had taken from your laboratory. At first I had neglected them; but now that I was able to decypher the characters in which they were written, I began to study them with diligence. It was your journal of the four months that preceded my creation. You minutely described in these papers every step you took in the progress of your work; this history was mingled with accounts of domestic occurrences. You, doubtless, recollect these papers. Here

---

5. Athenian statesman and reformer (c. 390–324 B.C.). Numa Pompilius (715–673 B.C.), second king of Rome. Solon (6th century B.C.), Athenian statesman and poet.
6. Legendary Athenian hero. Romulus, legendary founder (with Remus) of Rome.
7. Hierarchical, deferential.
8. Clothing. The same generic meaning of "dress" applies also on p. 124.

they are. Every thing is related in them which bears reference to my accursed origin; the whole detail of that series of disgusting circumstances which produced it is set in view; the minutest description of my odious and loathsome person is given, in language which painted your own horrors, and rendered mine ineffaceable. I sickened as I read. 'Hateful day when I received life!' I exclaimed in agony. 'Cursed creator! Why did you form a monster so hideous that even you turned from me in disgust? God in pity made man beautiful and alluring, after his own image; but my form is a filthy type[9] of your's, more horrid from its very resemblance. Satan had his companions, fellow-devils, to admire and encourage him; but I am solitary and detested.'

"These were the reflections of my hours of despondency and solitude; but when I contemplated the virtues of the cottagers, their amiable and benevolent dispositions, I persuaded myself that when they should become acquainted with my admiration of their virtues, they would compassionate me, and overlook my personal deformity. Could they turn from their door one, however monstrous, who solicited their compassion and friendship? I resolved, at least, not to despair, but in every way to fit myself for an interview with them which would decide my fate. I postponed this attempt for some months longer; for the importance attached to its success inspired me with a dread lest I should fail. Besides, I found that my understanding improved so much with every day's experience, that I was unwilling to commence this undertaking until a few more months should have added to my wisdom.

"Several changes, in the mean time, took place in the cottage. The presence of Safie diffused happiness among its inhabitants; and I also found that a greater degree of plenty reigned there. Felix and Agatha spent more time in amusement and conversation, and were assisted in their labours by servants. They did not appear rich, but they were contented and happy; their feelings were serene and peaceful, while mine became every day more tumultuous. Increase of knowledge only discovered to me more clearly what a wretched outcast I was. I cherished hope, it is true; but it vanished, when I beheld my person reflected in water, or my shadow in the moonshine, even as that frail image and that inconstant shade.

"I endeavoured to crush these fears, and to fortify myself for the trial which in a few months I resolved to undergo; and sometimes I allowed my thoughts, unchecked by reason, to ramble in the fields of Paradise, and dared to fancy amiable and lovely creatures sympathizing with my feelings and cheering my gloom; their angelic countenances breathed smiles of consolation. But it was all a dream: no Eve soothed my sorrows, or shared my thoughts; I was alone.

9. Version, manifestation. The language here derives from traditional theological typology.

I remembered Adam's supplication to his Creator;[1] but where was mine? he had abandoned me, and, in the bitterness of my heart, I cursed him.

"Autumn passed thus. I saw, with surprise and grief, the leaves decay and fall, and nature again assume the barren and bleak appearance it had worn when I first beheld the woods and the lovely moon. Yet I did not heed the bleakness of the weather; I was better fitted by my conformation[2] for the endurance of cold than heat. But my chief delights were the sight of the flowers, the birds, and all the gay apparel of summer; when those deserted me, I turned with more attention towards the cottagers. Their happiness was not decreased by the absence of summer. They loved, and sympathized with one another; and their joys, depending on each other, were not interrupted by the casualties that took place around them. The more I saw of them, the greater became my desire to claim their protection and kindness; my heart yearned to be known and loved by these amiable creatures: to see their sweet looks turned towards me with affection, was the utmost limit of my ambition. I dared not think that they would turn them from me with disdain and horror. The poor that stopped at their door were never driven away. I asked, it is true, for greater treasures than a little food or rest; I required kindness and sympathy; but I did not believe myself utterly unworthy of it.

"The winter advanced, and an entire revolution of the seasons had taken place since I awoke into life. My attention, at this time, was solely directed towards my plan of introducing myself into the cottage of my protectors. I revolved many projects; but that on which I finally fixed was, to enter the dwelling when the blind old man should be alone. I had sagacity enough to discover, that the unnatural hideousness of my person was the chief object of horror with those who had formerly beheld me. My voice, although harsh, had nothing terrible in it; I thought, therefore, that if, in the absence of his children, I could gain the good-will and mediation of the old De Lacy,[3] I might, by his means, be tolerated by my younger protectors.

"One day, when the sun shone on the red leaves that strewed the ground, and diffused cheerfulness, although it denied warmth, Safie, Agatha, and Felix, departed on a long country walk, and the old man, at his own desire, was left alone in the cottage. When his children had departed, he took up his guitar, and played several mournful, but sweet airs, more sweet and mournful than I had ever heard him play

1. Adam asks God for a "human consort" in *Paradise Lost* VIII.357ff.; see also n. 2, p. 3, above.
2. Constitution, design.
3. This name changes its spelling at this point in the 1818 edition.

before. At first his countenance was illuminated with pleasure, but, as he continued, thoughtfulness and sadness succeeded; at length, laying aside the instrument, he sat absorbed in reflection.

"My heart beat quick; this was the hour and moment of trial, which would decide my hopes, or realize my fears. The servants were gone to a neighbouring fair. All was silent in and around the cottage: it was an excellent opportunity; yet, when I proceeded to execute my plan, my limbs failed me, and I sunk to the ground. Again I rose; and, exerting all the firmness of which I was master, removed the planks which I had placed before my hovel to conceal my retreat. The fresh air revived me, and, with renewed determination, I approached the door of their cottage.

"I knocked. 'Who is there?' said the old man—'Come in.'

"I entered; 'Pardon this intrusion,' said I, 'I am a traveller in want of a little rest; you would greatly oblige me, if you would allow me to remain a few minutes before the fire.'

"'Enter,' said De Lacy; 'and I will try in what manner I can relieve your wants; but, unfortunately, my children are from home, and, as I am blind, I am afraid I shall find it difficult to procure food for you.'

"'Do not trouble yourself, my kind host, I have food; it is warmth and rest only that I need.'

"I sat down, and a silence ensued. I knew that every minute was precious to me, yet I remained irresolute in what manner to commence the interview; when the old man addressed me—

"'By your language, stranger, I suppose you are my countryman;—are you French?'

"'No; but I was educated by a French family, and understand that language only. I am now going to claim the protection of some friends, whom I sincerely love, and of whose favour I have some hopes.'

"'Are these Germans?'

"'No, they are French. But let us change the subject. I am an unfortunate and deserted creature; I look around, and I have no relation or friend upon earth. These amiable people to whom I go have never seen me, and know little of me. I am full of fears; for if I fail there, I am an outcast in the world for ever.'

"'Do not despair. To be friendless is indeed to be unfortunate; but the hearts of men, when unprejudiced by any obvious self-interest, are full of brotherly love and charity. Rely, therefore, on your hopes; and if these friends are good and amiable, do not despair.'

"'They are kind—they are the most excellent creatures in the world; but, unfortunately, they are prejudiced against me. I have good dispositions; my life has been hitherto harmless, and, in some degree, beneficial; but a fatal prejudice clouds their eyes, and where they ought to see a feeling and kind friend, they behold only a detestable monster.'

"'That is indeed unfortunate; but if you are really blameless, cannot you undeceive them?'

"'I am about to undertake that task; and it is on that account that I feel so many overwhelming terrors. I tenderly love these friends; I have, unknown to them, been for many months in the habits of daily kindness towards them; but they believe that I wish to injure them, and it is that prejudice which I wish to overcome.'

"'Where do these friends reside?'

"'Near this spot.'

"The old man paused, and then continued, 'If you will unreservedly confide to me the particulars of your tale, I perhaps may be of use in undeceiving them. I am blind, and cannot judge of your countenance, but there is something in your words which persuades me that you are sincere. I am poor, and an exile; but it will afford me true pleasure to be in any way serviceable to a human creature.'

"'Excellent man! I thank you, and accept your generous offer. You raise me from the dust by this kindness; and I trust that, by your aid, I shall not be driven from the society and sympathy of your fellow-creatures.'

"'Heaven forbid! even if you were really criminal; for that can only drive you to desperation, and not instigate you to virtue. I also am unfortunate; I and my family have been condemned, although innocent: judge, therefore, if I do not feel for your misfortunes.'

"'How can I thank you, my best and only benefactor? from your lips first have I heard the voice of kindness directed towards me; I shall be for ever grateful; and your present humanity assures me of success with those friends whom I am on the point of meeting.'

"'May I know the names and residence of those friends?'

"I paused. This, I thought, was the moment of decision, which was to rob me of, or bestow happiness on me for ever. I struggled vainly for firmness sufficient to answer him, but the effort destroyed all my remaining strength; I sank on the chair, and sobbed aloud. At that moment I heard the steps of my younger protectors. I had not a moment to lose; but, seizing the hand of the old man, I cried, 'Now is the time!—save and protect me! You and your family are the friends whom I seek. Do not you desert me in the hour of trial!'

"'Great God!' exclaimed the old man, 'who are you?'

"At that instant the cottage door was opened, and Felix, Safie, and Agatha entered. Who can describe their horror and consternation on beholding me? Agatha fainted; and Safie, unable to attend to her friend, rushed out of the cottage. Felix darted forward, and with supernatural force tore me from his father, to whose knees I clung: in a transport of fury, he dashed me to the ground, and struck me violently with a stick. I could have torn him limb from limb, as the lion rends the antelope. But my heart sunk within me as with bitter sickness, and I refrained. I saw him on the point of repeating his blow, when, overcome by pain and anguish, I quitted the cottage, and in the general tumult escaped unperceived to my hovel.

Chapter VIII.

"Cursed, cursed creator! Why did I live? Why, in that instant, did I not extinguish the spark of existence which you had so wantonly bestowed? I know not; despair had not yet taken possession of me; my feelings were those of rage and revenge. I could with pleasure have destroyed the cottage and its inhabitants, and have glutted myself with their shrieks and misery.

"When night came, I quitted my retreat, and wandered in the wood; and now, no longer restrained by the fear of discovery, I gave vent to my anguish in fearful howlings. I was like a wild beast that had broken the toils; destroying the objects that obstructed me, and ranging through the wood with a stag-like swiftness. Oh! what a miserable night I passed! the cold stars shone in mockery, and the bare trees waved their branches above me: now and then the sweet voice of a bird burst forth amidst the universal stillness. All, save I, were at rest or in enjoyment: I, like the arch fiend, bore a hell within me;[1] and, finding myself unsympathized with, wished to tear up the trees, spread havoc and destruction around me, and then to have sat down and enjoyed the ruin.

"But this was a luxury of sensation that could not endure; I became fatigued with excess of bodily exertion, and sank on the damp grass in the sick impotence of despair. There was none among the myriads of men that existed who would pity or assist me; and should I feel kindness towards my enemies? No: from that moment I declared everlasting war against the species, and, more than all, against him who had formed me, and sent me forth to this insupportable misery.

"The sun rose; I heard the voices of men, and knew that it was impossible to return to my retreat during that day. Accordingly I hid myself in some thick underwood, determining to devote the ensuing hours to reflection on my situation.

"The pleasant sunshine, and the pure air of day, restored me to some degree of tranquillity; and when I considered what had passed at the cottage, I could not help believing that I had been too hasty in my conclusions. I had certainly acted imprudently. It was apparent that my conversation had interested the father in my behalf,

---

1. Cf. Satan in *Paradise Lost*: "Me miserable! which way shall I fly / Infinite wrath, and infinite despair? / Which way I fly is Hell; myself am Hell" (IV.73–75).

and I was a fool in having exposed my person to the horror of his children. I ought to have familiarized the old De Lacy to me, and by degrees have discovered myself to the rest of his family, when they should have been prepared for my approach. But I did not believe my errors to be irretrievable; and, after much consideration, I resolved to return to the cottage, seek the old man, and by my representations win him to my party.[2]

"These thoughts calmed me, and in the afternoon I sank into a profound sleep; but the fever of my blood did not allow me to be visited by peaceful dreams. The horrible scene of the preceding day was for ever acting before my eyes; the females were flying, and the enraged Felix tearing me from his father's feet. I awoke exhausted; and, finding that it was already night, I crept forth from my hiding-place, and went in search of food.

"When my hunger was appeased, I directed my steps towards the well-known path that conducted to the cottage. All there was at peace. I crept into my hovel, and remained in silent expectation of the accustomed hour when the family arose. That hour past, the sun mounted high in the heavens, but the cottagers did not appear. I trembled violently, apprehending some dreadful misfortune. The inside of the cottage was dark, and I heard no motion; I cannot describe the agony of this suspence.

"Presently two countrymen passed by; but, pausing near the cottage, they entered into conversation, using violent gesticulations; but I did not understand what they said, as they spoke the language of the country,[3] which differed from that of my protectors. Soon after, however, Felix approached with another man: I was surprised, as I knew that he had not quitted the cottage that morning, and waited anxiously to discover, from his discourse, the meaning of these unusual appearances.

"'Do you consider,' said his companion to him, 'that you will be obliged to pay three months' rent, and to lose the produce of your garden? I do not wish to take any unfair advantage, and I beg therefore that you will take some days to consider of your determination.'

"'It is utterly useless,' replied Felix, 'we can never again inhabit your cottage. The life of my father is in the greatest danger, owing to the dreadful circumstance that I have related. My wife and my sister will never recover their horror. I entreat you not to reason with me any more. Take possession of your tenement,[4] and let me fly from this place.'

2. I.e., make him a partisan for me, get him on my side.
3. I.e., German.
4. Habitation.

"Felix trembled violently as he said this. He and his companion entered the cottage, in which they remained for a few minutes, and then departed. I never saw any of the family of De Lacy more. "I continued for the remainder of the day in my hovel in a state of utter and stupid[5] despair. My protectors had departed, and had broken the only link that held me to the world. For the first time the feelings of revenge and hatred filled my bosom, and I did not strive to controul them; but, allowing myself to be borne away by the stream, I bent my mind towards injury and death. When I thought of my friends, of the mild voice of De Lacy, the gentle eyes of Agatha, and the exquisite beauty of the Arabian, these thoughts vanished, and a gush of tears somewhat soothed me. But again, when I reflected that they had spurned and deserted me, anger returned, a rage of anger; and, unable to injure any thing human, I turned my fury towards inanimate objects. As night advanced, I placed a variety of combustibles around the cottage; and, after having destroyed every vestige of cultivation in the garden, I waited with forced impatience until the moon had sunk to commence my operations.

"As the night advanced, a fierce wind arose from the woods, and quickly dispersed the clouds that had loitered in the heavens: the blast tore along like a mighty avalanche, and produced a kind of insanity in my spirits, that burst all bounds of reason and reflection. I lighted the dry branch of a tree, and danced with fury around the devoted cottage, my eyes still fixed on the western horizon, the edge of which the moon nearly touched. A part of its orb was at length hid, and I waved my brand; it sunk, and, with a loud scream, I fired the straw, and heath, and bushes, which I had collected. The wind fanned the fire, and the cottage was quickly enveloped by the flames, which clung to it, and licked it with their forked and destroying tongues.

"As soon as I was convinced that no assistance could save any part of the habitation, I quitted the scene, and sought for refuge in the woods.

"And now, with the world before me, whither should I bend my steps?[6] I resolved to fly far from the scene of my misfortunes; but to me, hated and despised, every country must be equally horrible. At length the thought of you crossed my mind. I learned from your papers that you were my father, my creator; and to whom could I apply with more fitness than to him who had given me life? Among the lessons that Felix had bestowed upon Safie geography had not

---

5. "Characterized by stupor or insensibility" (*OED*).
6. Cf. the final lines of *Paradise Lost*, describing Adam and Eve in Eden: "The World was all before them, where to choose / Thir place of rest, and Providence thir guide: / They hand in hand with wand'ring steps and slow, / Through *Eden* took thir solitary way" (XII.646–69).

been omitted: I had learned from these the relative situations of the different countries of the earth. You had mentioned Geneva as the name of your native town; and towards this place I resolved to proceed.

"But how was I to direct myself? I knew that I must travel in a southwesterly direction to reach my destination; but the sun was my only guide. I did not know the names of the towns that I was to pass through, nor could I ask information from a single human being; but I did not despair. From you only could I hope for succour, although towards you I felt no sentiment but that of hatred. Unfeeling, heartless creator! you had endowed me with perceptions and passions, and then cast me abroad an object for the scorn and horror of mankind. But on you only had I any claim for pity and redress, and from you I determined to seek that justice which I vainly attempted to gain from any other being that wore the human form.

"My travels were long, and the sufferings I endured intense. It was late in autumn when I quitted the district where I had so long resided. I travelled only at night, fearful of encountering the visage of a human being. Nature decayed around me, and the sun became heatless; rain and snow poured around me; mighty rivers were frozen; the surface of the earth was hard, and chill, and bare, and I found no shelter. Oh, earth! how often did I imprecate curses on the cause of my being! The mildness of my nature had fled, and all within me was turned to gall and bitterness. The nearer I approached to your habitation, the more deeply did I feel the spirit of revenge enkindled in my heart. Snow fell, and the waters were hardened, but I rested not. A few incidents now and then directed me, and I possessed a map of the country; but I often wandered wide from my path. The agony of my feelings allowed me no respite: no incident occurred from which my rage and misery could not extract its food; but a circumstance that happened when I arrived on the confines of Switzerland, when the sun had recovered its warmth, and the earth again began to look green, confirmed in an especial manner the bitterness and horror of my feelings.

"I generally rested during the day, and travelled only when I was secured by night from the view of man. One morning, however, finding that my path lay through a deep wood, I ventured to continue my journey after the sun had risen; the day, which was one of the first of spring, cheered even me by the loveliness of its sunshine and the balminess of the air. I felt emotions of gentleness and pleasure, that had long appeared dead, revive within me. Half surprised by the novelty of these sensations, I allowed myself to be borne away by them; and, forgetting my solitude and deformity, dared to be happy. Soft tears again bedewed my cheeks, and I even raised my humid eyes with thankfulness towards the blessed sun which bestowed such joy upon me.

"I continued to wind among the paths of the wood, until I came to its boundary, which was skirted by a deep and rapid river, into which many of the trees bent their branches, now budding with the fresh spring. Here I paused, not exactly knowing what path to pursue, when I heard the sound of voices, that induced me to conceal myself under the shade of a cypress. I was scarcely hid, when a young girl came running towards the spot where I was concealed, laughing as if she ran from some one in sport. She continued her course along the precipitous sides of the river, when suddenly her foot slipt; and she fell into the rapid stream. I rushed from my hiding place, and, with extreme labour from the force of the current, saved her, and dragged her to shore. She was senseless; and I endeavoured, by every means in my power, to restore animation, when I was suddenly interrupted by the approach of a rustic, who was probably the person from whom she had playfully fled. On seeing me, he darted towards me, and, tearing the girl from my arms, hastened towards the deeper parts of the wood. I followed speedily, I hardly knew why; but when the man saw me draw near, he aimed a gun, which he carried, at my body, and fired. I sunk to the ground, and my injurer, with increased swiftness, escaped into the wood.

"This was then the reward of my benevolence! I had saved a human being from destruction, and, as a recompence, I now writhed under the miserable pain of a wound, which shattered the flesh and bone. The feelings of kindness and gentleness, which I had entertained but a few moments before, gave place to hellish rage and gnashing of teeth. Inflamed by pain, I vowed eternal hatred and vengeance to all mankind. But the agony of my wound overcame me; my pulses paused, and I fainted.

"For some weeks I led a miserable life in the woods, endeavouring to cure the wound which I had received. The ball had entered my shoulder, and I knew not whether it had remained there or passed through; at any rate I had no means of extracting it. My sufferings were augmented also by the oppressive sense of the injustice and ingratitude of their infliction. My daily vows rose for revenge—a deep and deadly revenge, such as would alone compensate for the outrages and anguish I had endured.

"After some weeks my wound healed, and I continued my journey. The labours I endured were no longer to be alleviated by the bright sun or gentle breezes of spring; all joy was but a mockery, which insulted my desolate state, and made me feel more painfully that I was not made for the enjoyment of pleasure.

"But my toils now drew near a close; and, two months from this time, I reached the environs of Geneva.

"It was evening when I arrived, and I retired to a hiding-place among the fields that surround it, to meditate in what manner I should apply to you. I was oppressed by fatigue and hunger, and far too unhappy to enjoy the gentle breezes of evening, or the prospect of the sun setting behind the stupendous mountains of Jura.

"At this time a slight sleep relieved me from the pain of reflection, which was disturbed by the approach of a beautiful child, who came running into the recess I had chosen with all the sportiveness of infancy. Suddenly, as I gazed on him, an idea seized me, that this little creature was unprejudiced, and had lived too short a time to have imbibed a horror of deformity. If, therefore, I could seize him, and educate him as my companion and friend, I should not be so desolate in this peopled earth.

"Urged by this impulse, I seized on the boy as he passed, and drew him towards me. As soon as he beheld my form, he placed his hands before his eyes, and uttered a shrill scream: I drew his hand forcibly from his face, and said, 'Child, what is the meaning of this? I do not intend to hurt you; listen to me.'

"He struggled violently; 'Let me go,' he cried; 'monster! ugly wretch! you wish to eat me, and tear me to pieces—You are an ogre—Let me go, or I will tell my papa.'

"'Boy, you will never see your father again; you must come with me.'

"'Hideous monster! let me go; My papa is a Syndic—he is M. Frankenstein—he would punish you. You dare not keep me.'

"'Frankenstein! you belong then to my enemy—to him towards whom I have sworn eternal revenge; you shall be my first victim.'

"The child still struggled, and loaded me with epithets which carried despair to my heart: I grasped his throat to silence him, and in a moment he lay dead at my feet.

"I gazed on my victim, and my heart swelled with exultation and hellish triumph: clapping my hands, I exclaimed, 'I, too, can create desolation; my enemy is not impregnable; this death will carry despair to him, and a thousand other miseries shall torment and destroy him.'

"As I fixed my eyes on the child, I saw something glittering on his breast. I took it; it was a portrait of a most lovely woman. In spite of my malignity, it softened and attracted me. For a few moments I gazed with delight on her dark eyes, fringed by deep lashes, and her lovely lips; but presently my rage returned: I remembered that I was for ever deprived of the delights that such beautiful creatures could bestow; and that she whose resemblance I contemplated would, in regarding me, have changed that air of divine benignity to one expressive of disgust and affright.

"Can you wonder that such thoughts transported me with rage? I only wonder that at that moment, instead of venting my sensations in exclamations and agony, I did not rush among mankind, and perish in the attempt to destroy them.

"While I was overcome by these feelings, I left the spot where I had committed the murder, and was seeking a more secluded hiding-place, when I perceived a woman passing near me. She was young, not indeed so beautiful as her whose portrait I held, but of an agreeable aspect, and blooming in the loveliness of youth and health. Here, I thought, is one of those whose smiles are bestowed on all but me; she shall not escape: thanks to the lessons of Felix, and the sanguinary[7] laws of man, I have learned how to work mischief. I approached her unperceived, and placed the portrait securely in one of the folds of her dress.

"For some days I haunted the spot where these scenes had taken place; sometimes wishing to see you, sometimes resolved to quit the world and its miseries for ever. At length I wandered towards these mountains, and have ranged through their immense recesses, consumed by a burning passion which you alone can gratify. We may not part until you have promised to comply with my requisition.[8] I am alone, and miserable; man will not associate with me; but one as deformed and horrible as myself would not deny herself to me. My companion must be of the same species, and have the same defects. This being you must create."

Chapter IX.

The being finished speaking, and fixed his looks upon me in expectation of a reply. But I was bewildered, perplexed, and unable to arrange my ideas sufficiently to understand the full extent of his proposition. He continued—

"You must create a female for me, with whom I can live in the interchange of those sympathies necessary for my being. This you alone can do; and I demand it of you as a right which you must not refuse."

The latter part of his tale had kindled anew in me the anger that had died away while he narrated his peaceful life among the cottagers, and, as he said this, I could no longer suppress the rage that burned within me.

"I do refuse it," I replied; "and no torture shall ever extort a consent from me. You may render me the most miserable of men, but you shall never make me base in my own eyes. Shall I create another like yourself, whose joint wickedness might desolate the world. Begone! I have answered you; you may torture me, but I will never consent."

7. Bloodthirsty.
8. Demand or requirement.

"You are in the wrong,' replied the fiend; "and, instead of threatening, I am content to reason with you. I am malicious because I am miserable; am I not shunned and hated by all mankind? You, my creator, would tear me to pieces, and triumph; remember that, and tell me why I should pity man more than he pities me? You would not call it murder, if you could precipitate me into one of those ice-rifts, and destroy my frame, the work of your own hands. Shall I respect man, when he contemns[1] me? Let him live with me in the interchange of kindness, and, instead of injury, I would bestow every benefit upon him with tears of gratitude at his acceptance. But that cannot be; the human senses are insurmountable barriers to our union. Yet mine shall not be the submission of abject slavery. I will revenge my injuries: if I cannot inspire love, I will cause fear; and chiefly towards you my arch-enemy, because my creator, do I swear inextinguishable hatred. Have a care: I will work at your destruction, nor finish until I desolate your heart, so that you curse the hour of your birth."

A fiendish rage animated him as he said this; his face was wrinkled into contortions too horrible for human eyes to behold; but presently he calmed himself, and proceeded—

"I intended to reason. This passion is detrimental to me; for you do not reflect that you are the cause of its excess. If any being felt emotions of benevolence towards me, I should return them an hundred and an hundred fold; for that one creature's sake, I would make peace with the whole kind! But I now indulge in dreams of bliss that cannot be realized. What I ask of you is reasonable and moderate; I demand a creature of another sex, but as hideous as myself: the gratification is small, but it is all that I can receive, and it shall content me. It is true, we shall be monsters, cut off from all the world; but on that account we shall be more attached to one another. Our lives will not be happy, but they will be harmless, and free from the misery I now feel. Oh! my creator, make me happy; let me feel gratitude towards you for one benefit! Let me see that I excite the sympathy of some existing thing; do not deny me my request!"

I was moved. I shuddered when I thought of the possible consequences of my consent; but I felt that there was some justice in his argument. His tale, and the feelings he now expressed, proved him to be a creature of fine sensations; and did I not, as his maker, owe him all the portion of happiness that it was in my power to bestow? He saw my change of feeling, and continued—

"If you consent, neither you nor any other human being shall ever see us again: I will go to the vast wilds of South America. My food is

1. Treats with contempt.

not that of man; I do not destroy the lamb and the kid, to glut my appetite; acorns and berries afford me sufficient nourishment. My companion will be of the same nature as myself, and will be content with the same fare. We shall make our bed of dried leaves; the sun will shine on us as on man, and will ripen our food. The picture I present to you is peaceful and human, and you must feel that you could deny it only in the wantonness of power and cruelty. Pitiless as you have been towards me, I now see compassion in your eyes; let me seize the favourable moment, and persuade you to promise what I so ardently desire."

"You propose," replied I, "to fly from the habitations of man, to dwell in those wilds where the beasts of the field will be your only companions. How can you, who long for the love and sympathy of man, persevere in this exile? You will return, and again seek their kindness, and you will meet with their detestation; your evil passions will be renewed, and you will then have a companion to aid you in the task of destruction. This may not be; cease to argue the point, for I cannot consent."

"How inconstant are your feelings! but a moment ago you were moved by my representations, and why do you again harden yourself to my complaints? I swear to you, by the earth which I inhabit, and by you that made me, that, with the companion you bestow, I will quit the neighbourhood of man, and dwell, as it may chance, in the most savage of places. My evil passions will have fled, for I shall meet with sympathy; my life, will flow quietly away, and, in my dying moments, I shall not curse, my maker."

His words had a strange effect upon me. I compassionated him, and sometimes felt a wish to console him; but when I looked upon him, when I saw the filthy mass that moved and talked, my heart sickened, and my feelings were altered to those of horror and hatred. I tried to stifle these sensations; I thought, that as I could not sympathize with him, I had no right to withhold from him the small portion of happiness which was yet in my power to bestow.

"You swear," I said, "to be harmless; but have you not already shewn a degree of malice that should reasonably make me distrust you? May not even this be a feint that will increase your triumph by affording a wider scope for your revenge?"

"How is this? I thought I had moved your compassion, and yet you still refuse to bestow on me the only benefit that can soften my heart, and render me harmless. If I have no ties and no affections, hatred and vice must be my portion; the love of another will destroy the cause of my crimes, and I shall become a thing, of whose existence every one will be ignorant. My vices are the children of a forced solitude that I abhor; and my virtues will necessarily arise when I live in communion with an equal. I shall feel the affections of a sensitive being, and become linked to the chain of existence and events, from which I am now excluded."

I paused some time to reflect on all he had related, and the various arguments which he had employed. I thought of the promise of virtues which he had displayed on the opening of his existence, and the subsequent blight of all kindly feeling by the loathing and scorn which his protectors had manifested towards him. His power and threats were not omitted in my calculations: a creature who could exist in the ice caves of the glaciers, and hide himself from pursuit among the ridges of inaccessible precipices, was a being possessing faculties it would be vain to cope with. After a long pause of reflection, I concluded, that the justice due both to him and my fellow-creatures demanded of me that I should comply with his request. Turning to him, therefore, I said—

"I consent to your demand, on your solemn oath to quit Europe for ever, and every other place in the neighbourhood of man, as soon as I shall deliver into your hands a female who will accompany you in your exile."

"I swear," he cried, "by the sun, and by the blue sky of heaven, that if you grant my prayer, while they exist you shall never behold me again. Depart to your home, and commence your labours: I shall watch their progress with unutterable anxiety; and fear not but that when you are ready I shall appear."

Saying this, he suddenly quitted me, fearful, perhaps, of any change in my sentiments. I saw him descend the mountain with greater speed than the flight of an eagle, and quickly lost him among the undulations of the sea of ice.

His tale had occupied the whole day; and the sun was upon the verge of the horizon when he departed. I knew that I ought to hasten my descent towards the valley, as I should soon be encompassed in darkness; but my heart was heavy, and my steps slow. The labour of winding among the little paths of the mountains, and fixing my feet firmly as I advanced, perplexed me, occupied as I was by the emotions which the occurrences of the day had produced. Night was far advanced, when I came to the half-way resting-place, and seated myself beside the fountain. The stars shone at intervals, as the clouds passed from over them; the dark pines rose before me, and every here and there a broken tree lay on the ground: it was a scene of wonderful solemnity, and stirred strange thoughts within me. I wept bitterly; and, clasping my hands in agony, I exclaimed, "Oh! stars, and clouds, and winds, ye are all about to mock me: if ye really pity me, crush sensation and memory; let me become as nought; but if not, depart, depart and leave me in darkness."

These were wild and miserable thoughts; but I cannot describe to you how the eternal twinkling of the stars weighed upon me, and how I listened to every blast of wind, as if it were a dull ugly siroc[2] on its way to consume me.

Morning dawned before I arrived at the village of Chamounix; but my presence, so haggard and strange, hardly calmed the fears of my family, who had waited the whole night in anxious expectation of my return.

The following day we returned to Geneva. The intention of my father in coming had been to divert my mind, and to restore me to my lost tranquillity; but the medicine had been fatal. And, unable to account for the excess of misery I appeared to suffer, he hastened to return home, hoping the quiet and monotony of a domestic life would by degrees alleviate my sufferings from whatsoever cause they might spring.

For myself, I was passive in all their arrangements; and the gentle affection of my beloved Elizabeth was inadequate to draw me from the depth of my despair. The promise I had made to the dæmon weighed upon my mind, like Dante's iron cowl on the heads of the hellish hypocrites.[3] All pleasures of earth and sky passed before me like a dream, and that thought only had to me the reality of life. Can you wonder, that sometimes a kind of insanity possessed me, or that I saw continually about me a multitude of filthy animals inflicting on me incessant torture, that often extorted screams and bitter groans?

By degrees, however, these feelings became calmed. I entered again into the every-day scene of life, if not with interest, at least with some degree of tranquillity.

END OF VOL. II.

---

2. Sirocco; a hot and blighting wind that blows from North Africa across the Mediterranean.
3. In canto XXIII of Dante's *Inferno* (see n. 2, p. 36, above), the hypocrites wear monks' hoods that are dazzling on the outside but inside are lined with lead.

Volume III

Chapter I.

Day after day, week after week, passed away on my return to Geneva; and I could not collect the courage to recommence my work. I feared the vengeance of the disappointed fiend, yet I was unable to overcome my repugnance to the task which was enjoined me. I found that I could not compose a female without again devoting several months to profound study and laborious disquisition.[1] I had heard of some discoveries having been made by an English philosopher, the knowledge of which was material to my success, and I sometimes thought of obtaining my father's consent to visit England for this purpose; but I clung to every pretence of delay, and could not resolve to interrupt my returning tranquillity. My health, which had hitherto declined, was now much restored; and my spirits, when unchecked by the memory of my unhappy promise, rose proportionably. My father saw this change with pleasure, and he turned his thoughts towards the best method of eradicating the remains of my melancholy, which every now and then would return by fits, and with a devouring blackness overcast the approaching sunshine. At these moments I took refuge in the most perfect solitude. I passed whole days on the lake alone in a little boat, watching the clouds, and listening to the rippling of the waves, silent and listless. But the fresh air and bright sun seldom failed to restore me to some degree of composure; and, on my return, I met the salutations of my friends with a readier smile and a more cheerful heart.

It was after my return from one of these rambles that my father, calling me aside, thus addressed me:—

"I am happy to remark, my dear son, that you have resumed your former pleasures, and seem to be returning to yourself. And yet you are still unhappy, and still avoid our society. For some time I was lost in conjecture as to the cause of this; but yesterday an idea struck me, and if it is well founded, I conjure you to avow it. Reserve on such a point would be not only useless, but draw down treble misery on us all."

1. Investigation, research.

I trembled violently at this exordium,[2] and my father continued—
"I confess, my son, that I have always looked forward to your
marriage with your cousin as the tie of our domestic comfort, and
the stay of my declining years. You were attached to each other
from your earliest infancy; you studied together, and appeared,
in dispositions and tastes, entirely suited to one another. But so
blind is the experience of man, that what I conceived to be the best
assistants to my plan may have entirely destroyed it. You, perhaps,
regard her as your sister, without any wish that she might become
your wife. Nay, you may have met with another whom you may
love; and, considering yourself as bound in honour to your cousin,
this struggle may occasion the poignant misery which you appear
to feel."

"My dear father, re-assure yourself. I love my cousin tenderly and
sincerely. I never saw any woman who excited, as Elizabeth does,
my warmest admiration and affection. My future hopes and prospects are entirely bound up in the expectation of our union."

"The expression of your sentiments on this subject, my dear Victor, gives me more pleasure than I have for some time experienced.
If you feel thus, we shall assuredly be happy, however present events
may cast a gloom over us. But it is this gloom, which appears to
have taken so strong a hold of your mind, that I wish to dissipate.
Tell me, therefore, whether you object to an immediate solemnization of the marriage. We have been unfortunate, and recent events
have drawn us from that every-day tranquillity befitting my years
and infirmities. You are younger; yet I do not suppose, possessed as
you are of a competent fortune, that an early marriage would at all
interfere with any future plans of honour and utility that you may
have formed. Do not suppose, however, that I wish to dictate happiness to you, or that a delay on your part would cause me any serious
uneasiness. Interpret my words with candour,[3] and answer me, I
conjure you, with confidence and sincerity."

I listened to my father in silence, and remained for some time
incapable of offering any reply. I revolved rapidly in my mind a multitude of thoughts, and endeavoured to arrive at some conclusion.
Alas! to me the idea of an immediate union with my cousin was one
of horror and dismay. I was bound by a solemn promise, which I had
not yet fulfilled, and dared not break; or, if I did, what manifold
miseries might not impend over me and my devoted family! Could I
enter into a festival with this deadly weight yet hanging round my
neck, and bowing me to the ground. I must perform my engagement,[4]

2. Beginning (of a discourse).
3. Kindliness, favorable disposition.
4. Promise, obligation.

and let the monster depart with his mate, before I allowed myself to enjoy the delight of an union from which I expected peace.

I remembered also the necessity imposed upon me of either journeying to England, or entering into a long correspondence with those philosophers of that country, whose knowledge and discoveries were of indispensable use to me in my present undertaking. The latter method of obtaining the desired intelligence was dilatory and unsatisfactory: besides, any variation was agreeable to me, and I was delighted with the idea of spending a year or two in change of scene and variety of occupation, in absence from my family; during which period some event might happen which would restore me to them in peace and happiness: my promise might be fulfilled, and the monster have departed; or some accident might occur to destroy him, and put an end to my slavery for ever.

These feelings dictated my answer to my father. I expressed a wish to visit England; but, concealing the true reasons of this request, I clothed my desires under the guise of wishing to travel and see the world before I sat down for life within the walls of my native town.

I urged my entreaty with earnestness, and my father was easily induced to comply; for a more indulgent and less dictatorial parent did not exist upon earth. Our plan was soon arranged. I should travel to Strasburgh, where Clerval would join me. Some short time would be spent in the towns of Holland, and our principal stay would be in England. We should return by France; and it was agreed that the tour should occupy the space of two years.

My father pleased himself with the reflection, that my union with Elizabeth should take place immediately on my return to Geneva. "These two years," said he, "will pass swiftly, and it will be the last delay that will oppose itself to your happiness. And, indeed, I earnestly desire that period to arrive, when we shall all be united, and neither hopes or fears arise to disturb our domestic calm."

"I am content," I replied, "with your arrangement. By that time we shall both have become wiser, and I hope happier, than we at present are." I sighed; but my father kindly forbore to question me further concerning the cause of my dejection. He hoped that new scenes, and the amusement of travelling, would restore my tranquillity.

I now made arrangements for my journey; but one feeling haunted me, which filled me with fear and agitation. During my absence I should leave my friends unconscious of the existence of their enemy, and unprotected from his attacks, exasperated as he might be by my departure. But he had promised to follow me wherever I might go; and would he not accompany me to England? This imagination was dreadful in itself, but soothing, inasmuch as it supposed the safety of my friends. I was agonized with the idea of the possibility that the reverse of this might happen. But through the whole period during which I was the slave of my creature, I allowed myself to be governed by the impulses of the moment; and my present sensations strongly intimated that the fiend would follow me, and exempt my family from the danger of his machinations.

It was in the latter end of August that I departed, to pass two years of exile. Elizabeth approved of the reasons of my departure, and only regretted that she had not the same opportunities of enlarging her experience, and cultivating her understanding. She wept, however, as she bade me farewell, and entreated me to return happy and tranquil. "We all," said she, "depend upon you; and if you are miserable, what must be our feelings?"

I threw myself into the carriage that was to convey me away, hardly knowing whither I was going, and careless of what was passing around. I remembered only, and it was with a bitter anguish that I reflected on it, to order that my chemical instruments should be packed to go with me: for I resolved to fulfil my promise while abroad, and return, if possible, a free man. Filled with dreary imaginations, I passed through many beautiful and majestic scenes; but my eyes were fixed and unobserving. I could only think of the bourne[5] of my travels, and the work which was to occupy me whilst they endured.

After some days spent in listless indolence, during which I traversed many leagues, I arrived at Strasburgh, where I waited two days for Clerval. He came. Alas, how great was the contrast between us! He was alive to every new scene; joyful when he saw the beauties of the setting sun, and more happy when he beheld it rise, and recommence a new day. He pointed out to me the shifting colours of the landscape, and the appearances of the sky. "This is what it is to live;" he cried, "now I enjoy existence! But you, my dear Frankenstein, wherefore are you desponding and sorrowful?" In truth, I was occupied by gloomy thoughts, and neither saw the descent of the evening star, nor the golden sun-rise reflected in the Rhine.—And you, my friend, would be far more amused with the journal of Clerval, who observed the scenery with an eye of feeling and delight, than to listen to my reflections. I, a miserable wretch, haunted by a curse that shut up every avenue to enjoyment.

We had agreed to descend the Rhine in a boat from Strasburgh to Rotterdam, whence we might take shipping for London. During this voyage, we passed by many willowy islands, and saw several beautiful towns. We staid a day at Manheim, and, on the fifth from our departure from Strasburgh, arrived at Mayence. The course of the Rhine below Mayence becomes much more picturesque. The river descends rapidly, and winds between hills, not high, but steep,

---

5. Goal, destination.

and of beautiful forms. We saw many ruined castles standing on the edges of precipices, surrounded by black woods, high and inaccessible. This part of the Rhine, indeed, presents a singularly variegated landscape. In one spot you view rugged hills, ruined castles overlooking tremendous precipices, with the dark Rhine rushing beneath; and, on the sudden turn of a promontory, flourishing vineyards, with green sloping banks, and a meandering river, and populous towns, occupy the scene.

We travelled at the time of the vintage, and heard the song of the labourers, as we glided down the stream. Even I, depressed in mind, and my spirits continually agitated by gloomy feelings, even I was pleased. I lay at the bottom of the boat, and, as I gazed on the cloudless blue sky, I seemed to drink in a tranquillity to which I had long been a stranger. And if these were my sensations, who can describe those of Henry? He felt as if he had been transported to Fairy-land, and enjoyed a happiness seldom tasted by man. "I have seen," he said, "the most beautiful scenes of my own country; I have visited the lakes of Lucerne and Uri, where the snowy mountains descend almost perpendicularly to the water, casting black and impenetrable shades, which would cause a gloomy and mournful appearance, were it not for the most verdant islands that relieve the eye by their gay appearance; I have seen this lake agitated by a tempest, when the wind tore up whirlwinds of water, and gave you an idea of what the water-spout must be on the great ocean, and the waves dash with fury the base of the mountain, where the priest and his mistress were overwhelmed by an avalanche, and where their dying voices are still said to be heard amid the pauses of the nightly wind; I have seen the mountains of La Valais, and the Pays de Vaud: but this country, Victor, pleases me more than all those wonders. The mountains of Switzerland are more majestic and strange; but there is a charm in the banks of this divine river, that I never before saw equalled. Look at that castle which overhangs yon precipice; and that also on the island, almost concealed amongst the foliage of those lovely trees; and now that group of labourers coming from among their vines; and that village half-hid in the recess of the mountain. Oh, surely, the spirit that inhabits and guards this place has a soul more in harmony with man, than those who pile[6] the glacier, or retire to the inaccessible peaks of the mountains of our own country."

Clerval! beloved friend! even now it delights me to record your words, and to dwell on the praise of which you are so eminently deserving. He was a being formed in the "very poetry of nature."[7]

6. Drive piles into (in order to build upon).
7. Leigh Hunt's "Rimini" [Mary Shelley's note]. *The Story of Rimini* (1816), a narrative poem by Leigh Hunt (1784–1859) about Paolo and Francesca, famous lovers in Dante's *Inferno*.

His wild and enthusiastic imagination was chastened by the sensibility of his heart. His soul overflowed with ardent affections, and his friendship was of that devoted and wondrous nature that the worldly-minded teach us to look for only in the imagination. But even human sympathies were not sufficient to satisfy his eager mind. The scenery of external nature, which others regard only with admiration, he loved with ardour:

> ———"The sounding cataract
> Haunted *him* like a passion: the tall rock,
> The mountain, and the deep and gloomy wood,
> Their colours and their forms, were then to him
> An appetite; a feeling, and a love,
> That had no need of a remoter charm,
> By thought supplied, or any interest
> Unborrowed from the eye."[8]

And where does he now exist? Is this gentle and lovely being lost for ever? Has this mind so replete with ideas, imaginations fanciful and magnificent, which formed a world, whose existence depended on the life of its creator; has this mind perished? Does it now only exist in my memory? No, it is not thus; your form so divinely wrought, and beaming with beauty, has decayed, but your spirit still visits and consoles your unhappy friend.

Pardon this gush of sorrow; these ineffectual words are but a slight tribute to the unexampled worth of Henry, but they soothe my heart, overflowing with the anguish which his remembrance creates. I will proceed with my tale.

Beyond Cologne we descended to the plains of Holland; and we resolved to post[9] the remainder of our way; for the wind was contrary, and the stream of the river was too gentle to aid us.

Our journey here lost the interest arising from beautiful scenery; but we arrived in a few days at Rotterdam, whence we proceeded by sea to England. It was on a clear morning, in the latter days of December, that I first saw the white cliffs of Britain. The banks of the Thames presented a new scene; they were flat, but fertile, and almost every town was marked by the remembrance of some story. We saw Tilbury Fort, and remembered the Spanish armada; Gravesend, Woolwich, and Greenwich, places which I had heard of even in my country.

At length we saw the numerous steeples of London, St. Paul's towering above all, and the Tower famed in English history.

---

8. Wordsworth's "Tintern Abbey" [Mary Shelley's note]. Lines 76–83 of "Lines composed a few miles above Tintern Abbey" (1798), by William Wordsworth (1770–1850); Mary Shelley has changed "me" to "him."
9. Travel by horse.

Chapter II.

London was our present point of rest; we determined to remain several months in this wonderful and celebrated city. Clerval desired the intercourse of[1] the men of genius and talent who flourished at this time; but this was with me a secondary object; I was principally occupied with the means of obtaining the information necessary for the completion of my promise, and quickly availed myself of the letters of introduction that I had brought with me, addressed to the most distinguished natural philosophers.

If this journey had taken place during my days of study and happiness, it would have afforded me inexpressible pleasure. But a blight had come over my existence, and I only visited these people for the sake of the information they might give me on the subject in which my interest was so terribly profound. Company was irksome to me; when alone, I could fill my mind with the sights of heaven and earth; the voice of Henry soothed me, and I could thus cheat myself into a transitory peace. But busy uninteresting joyous faces brought back despair to my heart. I saw an insurmountable barrier placed between me and my fellow-men; this barrier was sealed with the blood of William and Justine; and to reflect on the events connected with those names filled my soul with anguish.

But in Clerval I saw the image of my former self; he was inquisitive, and anxious to gain experience and instruction. The difference of manners which he observed was to him an inexhaustible source of instruction and amusement. He was for ever busy; and the only check to his enjoyments was my sorrowful and dejected mien. I tried to conceal this as much as possible, that I might not debar him from the pleasures natural to one who was entering on a new scene of life, undisturbed by any care or bitter recollection. I often refused to accompany him, alleging another engagement, that I might remain alone. I now also began to collect the materials necessary for my new creation, and this was to me like the torture of single drops of water continually falling on the head. Every thought that was devoted to it was an extreme anguish, and every word that I spoke in allusion to it caused my lips to quiver, and my heart to palpitate.

After passing some months in London, we received a letter from a person in Scotland, who had formerly been our visitor at Geneva. He mentioned the beauties of his native country, and asked us if those were not sufficient allurements to induce us to prolong our journey as far north as Perth, where he resided. Clerval eagerly desired to accept this invitation; and I, although I abhorred society,

1. Conversation with.

wished to view again mountains and streams, and all the wondrous works with which Nature adorns her chosen dwelling-places. We had arrived in England at the beginning of October, and it was now February. We accordingly determined to commence our journey towards the north at the expiration of another month. In this expedition we did not intend to follow the great road to Edinburgh, but to visit Windsor, Oxford, Matlock, and the Cumberland lakes, resolving to arrive at the completion of this tour about the end of July. I packed my chemical instruments, and the materials I had collected, resolving to finish my labours in some obscure nook in the northern highlands of Scotland.

We quitted London on the 27th of March, and remained a few days at Windsor, rambling in its beautiful forest. This was a new scene to us mountaineers; the majestic oaks, the quantity of game, and the herds of stately deer, were all novelties to us.

From thence we proceeded to Oxford. As we entered this city, our minds were filled with the remembrance of the events that had been transacted here more than a century and a half before. It was here that Charles I. had collected his forces. This city had remained faithful to him, after the whole nation had forsaken his cause to join the standard of parliament and liberty. The memory of that unfortunate king, and his companions, the amiable Falkland, the insolent Gower, his queen, and son,[2] gave a peculiar interest to every part of the city, which they might be supposed to have inhabited. The spirit of elder days found a dwelling here, and we delighted to trace its footsteps. If these feelings had not found an imaginary gratification, the appearance of the city had yet in itself sufficient beauty to obtain our admiration. The colleges are ancient and picturesque; the streets are almost magnificent; and the lovely Isis,[3] which flows beside it through meadows of exquisite verdure, is spread forth into a placid expanse of waters, which reflects its majestic assemblage of towers, and spires, and domes, embosomed among aged trees.

I enjoyed this scene; and yet my enjoyment was embittered both by the memory of the past, and the anticipation of the future. I was formed for peaceful happiness. During my youthful days discontent never visited my mind; and if I was ever overcome by *ennui*,[4] the sight of what is beautiful in nature, or the study of what is excellent and sublime in the productions of man, could always interest my heart, and communicate elasticity to my spirits. But I am a blasted

---

2. Henrietta Maria (1609–1669) and Charles (1630–1685), who became Charles II in 1660. *The amiable Falkland*: Lucius Cary, second Viscount Falkland (1610–1643), Royalist, killed in battle at Newberry. *The insolent Gower*: corrected to "Goring" in 1831; George Goring, Baron Goring (1608–1657), fought as a Royalist after twice switching sides.
3. The river Thames is known in Oxford as the Isis.
4. Weariness and dissatisfaction.

tree; the bolt has entered my soul; and I felt then that I should survive to exhibit, what I shall soon cease to be—a miserable spectacle of wrecked humanity, pitiable to others, and abhorrent to myself.

We passed a considerable period at Oxford, rambling among its environs, and endeavouring to identify every spot which might relate to the most animating epoch of English history. Our little voyages of discovery were often prolonged by the successive objects that presented themselves. We visited the tomb of the illustrious Hampden, and the field on which that patriot fell.[5] For a moment my soul was elevated from its debasing and miserable fears to contemplate the divine ideas of liberty and self-sacrifice, of which these sights were the monuments and the remembrancers. For an instant I dared to shake off my chains, and look around me with a free and lofty spirit; but the iron had eaten into my flesh, and I sank again, trembling and hopeless, into my miserable self.

We left Oxford with regret, and proceeded to Matlock, which was our next place of rest. The country in the neighbourhood of this village resembled, to a greater degree, the scenery of Switzerland; but every thing is on a lower scale, and the green hills want the crown of distant white Alps, which always attend on the piny mountains of my native country. We visited the wondrous cave, and the little cabinets of natural history, where the curiosities[6] are disposed in the same manner as in the collections at Servox and Chamounix. The latter name made me tremble, when pronounced by Henry; and I hastened to quit Matlock, with which that terrible scene was thus associated.

From Derby still journeying northward, we passed two months in Cumberland and Westmoreland.[7] I could now almost fancy myself among the Swiss mountains. The little patches of snow which yet lingered on the northern sides of the mountains, the lakes, and the dashing of the rocky streams, were all familiar and dear sights to me. Here also we made some acquaintances, who almost contrived to cheat me into happiness. The delight of Clerval was proportionably greater than mine; his mind expanded in the company of men of talent, and he found in his own nature greater capacities and resources than he could have imagined himself to have possessed while he associated with his inferiors. "I could pass my life here," said he to me; "and among these mountains I should scarcely regret Switzerland and the Rhine."

5. John Hampden (1594–1643), leader of the parliamentary opposition to Charles I, was killed on Chalgrove Field, near Oxford.
6. Rare or strange objects. *Cabinets*: rooms where works of art and natural wonders were displayed.
7. The Lake District, associated with the "Lake Poets" (Wordsworth, Coleridge, and Southey).

But he found that a traveller's life is one that includes much pain amidst its enjoyments. His feelings are for ever on the stretch;[8] and when he begins to sink into repose, he finds himself obliged to quit that on which he rests in pleasure for something new, which again engages his attention, and which also he forsakes for other novelties.

We had scarcely visited the various lakes of Cumberland and Westmoreland, and conceived an affection for some of the inhabitants, when the period of our appointment with our Scotch friend approached, and we left them to travel on. For my own part I was not sorry. I had now neglected my promise for some time, and I feared the effects of the dæmon's disappointment. He might remain in Switzerland, and wreak his vengeance on my relatives. This idea pursued me, and tormented me at every moment from which I might otherwise have snatched repose and peace. I waited for my letters with feverish impatience: if they were delayed, I was miserable, and overcome by a thousand fears; and when they arrived, and I saw the superscription[9] of Elizabeth or my father, I hardly dared to read and ascertain my fate. Sometimes I thought that the fiend followed me, and might expedite my remissness by murdering my companion. When these thoughts possessed me, I would not quit Henry for a moment, but followed him as his shadow, to protect him from the fancied rage of his destroyer. I felt as if I had committed some great crime, the consciousness of which haunted me. I was guiltless, but I had indeed drawn down a horrible curse upon my head, as mortal as that of crime.

I visited Edinburgh with languid eyes and mind; and yet that city might have interested the most unfortunate being. Clerval did not like it so well as Oxford; for the antiquity of the latter city was more pleasing to him. But the beauty and regularity of the new town of Edinburgh, its romantic castle, and its environs, the most delightful in the world, Arthur's Seat, St. Bernard's Well, and the Pentland Hills, compensated him for the change, and filled him with cheerfulness and admiration. But I was impatient to arrive at the termination of my journey.

We left Edinburgh in a week, passing through Coupar, St. Andrews, and along the banks of the Tay, to Perth, where our friend expected us. But I was in no mood to laugh and talk with strangers, or enter into their feelings or plans with the good humour expected from a guest; and accordingly I told Clerval that I wished to make the tour of Scotland alone. "Do you," said I, "enjoy yourself, and let this be our rendezvous. I may be absent a month or two; but do not interfere with my motions, I entreat you: leave me to peace and soli-

---

8. Tense.
9. The name or address at the head of a letter.

tude for a short time; and when I return, I hope it will be with a lighter heart, more congenial to your own temper."

Henry wished to dissuade me; but, seeing me bent on this plan, ceased to remonstrate. He entreated me to write often. "I had rather be with you," he said, "in your solitary rambles, than with these Scotch people, whom I do not know: hasten then, my dear friend, to return, that I may again feel myself somewhat at home, which I cannot do in your absence."

Having parted from my friend, I determined to visit some remote spot of Scotland, and finish my work in solitude. I did not doubt but that the monster followed me, and would discover himself to me when I should have finished, that he might receive his companion.

With this resolution I traversed the northern highlands, and fixed on one of the remotest of the Orkneys as the scene labours.[1] It was a place fitted for such a work, being hardly more than a rock, whose high sides were continually beaten upon by the waves. The soil was barren, scarcely affording pasture for a few miserable cows, and oatmeal for its inhabitants, which consisted of five persons, whose gaunt and scraggy limbs gave tokens of their miserable fare. Vegetables and bread, when they indulged in such luxuries, and even fresh water, was to be procured from the main land, which was about five miles distant.

On the whole island there were but three miserable huts, and one of these was vacant when I arrived. This I hired. It contained but two rooms, and these exhibited all the squalidness of the most miserable penury. The thatch had fallen in, the walls were unplastered, and the door was off its hinges. I ordered it to be repaired, bought some furniture, and took possession; an incident which would, doubtless, have occasioned some surprise, had not all the senses of the cottagers been benumbed by want and squalid poverty. As it was, I lived ungazed at and unmolested, hardly thanked for the pittance of food and clothes which I gave; so much does suffering blunt even the coarsest sensations of men.

In this retreat I devoted the morning to labour; but in the evening, when the weather permitted, I walked on the stony beach of the sea, to listen to the waves as they roared, and dashed at my feet. It was a monotonous, yet ever-changing scene. I thought of Switzerland; it was far different from this desolate and appalling landscape. Its hills are covered with vines, and its cottages are scattered thickly in the plains. Its fair lakes reflect a blue and gentle sky; and, when troubled by the winds, their tumult is but as the play of a lively infant, when compared to the roarings of the giant ocean.

1. Corrected in 1831 to "scene of my labours." *Orkneys*: islands off the north coast of Scotland.

In this manner I distributed my occupations when I first arrived; but, as I proceeded in my labour, it became every day more horrible and irksome to me. Sometimes I could not prevail on myself to enter my laboratory for several days; and at other times I toiled day and night in order to complete my work. It was indeed a filthy process in which I was engaged. During my first experiment, a kind of enthusiastic frenzy had blinded me to the horror of my employment; my mind was intently fixed on the sequel[2] of my labour, and my eyes were shut to the horror of my proceedings. But now I went to it in cold blood, and my heart often sickened at the work of my hands.

Thus situated, employed in the most detestable occupation, immersed in a solitude where nothing could for an instant call my attention from the actual scene in which I was engaged, my spirits became unequal;[3] I grew restless and nervous. Every moment I feared to meet my persecutor. Sometimes I sat with my eyes fixed on the ground, fearing to raise them lest they should encounter the object which I so much dreaded to behold. I feared to wander from the sight of my fellow-creatures, lest when alone he should come to claim his companion.

In the mean time I worked on, and my labour was already considerably advanced. I looked towards its completion with a tremulous and eager hope, which I dared not trust myself to question, but which was intermixed with obscure forebodings of evil, that made my heart sicken in my bosom.

Chapter III.

I sat one evening in my laboratory; the sun had set, and the moon was just rising from the sea; I had not sufficient light for my employment, and I remained idle, in a pause of consideration of whether I should leave my labour for the night, or hasten its conclusion by an unremitting attention to it. As I sat, a train of reflection occurred to me, which led me to consider the effects of what I was now doing. Three years before I was engaged in the same manner, and had created a fiend whose unparalleled barbarity had desolated my heart, and filled it for ever with the bitterest remorse. I was now about to form another being, of whose dispositions I was alike ignorant; she might become ten thousand times more malignant than her mate, and delight, for its own sake, in murder and wretchedness. He had sworn to quit the neighbourhood of man, and hide himself in deserts; but she had not; and she, who in all probability was to become a

2. Results.
3. Unbalanced.

thinking and reasoning animal, might refuse to comply with a compact made before her creation. They might even hate each other; the
creature who already lived loathed his own deformity, and might he
not conceive a greater abhorence for it when it came before his eyes
in the female form? She also might turn with disgust from him to the
superior beauty of man; she might quit him, and he be again alone,
exasperated by the fresh provocation of being deserted by one of his
own species.

Even if they were to leave Europe, and inhabit the deserts of the
new world, yet one of the first results of those sympathies for which
the dæmon thirsted would be children, and a race of devils would
be propagated upon the earth, who might make the very existence
of the species of man a condition precarious and full of terror. Had
I a right, for my own benefit, to inflict this curse upon everlasting
generations? I had before been moved by the *sophisms*[1] of the being
I had created; I had been struck senseless by his fiendish threats:
but now, for the first time, the wickedness of my promise burst
upon me; I shuddered to think that future ages might curse me as
their pest, whose selfishness had not hesitated to buy its own peace
at the price perhaps of the existence of the whole human race.

I trembled, and my heart failed within me; when, on looking up,
I saw, by the light of the moon, the dæmon at the casement. A
ghastly grin wrinkled his lips as he gazed on me, where I sat fulfilling the task which he had allotted to me. Yes, he had followed me in
my travels; he had loitered in forests, hid himself in caves, or taken
refuge in wide and desert heaths; and he now came to mark my
progress, and claim the fulfilment of my promise.

As I looked on him, his countenance expressed the utmost extent
of malice and treachery. I thought with a sensation of madness on
my promise of creating another like to him, and, trembling with passion, tore to pieces the thing on which I was engaged. The wretch
saw me destroy the creature on whose future existence he depended
for happiness, and, with a howl of devilish despair and revenge,
withdrew.

I left the room, and, locking the door, made a solemn vow in my
own heart never to resume my labours; and then, with trembling
steps, I sought my own apartment. I was alone; none were near me
to dissipate the gloom, and relieve me from the sickening oppression
of the most terrible reveries.

Several hours past, and I remained near my window gazing on
the sea; it was almost motionless, for the winds were hushed, and
all nature reposed under the eye of the quiet moon. A few fishing
vessels alone specked the water, and now and then the gentle breeze

1. Deceptive and misleading arguments.

wafted the sound of voices, as the fishermen called to one another. I felt the silence, although I was hardly conscious of its extreme profundity, until my ear was suddenly arrested by the paddling of oars near the shore, and a person landed close to my house.

In a few minutes after, I heard the creaking of my door, as if some one endeavoured to open it softly. I trembled from head to foot; I felt a presentiment of who it was, and wished to rouse one of the peasants who dwelt in a cottage not far from mine; but I was overcome by the sensation of helplessness, so often felt in frightful dreams, when you in vain endeavour to fly from an impending danger, and was rooted to the spot.

Presently I heard the sound of footsteps along the passage; the door opened, and the wretch whom I dreaded appeared. Shutting the door, he approached me, and said, in a smothered voice—

"You have destroyed the work which you began; what is it that you intend? Do you dare to break your promise? I have endured toil and misery: I left Switzerland with you; I crept along the shores of the Rhine, among its willow islands, and over the summits of its hills. I have dwelt many months in the heaths of England, and among the deserts of Scotland. I have endured incalculable fatigue, and cold, and hunger; do you dare destroy my hopes?"

"Begone! I do break my promise; never will I create another like yourself, equal in deformity and wickedness."

"Slave, I before reasoned with you, but you have proved yourself unworthy of my condescension. Remember that I have power; you believe yourself miserable, but I can make you so wretched that the light of day will be hateful to you. You are my creator, but I am your master;—obey!"

"The hour of my weakness is past, and the period[2] of your power is arrived. Your threats cannot move me to do an act of wickedness; but they confirm me in a resolution of not creating you a companion in vice. Shall I, in cool blood, set loose upon the earth a dæmon, whose delight is in death and wretchedness. Begone! I am firm, and your words will only exasperate my rage."

The monster saw my determination in my face, and gnashed his teeth in the impotence of anger. "Shall each man," cried he, "find a wife for his bosom, and each beast have his mate, and I be alone? I had feelings of affection, and they were requited by detestation and scorn. Man, you may hate; but beware! Your hours will pass in dread and misery, and soon the bolt will fall which must ravish from you your happiness for ever. Are you to be happy, while I grovel in the intensity of my wretchedness? You can blast my other passions; but revenge remains—revenge, henceforth dearer than light or food! I

2. Ending.

may die; but first you, my tyrant and tormentor, shall curse the sun that gazes on your misery. Beware; for I am fearless, and therefore powerful. I will watch with the wiliness of a snake, that I may sting with its venom. Man, you shall repent of the injuries you inflict."

"Devil, cease; and do not poison the air with these sounds of malice. I have declared my resolution to you, and I am no coward to bend beneath words. Leave me; I am inexorable."

"It is well. I go; but remember, I shall be with you on your wedding-night."

I started forward, and exclaimed, "Villain! before you sign my death-warrant, be sure that you are yourself safe."

I would have seized him; but he eluded me, and quitted the house with precipitation: in a few moments I saw him in his boat, which shot across the waters with an arrowy swiftness, and was soon lost amidst the waves.

All was again silent; but his words rung in my ears. I burned with rage to pursue the murderer of my peace, and precipitate him into the ocean. I walked up and down my room hastily and perturbed, while my imagination conjured up a thousand images to torment and sting me. Why had I not followed him, and closed[3] with him in mortal strife? But I had suffered him to depart, and he had directed his course towards the main land. I shuddered to think who might be the next victim sacrificed to his insatiate revenge. And then I thought again of his words—"I will be with you on your wedding-night." That then was the period fixed for the fulfilment of my destiny. In that hour I should die, and at once satisfy and extinguish his malice. The prospect did not move me to fear; yet when I thought of my beloved Elizabeth,—of her tears and endless sorrow, when she should find her lover so barbarously snatched from her,—tears, the first I had shed for many months, streamed from my eyes, and I resolved not to fall before my enemy without a bitter struggle.

The night passed away, and the sun rose from the ocean; my feelings became calmer, if it may be called calmness, when the violence of rage sinks into the depths of despair. I left the house, the horrid scene of the last night's contention, and walked on the beach of the sea, which I almost regarded as an insuperable barrier between me and my fellow-creatures; nay, a wish that such should prove the fact stole across me. I desired that I might pass my life on that barren rock, wearily it is true, but uninterrupted by any sudden shock of misery. If I returned, it was to be sacrificed, or to see those whom I most loved die under the grasp of a dæmon whom I had myself created.

3. Fought hand-to-hand.

I walked about the isle like a restless spectre, separated from all it loved, and miserable in the separation. When it became noon, and the sun rose higher, I lay down on the grass, and was overpowered by a deep sleep. I had been awake the whole of the preceding night, my nerves were agitated, and my eyes inflamed by watching and misery. The sleep into which I now sunk refreshed me; and when I awoke, I again felt as if I belonged to a race of human beings like myself, and I began to reflect upon what had passed with greater composure; yet still the words of the fiend rung in my ears like a death-knell, they appeared like a dream, yet distinct and oppressive as a reality.

The sun had far descended, and I still sat on the shore, satisfying my appetite, which had become ravenous, with an oaten cake, when I saw a fishing-boat land close to me, and one of the men brought me a packet; it contained letters from Geneva, and one from Clerval, entreating me to join him. He said that nearly a year had elapsed since we had quitted Switzerland, and France was yet unvisited. He entreated me, therefore, to leave my solitary isle, and meet him at Perth, in a week from that time, when we might arrange the plan of our future proceedings. This letter in a degree recalled me to life, and I determined to quit my island at the expiration of two days.

Yet, before I departed, there was a task to perform, on which I shuddered to reflect: I must pack my chemical instruments; and for that purpose I must enter the room which had been the scene of my odious work, and I must handle those utensils, the sight of which was sickening to me. The next morning, at day-break, I summoned sufficient courage, and unlocked the door of my laboratory. The remains of the half-finished creature, whom I had destroyed, lay scattered on the floor, and I almost felt as if I had mangled the living flesh of a human being. I paused to collect myself, and then entered the chamber. With trembling hand I conveyed the instruments out of the room; but I reflected that I ought not to leave the relics of my work to excite the horror and suspicion of the peasants, and I accordingly put them into a basket, with a great quantity of stones, and laying them up, determined to throw them into the sea that very night; and in the mean time I sat upon the beach, employed in cleaning and arranging my chemical apparatus.

Nothing could be more complete than the alteration that had taken place in my feelings since the night of the appearance of the dæmon. I had before regarded my promise with a gloomy despair, as a thing that, with whatever consequences, must be fulfilled; but I now felt as if a film had been taken from before my eyes, and that I, for the first time, saw clearly. The idea of renewing my labours did not for one instant occur to me; the threat I had heard weighed on my thoughts, but I did not reflect that a voluntary act of mine could avert it. I had resolved in my own mind, that to create another like the fiend I had first made would be an act of the basest and most atrocious selfishness; and I banished from my mind every thought that could lead to a different conclusion.

Between two and three in the morning the moon rose; and I then, putting my basket aboard a little skiff, sailed out about four miles from the shore. The scene was perfectly solitary: a few boats were returning towards land, but I sailed away from them. I felt as if I was about the commission of a dreadful crime, and avoided with shuddering anxiety any encounter with my fellow-creatures. At one time the moon, which had before been clear, was suddenly overspread by a thick cloud, and I took advantage of the moment of darkness, and cast my basket into the sea; I listened to the gurgling sound as it sunk, and then sailed away from the spot. The sky became clouded; but the air was pure, although chilled by the north-east breeze that was then rising. But it refreshed me, and filled me with such agreeable sensations, that I resolved to prolong my stay on the water, and fixing the rudder in a direct position, stretched myself at the bottom of the boat. Clouds hid the moon, every thing was obscure, and I heard only the sound of the boat, as its keel cut through the waves; the murmur lulled me, and in a short time I slept soundly.

I do not know how long I remained in this situation, but when I awoke I found that the sun had already mounted considerably. The wind was high, and the waves continually threatened the safety of my little skiff. I found that the wind was north-east, and must have driven me far from the coast from which I had embarked. I endeavoured to change my course, but quickly found that if I again made the attempt the boat would be instantly filled with water. Thus situated, my only resource was to drive before the wind. I confess that I felt a few sensations of terror. I had no compass with me, and was so little acquainted with the geography of this part of the world that the sun was of little benefit to me. I might be driven into the wide Atlantic, and feel all the tortures of starvation, or be swallowed up in the immeasurable waters that roared and buffeted around me. I had already been out many hours, and felt the torment of a burning thirst,[4] a prelude to my other sufferings. I looked on the heavens, which were covered by clouds that flew before the wind only to be replaced by others: I looked upon the sea, it was to be my grave. "Fiend," I exclaimed, "your task is already fulfilled!" I thought of Elizabeth, of my father, and of Clerval; and sunk into a reverie, so despairing and frightful, that even now, when the scene is on the point of closing before me for ever, I shudder to reflect on it.

4. Cf. Coleridge's "Ancient Mariner," lines 115ff.

Some hours passed thus; but by degrees, as the sun declined towards the horizon, the wind died away into a gentle breeze, and the sea became free from breakers. But these gave place to a heavy swell; I felt sick, and hardly able to hold the rudder, when suddenly I saw a line of high land towards the south.

Almost spent, as I was, by fatigue, and the dreadful suspense I endured for several hours, this sudden certainty of life rushed like a flood of warm joy to my heart, and tears gushed from my eyes.

How mutable are our feelings, and how strange is that clinging love we have of life even in the excess of misery! I constructed another sail with a part of my dress, and eagerly steered my course towards the land. It had a wild and rocky appearance; but as I approached nearer, I easily perceived the traces of cultivation. I saw vessels near the shore, and found myself suddenly transported back to the neighbourhood of civilized man. I eagerly traced the windings of the land, and hailed a steeple which I at length saw issuing from behind a small promontory. As I was in a state of extreme debility, I resolved to sail directly towards the town as a place where I could most easily procure nourishment. Fortunately I had money with me. As I turned the promontory, I perceived a small neat town and a good harbour, which I entered, my heart bounding with joy at my unexpected escape.

As I was occupied in fixing the boat and arranging the sails, several people crowded towards the spot. They seemed very much surprised at my appearance; but, instead of offering me any assistance, whispered together with gestures that at any other time might have produced in me a slight sensation of alarm. As it was, I merely remarked that they spoke English; and I therefore addressed them in that language: "My good friends," said I, "will you be so kind as to tell me the name of this town, and inform me where I am?"

"You will know that soon enough," replied a man with a gruff voice. "May be you are come to a place that will not prove much to your taste; but you will not be consulted as to your quarters, I promise you."

I was exceedingly surprised on receiving so rude an answer from a stranger; and I was also disconcerted on perceiving the frowning and angry countenances of his companions. "Why do you answer me so roughly?" I replied: "surely it is not the custom of Englishmen to receive strangers so inhospitably."

"I do not know," said the man, "what the custom of the English may be; but it is the custom of the Irish to hate villains."

While this strange dialogue continued, I perceived the crowd rapidly increase. Their faces expressed a mixture of curiosity and anger, which annoyed, and in some degree alarmed me. I inquired the way to the inn; but no one replied. I then moved forward, and a murmuring sound arose from the crowd as they followed and surrounded me; when an ill-looking man approaching, tapped me on the shoulder, and said, "Come, Sir, you must follow me to Mr. Kirwin's, to give an account of yourself."

"Who is Mr. Kirwin? Why am I to give an account of myself? Is not this a free country?"

"Aye, Sir, free enough for honest folks. Mr. Kirwin is a magistrate; and you are to give an account of the death of a gentleman who was found murdered here last night."

This answer startled me; but I presently recovered myself. I was innocent; that could easily be proved: accordingly I followed my conductor in silence, and was led to one of the best houses in the town. I was ready to sink from fatigue and hunger; but, being surrounded by a crowd, I thought it politic to rouse all my strength, that no physical debility might be construed into apprehension or conscious guilt. Little did I then expect the calamity that was in a few moments to overwhelm me, and extinguish in horror and despair all fear of ignominy or death.

I must pause here; for it requires all my fortitude to recall the memory of the frightful events which I am about to relate, in proper detail, to my recollection.

Chapter IV.

I was soon introduced into the presence of the magistrate, an old benevolent man, with calm and mild manners. He looked upon me, however, with some degree of severity; and then, turning towards my conductors, he asked who appeared as witnesses on this occasion.

About half a dozen men came forward; and one being selected by the magistrate, he deposed, that he had been out fishing the night before with his son and brother-in-law, Daniel Nugent, when, about ten o'clock, they observed a strong northerly blast rising, and they accordingly put in for port. It was a very dark night, as the moon had not yet risen; they did not land at the harbour, but, as they had been accustomed, at a creek about two miles below. He walked on first, carrying a part of the fishing tackle, and his companions followed him at some distance. As he was proceeding along the sands, he struck his foot against something, and fell all his length on the ground. His companions came up to assist him; and, by the light of their lantern, they found that he had fallen on the body of a man, who was to all appearance dead. Their first supposition was, that it was the corpse of some person who had been drowned, and was thrown on shore by the waves; but, upon examination, they found that the clothes were not wet, and even that the body was not then cold. They instantly carried it to the cottage of an old woman near the spot, and endeavoured, but in vain, to restore it to life. He appeared to be a handsome young man, about five and twenty years of age. He had apparently been strangled; for there was no sign of any violence, except the black mark of fingers on his neck.

The first part of this deposition did not in the least interest me; but when the mark of the fingers was mentioned, I remembered the murder of my brother, and felt myself extremely agitated; my limbs trembled, and a mist came over my eyes, which obliged me to lean on a chair for support. The magistrate observed me with a keen eye, and of course drew an unfavourable augury[1] from my manner.

The son confirmed his father's account: but when Daniel Nugent was called, he swore positively that, just before the fall of his companion, he saw a boat, with a single man in it, at a short distance from the shore; and, as far as he could judge by the light of a few stars, it was the same boat in which I had just landed.

A woman deposed, that she lived near the beach, and was standing at the door of her cottage, waiting for the return of the fishermen, about an hour before she heard of the discovery of the body, when she saw a boat, with only only one man in it, push off from that part of the shore where the corpse was afterwards found.

Another woman confirmed the account of the fishermen having brought the body into her house; it was not cold. They put it into a bed, and rubbed it; and Daniel went to the town for an apothecary, but life was quite gone.

Several other men were examined concerning my landing; and they agreed, that, with the strong north wind that had arisen during the night, it was very probable that I had beaten about for many hours, and had been obliged to return nearly to the same spot from which I had departed. Besides, they observed that it appeared that I had brought the body from another place, and it was likely, that as I did not appear to know the shore, I might have put into the harbour ignorant of the distance of the town of —— from the place where I had deposited the corpse.

Mr. Kirwin, on hearing this evidence, desired that I should be taken into the room where the body lay for interment, that it might be observed what effect the sight of it would produce upon me. This idea was probably suggested by the extreme agitation I had exhibited when the mode of the murder had been described. I was accordingly conducted, by the magistrate and several other persons, to the inn. I could not help being struck by the strange coincidences that had

1. Portent or foreboding.

taken place during this eventful night; but, knowing that I had been conversing with several persons in the island I had inhabited about the time that the body had been found, I was perfectly tranquil as to the consequences[2] of the affair.

I entered the room where the corpse lay, and was led up to the coffin. How can I describe my sensations on beholding it? I feel yet parched with horror, nor can I reflect on that terrible moment without shuddering and agony, that faintly reminds me of the anguish of the recognition. The trial, the presence of the magistrate and witnesses, passed like a dream from my memory, when I saw the lifeless form of Henry Clerval stretched before me. I gasped for breath; and, throwing myself on the body, I exclaimed, "Have my murderous machinations deprived you also, my dearest Henry, of life? Two I have already destroyed; other victims await their destiny: but you, Clerval, my friend, my benefactor"—

The human frame could no longer support the agonizing suffering that I endured, and I was carried out of the room in strong convulsions.

A fever succeeded to this. I lay for two months on the point of death: my ravings, as I afterwards heard, were frightful; I called myself the murderer of William, of Justine, and of Clerval. Sometimes I entreated my attendants to assist me in the destruction of the fiend by whom I was tormented; and, at others, I felt the fingers of the monster already grasping my neck, and screamed aloud with agony and terror. Fortunately, as I spoke my native language, Mr. Kirwin alone understood me; but my gestures and bitter cries were sufficient to affright the other witnesses.

Why did I not die? More miserable than man ever was before, why did I not sink into forgetfulness and rest? Death snatches away many blooming children, the only hopes of their doating parents: how many brides and youthful lovers have been one day in the bloom of health and hope, and the next a prey for worms and the decay of the tomb! Of what materials was I made, that I could thus resist so many shocks, which, like the turning of the wheel, continually renewed the torture.

But I was doomed to live; and, in two months, found myself as awaking from a dream, in a prison, stretched on a wretched bed, surrounded by gaolers,[3] turnkeys, bolts, and all the miserable apparatus of a dungeon. It was morning, I remember, when I thus awoke to understanding: I had forgotten the particulars of what had happened, and only felt as if some great misfortune had suddenly overwhelmed me; but when I looked around, and saw the barred windows,

2. Outcome.
3. Jailers.

and the squalidness of the room in which I was, all flashed across my memory, and I groaned bitterly.

This sound disturbed an old woman who was sleeping in a chair beside me. She was a hired nurse, the wife of one of the turnkeys, and her countenance expressed all those bad qualities which often characterize that class. The lines of her face were hard and rude, like that of persons accustomed to see without sympathizing in sights of misery. Her tone expressed her entire indifference; she addressed me in English, and the voice struck me as one that I had heard during my sufferings:

"Are you better now, Sir?" said she.

I replied in the same language, with a feeble voice, "I believe I am; but if it be all true, if indeed I did not dream, I am sorry that I am still alive to feel this misery and horror."

"For that matter," replied the old woman, "if you mean about the gentleman you murdered, I believe that it were better for you if you were dead, for I fancy it will go hard with you; but you will be hung when the next sessions[4] come on. However, that's none of my business, I am sent to nurse you, and get you well; I do my duty with a safe conscience, it were well if every body did the same."

I turned with loathing from the woman who could utter so unfeeling a speech to a person just saved, on the very edge of death; but I felt languid, and unable to reflect on all that had passed. The whole series of my life appeared to me as a dream; I sometimes doubted if indeed it were all true, for it never presented itself to my mind with the force of reality.

As the images that floated before me became more distinct, I grew feverish; a darkness pressed around me; no one was near me who soothed me with the gentle voice of love; no dear hand supported me. The physician came and prescribed medicines, and the old woman prepared them for me; but utter carelessness was visible in the first, and the expression of brutality was strongly marked in the visage of the second. Who could be interested in the fate of a murderer, but the hangman who would gain his fee?

These were my first reflections; but I soon learned that Mr. Kirwin had shewn me extreme kindness. He had caused the best room in the prison to be prepared for me (wretched indeed was the best); and it was he who had provided a physician and a nurse. It is true, he seldom came to see me; for, although he ardently desired to relieve the sufferings of every human creature, he did not wish to be present at the agonies and miserable ravings of a murderer. He came, therefore, sometimes to see that I was not neglected; but his visits were short, and at long intervals.

4. Judicial sittings.

One day, when I was gradually recovering, I was seated in a chair, my eyes half open, and my cheeks livid like those in death, I was overcome by gloom and misery, and often reflected I had better seek death than remain miserably pent up only to be let loose in a world replete with wretchedness. At one time I considered whether I should not declare myself guilty, and suffer the penalty of the law, less innocent than poor Justine had been. Such were my thoughts, when the door of my apartment was opened, and Mr. Kirwin entered. His countenance expressed sympathy and compassion; he drew a chair close to mine, and addressed me in French—

"I fear that this place is very shocking to you; can I do any thing to make you more comfortable?"

"I thank you; but all that you mention is nothing to me: on the whole earth there is no comfort which I am capable of receiving."

"I know that the sympathy of a stranger can be but of little relief to one borne down as you are by so strange a misfortune. But you will, I hope, soon quit this melancholy abode; for, doubtless, evidence can easily be brought to free you from the criminal charge."

"That is my least concern: I am, by a course of strange events, become the most miserable of mortals. Persecuted and tortured as I am and have been, can death be any evil to me?"

"Nothing indeed could be more unfortunate and agonizing than the strange chances that have lately occurred. You were thrown, by some surprising accident, on this shore, renowned for its hospitality; seized immediately, and charged with murder. The first sight that was presented to your eyes was the body of your friend, murdered in so unaccountable a manner, and placed, as it were, by some fiend across your path."

As Mr. Kirwin said this, notwithstanding the agitation I endured on this retrospect of my sufferings, I also felt considerable surprise at the knowledge he seemed to possess concerning me. I suppose some astonishment was exhibited in my countenance; for Mr. Kirwin hastened to say—

"It was not until a day or two after your illness that I thought of examining your dress, that I might discover some trace by which I could send to your relations an account of your misfortune and illness. I found several letters, and, among others, one which I discovered from its commencement to be from your father. I instantly wrote to Geneva: nearly two months have elapsed since the departure of my letter.—But you are ill; even now you tremble: you are unfit for agitation of any kind."

"This suspense is a thousand times worse than the most horrible event: tell me what new scene of death has been acted, and whose murder I am now to lament."

"Your family is perfectly well," said Mr. Kirwin, with gentleness; "and some one, a friend, is come to visit you."

I know not by what chain of thought the idea presented itself, but it instantly darted into my mind that the murderer had come to mock at my misery, and taunt me with the death of Clerval, as a new incitement for me to comply with his hellish desires. I put my hand before my eyes, and cried out in agony—

"Oh! take him away! I cannot see him; for God's sake, do not let him enter!"

Mr. Kirwin regarded me with a troubled countenance. He could not help regarding my exclamation as a presumption of my guilt, and said, in rather a severe tone—

"I should have thought, young man, that the presence of your father would have been welcome, instead of inspiring such violent repugnance."

"My father!" cried I, while every feature and every muscle was relaxed from anguish to pleasure. "Is my father, indeed, come? How kind, how very kind. But where is he, why does he not hasten to me?"

My change of manner surprised and pleased the magistrate; perhaps he thought that my former exclamation was a momentary return of delirium, and now he instantly resumed his former benevolence. He rose, and quitted the room with my nurse, and in a moment my father entered it.

Nothing, at this moment, could have given me greater pleasure than the arrival of my father. I stretched out my hand to him, and cried—

"Are you then safe—and Elizabeth—and Ernest?"

My father calmed me with assurances of their welfare, and endeavoured, by dwelling on these subjects so interesting to my heart, to raise my desponding spirits; but he soon felt that a prison cannot be the abode of cheerfulness. "What a place is this that you inhabit, my son!" said he, looking mournfully at the barred windows, and wretched appearance of the room. "You travelled to seek happiness, but a fatality seems to pursue you. And poor Clerval—"

The name of my unfortunate and murdered friend was an agitation too great to be endured in my weak state; I shed tears.

"Alas! yes, my father," replied I; "some destiny of the most horrible kind hangs over me, and I must live to fulfil it, or surely I should have died on the coffin of Henry."

We were not allowed to converse for any length of time, for the precarious state of my health rendered every precaution necessary that could insure tranquillity. Mr. Kirwin came in, and insisted that my strength should not be exhausted by too much exertion. But the appearance of my father was to me like that of my good angel, and I gradually recovered my health.

As my sickness quitted me, I was absorbed by a gloomy and black melancholy, that nothing could dissipate. The image of Clerval was for ever before me, ghastly and murdered. More than once the agitation into which these reflections threw me made my friends dread a dangerous relapse. Alas! why did they preserve so miserable and detested a life? It was surely that I might fulfil my destiny, which is now drawing to a close. Soon, oh, very soon, will death extinguish these throbbings, and relieve me from the mighty weight of anguish that bears me to the dust; and, in executing the award of justice, I shall also sink to rest. Then the appearance of death was distant, although the wish was ever present to my thoughts; and I often sat for hours motionless and speechless, wishing for some mighty revolution that might bury me and my destroyer in its ruins.

The season of the assizes[5] approached. I had already been three months in prison; and although I was still weak, and in continual danger of a relapse, I was obliged to travel nearly a hundred miles to the county-town, where the court was held. Mr. Kirwin charged himself with every care of collecting witnesses, and arranging my defence. I was spared the disgrace of appearing publicly as a criminal, as the case was not brought before the court that decides on life and death. The grand jury rejected the bill, on its being proved that I was on the Orkney Islands at the hour the body of my friend was found, and a fortnight after my removal I was liberated from prison.

My father was enraptured on finding me freed from the vexations of a criminal charge, that I was again allowed to breathe the fresh atmosphere, and allowed to return to my native country. I did not participate in these feelings; for to me the walls of a dungeon or a palace were alike hateful. The cup of life was poisoned for ever; and although the sun shone upon me, as upon the happy and gay of heart, I saw around me nothing but a dense and frightful darkness, penetrated by no light but the glimmer of two eyes that glared upon me. Sometimes they were the expressive eyes of Henry, languishing in death, the dark orbs nearly covered by the lids, and the long black lashes that fringed them; sometimes it was the watery clouded eyes of the monster, as I first saw them in my chamber at Ingolstadt.

My father tried to awaken in me the feelings of affection. He talked of Geneva, which I should soon visit—of Elizabeth, and Ernest; but these words only drew deep groans from me. Sometimes, indeed, I felt a wish for happiness; and thought, with melancholy delight, of my beloved cousin; or longed, with a devouring *maladie du pays*,[6] to see once more the blue lake and rapid Rhone,

5. Court sessions held periodically.
6. Homesickness.

that had been so dear to me in early childhood: but my general state of feeling was a torpor, in which a prison was as welcome a residence as the divinest scene in nature; and these fits were seldom interrupted, but by paroxysms of anguish and despair. At these moments I often endeavoured to put an end to the existence I loathed; and it required unceasing attendance and vigilance to restrain me from committing some dreadful act of violence.

I remember, as I quitted the prison, I heard one of the men say, "He may be innocent of the murder, but he has certainly a bad conscience." These words struck me. A bad conscience! yes, surely I had one. William, Justine, and Clerval, had died through my infernal machinations; "And whose death," cried I, "is to finish the tragedy? Ah! my father, do not remain in this wretched country; take me where I may forget myself, my existence, and all the world."

My father easily acceded to my desire; and, after having taken leave of Mr. Kirwin, we hastened to Dublin. I felt as if I was relieved from a heavy weight, when the packet[7] sailed with a fair wind from Ireland, and I had quitted for ever the country which had been to me the scene of so much misery.

It was midnight. My father slept in the cabin; and I lay on the deck, looking at the stars, and listening to the dashing of the waves. I hailed the darkness that shut Ireland from my sight, and my pulse beat with a feverish joy, when I reflected that I should soon see Geneva. The past appeared to me in the light of a frightful dream; yet the vessel in which I was, the wind that blew me from the detested shore of Ireland, and the sea which surrounded me, told me too forcibly that I was deceived by no vision, and that Clerval, my friend and dearest companion, had fallen a victim to me and the monster of my creation. I repassed, in my memory, my whole life; my quiet happiness while residing with my family in Geneva, the death of my mother, and my departure for Ingolstadt. I remembered shuddering at the mad enthusiasm that hurried me on to the creation of my hideous enemy, and I called to mind the night during which he first lived. I was unable to pursue the train of thought; a thousand feelings pressed upon me, and I wept bitterly.

Ever since my recovery from the fever I had been in the custom of taking every night a small quantity of laudanum;[8] for it was by means of this drug only that I was enabled to gain the rest necessary for the preservation of life. Oppressed by the recollection of my various misfortunes, I now took a double dose, and soon slept profoundly. But sleep did not afford me respite from thought and misery; my dreams presented a thousand objects that scared me.

7. Short for "packet-boat," a ship traveling at regular intervals between two ports.
8. An opium preparation.

Towards morning I was possessed by a kind of night-mare; I felt the fiend's grasp in my neck, and could not free myself from it; groans and cries rung in my ears. My father, who was watching over me, perceiving my restlessness, awoke me, and pointed to the port of Holyhead,[9] which we were now entering.

Chapter V.

We had resolved not to go to London, but to cross the country to Portsmouth, and thence to embark for Havre.[1] I preferred this plan principally because I dreaded to see again those places in which I had enjoyed a few moments of tranquillity with my beloved Clerval. I thought with horror of seeing again those persons whom we had been accustomed to visit together, and who might make inquiries concerning an event, the very remembrance of which made me again feel the pang I endured when I gazed on his lifeless form in the inn at ——.

As for my father, his desires and exertions were bounded to the[2] again seeing me restored to health and peace of mind. His tenderness and attentions were unremitting; my grief and gloom was obstinate, but he would not despair. Sometimes he thought that I felt deeply the degradation of being obliged to answer a charge of murder, and he endeavoured to prove to me the futility of pride.

"Alas! my father," said I, "how little do you know me. Human beings, their feelings and passions, would indeed be degraded, if such a wretch as I felt pride. Justine, poor unhappy Justine, was as innocent as I, and she suffered the same charge; she died for it; and I am the cause of this—I murdered her. William, Justine, and Henry—they all died by my hands."

My father had often, during my imprisonment, heard me make the same assertion; when I thus accused myself, he sometimes seemed to desire an explanation, and at others he appeared to consider it as caused by delirium, and that, during my illness, some idea of this kind had presented itself to my imagination, the remembrance of which I preserved in my convalescence. I avoided explanation, and maintained a continual silence concerning the wretch I had created. I had a feeling that I should be supposed mad, and this for ever chained my tongue, when I would have given the whole world to have confided the fatal secret.

9. On the Isle of Anglesey, Wales.
1. Le Havre, in France.
2. I.e., limited to a wish of.

Upon this occasion my father said, with an expression of unbounded wonder, "What do you mean, Victor? are you mad? My dear son, I entreat you never to make such an assertion again."

"I am not mad," I cried energetically; "the sun and the heavens, who have viewed my operations, can bear witness of my truth. I am the assassin of those most innocent victims; they died by my machinations. A thousand times would I have shed my own blood drop by drop, to have saved their lives but I could not, my father, indeed, could not sacrifice the whole human race."

The conclusion of this speech convinced my father that my ideas were deranged, and he instantly changed the subject of our conversation, and endeavoured to alter the course of my thoughts. He wished as much as possible to obliterate the memory of the scenes that had taken place in Ireland, and never alluded to them, or suffered me to speak of my misfortunes.

As time passed away I became more calm: misery had her dwelling in my heart, but I no longer talked in the same incoherent manner of my own crimes; sufficient for me was the consciousness of them. By the utmost self-violence, I curbed the imperious voice of wretchedness, which sometimes desired to declare itself to the whole world; and my manners were calmer and more composed than they had ever been since my journey to the sea of ice.

We arrived at Havre on the 8th of May, and instantly proceeded to Paris, where my father had some business which detained us a few weeks. In this city, I received the following letter from Elizabeth:—

"*To* VICTOR FRANKENSTEIN.

"MY DEAREST FRIEND,

"It gave me the greatest pleasure to receive a letter from my uncle dated at Paris; you are no longer at a formidable distance, and I may hope to see you in less than a fortnight. My poor cousin, how much you must have suffered! I expect to see you looking even more ill than when you quitted Geneva. This winter has been passed most miserably, tortured as I have been by anxious suspense; yet I hope to see peace in your countenance, and to find that your heart is not totally devoid of comfort and tranquillity.

"Yet I fear that the same feelings now exist that made you so miserable a year ago, even perhaps augmented by time. I would not disturb you at this period, when so many misfortunes weigh upon you; but a conversation that I had with my uncle previous to his departure renders some explanation necessary before we meet.

"Explanation! you may possibly say; what can Elizabeth have to explain? If you really say this, my questions are answered, and I have no more to do than to sign myself your affectionate cousin. But you are distant from me, and it is possible that you may dread, and yet be pleased with this explanation; and, in a probability of this being the case, I dare not any longer postpone writing what, during your absence, I have often wished to express to you, but have never had the courage to begin.

"You well know, Victor, that our union had been the favourite plan of your parents ever since our infancy. We were told this when young, and taught to look forward to it as an event that would certainly take place. We were affectionate playfellows during childhood, and, I believe, dear and valued friends to one another as we grew older. But as brother and sister often entertain a lively affection towards each other, without desiring a more intimate union, may not such also be our case? Tell me, dearest Victor. Answer me, I conjure[3] you, by our mutual happiness, with simple truth—Do you not love another?

"You have travelled; you have spent several years of your life at Ingolstadt; and I confess to you, my friend, that when I saw you last autumn so unhappy, flying to solitude, from the society of every creature, I could not help supposing that you might regret our connexion, and believe yourself bound in honour to fulfil the wishes of your parents, although they opposed themselves to your inclinations. But this is false reasoning. I confess to you, my cousin, that I love you, and that in my airy dreams of futurity you have been my constant friend and companion. But it is your happiness I desire as well as my own, when I declare to you, that our marriage would render me eternally miserable, unless it were the dictate of your own free choice. Even now I weep to think, that, borne down as you are by the crudest misfortunes, you may stifle, by the word *honour*, all hope of that love and happiness which would alone restore you to yourself. I, who have so interested an affection for you, may increase your miseries ten-fold, by being an obstacle to your wishes. Ah, Victor, be assured that your cousin and playmate has too sincere a love for you not to be made miserable by this supposition. Be happy, my friend; and if you obey me in this one request, remain satisfied that nothing on earth will have the power to interrupt my tranquillity.

"Do not let this letter disturb you; do not answer it to-morrow, or the next day, or even until you come, if it will give you pain. My uncle will send me news of your health; and if I see but one smile on your lips when we meet, occasioned by this or any other exertion of mine, I shall need no other happiness.

"Elizabeth Lavenza

"Geneva, May 18th, 17–."

3. Constrain by oath.

This letter revived in my memory what I had before forgotten, the threat of the fiend—"*I will be with you on your wedding-night!*" Such was my sentence, and on that night would the dæmon employ every art to destroy me, and tear me from the glimpse of happiness which promised partly to console my sufferings. On that night he had determined to consummate[4] his crimes by my death. Well, be it so; a deadly struggle would then assuredly take place, in which if he was victorious, I should be at peace, and his power over me be at an end. If he were vanquished, I should be a free man. Alas! what freedom? such as the peasant enjoys when his family have been massacred before his eyes, his cottage burnt, his lands laid waste, and he is turned adrift, homeless, pennyless, and alone, but free. Such would be my liberty, except that in my Elizabeth I possessed a treasure; alas! balanced by those horrors of remorse and guilt, which would pursue me until death.

Sweet and beloved Elizabeth! I read and re-read her letter, and some softened feelings stole into my heart, and dared to whisper paradisaical dreams of love and joy; but the apple was already eaten, and the angel's arm bared to drive me from all hope. Yet I would die to make her happy. If the monster executed his threat, death was inevitable; yet, again, I considered whether my marriage would hasten my fate. My destruction might indeed arrive a few months sooner; but if my torturer should suspect that I postponed it, influenced by his menaces, he would surely find other, and perhaps more dreadful means of revenge. He had vowed *to be with me on my wedding-night*, yet he did not consider that threat as binding him to peace in the mean time; for, as if to shew me that he was not yet satiated with blood, he had murdered Clerval immediately after the enunciation of his threats. I resolved, therefore, that if my immediate union with my cousin would conduce either to her's or my father's happiness, my adversary's designs against my life should not retard it a single hour.

In this state of mind I wrote to Elizabeth. My letter was calm and affectionate. "I fear, my beloved girl," I said, "little happiness remains for us on earth; yet all that I may one day enjoy is concentered in you. Chase away your idle fears; to you alone do I consecrate my life, and my endeavours for contentment. I have one secret, Elizabeth, a dreadful one; when revealed to you, it will chill your frame with horror, and then, far from being surprised at my misery, you will only wonder that I survive what I have endured. I will confide this tale of misery and terror to you the day after our marriage shall take place; for, my sweet cousin, there must be perfect confidence between us. But until then, I conjure you, do not mention or allude to it. This I most earnestly entreat, and I know you will comply."

4. Complete, perfect.

In about a week after the arrival of Elizabeth's letter, we returned to Geneva. My cousin welcomed me with warm affection; yet tears were in her eyes, as she beheld my emaciated frame and feverish cheeks. I saw a change in her also. She was thinner, and had lost much of that heavenly vivacity that had before charmed me; but her gentleness, and soft looks of compassion, made her a more fit companion for one blasted and miserable as I was.

The tranquillity which I now enjoyed did not endure. Memory brought madness with it; and when I thought on what had passed, a real insanity possessed me; sometimes I was furious, and burnt with rage, sometimes low and despondent. I neither spoke or looked, but sat motionless, bewildered by the multitude of miseries that overcame me.

Elizabeth alone had the power to draw me from these fits; her gentle voice would soothe me when transported by passion, and inspire me with human feelings when sunk in torpor. She wept with me, and for me. When reason returned, she would remonstrate, and endeavour to inspire me with resignation. Ah! it is well for the unfortunate to be resigned, but for the guilty there is no peace. The agonies of remorse poison the luxury there is otherwise sometimes found in indulging the excess of grief.

Soon after my arrival my father spoke of my immediate marriage with my cousin. I remained silent.

"Have you, then, some other attachment?"

"None on earth. I love Elizabeth, and look forward to our union with delight. Let the day therefore be fixed; and on it I will consecrate myself, in life or death, to the happiness of my cousin."

"My dear Victor, do not speak thus. Heavy misfortunes have befallen us; but let us only cling closer to what remains, and transfer our love for those whom we have lost to those who yet live. Our circle will be small, but bound close by the ties of affection and mutual misfortune. And when time shall have softened your despair, new and dear objects of care will be born to replace those of whom we have been so cruelly deprived."

Such were the lessons of my father. But to me the remembrance of the threat returned: nor can you wonder, that, omnipotent as the fiend had yet been in his deeds of blood, I should almost regard him as invincible; and that when he had pronounced the words, *"I shall be with you on your wedding-night,"* I should regard the threatened fate as unavoidable. But death was no evil to me, if the loss of Elizabeth were balanced with it; and I therefore, with a contented and even cheerful countenance, agreed with my father, that if my cousin would consent, the ceremony should take place in ten days, and thus put, as I imagined, the seal to my fate.

Great God! if for one instant I had thought what might be the hellish intention of my fiendish adversary, I would rather have banished myself for ever from my native country, and wandered a friendless outcast over the earth, than have consented to this miserable marriage. But, as if possessed of magic powers, the monster had blinded me to his real intentions; and when I thought that I prepared only my own death, I hastened that of a far dearer victim.

As the period fixed for our marriage drew nearer, whether from cowardice or a prophetic feeling, I felt my heart sink within me. But I concealed my feelings by an appearance of hilarity, that brought smiles and joy to the countenance of my father, but hardly deceived the ever-watchful and nicer[5] eye of Elizabeth. She looked forward to our union with placid contentment, not unmingled with a little fear, which past misfortunes had impressed, that what now appeared certain and tangible happiness, might soon dissipate into an airy dream, and leave no trace but deep and everlasting regret.

Preparations were made for the event; congratulatory visits were received; and all wore a smiling appearance. I shut up, as well as I could, in my own heart the anxiety that preyed there, and entered with seeming earnestness into the plans of my father, although they might only serve as the decorations of my tragedy. A house was purchased for us near Cologny, by which we should enjoy the pleasures of the country, and yet be so near Geneva as to see my father every day; who would still reside within the walls, for the benefit of Ernest, that he might follow his studies at the schools.

In the mean time I took every precaution to defend my person, in case the fiend should openly attack me. I carried pistols and a dagger constantly about me, and was ever on the watch to prevent artifice; and by these means gained a greater degree of tranquillity. Indeed, as the period approached, the threat appeared more as a delusion, not to be regarded as worthy to disturb my peace, while the happiness I hoped for in my marriage wore a greater appearance of certainty, as the day fixed for its solemnization drew nearer, and I heard it continually spoken of as an occurrence which no accident could possibly prevent.

Elizabeth seemed happy; my tranquil demeanour contributed greatly to calm her mind. But on the day that was to fulfil my wishes and my destiny, she was melancholy, and a presentiment of evil pervaded her; and perhaps also she thought of the dreadful secret, which I had promised to reveal to her the following day. My father was in the mean time overjoyed, and, in the bustle of preparation, only observed in the melancholy of his niece the diffidence of a bride.

After the ceremony was performed, a large party assembled at my father's; but it was agreed that Elizabeth and I should pass the afternoon and night at Evian, and return to Cologny the next morning.

5. More discriminating.

As the day was fair, and the wind favourable, we resolved to go by water. Those were the last moments of my life during which I enjoyed the feeling of happiness. We passed rapidly along: the sun was hot, but we were sheltered from its rays by a kind of canopy, while we enjoyed the beauty of the scene, sometimes on one side of the lake, where we saw Mont Salêve, the pleasant banks of Montalêgre, and at a distance, surmounting all, the beautiful Mont Blânc, and the assemblage of snowy mountains that in vain endeavour to emulate her; sometimes coasting the opposite banks, we saw the mighty Jura opposing its dark side to the ambition that would quit its native country, and an almost insurmountable barrier to the invader who should wish to enslave it.

I took the hand of Elizabeth: "You are sorrowful, my love. Ah! if you knew what I have suffered, and what I may yet endure, you would endeavour to let me taste the quiet, and freedom from despair, that this one day at least permits me to enjoy."

"Be happy, my dear Victor," replied Elizabeth; "there is, I hope, nothing to distress you; and be assured that if a lively joy is not painted in my face, my heart is contented. Something whispers to me not to depend too much on the prospect that is opened before us; but I will not listen to such a sinister voice. Observe how fast we move along, and how the clouds which sometimes obscure, and sometimes rise above the dome of Mont Blânc, render this scene of beauty still more interesting. Look also at the innumerable fish that are swimming in the clear waters, where we can distinguish every pebble that lies at the bottom. What a divine day! how happy and serene all nature appears!"

Thus Elizabeth endeavoured to divert her thoughts and mine from all reflection upon melancholy subjects. But her temper was fluctuating; joy for a few instants shone in her eyes, but it continually gave place to distraction and reverie.

The sun sunk lower in the heavens; we passed the river Drance, and observed its path through the chasms of the higher, and the glens of the lower hills. The Alps here come closer to the lake, and we approached the amphitheatre of mountains which forms its eastern boundary. The spire of Evian shone under the woods that surrounded it, and the range of mountain above mountain by which it was overhung.

The wind, which had hitherto carried us along with amazing rapidity, sunk at sunset to a light breeze; the soft air just ruffled the water, and caused a pleasant motion among the trees as we approached the shore, from which it wafted the most delightful scent of flowers and hay. The sun sunk beneath the horizon as we landed; and as I touched the shore, I felt those cares and fears revive, which soon were to clasp me, and cling to me for ever.

Chapter VI.

It was eight o'clock when we landed; we walked for a short time on the shore, enjoying the transitory light, and then retired to the inn, and contemplated the lovely scene of waters, woods, and mountains, obscured in darkness, yet still displaying their black outlines.

The wind, which had fallen in the south, now rose with great violence in the west. The moon had reached her summit in the heavens, and was beginning to descend; the clouds swept across it swifter than the flight of the vulture, and dimmed her rays, while the lake reflected the scene of the busy heavens, rendered still busier by the restless waves that were beginning to rise. Suddenly a heavy storm of rain descended.

I had been calm during the day; but so soon as night obscured the shapes of objects, a thousand fears arose in my mind. I was anxious and watchful, while my right hand grasped a pistol which was hidden in my bosom; every sound terrified me; but I resolved that I would sell my life dearly, and not relax the impending conflict until my own life, or that of my adversary, were extinguished.

Elizabeth observed my agitation for some time in timid and fearful silence; at length she said, "What is it that agitates you, my dear Victor? What is it you fear?"

"Oh! peace, peace, my love," replied I, "this night, and all will be safe: but this night is dreadful, very dreadful."

I passed an hour in this state of mind, when suddenly I reflected how dreadful the combat which I momentarily expected would be to my wife, and I earnestly entreated her to retire, resolving not to join her until I had obtained some knowledge as to the situation of my enemy.

She left me, and I continued some time walking up and down the passages of the house, and inspecting every corner that might afford a retreat to my adversary. But I discovered no trace of him, and was beginning to conjecture that some fortunate chance had intervened to prevent the execution of his menaces; when suddenly I heard a shrill and dreadful scream. It came from the room into which Elizabeth had retired. As I heard it, the whole truth rushed into my mind, my arms dropped, the motion of every muscle and fibre was suspended; I could feel the blood trickling in my veins, and tingling in the extremities of my limbs. This state lasted but for an instant; the scream was repeated, and I rushed into the room.

Great God! why did I not then expire! Why am I here to relate the destruction of the best hope, and the purest creature of earth. She was there, lifeless and inanimate, thrown across the bed, her head hanging down, and her pale and distorted features half covered by her hair. Every where I turn I see the same figure—her bloodless arms and relaxed form flung by the murderer on its bridal bier. Could I behold this, and live? Alas! life is obstinate, and clings closest where it is most hated. For a moment only did I lose recollection; I fainted.

When I recovered, I found myself surrounded by the people of the inn; their countenances expressed a breathless terror: but the horror of others appeared only as a mockery, a shadow of the feelings that oppressed me. I escaped from them to the room where lay the body of Elizabeth, my love, my wife, so lately living, so dear, so worthy. She had been moved from the posture in which I had first beheld her; and now, as she lay, her head upon her arm, and a handkerchief thrown across her face and neck, I might have supposed her asleep. I rushed towards her, and embraced her with ardour; but the deathly languor and coldness of the limbs told me, that what I now held in my arms had ceased to be the Elizabeth whom I had loved and cherished. The murderous mark of the fiend's grasp was on her neck, and the breath had ceased to issue from her lips.

While I still hung over her in the agony of despair, I happened to look up. The windows of the room had before been darkened; and I felt a kind of panic on seeing the pale yellow light of the moon illuminate the chamber. The shutters had been thrown back; and, with a sensation of horror not to be described, I saw at the open window a figure the most hideous and abhorred. A grin was on the face of the monster; he seemed to jeer, as with his fiendish finger he pointed towards the corpse of my wife. I rushed towards the window, and drawing a pistol from my bosom, shot; but he eluded me, leaped from his station, and, running with the swiftness of lightning, plunged into the lake.

The report of the pistol brought a crowd into the room. I pointed to the spot where he had disappeared, and we followed the track with boats; nets were cast, but in vain. After passing several hours, we returned hopeless, most of my companions believing it to have been a form conjured by my fancy. After having landed, they proceeded to search the country, parties going in different directions among the woods and vines.

I did not accompany them; I was exhausted: a film covered my eyes, and my skin was parched with the heat of fever. In this state I lay on a bed, hardly conscious of what had happened; my eyes wandered round the room, as if to seek something that I had lost.

At length I remembered that my father would anxiously expect the return of Elizabeth and myself, and that I must return alone. This reflection brought tears into my eyes, and I wept for a long time; but my thoughts rambled to various subjects, reflecting on my misfortunes, and their cause. I was bewildered in a cloud of wonder and horror. The death of William, the execution of Justine, the murder of Clerval, and lastly of my wife; even at that moment I knew not that my only remaining friends were safe from the malignity of the fiend; my father even now might be writhing under his grasp, and Ernest might be dead at his feet. This idea made me shudder, and recalled me to action. I started up, and resolved to return to Geneva with all possible speed.

There were no horses to be procured, and I must return by the lake; but the wind was unfavourable, and the rain fell in torrents. However, it was hardly morning, and I might reasonably hope to arrive by night. I hired men to row, and took an oar myself, for I had always experienced relief from mental torment in bodily exercise. But the overflowing misery I now felt, and the excess of agitation that I endured, rendered me incapable of any exertion. I threw down the oar; and, leaning my head upon my hands, gave way to every gloomy idea that arose. If I looked up, I saw the scenes which were familiar to me in my happier time, and which I had contemplated but the day before in the company of her who was now but a shadow and a recollection. Tears streamed from my eyes. The rain had ceased for a moment, and I saw the fish play in the waters as they had done a few hours before; they had then been observed by Elizabeth. Nothing is so painful to the human mind as a great and sudden change. The sun might shine, or the clouds might lour;[1] but nothing could appear to me as it had done the day before. A fiend had snatched from me every hope of future happiness: no creature had ever been so miserable as I was; so frightful an event is single in the history of man.

But why should I dwell upon the incidents that followed this last overwhelming event. Mine has been a tale of horrors; I have reached their *acme*, and what I must now relate can but be tedious to you. Know that, one by one, my friends were snatched away; I was left desolate. My own strength is exhausted; and I must tell, in a few words, what remains of my hideous narration.

I arrived at Geneva. My father and Ernest yet lived; but the former sunk under the tidings that I bore. I see him now, excellent and venerable old man! his eyes wandered in vacancy, for they had lost their charm and their delight—his niece, his more than daughter, whom he doated on with all that affection which a man feels, who, in the decline of life, having few affections, clings more earnestly to those that remain. Cursed, cursed be the fiend that brought misery on his grey hairs, and doomed him to waste in wretchedness! He could not live under the horrors that were accumulated around him; an apoplectic fit was brought on, and in a few days he died in my arms.

What then became of me? I know not; I lost sensation, and chains and darkness were the only objects that pressed upon me. Some-

1. Look dark or threatening.

times, indeed, I dreamt that I wandered in flowery meadows and pleasant vales with the friends of my youth; but awoke, and found myself in a dungeon. Melancholy followed, but by degrees I gained a clear conception of my miseries and situation, and was then released from my prison. For they had called me mad; and during many months, as I understood, a solitary cell had been my habitation.

But liberty had been a useless gift to me had I not, as I awakened to reason, at the same time awakened to revenge. As the memory of past misfortunes pressed upon me, I began to reflect on their cause— the monster whom I had created, the miserable dæmon whom I had sent abroad into the world for my destruction. I was possessed by a maddening rage when I thought of him, and desired and ardently prayed that I might have him within my grasp to wreak a great and signal revenge on his cursed head.

Nor did my hate long confine itself to useless wishes; I began to reflect on the best means of securing him; and for this purpose, about a month after my release, I repaired to a criminal judge in the town, and told him that I had an accusation to make; that I knew the destroyer of my family; and that I required him to exert his whole authority for the apprehension of the murderer.

The magistrate listened to me with attention and kindness: "Be assured, sir," said he, "no pains or exertions on my part shall be spared to discover the villain."

"I thank you," replied I; "listen, therefore, to the deposition that I have to make. It is indeed a tale so strange, that I should fear you would not credit it, were there not something in truth which, however wonderful,[2] forces conviction. The story is too connected to be mistaken for a dream, and I have no motive for falsehood." My manner, as I thus addressed him, was impressive, but calm; I had formed in my own heart a resolution to pursue my destroyer to death; and this purpose quieted my agony, and provisionally reconciled me to life. I now related my history briefly, but with firmness and precision, marking the dates with accuracy, and never deviating into invective or exclamation.

The magistrate appeared at first perfectly incredulous, but as I continued he became more attentive and interested; I saw him sometimes shudder with horror, at others a lively surprise, unmingled with disbelief, was painted on his countenance.

When I had concluded my narration, I said, "This is the being whom I accuse, and for whose detection and punishment I call upon you to exert your whole power. It is your duty as a magistrate, and I believe and hope that your feelings as a man will not revolt from the execution of those functions on this occasion."

2. I.e., to be wondered at.

This address caused a considerable change in the physiognomy of my auditor. He had heard my story with that half kind of belief that is given to a tale of spirits and supernatural events; but when he was called upon to act officially in consequence, the whole tide of his incredulity returned. He, however, answered mildly, "I would willingly afford you every aid in your pursuit; but the creature of whom you speak appears to have powers which would put all my exertions to defiance. Who can follow an animal which can traverse the sea of ice, and inhabit caves and dens, where no man would venture to intrude? Besides, some months have elapsed since the commission of his crimes, and no one can conjecture to what place he has wandered, or what region he may now inhabit."

"I do not doubt that he hovers near the spot which I inhabit; and if he has indeed taken refuge in the Alps, he may be hunted like the chamois,[3] and destroyed as a beast of prey. But I perceive your thoughts: you do not credit my narrative, and do not intend to pursue my enemy with the punishment which is his desert."

As I spoke, rage sparkled in my eyes; the magistrate was intimidated; "You are mistaken," said he, "I will exert myself; and if it is in my power to seize the monster, be assured that he shall suffer punishment proportionate to his crimes. But I fear, from what you have yourself described to be his properties, that this will prove impracticable, and that, while every proper measure is pursued, you should endeavour to make up your mind to disappointment."

"That cannot be; but all that I can say will be of little avail. My revenge is of no moment[4] to you; yet, while I allow it to be a vice, I confess that it is the devouring and only passion of my soul. My rage is unspeakable, when I reflect that the murderer, whom I have turned loose upon society, still exists. You refuse my just demand: I have but one resource; and I devote myself, either in my life or death, to his destruction."

I trembled with excess of agitation as I said this; there was a phrenzy in my manner, and something, I doubt not, of that haughty fierceness, which the martyrs of old are said to have possessed. But to a Genevan magistrate, whose mind was occupied by far other ideas than those of devotion and heroism, this elevation of mind had much the appearance of madness. He endeavoured to soothe me as a nurse does a child, and reverted to[5] my tale as the effects of delirium.

"Man," I cried, "how ignorant art thou in thy pride of wisdom! Cease; you know not what it is you say."

I broke from the house angry and disturbed, and retired to meditate on some other mode of action.

3. An Alpine antelope.
4. Importance.
5. Looked back at.

Chapter VII.

My present situation was one in which all voluntary thought was swallowed up and lost. I was hurried away by fury; revenge alone endowed me with strength and composure; it modelled my feelings, and allowed me to be calculating and calm, at periods when otherwise delirium or death would have been my portion.

My first resolution was to quit Geneva for ever; my country, which, when I was happy and beloved, was dear to me, now, in my adversity, became hateful. I provided myself with a sum of money, together with a few jewels which had belonged to my mother, and departed.

And now my wanderings began, which are to cease but with life. I have traversed a vast portion of the earth, and have endured all the hardships which travellers, in deserts and barbarous countries, are wont to meet. How I have lived I hardly know; many times have I stretched my failing limbs upon the sandy plain, and prayed for death. But revenge kept me alive; I dared not die, and leave my adversary in being.

When I quitted Geneva, my first labour was to gain some clue by which I might trace the steps of my fiendish enemy. But my plan was unsettled; and I wandered many hours around the confines of the town, uncertain what path I should pursue. As night approached, I found myself at the entrance of the cemetery where William, Elizabeth, and my father, reposed. I entered it, and approached the tomb which marked their graves. Every thing was silent, except the leaves of the trees, which were gently agitated by the wind; the night was nearly dark; and the scene would have been solemn and affecting even to an uninterested observer. The spirits of the departed seemed to flit around, and to cast a shadow, which was felt but seen not, around the head of the mourner.

The deep grief which this scene had at first excited quickly gave way to rage and despair. They were dead, and I lived; their murderer also lived, and to destroy him I must drag out my weary existence. I knelt on the grass, and kissed the earth, and with quivering lips exclaimed, "By the sacred earth on which I kneel, by the shades[1] that wander near me, by the deep and eternal grief that I feel, I swear; and by thee, O Night, and by the spirits that preside over thee, I swear to pursue the dæmon, who caused this misery, until he or I shall perish in mortal conflict. For this purpose I will preserve my life: to execute this dear revenge, will I again behold the sun, and tread the green herbage of earth, which otherwise should vanish from my eyes for ever. And I call on you, spirits of the dead; and on

1. Disembodied spirits.

you, wandering ministers of vengeance, to aid and conduct me in my work. Let the cursed and hellish monster drink deep of agony; let him feel the despair that now torments me."

I had begun my adjuration with solemnity, and an awe which almost assured me that the shades of my murdered friends heard and approved my devotion; but the furies possessed me as I concluded, and rage choked my utterance.

I was answered through the stillness of night by a loud and fiendish laugh. It rung on my ears long and heavily; the mountains re-echoed it, and I felt as if all hell surrounded me with mockery and laughter. Surely in that moment I should have been possessed by phrenzy, and have destroyed my miserable existence, but that my vow was heard, and that I was reserved for vengeance. The laughter died away, when a well-known and abhorred voice, apparently close to my ear, addressed me in an audible whisper—"I am satisfied: miserable wretch! you have determined to live, and I am satisfied."

I darted towards the spot from which the sound proceeded; but the devil eluded my grasp. Suddenly the broad disk of the moon arose, and shone full upon his ghastly and distorted shape, as he fled with more than mortal speed.

I pursued him; and for many months this has been my task. Guided by a slight clue, I followed the windings of the Rhone, but vainly. The blue Mediterranean appeared; and, by a strange chance, I saw the fiend enter by night, and hide himself in a vessel bound for the Black Sea. I took my passage in the same ship; but he escaped, I know not how.

Amidst the wilds of Tartary and Russia, although he still evaded me, I have ever followed in his track. Sometimes the peasants, scared by this horrid apparition, informed me of his path; sometimes he himself, who feared that if I lost all trace I should despair and die, often left some mark to guide me. The snows descended on my head, and I saw the print of his huge step on the white plain. To you first entering on life, to whom care is new and agony unknown, how can you understand what I have felt, and still feel. Cold, want, and fatigue, were the least pains which I was destined to endure. I was cursed by some devil, and carried about with me my eternal hell;[2] yet still a spirit of good followed and directed my steps, and, when I most murmured, would suddenly extricate me from seemingly insurmountable difficulties. Sometimes, when nature overcome by hunger, sunk under the exhaustion, a repast was prepared for me in the desert, that restored and inspirited me. The fare was indeed coarse, such as the peasants of the country ate; but I may not doubt that it was set there by the spirits that I had invoked to aid me.

2. See n. 1 on p. 95, above.

Often, when all was dry, the heavens cloudless, and I was parched by thirst, a slight cloud would bedim the sky, shed the few drops that revived me, and vanish.

I followed, when I could, the courses of the rivers; but the dæmon generally avoided these, as it was here that the population of the country chiefly collected. In other places human beings were seldom seen; and I generally subsisted on the wild animals that crossed my path. I had money with me, and gained the friendship of the villagers by distributing it, or bringing with me some food that I had killed, which, after taking a small part, I always presented to those who had provided me with fire and utensils for cooking.

My life, as it passed thus, was indeed hateful to me, and it was during sleep alone that I could taste joy. O blessed sleep! often, when most miserable, I sank to repose, and my dreams lulled me even to rapture. The spirits that guarded me had provided these moments, or rather hours, of happiness that I might retain strength to fulfil my pilgrimage. Deprived of this respite, I should have sunk under my hardships. During the day I was sustained and inspirited by the hope of night: for in sleep I saw my friends, my wife, and my beloved country; again I saw the benevolent countenance of my father, heard the silver tones of my Elizabeth's voice, and beheld Clerval enjoying health and youth. Often, when wearied by a toilsome march, I persuaded myself that I was dreaming until night should come, and that I should then enjoy reality in the arms of my dearest friends. What agonizing fondness did I feel for them! how did I cling to their dear forms, as sometimes they haunted even my waking hours, and persuade myself that they still lived! At such moments vengeance, that burned within me, died in my heart, and I pursued my path towards the destruction of the dæmon, more as a task enjoined by heaven, as the mechanical impulse of some power of which I was unconscious, than as the ardent desire of my soul.

What his feelings were whom I pursued, I cannot know. Sometimes, indeed, he left marks in writing on the barks of the trees, or cut in stone, that guided me, and instigated my fury. "My reign is not yet over," (these words were legible in one of these inscriptions); "you live, and my power is complete. Follow me; I seek the everlasting ices of the north, where you will feel the misery of cold and frost, to which I am impassive. You will find near this place, if you follow not too tardily, a dead hare; eat, and be refreshed. Come on, my enemy; we have yet to wrestle for our lives; but many hard and miserable hours must you endure, until that period shall arrive."

Scoffing devil! Again do I vow vengeance; again do I devote thee, miserable fiend, to torture and death. Never will I omit my search, until he or I perish; and then with what ecstacy shall I join my

Elizabeth, and those who even now prepare for me the reward of my tedious toil and horrible pilgrimage.

As I still pursued my journey to the northward, the snows thickened, and the cold increased in a degree almost too severe to support. The peasants were shut up in their hovels, and only a few of the most hardy ventured forth to seize the animals whom starvation had forced from their hiding-places to seek for prey. The rivers were covered with ice, and no fish could be procured; and thus I was cut off from my chief article of maintenance.

The triumph of my enemy increased with the difficulty of my labours. One inscription that he left was in these words: "Prepare! your toils only begin: wrap yourself in furs, and provide food, for we shall soon enter upon a journey where your sufferings will satisfy my ever-lasting hatred."

My courage and perseverance were invigorated by these scoffing words; I resolved not to fail in my purpose; and, calling on heaven to support me, I continued with unabated fervour to traverse immense deserts, until the ocean appeared at a distance, and formed the utmost boundary of the horizon. Oh! how unlike it was to the blue seas of the south! Covered with ice, it was only to be distinguished from land by its superior wildness and ruggedness. The Greeks wept for joy when they beheld the Mediterranean from the hills of Asia, and hailed with rapture the boundary of their toils.[3] I did not weep; but I knelt down, and, with a full heart, thanked my guiding spirit for conducting me in safety to the place where I hoped, notwithstanding my adversary's gibe, to meet and grapple with him.

Some weeks before this period I had procured a sledge and dogs, and thus traversed the snows with inconceivable speed. I know not whether the fiend possessed the same advantages; but I found that, as before I had daily lost ground in the pursuit, I now gained on him; so much so, that when I first saw the ocean, he was but one day's journey in advance, and I hoped to intercept him before he should reach the beach. With new courage, therefore, I pressed on, and in two days arrived at a wretched hamlet on the seashore. I inquired of the inhabitants concerning the fiend, and gained accurate information. A gigantic monster, they said, had arrived the night before, armed with a gun and many pistols; putting to flight the inhabitants of a solitary cottage, through fear of his terrific appearance. He had carried off their store of winter food, and, placing it in a sledge, to draw which he had seized on a numerous drove of trained dogs, he had harnessed them, and the same night, to the joy of the horror-struck villagers, had pursued his journey across the sea in a

---

3. A reference to the 401–399 B.C. Greek expedition to and from Persia, known as "the March of the Ten Thousand"; see book IV of the *Anabasis* of Xenophon (431–362 B.C.).

direction that led to no land; and they conjectured that he must speedily be destroyed by the breaking of the ice, or frozen by the eternal frosts.

On hearing this information, I suffered a temporary access of despair. He had escaped me; and I must commence a destructive and almost endless journey across the mountainous ices of the ocean,—amidst cold that few of the inhabitants could long endure, and which I, the native of a genial and sunny climate, could not hope to survive. Yet at the idea that the fiend should live and be triumphant, my rage and vengeance returned, and, like a mighty tide, overwhelmed every other feeling. After a slight repose, during which the spirits of the dead hovered round, and instigated me to toil and revenge, I prepared for my journey.

I exchanged my land sledge for one fashioned for the inequalities of the frozen ocean; and, purchasing a plentiful stock of provisions, I departed from land.

I cannot guess how many days have passed since then; but I have endured misery, which nothing but the eternal sentiment of a just retribution burning within my heart could have enabled me to support. Immense and rugged mountains of ice often barred up my passage, and I often heard the thunder of the ground sea, which threatened my destruction. But again the frost came, and made the paths of the sea secure.

By the quantity of provision which I had consumed I should guess that I had passed three weeks in this journey; and the continual protraction of hope, returning back upon the heart, often wrung bitter drops of despondency and grief from my eyes. Despair had indeed almost secured her prey, and I should soon have sunk beneath this misery; when once, after the poor animals that carried me had with incredible toil gained the summit of a sloping ice mountain, and one sinking under his fatigue died, I viewed the expanse before me with anguish, when suddenly my eye caught a dark speck upon the dusky plain. I strained my sight to discover what it could be, and uttered a wild cry of ecstacy when I distinguished a sledge, and the distorted proportions of a well-known form within. Oh! with what a burning gush did hope revisit my heart! warm tears filled my eyes, which I hastily wiped away, that they might not intercept the view I had of the dæmon; but still my sight was dimmed by the burning drops, until, giving way to the emotions that oppressed me, I wept aloud.

But this was not the time for delay; I disencumbered the dogs of their dead companion, gave them a plentiful portion of food; and, after an hour's rest, which was absolutely necessary, and yet which was bitterly irksome to me, I continued my route. The sledge was still visible; nor did I again lose sight of it, except at the moments when for a short time some ice rock concealed it with its intervening crags. I indeed perceptibly gained on it; and when, after nearly two days' journey, I beheld my enemy at no more than a mile distant, my heart bounded within me.

But now, when I appeared almost within grasp of my enemy, my hopes were suddenly extinguished, and I lost all trace of him more utterly than I had ever done before. A ground sea was heard; the thunder of its progress, as the waters rolled and swelled beneath me, became every moment more ominous and terrific. I pressed on, but in vain. The wind arose; the sea roared; and, as with the mighty shock of an earthquake, it split, and cracked with a tremendous and overwhelming sound. The work was soon finished: in a few minutes a tumultuous sea rolled between me and my enemy, and I was left drifting on a scattered piece of ice, that was continually lessening, and thus preparing for me a hideous death.

In this manner many appalling hours passed; several of my dogs died; and I myself was about to sink under the accumulation of distress, when I saw your vessel riding at anchor, and holding forth to me hopes of succour and life. I had no conception that vessels ever came so far north, and was astounded at the sight. I quickly destroyed part of my sledge to construct oars; and by these means was enabled, with infinite fatigue, to move my ice-raft in the direction of your ship. I had determined, if you were going southward, still to trust myself to the mercy of the seas, rather than abandon my purpose. I hoped to induce you to grant me a boat with which I could still pursue my enemy. But your direction was northward. You took me on board when my vigour was exhausted, and I should soon have sunk under my multiplied hardships into a death, which I still dread,—for my task is unfulfilled.

Oh! when will my guiding spirit, in conducting me to the dæmon, allow me the rest I so much desire; or must I die, and he yet live? If I do, swear to me, Walton, that he shall not escape; that you will seek him, and satisfy my vengeance in his death. Yet, do I dare ask you to undertake my pilgrimage, to endure the hardships that I have undergone? No; I am not so selfish. Yet, when I am dead, if he should appear; if the ministers of vengeance should conduct him to you, swear that he shall not live—swear that he shall not triumph over my accumulated woes, and live to make another such a wretch as I am. He is eloquent and persuasive; and once his words had even power over my heart: but trust him not. His soul is as hellish as his form, full of treachery and fiend-like malice. Hear him not; call on the manes[4] of William, Justine, Clerval, Elizabeth, my father, and of the wretched Victor, and thrust your sword into his heart. I will hover near, and direct the steel aright.

4. Spirits of the dead.

WALTON, in continuation.

August 26th, 17–.

You have read this strange and terrific story, Margaret; and do you not feel your blood congealed with horror, like that which even now curdles mine? Sometimes, seized with sudden agony, he could not continue his tale; at others, his voice broken, yet piercing, uttered with difficulty the words so replete with agony. His fine and lovely eyes were now lighted up with indignation, now subdued to downcast sorrow, and quenched in infinite wretchedness. Sometimes he commanded his countenance and tones, and related the most horrible incidents with a tranquil voice, suppressing every mark of agitation; then, like a volcano bursting forth, his face would suddenly change to an expression of the wildest rage, as he shrieked out imprecations on his persecutor.

His tale is connected,[5] and told with an appearance of the simplest truth; yet I own to you that the letters of Felix and Safie, which he shewed me, and the apparition of the monster, seen from our ship, brought to me a greater conviction of the truth of his narrative than his asseverations, however earnest and connected. Such a monster has then really existence; I cannot doubt it; yet I am lost in surprise and admiration. Sometimes I endeavoured to gain from Frankenstein the particulars of his creature's formation; but on this point he was impenetrable.

"Are you mad, my friend?" said he, "or whither does your senseless curiosity lead you? Would you also create for yourself and the world a demoniacal enemy? Or to what do your questions tend? Peace, peace! learn my miseries, and do not seek to increase your own."

Frankenstein discovered that I made notes concerning his history: he asked to see them, and then himself corrected and augmented them in many places; but principally in giving the life and spirit to the conversations he held with his enemy. "Since you have preserved my narration," said he, "I would not that a mutilated one should go down to posterity."

Thus has a week passed away, while I have listened to the strangest tale that ever imagination formed. My thoughts, and every feeling of my soul, have been drunk up by the interest for my guest, which this tale, and his own elevated and gentle manners have created. I wish to soothe him; yet can I counsel one so infinitely miserable, so destitute of every hope of consolation, to live? Oh, no! the only joy that he can now know will be when he composes his shattered feelings to peace and death. Yet he enjoys one comfort, the offspring of solitude and delirium: he believes, that, when in dreams he holds converse with

---

5. "Exhibiting proper sequence and coherence of thought" (*OED*).

his friends, and derives from that communion consolation for his miseries, or excitements to his vengeance, that they are not the creations of his fancy, but the real beings who visit him from the regions of a remote world. This faith gives a solemnity to his reveries that render them to me almost as imposing and interesting as truth.

Our conversations are not always confined to his own history and misfortunes. On every point of general literature he displays unbounded knowledge, and a quick and piercing apprehension. His eloquence is forcible and touching; nor can I hear him, when he relates a pathetic incident, or endeavours to move the passions of pity or love, without tears. What a glorious creature must he have been in the days of his prosperity, when he is thus noble and godlike in ruin. He seems to feel his own worth, and the greatness of his fall.

"When younger," said he, "I felt as if I were destined for some great enterprise. My feelings are profound; but I possessed a coolness of judgment that fitted me for illustrious achievements. This sentiment of the worth of my nature supported me, when others would have been oppressed; for I deemed it criminal to throw away in useless grief those talents that might be useful to my fellow-creatures. When I reflected on the work I had completed, no less a one than the creation of a sensitive and rational animal, I could not rank myself with the herd of common projectors.[6] But this feeling, which supported me in the commencement of my career, now serves only to plunge me lower in the dust. All my speculations and hopes are as nothing; and, like the archangel who aspired to omnipotence, I am chained in an eternal hell. My imagination was vivid, yet my powers of analysis and application were intense; by the union of these qualities I conceived the idea, and executed the creation of a man. Even now I cannot recollect, without passion, my reveries while the work was incomplete. I trod heaven in my thoughts, now exulting in my powers, now burning with the idea of their effects. From my infancy I was imbued with high hopes and a lofty ambition; but how am I sunk! Oh! my friend, if you had known me as I once was, you would not recognize me in this state of degradation. Despondency rarely visited my heart; a high destiny seemed to bear me on, until I fell, never, never again to rise."

Must I then lose this admirable being? I have longed for a friend; I have sought one who would sympathize with and love me. Behold, on these desert seas I have found such a one; but, I fear, I have gained him only to know his value, and lose him. I would reconcile him to life, but he repulses the idea.

"I thank you, Walton," he said, "for your kind intentions towards so miserable a wretch; but when you speak of new ties, and fresh affections, think you that any can replace those who are gone? Can

---

6. Schemers and speculators.

any man be to me as Clerval was; or any woman another Elizabeth? Even where the affections are not strongly moved by any superior excellence, the companions of our childhood always possess a certain power over our minds, which hardly any later friend can obtain. They know our infantine dispositions, which, however they may be afterwards modified, are never eradicated; and they can judge of our actions with more certain conclusions as to the integrity of our motives. A sister or a brother can never, unless indeed such symptoms have been shewn early, suspect the other of fraud or false dealing, when another friend, however strongly he may be attached, may, in spite of himself, be invaded with suspicion. But I enjoyed friends, dear not only through habit and association, but from their own merits; and, wherever I am, the soothing voice of my Elizabeth, and the conversation of Clerval, will be ever whispered in my ear. They are dead; and but one feeling in such a solitude can persuade me to preserve my life. If I were engaged in any high undertaking or design, fraught with extensive utility to my fellow-creatures, then could I live to fulfil it. But such is not my destiny; I must pursue and destroy the being to whom I gave existence; then my lot on earth will be fulfilled, and I may die."

September 2d.

MY BELOVED SISTER,

I write to you, encompassed by peril, and ignorant whether I am ever doomed to see again dear England, and the dearer friends that inhabit it. I am surrounded by mountains of ice, which admit of no escape, and threaten every moment to crush my vessel. The brave fellows, whom I have persuaded to be my companions, look towards me for aid; but I have none to bestow. There is something terribly appalling in our situation, yet my courage and hopes do not desert me. We may survive; and if we do not, I will repeat the lessons of my Seneca,[7] and die with a good heart.

Yet what, Margaret, will be the state of your mind? You will not hear of my destruction, and you will anxiously await my return. Years will pass, and you will have visitings of despair, and yet be tortured by hope. Oh! my beloved sister, the sickening failings of your heart-felt expectations are, in prospect, more terrible to me than my own death. But you have a husband, and lovely children; you may be happy: heaven bless you, and make you so!

My unfortunate guest regards me with the tenderest compassion. He endeavours to fill me with hope; and talks as if life were a possession which he valued. He reminds me how often the same

7. Lucius Annaeus Seneca (c. 4 B.C.–A.D. 65), Roman Stoic philosopher and poet (see n. 1, p. 48 above).

accidents have happened to other navigators, who have attempted this sea, and, in spite of myself, he fills me with cheerful auguries. Even the sailors feel the power of his eloquence: when he speaks, they no longer despair; he rouses their energies, and, while they hear his voice, they believe these vast mountains of ice are mole-hills, which will vanish before the resolutions of man. These feelings are transitory; each day's expectation delayed fills them with fear, and I almost dread a mutiny caused by this despair.

September 5th.
A scene has just passed of such uncommon interest, that although it is highly probable that these papers may never reach you, yet I cannot forbear recording it.

We are still surrounded by mountains of ice, still in imminent danger of being crushed in their conflict. The cold is excessive, and many of my unfortunate comrades have already found a grave amidst this scene of desolation. Frankenstein has daily declined in health: a feverish fire still glimmers in his eyes; but he is exhausted, and, when suddenly roused to any exertion, he speedily sinks again into apparent lifelessness.

I mentioned in my last letter the fears I entertained of a mutiny. This morning, as I sat watching the wan countenance of my friend— his eyes half closed, and his limbs hanging listlessly,—I was roused by half a dozen of the sailors, who desired admission into the cabin. They entered; and their leader addressed me. He told me that he and his companions had been chosen by the other sailors to come in deputation to me, to make me a demand, which, in justice, I could not refuse. We were immured in ice, and should probably never escape; but they feared that if, as was possible, the ice should dissipate, and a free passage be opened, I should be rash enough to continue my voyage, and lead them into fresh dangers, after they might happily have surmounted this. They desired, therefore, that I should engage with a solemn promise, that if the vessel should be freed, I would instantly direct my course southward.

This speech troubled me. I had not despaired; nor had I yet conceived the idea of returning, if set free. Yet could I, in justice, or even in possibility, refuse this demand? I hesitated before I answered; when Frankenstein, who had at first been silent, and, indeed, appeared hardly to have force enough to attend, now roused himself, his eyes sparkled, and his cheeks flushed with momentary vigour. Turning towards the men, he said—

"What do you mean? What do you demand of your captain? Are you then so easily turned from your design? Did you not call this a glorious expedition? and wherefore was it glorious? Not because the way was smooth and placid as a southern sea but because it was full of dangers and terror; because, at every new incident, your fortitude was to be called forth and your courage exhibited; because danger and death surrounded, and these dangers you were to brave and overcome. For this was it a glorious, for this was it an honourable undertaking. You were hereafter to be hailed as the benefactors of your species; your name adored, as belonging to brave men who encountered death for honour and the benefit of mankind. And now, behold, with the first imagination of danger, or, if you will, the first mighty and terrific trial of your courage, you shrink away, and are content to be handed down as men who had not strength enough to endure cold and peril; and so, poor souls, they were chilly, and returned to their warm fire-sides. Why, that requires not this preparation; ye need not have come thus far, and dragged your captain to the shame of a defeat, merely to prove yourselves cowards. Oh! be men, or be more than men. Be steady to your purposes, and firm as a rock. This ice is not made of such stuff as your hearts might be; it is mutable, cannot withstand you, if you say that it shall not. Do not return to your families with the stigma of disgrace marked on your brows. Return as heroes who have fought and conquered, and who know not what it is to turn their backs on the foe."

He spoke this with a voice so modulated to the different feelings expressed in his speech, with an eye so full of lofty design and heroism, that can you wonder that these men were moved. They looked at one another, and were unable to reply. I spoke; I told them to retire, and consider of what had been said: that I would not lead them further north, if they strenuously desired the contrary; but that I hoped that, with reflection, their courage would return.

They retired, and I turned towards my friend; but he was sunk in languor, and almost deprived of life.

How all this will terminate, I know not; but I had rather die, than return shamefully,—my purpose unfulfilled. Yet I fear such will be my fate; the men, unsupported by ideas of glory and honour, can never willingly continue to endure their present hardships.

September 7th.

The die is cast; I have consented to return, if we are not destroyed. Thus are my hopes blasted by cowardice and indecision; I come back ignorant and disappointed. It requires more philosophy than I possess, to bear this injustice with patience.

September 12th.

It is past; I am returning to England. I have lost my hopes of utility and glory;—I have lost my friend. But I will endeavour to detail these bitter circumstances to you, my dear sister; and, while I am wafted towards England, and towards you, I will not despond.

September 19th,[8] the ice began to move, and roarings like thunder were heard at a distance, as the islands split and cracked in every direction. We were in the most imminent peril; but, as we could only remain passive, my chief attention was occupied by my unfortunate guest, whose illness increased in such a degree, that he was entirely confined to his bed. The ice cracked behind us, and was driven with force towards the north; a breeze sprung from the west, and on the 11th the passage towards the south became perfectly free. When the sailors saw this, and that their return to their native country was apparently assured, a shout of tumultuous joy broke from them, loud and long-continued. Frankenstein, who was dozing, awoke, and asked the cause of the tumult. "They shout," I said, "because they will soon return to England."

"Do you then really return?"

"Alas! yes; I cannot withstand their demands. I cannot lead them unwillingly to danger, and I must return."

"Do so, if you will; but I will not. You may give up your purpose; but mine is assigned to me by heaven, and I dare not. I am weak; but surely the spirits who assist my vengeance will endow me with sufficient strength." Saying this, he endeavoured to spring from the bed, but the exertion was too great for him; he fell back, and fainted.

It was long before he was restored; and I often thought that life was entirely extinct. At length he opened his eyes, but he breathed with difficulty, and was unable to speak. The surgeon gave him a composing draught,[9] and ordered us to leave him undisturbed. In the mean time he told me, that my friend had certainly not many hours to live.

His sentence was pronounced; and I could only grieve, and be patient. I sat by his bed watching him; his eyes were closed, and I thought he slept; but presently he called to me in a feeble voice, and, bidding me come near, said—"Alas! the strength I relied on is gone; I feel that I shall soon die, and he, my enemy and persecutor, may still be in being. Think not, Walton, that in the last moments of my existence I feel that burning hatred, and ardent desire of revenge, I once expressed, but I feel myself justified in desiring the death of my adversary. During these last days I have been occupied in examining my past conduct; nor do I find it blameable. In a fit of enthusiastic madness I created a rational creature, and was bound towards him, to assure, as far as was in my power, his happiness and well-being. This was my duty; but there was another still paramount to that. My duties towards my fellow-creatures had greater claims to my attention, because they included a greater proportion of happiness or misery. Urged by this view, I refused, and I did right in refusing,

8. Corrected in 1831 to "September 9th."
9. Restorative liquid.

to create a companion for the first creature. He shewed unparalleled malignity and selfishness, in evil: he destroyed my friends; he devoted to destruction beings who possessed exquisite sensations, happiness, and wisdom; nor do I know where this thirst for vengeance may end. Miserable himself, that he may render no other wretched, he ought to die. The task of his destruction was mine, but I have failed. When actuated by selfish and vicious motives, I asked you to undertake my unfinished work; and I renew this request now, when I am only induced by reason and virtue.

"Yet I cannot ask you to renounce your country and friends, to fulfil this task; and now, that you are returning to England, you will have little chance of meeting with him. But the consideration of these points, and the well-balancing of what you may esteem your duties, I leave to you; my judgment and ideas are already disturbed by the near approach of death. I dare not ask you to do what I think right, for I may still be misled by passion.

"That he should live to be an instrument of mischief disturbs me; in other respects this hour, when I momentarily expect my release, is the only happy one which I have enjoyed for several years. The forms of the beloved dead flit before me, and I hasten to their arms. Farewell, Walton! Seek happiness in tranquillity, and avoid ambition, even if it be only the apparently innocent one of distinguishing yourself in science and discoveries. Yet why do I say this? I have myself been blasted in these hopes, yet another may succeed."

His voice became fainter as he spoke; and at length, exhausted by his effort, he sunk into silence. About half an hour afterwards he attempted again to speak, but was unable; he pressed my hand feebly, and his eyes closed for ever, while the irradiation[1] of a gentle smile passed away from his lips.

Margaret, what comment can I make on the untimely extinction of this glorious spirit? What can I say, that will enable you to understand the depth of my sorrow? All that I should express would be inadequate and feeble. My tears flow; my mind is overshadowed by a cloud of disappointment. But I journey towards England, and I may there find consolation.

I am interrupted. What do these sounds portend? It is midnight; the breeze blows fairly, and the watch on deck scarcely stir. Again; there is a sound as of a human voice, but hoarser; it comes from the cabin where the remains of Frankenstein still lie. I must arise, and examine. Good night, my sister.

Great God! what a scene has just taken place! I am yet dizzy with the remembrance of it. I hardly know whether I shall have the

---

1. Shining forth.

power to detail it; yet the tale which I have recorded would be incomplete without this final and wonderful catastrophe.

I entered the cabin, where lay the remains of my ill-fated and admirable friend. Over him hung a form which I cannot find words to describe; gigantic in stature, yet uncouth and distorted in its proportions. As he hung over the coffin, his face was concealed by long locks of ragged hair; but one vast hand was extended, in colour and apparent texture like that of a mummy. When he heard the sound of my approach, he ceased to utter exclamations of grief and horror, and sprung towards the window. Never did I behold a vision so horrible as his face, of such loathsome, yet appalling hideousness. I shut my eyes involuntarily, and endeavoured to recollect what were my duties with regard to this destroyer. I called on him to stay.

He paused, looking on me with wonder; and, again turning towards the lifeless form of his creator, he seemed to forget my presence, and every feature and gesture seemed instigated by the wildest rage of some uncontrollable passion.

"That is also my victim!" he exclaimed; "in his murder my crimes are consummated; the miserable series of my being is wound to its close! Oh, Frankenstein! generous and self-devoted being! what does it avail that I now ask thee to pardon me? I, who irretrievably destroyed thee by destroying all thou lovedst. Alas! he is cold; he may not answer me."

His voice seemed suffocated; and my first impulses, which had suggested to me the duty of obeying the dying request of my friend, in destroying his enemy, were now suspended by a mixture of curiosity and compassion. I approached this tremendous being; I dared not again raise my looks upon his face, there was something so scaring and unearthly in his ugliness. I attempted to speak, but the words died away on my lips. The monster continued to utter wild and incoherent self-reproaches. At length I gathered resolution to address him, in a pause of the tempest of his passion: "Your repentance," I said, "is now superfluous. If you had listened to the voice of conscience, and heeded the stings of remorse, before you had urged your diabolical vengeance to this extremity, Frankenstein would yet have lived."

"And do you dream?" said the dæmon; "do you think that I was then dead to agony and remorse?—He," he continued, pointing to the corpse, "he suffered not more in the consummation of the deed;—oh! not the ten-thousandth portion of the anguish that was mine during the lingering detail of its execution. A frightful selfishness hurried me on, while my heart was poisoned with remorse. Think ye that the groans of Clerval were music to my ears? My heart was fashioned to be susceptible of love and sympathy; and, when wrenched by misery to vice and hatred, it did not endure the violence of the change without torture, such as you cannot even imagine.

"After the murder of Clerval, I returned to Switzerland, heart-broken and overcome. I pitied Frankenstein; my pity amounted to horror: I abhorred myself. But when I discovered that he, the author at once of my existence and of its unspeakable torments, dared to hope for happiness; that while he accumulated wretchedness and despair upon me, he sought his own enjoyment in feelings and passions from the indulgence of which I was for ever barred, then impotent envy and bitter indignation filled me with an insatiable thirst for vengeance. I recollected my threat, and resolved that it should be accomplished. I knew that I was preparing for myself a deadly torture; but I was the slave, not the master of an impulse, which I detested, yet could not disobey. Yet when she died!—nay, then I was not miserable. I had cast off all feeling, subdued all anguish to riot in the excess of my despair. Evil thenceforth became my good.[2] Urged thus far, I had no choice but to adapt my nature to an element which I had willingly chosen. The completion of my demoniacal design became an insatiable passion. And now it is ended; there is my last victim!"

I was at first touched by the expressions of his misery; yet when I called to mind what Frankenstein had said of his powers of eloquence and persuasion, and when I again cast my eyes on the lifeless form of my friend, indignation was re-kindled within me. "Wretch!" I said, "it is well that you come here to whine over the desolation that you have made. You throw a torch into a pile of buildings, and when they are consumed you sit among the ruins, and lament the fall. Hypocritical fiend! if he whom you mourn still lived, still would he be the object, again would he become the prey of your accursed vengeance. It is not pity that you feel; you lament only because the victim of your malignity is withdrawn from your power."

"Oh, it is not thus—not thus," interrupted the being; "yet such must be the impression conveyed to you by what appears to be the purport of my actions. Yet I seek not a fellow-feeling in my misery. No sympathy may I ever find. When I first sought it, it was the love of virtue, the feelings of happiness and affection with which my whole being overflowed, that I wished to be participated.[3] But now, that virtue has become to me a shadow, and that happiness and affection are turned into bitter and loathing despair, in what should I seek for sympathy? I am content to suffer alone, while my sufferings shall endure: when I die, I am well satisfied that abhorrence and

2. Cf. Satan in *Paradise Lost*: "all Good to me is lost; / Evil be thou my Good" (IV.109–10).
3. Shared.

opprobrium should load my memory. Once my fancy was soothed with dreams of virtue, of fame, and of enjoyment. Once I falsely hoped to meet with beings, who, pardoning my outward form, would love me for the excellent qualities which I was capable of bringing forth. I was nourished with high thoughts of honour and devotion. But now vice has degraded me beneath the meanest animal. No crime, no mischief, no malignity, no misery, can be found comparable to mine. When I call over the frightful catalogue of my deeds, I cannot believe that I am he whose thoughts were once filled with sublime and transcendant visions of the beauty and the majesty of goodness. But it is even so; the fallen angel becomes a malignant devil. Yet even that enemy of God and man had friends and associates in his desolation; I am quite alone.

"You, who call Frankenstein your friend, seem to have a knowledge of my crimes and his misfortunes. But, in the detail which he gave you of them, he could not sum up the hours and months of misery which I endured, wasting in impotent passions. For whilst I destroyed his hopes, I did not satisfy my own desires. They were for ever ardent and craving; still I desired love and fellowship, and I was still spurned. Was there no injustice in this? Am I to be thought the only criminal, when all human kind sinned against me? Why do you not hate Felix, who drove his friend from his door with contumely?[4] Why do you not execrate the rustic who sought to destroy the saviour of his child? Nay, these are virtuous and immaculate beings! I, the miserable and the abandoned, am an abortion,[5] to be spurned at, and kicked, and trampled on. Even now my blood boils at the recollection of this injustice.

"But it is true that I am a wretch. I have murdered the lovely and the helpless; I have strangled the innocent as they slept, and grasped to death his throat who never injured me or any other living thing. I have devoted my creator, the select specimen of all that is worthy of love and admiration among men, to misery; I have pursued him even to that irremediable ruin. There he lies, white and cold in death. You hate me; but your abhorrence cannot equal that with which I regard myself. I look on the hands which executed the deed; I think on the heart in which the imagination of it was conceived, and long for the moment when they will meet my eyes, when it will haunt my thoughts, no more.

"Fear not that I shall be the instrument of future mischief. My work is nearly complete. Neither your's nor any man's death is needed to consummate the series of my being, and accomplish that which must be done; but it requires my own. Do not think that I

4. Humiliating contempt.
5. "Any dwarfed and misshapen product of generation" (*OED*).

shall be slow to perform this sacrifice. I shall quit your vessel on the ice-raft which brought me hither, and shall seek the most northern extremity of the globe; I shall collect my funeral pile, and consume to ashes this miserable frame, that its remains may afford no light to any curious and unhallowed wretch, who would create such another as I have been. I shall die. I shall no longer feel the agonies which now consume me, or be the prey of feelings unsatisfied, yet unquenched. He is dead who called me into being; and when I shall be no more, the very remembrance of us both will speedily vanish. I shall no longer see the sun or stars, or feel the winds play on my cheeks. Light, feeling, and sense, will pass away; and in this condition must I find my happiness. Some years ago, when the images which this world affords first opened upon me, when I felt the cheering warmth of summer, and heard the rustling of the leaves and the chirping of the birds, and these were all to me, I should have wept to die; now it is my only consolation. Polluted by crimes, and torn by the bitterest remorse, where can I find rest but in death?

"Farewell! I leave you, and in you the last of human kind whom these eyes will ever behold. Farewell, Frankenstein! If thou wert yet alive, and yet cherished a desire of revenge against me, it would be better satiated in my life than in my destruction. But it was not so; thou didst seek my extinction, that I might not cause greater wretchedness; and if yet, in some mode unknown to me, thou hast not yet ceased to think and feel, thou desirest not my life for my own misery. Blasted as thou wert, my agony was still superior to thine; for the bitter sting of remorse may not cease to rankle in my wounds until death shall close them for ever.

"But soon," he cried, with sad and solemn enthusiasm, "I shall die, and what I now feel be no longer felt. Soon these burning miseries will be extinct. I shall ascend my funeral pile triumphantly, and exult in the agony of the torturing flames. The light of that conflagration will fade away; my ashes will be swept into the sea by the winds. My spirit will sleep in peace; or if it thinks, it will not surely think thus. Farewell."

He sprung from the cabin-window, as he said this, upon the ice-raft which lay close to the vessel. He was soon borne away by the waves, and lost in darkness and distance.

THE END.

CONTEXTS

Circumstance, Influence, Composition, Revision

MARY SHELLEY

Introduction to *Frankenstein*, Third Edition (1831)[†]

The Publishers of the Standard Novels, in selecting 'Frankenstein' for one of their series, expressed a wish that I should furnish them with some account of the origin of the story. I am the more willing to comply, because I shall thus give a general answer to the question, so very frequently asked me— 'How I, then a young girl, came to think of, and to dilate upon, so very hideous an idea?' It is true that I am very averse to bringing myself forward in print; but as my account will only appear as an appendage to a former production, and as it will be confined to such topics as have connection with my authorship alone, I can scarcely accuse myself of a personal intrusion.

It is not singular that, as the daughter of two persons of distinguished literary celebrity, I should very early in life have thought of writing. As a child I scribbled; and my favourite pastime, during the hours given me for recreation, was to 'write stories.' Still I had a dearer pleasure than this, which was the formation of castles in the air—the indulging in waking dreams—the following up trains of thought, which had for their subject the formation of a succession of imaginary incidents. My dreams were at once more fantastic and agreeable than my writings. In the latter I was a close imitator— rather doing as others had done, than putting down the suggestions of my own mind. What I wrote was intended at least for one other eye—my childhood's companion and friend; but my dreams were all my own; I accounted for them to nobody; they were my refuge when annoyed—my dearest pleasure when free.

I lived principally in the country as a girl, and passed a considerable time in Scotland. I made occasional visits to the more picturesque parts; but my habitual residence was on the blank and dreary

---

[†] From *Frankenstein: or, The Modern Prometheus* (London: Henry Colburn and Richard Bentley, 1831), v–xii.

northern shores of the Tay, near Dundee. Blank and dreary on ret-
rospection I call them; they were not so to me then. They were the
eyry of freedom, and the pleasant region where unheeded I could
commune with the creatures of my fancy. I wrote then—but in a
most common-place style. It was beneath the trees of the grounds
belonging to our house, or on the bleak sides of the woodless mountains near, that my true compositions, the airy flights of my imagination, were born and fostered. I did not make myself the heroine
of my tales. Life appeared to me too common-place an affair as
regarded myself. I could not figure to myself that romantic woes or
wonderful events would ever be my lot; but I was not confined to
my own identity, and I could people the hours with creations far
more interesting to me at that age, than my own sensations.

After this my life became busier, and reality stood in place of fiction. My husband, however, was, from the first, very anxious that I
should prove myself worthy of my parentage, and enrol myself on
the page of fame. He was for ever inciting me to obtain literary reputation, which even on my own part I cared for then, though since I
have become infinitely indifferent to it. At this time he desired that
I should write, not so much with the idea that I could produce any
thing worthy of notice, but that he might himself judge how far I
possessed the promise of better things hereafter. Still I did nothing.
Travelling, and the cares of a family, occupied my time; and study,
in the way of reading, or improving my ideas in communication with
his far more cultivated mind, was all of literary employment that
engaged my attention.

In the summer of 1816, we visited Switzerland, and became the
neighbours of Lord Byron. At first we spent our pleasant hours on
the lake, or wandering on its shores; and Lord Byron, who was
writing the third canto of Childe Harold, was the only one among
us who put his thoughts upon paper. These, as he brought them
successively to us, clothed in all the light and harmony of poetry,
seemed to stamp as divine the glories of heaven and earth, whose
influences we partook with him.

But it proved a wet, ungenial summer, and incessant rain often
confined us for days to the house. Some volumes of ghost stories,
translated from the German into French, fell into our hands. There
was the History of the Inconstant Lover, who, when he thought to
clasp the bride to whom he had pledged his vows, found himself
in the arms of the pale ghost of her whom he had deserted. There
was the tale of the sinful founder of his race, whose miserable doom
it was to bestow the kiss of death on all the younger sons of his fated
house, just when they reached the age of promise. His gigantic, shadowy form, clothed like the ghost in Hamlet, in complete armour, but
with the beaver up, was seen at midnight, by the moon's fitful beams,

to advance slowly along the gloomy avenue. The shape was lost beneath the shadow of the castle walls; but soon a gate swung back, a step was heard, the door of the chamber opened, and he advanced to the couch of the blooming youths, cradled in healthy sleep. Eternal sorrow sat upon his face as he bent down and kissed the forehead of the boys, who from that hour withered like flowers snapt upon the stalk. I have not seen these stories since then; but their incidents are as fresh in my mind as if I had read them yesterday.

'We will each write a ghost story,' said Lord Byron; and his proposition was acceded to. There were four of us. The noble author began a tale, a fragment of which he printed at the end of his poem of Mazeppa. Shelley, more apt to embody ideas and sentiments in the radiance of brilliant imagery, and in the music of the most melodious verse that adorns our language, than to invent the machinery of a story, commenced one founded on the experiences of his early life. Poor Polidori had some terrible idea about a skull-headed lady, who was so punished for peeping through a key-hole—what to see I forget—something very shocking and wrong of course; but when she was reduced to a worse condition than the renowned Tom of Coventry, he did not know what to do with her, and was obliged to despatch her to the tomb of the Capulets, the only place for which she was fitted. The illustrious poets also, annoyed by the platitude of prose, speedily relinquished their uncongenial task.

I busied myself *to think of a story,*—a story to rival those which had excited us to this task. One which would speak to the mysterious fears of our nature, and awaken thrilling horror—one to make the reader dread to look round, to curdle the blood, and quicken the beatings of the heart. If I did not accomplish these things, my ghost story would be unworthy of its name. I thought and pondered—vainly. I felt that blank incapability of invention which is the greatest misery of authorship, when dull Nothing replies to our anxious invocations. *Have you thought of a story?* I was asked each morning, and each morning I was forced to reply with a mortifying negative.

Every thing must have a beginning, to speak in Sanchean phrase; and that beginning must be linked to something that went before. The Hindoos give the world an elephant to support it, but they make the elephant stand upon a tortoise. Invention, it must be humbly admitted, does not consist in creating out of void, but out of chaos; the materials must, in the first place, be afforded: it can give form to dark, shapeless substances, but cannot bring into being the substance itself. In all matters of discovery and invention, even of those that appertain to the imagination, we are continually reminded of the story of Columbus and his egg. Invention consists in the capacity of seizing on the capabilities of a subject, and in the power of moulding and fashioning ideas suggested to it.

Many and long were the conversations between Lord Byron and Shelley, to which I was a devout but nearly silent listener. During one of these, various philosophical doctrines were discussed, and among others the nature of the principle of life, and whether there was any probability of its ever being discovered and communicated. They talked of the experiments of Dr. Darwin, (I speak not of what the Doctor really did, or said that he did, but, as more to my purpose, of what was then spoken of as having been done by him,) who preserved a piece of vermicelli in a glass case, till by some extraordinary means it began to move with voluntary motion. Not thus, after all, would life be given. Perhaps a corpse would be re-animated; galvanism had given token of such things: perhaps the component parts of a creature might be manufactured, brought together, and endued with vital warmth.

Night waned upon this talk, and even the witching hour had gone by, before we retired to rest. When I placed my head on my pillow, I did not sleep, nor could I be said to think. My imagination, unbidden, possessed and guided me, gifting the successive images that arose in my mind with a vividness far beyond the usual bounds of reverie. I saw—with shut eyes, but acute mental vision,—I saw the pale student of unhallowed arts kneeling beside the thing he had put together. I saw the hideous phantasm of a man stretched out, and then, on the working of some powerful engine, show signs of life, and stir with an uneasy, half vital motion. Frightful must it be; for supremely frightful would be the effect of any human endeavour to mock the stupendous mechanism of the Creator of the world. His success would terrify the artist; he would rush away from his odious handy-work, horror-stricken. He would hope that, left to itself, the slight spark of life which he had communicated would fade; that this thing, which had received such imperfect animation, would subside into dead matter; and he might sleep in the belief that the silence of the grave would quench for ever the transient existence of the hideous corpse which he had looked upon as the cradle of life. He sleeps; but he is awakened; he opens his eyes; behold the horrid thing stands at his bedside, opening his curtains, and looking on him with yellow, watery, but speculative eyes.

I opened mine in terror. The idea so possessed my mind, that a thrill of fear ran through me, and I wished to exchange the ghastly image of my fancy for the realities around. I see them still; the very room, the dark *parquet*, the closed shutters, with the moonlight struggling through, and the sense I had that the glassy lake and white high Alps were beyond. I could not so easily get rid of my hideous phantom; still it haunted me. I must try to think of something else. I recurred to my ghost story,—my tiresome unlucky ghost story! O! if I could only contrive one which would frighten my reader as I myself had been frightened that night!

Swift as light and as cheering was the idea that broke in upon me. 'I have found it! What terrified me will terrify others; and I need only describe the spectre which had haunted my midnight pillow.' On the morrow I announced that I had *thought of a story*. I began that day with the words, *It was on a dreary night of November*, making only a transcript of the grim terrors of my waking dream.

At first I thought but of a few pages—of a short tale; but Shelley urged me to develope the idea at greater length. I certainly did not owe the suggestion of one incident, nor scarcely of one train of feeling, to my husband, and yet but for his incitement, it would never have taken the form in which it was presented to the world. From this declaration I must except the preface. As far as I can recollect, it was entirely written by him.

And now, once again, I bid my hideous progeny go forth and prosper. I have an affection for it, for it was the offspring of happy days, when death and grief were but words, which found no true echo in my heart. Its several pages speak of many a walk, many a drive, and many a conversation, when I was not alone; and my companion was one who, in this world, I shall never see more. But this is for myself; my readers have nothing to do with these associations.

I will add but one word as to the alterations I have made. They are principally those of style. I have changed no portion of the story, nor introduced any new ideas or circumstances. I have mended the language where it was so bald as to interfere with the interest of the narrative; and these changes occur almost exclusively in the beginning of the first volume. Throughout they are entirely confined to such parts as are mere adjuncts to the story, leaving the core and substance of it untouched.

M.W.S.

London, October 15, 1831

JOHN WILLIAM POLIDORI

Letter Prefaced to *The Vampyre* (1819)

It appears that one evening Lord B., Mr. P. B. Shelly, the two ladies and the gentleman before alluded to,[1] after having perused a German work, which was entitled Phantasmagoriana, began relating ghost stories; when his lordship having recited the beginning of Christabel, then unpublished, the whole took so strong a hold of Mr. Shelly's mind, that he suddenly started up and ran out of the room. The physician and Lord Byron followed, and discovered him leaning

---

1. Mary Shelley, Claire Clairmont, and Polidori himself.

against a mantle-piece, with cold drops of perspiration trickling down his face. After having given him something to refresh him, upon enquiring into the cause of his alarm, they found that his wild imagination // having pictured to him the bosom of one of the ladies with eyes (which was reported of a lady in the neighbourhood where he lived) he was obliged to leave the room in order to destroy the impression. It was afterwards proposed, in the course of conversation, that each of the company present should write a tale depending upon some supernatural agency, which was undertaken by Lord B., the physician, and Miss M. W. Godwin.[2] * * *

M. K. JOSEPH

The Composition of *Frankenstein*†

The volume of Mary Shelley's own journal covering the period 14 May 1815–20 July 1816, during which *Frankenstein* originated, is missing.

The earlier preface to the novel, dated September 1817, was written by Shelley.[1] It states simply that the story was begun in the summer of 1816, at Geneva; that, during a time of cold and rainy weather, the anonymous author and friends would meet of an evening by the fire; and would 'occasionally' read German ghost stories. Out of a 'playful desire of imitation', the author and two other friends (sc. Byron and Shelley) agreed each to write a supernatural tale; but the two friends left on 'a journey among the Alps', and the author's tale was the only one completed.

Mary Shelley's own account, written fourteen years later for the revised edition of 1831,[2] is much fuller, but is certainly inaccurate in some details. The sequence here is: the summer of 1816— fine weather and 'pleasant hours on the lake', followed by 'incessant rain' which 'often confined us for days to the house'; the reading of the book of German ghost stories; Byron's proposal, taken up by himself, Shelley, Mary, and Polidori, that each should write a ghost story; and the prolonged search for a story which, it is implied, went on for some days. Meantime Mary had been listening to 'many and long . . . conversations' between Byron and Shelley: one of these was the discussion on 'the nature of the principle of life', which led

---

2. Since published under the title of "Frankenstein; or, The Modern Prometheus." [*Polidori's note.*]

† From Mary Shelley, *Frankenstein*, ed. James Kinsley and M. K. Joseph (Oxford: Oxford UP, 1969), 224–27. Reprinted by permission.

1. See pp. 5–6, above. [*Editor's note.*]

2. See pp. 165–69, above. [*Editor's note.*]

immediately to Mary's dream and to the beginning of the novel on the very next day.

Byron's unfinished vampire-story, dated 17 June 1816, was published with *Mazeppa* in 1819, and suggested Polidori's novelette, *The Vampyre*, later published in dubious circumstances and attributed to Byron. Of Polidori's 'skull-headed lady', there is no further trace; his novel, *Ernestus Berchtold* (1819), has no reference to her.

Thomas Moore's account of these events in his *Life of Lord Byron* (1830) is slightly earlier, and presumably based largely on Mary Shelley's recollections. According to Moore, the regular routine while Byron was at Diodati included an evening excursion on the lake when the weather was fine; when it was bad, the Shelleys 'passed their evenings at Diodati; and, when the rain rendered it inconvenient for them to return home, remained there to sleep'. It was during 'a week of rain' that the party agreed to write their ghost stories, and *Frankenstein* resulted.[3]

The impression given by these accounts is of a leisurely time-scheme, yet it must in fact have been fairly brief: Byron met Shelley's party at Sécheron on 27 May, and did not move to the Villa Diodati until 10 June; the journey round Lake Leman began on 22 June, and the novel must have been started between these last two dates.

For more detailed information, we must turn to the brief and cryptic entries in the diary of Dr. Polidori. These confirm that Byron and Shelley's party met regularly in the evenings from 29 May onward, often for boating on the lake; these expeditions were interrupted for the first time by rain on 8 June. After the removal to Diodati on 10 June, evening meetings were resumed there. Then come three significant entries:

> June 15. . . . Shelley and I had a conversation about principles,— whether man was to be thought merely an instrument . . .
> June 16. . . . Shelley came, and dined and slept here, with Mrs. S[helley] and Miss Clare Clairmont . . .
> June 17. . . . The ghost-stories are begun by all but me.[4]

The 'conversation about principles' is likely to be the same as Mary's discussion on 'the principle of life', and it would be typical of Polidori to make himself a principal speaker rather than Byron. James Rieger, in an important article, would go further, and argue that in fact Mary gives the reverse order of events; that the 'conversation about principles' occurred first, followed next night by the stay at Diodati

---

3. Thomas Moore, *Letters and Journals of Lord Byron: With Notices of his Life* (1830), ii.31. [Moore, Irish poet, was a friend and biographer of Byron—*Editor*]
4. *The Diary of Dr. John William Polidori*, ed. W. M. Rossetti (1911), 122–25. [Polidori was Byron's twenty-year-old physician and traveling companion. Claire Clairmont was Mary Shelley's stepsister—*Editor*.]

and the beginning of the ghost stories (including Mary's) next morning. Certainly, Mary's memory for detail, especially of the *Fantasmagoriana* stories, can be shown to be imperfect; but is Polidori's record any more reliable? We have no certainty that the hasty entries were made day-by-day as they occurred, and soon after he makes errors in dates. Polidori was himself absent from Diodati on the nights of 12 and 13 June, and on the latter a thunderstorm occurred; it is possible that the scheme of writing ghost stories was proposed then, and that Polidori joined in later. This would agree with Mary's order of events and, at least minimally, with her time scheme.

Incidentally, one would like to know whether, by 'instrument', Polidori meant 'mechanism', and whether anyone in the party had read de la Mettrie's *L'Homme Machine*, which also uses the phrase 'a new Prometheus'.

Mary began her story with the words, 'It was a dreary night of November . . .', which now form the opening of Chapter V (Chapter IV in the 1818 edition). In late July occurred the excursion to Chamonix and the Mer de Glace which gave her the impressive scenery for Chapters IX and X; when her journal resumes, we find her writing at Chamonix on 24 July, and the work went on in earnest after her return to Geneva on the 27th.[5] What had been originally designed as a story of 'a few pages' was being developed, on Shelley's urging, into a full-length novel. Journal entries show her at work on at least half the days in August, and on one occasion discussing the story with Shelley. Writing was interrupted by their departure from Geneva and return to England, and possibly not resumed in earnest until mid-December; the work seems to have been virtually complete when it was suspended for the visit to London and her marriage to Shelley.[6]

Except for a few days early in 1817, Mary's journal gives no indications of further writing until late February or March. For a week from 10 April 1817, the entries read 'Correct "Frankenstein"'; transcription went on, with some interruptions, until about the middle of May. On 14 May, 'Shelley . . . corrects "Frankenstein"'; on the 22nd, the Shelleys went to London to submit the manuscript to John Murray. Murray refused—on Gifford's advice, or so Mary believed; Ollier also turned it down in August; but the book was accepted by Lackington, Allen and Company a month later. It was seen through the press, with some emendation, by Shelley, who wrote that he had 'paid considerable attention to the correction of such few instances of baldness of style as necessarily occur in the production of a very

5. *Mary Shelley's Journal*, ed. Frederick L. Jones (Norman: U of Oklahoma P, 1974), 53. For what follows, see subsequent entries in the journal.
6. *The Letters of Mary W. Shelley*, ed. Frederick L. Jones (Norman: U of Oklahoma P, 1944), i.14.

young writer'. He also busied himself in having copies sent out to friends and others whose opinions might be useful; and *Frankenstein* finally appeared in March 1818.[7] The reviewers were impressed in spite of themselves by a book which they found rather shocking; with partial truth, they sensed the Godwinian influence in it, but believed it to have been written by a man, possibly Shelley himself. Mary's authorship, which was at first intended to be a secret known only to a few friends like Moore and Byron, gradually became common knowledge.[8]

CHRIS BALDICK

[Assembling *Frankenstein*][†]

That Victor Frankenstein assembles his monster from parts of corpses collected from charnel-houses and dissecting rooms is one of the most memorable and enduring features of the story, even to those who have never read Mary Shelley's novel. The monstrosity of the creature is clearly enough the consequence of its assembly from different parts, but it still sets us a puzzle, which James Whale's 1931 film version evades by introducing a faulty component, the Abnormal Brain: why should a creature constructed from parts which Victor selects as perfect and indeed beautiful specimens turn out to be hideously repulsive? The novel provides no explanation for the creature's ugliness, and if we are tempted to account for it psychologically as a mere projection of Frankenstein's guilty revulsion from his deed, we run up against the evidence of the other characters' reactions. The monster appears frighteningly ugly not just to his creator but to all who see him, even to himself as he studies his reflection in water. By stressing clearly the beauty of the component parts and the ugliness of the finished combination, Mary Shelley is isolating and dramatizing a problem which was in her time central to philosophical, and by extension to aesthetic and political discussion; namely the question of the relation of parts to wholes.

Just as for Kant the mind had to be more than the sum of its sense-impressions, so for Coleridge, the British avatar of German Idealism, any living 'whole'—whether a plant, a poem, or a nation— was always more than a mere aggregation of its constituent parts. It

---

7. *Journal*, 78, 79, and 80; *Letters*, i.29, 31; *The Letters of Percy Bysshe Shelley*, ed. Frederick L. Jones (1964), i.564–65.
8. *Quarterly Review*, Jan. 1818; *Edinburgh Magazine*, Mar. 1818; *Blackwood's Edinburgh Magazine*, Mar. 1818. R. Glynn Grylls, *Mary Shelley*, 315–18.
† From *In* Frankenstein's *Shadow: Myth, Monstrosity, and Nineteenth-Century Writing* (New York: Oxford UP, 1987), 33–44. Reprinted by permission.

was upon this principle that Romantic Idealism founded its critique of the empiricist thought of the preceding century and set the terms of that central opposition between the mechanical and the organic which was to define so many of the conflicts within nineteenth-century culture.

In aesthetic theory, this opposition appears most clearly in Coleridge's own distinction between the Fancy, which merely reassembles ready-made memories and impressions, and the Imagination, which fuses and harmonizes into a new living entity not just images and sensations but the different faculties of the mind itself. In politics, a similar conviction is at work in the insistently organic imagery of Burke's writings, in which the organic integrity of the state is contrasted with the ridiculous and deadly artificial concoctions of the *philosophes*. And combining the political with the aesthetic, Friedrich Schiller's response to the French Revolution and the social fragmentation it threatened is to offer the harmonizing properties of art as a cure for the disintegrating tendencies of the age. Schiller's celebrated Sixth Letter in *The Aesthetic Education of Man* asserts that the development of human society has necessarily left behind it the noble simplicity of ancient Greek culture, 'but instead of rising to a higher form of organic existence it degenerated into a crude and clumsy mechanism'. Modern society is but 'an ingenious mechanism' made from 'the piecing together of innumerable but lifeless parts'.[1] In Schiller's diagnosis an advanced division of labour has dismembered the human personality so completely into distinct faculties that 'one has to go the rounds from one individual to another in order to piece together a complete image of the species'.[2] Now that the individual has become just a stunted fragment, society can be little more than a monstrous aggregation of incomplete parts.

From such diagnoses of the disorganization of European society, a whole tradition of culture-criticism was to develop in the nineteenth century. The fragmented society, the patchwork or clockwork individual—these become the themes of Romantic social analysis from Schiller through Carlyle and beyond. Mary Shelley's *Frankenstein* takes its place within this pattern of Romantic contrasts between lifeless parts and living wholes, partly as a dramatization of that principle of inorganic aggregation which Schiller saw as the modern disease. Viewed in this light, Victor Frankenstein's error is to have confused the beauty of the dead limbs he has collected with the beauty of a whole organism. According to the Idealist philosophy of

1. Friedrich Schiller, *On The Aesthetic Eduction of Man*, ed. and trans. Elizabeth M. Wilkinson and L. A. Willoughby (Oxford, 1967), 35.
2. Ibid., 23.

the Romantics, the beauty of the whole can arise only from a pure vital principle within, to which all subordinate parts and limbs will then conform. The parts, in a living being, can only be as beautiful as the animating principle which organizes them, and if this 'spark of life' proceeds, as it does in Victor's creation, from tormented isolation and guilty secrecy, the resulting assembly will only animate and body forth that condition and display its moral ugliness.

Among the self-reflexive peculiarities of *Frankenstein* which I have mentioned is the fact that the novel is part of the same problem. As Mary Shelley herself recognized in her Introduction of 1831, what we too often call literary 'creation' is really a process of assembling and combining pre-existing elements:

> Invention, it must be humbly admitted, does not consist in creating out of void, but out of chaos; the materials must, in the first place, be afforded: it can give form to dark, shapeless substances, but cannot bring into being the substance itself. (*F*, (226)/8)[3]

From here she goes on to reveal as her raw materials the conversations at the Villa Diodati about galvanism and Erasmus Darwin's wriggling vermicelli. These conversations are, however, only a small part of the stock of materials from which *Frankenstein* was assembled. In addition to—and in odd intimacy with—the distressing problems of Mary Shelley's own life, of which some elements go into the book, there is a fund of literary sources upon which *Frankenstein* cannibalistically feeds. To form an idea of the range of both kinds of constituent material, we should begin with Mary Shelley's immediate circle and proceed outwards from there.

To begin with, the names and status of some of the novel's characters are drawn from Mary Shelley's acquaintance: Elizabeth was the name of Percy Shelley's sister and his mother, and Victor was a name adopted in boyhood by Percy himself—a fact which has encouraged some commentators to identify him too hastily with Victor Frankenstein, when his portrait is given more clearly in the character of Henry Clerval. William was the name not just of Mary Shelley's father but also of her half-brother and of the son she was raising while writing the novel. The killing of William Frankenstein dramatizes perhaps some hidden sibling rivalries, while the recurrence of orphaned (in particular, of motherless) characters more clearly echoes the facts of her own childhood: Safie, indeed, is given a deceased mother who has championed the rights of women (*F*, 119/123–4), and the monster's sense of neglect seems to derive partly from William Godwin's paternal remoteness. Closer

---

3. All Baldick's references to F are to the M. K. Joseph edition (Oxford; OUP, 1969).

still to the author's own feelings at the time when the novel was written lies the trauma of her own motherhood, as Ellen Moers has established. The fantasy of reanimating the dead occurred to Mary Godwin not just as a second-hand scientific speculation overheard from Byron, but as a most disturbing dream recorded in her journal of March 1815, in which her first dead child was brought back to life by being rubbed before a fire. The Alpine setting of the novel draws, obviously enough, upon the 1816 holiday which also inspired Percy Shelley's 'Mont Blanc' and Byron's *Manfred*; and the University of Ingolstadt appears as a result of Percy's interest in the alleged Illuminati conspiracy which Barruel traced to that town. Such lived 'sources' should not be forgotten, particularly those closest to Mary Shelley's personal troubles, but as a literary composition *Frankenstein* is constituted more fully by its written sources.

Mary Godwin kept quite extensive records of her reading from 1814 onwards, so the identification of literary borrowings has plentiful possibilities, ranging from the German ghost stories mentioned in the 1831 Introduction, through the novels of the American Godwinian Charles Brockden Brown, to William Beckford's *Vathek* (1786), whose hero is driven by his restless curiosity to 'penetrate the secrets of heaven'.[4] The major influences, though, can be reduced to a handful, among them being the works of the author's own parents.

The Frankensteinian elements latent in some of their political writings and in Godwin's *Caleb Williams* have been touched on above [in an earlier chapter of the book here excerpted]; but in some ways just as suggestive a source is another of Godwin's novels, *St. Leon, A Tale of the Sixteenth Century* (1799). The hero of this tale discovers the secrets of the philosopher's stone and the elixir of life, only to be disappointed in his fruitless efforts to benefit mankind by their means. As his project inadvertently brings about the deaths of his loved ones and other innocents, he exclaims:

> Fatal legacy! Atrocious secrets of medicine and chemistry! Every day opened to my astonished and terrified sight a wider prospect of their wasteful effects! A common degree of penetration might have shown me, that secrets of this character cut off their possessor from the dearest ties of human existence, and render him a solitary, cold, self-centered individual; his heart no longer able to pour itself into the bosom of a mistress or a friend; his bosom no longer qualified to receive upon equal terms the overflowing of a kindred heart. But no mere exercise of imagination . . . could have adequately represented the mis-

4. William Beckford, *Vathek*, ed. Roger Lonsdale (Oxford, 1970), 4.

chiefs of a thousand various names, that issued from this Pandora's box, this extract of a universal panacea. . . . I felt as truly haunted with the ghosts of those I had murdered, as Nero or Caligula might have been; my wife, my son, my faithful negro; and now, in addition to these, the tender Julia and her unalterable admirer. I possessed the gift of immortal life, but I looked on myself as a monster that did not deserve to exist.[5]

St. Leon's bafflement would seem to be another fictional exploration of the disappointments suffered by the rationalist radicals of Godwin's circle, a reworking of the frustrations embodied in the predicament of Caleb Williams: 'Why', St. Leon asks himself, 'was every power of the social constitution, every caprice of the multitude, every insidious project of the noble, thus instantly in arms against so liberal and grand an undertaking?'[6] St. Leon abandons his experiments, having learned that his obsession with them has destroyed his familial loyalties, and he turns instead to cultivate the 'dearest ties of human existence'—a conversion which even Godwin's sworn enemy the *Anti-Jacobin Review* had to applaud as a welcome sign.[7] The same novel even contains a hideous giant named Bethlem Gabor, whose sufferings have made him a misanthrope. 'I hate mankind', declares Gabor; 'I was not born to hate them. . . . But they have forced me to hate them.'[8] There is more than a hint of Frankenstein's monster here, as there is of its creator in the disastrous scientific career of St. Leon.

From her mother's writings Mary Shelley undoubtedly derived an interest in the theory of education, and a tendency (prominent in many digressive passages of her novel) to stress the influence of a character's upbringing and early impressions. Mary Wollstonecraft, herself a governess and schoolteacher, repeatedly explored these issues in her work, especially in the celebrated *Vindication of the Rights of Woman* (1792), which is in part an extension—and critique—of Rousseau's educational doctrines, redirected against the artificiality with which young women were 'formed' by their upbringing. In the pages of the *Vindication* at least two incidental reflections can be found which seem to anticipate the themes of *Frankenstein*. In one, Mary Wollstonecraft defends herself against her contemporaries' horror of rational innovation and experiment:

> Everything new appears to them wrong; and not able to distinguish the possible from the monstrous, they fear where no fear should find a place, running from the light of reason, as if it

5. William Godwin, *St. Leon, A Tale of the Sixteenth Century* (London, 1831), 362–63.
6. Ibid., 424.
7. *Anti-Jacobin Review and Magazine*, v (1800), 152.
8. Godwin, *St. Leon*, 415.

were a firebrand; yet the limits of the possible have never been defined to stop the sturdy innovator's hand.[9]

In the reactionary climate of the 1790s rationalist innovation and reform had been successfully identified with the 'monstrous',[1] and Mary Wollstonecraft herself came to be displayed as a monstrous figure: when Godwin's posthumous memoir of her revealed that she had once attempted suicide when abandoned by a lover, the fact was deemed to illustrate the dire consequences of straying from virtue's path and woman's lot, just as Percy Shelley's drowning was later interpreted as a fitting judgement upon his atheism. Mary Godwin's strong identification with her mother's memory taught her to question the category of the 'monstrous' and to sympathize with moral outcasts; as an unmarried mother herself (she became Mary Shelley only in December 1816), she needed little reminding.

A second Frankensteinian theme adumbrated in the *Vindication* is the questioning of heroic exertion. While agreeing with Bacon that the greatest human achievements are made by those who are unmarried, Wollstonecraft insists that she shall not therefore recommend all women to abandon marriage and domestic life, since 'the welfare of society is not built on extraordinary exertions; and were it more reasonably organized, there would be still less need of great abilities, or heroic virtues'.[2] She is no more impressed by masculine heroism than she is by other ingredients of aristocratic ideology; rational and democratic reform could bring it down to its true size. Like Godwin in his treatment of Falkland's inflated honour, Wollstonecraft recognizes the danger and the redundancy of the heroic ideal, particularly in its artificial divorce from the domestic. *Frankenstein* too investigates the same problem, from its opening contrast between the ardent but isolated adventurer Robert Walton and his sister's settled sanity, to Victor's closing speech against the alleged cowardice of Walton's crew.

To these parental influences we may add some of the more important sources in Mary Shelley's early reading. One story of her girlhood has her hiding behind a sofa while Coleridge himself read to Godwin his 'Rime of the Ancient Mariner'. Coleridge's hypnotic tale of guilt and isolation is clearly a significant source for the ice-bound voyage of *Frankenstein*'s frame-narrative, and possibly for its doomed

---

9. Mary Wollstonecraft, *Vindication of the Rights of Woman*, ed. Miriam Brody Kramnick (Harmondsworth, 1975), 265.
1. The *Anti-Jacobin Review* (v. 427) called Godwin's followers 'spawn of the same monster'; and Thomas De Quincey recalled in 1837 that 'most people felt of Mr Godwin with the same alienation and horror as of a ghoul, or a bloodless vampyre, or the monster created by Frankenstein'. *The Collected Writings of Thomas De Quincey*, ed. David Masson (Edinburgh, 1890), iii.25.
2. Wollstonecraft, *Vindication*, 155.

and transgressing hero too. Mary Shelley was careful to emphasize the connection herself, by having Frankenstein quote (anachronistically) the 'Rime' to express his fear of the monster (*F*, 54/59). In her revisions of 1831 she reinforced the allusions to the poem by both Victor and Walton, making the latter attribute his enthusiasm for polar exploration to Coleridge's inspiration (*F*, (231)/21). It seems that in the confessional mode of the 'Rime', especially in its contrast between the Mariner and the Wedding-Guest, Mary Shelley found some hints towards a narrative structure which could frame and partly domesticate the trials of the Romantic outcast.

There is some evidence, as Burton R. Pollin has suggested,[3] that the myth of Pygmalion and his animated statue Galatea helped to stimulate the Frankenstein story, particularly in the form given to it by Mme de Genlis in a dramatic sketch, 'Pygmalion et Galatée', from her *Nouveaux contes moraux* (1802–3), which Mary Shelley read in the summer of 1816. 'Pygmalion et Galatée' uses the device of the naïve creature's initiation into human customs as a vehicle of social criticism, showing its heroine's horror upon learning of slavery, tyranny, poverty, and human guile, just as Mary Shelley has the monster respond to Safie's history lessons in the De Lacey cottage.

By far the most important literary source for *Frankenstein*, though, is Milton's *Paradise Lost*, as repeated allusions in the novel remind us, beginning with the title-page itself and culminating in the monster's own avid reading of the epic poem, which he takes to be true history. As the monster reflects upon his reading, he first compares his condition with Adam's, but then feels a frustration akin to Satan's, if not worse (*F*, 125–7 / 129–31). Victor, who ought to correspond to God in this new creation, comes also to feel like Satan; he too bears a hell within him. The monster's earliest memories resemble those of Adam in *Paradise Lost* Book VIII, while his first sight of his own reflection in water is a travesty of Eve's similar revelation in Book IV. Likewise, the monster's vengeful declaration of war against human kind arises from a bitter feeling of exclusion from human joys, a hopeless envy described in terms similar to Satan's (*Paradise Lost*, iv.505 ff.; ix.114 ff.).

Frankenstein's relationship to Milton's epic is, however, more than a matter of incidental borrowings. Unlike the story of Pygmalion, the subject-matter of *Paradise Lost* happens to be the most powerfully authorized creation myth in Western culture. Moreover, it elaborates upon the connections between *two* kinds of myth: a myth of creation and a myth of transgression. *Frankenstein* does this too, but its sinister travesty collapses the two kinds of myth together so

---

3. Burton R. Pollin, 'Philosophical and Literary Sources of *Frankenstein*', *Comparative Literature* xvii (1965), 100–1.

that now creation and transgression appear to be the same thing, as they are also in William Blake's *Book of Urizen*. The accusations of impiety which greeted the publication of *Frankenstein* may surprise us today, but it seemed to some of Mary Shelley's first readers that the novel was calling into question the most sacred of stories, equating the Supreme Being with a blundering chemistry student. The particular impiety of Mary Shelley's Miltonic travesty forms part of that common Romantic reinterpretation of *Paradise Lost* which follows the Gnostic heresy in elevating Satan to the role of sublimely heroic rebel.[4] Blake's remark in *The Marriage of Heaven and Hell*, that Milton was unwittingly of the Devil's party, and Percy Shelley's qualified admiration for Satan in his Preface to *Prometheus Unbound* are well-known instances, but William Godwin too conducted a defence of Satan's principled opposition to tyranny in his *Political Justice* (*EPJ*, 309), while Mary Shelley herself, in one of her unpublished corrections to the 'Thomas' copy of *Frankenstein*, refers to Satan's 'sublime defiance' (*F*, 125/—). The widespread cult of Prometheus in Romantic literature is often only a slightly Hellenized variant of the same heretical tendency.

As many commentators have pointed out, Milton had, by submitting God's providence to rational debate, inadvertently exposed the foundations of his religion to subversion. Nowhere is this clearer than in the very speech which Mary Shelley uses as her epigraph to *Frankenstein*, in which Adam bewails the injustice of his position:

> Did I request thee, Maker, from my clay
> To mould me man? Did I solicit thee
> From darkness to promote me?
>
> (*Paradise Lost*, x.743–45)

As Adam complains a few lines later, God's justice seems 'inexplicable'. In the full context of Milton's poem, Adam's complaint can be discredited on several theological grounds, and the Christian readings are in the literal sense the authorized ones; but the Romantic revision of Milton is precisely a decontextualizing movement which, in plundering *Paradise Lost* for meanings, tears elements of the poem free from their doctrinal framework. *Frankenstein* takes part in this desecration by dramatizing Romanticism's sympathy for the Devil.

Actual devils, however, do not appear in *Frankenstein*. Victor calls his creature a devil and a demon, but he knows better than anyone in the tale that the monster is not literally a paid-up and fork-

---

4. See Paul A. Cantor, *Creature and Creator: Myth-Making and English Romanticism* (Cambridge, 1984).

carrying member of that order. This absence of any demonic tempter behind Victor's transgression is the main reason why we have to eliminate the Faust myth from our list of sources (Mary Shelley appears not to have known Goethe's recent version, at least until after *Frankenstein*'s composition); it is also the factor that most clearly marks the story's distance from Milton. It is tempting to jump from the continuing significance of the Faust myth in Western culture[5] to the hasty conclusion that all modern stories of transgression are derivatives of it, but to do this with *Frankenstein* would be to obscure a vital feature of the novel's modernity. While Faust's damnation and the Fall of Adam and Eve are brought about by the machinations of Mephistopheles and Satan, Victor Frankenstein has no serious tempter other than himself, his chemistry professor remaining a minor, innocent figure. If Frankenstein is any kind of Faust, he is a Faust without a Mephisto, that is, hardly a Faust at all; and if he is a Prometheus, as the novel's subtitle suggests, then he is a Prometheus without a Jove.

The novelty of *Frankenstein* which sets it apart from the phantasmagoria of Faust and of the Gothic novel is, as George Levine rightly insists, its starkly secular nature.[6] Eschewing the *geistig* world of Germanic mythology, it belongs in many ways with the more earthbound materiality of that other English myth, *Robinson Crusoe*. The gross physical insistence of *Frankenstein*'s central figure cruelly mocks the emptiness of spiritual aspiration, in what can be read as an ironic commentary upon Romantic idealism's 'angelic' transcendence of the flesh.[7] At the same time, the narrative logic of the novel observes (perhaps even invents) the rules of what we now call science fiction, tracing a chain of probable consequences from a single implausible premiss without resort to magical interventions. The impiety which early readers found in *Frankenstein* lies partly in the fact that its story is, as Levine says, 'acted out in the absence of God',[8] that it follows the logic of a godless world; its tensions interest us because they thrive upon that disorientation which follows the subtraction of God and Mephistopheles from the known creation. Mary Shelley's impiety goes a step further than many of Romanticism's Satanic heresies, revising *Paradise Lost* in so decontextualized a manner that the great context Himself is removed, turning the novel into 'a *Paradise Lost* without angels, or devils, or God'.[9]

5. On the modernity of Faust see Marshall Berman, *All That Is Solid Melts Into Air: The Experience of Modernity* (New York, 1982).
6. Levine and Knoepflmacher, eds., *Endurance of 'Frankenstein'*, 6–7.
7. On *Frankenstein*'s critique of 'angelism' see Gerhard Joseph, 'Frankenstein's Dream: The Child as Father of the Monster', *Hartford Studies in Literature*, vii (1975), 97–115.
8. Levine and Knoepflmacher, eds., *Endurance of 'Frankenstein'*, 7.
9. Ibid., 7.

God is mentioned in the novel only as a minor character in Milton's epic, or in blasphemous exclamations, and the only character to invoke His name piously ends up on the gallows, hanged for a crime she never committed, having made a false confession at the prompting of her priest.

Among the simpler interpretations of *Frankenstein* as a moral fable of presumption, it is often asserted that Victor Frankenstein is trying to 'play God' or usurp divine powers. Although Mary Shelley's 1831 Introduction hints at such a view, the novel offers very limited grounds for it: Victor aims at first not to rival God but to be useful to humanity by eliminating disease, and all he creates is a single living creature. If this is a blasphemous crime, then all parents stand condemned for it too. From the monster's point of view, though, Victor is a 'god' of sorts, and it is through this perspective that the novel's impieties emerge, the most mischievous of them being the incident in which the monster swears to Victor a solemn oath 'by you that made me' (*F*, 143/147). The monster's 'god' comes to be seen as an ineptly negligent creator whose conduct towards his creation is callously unjust. If Adam's complaint in the epigraph is borne in mind as well, the novel begins to look like a nightmarish parody of patriarchal religion, in which the Son is made, not begotten, the Flesh is made Word,[1] and women cede the power of Conception to men while being legally framed as criminals (like Eve) or torn to pieces. It is not too hard to imagine the pious readers of 1818 feeling that their God and His creation were being grimly mocked.

Lowry Nelson Jr. has suggested that *Frankenstein* inaugurates a line of 'unchristian' or diabolical novels of a distinctive Romantic or mythic cast, which includes *Wuthering Heights* and *Moby Dick* (and, we could add, *Heart of Darkness* among others), and which is remarkable for its common use of complex narrative frames surrounding a central transgressing anti-hero.[2] In *Frankenstein* as in these other works the diabolical nature of the narrative form inheres in what we could call its 'dialogical' openness. Since there is no Mephisto or recognizably evil tempter, and no Jove for the modern Prometheus to offend, the moral framework of the novel is dissolved into an open contest or debate between Victor and the monster, in which the reassuring categories of Good, Evil, Guilt, and Justice can never be allotted a settled place. Other Gothic or Godwinian writers of this period, like Charles Brockden Brown in *Wieland* (1798) and James Hogg in *Confessions of a Justified Sinner* (1824), found double or multiple narration to be an ideal device for under-

---

1. See Milton A. Mays, '*Frankenstein*, Mary Shelley's Black Theodicy', *Southern Humanities Review* iii (1969), 146–59; and Judith Wilt, '*Frankenstein* as Mystery Play', in Levine and Knoepflmacher (eds.), *Endurance of 'Frankenstein'*, 31–48.
2. Nelson, 'Night Thoughts', 251. ff.

mining the certainties of religious delusion; Mary Shelley achieves a similar effect in the narrative design of *Frankenstein*. As most readers of the novel attest, its most challenging effect comes from the reversal of sympathies demanded by the monster's narrative. This jolt is reinforced by the 'doubling' in the relationship between the monster and Victor (and in Victor's resemblance to Walton too), so that all identities in the novel are unstable and shifting, the roles of master and slave, pursuer and pursued alternating or merging. As in the Revolution debates, the accuser of monstrous offspring is himself accused of being a monstrously negligent parent. When Victor and his monster refer themselves back to *Paradise Lost*—a guiding text with apparently fixed moral roles—they can no longer be sure whether they correspond to Adam, to God, or to Satan, or to some or all of these figures. Like the iceberg on which Frankenstein makes his first appearance in the novel, their bearings are all adrift. Interpretation of the novel encounters much the same problem.

RICHARD HOLMES

[Mary Shelley and the Power of Contemporary Science][†]

* * *

Mary Shelley's preliminary ideas for the novel can be dated back remarkably early, to the year 1812, when her father William Godwin took her to hear Humphry Davy give his public lectures on chemistry at the Royal Institution. She was then only fourteen. Her young Victor Frankenstein would also begin as an idealistic and dedicated medical student, inspired by the lectures of the visionary Professor Waldman at Ingolstadt. Mary Shelley would eventually draw directly on the published text of Davy's famous 'Introductory Discourse', in which he spoke of those future experiments in which man would 'interrogate Nature with Power . . . as a master, active, with his own instruments.'[1]

Waldman's lecture on chemistry expands Davy's claims, and has an electric effect on the young Victor Frankenstein.

> 'The ancient teachers of this science,' said he, 'promised impossibilities and performed nothing. The modern masters promise very little; they know that metals cannot be transmuted, and

† From *The Age of Wonder: How the Romantic Generation Discovered the Beauty and Terror of Science* (London: HarperPress, 2008), 325–36. Reprinted by permission.
1. [Sir Humphry] Davy, 'Discourse Introductory to Lectures on Chemistry,' 1802, HD Works 2, 311–26

that the elixir of life is a chimera. But these philosophers, whose hands seem only to dabble in dirt, and their eyes to pore over the microscope or crucible, have indeed performed miracles. They penetrate into the recesses of Nature, and show how she works in her hiding-places. They ascend into the heavens; they have discovered how the blood circulates, and the nature of the air we breathe. They have acquired new and almost unlimited Powers: they can command the thunders of heaven, mimic the earthquake, and even mock the invisible world with its own shadow.'

Such were the Professor's words—rather let me say such the words of Fate—enounced to destroy me. As he went on I felt as if my soul were grappling with a palpable enemy; one by one the various keys were touched which formed the mechanism of my being. Chord after chord was sounded, and soon my mind was filled with one thought, one conception, one purpose. So much has been done!—exclaimed the soul of Frankenstein: more, far more will I achieve! Treading in the steps already marked, I will pioneer a new way, explore unknown Powers, and unfold to the world the deepest mysteries of Creation.[2]

When Mary eloped with Shelley to France and Switzerland in 1814, their shared journal indicates that they were already discussing notions of creating artificial life. As they returned penniless, by public riverboat down the Rhine, they remarked on the monstrous, inhuman appearance of several of the huge German labourers on board, and noticed that they sailed beneath a lowering *schloss* known as 'Castle Frankenstein'.[3] On their return Shelley began writing the first of his series of speculative and autobiographical essays, mixing scientific ideas with psychology, under such titles as 'On the Science of Mind', 'On a Catalogue of the Phenomenon of Dreams' and 'On Life'. He evidently discussed these disturbing ideas with Mary, for she remembered on one occasion how he broke off from writing one of them, 'overcome by thrilling horror.'[4]

Mary's brilliance was to see that these weighty and often alarming ideas could be given highly suggestive, imaginative and even playful form. In a sense, she would treat male concepts in a female style. She would develop exactly what William Lawrence had dismissed in his lectures as a 'hypothesis or fiction'. Indeed, it was to be an utterly new form of fiction—the science fiction novel. Mary plunged instinctively into the most extreme implications of Vitalism. In effect, she would take up where Aldini had been forced to leave off. She would pursue the controversial—and possibly blasphemous—idea that

2. *Frankenstein*, 1818, Chapter 2, Penguin Classics
3. *Mary Shelley's Journal*, 25 August–5 September 1814
4. In September 1815 at Great Marlow; see Holmes, *Shelley*, 296

vitality, like electricity, might be used to reanimate a dead human being. But she would go further, much further. She would imagine an experiment in which an entirely new human being was 'created' from dead matter. *She would imagine a surgical operation, a corpse dissection, in reverse.* She would invent a laboratory in which limbs, organs, assorted body parts were not separated and removed and thrown away, but assembled and sewn together and 'reanimated' by a 'powerful machine', presumably a voltaic battery.[5] Thus they would be given organic life and vitality. But whether they would be given a soul as well was another question.

This extraordinary fiction was begun at the Villa Diodati on Lake Geneva in the summer of 1816, in a holiday atmosphere of dinner parties and late-night talk. . . . The talk was quick, clever, sceptical, teasing and flirtatious. Mary Shelley records that she, Shelley and Byron, inspired by Dr Polidori (himself only twenty-two), discussed the galvanic experiments of Aldini, and various speculations about the artificial generation of life by Erasmus Darwin. They then, famously, set themselves a ghost-story-writing competition.

Byron scrawled a fragment about a dying explorer, 'Augustus Darvell' (dated 17 June 1816); Shelley composed his atheist poem 'Mont Blanc'; Polidori dashed off a brief gothic bagatelle, 'The Vampyre', which he later tried to pretend was actually Byron's (so he could sell it), while Mary Shelley wrote—but very slowly, over the next fourteen months—an intricately constructed 90,000-word fiction, which gradually became, draft crafted upon draft, *Frankenstein, or The Modern Prometheus.* She handed in the completed manuscript to Lackington, Allen & Co. in August 1817, just three weeks before her baby Clara was born on 2 September.

The actual writing of Mary's novel can be followed fairly closely from her journal in Switzerland, and then back in England at Great Marlow on the Thames. What is less clear is where she gathered her ideas and materials from, and how she created her two unforgettable protagonists: Dr Frankenstein and his Creature. One is tempted to say that the Creature—who is paradoxically the most articulate person in the whole novel—was a pure invention of Mary's genius. But in Victor Frankenstein of Ingolstadt she had created a composite figure who in many ways was typical of a whole generation of scientific men. The shades of 'inflammable' Priestley, the deeply eccentric Cavendish, the ambitious young Davy, the sinister Aldini and the glamorous, iconoclastic William Lawrence may all have contributed something to the portrait.

Yet Frankenstein is essentially a European figure, a Genevan—perhaps of German Jewish ancestry—studying and working at

5. Mary Shelley, 'Introduction' to *Frankenstein* 1831 text

Ingolstadt in Germany.[6] The importance of the German connection, and the experiments already done there, was pointed out by Percy Shelley in the very first sentence of his anonymous 'Preface' to the original 1818 edition of the novel. 'The event on which this fiction is founded, has been supposed, by Dr Darwin, and some of the physiological writers of Germany, as not impossible of occurrence.'

So who had Mary Shelley been thinking of? The outstanding young German physiologist known in British scientific circles at this time was Johann Wilhelm Ritter (1776–1810). His work at the university of Jena had been reported to Banks regularly at the turn of the century, and his election and move to the Bavarian Academy of Sciences in Munich in 1804, when still only twenty-eight, was closely followed.[7] Banks and Davy kept a particularly keen eye on his work, since Ritter had anticipated Davy's improvements on the voltaic battery, had invented a dry-cell storage battery, and had followed up Herschel's work on infra-red radiation from the sun, by identifying ultraviolet rays in 1803. He was also known for certain undefined 'galvanic' experiments with animals, which were the talk of the Royal Society, although amidst a certain amount of head-shaking.[8] But among his colleagues at Jena he was regarded as a portent. The young poet Novalis (Frederick von Hardenburg, also a mining engineer) exclaimed: 'Ritter is indeed searching for the real *Soul of the World* in Nature! He wants to decipher her visible and tangible language, and explain the emergence of the Higher Spiritual Forces.'[9]

In September 1803 Banks received a confidential report from the chemist Richard Chenevix, a Fellow of the Royal Society and the recipient of the Copley Medal in 1803, who was on a scientific tour of German cities. Writing from Leipzig, Chenevix noted that the 'most interesting' work at Jena was being done by Ritter, who was using a huge voltaic battery to obtain 'most capital results', having 'a very powerful effect upon the animal economy' but without damaging 'the most delicate organs'. Apparently holding back further details for a separate paper, Chenevix added to Banks: 'In communicating these experiments to you who *are at the centre*, they will immediately find their way to other Philosophers of London. Mr Davy I am sure will be particularly interested.'[1]

But by August of the following year, when Ritter had moved to Munich, Chenevix's reports had taken on a rather different tone.

6. *Frankenstein*, 1818, Chapter 1, Penguin Classics
7. JB Correspondence 5, no. 1804
8. J.H. Ritter as featured in www.CorrosionDoctors
9. Walter Wetzels, 'Ritter and Romantic Physics', in *Romanticism and the Sciences*, edited by Cunningham and Jardine, 1990. The best account of the extraordinary writer Novalis appears in Penelope Fitzgerald's inspired novel *The Blue Flower*, 1995
1. JB Correspondence 5, no. 1748, 316–17

'Ritter the galvanist is the only man of real talent I have met with; and his head and morals are overturned by the new philosophy of Schelling. I have declared open war against these absurdities.'[2] Chenevix's final report, of 7 November 1804, while still praising Ritter, now has an openly sarcastic edge, and ends on a disturbing note, as if he had witnessed something terrible which he cannot quite bring himself to describe: 'You may remember that I mentioned to you Ritter's experiments with a Galvanic pile . . . Ritter is experimenter in chief, or as they term him, *Empyrie of the New Transcendent School.* I saw him repeat his experiments; and they appeared most convincing. Whether there was any trick in them or not I cannot pretend to say . . . Ritter with a large body of Professors and pupils, is gone from Jena; and Bavaria is now enlightened by their Doctrines. It is impossible to conceive anything so disgusting and humiliating for the human understanding as their dreams.'[3]

That these 'dreams' are related to those of the fictional Dr Frankenstein seems more than possible. Experiments that had been forbidden by the Prussian government in Jena were taken up again when Ritter moved to the traditionally more libertarian atmosphere of Munich. From his desultory and posthumous memoirs, *Fragments of a Young Physicist* (1810), it would seem that in Munich Ritter fell fatally under the influence of one of the wildest of the *Naturphilosophie* practitioners, a certain Franz von Baader. Experiments that began with water divining, 'geoelectrical' mapping and 'metal witching' turned to the revival of dead animals by electrical action, and possibly the 'disgusting and humiliating' revival of dead human beings, although there is no definitive evidence of this. At all events, Ritter's Bavarian colleagues were gradually alienated, his students abandoned him, and his mental stability became increasingly fragile. He neglected his family (he had three children), withdrew into his laboratory, and grew increasingly remote and obsessive. Finally, his promising career was destroyed, and he died penniless and insane in 1810, aged thirty-three. In other circumstances his *Memoirs* might have been those of young Victor Frankenstein.[4]

Ritter's tragic story was clearly known to Banks, to Davy, and very probably to Lawrence after his time in Göttingen with Blumenbach. Whether it was known to Dr Polidori, and whether it was he who told it to the Shelleys in 1816, is speculation. But they clearly knew from some source about 'the physiological writers of Germany'. Moreover, the novel owes something else to Germany. Mary Shelley chose to narrate Frankenstein's act of electrical reanimation, or

2. Ibid., no. 1790, 368
3. Ibid., no. 1799, 387
4. For a wider perspective see 'Death, Dying and Resurrection', in Peter Hanns Reill, *Vitalizing Nature in the Enlightenment*, California UP, 2005, 171–6

blasphemous 'creation', in a gothic style that owes nothing to the cool British manner of the Royal Society reports, but everything to German ballads and folk tales.

> It was on a dreary night of November, that I beheld the accomplishment of my toils. With an anxiety that almost amounted to agony, I collected the instruments of life around me, that I might infuse a spark of being into the lifeless thing that lay at my feet. It was already one in the morning; the rain pattered dismally against the panes, and my candle was nearly burnt out, when by the glimmer of the half extinguished light, I saw the dull yellow eye of the creature open. It breathed hard, and a convulsive motion agitated its limbs.
>
> How can I describe my emotions at this catastrophe, or how delineate the Wretch whom with such infinite pains and care I had endeavoured to form? His limbs were in proportion, and I had selected his features as beautiful. Beautiful!—Great God! His yellow skin scarcely covered the work of muscles and arteries beneath. His hair was lustrous black and flowing; his teeth of pearly whiteness. But these luxuriances only formed a more horrid contrast with his watery eyes, that seemed almost of the same colour as his dun-white sockets in which they were set, his shrivelled complexion and straight black lips.[5]

*   *   *

As her novel developed, Mary Shelley began to ask in what sense Frankenstein's new 'Creature' would be human. Would it have language, would it have a moral conscience, would it have human feelings and sympathies, *would it have a soul?* (It should not be forgotten that Mary was pregnant with her own baby in 1817.) Many of Lawrence's reflections on the metaphysics of the dissecting room and the theory of brain development seem to be echoed in ideas and even complete phrases used in *Frankenstein*. Here again it seems that Shelley, who was attending medical consultations with Lawrence throughout spring 1817, and may sometimes have been accompanied by Mary, made an opportunity for all three of them to explore these specialist themes.[6]

Mary Shelley's idea of the mind was, like Lawrence's, based on the notion of the strictly physical evolution of the brain. This is how Lawrence was provocatively challenging his fellow members of the Royal College of Surgeons in his lectures of 1817: 'But examine the "mind", the grand prerogative of man! Where is the "mind" of the foetus? Where is that of a child just born? Do we not see it actually built up before our eyes by the actions of the five external

5. *Frankenstein*, 1818, vol 1, Chapter 5, Penguin Classics, 56
6. These connections are further traced by Ruston, 86–95

senses, and of the gradually developed internal faculties? Do we not trace it advancing by a slow progress from infancy and childhood to the perfect expansion of its faculties in the adult . . .'[7]

Frankenstein's Creature has been constructed as a fully developed man, from adult body parts, but his mind is that of a totally undeveloped infant. He has no memory, no language, no conscience. He starts life as virtually a wild animal, an orangutan or an ape. Whether he has sexual feelings, or is capable of rape, is not immediately clear. Although galvanised into life by a voltaic spark, the Creature has no 'divine spark' from Heaven. Yet perhaps his life could be called, in a phrase of the medical student John Keats, a 'vale of soul-making'.

Almost his first conscious act of recognition, when he has escaped the laboratory into the wood at night, is his sighting of the moon, an object that fills him with wonder, although he has no name for it: 'I started up and beheld a radiant form rise from among the trees.[8] I gazed with a kind of wonder. It moved slowly, but it enlightened my path . . . It was still cold . . . No distinct ideas occupied my mind; all was confused. I felt light, and hunger, and thirst, and darkness; innumerable sounds rung in my ears and on all sides various scents saluted me. . . . Sometimes I tried to imitate the pleasant songs of the birds, but was unable. Sometimes I wished to express sensations in my own mode, but the uncouth and inarticulate sounds which broke from me frightened me into silence again . . . Yet my mind received, every day, additional ideas.'[9]

From this moment the Creature evolves rapidly through all the primitive stages of man. Mary's account is almost anthropological, reminiscent of Banks's account of the Tahitians. First he learns to use fire, to cook, to read. Then he studies European history and civilisation, through the works of Plutarch, Milton and Goethe. Secretly listening to the cottagers in the woods, he learns conceptual ideas such as warfare, slavery, tyranny. His conscience is aroused, and his sense of justice. But above all, he discovers the need for companionship, sympathy and affection. And this is the one thing he cannot find, because he is so monstrously ugly: 'The cold stars shone in their mockery, and the bare trees waved their branches above me, the sweet voice of a bird burst forth amidst the universal stillness. All, save I, were at rest . . . I, like the arch-fiend, bore a hell within me, and finding myself unsympathised with, wished to tear up the trees, spread havoc and destruction around me, and then to have sat down and enjoyed the ruin.'[1]

On the bleak Mer de Glace glacier in the French Alps, the Creature appeals to his creator Frankenstein for sympathy, and for love.

7. Lawrence, *Lectures*, 1817, 6–7
8. Mary Shelley adds as her own footnote in the novel: '*the moon'.
9. *Frankenstein*, 1818, vol 2, Chapter 3, Penguin Classics, 99–100
1. Ibid., Chapter 8, 132

'I am malicious because I am miserable. Am I not shunned and hated by all mankind? You, my creator would not call it murder, if you could precipitate me into one of those ice-rifts . . . Oh! My creator, make me happy! Let me feel gratitude towards you for *one* benefit! Let me see that I excite the sympathy of *one* existing thing. Do not deny me my request!'[2]

This terrible corrosive and destructive solitude becomes the central theme of the second part of Mary Shelley's novel. Goaded by his misery, the Creature kills and destroys. Yet he also tries to take stock of his own violent actions and contradictory emotions. He concludes that his one hope of happiness lies in sexual companionship. The scene on the Mer de Glace in which he begs Frankenstein to create a wife for him is central to his search for human identity and happiness. The clear implication is that a fully human 'soul' can only be created through friendship and love: 'If you consent [to make me a wife], neither you nor any other human being shall ever see us again. I will go to the vast wilds of South America. My food is not that of man. I do not destroy the lamb and the kid to glut my appetite; acorns and berries afford me sufficient nourishment. My companion will be of the same nature as myself, and will be content with the same fare. We shall make our bed of dried leaves; the sun will shine on us as on man, and will ripen our food. The picture I present to you is peaceful and human, and you must feel that you could deny it only in the wantonness of power and cruelty.'[3]

The Creature is here offering to go westwards to South America or the Pacific, and to return to that primitive Edenic state glimpsed by Cook and Banks. He and his mate will live as vegetarians, kill nothing, cook nothing, build nothing, and reject everything that European civilisation stands for. They will become, in fact, Noble Savages.

In response, Frankenstein goes to London (rather than Paris) to study the latest surgical techniques. He consults with 'the most distinguished natural philosopher' of the day in this 'wonderful and celebrated city', though this man is not named.[4] He then sets up a second laboratory in Scotland, in the remote Orkney islands, where he plans to create a second Creature, a woman. Her companionship will satisfy the male Creature.

But Frankenstein is overcome with doubts. 'Even if they were to leave Europe, and inhabit the deserts of the New World, yet one of the first results of those sympathies for which the Demon thirsted would be children, and a race of devils would be propagated on earth . . . Had I the right, for my own benefit, to inflict this curse

2. Ibid., Chapter 9, 140–1
3. Ibid., Chapter 9, 141
4. Ibid., vol 3, Chapter 2, 160

upon everlasting generations?'[5] His eventual decision to destroy his handiwork is perhaps the grimmest scene in the novel. The laboratory is revealed as a place of horror and blasphemy: 'I summoned sufficient courage, and unlocked the door of my laboratory. The remains of the half-finished creature, whom I had destroyed, lay scattered on the floor, and I almost felt as if I had mangled the flesh of a human being . . . With trembling hand I conveyed the instruments out of the room, cleaned my chemical apparatus, and put the relics of my work into a basket with a great quantity of stones.'[6] There is something more than deathly about those stones. It is as if Frankenstein is burying scientific hope itself beneath the earth.

In his grief and fury the Creature revenges himself on his creator by destroying Frankenstein's friend Clerval, and then his bride, Elizabeth. From thenceforth both are locked in a pact of mutual destruction, which eventually leads pursuer and pursued to the frozen wastes of the North Pole—the antithesis of the warm, Pacific paradise. In a sense, both have lost their own souls. Drawing on the Miltonic imagery of *Paradise Lost*, both see themselves as fallen angels, doomed to eternal solitude and destruction. The dying Frankenstein remains unrepentant as he gasps: 'All my speculations and hopes are as nothing. Like the archangel who aspired to omnipotence, I am chained in eternal hell . . . I have myself been blasted in all my hopes . . . *Yet another may succeed.*'[7]

But the Creature has attained a kind of self-knowledge, and even humility: 'When I call over the frightful catalogue of my deeds, I cannot believe that I am he whose thoughts were once filled with sublime and transcendent visions of the beauty of the world. But it is even so. The fallen angel becomes a malignant devil. Yet even that enemy of God and man had friends and associates in his desolation. I am quite alone . . . He is dead who called me into being; and when I shall be no more, the very remembrance of us both will speedily vanish . . . I shall no longer see the sun or stars, or feel the winds play on my cheeks.'[8]

*   *   *

Victor Frankenstein's experiment in soul-making had ended in disaster. The novel itself disappeared into temporary obscurity, and fewer than 500 copies were sold of the first edition. But it was made famous, if not notorious, in the 1820s by no less than five adaptations for the stage. These caused widespread controversy. The first was staged in London in July 1823, at the English Opera House in

5. Ibid., Chapter 3, 160
6. Ibid., 164–5
7. *Frankenstein*, 1831 text, 178, 180, 186. My italics [Editor]
8. Ibid., 189

The Strand. It was entitled portentously *Presumption: or The Fate of Frankenstein*. From the start there was sensational publicity:

> Do not go to the Opera House to see the Monstrous Drama, founded on the improper work called FRANKENSTEIN!!! Do not take your wives, do not take your daughters, do not take your families!!!—The novel itself is of a decidedly immoral tendency; it treats of a subject which in nature cannot occur. This subject is PREGNANT with mischief; and to prevent the ill-consequences which may result from the promulgation of such dangerous Doctrines, a few zealous friends of morality, and promoters of the Posting-bill (and who are ready to meet the consequences thereof) are using their strongest endeavours.[9]

The part of 'The Creature', which was cleverly and sinisterly left *blank* in the programme, made the actor T. P. Cooke famous (despite his terrible gout)—just as it later made Boris Karloff famous. Over the next four years there were fourteen separate productions, mounted in London, Bristol, Paris and New York.

Presumption made several fundamental changes to Mary Shelley's novel, all without her permission. Nor did she receive any copyright fees. Curiously she did not seem to mind, and when she herself went to see the play in September 1823 she loved it. 'But lo & behold! I found myself famous! Frankenstein had prodigious success as a drama at the English Opera House . . . Mr. Cooke played the *"blank's"* part extremely well—his trying to grasp at the sounds he heard—all he does was well imagined and executed . . . it appears to excite a breathless eagerness in the audience . . . in the early performances all the ladies fainted and hubbub ensued! . . . They continue to play it even now.'[1]

Yet the changes have influenced almost all subsequent stage and film productions. They altered the scientific and moral themes of the book, and shifted it permanently towards a mixture of gothic melodrama and black farce. Victor Frankenstein is made the archetypal mad and evil scientist. He has stood for this role ever since. But in the original novel he is also a romantic and idealistic figure, obsessive rather than evil, and determined to benefit mankind. His demoniac laboratory becomes the centre of dramatic interest, with fizzing electrical generators, sinister bubbling vats and violent explosions. But no such laboratory is described in the novel: Frankenstein works by candlelight at a surgical table. He is also given a comic German assistant called Fritz, who adds gothic farce to the whole

9. Text from 1823 leaflet about *Presumption*; see Fred Botting (editor), *New Casebooks: Frankenstein*, Palgrave, 1995. The evolution and impact of the novel is brilliantly disclosed by William St Clair in *The Reading Nation in the Romantic Period*, (OUP, 2004).
1. Mary Shelley, *The Letters of Mary Shelley*, vol 1, edited by Betty T. Bennett (Johns Hopkins UP, 1988, 369, 378).

proceedings. There is no such assistant in the novel: Frankenstein's work is essentially solitary and dedicated, like that of an artist.

But the most important change of all is this. Mary Shelley's unnamed Creature is transformed into the 'Monster', and made completely dumb. He is deprived of all words, whereas in the novel he is superbly and even tragically articulate: 'And what was I? Of my creation and my creator I was absolutely ignorant . . . Where were my friends and relations? No father had watched my infant days, no mother had blessed me with smiles and caresses; or if they had, all my past life was now a blot, a blind vacancy in which I distinguished nothing . . . I was, besides, endued with a figure hideously deformed and loathsome. I was not even of the same nature as man . . . When I looked around I saw and heard of none like me. Was I, then, a Monster, a blot upon the earth, from which all men fled and whom all men disowned? I cannot describe the agony that these reflections inflicted upon me . . . Oh, that I had forever remained in my native wood, nor known nor felt beyond the sensations of hunger, thirst and heat!'[2]

* * *

William Lawrence's experiment ended in an altogether different way. At the end of 1819 he withdrew his *Natural History of Man*, yielding to pressure from the Royal College of Surgeons and a number of medical institutions. But he continued to speak out in favour of scientific freedom. 'I take the opportunity of protesting, in the strongest possible terms . . . against the attempt to stifle impartial enquiry by an outcry of pernicious tendency; and against perverting science and literature, which naturally tend to bring mankind acquainted with each other, to the anti-social purpose of inflaming and prolonging national prejudice and animosity.'[3]

Lawrence allowed the radical publisher Richard Carlile to reissue a pirate edition of the *Natural History* in 1822, which ran to nine editions (Carlile also successfully pirated Shelley's *Queen Mab*). Carlile wrote his own pamphlet, *Address to the Men of Science* (1821), in which he urged Lawrence and others to retain their intellectual independence. When Carlile died, in a final gesture of support, he gave Lawrence his corpse for dissection, an almost unheard-of bequest.[4]

Lawrence was also supported by Thomas Wakley, mercurial editor of the newly founded medical journal the *Lancet*. In scintillating and lively articles, Wakley attacked the old guard of the Royal College, and satirised the attempts of Abernethy and others to bring theology into the surgical theatre. Whenever they dissected some

2. *Frankenstein*, 1818, vol 2, Chapter 5, Penguin Classics, 116–17
3. Lawrence, *On the Natural History of Man*, 1819, 150
4. Ruston, 71

haemorrhaging organ, or pulsating artery, Wakley mocked, they would exclaim 'with uplifted eye, and most reverentially contracted mouth: "*Gintilmen*, behold the *winderful* evidence of *Desin!*"'[5]

But in 1829 William Lawrence stood for the Council of the Royal College of Surgeons, a body famous for its conservatism. Silently renouncing his radical and 'materialist' views, he went to see his old patron and enemy John Abernethy. It was not a meeting on the Mer de Glace. After long discussions, Lawrence received forgiveness and wholehearted support from his old mentor. Lawrence was unanimously elected, and when his old comrade-in-arms Thomas Wakley came to protest on behalf of the *Lancet*, Lawrence helped to physically manhandle him out of the Council chamber. Sir William Lawrence finished his career as Surgeon-General to Queen Victoria, and was created a baronet. But perhaps he had lost his own soul.

CHRISTA KNELLWOLF AND JANE GOODALL

[The Significance of Place: Ingolstadt][†]

* * *

The locations of *Frankenstein* have been chosen with utmost care. Victor's birthplace in Geneva positions him in the stronghold of Calvinism. At the same time, it alludes to the fact that Jean Jacques Rousseau (1712–78) returned to this small republic on Lake Geneva as a refuge from the vices of France. Another significant setting for the formation of Victor's mind is Ingolstadt, a Bavarian town with a recently founded university (1759) that adopted progressive principles and aimed to achieve social reform. Ingolstadt became famous throughout Europe in the early 1780s for a particular brand of Enlightenment: the order of the Illuminati who describe themselves simply by the Latin word for Enlightenment. It is true that *Frankenstein* does not contain any direct references to the Illuminism, or its founder Adam Weishaupt (1748–1811), but it is telling that the dates of Walton's letters to his sister, '17–', refer its action back to an anonymous time of the eighteenth century. It therefore seems to be fair to conclude that the pursuit of superhuman objectives must be located in the decade before the French Revolution, when all of Europe was intoxicated with a heady ferment of reformatory ideas and utopian visions.

---

5. Adrian Desmond, *The Politics of Evolution: Medicine in Radical London*, Chicago, 1989, 112
† From *Frankenstein's Science: Experimentation and Discovery in Romantic Culture, 1780–1830* (Burlington, VT: Ashgate, 2008), 4–7. Reprinted by permission.

Weishaupt had been educated as a Jesuit but rejected this rigid form of Catholicism and became the first layman to be appointed for the chair of canon law at the University of Ingolstadt (1773). The contribution to the intellectual life of his university, though, was not sufficient for him. Sharing Victor Frankenstein's immense craving to better the lot of mankind, he embarked on negotiations with the Freemasons. His unyielding temper rendered such a rapprochement difficult, so that he founded a new secret society, which was, however, modelled on this society.[1] The joint efforts between Weishaupt and Adolf von Knigge (1752–96) guaranteed the enormous success of the new society between 1780 and 1782. Disagreement between the two leaders, along with public scandals and denunciations that the society was aiming for political sedition rather than the advancement of human welfare and scientific knowledge, caused serious suspicions. In 1787, the Bavarian government went so far as to forbid it under penalty of death.

The stated goals of the society of the Illuminati were to improve society through the cultivation of sensibility and the practice of scientific research. These objectives were shared by most contemporary intellectuals and it, therefore, attracted the leading lights of German intelligentsia, including Johann Wolfgang Goethe (1749–1832), Johann Gottfried von Herder (1744–1803) and Friedrich Nicolai (1733–1811). They joined as a means of dedicating themselves to an organised study and cultivation of human nature. The initiatory oath of new members of the order revolves around humanitarian principles: 'I profess, and also pledge, that I will eagerly grasp every opportunity of serving humankind, will improve my knowledge and willpower, and will make generally available my useful recognitions, in so far as the welfare and statutes of this particular society will demand it of me.'[2]

While pursuing similar goals as the *philosophes*, a group of French intellectuals dedicated themselves to the compilation of comprehensive information about the arts and the sciences to be collected in the one reference work of the *Encyclopédie* (1751–72).[3] The group of intellectuals around Denis Diderot (1713–84) and Jean D'Alembert (1717–83) aimed to spread knowledge as a means of breaking down

1. For a historical background of eighteenth-century freemasonry, see Margaret Jacob, *Living the Enlightenment: Freemasonry and Politics in Eighteenth-Century Europe* (New York: Oxford UP, 1991).
2. For a detailed historical analysis of Illuminism, see Richard van Dülmen, *Der Geheimbund der Illuminaten: Darstellung, Analyse, Dokumentation*, trans. Christa Knellwolf (Stuttgart: F. Frommann, 1975), 159.
3. Denis Diderot and Jean D'Alembert Le Rond, eds, *L'Encyclopédie, ou Dictionnaire raisonné des art et des sciences* (Paris: Le Breton, 1751–72). For a discussion of the cultural context and objectives of the *philosophes*, see David Garrioch, 'The party of the *Philosophes*', in *The Enlightenment World*, eds Martin Fitzpartick, Peter Jones, Christa Knellwolf and Iain McCalman (London: Routledge, 2004), 426–41.

privileges and abuses by church and nobility, which is why they advocated a strictly empiricist approach to science. While Weishaupt admired these spokespeople for reason and rationality, his own society embedded the practice of rationality and benevolence in an atmosphere of ritual. He also combined his commitment to pioneering scientific exploration with the exploration of the more esoteric borderlines between material and non-material phenomena.

The emotional dimension to his practice of reason and rationality, for instance, consisted of the adoption of classical names for all members of the society. Weishaupt called himself Spartacus and Knigge was Philo. Weishaupt's taste for secrecy led him to refer even to places by pseudonyms, 'Athens', for instance, standing for Munich and 'Thessalonica' for Mannheim. The veil of mystery also provided a cover for some serious agitations for the 'elaboration and propagation of a new popular religion and . . . the gradual establishment of a universal democratic republic'.[4] It was also a fertile environment for the observation of phenomena of psyche and soul.

Although Weishaupt and Knigge are not directly recognisable in Shelley's imaginary depiction of Ingolstadt, there are some revealing links between the heyday of Illuminism and the novel's scientific culture. A striking coincidence is that the jubilant vision of scientific progress expressed by Professors Krempe and Waldheim positions them in the decade of the 1780s, which was also the time when Antoine de Lavoisier (1743–94) ousted the long-established belief that combustion was a process that released phlogiston—a colourless, tasteless and weightless substance believed to be present in every object as a latent principle waiting to be released. Lavoisier demonstrated the inconsistencies of the phlogiston theory in 1783 and published his own theories in 1789, demonstrating that conservation of mass is a fundamental principle not just in mechanical physics but also in chemistry. Lavoisier, importantly, proved the viability of quantitative approaches to chemical processes, including respiration and other vital processes of the human body.[5]

In *Frankenstein* the clash between the old and the new theories is pitched as a contrast between the 'modern masters' and old alchemists.[6] After Krempe's scornful response to Victor's interest in their 'exploded systems', the benevolent Waldman explains that 'these were men to whose indefatigable zeal modern philosophers were

4. Compare the entry for 'Illuminati' in the *Catholic Encyclopaedia* online: http://www .newadvent.org/cathen/07661b.htm (accessed 10 October 2007).
5. Antoine Lavoisier, *Traité élémentaire de chimie, présenté dans un ordre nouveau et d'après les découvertes modernes*, 2 vols (Paris: Chez Cuchet, 1789; repr. Bruxelles: Cultures et Civilisations, 1965).
6. Mary Shelley, *Frankenstein or The Modern Prometheus: The 1818 Text* (Oxford: Oxford UP, 1993), 30. All further references are from this text and are cited parenthetically.

indebted for most of the foundations of knowledge' (31). The key figures in the alchemical tradition mentioned in the novel—Albertus Magnus (c. 1206–80), Cornelius Agrippa von Nettesheim (1486–1535), and Paracelsus (Theophrastus von Hohenheim, 1493–1541)—do not simply feature as scholars who made groundbreaking contributions to the history of science. Once he has lost his fascination for the old alchemists, Victor Frankenstein rationalises his attraction to their ideas as a craving for 'boundless grandeur'. Prior to studying at Ingolstadt, he describes his early quests for the 'philosopher's stone and the elixir of life', and goes on to flesh out the moment of success: 'what glory would attend the discovery, if I could banish disease from the human frame, and render man invulnerable to any but a violent death'. If he has really studied the writings of these authors, he must have a more complex understanding of the symbolic qualities of key alchemical concepts, like the philosopher's stone. The text of the novel is quiet about whether he ever pondered the capacity of this most cherished of substances to enable a mystic union between self and world. We can, therefore, only speculate if he was initially attracted to the authors of alchemical works because they embraced a holistic view of nature, which foregrounded strong resemblances between physical and metaphysical phenomena.

It should also be noted that many scholars who broadly belong in the alchemical tradition explored the borderlines between mind and matter. Striking investigations of topics as diverse as social deviance, the origin of the Devil, the true skills of magicians, black and white magic, witchcraft, and the power of poisons and remedies are collected in the work of Johann Weyer, Agrippa's most prominent disciple.[7] If stripped of its religious-demonic framework, Weyer's insight into the psychology of delusions, obsessions, sexual deviance, as well as a whole range of ailments that would come to be classified as nervous diseases during the Romantic period, is truly remarkable. It, therefore, is no surprise that Romantic writers had a certain penchant for the works of the old alchemists. Mary Shelley's father, William Godwin, himself embarked on a book-length study entitled *Lives of the Necromancers* (1834),[8] in which he assessed their true achievements in a strictly secular light. As a stolid rationalist, Godwin must have wanted to cool his period's enthusiasm for what he would have described as irrational obfuscation.

7. Johann Weyer, *De praestigiis daemonum*, trans. John Shea, in *Witches, Devils, and Doctors in the Renaissance* (Binghamton, NY: Medieval & Renaissance Texts & Studies, 1991 [1583]).
8. For the details of Godwin's study, see *Lives of the Necromancers: or, An Account of the Most Eminent Persons in Successive Ages, Who Have Claimed for Themselves, or to Whom Has Been Imputed by Others, the Exercise of Magical Power* (London: Frederick J. Mason, 1834).

Interest in the principles of life—the nervous system, the psyche and the soul—however, provides a connection between Weishaupt's Illuminati, the 'modern masters' and the old alchemists. But as is illustrated by the fact that Weishaupt fell into general disgrace while Lavoisier came to be hailed as the founder of modern chemistry, the line between respectable pursuits and politically and otherwise suspect explorations of the non-material aspects of human existence was easily crossed.[9] Nowhere was this boundary more richly confused than in the dramas of intellectual adventure conceived by Coleridge, Goethe, Shelley, Byron and other leading poets of the Romantic movement, in whose imaginative company Mary Shelley's story was conceived.

* * *

CHARLES E. ROBINSON

Texts in Search of an Editor: Reflections on *The Frankenstein Notebooks* and on Editorial Authority[†]

Every novel exists in a plurality of texts, and none dramatizes this fact more than Mary Shelley's *Frankenstein*, the Draft and Fair-Copy Notebooks of which I have recently edited for Garland Press.[1] My editorial labors on this famous novel have made me painfully aware of how it developed through its various texts, from its original conception on ?17 June 1816 through its gestation, quickening, lightening, birth, and development into the novel (or novels) that so many of us now read. I here take the liberty of applying a creative metaphor to describe this developmental process because the novel itself concerns creativity and because both Mary Shelley and her persona Robert Walton took nine months to write their narratives: Robert Walton wrote his series of letters and journals over a period of 276 days between 11 December 17[96] and 12 September 17[97]; and, although Mary Shelley took eleven months between conceiving the story and finishing the Fair Copy (?17 June 1816 through 10/13 May 1817), it appears that the first two months were spent in

9. Also compare Robert Darnton, *Mesmerism and the End of the Enlightenment in France* (Cambridge, MA: Harvard UP, 1968); and Auguste Viatte, *Les sources occultes du romanticism, illuminism, théosophie, 1770–1820* (Paris: Champion, 1965).

† From *Textual Studies and the Common Reader: Essays on Editing Novels and Novelists*, ed. Alexander Pettit (Athens: U of Georgia P, 2000), 91–97. Reprinted by permission.

1. *The Frankenstein Notebooks: A Facsimile of Mary Shelley's Manuscript Novel, 1816–17 (with alterations in the hand of Percy Bysshe Shelley) as it survives in Draft and Fair Copy deposited by Lord Abinger in the Bodleian Library, Oxford (Dep. c. 477/1 and Dep. c. 534/1–2),* ed. Charles E. Robinson, parts 1 and 2 (New York: Garland, 1996); hereafter cited as *1816–17 Robinson*.

writing the ur-text of the novel and that she therefore devoted the
next nine months to expanding, drafting, and fair-copying her
novel. What happened in the novel, therefore, can be seen to parallel or "figure" what happened outside of the novel.[2]
It would be fair to say further that Walton's writing *in* the novel
and Mary Shelley's writing *of* the novel are also "figured" by the
creative work of Victor Frankenstein himself. Victor's assembling of
disparate body parts into his monster is not that different from Walton's assembling his discrete notes about Victor into a narrative; and
both these creative acts may be compared to Mary Shelley's esem-
plastic fusing of words and images and symbols and punctuation
into the text of her novel. Mary Shelley herself encouraged this kind
of comparison when she bade her novel, her "hideous progeny," to
"go forth and prosper," suggesting that her monster was a metaphor
for her novel and that both creations would be altered by their experiences in the world.[3] Because of these alterations, it would also be
fair to say that the monster and the text were not only "authored"
but also "edited"—both words in their etymologies denote a bringing forth, a giving birth to something new.

If we pursue the editing metaphor further, we encounter another
collaborator who assisted in the development of *Frankenstein,*
namely, the midwife Percy Bysshe Shelley who helped bring Mary
Shelley's novel to its full term and then helped present it to an audience on publication day, 1 January 1818. This assistance, as evi-
denced by his no fewer than 4,000 words in this 72,000-word novel,
resulted from his correcting and augmenting portions of the Draft
and the Fair Copy (and the proofs and the revises) of the novel. The
nature of his editorial labors, which are made manifest in my edition
of *The Frankenstein Notebooks,* will be briefly discussed below, but
for the moment I wish to draw one more parallel between the actions
inside and outside the novel: what Percy Shelley did to (or for) the
novel is "figured" by both Walton and Victor Frankenstein serving as
editors of each other's narratives. Indeed, the more we look at the
novel, the more we are led to the conclusion that *Frankenstein* is a
series of texts in search of an editor, one who will ultimately give
form and shape to the novel.

2. It can even be argued that Walton's dates of writing from 11 December 17[96] to 12
   September 17[97] (the years arrived at with the help of a perpetual calendar) are very
   close to the dates when Mary Shelley was conceived and born; see *1816–17 Robinson,*
   1:lxv–lxvi and nn.
3. [Mary W. Shelley], *Frankenstein: or, The Modern Prometheus,* rev. ed. (London: Henry
   Colburn and Richard Bentley, 1831), xii; hereafter cited as *1831.* Other editions will be
   similarly cited in this essay: thus, for example, *1818* provides a shorthand for *Frankenstein; or, The Modern Prometheus,* 3 vols. (London: Lackington, Hughes, Harding,
   Mavor, & Jones, 1818).

Frankenstein is a frame tale and, as such, is very much about the question of authorial and editorial control. That is, the device of a frame tale enabled Mary Shelley to write as if she were Robert Walton writing the narrative of Victor Frankenstein, in which was embedded the story of the monster who recounted not only his adventures but also those of the De Laceys and the Arabian Safie. These interlocked narratives seem to make Mary Shelley's the dominant voice until we realize that Walton is her persona, and it is his voice we hear. After explaining to his sister Margaret that Victor "would commence his narrative the next day" on 20 August 17[97], Walton described how he would serve as both amanuensis and editor for Victor's words:

> I have resolved every night, when I am not engaged, to record, as nearly as possible in his own words, what he has related during the day. If I should be engaged, I will at least make notes. This manuscript will doubtless afford you the greatest pleasure: but to me, who know him, and who hear it from his own lips, with what interest and sympathy shall I read it in some future day! (*1818*, 1:37–38)

We as readers, of course, are the ones who are destined for the "greatest pleasure" if, like Margaret, we read Victor's narration as edited by Walton. But was Walton the editor who brought forth Victor's tale? It is equally valid to argue that Victor Frankenstein edited the "notes" that Walton made about Victor's history of Victor:

> Frankenstein discovered that I made notes concerning his history: he asked to see them, and then himself corrected and augmented them in many places; but principally in giving the life and spirit to the conversations he held with his enemy. "Since you have preserved my narration," said he, "I would not that a mutilated one should go down to posterity." (*1818*, 3:157)

Victor, it seems, expressed greater concern for his text than he did for his monster. And although it appears that Victor had the last word in his own novel about himself, it was Walton who ultimately voiced Victor's concern for editorial authority. If, however, we privilege author over character and claim that Mary Shelley was the ultimate authority here, the manuscript versions of this passage reveal that Mary Shelley miscopied a phrase when she transcribed the Draft into the Fair Copy and that the error required a later correction by a hand that seems different from that of either of the Shelleys.[4]

The question of editorial authority in this novel gets even more complex if we ask in what form we read Victor's story as edited by Walton edited by Victor edited by Walton—because the question of

---

4. See *1816–17 Robinson*, 2:606–7, 2:736–37, 2:806.

form potentially introduces yet another collaborator in the editorial process. Do we read the manuscript written out by Walton for Margaret's eyes only—or do we read a version of that manuscript that his sister Margaret received and then edited for the press? Mary Shelley provides no answer to this question, but in either case Margaret acts as a surrogate for the reader. But is Margaret Walton Saville a surrogate only for the reader—or do her initials, MWS, force us to read her as a surrogate for Mary Wollstonecraft Shelley? If these initials are purposeful, then we have a novel written by MWS as if she were Walton writing to MWS—and the silent MWS stands in the corner of this narrative, teasing us to see her as both author and reader (and author and editor) of her own work.

If the questions of editorial authority inside the novel tease us out of thought, even more complex and teasing questions await us outside the novel as we encounter no fewer than ten texts that go into the making of *Frankenstein*, texts that have been edited by Mary Shelley herself (more than once), Percy Shelley (more than once), William Godwin, various publishers' readers and printers, and then the long list of nineteenth- and twentieth-century scholars who have printed and edited and otherwise disseminated the novel to millions of readers, each of whom may be said to "edit" the text while assembling and re-assembling the ideas, words, and punctuation that make up the spirit and matter of the thing we call a novel (which exists, as Percy Shelley would have it, only as it is perceived by the reader).[5] When I was invited to join this editorial procession, I anticipated doing little more than creating a useful "diplomatic" edition of *The Frankenstein Notebooks*, one that would faithfully represent the text of the extant Draft and Fair Copy by reproducing photographs of the manuscript pages, each of which would be faced by a type facsimile of the manuscript of that page. I was familiar with Mary Shelley's hand, having published a similar albeit simpler edition of the Fair Copies of her mythological dramas *Proserpine* and *Midas*,[6] I could recognize Percy Shelley's hand in the manuscript, and I planned somehow to distinguish his hand from that of Mary Shelley. In short, I would serve the scholarly community by bringing empirical and hard evidence into the various debates on Mary Shelley's most famous novel. What I did not anticipate was how much the editing of these Notebooks would force me to contextualize the extant

5. Percy Shelley more than once remarked that "all things exist as they are perceived"; see, for example, "A Defence of Poetry," in *Shelley's Poetry and Prose: Authoritative Texts, Criticism*, ed. Donald H. Reiman and Sharon B. Powers (New York: Norton, 1977), 505; see also "nothing exists but as it is perceived" (Percy Shelley, "On Life," in *Shelley's Poetry and Prose*, 476).
6. Mary Shelley, *Mythological Dramas: Proserpine and Midas*, Bodleian MS. Shelley d. 2, ed. Charles E. Robinson (New York: Garland, 1992).

manuscripts by reference to other manuscripts, proofs, revises, printed texts, and editions of *Frankenstein*.

My first step down that road of contextualization resulted from three circumstances that determined the character of my edition: a Garland policy (worked out in collaboration with Donald H. Reiman and the Bodleian Library) to reproduce in photofacsimile all extant manuscript pages, each of which would be faced by a type facsimile of the manuscript; a set of *Frankenstein* manuscripts in which Mary Shelley wrote fewer than ten words in each line; and Garland's predetermined nine-by-twelve-inch format that enabled me to print on each recto not only the type facsimile of the manuscript (with different fonts to distinguish Mary Shelley's hand from Percy Shelley's) but also, in tandem with the manuscript, a literal transcript of the 1818 first edition (all glossed by footnotes at the bottom of each page).[7] On one page, the reader could see what Mary Shelley originally wrote, then what she and Percy Shelley corrected, then what was printed a few months later, and finally the footnotes that addressed not only anomalies in the manuscript but also errors in the text of *1818*. These anomalies and errors forced me to extend my study of the transmission of the text in two directions: backward from *1818* through revises and proofs and Fair Copy and Draft to the ur-text that I hypothetically reconstructed; and forward from the first edition of 1818 through to the third and revised edition of 1831 (and also through to some recent critical editions of the novel). New discoveries about the meaning and form of the novel awaited me at every step in this sequence of texts, the interrelations of which I have discussed in the introduction, chronology, and footnotes in *The Frankenstein Notebooks*. Here, however, I will rely on the following outline to indicate how one text leads directly to another between the years of 1816 and 1831. The two exceptions to this direct sequence are *1818 Thomas* and [*1826*], both of which have been indented to allow the stemma arrows to pass by them.

The Texts of Frankenstein

> *1816* **Ur-text**: A novella-length narrative written between ?17 June and ?August 1816—not extant: certainly in the hand of Mary Shelley, but no evidence one way or the other of
> ↓ Percy Shelley's direct involvement.
>
> *1816–17* **Draft**: A two-volume novel in two hard-cover notebooks written between ?August 1816 and 17 April 1817— most of the now disbound Notebooks A and B survive in

---

7. The terms "photofacsimile," "type facsimile," and "literal transcript" are adapted from D. C. Greetham, *Textual Scholarship: An Introduction* (New York: Garland, 1994), 350.

152 leaves (with text on 301 pages) together with three insert leaves and two insert slips (with text on a total of eight pages), all of which are reproduced in *The Frankenstein Notebooks* and account for approximately 87 percent of the *1818* text: in the hand of Mary Shelley, with altera-↓ tions in the hand of Percy Shelley.

1817 **Fair Copy:** A three-volume novel in ?eleven soft-cover notebooks written between 18 April and 10/13 May 1817—parts of now disbound Notebooks c1 and c2 survive in twenty-nine leaves (with text on fifty-eight pages) together with one insert leaf (with text on one page) as well as one substitute leaf (with text on two pages), all of which are reproduced in *The Frankenstein Notebooks* and contain approximately 12 percent of the *1818* text: in the hand of Mary Shelley, with the last twelve and three-quarters pages of Notebook c2 in the hand of Percy Shelley. There is additional evidence that Percy Shelley corrected other parts ↓ of the Fair Copy.

Proofs: A three-volume novel issued between ?23 September and ?3 November 1817—not extant, but there is evidence that both Shelleys read and corrected the proofs and that Mary and/or Percy made three major additions to the text, ↓ one in September and two in October.

Revises: Three or more sheets of revised proofs printed between ?23 September and ?20 November 1817—not extant, but the three major additions to the proofs would certainly have resulted in revises that Mary and/or Percy Shelley would ↓ have read.

1818: A three-volume novel (1st ed.) published anonymously on 1 January 1818 in 500 copies by Lackington, Hughes, Harding, Mavor, & Jones.

↓ *1818 Thomas:* Copy of first edition (*1818*) corrected by Mary Shelley and given to a Mrs. Thomas in Genoa by July 1823—survives at the Pierpont Morgan Library in New York City.

1823: A two-volume novel (2nd ed.) published on 11 August 1823 in an unknown number of copies by G. and W. B. Whittaker (set from *1818* rather than from *1818 Thomas*)—William Godwin rather than Mary Shelley made the arrangements for this edition, the copy-text for which would have been either *1818* or a proof copy that Godwin may have possessed. Godwin, it appears, was the one responsible for the 123 substantive variants introduced into this edition, almost all of which were carried over to *1831*, suggesting that *1823* was

used as the copy-text for *1831* and that Mary Shelley no
longer possessed a copy of *1818* to use for this purpose.

↓   **[*1826*]: [?Re-issue of 2nd ed.** (*1823*)] "published" on 4
April 1826 by Henry Colburn. Because no copy of an 1826
edition has ever been located or described, Colburn appears
to have purchased and offered for sale the unsold sheets of
1823 without printing a new title page, but no collation of
multiple copies of *1823* has been done to determine if there
was in fact a distinct *1826* re-issue of *1823*.

1831: A one-volume novel (3rd or revised ed.) published on 31
October 1831 in 4,020 stereotyped copies by Henry Colburn
and Richard Bentley in the "Standard Novels" series: Mary
Shelley was responsible for the substantial changes made to
the text, and she apparently used *1823* as copy-text.

This brief outline of the texts of *Frankenstein* should suggest that
there were at least three major editorial hands (of the two Shelleys
and of Godwin) in the versioning of the novel between the time it
was "finished" and fair-copied for the publisher and printer in April/
May 1817 and the time it was revised in 1831; this of course does not
count the publishers and their readers, or the printers and their com-
positors, who also exercised some influence on the text. A glance at
the extant Fair Copy (which was also printer's copy), for example, will
show that more than one unidentified hand made small alterations to
the text that had been transcribed by Mary and Percy Shelley.

All these interventions should help to dispel the still-persistent
myth of the solitary artist who has total control over a text. * * *

* * *

ANNE K. MELLOR

Choosing a Text of *Frankenstein* to Teach[†]

Which edition of *Frankenstein* should I teach? This question is
more complicated than it might at first appear. There are critically
significant differences among the manuscript of *Frankenstein* in the
Bodleian Library, the first edition of the novel in 1818, and the second and heavily revised edition of 1831. Since current text-editing
theory and practice no longer assume that the author's final word is
definitive, we cannot select the final edition for that reason alone.

† From *Approaches to Teaching Shelley's* Frankenstein, ed. Stephen C. Behrendt (New
York: Modern Language Association of America, 1990) 31–37. Reprinted by permission of the Modern Language Association of America.

Nor should we be unduly swayed by the fact that the 1831 edition in the Signet-NAL paperback costs less than two dollars.

I strongly believe that the text of preference should be the 1818 edition, for the same reasons that students of Romanticism prefer the 1805 edition of Wordsworth's *Prelude* to the final 1850 edition. The first completed versions of both works have greater internal philosophical coherence, are closest to the authors' original conceptions, and are more convincingly related to their historical contexts. In *Frankenstein*, these contexts are biographical (the recent death of Mary Shelley's first baby and her dissatisfactions with Percy Shelley's Romantic ideology), political (her observations of the aftermath of the French Revolution in 1814–16), and scientific (the experiments with galvanic electricity in the first decade of the nineteenth century).

The most striking thematic differences between the two published versions of the novel concern the role of fate, the degree of Frankenstein's responsibility for his actions, the representation of nature, the role of Clerval, and the representation of the family. I discuss these issues in more detail later in this essay, but here I must make two preliminary observations. Even the first published text of *Frankenstein* has moved away from Mary Shelley's original style and conception, insofar as we can determine these from the surviving sections of the manuscript in the Abinger Shelley Collection in the Bodleian Library (these sections constitute page 30, line 13, through page 109, line 9, plus page 117, line 17, to page 221, line 12, in the Rieger edition of the 1818 text). Furthermore, the account given of this manuscript by James Rieger, the editor of the only available reprint of the 1818 text of *Frankenstein*,[1] is so inaccurate and so prejudiced in favor of Percy Shelley that students must be warned against its misleading combination of truths, half-truths, and unwarranted speculations.

As Mary Shelley wrote her story of Frankenstein, she gave it to her husband to edit. She rightly claimed that she "did not owe the suggestion of one incident, nor scarcely of one train of feeling" to Percy Shelley (Rieger 229), with one minor exception: it was Percy who suggested that Frankenstein's trip to England be proposed by Victor himself, rather than by his father. Yet Percy Shelley made numerous corrections, about a thousand in all, on the surviving manuscript pages, almost all of which Mary Shelley accepted.

James Rieger credits Percy Shelley with wording the descriptions of contrasts between the personalities of Frankenstein and Elizabeth and between the governments of the Swiss republic and less fortunate nations, with coining the metaphoric description of the power within Mont Blanc, with conceiving the "idea that Frankenstein

---

1. Originally published by Bobbs-Merrill (Indianapolis) in 1974 and reprinted by U of Chicago P in 1982. [*Editor's note.*]

journey to England for the purpose of creating a female Monster," with making the "final revisions" of the last pages, and with correcting Mary Shelley's "frequent grammatical solecisms, her spelling, and her awkward phrasing." He then concludes that Percy Shelley's "assistance at every point in the book's manufacture was so extensive that one hardly knows whether to regard him as editor or minor collaborator" (Rieger xviii).

Close examination of the surviving manuscript fragments shows that Percy Shelley's numerous revisions of Mary's original text damaged as well as improved it. To dispose of Rieger's misinformation, Percy did expand, although he did not initiate, the comparison of Elizabeth's character to Victor Frankenstein's; and he did interpolate a favorable comparison of Switzerland's republicanism with the tyranny of other nations. However, the descriptions of Mont Blanc and the Mer de Glace in the novel are based primarily on Mary Shelley's own observations, which she made in July 1816 and recorded both in her journal entries for 22–26 July and in her letters to Fanny Imlay; these letters were later published in her *History of a Six Weeks' Tour* (1817). As already noted, Percy suggested merely that Victor rather than Alphonse Frankenstein propose the trip to England. We might pass over Rieger's annoying habit of referring to Percy Shelley only by his last name and to Mary Shelley by her first, or his failure to acknowledge, in his assertion that Percy corrected "her frequent grammatical solecisms, her spelling, and her awkward phrasing," that Mary's grammatical errors or misspellings were infrequent, while her phrasings were often more graceful than her husband's revised versions. Rieger's concluding suggestion that Percy Shelley can be regarded as a "minor collaborator" or even as one of the two authors of the novel (xliv) is not only unjustified by the evidence. It is also, as we can now recognize, explicitly sexist, since it implies that Mary Shelley could not have created her story alone. Rieger thus does a great disservice to Mary Shelley's genius.

Percy Shelley did improve the manuscript of *Frankenstein* in several minor ways: he corrected three factual errors, eliminated a few grammatical mistakes, occasionally clarified the text, substituted more precise technical terms for Mary's cruder ones, smoothed out a few paragraph transitions, and enriched the thematic resonance of the text. But Percy Shelley misunderstood his wife's intentions. He tended to see the Creature as more monstrous and less human than Mary did, and he frequently underestimated the flaws in Victor Frankenstein's personality. Furthermore, he introduced into the text his own philosophical and political opinions, opinions that were often at variance with his wife's beliefs. For instance, throughout her manuscript Mary assumes the existence of a sacred animating principle, call it Nature or Life or God, which Frankenstein usurps at his peril. But Percy undermined her notion that Frankenstein's pursuit of his Creature was "a task enjoined by heaven" by adding his atheistic concept of a universe mechanistically determined by necessity or power, "the mechanical impulse of some power of which I was unconscious" (Rieger 202). Percy also introduced all the references to Victor Frankenstein as the "author" of the Creature (see Rieger 87, 96) and thus may be largely responsible for recent discussions of Mary Shelley's anxiety of authorship (see Gilbert and Gubar 49; Mary Poovey, *The Proper Lady and the Woman Writer* [Chicago: UCP, 1982], chs. 4 and 5).

More important, Percy changed the last line of the novel in a way that potentially alters its meaning. Mary had penned Walton's final vision of the Creature thus:

> He sprung from the cabin window as he said this upon an ice raft that lay close to the vessel & pushing himself off he was carried away by the waves and I soon lost sight of him in the darkness and distance.

But Percy changed this to

> He sprung from the cabin-window, as he said this, upon the ice-raft which lay close to the vessel. He was soon borne away by the waves, and lost in darkness and distance. (Rieger 221)

Mary's version, by suggesting that Walton has only lost sight of the Creature, leaves open the troubling possibility that the Creature may still be alive, while Percy's flat assertion that the Creature is lost provides the reader a more comforting closure of the novel's monstrous threats.

By far the largest number of Percy's revisions were stylistic. He typically changed Mary's simple, Anglo-Saxon diction and straightforward or colloquial sentence structures into more refined, complex, and Latinate equivalents. He is thus largely responsible for the stilted, ornate, putatively Ciceronian prose style about which so many students complain. Mary's voice tended to utter a sentimental, rather abstract, and generalized rhetoric, typically energized with a brisk stylistic rhythm. Here, for instance, is Mary on Frankenstein's fascination with supernatural phenomena:

> Nor were these my only visions. The raising of ghosts or devils was also a favorite pursuit and if I never saw any I attributed it rather to my own inexperience and mistakes than want of skill in my instructors.

And here is Percy's revision:

> Nor were these my only visions. The raising of ghosts or devils was a promise liberally accorded by my favourite authors, the fulfillment of which I most eagerly sought; and if my

incantations were always unsuccessful, I attributed the failure rather to my own inexperience and mistakes, than to a
want of skill or fidelity in my instructors. (Rieger 34)

Percy's preference for more learned, polysyllabic terms was obsessive; in addition, he rigorously eliminated Mary's colloquial phrases,
as the following lists indicate.

Mary Shelley's manuscript	*Percy Shelley's revision*
have	possess
wish	desire, purpose
caused	derive their origin from
a painting	a representation
place	station
plenty of	sufficient
time	period
felt	endured
hope	confidence
had	experienced
stay	remain
took away	extinguish
talked	conversed
hot	inflamed
smallness	minuteness
end	extinction
inside	within
tired	fatigued
die	perish
leave out	omit
add to	augment
poverty	penury
mind	understanding
ghost-story	a tale of superstition
about on a par	of nearly equal interest and utility
we were all equal	neither of us possessed the slightest pre-eminence over the other
it was safe	the danger of infection was past
bear to part	be persuaded to part
the use I should make of it	the manner in which I should employ it
eyes were shut to	eyes were insensible to
do not wish to hate you	will not be tempted to set myself in opposition to thee

Mary Shelley's manuscript	Percy Shelley's revision
wrapping the rest	depositing the remains
it was a long time	a considerable period elapsed
had a means	possessed a method
how my disposition and	the alteration perceptible in my
habits were altered	disposition and habits
whatever I should	whatever course of conduct I
afterwards think it	might hereafter think it right
right to do	to pursue
what to say	what manner to commence the
	interview

I wish to claim not that Mary Shelley is a great prose stylist but only that her language, despite its tendency toward the abstract, sentimental, and even banal, is more direct and forceful than her husband's. (For a more detailed discussion of Percy Shelley's revisions of the manuscript of *Frankenstein*, see Mellor, *Mary Shelley*, ch. 3 and app.)[2]

Turning now to the differences between the first and second published editions of *Frankenstein*, we must recognize that between 1818 and 1831, Mary Shelley's philosophical views changed radically, primarily as a result of the pessimism generated by the deaths of Clara, William, and Percy Shelley; by the betrayals of Byron and Jane Williams; and by her severely straitened economic circumstances. These events convinced Mary Shelley that human events are decided not by personal choice or free will but by an indifferent destiny or fate. The values implicitly espoused in the first edition of *Frankenstein*—that nature is a nurturing and benevolent life force that punishes only those who transgress against its sacred rights, that Victor is morally responsible for his acts, that the Creature is potentially good but driven to evil by social and parental neglect, that a family like the De Laceys that loves all its children equally offers the best hope for human happiness, and that human egotism causes the greatest suffering in the world—are all rejected in the 1831 revisions.

In the 1818 version, Victor Frankenstein possessed free will: he could have abandoned his quest for the "principle of life," he could have cared for his Creature, he could have protected Elizabeth. But in the 1831 edition, he is the pawn of forces beyond his knowledge or control. As he comments, "Destiny was too potent, and her immutable laws had decreed my utter and terrible destruction" (Rieger, app. 239). Elizabeth also subscribes to this rhetoric of

2. Anne Kostelanetz Mellor, *Mary Shelley: Her Life, Her Fiction, Her Monsters* (New York: Methuen, 1988). [*Editor's note.*]

fatalism: "I think our placid home, and our contented hearts are regulated by the same immutable laws" (Rieger, app. 243).

In the 1831 edition, Mary Shelley replaces her earlier organic conception of nature with a mechanistic one. She now portrays nature as a mighty machine, a juggernaut, an "imperial" tyrant (Rieger, app. 249). Since human beings are now but puppets ("one by one the various keys were touched which formed the mechanism of my being," says Victor [Rieger, app. 241]), Victor's downfall is caused not so much by his egotistical "presumption and rash ignorance" as by bad influences, whether his father's ignorance or Professor Waldman's Mephistophelian manipulations. Victor's only sin is not his failure to love and care for his Creature but his original decision to construct a human being. His scientific experiments themselves are now described as "unhallowed arts" (Rieger, app. 247).

Not only is Frankenstein portrayed in 1831 as a victim rather than an originator of evil, but Clerval—who had functioned in the first edition as the touchstone of moral virtue against which Victor's fall was measured—is now portrayed as equally ambitious of fame and power, as a future colonial imperialist who will use his "mastery" of Oriental languages to exploit the natural resources of the East (Rieger, app. 243, 253). Furthermore, the ideology of the egalitarian and loving bourgeois family that Mary Shelley had inherited from her mother's writings and that sustained the first edition of *Frankenstein* is now undercut. Maternal love is identified with self-destruction when Caroline Beaufort deliberately sacrifices her life to nurse Elizabeth. And Elizabeth Lavenza has become a passive "angel in the house," no longer able to speak out in the law courts against Justine's execution.

By coming to construe nature in the 1831 edition as only Waldman and Frankenstein had done in the first edition, as a mighty and amoral machine, Mary Shelley significantly decreased the critical distance between herself and her protagonist. In the "Author's Introduction" added to the novel in 1831, Mary Shelley presents herself as she now represents Frankenstein, as a victim of destiny. She is "compelled" to write (Rieger 222); her imagination "unbidden" possessed and guided her (Rieger 227). She ends with a defensive lie: "I have changed no portion of the story, nor introduced any new ideas or circumstances" (Rieger 229). Thus in the final version of her novel, Mary Shelley disclaims responsibility for her hideous progeny and at the same time insists that she has remained passive before it, "leaving the core and substance of it untouched" (Rieger 229). For invention "can give form to dark, shapeless substances, but cannot bring into being the substance itself" (Rieger 226). Imperial nature, the thing-in-itself, is now triumphant. Before it, Mary Shelley's human imagination can only mold shapeless darkness into a hideous monster. Like Victor Frankenstein, she has become the unwilling "author of unalterable evils." (For a more detailed description of Mary Shelley's revisions of *Frankenstein* in 1831, see Mellor, *Mary Shelley*, ch. 9.) The remarkable shifts in both diction and philosophical conception between the three versions of *Frankenstein*—the manuscript, the 1818 edition, and the 1831 edition—make this an ideal text for use in courses in either text editing or the theory of the text itself. From the perspective of deconstructive literary criticism, *Frankenstein* exemplifies what Julia Kristeva has called "the questionable subject-in-process," both a text and an author without stable boundaries. For students who have time to consult only one text, the 1818 text alone presents a stable and coherent conception of the character of Victor Frankenstein and of Mary Shelley's political and moral ideology. It is a pity that the significantly higher price of the Rieger edition often proves decisive in persuading teachers to opt for the cheaper editions of the revised 1831 *Frankenstein*, editions that cannot do justice to Mary Shelley's powerful originating vision.

Reception, Impact, Adaptation

PERCY BYSSHE SHELLEY

On *Frankenstein*†

The novel of 'Frankenstein; or, the Modern Prometheus,' is undoubt-edly, as a mere story, one of the most original and complete productions of the day. We debate with ourselves in wonder, as we read it, what could have been the series of thoughts—what could have been the peculiar experiences that awakened them—which conduced, in the author's mind, to the astonishing combinations of motives and incidents, and the startling catastrophe, which compose this tale. There are, perhaps, some points of subordinate importance, which prove that it is the author's first attempt. But in this judgment, which requires a very nice discrimination, we may be mistaken; for it is conducted throughout with a firm and steady hand. The interest gradually accumulates and advances towards the conclusion with the accelerated rapidity of a rock rolled down a mountain. We are led breathless with suspense and sympathy, and the heaping up of incident on incident, and the working of passion out of passion. We cry "hold, hold! enough!"—but there is yet something to come; and, like the victim whose history it relates, we think we can bear no more, and yet more is to be borne. Pelion is heaped on Ossa, and Ossa on Olympus. We climb Alp after Alp, until the horizon is seen blank, vacant, and limitless; and the head turns giddy, and the ground seems to fail under our feet.

This novel rests its claim on being a source of powerful and profound emotion. The elementary feelings of the human mind are exposed to view; and those who are accustomed to reason deeply on their origin and tendency will, perhaps, be the only persons who can sympathize, to the full extent, in the interest of the actions which are their result. But, founded on nature as they are, there is perhaps no reader, who can endure anything beside a new love story, who will not feel a responsive string touched in his inmost soul. The

† Written in 1817; published (posthumously) in *The Athenæum Journal of Literature, Science and the Fine Arts,* Nov. 10, 1832.

sentiments are so affectionate and so innocent—the characters of the subordinate agents in this strange drama are clothed in the light of such a mild and gentle mind—the pictures of domestic manners are of the most simple and attaching character: the father's is irresistible and deep. Nor are the crimes and malevolence of the single Being, though indeed withering and tremendous, the off-spring of any unaccountable propensity to evil, but flow irresistibly from certain causes fully adequate to their production. They are the children, as it were, of Necessity and Human Nature. In this the direct moral of the book consists; and it is perhaps the most impor-tant, and of the most universal application, of any moral that can be enforced by example. Treat a person ill, and he will become wicked. Requite affection with scorn;—let one being be selected, for what-ever cause, as the refuse of his kind—divide him, a social being, from society, and you impose upon him the irresistible obligations— malevolence and selfishness. It is thus that, too often in society, those who are best qualified to be its benefactors and its ornaments, are branded by some accident with scorn, and changed, by neglect and solitude of heart, into a scourge and a curse.

The Being in 'Frankenstein' is, no doubt, a tremendous creature. It was impossible that he should not have received among men that treatment which led to the consequences of his being a social nature. He was an abortion and an anomaly; and though his mind was such as its first impressions framed it, affectionate and full of moral sensi-bility, yet the circumstances of his existence are so monstrous and uncommon, that, when the consequences of them became developed in action, his original goodness was gradually turned into inextin-guishable misanthropy and revenge. The scene between the Being and the blind De Lacey in the cottage, is one of the most profound and extraordinary instances of pathos that we ever recollect. It is impossible to read this dialogue,—and indeed many others of a somewhat similar character,—without feeling the heart suspend its pulsations with wonder, and the "tears stream down the cheeks." The encounter and argument between Frankenstein and the Being on the sea of ice, almost approaches, in effect, to the expostulations of Caleb Williams with Falkland. It reminds us, indeed, somewhat of the style and character of that admirable writer, to whom the author has dedi-cated his work, and whose productions he seems to have studied.

There is only one instance, however, in which we detect the least approach to imitation; and that is the conduct of the incident of Frankenstein's landing in Ireland. The general character of the tale, indeed, resembles nothing that ever preceded it. After the death of Elizabeth, the story, like a stream which grows at once more rapid and profound as it proceeds, assumes an irresistible solemnity, and the magnificent energy and swiftness of a tempest.

The churchyard scene, in which Frankenstein visits the tombs of his family, his quitting Geneva, and his journey through Tartary to the shores of the Frozen Ocean, resemble at once the terrible reanimation of a corpse and the supernatural career of a spirit. The scene in the cabin of Walton's ship—the more than mortal enthusiasm and grandeur of the Being's speech over the dead body of his victim—is an exhibition of intellectual and imaginative power, which we think the reader will acknowledge has seldom been surpassed.

[JOHN CROKER]

From the *Quarterly Review* (January 1818)[†]

Frankenstein, a Swiss student at the university of Ingolstadt, is led by a peculiar enthusiasm to study the structure of the human frame, and to attempt to follow to its recondite sources 'the stream of animal being.' In examining the causes of *life*, he informs us, antithetically, that he had first recourse to *death*.—He became acquainted with anatomy; but that was not all; he traced through vaults and charnel-houses the decay and corruption of the human body, and whilst engaged in this agreeable pursuit, examining and analyzing the minutiæ of mortality, and the phenomena of the change from life to death and from death to life, a sudden light broke in upon him—

> 'A light so brilliant and wondrous, yet so simple, that while I became dizzy with the immensity of the prospect which it illustrated, I was surprized that among so many men of genius, who had directed their inquiries towards the same science, I alone should be reserved to discover so astonishing a secret.
>
> 'Remember, I am NOT recording the vision of a madman. The sun does not more certainly shine in the heavens, than that which I now affirm is true. Some miracle might have produced it, yet the stages of the discovery were distinct and probable. After days and nights of incredible labour and fatigue, I succeeded in discovering the cause of generation and life; nay, more, I became myself capable of bestowing animation upon lifeless matter.'

Having made this wonderful discovery, he hastened to put it in practice; by plundering graves and stealing, not bodies, but parts of bodies, from the church-yard: by dabbling (as he delicately expresses it) with the unhallowed damps of the grave, and torturing the living animal to animate lifeless clay, our modern Prometheus formed a

† 36 (January 1818): 379–85.

filthy image to which the last step of his art was to communicate being:—for the convenience of the process of his animal manufacture, he had chosen to form his figure about eight feet high, and he endeavoured to make it as handsome as he could—he succeeded in the first object and failed in the second; he made and animated his giant; but by some little mistake in the artist's calculation, the intended beauty turned out the ugliest monster that ever deformed the day. The creator, terrified at his own work, flies into one wood, and the work, terrified at itself, flies into another. Here the monster, by the easy process of listening at the window of a cottage, acquires a complete education: he learns to think, to talk, to read prose and verse; he becomes acquainted with geography, history, and natural philosophy, in short, 'a most delicate monster.' This credible course of study, and its very natural success, are brought about by a combination of circumstances almost as natural. In the aforesaid cottage, a young *Frenchman* employed his time in teaching an *Arabian* girl all these fine things, utterly unconscious that while he was

'whispering soft lessons in his fair one's ear,'

he was also tutoring Frankenstein's hopeful son. The monster, however, by due diligence, becomes highly accomplished: he reads Plutarch's Lives, Paradise Lost, Volney's Ruin of Empires, and the Sorrows of Werter. Such were the works which constituted the Greco-Anglico-Germanico-Gallico-Arabic library of a Swabian hut, which, if not numerous, was at least miscellaneous, and reminds us, in this particular, of Lingo's famous combination of historic characters—'Mahomet, Heliogabalus, Wat Tyler, and Jack the Painter.' He learns also to decypher some writings which he carried off from the laboratory in which he was manufactured; by these papers he becomes acquainted with the name and residence of Frankenstein and his family, and as his education has given him so good a taste as to detest himself, he has also the good sense to detest his creator for imposing upon him such a horrible burden as conscious existence, and he therefore commences a series of bloody persecutions against the unhappy Frankenstein—he murders his infant brother, his young bride, his bosom friend; even the very nursery maids of the family are not safe from his vengeance, for he contrives that they shall be hanged for robbery and murder which he himself commits.

The monster, however, has some method in his madness: he meets his Prometheus in the valley of Chamouny, and, in a long conversation, tells him the whole story of his adventures and his crimes, and declares, that he will 'spill much more blood and become worse,' unless Frankenstein will *make* (we should perhaps say *build*) a wife for him; the Sorrows of Werter had, it seems, given him a strange longing to find a Charlotte, of a suitable size, and it is plain that none of Eve's daughters, not even the enormous Charlotte[1] of the Variétés herself, would have suited this stupendous fantoccino. A compliance with this natural desire his kind-hearted parent most reasonably promises; but, on further consideration, he becomes alarmed at the thoughts of reviving the race of Anak, and he therefore resolves to break his engagement, and to defeat the procreative propensities of his ungracious child—hence great wrath and new horrors—parental unkindness and filial ingratitude. The monster hastens to execute his promised course of atrocity, and the monster-maker hurries after to stab or shoot him, and so put an end to his proceedings. This chase leads Frankenstein through Germany and France, to England, Scotland, and Ireland, in which latter country, he is taken up by a constable called Daniel Nugent, and carried before Squire Kirwan a magistrate, and very nearly hanged for a murder committed by the monster. We were greatly edified with the laudable minuteness which induces the author to give us the names of these officers of justice; it would, however, have been but fair to have given us also those of the impartial judge and enlightened jury who acquitted him, for acquitted, as our readers will be glad to hear, honourably acquitted, he was at the assizes of Donegal.—Escaped from this peril, he renews the chase, and the monster, finding himself hard pressed, resolves to fly to the most inaccessible point of the earth; and, as our Review had not yet enlightened mankind upon the real state of the North Pole, he directs his course thither as a sure place of solitude and security; but Frankenstein, who probably had read Mr. Daines Barrington and Colonel Beaufoy on the subject, was not discouraged, and follows him with redoubled vigour, the monster flying on a sledge drawn by dogs, according to the Colonel's proposition, and Prometheus following in another—the former, however, had either more skill or better luck than the latter, whose dogs died, and who must have been drowned on the breaking up of the ice, had he not been fortunately picked up in the nick of time by Mr. Walton, the master of an English whaler, employed on a voyage of discovery towards the North Pole. On board this ship poor Frankenstein, after telling his story to Mr. Walton, who has been so kind as to write it down for our use, dies of cold, fatigue, and horror; and soon after, the monster, who had borrowed (we presume from the flourishing colony of East Greenland) a kind of raft, comes alongside the ship, and notwithstanding his huge bulk, jumps in at Mr. Walton's cabin window, and is surprized by that gentleman pronouncing a funeral oration over the departed Frankenstein; after which, declaring that he will go back to the Pole, and there burn himself on a funeral pyre

---

1. In the parody of Werter, at the Variétés in Paris, the Charlotte is ludicrously corpulent.

(of ice, we conjecture) of his own collecting, he jumps again out of the window into his raft, and is out of sight in a moment.

Our readers will guess from this summary, what a tissue of horrible and disgusting absurdity this work presents.—It is piously dedicated to Mr. Godwin, and is written in the spirit of his school. The dreams of insanity are embodied in the strong and striking language of the insane, and the author, notwithstanding the rationality of his preface, often leaves us in doubt whether he is not as mad as his hero. Mr. Godwin is the patriarch of a literary family, whose chief skill is in delineating the wanderings of the intellect, and which strangely delights in the most afflicting and humiliating of human miseries. His disciples are a kind of *out-pensioners of Bedlam*, and, like 'Mad Bess' or 'Mad Tom,' are occasionally visited with paroxysms of genius and fits of expression, which make soberminded people wonder and shudder.

We shall give our readers a very favourable specimen of the vigour of fancy and language with which this work is written, by extracting from it the three passages which struck us the most on our perusal of it. The first is the account of the animation of the image.[2]

The next is the description of the meeting in the valley of Chamouny.[3]

The last with which we shall agitate the nerves of our readers is Captain Walton's description of the monster he found in his cabin.[4]

It cannot be denied that this is nonsense—but it is nonsense decked out with circumstances and clothed in language highly terrific: it is, indeed,

> _____'a tale
> Told by an ideot, full of sound and fury,
> Signifying nothing—'

but still there is something tremendous in the unmeaning hollowness of its sound, and the vague obscurity of its images.

But when we have thus admitted that Frankenstein has passages which appal the mind and make the flesh creep, we have given it all the praise (if praise it can be called) which we dare to bestow. Our taste and our judgment alike revolt at this kind of writing, and the greater the ability with which it may be executed the worse it is—it inculcates no lesson of conduct, manners, or morality; it cannot mend, and will not even amuse its readers, unless their taste have been deplorably vitiated—it fatigues the feelings without interesting

2. See p. 36, above. [*Editor's note.*]
3. See p. 67, above. [*Editor's note.*]
4. See p. 158, above. [*Editor's note.*]

the understanding; it gratuitously harasses the heart, and wantonly adds to the store, already too great, of painful sensations. The author has powers, both of conception and language, which employed in a happier direction might, perhaps, (we speak dubiously,) give him a name among those whose writings amuse or amend their fellow-creatures; but we take the liberty of assuring him, and hope that he may be in a temper to listen to us, that the style which he has adopted in the present publication merely tends to defeat his own purpose, if he really had any other object in view than that of leaving the wearied reader, after a struggle between laughter and loathing, in doubt whether the head or the heart of the author be the most diseased.

SIR WALTER SCOTT

From *Blackwood's Edinburgh Magazine* (March 1818)[†]

> Did I request thee, Maker, from my clay
> To mould me man? Did I solicit thee
> From darkness to promote me?—
> *Paradise Lost.*

This is a novel, or more properly a romantic fiction, of a nature so peculiar, that we ought to describe the species before attempting any account of the individual production.

The first general division of works of fiction, into such as bound the events they narrate by the actual laws of nature, and such as, passing these limits, are managed by marvellous and supernatural machinery, is sufficiently obvious and decided. But the class of marvellous romances admits of several subdivisions. In the earlier productions of imagination, the poet, or tale-teller does not, in his own opinion, transgress the laws of credibility, when he introduces into his narration the witches, goblins, and magicians, in the existence of which he himself, as well as his hearers, is a firm believer. This good faith, however, passes away, and works turning upon the marvellous are written and read merely on account of the exercise which they afford to the imagination of those who, like the poet Collins, love to riot in the luxuriance of oriental fiction, to rove through the meanders of enchantment, to gaze on the magnificence of golden palaces, and to repose by the water-falls of Elysian gardens. In this species of composition, the marvellous is itself the principal and most important object both to the author and reader.

† Vol. ii, no. xii (March 1818), 613–20.

To describe its effect upon the mind of the human personages engaged in its wonders, and dragged along by its machinery, is comparatively an inferior object. The hero and heroine, partakers of the supernatural character which belongs to their adventures, walk the maze of enchantment with a firm and undaunted step, and appear as much at their case, amid the wonders around them, as the young fellow described by the Spectator, who was discovered taking a snuff with great composure in the midst of a stormy ocean, represented on the stage of the Opera.

A more philosophical and refined use of the supernatural in works of fiction, is proper to that class in which the laws of nature are represented as altered, not for the purpose of pampering the imagination with wonders, but in order to shew the probable effect which the supposed miracles would produce on those who witnessed them. In this case, the pleasure ordinarily derived from the marvellous incidents is secondary to that which we extract from observing how mortals like ourselves would be affected.

By scenes like these which, daring to depart
From sober truth, are still to nature true.

Even in the description of his marvels, however, the author who manages this stile of composition with address, gives them an indirect importance with the reader, when he is able to describe with nature, and with truth, the effects which they are calculated to produce upon his dramatis personæ. It will be remembered, that the sapient Partridge was too wise to be terrified at the mere appearance of the ghost of Hamlet, whom he knew to be a man dressed up in pasteboard armour for the nonce—it was when he saw the "little man," as he called Garrick, so frightened, that a sympathetic horror took hold of him. Of this we shall presently produce some examples from the narrative before us. But success in this point is still subordinate to the author's principal object, which is less to produce an effect by means of the marvels of the narrations, than to open new trains and channels of thought, by placing men in supposed situations of an extraordinary and preternatural character, and then describing the mode of feeling and conduct which they are most likely to adopt.

To make more clear the distinction we have endeavoured to draw between the marvellous and the effects of the marvellous, considered as separate objects, we may briefly invite our readers to compare the common tale of Tom Thumb with Gulliver's Voyage to Brobdingnag; one of the most childish fictions, with one which is pregnant with wit and satire, yet both turning upon the same assumed possibility of the existence of a pigmy among a race of giants. In the former case, when the imagination of the story-teller has exhausted itself in every species of hyperbole, in order to describe the diminutive size of his hero, the interest of the tale is at an end; but in the romance of the Dean of St Patrick's, the exquisite humour with which the natural consequences of so strange and unusual a situation is detailed, has a canvass on which to expand itself, as broad as the luxuriance even of the author's talents could desire. Gulliver stuck into a marrow bone, and Master Thomas Thumb's disastrous fall into the bowl of hasty-pudding, are, in the general outline, kindred incidents; but the jest is exhausted in the latter case, when the accident is told; whereas in the former, it lies not so much in the comparatively pigmy size which subjected Gulliver to such a ludicrous misfortune, as in the tone of grave and dignified feeling with which he resents the disgrace of the incident.

In the class of fictitious narrations to which we allude, the author opens a sort of account-current with the reader; drawing upon him, in the first place, for credit to that degree of the marvellous which he proposes to employ; and becoming virtually bound, in consequence of this indulgence, that his personages shall conduct themselves, in the extraordinary circumstances in which they are placed, according to the rules of probability, and the nature of the human heart. In this view, the *probable* is far from being laid out of sight even amid the wildest freaks of imagination; on the contrary, we grant the extraordinary postulates which the author demands as the foundation of his narrative, only on condition of his deducing the consequences with logical precison.

We have only to add, that this class of fiction has been sometimes applied to the purposes of political satire, and sometimes to the general illustration of the powers and workings of the human mind. Swift, Bergerac, and others, have employed it for the former purpose, and a good illustration of the latter is the well known Saint Leon of William Godwin. In this latter work, assuming the possibility of the transmutation of metals, and of the *elixir vita*, the author has deduced, in the course of his narrative, the probable consequences of the possession of such secrets upon the fortunes and mind of him who might enjoy them. Frankenstein is a novel upon the same plan with Saint Leon; it is said to be written by Mr Percy Bysshe Shelley, who, if we are rightly informed, is son-in-law to Mr Godwin; and it is inscribed to that ingenious author.

In the preface, the author lays claim to rank his work among the class which we have endeavoured to describe.

> The event on which this fiction is founded has been supposed by Dr Darwin, and some of the physiological writers of Germany, as not of impossible occurrence. I shall not be supposed as according the remotest degree of serious faith to such

an imagination; yet, in assuming it as the basis of a work of fancy, I have not considered myself as merely weaving a series of supernatural terrors. The event on which the interest of the story depends is exempt from the disadvantages of a mere tale of spectres or enchantment. It was recommended by the novelty of the situations which it developes; and, however impossible as a physical fact, affords a point of view to the imagination for the delineating of human passions more comprehensive and commanding than any which the ordinary relations of existing events can yield.

I have thus endeavored to preserve the truth of the elementary principles of human nature, while I have not scrupled to innovate upon their combinations. The *Iliad*, the tragic poetry of Greece,—Shakespeare, in the *Tempest* and *Midsummer Night's Dream*,—and most especially Milton, in *Paradise Lost*, conform to this rule; and the most humble novellist, who seeks to confer or receive amusement from his labours, may, without presumption, apply to prose fiction a license, or rather a rule, from the adoption of which so many exquisite combinations of human feeling have resulted in the highest specimens of poetry.

We shall, without farther preface, detail the particulars of the singular story, which is thus introduced.

A vessel, engaged in a voyage of discovery to the North Pole, having become embayed among the ice at a very high latitude, the crew, and particularly the captain or owner of the ship, are surprised at perceiving a gigantic form pass at some distance from them, on a car drawn by dogs, in a place where they conceived no mortal could exist. While they are speculating on this singular apparition, a thaw commences, and disengages them from their precarious situation. On the next morning they pick up, upon a floating fragment of the broken ice, a sledge like that they had before seen, with a human being in the act of perishing. He is with difficulty recalled to life, and proves to be a young man of the most amiable manners and extended acquirements, but, extenuated by fatigue, wrapped in dejection and gloom of the darkest kind. The captain of the ship, a gentleman whose ardent love of science had engaged him on an expedition so dangerous, becomes attached to the stranger, and at length extorts from him the wonderful tale of his misery, which he thus attains the means of preserving from oblivion.

Frankenstein describes himself as a native of Geneva, born and bred up in the bosom of domestic love and affection. His father—his friend Henry Clerval—Elizabeth, an orphan of extreme beauty and talent, bred up in the same house with him, are possessed of all the qualifications which could render him happy as a son, a friend, and a lover. In the course of his studies he becomes acquainted with the works of Cornelius Agrippa, and other authors treating of occult philosophy, on whose venerable tomes modern neglect has scattered no slight portion of dust. Frankenstein remains ignorant of the contempt in which his favourites are held, until he is separated from his family to pursue his studies at the university of Ingolstadt. Here he is introduced to the wonders of modern chemistry, as well as of natural philosophy in all its branches. Prosecuting these sciences into their innermost and most abstruse recesses, with unusual talent and unexampled success, he at length makes that discovery on which the marvellous part of the work is grounded. His attention had been especially bound to the structure of the human frame and of the principle of life. He engaged in physiological researches of the most recondite and abstruse nature, searching among charnel vaults and in dissection rooms, and the objects most insupportable to the delicacy of human feelings, in order to trace the minute chain of causation which takes place in the change from life to death, and from death to life. In the midst of this darkness a light broke in upon him.

"Remember," says his narrative, "I am not recording the vision of a madman. The sun does not more certainly shine in the heavens than that which I now affirm is true. Some miracle might have produced it, yet the stages of the discovery were distinct and probable. After days and nights of incredible labour and fatigue, I succeeded in discovering the cause of generation and life; nay, more, I became myself capable of bestowing animation upon lifeless matter."

This wonderful discovery impelled Frankenstein to avail himself of his art by the creation (if we dare to call it so), or formation of a living and sentient being. As the minuteness of the parts formed a great difficulty, he constructed the figure which he proposed to animate of a gigantic size, that is, about eight feet high, and strong and large in proportion. The feverish anxiety with which the young philosopher toils through the horrors of his secret task, now dabbling among the unhallowed reliques of the grave, and now torturing the living animal to animate the lifeless clay, are described generally, but with great vigour of language. Although supported by the hope of producing a new species that should bless him as his creator and source, he nearly sinks under the protracted labour, and loathsome details, of the work he had undertaken, and scarcely is his fatal enthusiasm sufficient to support his nerves, or animate his resolution. The result of this extraordinary discovery it would be unjust to give in any words save those of the author. We shall give it at length as an excellent specimen of the style and manner of the work.

It was on a dreary night of November that I beheld the accomplishment of my toils. With an anxiety that almost amounted to agony, I collected the instruments of life around me, that I might infuse a spark of being into the lifeless thing that lay at my feet. It was already one in the morning; the rain pattered dismally against the panes, and my candle was nearly burnt out, when, by the glimmer of the half-extinguished light, I saw the dull yellow eye of the creature open; it breathed hard, and a convulsive motion agitated its limbs.

How can I describe my emotions at this catastrophe, or how delineate the wretch whom with such infinite pains and care I had endeavoured to form? His limbs were in proportion, and I had selected his features as beautiful. Beautiful!—Great God! His yellow skin scarcely covered the work of muscles and arteries beneath; his hair was of a lustrous black, and flowing; his teeth of a pearly whiteness; but these luxuriances only formed a more horrid contrast with his watery eyes, that seemed almost of the same colour as the dun white sockets in which they were set—his shrivelled complexion, and straight black lips.

The different accidents of life are not so changeable as the feelings of human nature. I had worked hard for nearly two years, for the sole purpose of infusing life into an inanimate body. For this I had deprived myself of rest and health. I had desired it with an ardour that far exceeded moderation; but now that I had finished, the beauty of the dream vanished, and breathless horror and disgust filled my heart. Unable to endure the aspect of the being I had created, I rushed out of the room, and continued a long time traversing my bed-chamber, unable to compose my mind to sleep. At length lassitude succeeded to the tumult I had before endured; and I threw myself on the bed in my clothes, endeavouring to seek a few moments of forgetfulness. But it was in vain; I slept indeed, but I was disturbed by the wildest dreams. I thought I saw Elizabeth, in the bloom of health, walking in the streets of Ingolstadt. Delighted and surprised, I embraced her; but as I imprinted the first kiss on her lips, they became livid with the hue of death; her features appeared to change, and I thought that I held the corpse of my dead mother in my arms; a shroud enveloped her form, and I saw the grave-worms crawling in the folds of the flannel. I started from my sleep with horror; a cold dew covered my forehead, my teeth chattered, and every limb became convulsed; when, by the dim and yellow light of the moon, as it forced its way through the window-shutters, I beheld the wretch—the miserable monster whom I had created. He held up the curtain of the bed; and his eyes, if eyes they may be called, were fixed on me. His jaws opened, and he muttered some inarticulate sounds, while a grin wrinkled his cheeks. He might have spoken, but I did not hear; one hand was stretched out, seemingly to detain me, but I escaped, and rushed down stairs. I took refuge in the court-yard belonging to the house which I inhabited; where I remained during the rest of the night, walking up and down in the greatest agitation, listening attentively, catching and fearing each sound as if it were to announce the approach of the demoniacal corpse to which I had so miserably given life. Oh! no mortal could support the horror of that countenance. A mummy again endued with animation could not be so hideous as that wretch. I had gazed on him while unfinished; he was ugly then; but when those muscles and joints were rendered capable of motion, it became a thing such as even Dante could not have conceived.

I passed the night wretchedly. Sometimes my pulse beat so quickly and hardly, that I felt the palpitation of every artery; at others. I nearly sank to the ground through languor and extreme weakness. Mingled with this horror, I felt the bitterness of disappointment; dreams, that had been my food and pleasant rest for so long a space, were now become a hell to me; and the change was so rapid, the overthrow so complete!

Morning, dismal and wet, at length dawned, and discovered, to my sleepless and aching eyes, the church of Ingolstadt, its white steeple and clock, which indicated the sixth hour. The porter opened the gates of the court, which had that night been my asylum, and I issued into the streets, pacing them with quick steps, as if I sought to avoid the wretch whom I feared every turning of the street would present to my view. I did not dare return to the apartment which I inhabited, but felt impelled to hurry on, although wetted by the rain, which poured from a black and comfortless sky.

I continued walking in this manner for some time, endeavouring, by bodily exercise, to ease the load that weighed upon my mind. I traversed the streets without any clear conception of where I was or what I was doing. My heart palpitated in the sickness of fear; and I hurried on with irregular steps, not daring to look about me:

> Like one who, on a lonely road,
>   Doth walk in fear and dread,
> And, having once turn'd round, walks on,
>   And turns no more his head;
> Because he knows a frightful fiend
>   Doth close behind him tread.[1]

He is relieved by the arrival of the diligence from Geneva, out of which jumps his friend Henry Clerval, who had come to spend a season at the college. Compelled to carry Clerval to his lodgings, which, he supposed, must still contain the prodigious and hideous specimen of his Promethean art, his feelings are again admirably

---

1. Coleridge's "Ancient Mariner."

described, allowing always for the extraordinary cause supposed to give them birth.

I trembled excessively; I could not endure to think of, and far less to allude to, the occurrences of the preceding night. I walked with a quick pace, and we soon arrived at my college. I then reflected, and the thought made me shiver, that the creature whom I had left in my apartment might still be there, alive, and walking about. I dreaded to behold this monster; but I feared still more that Henry should see him. Entreating him therefore to remain a few minutes at the bottom of the stairs, I darted up towards my own room. My hand was already on the lock of the door before I recollected myself. I then paused; and a cold hovering came over me. I threw the door forcibly open, as children are accustomed to do when they expect a spectre to stand in waiting for them on the other side; but nothing appeared. I stepped fearfully in the apartment was empty; and my bed-room was also freed from its hideous guest. I could hardly believe that so great a good fortune could have befallen me; but when I became assured that my enemy had indeed fled, I clapped my hands for joy, and ran down to Clervair.

The animated monster is heard of no more for a season. Frankenstein pays the penalty of his rash researches into the *arcana* of human nature, in a long illness, after which the two friends prosecute their studies for two years in uninterrupted quiet. Frankenstein, as may be supposed, abstaining, with a sort of abhorrence, from those in which he had once so greatly delighted. At the lapse of this period, he is made acquainted with a dreadful misfortune which has befallen his family, by the violent death of his youngest brother, an interesting child, who, while straying from his keeper, had been murdered by some villain in the walks of Plainpalais. The marks of strangling were distinct on the neck of the unfortunate infant, and a gold ornament which it wore, and which was amissing, was supposed to have been the murderer's motive for perpetrating the crime. At this dismal intelligence Frankenstein flies to Geneva, and impelled by fraternal affection, visits the spot where this horrid accident had happened. In the midst of a thunder-storm, with which the evening had closed, and just as he had attained the fatal spot on which Victor had been murdered, a flash of lightning displays to him the hideous demon to which he had given life, gliding towards a neighbouring precipice. Another flash shows him hanging among the cliffs, up which he scrambles with far more than mortal agility, and is seen no more. The inference, that this being was the murderer of his brother, flashed on Frankenstein's mind as irresistibly as the lightning itself, and he was tempted to consider the creature whom he had cast among mankind to work, it would seem, acts of horror and depravity, nearly in the light of his own vampire let loose from the grave, and destined to destroy all that was dear to him. Frankenstein was right in his apprehensions. Justine, the maid to whom the youthful Victor had been intrusted, is found to be in possession of the golden trinket which had been taken from the child's person; and by a variety of combining circumstances of combined evidence, she is concluded to be the murtheress, and, as such, condemned to death and executed. It does not appear that Frankenstein attempted to avert her fate, by communicating his horrible secret; but, indeed, who would have given him credit, or in what manner could he have supported his tale?

In a solitary expedition to the top of Mount Aveyron, undertaken to dispel the melancholy which clouded his mind, Frankenstein unexpectedly meets with the monster he had animated, who compels him to a conference and a parley. The material demon gives an account, at great length, of his history since his animation, of the mode in which he acquired various points of knowledge, and of the disasters which befell him, when, full of benevolence and philanthropy, he endeavoured to introduce himself into human society. The most material part of his education was acquired in a ruinous pig-stye—a Lyceum which this strange student occupied, he assures us, for a good many months undiscovered, and in constant observance of the motions of an amiable family, from imitating whom he learns the use of language, and other accomplishments, much more successfully than Caliban, though the latter had a conjuror to his tutor. This detail is not only highly improbable, but it is injudicious as its unnecessary minuteness tends rather too much to familiarize us with the being whom it regards, and who loses, by this *lengthy* oration, some part of the mysterious sublimity annexed to his first appearance. The result is, this monster, who was at first, according to his own account, but a harmless monster, becomes ferocious and malignant, in consequence of finding all his approaches to human society repelled with injurious violence and offensive marks of disgust. Some papers concealed in his dress acquainted him with the circumstances and person to whom he owed his origin; and the hate which he felt towards the whole human race was now concentrated in resentment against Frankenstein. In this humour he murdered the child, and disposed the picture so as to induce a belief of Justine's guilt. The last is an inartificial circumstance: this indirect mode of mischief was not likely to occur to the being the narrative presents to us. The conclusion of this strange narrative is a peremptory demand on the part of the demon, as he is usually termed, that Frankenstein should renew his fearful experiment, and create for him an helpmate hideous as himself, who should have no pretence for shunning his society. On this condition he promises to withdraw to some distant desert, and shun the human race for ever. If his creator shall refuse him this consolation, he vows the prosecution of the most frightful vengeance. Frankenstein, after a long pause of reflection, imagines he sees that the justice due to the miserable being, as well as to mankind, who might be exposed to so much misery, from the power and evil dispositions of a creature who could climb perpendicular cliffs and exist among glaciers, demanded that he should comply with the request; and granted his promise accordingly.

Frankenstein retreats to one of the distant islands of the Orcades, that in secrecy and solitude he might resume his detestable and ill-omened labours, which now were doubly hideous, since he was deprived of the enthusiasm with which he formerly prosecuted them. As he is sitting one night in his laboratory, and recollecting the consequences of his first essay in the Promethean art, he begins to hesitate concerning the right he had to form another being as malignant and blood-thirsty as that he had unfortunately already animated. It is evident that he would thereby give the demon the means of propagating a hideous race, superior to mankind in strength and hardihood, who might render the very existence of the present human race a condition precarious and full of terror. Just as these reflections lead him to the conclusion that his promise was criminal, and ought not to be kept, he looks up, and sees, by the light of the moon, the demon at the casement.

> A ghastly grin wrinkled his lips as he gazed on me, where I sat fulfilling the task which he allotted to me. Yes, he had followed me in my travels; he had loitered in forests, hid himself in caves, or taken refuge in wide and desert heaths; and he now came to mark my progress, and claim the fulfilment of my promise.
>
> As I looked on him, his countenance expressed the utmost extent of malice and treachery. I thought with a sensation of madness on my promise of creating another like to him, and, trembling with passion, tore to pieces the thing on which I was engaged. The wretch saw me destroy the creature on whose future existence he depended for happiness, and, with a howl of devilish despair and revenge, withdrew.

At a subsequent interview, described with the same wild energy, all treaty is broken off betwixt Frankenstein and the work of his hands, and they part on terms of open and declared hatred and defiance. Our limits do not allow us to trace in detail the progress of the demon's vengeance. Clerval falls its first victim, and under circumstances which had very nearly conducted the new Prometheus to the gallows as his supposed murderer. Elizabeth, his bride, is next strangled on her wedding-night; his father dies of grief; and at length

Frankenstein, driven to despair and distraction, sees nothing left for him in life but vengeance on the singular cause of his misery. With this purpose he pursues the monster from clime to clime, receiving only such intimations of his being on the right scent, as served to shew that the demon delighted in thus protracting his fury and his sufferings. At length, after the flight and pursuit had terminated among the frost-fogs, and icy islands of the northern ocean, and just when he had a glimpse of his adversary, the ground sea was heard, the ice gave way, and Frankenstein was placed in the perilous situation in which he is first introduced to the reader.

Exhausted by his sufferings, but still breathing vengeance against the being which was at once his creature and his persecutor, this unhappy victim to physiological discovery expires just as the clearing away of the ice permits Captain Walton's vessel to hoist sail for their return to Britain. At midnight, the dæmon, who had been his destroyer, is discovered in the cabin, lamenting over the corpse of the person who gave him being. To Walton he attempts to justify his resentment towards the human race, while, at the same time, he acknowledges himself a wretch who had murdered the lovely and the helpless, and pursued to irremediable ruin his creator, the select specimen of all that was worthy of love and admiration.

"Fear not," he continues, addressing the astonished Walton, "that I shall be the instrument of future mischief. My work is nearly complete. Neither yours nor any man's death is needed to consummate the series of my being, and accomplish that which must be done; but it requires my own. Do not think that I shall be slow to perform this sacrifice. I shall quit your vessel on the ice-raft which brought me hither, and shall seek the most northern extremity of the globe I shall collect my funeral pile, and consume to ashes this miserable frame, that its remains may afford no light to any curious and unhallowed wretch, who would create such another as I have been.———"

He sprung from the cabin-window, as he said this, upon the ice-raft which lay close to the vessel. He was soon borne away by the waves, and lost in darkness and distance.

Whether this singular being executed his purpose or no must necessarily remain an uncertainty, unless the voyage of discovery to the north pole should throw any light on the subject.

So concludes this extraordinary tale, in which the author seems to us to disclose uncommon powers of poetic imagination. The feeling with which we perused the unexpected and fearful, yet, allowing the possibility of the event, very natural conclusion of Frankenstein's experiment, shook a little even our firm nerves; although such and so numerous have been the expedients for exciting terror employed by the romantic writers of the age, that the reader may adopt Macbeth's words with a slight alteration:

"We have supp'd full with horrors:
Direness, familiar to our "callous" thoughts,
Cannot once startle us.

It is no slight merit in our eyes, that the tale, though wild in incident, is written in plain and forcible English, without exhibiting that mixture of hyperbolical Germanisms with which tales of wonder are usually told, as if it were necessary that the language should be as extravagant as the fiction. The ideas of the author are always clearly as well as forcibly expressed; and his descriptions of landscape have in them the choice requisites of truth, freshness, precision, and beauty. The self-education of the monster, considering the slender opportunities of acquiring knowledge that he possessed, we have already noticed as improbable and overstrained. That he should have not only learned to speak, but to read, and, for aught we know, to write— that he should have become acquainted with Werter, with Plutarch's Lives, and with Paradise Lost, by listening through a hole in a wall, seems as unlikely as that he should have acquired, in the same way, the problems of Euclid, or the art of book-keeping by single and double entry. The author has however two apologies—the first, the necessity that his monster should acquire those endowments, and the other, that this neighbours ware engaged in teaching the language of the country to a young foreigner. His progress in self-knowledge, and the acquisition of information, is, after all, more wonderful than that of Hai Eben Yokhdan, or Automathes, or the hero of the little romance called The Child of Nature, one of which works might perhaps suggest the train of ideas followed by the author of Frankenstein. We should also be disposed, in support of the principles with which we set out, to question whether the monster, how tall, agile, and strong however, could have perpetrated so much mischief undiscovered, or passed through so many countries without being secured, either on account of his crimes, or for the benefit of some such speculator us Mr. Polito, who would have been happy to have added to his museum to curious a specimen of natural history. But as we have consented to admit the leading incident of the work, perhaps some of our readers may be of opinion, that to stickle upon lesser improbabilities, is to incur the censure bestowed by the Scottish proverb on those who start at straws after swallowing *windlings*.

The following lines, which occur in the second volume, mark, we think, that the author possesses the same facility in expressing himself in verse as in prose.

We rest; a dream has power to poison sleep.
We rise; one wand'ring thought pollutes the day.
We feel, conceive, or reason; laugh, or weep,
  Embrace fond woe, or cast our cares away;
It is the same: for, be it joy or sorrow,
The path of its departure still is free.
Man's yesterday may ne'er belike his morrow;
Nought may endure but mutability!

Upon the whole, the work impresses us with a high idea of the author's original genius and happy power of expression. We shall be delighted to hear that he has aspired to the *paullo majora*; and in the meantime, congratulate our readers upon a novel which excites new reflections and untried sources of emotion. If Gray's definition of Paradise, to lie on a couch, namely, and read new novels, come any thing near truth, no small praise is due to him, who, like the author of Frankenstein, has enlarged the sphere of that fascinating enjoyment.

EDINBURGH MAGAZINE

[On *Frankenstein*] (March 1818)[†]

Here is one of the productions of the modern school in its highest style of caricature and exaggeration. It is formed on the Godwinian manner, and has all the faults, but many likewise of the beauties of that model. In dark and gloomy views of nature and of man, bordering too closely on impiety,—in the most outrageous improbability,—in sacrificing everything to effect,—it even goes beyond its great prototype; but in return, it possesses a similar power of fascination, something of the same mastery in harsh and savage delineations of passion, relieved in like manner by the gentler features of domestic and simple feelings. There never was a wilder story imagined, yet, like most of the fictions of this age, it has an air of reality attached to it, by being connected with the favourite projects and passions of the times. The real events of the world have, in our day, too, been of so wondrous and gigantic a kind,—the shiftings of the scenes in our stupendous drama have been so rapid and various, that Shakespeare himself, in his wildest flights, has been completely distanced by the eccentricities of actual existence. Even he would scarcely have dared to have raised, in one act, a private adventurer to the greatest of European thrones,—to have conducted him, in the next, victorious

† March 1818: 249–53.

over the necks of emperors and kings, and then, in a third, to have shewn him an exile, in a remote speck of an island, some thousands of miles from the scene of his triumphs; and the chariot which bore him along covered with glory, quietly exhibited to a gaping mechanical rabble under the roof of one of the beautiful buildings on the North Bridge of Edinburgh,—(which buildings we heartily pray may be brought as low as the mighty potentate whose Eagles are now to be seen looking out of their windows, like the fox from the ruins of Balclutha.) Our appetite, we say, for every sort of wonder and vehement interest, has in this way become so desperately inflamed, that especially as the world around us has again settled into its old dull state of happiness and legitimacy, we can be satisfied with nothing in fiction that is not highly coloured and exaggerated; we even like a story the better that it is disjointed and irregular, and our greatest inventors, accordingly, have been obliged to accommodate themselves to the taste of the age, more, we believe, than their own judgment can, at all times, have approved of. The very extravagance of the present production will now, therefore, be, perhaps, in its favour, since the events which have actually passed before our eyes have made the atmosphere of miracles that in which we most readily breathe.

The story opens with a voyage of discovery to the North Pole. A young Englishman, whose mind had long been inflamed with this project, sets sail from Archangel, soon gets inclosed, as usual, among ice mountains, and is beginning to despair of success, when all his interest and thoughts are diverted suddenly into another channel, in consequence of a very singular adventure. One day a gigantic figure was seen moving northwards on a sledge, drawn by dogs, and a short time afterwards a poor emaciated wretch was picked up from a sledge that drifted close to the vessel. The Englishman soon formed a violent friendship for this stranger, and discovers him to be a person of the greatest virtues, talents, and acquirements, which are only rendered the more admirable and interesting, from the deep cloud of melancholy which frequently overshadowed them. After a time, he gets so far into his confidence, as to obtain from him the story of his life and misfortunes. His name was Frankenstein, son of a Syndic of Geneva, and of an amiable mother, who very properly dies at the beginning of the book, to leave her son and a young female cousin, who resided in the family, so disconsolate, that they could find no comfort except by falling in love. Frankenstein had been left much to his own disposal in the conduct of his studies, and, at a very early period, he had become quite *entêté* with some of the writings of the alchemists, on which he accidentally lighted; and we were at first in expectation that, like St Leon, he was to become possessed of the philosopher's stone, or of the *elixir vitae*. He is destined, however, to obtain a still more extraordinary power, but not from the alchemists, of the futility of whose speculations he soon became convinced, but whose wild conceptions continued to give to his mind a strong and peculiar bias. At the university, stimulated by the encouragement of some distinguished philosophers, he applied himself, with the utmost perseverance and ability, to every department of natural science, and soon became the general object of envy and admiration. His researches led him to investigate the principle of life, which he did in the old and approved manner by dissecting living animals, groping into all the repositories of the dead, and making himself acquainted with life and death in all their forms. The result was a most wonderful discovery,—quite simple, he says, when it was made, but yet one which he very wisely does not communicate to his English acquaintance, and which, of course, must remain a secret to the world,—no less than the discovery of the means of communicating life to an organized form. With this our young philosopher sets himself to make a man, and that he might make no blunder from taking too small a scale, unfortunately, as it turns out, his man is a giant. In a garret of his apartments, to which none but himself was ever admitted, he employs four months on this wonderful production. Many of the ingredients seem to have been of a very disgusting description, since he passed whole nights in sepulchres raking them out; he thought, however, that he had succeeded in making a giant, as gainly in appearance at least as O'Brien, or the Yorkshire Boy, and every thing was now ready for the last touch of the master, the infusion of life into the inanimate mass. In breathless expectation, in the dead of night, he performed this last momentous act of creation; and the creature opened upon him two immense ghastly yellow eyes, which struck him with instant horror. He immediately hated himself and his work, and flew, in a state of feverish agony, to his room below; but, finding himself followed thither by the monster, he rushed out into the streets, where he walked about in fearful agitation, till the morning dawned, and they began to be frequented by their inhabitants. Passing along, he saw step from a coach an intimate friend of his from Geneva. For the moment he forgot every thing that had happened, was delighted to find that his friend had come to pursue his studies along with him, and was conducting him to his apartments, when on a sudden he recollected the dreadful inmate who would probably be found in them. He ran up and examined them, and, on finding that the monster had disappeared, his joy became quite foolish and outrageous; he danced about like a madman, and his friend was not surprised when immediately after he was seized by a delirious fever, which confined him for some weeks, alleviated, however, by all the attentions which friendship could bestow.

Scarcely had he recovered, when a sad piece of intelligence arrives from home. His father writes him that his little brother had strayed from them in an evening walk, and was at last found dead, and apparently strangled. He flies home to comfort his family, but it is night ere he reaches Geneva, and the gates being shut, he remains in the neighbourhood, and walks out in the dark towards the hills. The monster on a sudden stalks past him, and moving with inconceivable rapidity, is seen by him perched on one of the highest cliffs. The thought instantly strikes him, that this fiend, the creation of his own hand, must have been the murderer of his brother, and he feels all the bitterness of despair. Very ill able to comfort others, he next morning went to his father's house, and learns, as an additional misery, that a young servant girl, who had been beloved as a friend in the family, was taken up on suspicion of the murder, and was to be tried for her life. A picture, which the child had worn on the fatal night, was found in her pocket. Though, in his own mind, he could not doubt of the real author of the murder, and his beloved Elizabeth was equally convinced that it could not be her favourite Justine, still circumstances were so strong against her, that the poor girl was condemned and executed. No wonder that Frankenstein now fell into a deep melancholy; to relieve him from which, his father took him and Elizabeth on a tour to the valley of Chamounix. This part of the book is very beautifully written; the description of the mountain scenery, and of its effect on Frankenstein's mind, is finely given. One rainy day they did not proceed on their journey, but Frankenstein, in a state of more than common depression, left them early in the inn, for the purpose of scaling the summit of Montarvet.[1]

Frankenstein at first addresses him in words of violent rage,—the monster, however, endeavours to soften him.[2]

The monster now begins his story, and a very amiable personage he makes himself to be. The story is well fancied and told. Immediately on his creation he wandered out into the forest of Ingolstadt, where he remained for some days, till his different senses learnt to perform their appropriate functions, and he discovered the use of fire and various other rudiments of knowledge; and thus accomplished, he ventured forth into the great world. But in the first village that he reached he was hooted and stoned, and was obliged to take shelter in a hovel at the back of a cottage. Through a crevice in the wall, he soon became intimate with all the operations in the cottage, the inhabitants of which were an old blind man, his son and daughter. After the reception he had met with in the village, he kept himself very snug in his hole through the day, but being really a good-natured monster, and finding the young man was much overwrought in cutting fuel for the family, what does he, but betake

1. See pp. 65–66, above. [Editor's note.]
2. See p. 67, above. [Editor's note.]

him to the wood in the night time, and collect quantities of fuel, which he piles up beside the door? The good people think themselves the favourites of some kind spirit or *brownie*. In the mean time, he learns how to apply their language, which he found he could imitate tolerably well. He gradually, too, becomes acquainted with more of their circumstances and feelings; and there was so much affection between the venerable blind man (who moreover played beautifully on a musical instrument) and his children, and they were so loving to each other,—and they were so interesting withal from their poverty, that the worthy monster took a vehement passion for them, and had the greatest inclination to make himself agreeable to them. By close study, and the occurrence of favourable opportunities, he also acquires a knowledge of written language; and one day on his rambles, lighting on a portmanteau, which contained the Sorrows of Werter, a volume of Plutarch, and Milton's Paradise Lost,—he becomes quite an adept in German sentiment, ancient heroism, and Satanic sturdiness. He now thought himself qualified to make himself acquainted with the family,—though aware of his hideous appearance, he very wisely began with the blind gentleman, on whom he ventured to make a call when the rest of the family were out of doors. He had just begun to interest the old man in his favour, when their *tête-a-tête* is unluckily interrupted, and the poor monster is abused and maltreated as heretofore by the villagers. He flies to the woods, furious with rage, and disappointed affection; and, finding on his return that the cottagers had forsaken the place, scared by his portentous visit, he amuses himself in his rage with setting it on fire, and then sets out in search of his creator. Other circumstances occur in his journey to give him a greater antipathy to the human race. He confesses the murder of the boy, whom, lighting upon, he wished to carry off, in the hope that he might find in him an object to attach himself to;—the murder was partly accidental,—but the slipping the picture into Justine's pocket was a piece of devilish malice. He concludes with denouncing vengeance against Frankenstein and all his race, if he does not agree to one request, to create a female companion for him like himself, with whom he proposes to retire to the wilds of North America, and never again to come into contact with man.

It is needless to go minutely through the remainder of this wild fiction. After some demurring, Frankenstein at last accedes to the demand, and, begins a second time the abhorred creation of a human being,—but again repents, and defies the demon; who thenceforth recommences his diabolical warfare against the unhappy philosopher,—destroys his friends and relations one by one, and finally murders his beloved Elizabeth, on the very evening of their marriage. Frankenstein, alive only to vengeance, now pursues the fiend over the world,—and it was in this chace that he had got into the neighbourhood of the North Pole, where he was but a little way behind him, but had quite spent himself in the pursuit. So ends the narrative of Frankenstein, and worn out nature soon after yields to the bitterness of his thoughts and his exhausted frame. He dies, and, to the astonishment of our Englishman and the crew, the monster makes his appearance,—laments the fate of his creator,—says that his feelings of vengeance are for ever at an end,—departs, and is heard of no more.

Such is a sketch of this singular performance, in which there is much power and beauty, both of thought and expression, though, in many parts, the execution is imperfect, and bearing the marks of an unpractised hand. It is one of those works, however, which, when we have read, we do not well see why it should have been written;—for a *jeu d'esprit* it is somewhat too long, grave, and laborious,—and some of our highest and most reverential feelings receive a shock from the conception on which it turns, so as to produce a painful and bewildered state of mind while we peruse it. We are accustomed, happily, to look upon the creation of a living and intelligent being as a work that is fitted only to inspire a religious emotion, and there is an impropriety, to say no worse, in placing it in any other light. It might, indeed, be the author's view to shew that the powers of man have been wisely limited, and that misery would follow their extension,—but still the expression "Creator," applied to a mere human being, gives us the same sort of shock with the phrase, "the Man Almighty," and others of the same kind, in Mr Southey's "Curse of Kehama." All these monstrous conceptions are the consequences of the wild and irregular theories of the age; though we do not at all mean to infer that the authors who give into such freedoms have done so with any bad intentions. This incongruity, however, with our established and most sacred notions, is the chief fault in such fictions, regarding them merely in a critical point of view. Shakespeare's Caliban (though his simplicity and suitableness to the place where he is found are very delightful) is, perhaps, a more *hateful* being than our good friend in this book. But Caliban comes into existence in the received way which common superstition had pointed out; we should not have endured him if Prospero had created him. Getting over this original absurdity, the character of our monster is in good keeping;—there is a grandeur, too, in the scenery in which he makes his appearances,—the ice-mountains of the Pole, or the glaciers of the Alps;—his natural tendency to kind feelings, and the manner in which they were blighted,—and all the domestic picture of the cottage, are very interesting and beautiful. We hope yet to have more productions, both from this author and his great model, Mr Godwin; but they would make a great improvement in their writings, if they would rather study the established order of nature as it appears, both in the world of matter and of mind, than continue to revolt our feelings by hazardous innovations in either of these departments.

GENTLEMAN'S MAGAZINE

[On *Frankenstein*] (April 1818)†

This Tale [*Frankenstein*] is evidently the production of no ordinary Writer; and, though we are shocked at the idea of the event on which the fiction is founded, many parts of it are strikingly good, and the description of the scenery is excellent.

In the pride of Science, the Hero of the Tale presumes to take upon himself the structure of a human being; in which, though he in some degree is supposed to have succeeded, he forfeits every comfort of life, and finally even life itself.

"The event," we are told, "has been supposed, by Dr. Darwin, and some of the physiological writers of Germany, as not of impossible occurrence. I shall not be supposed as according the remotest degree of serious faith to such an imagination; yet, in assuming it as the basis of a work of fancy, I have not considered myself as merely weaving a series of supernatural terrors. The event on which the interest of the story depends is exempt from the disadvantages of a mere tale of spectres or enchantment. It was recommended by the novelty of the situations which it developes; and, however impossible as a physical fact, affords a point of view to the imagination for the delineating of human passions more comprehensive and commanding than any which the ordinary relations of existing events can yield.—The story was begun in the majestic region where the scene is principally laid, and in society which cannot cease to be regretted. I passed the summer of 1816 in the environs of Geneva. The season was cold and rainy, and in the evenings we crowded around a blazing wood fire, and occasionally amused ourselves with some German stories of ghosts, which happened to fall into our hands. These tales excited in us a playful desire of imitation. Two other friends (a tale from the pen of one of whom would be far more acceptable to the publick than any thing I can ever hope to produce) and myself agreed to write each a story, founded on some supernatural occurrence. The weather, however, suddenly became serene; and my two friends left me on a journey among the Alps, and lost, in the magnificent scenes which they present, all

† April 1818: 334–35.

memory of their ghostly visions. The following tale is the only one which has been completed."

If we mistake not, this friend was a Noble Poet.

KNIGHT'S QUARTERLY

[On *Frankenstein*] (August–November 1824)[†]

I do not think I ever was so much disappointed in any book as in Valperga;[1] I had the very highest expectations of the maturing of the genius which could produce such a work as Frankenstein. The faults of Frankenstein were occasional extravagance and *over-writing*;—it was, therefore, natural to suppose that the interval of between four and five years would correct this, without impairing its freshness, force, and vigour. But in Valperga there is not the slightest trace of the same hand—instead of the rapidity and enthusiastic energy which hurries you forward in Frankenstein, every thing is cold, crude, inconsecutive, and wearisome;—not one flash of imagination, not one spark of passion—opening it as I did, with eager expectation, it must indeed have been bad for me after toiling a week to send the book back without having finished the first volume. This induced me to read Frankenstein again—for I thought I must have been strangely mistaken in my original judgment. So far, however, from this, a second reading has confirmed it. I think Frankenstein possesses extreme power, and displays *capabilities* such as I did hope would have produced far different things from Castruccio.

* * *

Frankenstein is, I think, the best instance of natural passions applied to supernatural events that I ever met with. Grant that it is possible for one man to create another, and the rest is perfectly natural and in course. I do not allude to the incidents, for they are thrown together with a haste and carelessness so apparent as to be almost confessed; but the sentiments—both of thought and passion—are given with a truth which is equal to their extraordinary vigour. I am surprised to see by the preface that Dr. Darwin, and some of the physiological writers of Germany supposed the creation of a human being "as not of impossible occurrence." I can understand that it might be possible to put together a human frame—though with the very greatest

† 3 (Aug.–Nov. 1824): 195–99.
1. A later (1823) historical novel by Mary Shelley.

difficulty—both from the intricacy and minuteness of the conformation, the most trifling error in which would be fatal, and from the
difficulty of preventing putrescence during the process, without dry-
ing up the form like a mummy, which would incapacitate it from all
purposes of *life*. But, granting that a frame could be so constructed,
I cannot conceive how Dr. Darwin, who, however over-rated by
his friends, was certainly a man of considerable powers of mind, I
cannot conceive, I say, how he could contemplate the possibility of
infusing the principle of life, when of such principle we are wholly
ignorant. Many attempts have been made to say where life dwells—to
prove that such or such a part is infallibly vital; but whoever could
say what life itself was? This is one of the most strange of those mysteries which are hidden from human reason. The simplest operations
of nature are, in their cause and process, equally inscrutable;—the
whole progress and vegetation from the seed rotting in the earth, to
the shoot, the sapling, the tree, the blossom, the fruit—is as utterly
inscrutable by man as are the causes of his own production and
existence.

The most unskilful thing in the book is the extreme ugliness of the
being whom Frankenstein creates. It is not natural, that to save himself additional trouble from the minuteness of the parts, he should
create a giant. He must have known the vast danger of forming one
of such bodily power, whose mind it would take a considerable time
to mould into humanity. Besides, though it is highly natural that the
features which had been chosen individually as perfect, and which
appeared so even when conjoined in the lifeless figure, should, on
their being vivified, have an incongruous and unearthly aspect; yet,
it is not at all probable, that one with Frankenstein's science should
have formed a creature of such "appalling hideousness." It is utterly
inconceivable also, that he should have let the monster (as he is
somewhat unfairly called) escape;—one of the thoughts which must,
one would imagine, have been uppermost in his mind during his
labours, would have been the instructing his creature intellectually
as he had formed him physically.

In the account which the creature gives of his instruction by
means of watching the polished cottagers, the hastiness of the composition is the most apparent. Indeed, nothing would require such
extreme trouble and carefulness as a correct representation of the
mind of one who had (from whatever circumstances) reached maturity without any acquired knowledge. Those things which, from having been known to us before the period to which our remembrances
reach, appear to be part of our innate consciousness, would be perfect novelty to such a being. Not only speech would be non-existent
but even sight would be imperfect in him. In short, it would require

much thought and some physical knowledge, joined (as I before said) to the greatest care, to render such a description at once full and accurate. In Frankenstein what there is of it is sufficiently interesting in itself, but it suggests so frequently how much more it might be wrought out, that it brings strongly into view its own imperfectness.

For my own part, I confess that *my* interest in the book is entirely on the side of the monster. His eloquence and persuasion, of which Frankenstein complains, are so because they are truth. The justice is indisputably on his side, and his sufferings are, to me, touching to the last degree. Are there are any sufferings, indeed, so severe as those which arise from the sensation of dereliction, or, (as in this case) of isolation? Even the slightest tinge of those feelings, arising as they often do from trivial circumstances, as from passing a solitary evening in a lone and distant situation—even these, are bitter to a severe degree. What it must be, then,—what *is* it to feel oneself *alone in the world!* Fellow-feeling is the deepest of all the needs which Nature has implanted within us. The impulses which lead us to the physical preservation of our life are scarcely stronger than those which impel us to communion with our fellows. Alas! then to have no fellows!—to be, with feelings of kindliness and beneficence, the object of scorn and hate to every one whose eyes lighted on us!—to be repaid with blows and wounds for the very benefits we confer!—The poor monster always, for these reasons, touched me to the heart. Frankenstein ought to have reflected on the means of giving happiness to the being of his creation, before he *did* create him. Instead of that, he heaps on him all sorts of abuse and contumely for his *ugliness*, which was directly *his* work, and for his crimes to which his neglect gave rise.

But whence arises the extreme inferiority of Valperga? I can account for it only by supposing that Shelley wrote the first, though it was attributed to his wife,—and that she really wrote the last. Still I should not, from internal evidence, suppose Frankenstein to be the work of Shelley. It has much of his poetry and vigour—but it is wholly free from those philosophical opinions from which scarcely any of his works *are* free, and for which there are many fair openings in Frankenstein. It is equally to be observed that there are no religious reflections—and that there are many circumstances in which a mind at all religiously inclined would not have failed to have expressed some sentiments of that nature. It may be, that Mrs. Shelley wrote Frankenstein—but, knowing that its fault was extravagance, determined to be careful and correct in her next work; and, thence, as so many do from the same cause, became cold and common-place. At all events, the difference of the two books is very remarkable.

HUGH REGINALD HAWEIS

Introduction to the Routledge
World Library Edition (1886)

I issue "Frankenstein" with some degree of hesitation, but after mature reflection. The subject is somewhat revolting, the treatment of it somewhat hideous. The conception is powerful, but the execution very unequal. The *mise-en-scène* of this appalling story is admirable. It ranges from the ice drifts in Polar seas to Alpine valleys and the steppes of Asia; but the local outlines are sharp, the colouring is faithful.

It is in her natural descriptions, as well as her subtle analysis of moods, that Mrs. Shelley proves herself to be an imaginative writer of no mean order.

It is in her construction and plot that she is weak.

The manufacturer of the human monster, since no mortal could say how such a thing should be done, is slurred over in a few hasty but ghastly paragraphs.

When this nameless demon stalks forth and is shunned by his terrified creator, what becomes of him, how he develops, why he is let go free, is not sufficiently made clear.

When the figure begins to talk, all the show of probability at once vanishes, more completely than in "Gulliver's Travels" or the "Arabian Nights' Entertainments."

The general conception of a creature created non-natural by the appliance of art and science, and impelled into crime after crime simply by a despairing contest with a world into which he should never have been introduced at all, is certainly powerful; but the tale of horror is unrelieved by any real poetical justice, and the moral threat—if there is any—is vague and indeterminate.

Still "Frankenstein" retains its popularity as the first of a class of fiction—not of a very high order—to which the genius of Edgar Allan Poe has given an importance somewhat out of proportion to its merits.

The handling of horrors, like the practice of anatomy and vivisection, can only be justified by the supposed benefits conferred.

In the case of anatomy those benefits are physical, in the case of action they are moral. In cases where neither physical nor moral interests are furthered, many people think that such things had best be left alone.

"Frankenstein," with all its undoubted power, with its exquisite descriptions, its subtle analysis of feeling, its continual attempts at a moral, falls short of a *chef d-oeuvre* for want of workmanship and constructive power, or those qualities which reconcile us to the horrors of Poe's "M. Valdemar" and the ghastly solution of the "Murders in the Rue Morgue."

Still the reader will begin "Frankenstein" excited by the leading idea, and he will read it to the end, not only on account of its accumulation of horrors, but for the sake of its fine and varied scenes—I had almost said atmospheric effects—and its deep insight into the natural workings of the human heart.

* * *

The actual occasion which gave rise to "Frankenstein" was this. One day Shelley and his wife, Lord Byron and Polidori, had been talking together, apparently about ghosts, when Lord Byron, before they separated, exclaimed, "We will each write a ghost story!" Although Lord Byron's "Vampire" remains an uncouth fragment of no great merit in prose, neither Shelley's nor Polidori's compositions seem to have come to anything; but Mrs. Shelley, who had always been what she calls a "scribbler" from her early girlhood, was more tenacious of the project, and urged on by both Shelley and Byron, she at last completed the ghastly and powerful narrative which, in spite of its technical imperfections, is certainly worth preserving, and will be undoubtedly read through by everyone who gets as far as the second letter. In that letter "so strange an accident happens," that a curiosity is then and there excited which is not finally satisfied until the horrid figure which haunts the remaining pages finally springs through the window of the ship's cabin "upon the ice-raft which lay close to the vessel, and is soon borne away by the waves and lost in darkness and distance."

CHRIS BALDICK

[The Reception of *Frankenstein*]†

The reception of literary works is no straightforward matter of 'the reader' either consuming or producing the text's meanings, but a struggle which takes place among and between *different* readers who are already disposed in various camps, constituencies, and cultural factions, as *Frankenstein*'s early reception shows quite clearly. The novel did not appear under Mary Shelley's own name until the second edition of 1823, so the only clue which readers had in 1818 about the anonymous author lay in the dedication to William

† From *In* Frankenstein's *Shadow: Myth, Monstrosity, and Nineteenth-Century Writing* (New York: Oxford UP, 1987), 56–62. Reprinted by permission.

Godwin. This was quite enough for the Tory *Quarterly Review* to damn it, while others were put on their guard against *Frankenstein*'s possibly subversive and atheistic content. William Beckford, a pioneer of the Gothic novel in England, recoiled in disgust from this latest of his offspring, writing in the flyleaf of his copy: 'This is, perhaps, the foulest Toadstool that has yet sprung up from the reeking dunghill of the present times.'[1] The *Quarterly Review*, along with the *Edinburgh Magazine*, drew attention to the novel's affinities with Godwin, and denounced it as 'a tissue of horrible and disgusting absurdity'. The objection continued:

> Our taste and our judgement alike revolt at this kind of writing, and the greater the ability with which it is executed the worse it is—it inculcates no lesson of conduct, manners, or morality; it cannot mend, and will not even amuse its readers, unless their taste have been deplorably vitiated . . . [2]

This reader at least, although seething with moral indignation, discerned no cautionary fable in the book; on the contrary, the basis of his objection is just this absence of a guiding 'moral'.

The *Edinburgh Magazine* likewise found the views expressed in *Frankenstein* to be 'bordering too closely on impiety', even more dangerously than Godwin's novels.[3] More astutely, this reviewer recognizes that *Frankenstein* 'has an air of reality attached to it, by being connected with the favourite projects and passions of the times'; it calls contemporary events 'wondrous and gigantic', presumably referring to the French Revolution and the Napoleonic wars. This review also carries the first attempt at the now established 'moral' reading: 'It might, indeed, be the author's view to shew that the powers of man have been wisely limited; and that misery would follow their extension.' It is worth noting that this remark is offered tentatively as a guess at the author's intention, to offset the more powerful feeling of *Frankenstein*'s disturbing impiety ('some of our highest and most reverential feelings receive a shock from the conception on which it turns', particularly the idea of a mere man as creator). Sir Walter Scott in *Blackwood's* was kinder, admitting that *Frankenstein* showed 'uncommon powers of poetic imagination', although it 'shook a little even our firm nerves'.[4]

The conservative reviewers were not alone in emphasizing the Godwinian heresies of *Frankenstein*. Percy Shelley also wrote an appreciation which (although unpublished until 1832) was obviously intended to appear as an anonymous review, since it pretends igno-

1. Cited by Howard B. Gotlieb, *William Beckford of Fonthill* (New Haven, 1960), 61.
2. *The Quarterly Review*, xviii (1818), 385.
3. *The Edinburgh Magazine and Literary Miscellany*, ii (1818), 249–53.
4. *Blackwood's Edinburgh Magazine*, ii (1817–18), 619.

rance of the author's identity and sex. In it he draws attention to the novel's similarities to Godwin in style and subject, admiring the way the monster's crimes are explained by definite causes rather than by any unaccountably evil propensity. For Percy Shelley the moral of *Frankenstein* is clear: 'Treat a person ill, and he will become wicked.'[5] Another heretic, whose taste the *Quarterly Review* would have regarded as vitiated, was the reviewer of *Frankenstein*'s second edition in *Knight's Quarterly Magazine*, who enthused about the book's 'extreme power', and continued:

> For my own part, I confess that *my* interest in the book is entirely on the side of the monster. His eloquence and persuasion, of which Frankenstein complains, are so because they are truth. The justice is indisputably on his side, and his sufferings are, to me, touching to the last degree.[6]

So far there is little sign, from either the horrified or the enthusiastic, of *Frankenstein* being received as a conservative parable of presumption. The novel appeared to these early readers to inculcate, in the *Quarterly Review*'s words, 'no lesson', unless it were the radical Godwinian critique of injustice.

The moral outrage provoked among *Frankenstein*'s more pious readers did, however, help to resolve this problem of interpretation by influencing the story's adaptation for the stage. The first dramatic version of *Frankenstein* appeared in 1823 with the staging of Richard Brinsley Peake's *Presumption: or the Fate of Frankenstein* at the English Opera House, T. P. Cooke playing the part of the monster. Mary Shelley herself went to see a performance, and although she was amused by it and impressed by Cooke's acting, she decided that 'The story is not well managed.'[7] This is a remarkable understatement. The tendency of Peake's management of the tale can be guessed at from the title alone, which so baldly advertises the morally improving nature of the adaptation. What is more interesting is that, according to Elizabeth Nitchie's 'Stage History of *Frankenstein*', the production had to face what the playbills described as 'abortive attempts . . . to prejudice the Publick' in the form of placards apparently displayed by certain 'friends of humanity' who appealed to fathers of families to boycott the play. Under the pressure of this moral campaign, the theatre management went out of its way to announce that 'The striking moral exhibited in this story, is the fatal consequence of that presumption which attempts to pen-

5. *The Prose Works of Percy Bysshe Shelley*, ed. R. H. Shepherd, 2 vols. (London, 1888), i. 418.
6. *Knight's Quarterly Magazine*, iii (1824), 198.
7. *The Letters of Mary Wollstonecraft Shelley*, ed. Betty T. Bennett, 2 vols. (Baltimore, 1980–3), i. 378 (to Leigh Hunt, 9 Sept. 1823).

etrate, beyond prescribed depths, into the mysteries of nature.'[8] One may well understand that Peake's play had to pander to the conscience of the churchgoing paterfamilias. The same seems to apply to H. M. Milner's version, *The Daemon of Switzerland*, which was produced in the same year and was advertised as the illustration of an 'Instructive Lesson'.

A glance at Peake's adaptation (later retitled *Frankenstein, A Romantic Drama*) will show how the moralizing of the tale works. After creating the monster off-stage, Victor appears before the audience and describes his creature's ugliness in terms which are lifted verbatim from the novel, but then he suddenly departs from his literary source by announcing that 'a flash breaks in upon my darkened soul, and tells me my attempt was impious'.[9] He goes on to cry, 'Oh that I could recall my impious labour, or suddenly extinguish the spark which I have so presumptuously bestowed.' (*FRD*, 7.) Earlier in the play Peake has introduced the comic character of Fritz, the country bumpkin who acts as Victor's assistant and who prepares the audience to interpret the tale according to received Christian notions of sin and damnation by telling them that 'like Dr Faustus, my master is raising the Devil' (*FRD*, 3). Peake makes several minor alterations in the story (Elizabeth becomes Victor's sister and is engaged to Clerval, while Victor is enamoured of Agatha De Lacey, who becomes the monster's victim), but the important changes are the dropping of Walton's frame-narrative and above all the silencing of the monster, who in this version has, as Frankenstein tells us, 'the mind of an infant' (*FRD*, 7). The monster is still responsive to music, he discovers the mixed blessings of fire, and he chops wood for the De Laceys, but he is never allowed to develop beyond blind power and rage, still less to learn of human language and customs before he is buried with his creator in an avalanche. From a sensitive critic of social institutions, the monster has been transformed into a rampaging embodiment of Victor's unleashed 'impiety', who is never given a hearing. In short, he is assimilated firmly into the traditional role of the monster as a visible image of presumptuous vice.

Peake's adaptation of the tale, and the fame of Cooke's rendering of the inarticulate monster (or '———' as he was called in the theatre programme), set the pattern for nearly all subsequent stage versions, and eventually for the 1931 screen version too, which even preserves Fritz along with the virtually silenced monster. As Nitchie's stage history records, the formula was successful and recognizable

8. Cited by Elizabeth Nitchie, *Mary Shelley, Author of 'Frankenstein'* (Westport, Conn., 1953), 221. This section of Nitchie's book is reprinted from her article 'The Stage History of *Frankenstein*', *South Atlantic Quarterly*, xli (1942), 384–98.
9. Richard Brinsley Peake, *Frankenstein, A Romantic Drama in Three Acts* (London, 1884), 7. Subsequent page references in the text are to this edition, abbreviated as *FRD*.

enough to spawn several burlesques—tributes to its possibilities as
an established myth:

> The laboratory at the top of a staircase leading from the back of
> the stage, with a door for the monster to break down and a win-
> dow for the frightened servant to peer through, was part of the
> setting for each play. There was almost invariably a cottage to
> be burnt. The monster always leaped the railing of the staircase;
> he always seized and snapped Frankenstein's sword; he always
> experienced wonder at sounds and was charmed by music. He
> was always nameless. He was always painted blue.[1]

While the monster was being recuperated into the traditional form
of visible monstrosity in this congealing of a dramatic cliché, he was
also beginning his career as an object of rhetorical allusion. In the
year after the first stage productions of the story, the Foreign Secre-
tary George Canning spoke in the House of Commons in a debate on
West Indian slave emancipation, remarking of the slave that 'To turn
him loose in the manhood of his physical strength, in the maturity of
his physical passion, but in the infancy of his uninstructed reason,
would be to raise up a creature resembling the splendid fiction of a
recent romance.'[2] Mary Shelley felt flattered by the attention shown
to her tale in such quarters, but seems not to have noticed how *Frankenstein* was being used by nervous liberal statesmen to delay reform,
nor how the monster (and worse, the slave) was being transformed by
such rhetoric into a mindless brute. Canning, a former contributor to
the *Anti-Jacobin Review* and a founder of the *Quarterly Review*, was
clearly reclaiming the monster as a Burkean bogy figure to illustrate
the danger of reform turning into rebellion. The same tradition of
colourful rhetoric was maintained by the radical Tories of *Fraser's
Magazine*, for whom Thomas Carlyle wrote in his early days. *Fraser's*
seems to have invented the problem of the monster's 'soul' before
even Mary Shelley herself did:

> A state without religion is like a human body without a soul, or
> rather like an unnatural body of the species of the Franken-
> stein monster, without a pure and vivifying principle; for the
> limbs are of different natures, and form a horrible heteroge-
> neous compound, full of corruption and exciting our disgust.[3]

The allusion here not only absorbs the monster into the old image
of the body politic, but provides retrospectively a pious explanation
for Victor Frankenstein's disastrous failure.

---

1. Nitchie, *Mary Shelley*, 225.
2. *Hansard's Parliamentary Debates*, 2nd ser., x (London, 1824), col. 1103. See Mary Shelley's *Letters*, i. 417, 564.
3. *Fraser's Magazine* (Nov. 1830), 481. Cited by Sterrenburg, 'Mary Shelley's Monster', 166.

When Mary Shelley came to revise her novel for the third edition of 1831, on which virtually all modern editions have been based, she incorporated several of the more conservative readings implied in the dramatic and rhetorical uses to which the story had been put since 1818. Now distancing herself from her radical past, the author strengthened the cautionary element of the novel to the point where it could be read as an 'improving' work. Despite her misgivings about Peake's handling of the story, she even introduced his title into the book: the word 'presumption' appears for the first time in a new speech given to Victor, who now describes the monster as 'the living monument of presumption and rash ignorance which I had let loose upon the world' (*F*, (245)/80). Victor is twice made to describe his action in creating the monster as 'unhallowed' (*F*, (247)/89; (256)/185), and is given a chance to mention, for the first time, the problem of 'the mockery of a soul' with which he has endued his creature (*F*, (255)/183). Galvanism, unmentioned in 1818, also creeps into the text along with occasional phrases which stress the unhallowed nature of Victor's transgression, like the reference to his 'fervent longing to penetrate the secrets of nature' (*F*, (238)/39). Elizabeth's radical speech against retributive justice, in the dialogues before Justine's execution, is excised and replaced, absurdly, with some saintly advice from Justine, who now tells Elizabeth: 'Learn from me, dear lady, to submit in patience to the will of Heaven!' (*F*, (246)/88.)

The figure of Walton is adapted to this process of conservative revision, turned into a far more deluded explorer than he was in 1818 so as to correspond to the new 'presumptuous' Frankenstein. 'I would sacrifice my fortune, my existence, my every hope,' declares this revised Walton, 'to the furtherance of my enterprise. One man's life or death were but a small price to pay for the acquirement of the knowledge which I sought.' (*F*, (231–2)/28.) In reply Victor hints strongly at the similarity of their presumptuous endeavours: 'Unhappy man! do you share my madness? Have you drank also of the intoxicating draught? Hear me—let me reveal my tale, and you will dash the cup from your lips!' (*F*, (232)/28.) By the end of the novel Walton accordingly comes to regret his own 'mad schemes' (*F*, (258)/212). This revision of *Frankenstein*'s narrative frame effects a decisive adjustment of the sense in which the central episodes are to be understood. In the 1818 text Victor tells Walton his story because he thinks his rescuer might find it interesting and useful. In the 1831 version, though, the similarities between the respective enterprises of the two men are drummed home in order to give Frankenstein's narrative a fully cautionary status: 'when I reflect', Victor tells Walton, 'that you are pursuing the same course, exposing yourself to the same dangers which have rendered me what I am, I imagine that you may deduce an apt moral from my tale.' (*F*, (232–3)/30.)

Provided thus with a moral, *Frankenstein* at last became an acceptable text, its meanings brought into line with the improving lessons of its dramatic versions. But while the developing tradition of stage, cartoon, and—eventually—screen *Frankenstein*s managed more successfully to rein in the excesses of the story's multiple significance by exhibiting the monster as an awful warning, there remained a sphere in which the monster could live on in the less prejudicial condition of eloquent invisibility: the literary tradition. In this chapter I have sought to fend off the intrusion of later mythic developments into the reading of the 1818 novel, isolating the text from its offspring all the better to highlight the subsequent process of transformation from text to myth. * * *

WILLIAM ST. CLAIR

[*Frankenstein*'s Impact][†]

* * *

Like all the books written by members of the Godwin and Shelley families, *Frankenstein* had a political and ethical purpose. In accordance with the Godwinian theory of progress, *Frankenstein* would, they hoped, help to change the perceptions, the knowledge, the understanding, and therefore the behaviour, of those who read or otherwise encountered it. The reading of the book would, they hoped, contribute, in its small way, to the general intellectual and moral improvement of society in its slow, much interrupted, progress towards perfection.[1]

Shelley told publishers that he was acting for a friend abroad, a pretence which authors often adopt to protect themselves from disappointment. A phrase in the preface implied that the author was a man.[2] But if publishers thought that Shelley was himself the author, that was no advantage in the negotiations. Both *Queen Mab* and *Alastor* had been printed 'on commission', and the same was to be true of *Laon and Cythna* which was being turned down when Shelley was negotiating for *Frankenstein*. Until the pirate reprinting of *Queen Mab* in 1821, Shelley was just one of the many scarcely known and commercially unsuccessful authors whose books could

---

† From *The Reading Nation in the Romantic Period* (New York: Cambridge UP, 2004), 358–73. Copyright © 2004 William St. Clair. Reprinted with the permission of Cambridge University Press.
1. See, for example, William St Clair, *The Godwins and the Shelleys: The Biography of a Family* (New York: Norton, 1989), 434–39.
2. 'his labours.' In the usage of the time the phrase might also be read as gender neutral.

only be published at his own expense, if at all.[3] *Frankenstein* was rejected by the leading publishers.[4] Ollier, Shelley's publisher, took only three days to say 'no'. The reason why *Frankenstein* was turned down so decisively was probably more to do with self-censoring doubts about its subject matter than with any fears about its innovative literary quality or its commercial prospects. Publishers and circulating-library owners were well aware that the narrow constituency of readers upon whom their livelihoods depended was, for the most part, conservative, indeed reactionary, in its political and religious opinions.

Shelley then turned to the outsider firm of Lackington, and in August they contracted to publish an edition of 500 copies, dividing the net profits, one third to the author, two thirds to the publisher. *Frankenstein, or, The Modern Prometheus*, went on sale later in the year. Like most novels of the time it was anonymous, in three volumes, and expensive, a book intended to be sold primarily to commercial circulating libraries, with perhaps less than half the edition expected to go to individual buyers.[5] *Frankenstein* was only stretched to three volumes by printing few words to the line, few lines to the page, and few pages to the volume.

Lackington specialised in magic, the illegitimate supernatural, and horror, a fact emphasised by advertisements.[6] For many readers therefore Lackington's printed advertisements tipped into the book acted as an optional disposable extra paratext whose effect was to offset the authorial paratext, and the plea for the book to be taken seriously was largely ignored when the book was reviewed in the literary press.[7] The notion that the dead could be made to live again by manmade agency was, it was suggested, atheistical and blasphemous, a secret attack on a central tenet of Christianity. 'These volumes have neither principle, object, nor moral', thundered the *British Critic*. 'The horror which abounds in them is too grotesque and

3. See Charles E. Robinson, "Percy Bysshe Shelley, Charles Ollier, and William Blackwood" in Kevin Everest, ed., *Shelley Revalued. Papers from the Gregynog Conference*, Leicester, 1983.
4. See the remark and editor's note in Shelley *Letters*, i, 551. Another candidate for the third publisher known to have said 'no' is Hookham who published Thomas Love Peacock's novels.
5. The book is dated 1818 on the title page, but most copies appear to have been already sold to the retail distributors late in 1817.
6. The copy in the Codrington Library, All Souls College, Oxford, carries a long advertisement description of Lackington's other publications in the associated genres, including *The Magus or Celestial Intelligencer, Lives of the Alchemystical Philosophers, Apparitions, or The Mysteries of Ghosts, Hobgoblins, and Haunted Houses, The Life, Prophecies and Predictions of Merlin Interpreted*, Toland's *Critical History of the Celtic Religion, Tales of the Dead*.
7. The reviews, from which the quotations are taken, are noted and summarised in W.H. Lyles, *Mary Shelley, An Annotated Bibliography* (New York 1975) 168.

bizarre ever to approach the sublime.' The young Thomas Carlyle, who had only read a review, reported that 'Frankenstein, by Godwin's son in law, seems to be another unnatural disgusting fiction.'[8] According to William Beckford, *Frankenstein* was 'perhaps the foulest Toadstool that has yet sprung from the reeking dunghill of present times'.[9]

The whole edition of 500 copies was sold to the retail booksellers as soon as the copies were printed, so passing all the remaining sales risks to them, and the book reached its initial readers over the following months and years.[1] The net profit declared to the author was more than the total cost of manufacturing, advertising, and selling the book. In 1818 Mary Shelley, with her third share, was commercially a far more successful author than Shelley. The first edition of *Frankenstein* outsold all the works of her husband put together. It made more money than all Shelley's works were to fetch in his lifetime. The gross rate of return to the publisher cannot have been less than about 300 per cent at an annual rate. With such high and immediate profits on small sales, and with plenty of publicity already obtained, it might have been expected that the publisher would have wanted to build on his success, especially as the possibility of a second edition had been discussed. But for Lackington, the selling out of the first edition was the end of the matter. In making that decision Lackington was following the usual practice. Publishers' archives record the publication of dozens of novels in three volumes in editions of 500 or 750, many without a spark of originality.[2]

In 1823, five years after the first publication, Godwin wrote to tell his daughter that he had heard that a stage version was to be produced.[3] Godwin was able to negotiate for a second edition from another publisher which included some textual changes, this time in two volumes, still in a lavish format, and still at a high retail price. Perhaps in an attempt to exploit the notoriety of the name that had now been publicly revealed, the second edition was advertised as by Mary Wollstonecraft Shelley.[4] Copies were still available at full price in the 1830s and probably later.[5] In 1831, however, again as a result of the interest caused by stage versions, Mary Shelley was able to sell the copyright to Richard Bentley for inclusion in

8. *The Collected Letters of Thomas and Jane Welsh Carlyle* (Durham, NC 1970) i, 124, 30 April 1818.
9. Forry ix.
1. The account is transcribed in SC v, 397, from the manuscript in the Bodleian, and in appendix 5, 509.
2. *Shelley and His Circle, 1773–1822*, ed. K. N. Cameron and others (Cambridge, MA) v, 397.
3. Godwin to Mary Shelley, 22 July 1823. Quoted by Forry 3, from an unpublished letter in the Huntington Library, California.
4. *Morning Post*, 23 August 1823, quoted by Forry 37.
5. Still advertised in the *London Catalogue* (1835).

Bentley's Standard Novels for £30, the last financial benefit she or her family was ever to receive.[6]

In the late 1820s, Richard Bentley, like the publishers of the Waverley novels, had understood the implications of the sharp increase in the price of three-decker novels brought about in the previous decade. Bentley realised that, if he could buy the tail-ends of copyrights of out-of-print novels cheaply, he could start a uniform series which would take a second tranche from libraries and individuals who had not bought first time round. *Bentley's Standard Novels*, which began in the 1830s, included works by many excellent recent authors whose works had then become unavailable: Austen, Beckford, Burney, Edgeworth, Ferrier, Gait, Godwin, Peacock, and others. With the exception of the Waverley novels, Bentley made himself the owner of almost all the best fiction of the romantic period and later of the 1830s. With a new title coming out every few weeks, *Bentley's Standard Novels* provided several years' worth of continuous serial reading, a delayed, carefully selected, series of most of the best fictional writing of recent times. Since Bentley arranged the series by name of the author, for the first time, the names of Jane Austen, Susan Ferrier, John Galt, and others appeared on the title pages. Bentley did for romantic-period novels what the editors of the initial old-canon series had done at the end of the previous century. Novels such as Hogg's *Justified Sinner* and Godwin's *Mandeville*, which failed to be selected, disappeared from public attention until the twentieth century.

Bentley insisted that the author should correct errors and supply new material either in the text or as a paratextual preface or notes. Even if the changes were minimal, the revisions allowed him to claim a new copyright which, if not valid in law, would normally be respected within the industry. If authors were reluctant to revise their texts, Bentley would provide a professional reviser to do the work.[7] If, as in the case of Austen, the author was dead, Bentley asked a member of the family to write a memoir. In accepting Bentley's offer to republish *Frankenstein*, Mary Shelley was happy to comply with his conditions. She made changes to the text, some substantial, and added an autobiographical introduction, explaining how and when the book came to be written. The new introduction, which was printed alongside the original 1817 preface, emphasised that in essentials, the story was unchanged and that the composition had been written in collaboration with Shelley, but it said little

6. Bentley archives, BL. See also Gettman, although some of the figures he offers are not borne out by the archival record.

7. As he told Fanny Burney, some of whose works had already come out of copyright and been reprinted in cheap editions, he had to insist. See his letter of 12 October 1835 quoted in Joyce Hemlow, general ed., *The Journals and Letters of Fanny Burney* (Oxford 1984) xii, 879.

further about the book's political and moral purpose. *Frankenstein*, like many books in the series, was described as 'Revised, Corrected, and Illustrated, with a New Introduction by the Author'.

The books were tightly printed in one volume, and sold already bound in cloth, so saving customers the usual further cost of rebinding, and they each included an engraved frontispiece. The texts of some titles had to be cut back in order to fit the one-volume format.[8] Almost all were stereotyped. Although, over time, the plates became worn and the books became harder to read, the plates could occasionally be repaired to prolong their useful life.[9] The *Bentley's Standard Novels Frankenstein* is found with four different title pages, dated 1831, 1832, 1839, and 1849. But, the archives show, this does not mean that there were four editions or four printings from the stereotype plates, as has been assumed in bibliographies. With *Frankenstein*, as with the other books in the series, Bentley's decisions on when to create a new title page were not timed to the selling out of previously printed stocks, but to his policies for occasionally reannouncing and repricing the series as a whole.[1] Although, at an initial price of 6 shillings, *Bentley's Standard Novels* were less than a fifth of the price of new novels, they were not cheap by absolute terms. In the 1830s, a single *Bentley's Standard Novel* cost about half the weekly wage of a clerk or skilled manual worker. Bentley's novels were more expensive than Waverley novels whose sales were far higher.[2] They were twice as expensive as reprints of out-of-copyright novels of similar length.[3] Within his chosen market, Bentley positioned himself as far upmarket as he could go.

When he bought *Frankenstein*, Bentley could, as the law stood at the time, have expected to keep his monopoly until 1846, and, if the revised version was respected within the book industry, until 1859.[4] If the old pre-1842 regime had continued, Bentley could have extended his list almost indefinitely, adding say, Dickens, Trollope, Thackeray, and the other mid-Victorian novelists to his list as their works went

---

8. Examples in Gettman.
9. In the case of *Frankenstein*, a repair, effected by soldering in a plug which is not quite aligned, can be seen on page 35, where, in the 1849 reimpression, the word MODERN in the running title has been replaced. This appears to have been an error on the part of the repairer for it is the word PROMETHEUS which had become worn. The engraved title page was also dropped in the later reimpressions, perhaps because the plates had become too worn.
1. For prices see Gettman 51, and Michael Sadleir, *Nineteenth-Century Fiction, A Bibliographical Record* (1951) ii, 97. The prices noted in these books are however mainly for new volumes appearing in the series for the first time. The dates when the prices of existing titles such as *Frankenstein* were reduced are not all known.
2. The Waverley novels, sold to the trade at 3s 10d (3.8 shillings) for retailing at 5 shillings were often 'undersold' at 4 shillings. James J. Barnes, *Free Trade in Books* (Oxford 1964) 6.
3. See for example the English Classics produced by Dove, Scott and Webster, and other publishers at this time, noted in appendix 6.
4. As I calculate, twenty-eight years from 1818, or twenty-eight years from 1831.

out of copyright. But after the ending of the brief copyright window in 1842, he was boxed in. With the new longer copyright regime, publishers were no longer willing to let him have copyrights cheap—they wanted to exploit them themselves. The supply of tail-end copyrights fell to a trickle and the latter titles of *Bentley's Standard Novels* were less distinguished than their predecessors. At the same time, as events turned out, Mary Shelley and other authors were still alive at the time of the Copyright Act of 1842. Bentley and his heirs thus found themselves windfall owners of a copyright in *Frankenstein* which they could enjoy at least until 1866 and with luck until 1879. Bentley was the monopoly owner of a range of excellent, but increasingly obsolete, intellectual properties and also of the increasingly obsolescent plant from which copies could be manufactured.

In 1838, before the copyright change, William Hazlitt Junior, the essayists son, asked Mary Shelley's permission to include *Frankenstein* in his series, *The Romancist and Novelist's Library, The Best Works by the Best Authors*. By this time, as a result of mechanisation of manufacturing methods and reductions in the taxed price of paper, a new branch of the book industry had grown up, able to use newspaper manufacturing technologies to offer fiction at prices far lower than anything that had been possible even a few years before. *The Romancist* was cheap not only in relation to new, three volume, novels and to Bentley's reprints, but in absolute terms in relation to incomes. 'It is astonishing to me how much can be got for 2d [two pence].' Mary Shelley replied to Hazlitt. 'I must have every Wednesday enlivened by your sheet.'[5] But, having sold the copyright, it was not Mary Shelley's decision. The owners, protecting their high prices, said 'no', and they apparently refused permission for any of the titles in *Bentley's Standard Novels* to be reprinted.[6] Other publishers of other copyrighted novels seem to have done the same. The sharp fall in the price of recently published books which, before the copyright change of 1842, would have occurred in the 1840s was postponed for a generation.

Most of *Bentley's Standard Novels* were kept continuously in print for twenty years, with supply kept closely in line with demand. Bentley and his successors brought the price down from 6 shillings to 3s 6d to 2s 6d (3.5 to 2.5 shillings), but then stopped. Why they did not tranche down further, as the publishers of the Waverley novels did with success, is not known, but the effects of this single publishing decision on the reading of the novels of the romantic

---

5. Mary Shelley, *Letters* ii, 299.
6. The Hodgson Parlour Library edition is a possible exception. I have found no record among the Bentley archives either of permission having been given or of a complaint of piracy. Since Hodgson's edition is taken from the 1831 version, it would have been hard for him to claim that he was not infringing copyright.

period were enormous. Whereas, in the case of the Waverley novels, the further lowering of price took the texts to a reading nation of several millions, in the case of the other novels of the period, readerships remained confined to the upper tranches. Cumulative production, even of Austen, never reached more than about 8,000 per title over the twenty years before the plates were melted, a sales figure reached by several of Scott's novels in the first month.[7] By the mid 1850s, when the price of *Frankenstein* was down to 2s 6d, demand had fallen to a trickle and the series was allowed to die. Some time before 1861, by which time most of the copyrights were expiring, all the stereotype plates from the series, other than those of Austen and Ferrier, were melted as scrap.[8] After that, with only a few exceptions, little of the prose fiction of the romantic period other than Waverley novels was selected to be reprinted in the vast late-Victorian sixpenny-fiction paperback market.[9]

With one exception, for most of the 1850s, 1860s, and 1870s, *Frankenstein* was out of print. It had also disappeared from the circulating libraries.[1] As a novel, as a text, as a piece of writing in fixed form in which a property right had been established by law, *Frankenstein* was condemned to a long period of catalepsy, neither quite dead nor quite alive. Unable to think of a way of enjoying the intellectual property themselves, the then owners were determined, like a dog in the manger, to deny others the opportunity. While in copyright, *Frankenstein* was never issued as a yellow back, as a shilling shocker, never abridged, turned into a chapbook, or otherwise adapted for the lower-income readers who were joining the reading nation in the middle nineteenth century.

For the first fourteen years of its life in print *Frankenstein* existed in about a thousand copies, fewer than most of the works of Byron and Scott sold on publication day.[2] During its first forty years, a total of between 7,000 and 8,000 copies were printed and sold, still fewer than Byron and Scott commonly sold in the first week. Although copies were frequently bought by circulating libraries, the total read-

---

7. I exclude the sea stories of Marryat which were first published after the end of the romantic period and sold more. See appendix 7.
8. Inventory of stereotypes 1861, Bentley archives.
9. See the lists of reprint collections in the *English Catalogue of Books, 1881–1889* (1891).
1. It does not appear, for example, in the *Catalogue of W. H. Smith's Subscription Library* (1872). John Johnson collection, Bodleian.
2. See 'Mary Shelley', appendix 9, 644. Many currently available editions still spread the error that the book sold well from the beginning. 'The novel was an instant success', Mary Wollstonecraft Shelley, *Frankenstein, The Original 1818 Text*, edited by James Rieger (New York 1974) xx. '*Frankenstein* became an immediate best-seller', Mary Shelley, *Frankenstein*, edited with an introduction by Maurice Hindle (London 1985) 8. 'Immediately became a best seller', Mary Shelley, *Frankenstein, Or, The Modern Prometheus*, Modern Library (New York 1993) ix. '. . . enjoyed enormous success'. Mary Wollstonecraft Shelley, *Frankenstein, The Original 1818 Text*, edited by D. L. Macdonald and Kathleen Scherf (Peterborough: Ontario, 1994) 35.

ership cannot have been large on such a small base.[3] Nor was *Frankenstein* unusual in this regard. The figures for Austen show a similarly modest success. The cumulative sales over half a century of none of the other novels of the romantic period reached the readership levels of half-a-dozen Waverley novels in their first week. During the first fifty years of *Frankenstein's* existence, the readership was largely confined to a narrow constituency of men and women at the topmost end of the income scale.

The main change occurred in late-Victorian times. As soon as *Frankenstein* came incontrovertibly out of all copyright restrictions and trade courtesies in about 1880, the reprinting began. The demand that had been held back after 1842 could at last be satisfied. The price plummeted and the print runs soared. In its first year the first reprint of *Frankenstein* sold more copies than all of the previous editions put together. By the end of the century *Frankenstein* was available in a range of editions adapted to different groups of book buyers. You could buy it, in full, with illustrations, at one per cent of the original price, and there were abridgements and books in parts, as well as a few more expensive versions. At the turn of the nineteenth century, eighty years after its first appearance, *Frankenstein* at last became accessible to the whole reading nation.

Some of the late-nineteenth-century reprints were intended for the poor and the poorly educated, offered with well intentioned condescension to men and women who had previously lived largely without books. *Routledge's World Library*, a paperback series, set out the publisher's aims of the series, and described the implied and expected readership, in a printed paratextual advertisement:

> When I think of the long, gossiping, yawning, gambling hours of grooms, valets, coachmen, and cabmen; the railway stations conveniently provided with book-stalls, and crowded every morning and evening with workmen's trains—the winter evenings in thousands of villages, wayside cottages, and scattered hamlets—the brief, but not always well spent leisure of factory hands in the north—the armies of commercial and uncommercial travellers with spare half hours—the shop assistants—the city offices with their hangers on—the Board Schools—the village libraries—the Army and Navy—the barrack or the dockyard—again the vision of Routledge's World Library rises before me, and I say, 'This, if not a complete cure for indolence and vice, may at least prove a powerful counter charm.'[4]

3. From a sample of circulating-library catalogues in the Bodleian Library.
4. Advertisement by the editor, the Reverend H. R. Haweis, MA, in copies of books published in *Routledge's World Library*.

'I issue "Frankenstein" with some degree of hesitation', the editor confessed, 'The subject is somewhat revolting, the treatment of it is somewhat hideous.' *Frankenstein* remained morally (and perhaps politically) suspect, and even after the texts passed out of private ownership, it was seldom reprinted for a middle-class readership. The late nineteenth-century campaigners for women's suffrage, who wanted to promote Mary Shelley as a woman of achievement in her own right, found her book an embarrassment. 'Everyone now knows the story of "The Modern Prometheus", wrote Mrs Marshall in her biography in 1889, but she appears ashamed to admit that Mary Shelley wrote 'the ghastly but powerful allegorical romance'.[5] Richard Church, who wrote the Mary Shelley volume for the *Representative Women* series, blames Shelley for not discouraging Mary's 'girlish romanticism' and so allowing the book to be 'marred very seriously by a certain haste, an indolence, a vagueness of construction'. 'Mary Shelley', he remarks, picking up the ancient warnings to be found in conduct literature, 'suffered from an overtrained intellectual conscience.'[6]

These attitudes seem to have continued for most of the first half of the twentieth century. Although, with this period too, it is frequently assumed that the book sold well, the archival record shows a different picture. At a time when the United Kingdom had a population of about fifty million, was fully literate, and reading was the main entertainment, the total annual sales of the main edition, that of *Everyman's Library*, to the whole British market, which included India, Australia, South Africa, New Zealand, and other English-speaking countries overseas other than North America, were only rarely above 500 a year.

During most of the nineteenth century, it was not the reading of the text of the book, but seeing adaptations of the story on the stage which kept *Frankenstein* alive in the culture, and here we have another example of how the nature of cultural production and reception was decisively influenced by the regulatory regime of intellectual property and textual controls. Since 1737, only two theatres in London, Covent Garden and Drury Lane, and a few in other cities, were licensed to perform plays, whether they were newly written pieces, old favourites, or Shakespeare. The consolidation of a state-enforced monopoly in theatrical performance, from which the state benefited through the capitalised fee for the patent, ensured

5. Mrs Julian Marshall, *The Life and Letters of Mary Wollstonecraft Shelley* (1889) i, 139, 143.
6. Richard Church, *Mary Shelley* (n.d. c. 1895) 52.

that admission prices remained higher than they would otherwise have been, and during the seventeenth century the size of the theatre audience, like the size of the reading nation, may have fallen relative to the size of the population.

During the eighteenth century the regulatory regime also seems to have brought about many of the same effects as we see in the case of printed books, rising financial returns to the producers (playwrights, theatrical owners, and perhaps other workers in the industry), but also a tendency to entrench the obsolete, as producers preferred to recycle older, well-tried, theatrical texts for which the capital costs had been amortised, rather than to invest in new compositions.[7] In other respects, the eighteenth-century London theatre continued the regime of the state licensing period of the late seventeenth century as it had been applied to printed books, a limit on the absolute size of the industry, access to the cultural production restricted to elites, and pre-censorship controls on textual content. In these respects the determinants of theatrical production in the eighteenth century were very different from those governing the production of printed books.

In the romantic period, every stage performance was individually licensed by the Lord Chamberlain, the state censor. Besides controlling the patented theatres, the censor was empowered to grant licences for performances such as opera, pantomime, and other spectacles which were less likely than straight plays to contain material which the state found ideologically threatening, and since 1788 a large theatre/entertainment industry supplying such performances had grown up in London and elsewhere. All performances in such theatres also needed a licence from the Lord Chamberlain which would not be granted if the submitted texts offended against certain criteria. The adaptations of *Frankenstein*, like those of most adaptations, were, we can say, officially pre-censored not only to check that they were ideologically acceptable to the political and religious authorities but to ensure that they were not legitimate drama.

Although the direct textual controls were tighter than for printed texts, there was no regime of intellectual property. Until the Dramatic Copyright Act of 1833 a theatre wishing to put on a commercial production did not need to obtain the permission of the holder of the copyright in a printed play. In 1822, for example, Murray brought an action against the Theatre Royal, Drury Lane, for putting on a performance of Byron's recently published play, *Marino Faliero*, abridged and adapted, without permission. In the contract Byron

7. See Judith Milhous and Robert D. Hume, 'Playwrights', Remuneration in Eighteenth-Century London', in *Harvard Library Bulletin*, vol. 10 (1999 but actually 2001).

had sold Murray 'the tragedy and poem and copyright thereof, and the exclusive right of printing and publishing, and all benefit and advantage thereof', an indisputable assignment of all his intellectual property rights as the author. However, the court confirmed that no intellectual property rights had been infringed. The Copyright Acts, the court decided, protected only the printing of a text, they did not prevent a printed text from being performed.[8] At the time when *Frankenstein* was first adapted for the stage, theatres were also able to make adaptations of printed texts without the need for permission either from the author or the owner of the intellectual property. However, all such adaptations had to include a good deal of music to pretend to be operas or pantomimes, not straight plays.

In the novel the being created by Frankenstein comes into the world full of natural human sympathy which is refined by his education, including his reading of one of the works of the radical canon, Volney's *The Ruins of Empires*.[9] It is only when he is misjudged and mistreated by unfair, unenlightened, human beings that he is corrupted into violence. Treat other people as you would like them to treat you is the explicit message, a Christian as well as a humanist sentiment. The many stage versions which were put on after 1823 are also scarcely subversive—if they had been, they would not have been licensed. The first, as its title, *Presumption, or the Fate of Frankenstein*, emphasised, saw the story as a warning against human pride. But, as had happened with the reviewers of the book, others feared something more sinister. The *Morning Post* led the attack:

> To Lord Byron, the late Mr Shelley, and philosophers of that stamp, it might appear a very fine thing to attack the Christian religion . . . and burlesque the resurrection of the dead . . . but we would prefer the comparatively noble assaults of VOLNEY, VOLTAIRE and PAINE.[1]

Other reviews of the play linked it with the hated names of the two authors whose books, Queen Mab and Don Juan, were at that very time becoming available to the same literate urban clerical and working classes whom conservatives most feared. The play, according to *John Bull*, was taken from the novel by 'one of the coterie of that self-acknowledged Atheist Percy B. Shelley'.[2] By the time *Presumption, or the Fate of Frankenstein* reached Birmingham in 1824, it had become part of the surrounding ritual of the performance that warning posters were circulated by local upholders of public

---

8. Gavin McFarlane, *Copyright: the Development and Exercise of the Performing Right* (1980) 37.
9. In volume ii, chapter 5 of the 1818 version.
1. Quoted by Forry 5.
2. For 29 July 1823, quoted by Forry 5.

morality, denials were issued by the theatre, and threats of legal action thrown about by both sides.

The English Opera House, where *Presumption* opened in 1823, was able to hold about 1,500 persons.[3] The Coburg Theatre, where *Frankenstein or the Demon of Switzerland* opened shortly afterwards, held over 3,800.[4] Admission to the English Opera House cost 5 shillings for a box, 3 for the pit, 2 for the gallery, and 1 shilling for the upper gallery, and, if the house was not full, the prices were reduced.[5] Midweek was for 'the better classes', Monday for 'the higher working classes'.[6] Every single night when one of the *Frankenstein* plays was performed brought a version of the story of the manmade monster to more men and women than the book did in ten or twenty years.

Some managers asked authors to write their own adaptations, and Scott, most of whose works were dramatised, for one, cooperated. On the whole, however, stage versions were prepared by professional adapters. When in 1833 the law was changed to grant an exclusive right to publishers to put on performances of plays that they had printed, there was still no provision for an author or text owner to claim an intellectual property right over performed adaptations.[7] If anything, the new regime encouraged a widening of the gap between original text and the theatrical adaptation, for the further the adapter departed from the original, the more free the theatre was from any intellectual property claim. The theatrical versions are, therefore, not so much attempts to turn a good printed text into dramatic form, but misshapen creatures designed to fit into the complex regulatory regime. In the adaptations of *Frankenstein* the location was moved to wicked Venice, to icy Swiss forests, or to burning Sicilian mountains. Names, such as Manfred, were taken from more familiar stories, and Ratzbaen, Tiddliwincz, and Captain Risotto invented for laughs. Fritz, the hunchback, who is not in the book, stole the show so often that he became indispensable.[8] Turbans, veils, and turned-up slippers gave a hint of the east, and there were plenty of Italian banditti. Early in its stage life *Frankenstein* frequently amalgamated with *The Vampyre*, not because that piece had been written on the same occasion in 1816, but as part of a general muddling of gothic, of horror, and of laughs. From the start, the

3. I have been unable to find a more exact figure. Capacity at the time was normally measured in money terms, gross nightly takings. It is however clear from figures given by witnesses to the House of Commons *Report of the Select Committee on Dramatic Literature* (1832) that the English Opera House was comparable in size to the Haymarket which held between 1,600 and 1,700.
4. The boxes held 1,230 persons, the pit 1,090, and the galleries 1,512.
5. 'Second prices': boxes 3 shillings; pit is 6d (1.5); lower gallery 1 shilling. Information from a playbill for a performance on 27 August 1828.
6. Evidence by the theatre managers to the Select Committee on Dramatic Literature 1832.
7. McFarlane, *Copyright* 51.
8. In film versions he was renamed Egor and made famous by Marty Feldman.

stage *Frankensteins* mocked themselves. They are full of topical allusions and jokes, mostly probably now irretrievable. In the late-Victorian version, for example, the Monster wore a hat which, copying Gilbert and Sullivan in *Patience*, brought a laugh at the expense of Oscar Wilde. The story was cut, added to, transformed into pantomime or farce, amalgamated with other stories, parodied, burlesqued, and reduced to cliché, tag, and catchphrase.

The playbills of the first 1823 version advertised *Presumption*, a new romance, with no mention of Frankenstein in the title.[9] But the name itself was soon a magic word, a vital part of the appeal. In both favourite early stage versions, the primary and secondary titles were soon reversed. *Presumption, or the Fate of Frankenstein* became *Frankenstein, or, The Danger of Presumption. The Man and the Monster* became *Frankenstein, or, The Monster*. By 1824 it was already common for the unnamed monster to be called 'Frankenstein' instead of the scientist who constructed him, a confusion put about by the actors. By the end of the century the reversal of the names had become so common that Fowler's *Modern English Usage* felt able to call it 'a blunder almost, but surely not quite, sanctioned by custom'. Comparing the dates of the printed books and the main stage and film adaptations, we can see how they interacted.[1] In 1823, and again in 1831, the printed novel was revived by the stage versions. The stage versions of the 1850s were stimulated by the Hodgson edition. In the 1880s the large-scale reprinting of the novel when the copyright expired led to the putting on of a new play version, which in its turn stimulated more reprints.[2] *Frankenstein* did not become part of popular culture with the cinema: the film industry picked it up from the stage where it was already vigorous. There is an episode in the 1931 classic where the as yet uncorrupted creature, acted by Boris Karloff, plays happily with the innocent little girl. But such survivals of the original moral purpose are rare. The *Frankenstein* films in both Britain and the United States are as unstable as the stage versions. Continuing the tradition of their stage predecessors they laughed at themselves and chased every passing fashion.[3] Far into the twentieth century Frankenstein and his monster continued to live largely independently of books. In so far as they had a printed or material existence at all, it was in films, posters, comics, and funny masks of Boris Karloff.

Almost every book published in early nineteenth-century London which achieved any kind of popularity as a book was adapted and transformed for the stage. Every Waverley novel was followed by at

9. E.g. in *The Theatrical Observer* for 2 August 1823.
1. See the list in appendix 9.
2. Summarised in 'Mary Shelley', appendix 9, 644–6.
3. See the list in appendix 9, 647.

least one stage version, often by several.[4] Byron was often adapted and performed in versions such as *The Corsair, The Corsair's Son, The Corsair's Bride*. On the early nineteenth-century stage the romance of Scott's Scotland might be conjured up by a glimpse of tartan, the spirit of Byron by an extravagant open necked shirt, and the oriental fantasies of Moore by a whirl of silk over pointed slippers. The stage versions lived (and mostly soon died) alongside the printed texts of the original works, which continued to be readily available and to be widely read. The mutating stage versions came and went, collectively influential and infiltrating themselves in innumerable irrecoverable ways into popular oral culture, memory, and myth.

Charles Dickens, who hated to see his work mangled, realised that stage adaptation was an intrinsic part of the reception of his books. He invented a conversation between Nicholas Nickleby, the aspiring author, and an adapter for the stage who is modelled on R. B. Peake and H. M. Milner who had each adapted *Frankenstein*.

> . . . there was a literary gentleman present who had dramatised in his time two hundred and forty seven novels as fast as they came out—some of them faster than they had come out—and who *was* a literary gentleman in consequence.[5]

Since, in most cases, the printed texts were easily available to readers and audiences, any new mutated stage version had to compete anew with a knowledge of the original printed text. The printed texts stood like fixed beacons, circumscribing the limits to the range of possible mutation, and ready at all times to draw audiences and new adapters back to the originals. In the case of *Frankenstein*, on the other hand, with long periods with no easily accessible printed version, new stage versions tended to mutate from other earlier mutations rather than directly from the original. Parodies parodied parodies, moving in any direction that the moment made promising. Refused a life in the reasonably stable culture of print and reading, *Frankenstein* survived in a free-floating popular oral and visual culture, with only the central episode of the making of the creature holding it tenuously to its original.

In Victorian times, even when *Frankenstein* was not in print and when there was no play on the stage, the story was alive in the nation's memory. All through the nineteenth century we find allusions in literature, journalism, and politics.[6] Scholarly books have used hermeneutic and psychoanalytical techniques to explore the

---

4. See Richard Ford, *Dramatisations of Scott's novels: A Catalogue* (Oxford 1979), and H. Philip Bolton, *Scott Dramatised* (1992).
5. *Nicholas Nickleby*, chapter 48, quoted by Altick 456.
6. See 'Mary Shelley', appendix 9.

Frankenstein monsters lurking in the Victorian mind.[7] Such allusions are, it is suggested, the occasional visible manifestations of
deeper myths. No doubt the Victorians suffered from monsters like
everybody else. But such claims rest on assumptions that the novel
was being read, or that its text had somehow emanated from or infil-
trated into the collective subconscious and had stayed there, and that
the collective unconscious can be recovered by modern critical reading of texts. In fact, most of those who used, heard, and understood
Frankenstein expressions in Victorian times are unlikely to have read
the book, and if they saw a stage version, they could have had only
the sketchiest idea of the rich layers of meaning of the book.

The word 'Frankenstein' in Victorian culture is a cliché, a conve-
nient tag for those who fear change.[8] If you free the slaves, reform
parliament, give votes to the working class or independence to the
Irish, you will create a Frankenstein monster which will destroy you.
Already by 1824, within a year of the first stage version, that had
become the single, simple, unvaried meaning. By the end of the century, the simplicities of the stage versions had decisively defeated the
complexities of the literary text. Anyone who took a different meaning was reading against the grain and against the norm. So universal was the accepted meaning that the editor of the Penny Novels
abridgement dropped the author's preface, and provided a preface
of his own to ram home the perverse interpretation.

Frankenstein thus stands in contrast to Shelley's Queen Mab and
Byron's Don Juan. In the 1820s, 1830s, and for many years later,
there was a clear demand for access to all three books particularly
by readers for whom all books were expensive and largely inaccessible, but who often went to the theatre. But whereas, owing to
quirks in the copyright law, Queen Mab and Don Juan were freed
from private ownership, their price plummeted, their readerships
soared, and the cultural influence of both was enormous, the original Frankenstein, as a result of other quirks, was held back from
most of its potential readers. A gripping tale with a reformist moral
message, the book might have taken its place alongside other famous
works of the radical canon which helped to shape a new sceptical,
reformist, urban culture. As events turned out, the Frankenstein
story, for most of those who encountered it, conveyed a message
which was contrary to the plain meaning of the original text. The
impact has been, for the most part, the opposite of what the author
and her collaborator had hoped for and intended.

---

7. Notably Baldick.
8. The full list of examples in appendix 9.

SUSAN TYLER HITCHCOCK

[The Monster Lives On]†

By the middle of the nineteenth century, propelled as much by adaptations as by the novel itself, the myth of Frankenstein and his monster had entered the vernacular. The name "Frankenstein" had become a code word for misguided ambition, for new ideas conjured up with good intentions but destined to grow and change beyond all reckoning, ultimately overwhelming those who conceived them. With a swing away from Romantic idealism toward the conservative and pragmatic, the Victorians doubted that the human intellect could understand, control, replicate, or improve the world, whether that world meant natural phenomena or the social sphere. The Frankenstein myth gave them an icon for mistaken idealisms. Variations on the Frankenstein message entered politics, in new incarnations quite different from Canning's comments of 1824 about emancipating the slaves of the West Indies.

The myth fit well, for example, into arguments against the 1832 Reform Bill. The rules by which members of Parliament were elected, based on property ownership and ancient geographical boundaries, disenfranchised the middle and working classes in fast-growing industrial cities like Manchester and Birmingham. Liberal politicians sought to change the law to give more voting power to the masses. George IV and William IV, Victoria's predecessors, had favored Whig calls for social reform, but Tory conservatives fought it all the way. An odd couple—the Scottish radical Henry Brougham and the elegant prime minister, the Second Earl Grey—advocated a compromise bill that would extend the vote to half again as many Britons as before. The situation brought a recently reissued novel to mind, and in 1832 and 1833 several cartoonists referred to the familiar story in comments on the political scene. Brougham became a Frankenstein, the wigged Lord Grey his demented assistant. Together they were bringing to life a monster, a new voting population with the potential of rising up and destroying them—and with them, the old social order.

Cartoonists grabbed hold of the Frankenstein imagery to symbolize a good idea gone wrong. John Tenniel, today revered for his illustrations of *Alice in Wonderland* and *Through the Looking-Glass*, was better known by his contemporaries for political cartoons that appeared in the magazine *Punch* from 1850 to 1901. With his delicate touch and literary sophistication, Tenniel used the myth of

† From Frankenstein: *A Cultural History* (New York: Norton, 2007), 106–16. Copyright © 2007 by Susan Tyler Hitchcock. Used by permission of W. W. Norton & Company, Inc.

THE BRUMMAGEM FRANKENSTEIN.

JOHN BRIGHT. *"I have no fe—fe—fear of ma—manhood suffrage!"*

[MR. BRIGHT's Speech at Birmingham.

"Frankenstein's monster," meaning the newly empowered and now threatening working classes, became a familiar political sobriquet in the mid-nineteenth century, as in this 1866 cartoon parodying Birmingham's newly enlarged voting population. Print Collection, Miriam and Ira D. Wallach Division of Art, Prints, and Photographs. The New York Public Library, Astor, Lenox and Tilden Foundations.

Frankenstein over and over. In his "Brummagem Frankenstein," September 1866, he portrayed populist leader John Bright as a tiny figure, tiptoeing by a giant—an unshorn, pipe-smoking, fist-clenching, working-class man. Typifying citizens of Birmingham (nicknamed "Brummagem"), he glares down at his erstwhile creator. It was Tenniel's response to further efforts to extend voting rights, which he feared would create a working-class monster of unknown strength and disastrous proportions. Similarly, in 1882 Tenniel used Frankenstein imagery to comment on Charles Stewart Parnell and his campaign for Irish nationalism. Here the monster created is the Irish populace, now empowered, yet endowed—thanks to Tenniel's conservative English opinion—with unkempt hair, unshaven chin, predatory fangs, and a simian upper lip, atavistic and threatening. These cartoons settled in on a familiar political theme: Well-meaning reforms often create monsters. In Tenniel's imagination—and presumably that of his Victorian audience—the creature stood in for the Other—the dangerous unknown future force present in a population that is lower-class, newly enfranchised, and potentially threatening to those who have long held power and influence.

Other cartoonists, continuing into the twentieth century, used the Frankenstein myth to comment on war. Tenniel may have been the first, drawing "The Russian Frankenstein and His Monster" for *Punch* in July 1854, three months after Britain and France declared war on Russia in the Crimea. Dominating the frame is a giant figure, a war machine—cannons for legs, a mortar for a body. The monster charges, soulless eyes wide open, bloodied sword and torch held high, as uniformed British soldiers cower. The decision to go to war has made a monster, Tenniel implied: huge, powerful, inhuman, overwhelming.

Most references through the nineteenth century used Frankenstein's creation to symbolize a monstrous mistake, but radical philosophers in the late 1800s championed the monster, not the creator. On the one hand, the Fabian Socialist movement of the late nineteenth century was the offspring of the Reform Movement half a century earlier, seeking power for the working class; on the other, it entirely reversed the early-nineteenth-century rage against industrial technology, seeing machinery as the friend, not the enemy, of the worker. Members of the Fabian Society tagged playwright George Bernard Shaw to edit a collection of essays, spelling out their argument and social plan. Illustrious radical thinkers each contributed to the book, including Sidney Webb, a barrister and economist who with his wife, Beatrice, helped found the London School of Economics.

In early-eighteenth-century England, Webb wrote, a medieval economy still prevailed. The worker "was apparently better off in

Through the nineteenth century the monster remained
a malleable metaphor. In 1854 cartoonist John Tenniel
created "the Russian Frankenstein," his monster made
of weaponry, as a comment on the Crimean War.

1750 than at any other time between 1450 and 1850," even though
the simple, rural, unmechanized world that workers lived in was "a
world still mainly mediaeval," "a world of status and of permanent
social inequalities." New towns, new classes, new kinds of work had
all destroyed those feudal ways. The Industrial Revolution meant
"the final collapse of Mediaevalism," and it held hidden promise for
the working classes. "Within a couple of generations the squire faded
away before the mill-owner," wrote Webb, and now "new motors" are
"destroying the individualist conception of property. The landlord
and the capitalist are both finding that the steam-engine is a Frankenstein which they had better not have raised; for with it comes

inevitably urban Democracy, the study of Political Economy and Socialism."[1]

In this conceit the villainous pair of landlord and capitalist plays the creator, while the steam engine is the monster, capable of shifting power into the hands of the working class, which will then grow in strength and power beyond the creator's wildest imagining. To the Fabian Socialist, the monster, not the creator, is the hero, with his capacity to overturn the old order and grant wealth and power to the working class. Returning to a radical model, the Fabian philosophers of the late nineteenth century picked up the Godwinian strands in Mary Shelley's story—the portrayal of the creature as a victim of social forces, antagonistic because powerless, hostile because unloved. As a champion of the underdog, Webb reorients the moral from a Victorian caution to a socialist ideal. Unknowing creators have brought to life a monster, but he will stand tall and bring forth a brighter day in which the disenfranchised will come to power.

American Monsters

It did not take long for the imagery of the Frankenstein myth to appear in political commentaries on the other side of the Atlantic. Stage versions of the story had appeared in New York as early as 1825, an American edition of the novel as early as 1833. In the United States, as in Britain and on the Continent, the Frankenstein story first served as code language for mistaken political intentions. Reviewing "a sensible treatise on 'Popular Education,'"[2] a New York Daily Times writer in 1852 called adult students—that "host of uneducated human souls"—"as pernicious as the giant of Frankenstein Creation, potent in the capacity for evil; and without sufficient intellectual culture to control the exercise of his physical passions and powers." The educators, this writer implied, must do better than the original Frankenstein and "devise a plan for bringing these people under educational influences. The need is urgent." Seeing the metaphor come to life at a national level, abolitionist Charles Sumner predicted that the Confederacy would operate like "the soulless monster of Frankenstein."[3]

Malleable in its meaning, in 1900 the myth fit the times in other ways. The United States was waging its first colonial war on the other side of the globe, in the Philippines. Many decried the

1. Webb, "The Disintegration of the Old Synthesis," in Fabian Essays on Socialism, ed. George Bernard Shaw (London: The Walter Scott Publishing Co., 1908), pp. 54–55.
2. New York Daily Times, 14 December 1842. This and most subsequent references to newspaper articles researched through ProQuest Historical Newspapers.
3. Reported in E. Cobham Brewer, Dictionary of Phrase and Fable, 1898, as listed on http://www.bartelby.com/.

"Our Frankenstein," a political cartoon published in *Life* in 1900, shows the monster of European imperialism coming across the Atlantic to American shores.

government's imperialist intentions, seeing them as anathema to republicanism, isolationism, and the American commitment to free peoples everywhere. The November 1, 1900, issue of *Life* magazine included an oversize page that folded out to reveal a cartoon titled "Our Frankenstein." A giant crowned monarch, ermine cape flying, lurches ashore, menacing a small and startled Uncle Sam. In the distance, across the ocean, a city goes up in flames; on a nearby hilltop, a Greek temple bearing on its pediment one word—"Peace"—stands in ruins. Civilization is crumbling, and the monster causing such ruin is the embodiment of imperialism, clothed in European monarchic garb but arriving on Uncle Sam's shores.

* * *

References to Frankenstein and his monster seemed to shift from usage to usage, flinging associations hither and yon. In 1879 a tongue-in-cheek article about America's wealthiest citizenry described A. T. Stewart, founder of New York's first department store, as "a sort of *Frankenstein*, who had constructed a vast machine that was self-moving; but he fell into it, became himself only the central wheel of it, and died when he had worn out."[4] Defending Justus H. Schwab, an outspoken advocate for New York's working class, against charges of inciting a riot in February 1885, a lawyer argued that "Schwab was not the black Frankenstein that

4. *New York Times*, 19 May 1879, 4.

he had been painted, but he was an estimable citizen, with theories and pronunciamentos abreast of the able thought of the age."[5] In an 1887 commentary on the present force of munitions, thankfully in the hands of governments and not insurgents, a writer imagined what might happen if "Pekin [sic], or Mecca . . . forges Excaliburs successfully!" In his view, "a Chinaman with a repeating rifle which he knew fully how to use would be a Frankenstein against whom the human race might be obliged to unite in order to destroy him."[6] In an Indianapolis campaign speech in 1896, a legislative candidate mixed myths, stirring in Frankenstein with the Greeks for full effect, and promised:

> We deem it wise to pursue an aggressive rather than a negative policy, to be Achilles dragging Hector around the walls of Troy rather than Achilles sulking in his tent. We proposed to make a funeral pyre of the cadavers of Populism and Anarchy. We propose to drag behind our triumphant chariot wheels, in defeat and disgrace, around the National Capitol, the dead Frankenstein personifying their pernicious creed and their turbulent fanaticism.[7]

The more the references, the vaguer the meaning. The name of Frankenstein could refer to creator or creature. The confusion annoyed some readers. One wrote a letter to the editor of the *New York Times* in October 1902:

> The mistake is frequently made by writers and orators of describing a monster constructed by man as a "Frankenstein." Mr. James W. Osborne [an attorney] is reported in today's *Times* as being the latest offender in this respect. . . . A reference to Mrs. Shelley's gruesome book will assure the reader that Frankenstein was the man who made the monster and not the monster that was made.[8]

As this correspondent suggested, few of those alluding to the myth of Frankenstein had even read the novel. Indeed, references to Frankenstein proliferated wildly in Europe and the United States through decades when editions of the novel were difficult to find. In England few copies of the novel circulated in the decades between Mary Shelley's death and the 1880s. The last of its editions as one of Bentley's Standard Novels, still priced low at two shillings sixpence, came out in the early 1850s. By 1860 the plates for the novel, as well as others in the series, had been destroyed, but the publisher's copyright

5. Ibid., 20 May 1885, 3.
6. Ibid., 6 March 1887, 12.
7. Ibid., 3 September 1896, 3.
8. Ibid., 22 October 1902, 8.

kept others from reprinting it for another two decades. Once Bentley's copyright expired, the novel became more widely available, included in series such as the Ideal Library, Gem Classics, and, in 1912, Everyman's Library, published by Dent in Britain and Dutton in the United States, a standard edition still in print today. "Eighty years after its first appearance," writes reading historian William St. Clair, "*Frankenstein* at last became accessible to the whole reading nation,"[9] not only in its home country of Britain but in the United States as well.

"The number of writers who should have read 'Frankenstein,' and yet have not read it, is appalling,"[1] wrote a *New York Times* book critic in 1901, commenting on the novel's inclusion in the Gem Classics series.

> Rarely is any reference made to the book but we hear about "that monster Frankenstein." Now, poor Frankenstein was not the monster at all, yet for years he has done rhetorical service as such. It can only be fervently hoped that the successive editions of Mrs. Shelley's fantastic and tiresome tale may at last stamp out the fallacy.

After decades out of print, now the novel was everywhere. "Apparently no series of English classics, however limited, is considered distinctive or representative unless it includes a copy of 'Frankenstein,'" wrote the same critic, snidely adding, "Why, we are unable to say." Publishers may have wanted to convince the reading public that *Frankenstein* belonged in everyone's library—it was a gem, it was a classic—but for this critic at least, its literary merit was still in question.

ELIZABETH YOUNG

[Frankenstein as Historical Metaphor][†]

You can teach an old metaphor new tricks. In the Frankenstein story, first introduced in the novel by Mary Shelley in 1818 and made famous on film by James Whale in 1931, a monster, assembled from corpses and reanimated, rebels violently against his creator. The Frankenstein story has a long history of being used as a political metaphor, and at the start of the twenty-first century, it continues to shape political debate. Consider, for example, critiques of U.S.

---

9. St. Clair, *The Reading Nation in the Romantic Period*, 365.
1. *New York Times*, 28 September 1901, BR4.
† From *Black Frankenstein: The Making of an American Metaphor* (New York: NYU Press, 2008), 1–5. Reprinted by permission.

foreign policy in the wake of 9/11. In "We Finally Got Our Franken-stein," filmmaker Michael Moore compares Iraqi leader Saddam Hussein to the Frankenstein monster: "We had a virtual love fest with this Frankenstein whom we (in part) created. And, just like the mythical Frankenstein, Saddam eventually spun out of control. He would no longer do what he was told by his master. Saddam had to be caught." Moore considers Hussein one of many monsters cre-ated by the U.S. government, including Osama bin Laden—"Our other Frankenstein"—and a roster of right-wing dictators: "We liked playing Dr. Frankenstein. We created a lot of monsters—the Shah of Iran, Somoza of Nicaragua, Pinochet of Chile—and then we expressed ignorance or shock when they ran amok and massacred people."[1] Moore uses the Frankenstein metaphor to condemn the U.S. government for "playing Dr. Frankenstein," conducting a scientific experiment that is also a "love fest" gone wrong. Novelist Carlos Fuentes offers a similar cautionary tale but links the monster to a familial metaphor: "Saddam Hussein was Saddam Hussein because the United States gave him all possible support. The United States is extraordinarily gifted in creating monsters like Frankenstein. Then one fine day they discover that these Frankensteins are dreadful. However, for twenty years they were the spoilt children, their prote-ges, and the babies of the United States."[2] Journalist Maureen Dowd invokes the idea of religious overreaching when she condemns Vice President Dick Cheney "and his crazy-eyed Igors at the Pentagon [for] their hunger to remake the Middle East. It's often seen in scary movies: you play God to create something in your own image, and the monster you make ends up coming after you." She renames the vice president "Dr. Cheneystein."[3]

Even when the metaphor is not directly named, *Frankenstein* informs contemporary critiques of U.S. foreign policy. "Blowback" is the term popularized by Chalmers Johnson to describe contem-porary violence against the United States that results from its for-eign policy: "The most direct and obvious form of blowback often

1. Michael Moore, "We Finally Got Our Frankenstein . . . and He Was in a Spider Hole!" Michael Moore website, 14 December 2003, www.michaelmoore.com/words/message/index.php?messageDate=2003-12-14.
2. Carlos Fuentes, "The Invention of the Frankenstein Monster: Interview with Carlos Fuentes," originally published in *Freitag* 31, 23 July 2004, available in English at http://portland.indymedia.org/en/2004/07/293671.shtml.
3. Maureen Dowd, "White House of Horrors," *New York Times*, 28 October 2004, A29. There are many other explicit uses of Frankenstein imagery in contemporary political discourse; see, for example, Craig Unger, in *House of Bush, House of Saud: The Secret Relationship between the World's Two Most Powerful Dynasties* (New York: Scribner, 2004), who entitles a chapter "Another Frankenstein" and quotes former Pakistani prime minister Benazir Bhutto criticizing the first President Bush for his support of extremist groups: "You are creating a veritable Frankenstein" (111).

occurs when the victims fight back after a secret American bombing, or a U.S.-sponsored campaign of state terrorism, or a CIA-engineered overthrow of a foreign political leader."[4] With its plot of boomerang violence, *Frankenstein* is the embodiment of blowback, or as another commentator summarizes the theory, "Now the monster has turned on its creator."[5] In *Multitude: War and Democracy in the Age of Empire* (2004), Antonio Hardt and Michael Negri extract a different political lesson from *Frankenstein*. They open the volume, the sequel to their influential *Empire* (2000), with a discussion of the Frankenstein monster and the golem, another fictional monster who rebels against his creator. Writing "under the cloud of war . . . between September 11, 2001, and the 2003 Iraq War," Hardt and Negri suggest that both monster and golem are "whispering to us secretly under the din of our global battlefield . . . a lesson about the monstrosity of war and our possible redemption through love."[6] Later in the volume, Hardt and Negri use the Frankenstein monster as the affirmative symbol of the "multitude," their model of a global democratic proletariat. Since "Frankenstein is now a member of the family," they assert, "[t]he new world of monsters is where humanity has to grasp its future."[7] Hardt and Negri are vague on the details of this vision, but they are clearly faithful to Mary Shelley's own depiction of the monster as a sympathetic figure. The "love fest" of Moore's "We Finally Got Our Frankenstein" has become the "redemption through love" prompted by monsters.

These are disparate examples, varying in tone, sophistication, and target. My interest is in the metaphoric figure they employ as much as the political ground they occupy—or rather, in the way the figure shapes the ground. Metaphors matter to culture and thought, and these examples all suggest the continuing vitality of the Frankenstein metaphor for shaping contemporary political critique and, in particular, for voicing dissent against elites whose policies are seen as misguided in intention and disastrous in effect. Critiques of U.S. power are one inheritance of the Frankenstein story in a post-9/11 world; expressions of sympathy for the monstrous violence that defines that world are another. What we might call the "blowback" and "sympathy" themes of the Frankenstein story extract different

---

4. Chalmers Johnson, *Blowback: The Costs and Consequences of American Empire*, 2nd ed. (New York: Henry Holt, 2004), 9. This term has a longer history; see Patricia M. Thornton and Thomas F., Thornton, "Blowback," in *Collateral Language: A User's Guide to America's New War*, ed. John Collins and Ross Glover (New York: NYU Press, 2002), 27–38.
5. Louis Menand, "Faith, Hope, and Clarity," *New Yorker*, 16 September 2002, 98.
6. Michael Hardt and Antonio Negri, *Multitude: War and Democracy in the Age of Empire* (New York: Penguin, 2004), xviii, 12.
7. Ibid., 196.

but complementary meanings from it, using it to criticize monster-makers and to explain monstrous violence, if not to defend monsters themselves.

Highlighting some contemporary political uses of the Frankenstein metaphor, these examples also suggest some ambiguities intrinsic to this metaphor. Moore employs "Frankenstein" to signal both monster and monster-maker, whereas in Shelley's novel "Frankenstein" refers only to the maker, who is a university student, not a doctor; Fuentes's image of Hussein as a long-time "spoilt baby" has no correspondence to the plot of the novel, in which the creature is abandoned from birth; Dowd's reference to Igor, the scientist's assistant, is to the film version of *Frankenstein*. Such changes themselves have a long history: the term "Frankenstein" migrated from creator to monster as early as the 1830s, and the assistant character was added to theatrical productions in the 1820s.[8] Combining different elements of the Frankenstein story, these writers do not so much replace older versions with newer ones as reanimate elements in place since the early nineteenth century. In these processes of recombination and reanimation, they mimic the actions of Victor Frankenstein within the story, a self-reflexivity that Mary Shelley had set in motion in her 1831 preface to the novel, in which she aligned monster and book: "I bid my hideous progeny go forth and prosper."[9] The piecing-together process by which "Frankenstein" becomes "Cheneystein" is part of a longer, and indeed prosperous, history in which commentators on *Frankenstein* reprise the monster-making in the novel itself.

There are, of course, many other strands of Frankenstein imagery in contemporary political culture, including references to the story in discussions of stem-cell research, cloning, cosmetic surgery, and genetically modified foods.[1] These discussions draw on the implications of the idea of "Frankenstein" as monstrous creation, an idea embodied in the neologisms drawn from the word itself. Thus, a judge ruling in a lawsuit against McDonald's Chicken McNuggets condemns this product as "a McFrankenstein creation"; opponents

8. On the origins of the nominal confusion over "Frankenstein," see Steven Earl Forry, *Hideous Progenies: Dramatizations of Frankenstein from Mary Shelley to the Present* (Philadelphia: U of Pennsylvania P, 1990), 36–37.
9. Mary Shelley, *Frankenstein*, ed. J. Paul Hunter (New York: Norton, 1996), 173.
1. On the use of Frankenstein imagery in discussions of reproductive technologies, see Jon Turney, *Frankenstein's Footsteps: Science, Genetics, and Popular Culture* (New Haven, CT: Yale UP, 1998); in discussions of cosmetic surgery, see Virginia L. Blum, *Flesh Wounds: The Culture of Cosmetic Surgery* (Berkeley: U of California P, 2003), esp. chap. 4; and in discussions of cadavers, see Mary Roach, *Stiff: The Curious Lives of Human Cadavers* (New York: Norton, 2003), esp. 197. For a survey of recent examples of Frankenstein imagery, see Susan Tyler Hitchcock, *Frankenstein: A Cultural History* (New York: Norton, 2007), 264–322.

of a cellphone tower designed to look like a fir tree term it "Frankenpine."[2] Whereas these examples provide a verbal analogue to hybrid monsters, others also make the connection to monster-makers. For example, campaigners against "frankenfoods" attack genetically modified foods as monstrous creations, while also targeting the corporations that produce these foods, like Monsanto, as both monster-makers and monsterlike agribusiness giants.[3] Moreover, the metaphor is used by those on the political right as well as the left. For example, Leon Kass, former chairman of President Bush's Council of Bioethics, has excoriated cloning for what he sees as its place on a slippery slope of social wrongs including feminism, single-parenting, gay rights, sex with animals, cannibalism, and the desecration of corpses. Counseling "the wisdom of repugnance" against cloning, Kass condemns "the Frankensteinian hubris to create human life and increasingly to control its destiny."[4]

But if the Frankenstein metaphor is so protean that it sometimes seems to defy categorization, it does have particularly significant forms. I have chosen to begin with examples from left-wing discussions of U.S. foreign policy because they highlight the vitality of the Frankenstein metaphor, in a context far removed from its specific plot of bodily animation, as a contemporary language of political dissent. This book investigates one prehistory of such political critiques, tracking the Frankenstein metaphor in U.S. literature, film, and culture of the past two centuries in relation to the interdependent themes of race and nation. These themes converge in the sustained, multivalent, and revelatory imagery of a black American Frankenstein monster.

Writing in 1860 on the eve of Civil War, Frederick Douglass declared, "Slavery is everywhere the pet monster of the American

2. On "McFrankenstein," see Benjamin Weiser, "Your Honor, We Call Our Next Witness: McFrankenstein," *New York Times*, 26 January 2003, Week in Review section, 5. On "Frankenpine," see Eleanor Randolph, "The Cell Tower Blight: Text-Message Calder, ASAP," *New York Times*, 26 February 2005, A26. For commentary on recent permutations of the word, see William Safire, "On Language," *New York Times Magazine*, 13 August 2000, 23, reprinted as "Franken-A Monstrous Prefix is Stalking Europe," in *Genetically Modified Foods: Debating Biotechnology*, ed. Michael Ruse and David Castle (Amherst, NY: Prometheus Books, 2002), 133–34.
3. For a description of the movement against "frankenfoods," see Bill Lambrecht, *Dinner at the New Gene Café: How Genetic Engineering Is Changing What We Eat, How We Live, and the Global Politics of Food* (New York: Thomas Dunne/St. Martins, 2001), 232–36; for analysis of the concept, see Elaine L. Graham, *Representations of the Post/Human: Monsters, Aliens and Others in Popular Culture* (New Brunswick, NJ: Rutgers University Press, 2002), 13–14, 25–26.
4. Leon R. Kass, "The Wisdom of Repugnance," in Leon R. Kass and James Q. Wilson, *The Ethics of Human Cloning* (Washington, DC: American Enterprise Institute Press, 1998), 18; the essay was first published in the *New Republic* in 1997. For a critique of this essay, see Chris Mooney, "Irrationalist in Chief," *American Prospect*, 24 September 2001, 10–13. For a more sympathetic view of Kass, see Hitchcock, *Frankenstein*, 297–303.

people."⁵ A century later, in the midst of the second Civil War launched by the civil rights movement, comedian and activist Dick Gregory specified the legacy of that "pet monster." When he saw James Whale's *Frankenstein* as a child, Gregory remembered, he realized that "[h]ere was a monster, created by a white man, turning upon his creator. The horror movie was merely a parable of life in the ghetto. The monstrous life of the ghetto has been created by the white man. Only now in the city of chaos are we seeing the monster created by oppression turn upon its creator."⁶ In the "now" of 1968, Gregory saw the African American urban uprisings of the era in terms of the monster's revenge against his creator. In the sphere of domestic U.S. race relations, as in that of U.S. foreign policy, *Frankenstein* was the story of blowback.

[T]he genealogy [runs] from Douglass to Gregory and beyond, [indicating] the importance of the metaphor of the black Frankenstein monster in nineteenth- and twentieth-century U.S. culture. *Frankenstein* and its legacy have been the subject of substantial amounts of scholarly and popular writing, but little serious attention has been paid to the historical specificities of its place in American culture, and virtually none to its racial resonances in the United States.⁷ I take up the question of what happens to the Frankenstein story in America, defining that story in its most basic form as having three distinct elements: a monster is amalgamated from body parts; a monster is reanimated from corpses; and a monster engages in revolt against a creator. Drawn from these elements, the figure of a black Frankenstein monster appears frequently throughout nineteenth- and twentieth-century American culture, in fiction, essays, oratory, film, painting, and other media, and in works by both whites and African Americans. Described as yellow in the novel, painted blue in nineteenth-century stage incarnations, and tinted green in twentieth-century cinematic ones, the monsters color nonetheless signifies symbolically, on the domestic American scene, as black.

In this genealogy of black Frankenstein stories, the figure of the monster is consistently intertwined with fantasies and anxieties about masculinity, relations between men, and the male iconography of the American nation. Within this terrain of masculinity, the Frankenstein metaphor is mutable in its politics. It is sometimes invoked by political conservatives, but it has tended to serve more

5. Frederick Douglass, "Slavery and the Irrepressible Conflict" (1860), in *The Frederick Douglass Papers*, ed. John W. Blassingame et al. (New Haven, CT: Yale University Press, 1985), ser. 1, 3:370.
6. Dick Gregory, *The Shadow That Scares Me*, ed. James R. McGraw (New York: Pocket, 1968), 168.
7. The modern revival of scholarly interest in Frankenstein was initiated by U. C. Knoepflmacher and George Levine, eds., *The Endurance of Frankenstein: Essays on Mary Shelley's Novel* (Berkeley: U of California P, 1979).

effectively as a radical condemnation of those in power for making monsters or as a defense of monsters themselves. In a racist culture that already considered black men monstrous and contained them within paternalist rhetoric, the Frankenstein story, with its focus on the literal making of monsters and the unmaking of fathers, provided a stylized rhetoric with which to turn an existing discourse of black monstrosity against itself. Black Frankenstein stories, I argue, effected four kinds of antiracist critique: they humanized the slave; they explained, if not justified, his violence; they condemned the slaveowner; and they exposed the instability of white power.

* * *

DAVID PIRIE

Approaches to *Frankenstein* [in Film]†

How can I describe my emotions at this catastrophe, or how delineate the wretch whom with such infinite pains and care I had endeavoured to form? His limbs were in proportion, and I had selected his features as beautiful. Beautiful!—Great God! His yellow skin scarcely covered the work of muscles and arteries beneath. His hair was of a lustrous black and flowing. His teeth of a pearly whiteness. But these luxuriances only formed a more horrid contrast with his watery eyes, that seemed almost of the same colour as the dun white sockets in which they were set, his shrivelled complexion and straight black lips.
Mary Shelley: *Frankenstein or the Modern Prometheus*

'In short, the man I once loved is dead. This is a vampire.'
Harriet Shelley in a letter to Catherine Nugent,
20 November 1819

The summer house-party which took place in 1816 at Lord Byron's villa by Lake Geneva has been justly celebrated as a key moment in the history of English Romantic art. Together with Shelley and Byron were Mary Godwin (later to become Mary Shelley), Dr. Polidori, Byron's personal Italian physician, and Jane Clairmont, Mary's hysterical but beautiful stepsister who was in the process of conducting a sporadic affair with Byron.

The combination was in any sense an electric one and Mary Shelley's account of it, in her much quoted preface to the novel (written ten years after Shelley's death), is understandably restrained and tactful. A better understanding of the milieu in which *Frankenstein*

† From *A Heritage of Horror: The English Gothic Cinema, 1946–1972* (London: Gordon Fraser, 1973), 66–81.

was created may be derived from Shelley's own diary. Eighteen months before the occasion in Geneva he wrote this long but not untypical account of a night spent with Jane and Mary in London which gives an excellent idea of the way in which he was prone to conduct these nightly sessions:

> Friday, October 7th (Shelley's entry):
> Mary goes to bed at half past eight; Shelley sits up with Jane. At one o'clock Shelley observes that it is the witching hour of night: he enquires soon after if it is not horrible to feel the silence of night tingling in our ears; in half an hour the question is repeated in a different form; at two they retire awestruck and hardly dare to breathe. Shelley says to Jane 'Good Night'; his hand is leaning on the table; he is conscious of an expression in his countenance which he cannot repress. Jane hesitates. 'Good Night' again. She still hesitates. 'Did you ever read the tragedy of Orra?' said Shelley. 'Yes. How horribly you look!—Turn your eyes off.' 'Good Night', again, and Jane runs to her room. Shelley unable to sleep kisses Mary, and prepares to sit beside her and read till morning when rapid footsteps descend the stairs. Jane was there; her countenance was distorted most unnaturally by horrible dismay—it beamed with a whiteness that seemed almost like light; her lips and cheeks were of one deadly hue; the skin of her face and forehead was drawn into innumerable wrinkles—the lineaments of terror which could not be contained; her hair came prominent and erect; her eyes were wide and staring drawn almost from the sockets by the convulsion of the muscles; the eyelids were forced in, and the eyeballs, without any relief, seemed as if they had been newly inserted, in ghastly sport, in the sockets of a lifeless head. This frightful spectacle endured but for a few moments—it was displaced by terror and confusion, violent indeed, and full of dismay, but human. She asked me if I had touched her pillow (her tone was that of dreadful alarm). I said 'No, no! If you will come into the room I will tell you'. I informed her of Mary's pregnancy; this seemed to check her violence. She told me that a pillow placed upon her bed had moved, in the moment that she turned her eyes away to a chair at some distance, and evidently by no human power. She was positive as to the facts of her self-possession and calmness. Her manner convinced me that she was not deceived. We continued to sit by the fire, at intervals indulging in awful conversation relative to the nature of these mysteries. I read parts of 'Alexy'; I repeated one of my own poems. Our conversation, although intentionally directed to other topics, irresistibly recurred to these. Our candles burned low; we feared they would not last until daylight. Just as the dawn was struggling with moonlight,

Jane remarked in me that unutterable expression which had
affected her with so much horror before; she described it as
expressing a mixture of deep sadness and conscious power over
her. I covered my face with my hands, and spoke to her in the
most studied gentleness. It was ineffectual; her horror and
agony increased even to the most dreadful convulsions. She
shrieked and writhed on the floor. I ran to Mary; I communicated in a few words the state of Jane. I brought her to Mary.
The convulsions gradually ceased, and she slept. At daybreak
we examined her apartment and found her pillow on the chair.

This passage sums up admirably the kind of charged hyper-
emotional atmosphere in which the Shelley ménage (especially when
it included Jane) existed day after day, and by all accounts the time
spent at Byron's villa Diodati, where Mary first conceived *Frankenstein*, was particularly fraught. It is certainly no coincidence that the
little gathering resulted in *both* of the central English Gothic myths
(Polidori's enormously influential short story *The Vampire* was the
first prose account of vampirism in English and undoubtedly supplied primary source material for Bram Stoker some seventy-eight
years later).

A close reading of the novel which Mary Shelley conceived that
wet summer as a result of Byron's suggestion that they should all
write a ghost story quickly reveals that it never has been—and is
never likely to be—faithfully adapted to the screen. Based on a brilliant and disturbing central idea, that of a man who creates an innocent and intelligent but ugly creature which is shunned by humanity
and gradually becomes its creator's *doppelganger*, the difficulties in
adapting it as it stands are more or less insuperable. There is simply
no way in which the kind of 'noble savage' monster which Mary
Shelley envisaged, reading *Paradise Lost* and expounding moral
principles to its creator, *could* be presented in the cinema without immediately becoming ludicrous. In order to make *Frankenstein*
believable, the filmmaker has regrettably almost always had to dis-
pense with the monster's intellectual equipment and this is true of
every single film bearing the title except one (Fisher's extraordinary
Frankenstein Must Be Destroyed which will be discussed at some
length later in this chapter). What is more surprising is that the
films have also seen fit to omit many of the novel's descriptive set
pieces, even those—like Frankenstein's nightmarish laboratory in
a deserted Orkney croft—which would seem absolutely ideal for
their purposes. As in the case of *Dracula* there has often been little
attempt to keep the narrative of the original intact, but this is not
nearly so serious as might be supposed for, as with any real myth,
the essential structure of *Frankenstein* (a man creating life out of

death but being destroyed by his creation) is practically inviolable. It is more frustrating perhaps that so little interpretation has been attempted by film-makers, for much of the power and durability of the Frankenstein myth would seem to lie in the fact that it depicts in cruel symbolic images the basic processes of human reproduction followed by the inevitable power struggle between father and son, in which the father is always destined to be destroyed.

Mary Shelley's novel was first properly adapted for the screen in 1931, and one of the minor alterations that Universal made was to elevate its leading character to the nobility. Perhaps they wished to be certain of repeating their success of a year earlier with the aristocratic Count Dracula, but this almost accidental alteration was to have far-reaching implications when it was taken up by Hammer twenty-five years later. In the meantime the Henry Frankenstein character as Universal portrayed him, together with certain aspects of the script, greatly weakened James Whale's remarkable film. In the part Colin Clive alternates unconvincingly between extravagant monomania and wooden riding-booted heroics, while Robert Florey's ridiculous idea of giving the monster an accidental 'criminal brain' renders much of the story pointless and seriously undermines Karloff's magnificent performance. Even so, in spite of these blunders, the overall effect of Whale's stunning expressionist photography and Karloff's interpretation of the monster remains extremely potent. Most of the Universal horror films (in particular Browning's overrated and tedious *Dracula*) cannot compare with the robust consistency of Terence Fisher's work, but Whale's *Frankenstein* (and its sequel *The Bride of Frankenstein*) are the exceptions. They remain magnificent examples, not of the Gothic, but of a particularly baroque form of American expressionism, and they have dated very little over the years.

The significance of the critical outrage which greeted Hammer's *The Curse of Frankenstein* when it appeared in 1957 has already been discussed. It is by now well known that, although Mary Shelley's book was in the public domain, the original monster make-up was copyright and Hammer were fortunately obliged to mount an entirely new conception of the whole myth. In retrospect it is bizarre that so much critical attention should have centred on the monster (especially its failure to compare with Karloff) for, whatever else may be said about *The Curse of Frankenstein*, the *physical* appearance of the monster conforms extremely closely to Mary Shelley's description: '. . . his yellow skin scarcely covered the work of muscles and arteries beneath. His hair was of a lustrous black and flowing. But these luxuriances only formed a more horrid contrast with his watery eyes, that seemed almost of the same colour as the dun white sockets in which they were set, his shrivelled complexion and straight black lips.'

What Hammer *did* substantially alter was the weakest aspect of
the Universal series: the character of the Baron himself. Rejecting
the bland and self-pitying martyr of fate, whom Mary Shelley originally envisaged, Terence Fisher and his collaborators transformed
the Baron into a magnificently arrogant aristocratic rebel, in the
direct Byronic tradition, who never relinquishes his explorations for
one moment, even reviving the monster after it has been killed once,
and conducting himself throughout with an utterly unscrupulous
and authoritative elegance: he dresses with an extravagant attention
to detail, enjoys food, wine and women, pursues studies in countless
diverse fields and even sings softly in the laboratory as he works. But
his will at the same time remains absolutely inflexible. In fact, as one
examines the minutiae of Peter Cushing's performance, it is scarcely
possible to resist the impression that this is Frankenstein as he would
have been seen through the eyes of Baudelaire or Oscar Wilde, in the
latter part of the nineteenth century. For Cushing conforms almost
exactly to Baudelaire's complex definition of the 'dandy': 'Above all
else it is the burning need to create an originality for oneself, a
need contained within the exterior limit of convention. . . . It is the
pleasure of astonishing and the proud satisfaction of never being
astonished . . . they all participate in the same characteristics of
opposition and revolt; they are all representative of what is best in
human pride, in that need which is too rare in the men of today, *of
opposing and demolishing triviality.*'

Baudelaire's 'dandy', as his account suggests, is an extravagant
rebel who alternates between noble defiance and detached cruelty.
He is authoritarian, diligent and creative but utterly single-minded
and unscrupulous and Cushing's portrayal of the Baron, in precisely
this mould, was nicely complemented by Fisher's colourful and precise direction. Quite correctly in the circumstances, Fisher brings
no expressionism to the piece at all, but instead uses all the resources
at his disposal to depict the extravagant contrasts which punctuate
the Baron's world. His direction continually juxtaposes the elegant,
shiny décor of the Victorian drawing-room, full of polished mahog-
any and over-dressed women with the grisly appendages of the laboratory, and we watch Cushing glide easily from one to the other,
sitting down to an excellent breakfast, for example, shortly after he
has seen his monster murder a girl. Fisher also goes to enormous
trouble in his use of the technique—so popular in Gothic novels—of
contrasting beautiful natural scenery with human depravity and
corruption. The monster's slaughter of an old man and its first
destruction takes place by the side of an autumnal wood in a series
of compositions which employ green and gold to maximum effect.

Perhaps the most spectacular scene of all in Hammer's first *Frankenstein* is the birth of the monster. As a general rule, the laborato-

ries of Fisher's *Frankenstein* films are an aesthetic delight, full of bizarre colour effects and mysterious noises, so that it is often as though Cushing was conducting some kind of elaborate symphony in sound and light as he moves delicately back and forth through the rows of equipment. In *The Curse of Frankenstein,* he is forced at the last moment to leave the laboratory for help and as he runs back Fisher tracks through the door to reveal with terrible suddenness in mid-long shot an enormously grotesque figure, swathed in white bandages, staggering forward towards him. Christopher Lee's monster, which comes into the world so abruptly, late in the film, and attempts to strangle its creator as soon as it is born, is certainly the most brutal and depraved in any Frankenstein film. Yet Lee still somehow contrives to make it seem pitiful and wretched, so that he is one of the tiny number of actors who can be said to have given the part depth and subtlety, despite the fact that the monster's appearances are extremely brief. His performance may be ultimately less moving than Karloff's, but it is no less brilliant or disturbing, with its jerky, kinetic, puppet-like walk, which suggests a deformed animal in pain.

The change of emphasis that Hammer had made in the Frankenstein myth—making the Baron, rather than the monster, its central character—turned out to be fully justified in box-office terms, for, just as public demand forced Universal to revive the Frankenstein monster, in Hammer's version it was his *creator* who had conquered audiences. Cushing was in fact the hero (or anti-hero) of the film (just as Karloff had been the hero of the first *Frankenstein*), and it was thus necessary to save him from the oddly incongruous execution that he had suffered at its climax. (The Baron's plea for mercy at the end of *The Curse of Frankenstein* is the single jarring note in any part of the characterisation and perhaps reflects a slight uncertainty on Hammer's part about public reaction.) *The Revenge of Frankenstein,* which followed, contains no such hesitation and the tone of the Frankenstein character was by now completely and unfalteringly established. The film begins with his execution, but as is soon made clear, Frankenstein's henchmen have complied with their master's satanically humorous instructions by guillotining the priest instead. Shortly afterwards the flamboyant and brilliant Doctor Stein, an alias of Frankenstein, begins to practice in Carlsbruck and outrages the stuffy local doctors by his generosity and his skill.

Several of Fisher's heroes thrive on ambiguity, but none more so than the Baron Frankenstein and the central ambiguity in his character is most fully elaborated in *The Revenge of Frankenstein.* Here the Baron works diligently and mercifully at the local poor hospital in Carlsbruck, but is at the same time using it as a means of augmenting his supply of human limbs not in order to create an independent entity, but simply to give his crippled hunchback assistant

Hans a new body and so cure him of his suffering. The sadistic and noble elements in his character thus exist side by side and, as in *The Curse of Frankenstein*, the operation is finally frustrated, not by an arbitrary mechanism (Universal's 'criminal brain'), but by the contempt and fear in which his activities are held by the populace, including the bourgeois local doctors and the ignorant patients in his own hospital. It is in this respect that the character comes closest to being a victimised scientific pioneer in the tradition of Galileo or Freud, for there can be no doubt that by the time the patients of his hospital turn on him (in an extraordinary scene strongly reminiscent of *Marat-Sade*), he has begun to take on the role not only of a hero but of a martyr. One of the other most impressive elements in the film is exemplified by the scene in which Frankenstein's hated identity is revealed to the society of Carlsbruck. Hans, who has been given his new body, is desperately in heed of help after being beaten up by a brutal janitor (George Woodbridge). His form is beginning to twist and turn with gruesome realism into its original deformity as he stumbles across the grass towards the large house where Frankenstein is attending a ball with the local gentry. Windows undoubtedly have a special importance in Fisher's work as the means by which chaos and dream overtake reality (cf. *Dracula*), and in this particular instance the French windows of the house become a focus for the mutual collision of two opposite worlds, one of superficial politeness and opulence and grace, the other of death and insanity and ugliness. As the Baron is engaged in some polite conversation with his hostess Hans crashes through the French windows—his body further disfigured by glass and mud—and careers into the terrified guests shouting 'Frankenstein, help me!'. In no specific political sense is it possible to call Fisher's art revolutionary, but it does have revolutionary moments and this astonishing image of the forces of chaos and disorder erupting into a repressive community is certainly one of them.

Both *The Curse of Frankenstein* and *The Revenge of Frankenstein* represent imaginative extensions of the schema I have already analysed in Fisher's work. Frankenstein's complex and ambiguous character becomes a host for two distinct opposing forces, the one of generosity, self-sacrifice and exploration, the other of greed, cruelty and blasphemy. Fisher even contrives to exemplify this tension through his camera movements as in one of the confrontations between Victor and his assistant Paul in *The Curse* shortly after the monster has come to life. Frankenstein says: 'That's the brain, when you attacked me it was damaged. That makes it your fault, Paul,' and as he says it, the camera tracks forward to a mid-long shot of Paul, underlining the truth of his words. As in practically all Fisher's movies, it *is* to a large extent outside interference that prevents Frankenstein from succeeding. But on the other hand this view does not take into account the other side of the Baron's character; and in order to show this, Fisher closes the sequence by tracking in ominously to hold a close two-shot of Victor alone with his grotesque creation, which explicitly identifies him with it. The identification reaches its ultimate imaginative extension in the extraordinary climax of *The Revenge* where the Baron actually inhabits the body he has created and literally *becomes* his own creation. The first two Frankenstein films also contain the comic characterisation, which gives them their slight Dickensian flavour (in this instance Paul Hardtmuth and Lionel Jeffries) and the strictly linear handling of narrative which we have come to expect. But unfortunately at this point Fisher's Frankenstein series was interrupted for very nearly ten years. *The Revenge of Frankenstein* was not as successful as its forerunner, and it was not until 1963 that Hammer decided to make another in the series, this time with Freddie Francis directing.

The Evil of Frankenstein, written by John Elder (Anthony Hinds), turned out to be a most disappointing film whose only real merit was that it indicated, beyond a shadow of a doubt, how great Fisher's contribution to the series had been. Francis and his collaborators apparently went all out to ignore the earlier Hammer films and took their inspiration from Universal, but the attempt was a dire failure which resulted in a thoroughly pedestrian and cardboard thriller. In the first place, they were unable to abandon the essential points of Peter Cushing's characterisation of the Baron which by this time was far too well entrenched in the public imagination and instead had to concentrate on a futile effort to make Kiwi Kingston look like Boris Karloff. Meanwhile the Baron's laboratory, which had reached a peak of abstract colourful perfection in *The Revenge*, was reduced to a sorry remnant of wires and lightning conductors. The plot which might possibly have contained some pleasing nostalgia for the old Universal days is a repetitive and tedious accumulation of accidents, involving a hypnotist who uses a lumbering and unimpressive monster for his own ends. It is better to pass on to the happier occasion of 1966, when once again Fisher took up the reins of a Frankenstein film: *Frankenstein Created Woman*.

If the *Evil of Frankenstein* had unsuccessfully plagiarised the Universal approach, *Frankenstein Created Woman* takes us just about as far away from anything that Universal could have concocted as it is possible to go. Again, the preoccupation of the script and direction lie to some extent with the Baron, who appears as a kind of philosophical explorer, but on this occasion he is less in evidence than before and the strong undercurrent of sexual imagery which runs through so much of Fisher's work is completely dominant. The film rapidly develops into an extravagant fairy-tale full of decadent romantic imagery, with Fisher using the spurious scientific contrivance of soul transplants to take the recurrent nineteenth-century image of the Fatal Woman to its logical conclusion. In retrospect, bearing in mind the discussion in the chapter on Fisher, it seems inevitable that Frankenstein's female creation should, in Fisher's world, turn out to be not some fiend, but, instead, a deadly seductress. The monster in *Frankenstein Created Woman* is the soul of a man imprisoned in the outer physical shell of a woman's body and (as in Fisher's most recent Frankenstein, *Frankenstein Must Be Destroyed*), it is precisely this tension between matter and spirit that causes the final destruction.

The central character of the film is Christina, a pretty girl who is seriously deformed on one side of her face and body. The 'Beauty of the Medusa' theme is fully indulged here when, for example, Christina's lover Hans touches her scar admiringly while the camera lingers, and Fisher even juxtaposes their lovemaking with Frankenstein's magical (and phallic) energy machine ('You see the energy . . . the force trapped in cells being released'). The scene is thus set for the miraculous series of sexual events which are to occur: in a succession of incidents, for which three young men are responsible, both Christina and Hans are killed, and Frankenstein, unashamedly in the role of an enchanter on the side of justice, employs his energy machine to merge the two of them into Christina's rejuvenated and healed body. Now given an utterly sensual, hermaphroditic and polymorphous-perverse rejuvenation, Christina sets about seducing and murdering the men who previously killed her father and had Hans hanged. Like Keats's Lamia, she is the illusory incarnation of female beauty who has only recently been transformed from her true hideous shape, and in fact some of the lines which Keats uses in *Lamia* are perfectly appropriate here, just as the images with which Fisher mounts the whole thing have a strong echo of Keats's highly fanciful medievalism:

> A virgin purest lipp'd yet in the lore
> Of love deep learned to the red heart's core:
> Not one hour old, yet of sciential brain
> To unperplex bliss from its neighbour, pain;

In scene after scene of cloying beauty, Christina stalks and lures her victims with a kind of vampiric power continually acting out the fears of all sexual fantasy by metamorphosing into a vengeful beast at the moment of intercourse. Finally, Christina and her third victim, John, go for a picnic, and the situation is less straightforward here in that John is the nicest and least culpable of the three men responsible (indirectly) for her death. The scene is constructed with some beauty in a setting of grass and trees and John's green suit matches the landscape while Christina in a black and purple cape violates it like some aggressive animal. The mythological associations are immediately obvious. Meanwhile Frankenstein, who has realised what has been happening and is searching for her, finally stumbles on the clearing to find (in a shot that has been put together with tremendous care) that John is already Christina's victim and she is holding Hans's head in her hands, talking to it in Hans's voice. The head replies in her own voice, thus the confusion and intermingling of her spiritual identity with his is complete whereupon she drowns herself so that she can be free of the imprisoning body. It should be emphasised that what could have so easily degenerated into cheap sensationalism becomes in Fisher's hands a measured and convincing fusion of myth and nightmare. As this account clearly indicates the plot of *Frankenstein Created Woman* is, on any thematic level, absurd, but then that can be said of a great many works which generate a considerable force within their dream-like atmosphere. It is not as intellectually satisfying as Fisher's two earlier Frankenstein films, but in one respect—the sheer beauty and poetry of its images—it certainly excels them.

Following *Frankenstein Created Woman*, there is a three-year lull until Fisher's final Frankenstein film which has a special place for a number of reasons, the most important being that it is his last film to date. Made in 1969 and written by Bert Batt, a Hammer staff assistant director, it marked a further departure from the simple 'monster' theme, and again concerned a conflict between spirit and body via the—by 1969—topical subject of brain transplantation. Peter Cushing, in his last performance to date as the Baron, began by recalling the full flexibility and ambiguity that he had first introduced to the character in 1956. Still well within the complex role which he has used so brilliantly over the years, he chose in this last performance to isolate some of its cruellest and most unscrupulous components and so perhaps to finally implicate the audience in their own sympathy for him and arouse their guilt. Certainly it is this Hitchcockian mechanism which makes Hammer's use of the Baron since *The Curse* so intriguing, with the result that when one considers the films as a whole his character reaches a level of subtlety that can be compared interestingly with the most equivocal of nineteenth-century anti-heroes.

Frankenstein Must Be Destroyed begins with the Baron murdering a passer-by in order to procure material for his experiments and, after a spirited fight with a burglar amidst the ghoulish apparatus of his secret laboratory (which is utterly wrecked in the process), he is forced to blackmail a young couple into assisting him with his experiments ('I need her to make coffee' he says at one point). In all these early scenes, Fisher is at pains to juxtapose the Baron's deft courtesy and elegance with his brutality exemplified in symbolic terms by a shock cut from the bourgeois drawing-room milieu ('You will find it very quiet here') to a lunatic screaming in his cell. On another occasion—somewhat reminiscent of the final cut in *Psycho* and almost as effective—he closely follows a shot of the Baron buying a flower for his buttonhole in the market with the sudden bursting of a water-pipe in his garden which causes one of his victims' bodies to jet up through the mud, In due course the Baron and his new assistants abduct his former colleague, Brandt, from an insane asylum in order to obtain information from him and, when he dies of a heart attack, Frankenstein transplants his brain into the body of the distinguished Professor Richter. Then in a moment of superb irony and cruelty, Brandt's wife, who has no way of knowing about the transformation Frankenstein has initiated, is taken on her own insistence to see her husband who is wrapped in bandages. The horror of this scene in which the wife ecstatically recognises her now sane husband from his whispered words is amplified, not only because Fisher cuts almost directly from it to the macabre spectacle of Brandt in a carriage at night being fed through a tube, but by the fact that the audience is again being forced to make a complex moral judgement about Frankenstein's character and actions. He has performed a grotesque operation on his colleague and yet we know that he has also saved his life and his sanity. Beyond this, the situation is immediately relevant to Fisher's dualism. Brandt's brain is now in another body, and consequently inhabits a kind of limbo, sealed off from communication by a shell of alien matter. Finally, in a scene of agonising romantic significance (which echoes the scene in *The Revenge* in which Hans crashes for help through the drawing-room window), Brandt's pathetic half-disintegrated form returns to walk silently through his former home and mounts the stairs to cry as he watches his wife sleeping. When she wakes up, he tries to explain from behind a screen what has happened, but she completely fails to understand or believe in him and there is no way in which his brain can make contact with her or pierce the shell in which it is contained. He is a lost soul, in the most graphic sense. Finally Frankenstein tracks Brandt to the house where he finds an agonised monster who is concerned only with destroying him. In a protracted struggle the house is set on fire and the last image shows the monster carrying his master through the door of the house back into the inferno which rages within.

So, for what was to prove for several years his last film in the series Fisher had reserved a marvellous surprise. Always a Romantic in the fullest sense, he contrived to make *Frankenstein Must Be Destroyed* into a positively inspired essay on the whole theme of change and nostalgia, using the science-fiction element as a mere pretext to create with Freddie Jones's help, one of the most overtly sympathetic and moving Frankenstein monsters in the history of the cinema. It is completely fitting that this particular creation was the only one of Fisher's monsters to finally threaten and destroy its maker in the traditional fashion; for it represented a degree of emotional complexity with which even Cushing's Baron could not compete.

In the circumstances it would be appropriate if one could leave the Hammer Frankenstein movies at this climax, but there is a further film to discuss. Realising, quite correctly, that *Frankenstein Must Be Destroyed* represented the grand finale to the rich vein they had been mining throughout the 1960s, Hammer chose in 1970 to try a completely new approach to the series. Presumably with one eye on the success of the various 'tongue in cheek' black comedies that were currently fashionable, they hired Jimmy Sangster to shoot a camped-up re-make of the film he had scripted for Fisher in 1956: *The Horror of Frankenstein*. Sangster produced, directed and wrote the new film while Ralph Bates, a talented newcomer to the Hammer ranks, played the Baron.

The results, as it happened, were disastrous but extremely revealing. Sangster (whose talent is beyond question and who played a major part in many of Hammer's greatest films including the first two Frankensteins) seems to have failed to realise that the early movies already contained a strong element of black humour, for, sequence by sequence, he proceeded to obliterate every nuance and subtlety in the original, even returning to Universal's idea of the clumsy 'assistant'. As the Baron, Ralph Bates, who is normally an excellent actor, floundered helplessly in the wake of Cushing, caricaturing the Byronic pose to the point where it loses any weight at all, while David Smith as the monster remained hopelessly unconvincing. But, since *The Horror of Frankenstein* was made, Sangster has made a much better film (*Lust for a Vampire*) in his own right, and perhaps the exercise did in its way achieve some good. It is certainly the most positive and gratifying indication of just how great Fisher's (and Cushing's) contributions to the Frankenstein series had been. One does not often have the opportunity of *detaching* a screen writer and director in this way, but in view of the fact that *The Horror of Frankenstein* was directed and written by the man who had scripted the earliest Frankenstein movies, it leaves one with the absolute conviction that Fisher's presence had previously been responsible for transforming the whole conception. The ugliness and self-parody of *The Horror of Frankenstein* remains an absolute testament to the grace and conviction that Fisher had previously brought to the series and it is a final confirmation—if any were needed—of his greatness as a film-maker.

Sources, Influences, Analogues

[Biblical Account of Creation]

From Genesis 2.4–23 *(King James translation)*

4 "These are the generations of the heaven and of the earth when they were created, in the day that the LORD God made earth and heaven. 5 And no plant of the field was yet in the earth, and no herb of the field had yet sprung up: for the LORD God had not caused it to rain upon the earth, and there was not a man to till the ground; 6 but there went up a mist from the earth, and watered the whole face of the ground. 7 And the LORD GOD formed man of the dust of the ground, and breathed into his nostrils the breath of life; and man became a living soul. 8 And the LORD God planted a garden eastward, in Eden; and there he put the man whom he had formed. 9 And out of the ground made the LORD God to grow every tree that is pleasant to the sight, and good for food: the tree of life also in the midst of the garden, and the tree of the knowledge of good and evil. 10 And a river went out of Eden to water the garden; * * * 15 And the LORD God took the man, and put him into the garden of Eden to dress it and to keep it. 16 And the LORD God commanded the man, saying, Of every tree of the garden thou mayest freely eat: 17 but of the tree of the knowledge of good and evil, thou shall not eat of it: for in the day that thou eatest thereof thou shalt surely die.

18 And the LORD God said, It is not good that the man should be alone; I will make him an help meet, for him. 19 And out of the ground the LORD God formed every beast of the field, and every fowl of the air; and brought them unto the man to see what he would call them: and whatsoever the man called every living creature, that was the name thereof. 20 And the man gave names to all cattle, and to the fowl of the air, and to every beast of the field; but for man there was not found an help meet for him. 21 And the LORD God caused a deep, sleep to fall upon the man, and he slept; and he took one of his ribs, and closed up the flesh instead thereof: 22 and the rib, which the LORD God had taken from the man, made he a woman, and brought her unto the man. 23 And the man

said, This is now bone of my bones, and flesh of my flesh: she shall
be called Woman, because she was taken out of Man.

JOHN MILTON

From Paradise Lost[†]

From Book One

[DESCRIPTION OF SATAN AFTER HIS EXPULSION]

Against the throne and monarchy of God
Raised impious war in Heav'n and battle proud
With vain attempt. Him the Almighty Pow'r
Hurled headlong flaming from th' ethereal sky   45
With hideous ruin and combustion down
To bottomless perdition, there to dwell
In adamantine chains and penal fire
Who durst defy th' Omnipotent to arms.
Nine times the space that measures day and night   50
To mortal men he with his horrid crew
Lay vanquished rolling in the fiery gulf
Confounded though immortal. But his doom
Reserved him to more wrath, for now the thought
Both of lost happiness and lasting pain   55
Torments him. Round he throws his baleful eyes
That witnessed huge affliction and dismay
Mixed with obdurate pride and steadfast hate.
At once as far as angels' ken he views
The dismal situation waste and wild: 60
A dungeon horrible on all sides round
As one great furnace flamed yet from those flames
No light but rather darkness visible
Served only to discover sights of woe,

---

† From *Paradise Lost : A Norton Critical Edition* by John Milton, edited by Gordon Teskey; Book I, lines 54–75; Book IV, lines 93–110; Book X, lines 741–54, Book XII, lines 646–49. Copyright © 2005 by W. W. Norton & Company, Inc. Used by permission of W. W. Norton & Company, Inc.

44. *Pow'r*: power, pronounced with one syllable: 'paar.'
45. *ethereal*: has three syllables: 'eth-ear-yal.'
46. *hideous* has two syllables: 'hid-jus.'
48. *adamantine*: made of the legendary hardest substance, *adamant*. The word is from a Homeric epithet of the king of the underworld, Hades (*Iliad* 9.158): *adamastos*, "untamable, incapable of being overpowered" (*a* "un" + *damnaô* "to overpower, subjugate, master").
50. *Nine times*: recalls the titans in Greek myth (Hesiod, *Theogony* 720f.), who fell nine days to earth and nine more into the pit of Tartarus. Milton's rebel angels are not the devils of medieval myth but huge cosmic powers. See lines 197–200.

Regions of sorrow, doleful shades, where peace   65
And rest can never dwell, hope never comes
That comes to all but torture without end
Still urges and a fiery deluge fed
With ever-burning sulfur unconsumed.
Such place Eternal Justice had prepared   70
For those rebellious, here their pris'n ordained
In utter darkness and their portion set
As far removed from God and light of Heav'n
As from the center thrice to th' utmost pole.
O how unlike the place from whence they fell!   75

From Book Four

[SATAN SPEAKING]

Still threat'ning to devour me opens wide,
To which the Hell I suffer seems a Heav'n.
O then at last relent! Is there no place
Left for repentance, none for pardon left?   80
None left but by submission and that word
Disdain forbids me and my dread of shame
Among the spirits beneath whom I seduced
With other promises and other vaunts
Than to submit, boasting I could subdue   85
Th' Omnipotent. Ay me! they little know
How dearly I abide that boast so vain,
Under what torments inwardly I groan
While they adore me on the throne of Hell
With diadem and scepter high advanced   90
The lower still I fall, only supreme
In misery. Such joy ambition finds.
But say I could repent and could obtain
By act of grace my former state. How soon
Would heighth recall high thoughts? How soon unsay   95
What feigned submission swore? Ease would recant
Vows made in pain as violent and void

---

59. *ken*: sight. Possibly a verb ("can see"), probably a noun.
74. *center*: of the earth. *pole*: of the created universe, not of the earth. Milton's Hell
    is situated not in the interior of the earth but outside the created universe alto-
    gether, far off in Chaos. The distance referred to here would be many times the
    distance from the center of the earth to the upper pole of the cosmos.
88–92. An example of Milton's compressed syntax, where two distinct sentences coincide
    in one: 'I groan while they adore me with my diadem and scepter raised' and 'the
    higher my diadem and scepter are raised the lower I fall.'
90. *diadem*: crown. *scepter*: a rod borne in the hand as an emblem of royal authority.
96–97. Once restored to blessedness, I would recant my vow of faith as invalid, since it
    was made under duress.

(For never can true reconcilement grow
Where wounds of deadly hate have pierced so deep)
Which would but lead me to a worse relapse   100
And heavier fall. So should I purchase dear
Short intermission bought with double smart.
This knows my punisher. Therefore as far
From granting He as I from begging peace.
All hope excluded thus, behold instead   105
Of us outcast, exiled, His new delight:
Mankind created and for him this world.
So farewell hope and with hope farewell fear!
Farewell remorse! All good to me is lost.
Evil, be thou my good. By thee at least   110
Divided empire with Heav'n's King I hold
By thee, and more than half perhaps will reign,
As man ere long and this new world shall know.
    Thus while he spake each passion dimmed his face
Thrice changed with pale ire, envy and despair,   115
Which marred his borrowed visage and betrayed
Him counterfeit if any eye beheld,
For Heav'nly minds from such distempers foul
Are ever clear. Whereof he soon aware
Each perturbation smoothed with outward calm,   120
Artificer of fraud, and was the first
That practiced falsehood: under saintly show
Deep malice to conceal couched with revenge.
Yet not enough had practiced to deceive
Uriel once warned, whose eye pursued him down   125
The way he went and on th' Assyrian mount
Saw him disfigured more than could befall
Spirit of happy sort. His gestures fierce
He marked and mad demeanor, then alone,
As he supposed, all unobserved, unseen.   130
So on he fares and to the border comes
Of Eden where delicious Paradise,

102. *double smart*: redoubled agony.
110. Isaiah 5:20: "Woe unto them that call evil good, and good evil!"
110 and 112. *By thee*: by evil. The ungrammatical repetition of the phrase *by thee* perhaps
    indicates a minor lapse in transmission: the poet began the sentence with "By thee"
    and then moved the phrase behind the principal clause without eliminating the first
    appearance.
116. *borrowed visage*: Satan is still disguised as the *stripling cherub* of 3.636.
126. *Assyrian mount*: Niphates (3.742).
129. *He*: Uriel.
130. *he*: Satan.
131. *he*: Satan.

Now nearer, crowns with her enclosure green
As with a rural mound the champaign head
Of a steep wilderness whose hairy sides   135
With thicket overgrown, grotesque and wild,
Access denied. And overhead up grew
Insuperable heighth of loftiest shade,
Cedar and pine and fir and branching palm,
A sylvan scene, and as the ranks ascend   140
Shade above shade, a woody theater
Of stateliest view. Yet higher than their tops
The verdurous wall of Paradise up sprung
Which to our gen'ral sire gave prospect large

From Book Ten

[ADAM SPEAKING]

Now death to hear! For what can I increase
Or multiply but curses on my head?
Who of all ages to succeed but, feeling
The evil on him brought by me, will curse
My head: "ill fare our ancestor impure,   735
For this we may thank Adam." But his thanks
Shall be the execration. So besides
Mine own that bide upon me, all from me
Shall with a fierce reflux on me redound,
On me as on their natural center light,   740
Heavy though in their place. O fleeting joys

132. *Eden* and *Paradise.*
132–35. I.e., The garden, *Paradise*, enclosed with trees, lies on the broad plain (*cham-paign*) that surmounts a steep hill overgrown with thickets.
136. *grotesque*: full of caves (grottos) as well as like the decorative, tangled growth depicted on Roman wall paintings.
137. *Access* is the direct object of *wilderness.* The wilderness on the side of the para-disal mountain denied access to Paradise at the top.
137–42. *overhead*: As ranks of trees *ascend* the mountainside, each rank overshadows the last (*shade above shade*) so that the trees appear to form a kind of theater. Milton follows closely a description of trees in the *Aeneid* 1.164–65, capturing the phrase *silvis scaena* in *sylvan scene* (line 140).
143. *verdurous*: green. The wall is overgrown with plants.
144. *our general sire*: the father of us all, Adam. *general* has two syllables: 'gen-ral.'
738. *Mine own*: evils, curses.
741. *Heavy though in their place*: In pre-Newtonian physics objects are not moved by external forces but are drawn to their natural places, where they are at rest. Fire rises, seeking its home above the air, and earth sinks, seeking its home beneath the water. The principle has been invoked by Moloch: "in our proper motion we ascend / Up to our native seat. Descent and fall / To us is adverse" (2.75–77). The evils and curses find their natural place in Adam, their origin and center, but they are still heavy, crushing him with their weight.
762. A hypermetrical line.

Of Paradise dear bought with lasting woes!
Did I request Thee, Maker, from my clay
To mold me Man? Did I solicit Thee
From darkness to promote me or here place   745
In this delicious garden? As my will
Concurred not to my being it were but right
And equal to reduce me to my dust,
Desirous to resign and render back
All I received, unable to perform   750
Thy terms too hard by which I was to hold
The good I sought not. To the loss of that,
Sufficient penalty, why hast thou added
The sense of endless woes? Inexplicable
Thy justice seems! Yet to say truth too late   755
I thus contést. Then should have been refused
Those terms whatever when they were proposed.
Thou didst accept them: wilt thou enjoy the good,
Then cavil the conditions? And though God
Made thee without thy leave, what if thy son   760
Prove disobedient and, reproved, retort
"Wherefore didst thou beget me? I sought it not."
Wouldst thou admit for his contempt of thee
That proud excuse? Yet him not thy election
But natural necessity begot.   765
God made thee of choice His own and of His own

From Book Twelve

[FINAL LINES OF THE POEM, DESCRIBING ADAM AND
EVE LEAVING THE GARDEN OF EDEN]

Who for my willful crime art banished hence.
This further consolation yet secure   620
I carry hence: though all by me is lost,
Such favor I unworthy am vouchsafed,
By me the promised Seed shall all restore.
    So spake our mother Eve and Adam heard
Well pleased but answered not. For now too nigh   625
Th' archangel stood and from the other hill
To their fixed station all in bright array
The cherubim descended, on the ground

---

762. A hypermetrical line.
766. *thee* and *of* are elided.
766–68. I.e., Because God made you, you owe him absolute service (as an implement is
    made only for the use of its maker). But God gave you a reward for your service:
    your freedom. Your punishment, therefore, is entirely up to him.

Gliding meteorous as evening mist
Ris'n from a river o'er the marish glides   630
And gathers ground fast at the laborer's heel
Homeward returning. High in front advanced,
The brandished sword of God before them blazed
Fierce as a comet which with torrid heat
And vapor as the Libyan air adust   635
Began to parch that temperate clime. Whereat
In either hand the hast'ning angel caught
Our ling'ring parents and to the eastern gate
Led them direct and down the cliff as fast
To the subjected plain, then disappeared.   640
They, looking back, all th' eastern side beheld
Of Paradise, so late their happy seat,
Waved over by that flaming brand. The gate
With dreadful faces thronged and fiery arms.
Some natural tears they dropped but wiped them soon.   645
The world was all before them, where to choose
Their place of rest, and Providence their guide.
They hand in hand with wand'ring steps and slow
Through Eden took their solitary way.

PERCY BYSSHE SHELLEY

Mont Blanc†

Lines Written in the Vale of Chamouni

I.

The everlasting universe of things
Flows through the mind, and rolls its rapid waves,
Now dark—now glittering—now reflecting gloom—
Now lending splendour, where from secret springs

---

629. *meteorous*: in midair (the Greek etymological sense of the word). It is possible but
not necessary to accent the second syllable, *metéorous*. Doing so gives the interesting rhythm of two dactyls opening the line (∕⌣⌣) and improves an otherwise
abrupt caesura. Accenting the first and third syllables gives a more regular rhythm
of three trochees (∕⌣∕⌣).
635. *adust*: dry from having been burned by the sun.
640. *subjected*: lying below.
649. *through Eden*: Eden is not the garden paradise but the large country in which
that paradise is contained. Outside the garden, on the plain beneath it, Adam
and Eve move through the country of Eden.
   † From the 1816 version. Mont Blanc is the highest peak in Europe. Its snows melt
into the River Arve and the Chamonix Valley in France, near the borders of Switzerland and Italy.

The source of human thought its tribute brings
Of waters,—with a sound but half its own,
Such as a feeble brook will oft assume
In the wild woods, among the mountains lone,
Where waterfalls around it leap for ever,
Where woods and winds contend, and a vast river
Over its rocks ceaselessly bursts and raves.

II.

Thus thou, Ravine of Arve—dark, deep Ravine—
Thou many-coloured, many-voiced vale,
Over whose pines and crags and caverns sail
Fast clouds, shadows, and sunbeams; awful scene,
Where Power in likeness of the Arve comes down
From the ice-gulfs that gird his secret throne,
Bursting through these dark mountains like the flame
Of lightning through the tempest;—thou dost lie,
The giant brood of pines around thee clinging,
Children of elder time, in whose devotion
The chainless winds still come and ever came
To drink their odours, and their mighty swinging
To hear—an old and solemn harmony:
Thine earthly rainbows stretched across the sweep
Of the ethereal waterfall, whose veil
Makes some unsculptured image; the strange sleep
Which, when the voices of the desert fail,
Wraps all in its own deep eternity;—
Thy caverns echoing to the Arve's commotion
A loud, lone sound, no other sound can tame;
Thou art pervaded with that ceaseless motion,
Thou art the path of that unresting sound—
Dizzy Ravine! and when I gaze on thee
I seem as in a trance sublime and strange
To muse on my own separate fantasy,
My own, my human mind, which passively
Now renders and receives fast influencings,
Holding an unremitting interchange
With the clear universe of things around;
One legion of wild thoughts, whose wandering wings
Now float above thy darkness, and now rest
Where that or thou art no unbidden guest,
In the still cave of the witch Poesy,
Seeking among the shadows that pass by
Ghosts of all things that are, some shade of thee,

Some phantom, some faint image; till the breast
From which they fled recalls them, thou art there!

III.

Some say that gleams of a remoter world
Visit the soul in sleep,—that death is slumber,
And that its shapes the busy thoughts outnumber
Of those who wake and live.—I look on high;
Has some unknown omnipotence unfurled
The veil of life and death? or do I lie
In dream, and does the mightier world of sleep
Speed far around and inaccessibly
Its circles? For the very spirit fails,
Driven like a homeless cloud from steep to steep
That vanishes among the viewless[1] gales!
Far, far above, piercing the infinite sky,
Mount Blanc appears,—still, snowy, and serene—
Its subject mountains their unearthly forms
Pile around it, ice and rock; broad vales between
Of frozen floods, unfathomable deeps,
Blue as the overhanging heaven, that spread
And wind among the accumulated steeps;
A desert peopled by the storms alone,
Save when the eagle brings some hunter's bone,
And the wolf tracks her there—how hideously
Its shapes are heaped around! rude, bare, and high,
Ghastly, and scarred, and riven.—Is this the scene
Where the old Earthquake-demon taught her young
Ruin? Were these their toys? or did a sea
Of fire envelope once this silent snow?[2]
None can reply—all seems eternal now.
The wilderness has a mysterious tongue
Which teaches awful doubt, or faith so mild,
So solemn, so serene, that man may be
But for such faith with nature reconciled;
Thou hast a voice, great Mountain, to repeal
Large codes of fraud and woe; not understood,
By all, but which the wise, and great, and good,
Interpret, or make felt, or deeply feel.

1. Invisible.
2. According to scientific theories of Shelley's time, the earth was originally round and
   smooth, and mountains resulted from floods, earthquakes, or fires erupting from the
   earth's center.

IV.

The fields, the lakes, the forests, and the streams,
Ocean, and all the living things that dwell
Within the dædal[3] earth; lightning, and rain,
Earthquake, and fiery flood, and hurricane,
The torpor of the year when feeble dreams
Visit the hidden buds, or dreamless sleep
Holds every future leaf and flower;—the bound
With which from that detested trance they leap;
The works and ways of man, their death and birth,
And that of him and all that his may be;
All things that move and breathe with toil and sound
Are born and die, revolve, subside, and swell.
Power dwells apart in its tranquillity
Remote, serene, and inaccessible:
And *this*, the naked countenance of earth,
On which I gaze, even these primæval mountains,
Teach the adverting mind. The glaciers creep
Like snakes that watch their prey, from their far fountains,
Slowly rolling on; there, many a precipice
Frost and the Sun in scorn of mortal power
Have piled—dome, pyramid, and pinnacle,
A city of death, distinct with many a tower
And wall impregnable of beaming ice.
Yet not a city, but a flood of ruin
Is there, that from the boundaries of the sky
Rolls its perpetual stream; vast pines are strewing
Its destined path, or in the mangled soil
Branchless and shattered stand; the rocks, drawn down
From yon remotest waste, have overthrown
The limits of the dead and living world,
Never to be reclaimed. The dwelling-place
Of insects, beasts, and birds, becomes its spoil;
Their food and their retreat for ever gone,
So much of life and joy is lost. The race
Of man flies far in dread; his work and dwelling
Vanish, like smoke before the tempest's stream,
And their place is not known. Below, vast caves
Shine in the rushing torrent's restless gleam,
Which from those secret chasms in tumult welling
Meet in the vale, and one majestic River,
The breath and blood of distant lands, for ever

3. Varied.

Rolls its loud waters to the ocean waves,
Breathes its swift vapours to the circling air.

v.

Mont Blanc yet gleams on high:—the power is there,
The still and solemn power of many sights
And many sounds, and much of life and death.
In the calm darkness of the moonless nights,
In the lone glare of day, the snows descend
Upon that Mountain; none beholds them there,
Nor when the flakes burn in the sinking sun,
Or the star-beams dart through them:—Winds contend
Silently there, and heap the snow with breath
Rapid and strong, but silently! Its home
The voiceless lightning in these solitudes
Keeps innocently, and like vapour broods
Over the snow. The secret strength of things
Which governs thought, and to the infinite dome
Of heaven is as a law, inhabits thee!
And what were thou, and earth, and stars, and sea,
If to the human mind's imaginings
Silence and solitude were vacancy?

SWITZERLAND, *June 23, 1816.*

[The Sea of Ice]†

Chamouni, July 25th [1817].
We have returned from visiting the glacier of Montanvert, or as it is
called, the Sea of Ice, a scene in truth of dizzying wonder. The path
that winds to it along the side of a mountain, now clothed with
pines, now intersected with snowy hollows, is wide and steep. The
cabin of Montanvert is three leagues from Chamouni, half of which
distance is performed on mules, not so sure footed but that on the
first day the one which I rode fell in what the guides call a *mauvais
pas*, so that I narrowly escaped being precipitated down the mountain. We passed over a hollow covered with snow, down which vast
stones are accustomed to roll. One had fallen the preceding day, a
little time after we had returned: our guides desired us to pass
quickly, for it is said that sometimes the least sound will accelerate
their descent. We arrived at Montanvert, however, safe.

† From *History of a Six Weeks' Tour* (London: T. Hookham & C. & J. Oliver, 1817).

On all sides precipitous mountains, the abodes of unrelenting frost, surround this vale: their sides are banked up with ice and snow, broken, heaped high, and exhibiting terrific chasms. The summits are sharp and naked pinnacles, whose overhanging steepness will not even permit snow to rest upon them. Lines of dazzling ice occupy here and there their perpendicular rifts, and shine through the driving vapours with inexpressible brilliance: they pierce the clouds like things not belonging to this earth. The vale itself is filled with a mass of undulating ice, and has an ascent sufficiently gradual even to the remotest abysses of these horrible desarts. It is only half a league (about two miles) in breadth, and seems much less. It exhibits an appearance as if frost had suddenly bound up the waves and whirlpools of a mighty torrent. We walked some distance upon its surface. The waves are elevated about 12 or 15 feet from the surface of the mass, which is intersected by long gaps of unfathomable depth, the ice of whose sides is more beautifully azure than the sky. In these regions every thing changes, and is in motion. This vast mass of ice has one general progress, which ceases neither day nor night; it breaks and bursts for ever: some undulations sink while others rise; it is never the same. The echo of rocks, or of the ice and snow which fall from their overhanging precipices, or roll from their aerial summits, scarcely ceases for one moment. One would think that Mont Blanc, like the god of the Stoics, was a vast animal, and that the frozen blood for ever circulated through his stony veins.

We dined (M * * *, C * * *,[1] and I) on the grass, in the open air, surrounded by this scene. The air is piercing and clear. We returned down the mountain, sometimes encompassed by the driving vapours, sometimes cheered by the sunbeams, and arrived at our inn by seven o'clock.

Mutability[†]

We are as clouds that veil the midnight moon;
    How restlessly they speed, and gleam, and quiver,
Streaking the darkness radiantly!—yet soon
    Night closes round, and they are lost for ever:

Or like forgotten lyres, whose dissonant strings   5
    Give various response to each varying blast,
To whose frail frame no second motion brings
    One mood or modulation like the last.

1. Mary, Claire [Claremont].
† Published with *Alastor* in 1816. From *The Complete Poetical Works of Percy Bysshe Shelley*, ed. Thomas Hutchinson (London: Oxford UP, 1921).

We rest.—A dream has power to poison sleep;
   We rise.—One wandering thought pollutes the day;   10
We feel, conceive or reason, laugh or weep;
   Embrace fond woe, or cast our cares away:

It is the same!—For, be it joy or sorrow,
   The path of its departure still is free:
Man's yesterday may ne'er be like his morrow;   15
   Nought may endure but Mutability.

GEORGE GORDON, LORD BYRON

Prometheus†

1

Titan! to whose immortal eyes
   The sufferings of mortality,
   Seen in their sad reality,
Were not as things that gods despise;
What was thy pity's recompense?   5
A silent suffering, and intense;
The rock, the vulture, and the chain,
All that the proud can feel of pain,
The agony they do not show,
The suffocating sense of woe,   10
   Which speaks but in its loneliness,
And then is jealous lest the sky
Should have a listener, nor will sigh
   Until its voice is echoless.

2

Titan! to thee the strife was given   15
   Between the suffering and the will,
   Which torture where they cannot kill;
And the inexorable Heaven,
And the deaf tyranny of Fate,
The ruling principle of Hate,   20
Which for its pleasure doth create
The things it may annihilate,
Refused thee even the boon to die:
The wretched gift eternity   24

---

† From *The Prisoner of Chillon and Other Poems* (1816).

Was thine—and thou hast borne it well.
All that the Thunderer wrung from thee
Was but the menace which flung back
On him the torments of thy rack;
The fate thou didst so well foresee,
But would not to appease him tell;   30
And in thy Silence was his Sentence,
And in his Soul a vain repentance,
And evil dread so ill dissembled,
That in his hand the lightnings trembled.

3

Thy Godlike crime was to be kind,   35
   To render with thy precepts less
   The sum of human wretchedness,
And strengthen Man with his own mind;
But baffled as thou wert from high,
Still in thy patient energy,   40
In the endurance, and repulse
   Of thine impenetrable Spirit,
Which Earth and Heaven could not convulse,
   A mighty lesson we inherit:
Thou art a symbol and a sign   45
   To Mortals of their fate and force;
Like thee, Man is in part divine,
   A troubled stream from a pure source;
And Man in portions can foresee
His own funereal destiny;   50
His wretchedness, and his resistance,
And his sad unallied existence:
To which his Spirit may oppose
Itself—an equal to all woes,
   And a firm will, and a deep sense,   55
Which even in torture can descry
   Its own concenter'd recompense,
Triumphant where it dares defy,
And making Death a Victory.
                    Diodati, July 1816.

Darkness†

I had a dream, which was not all a dream.
The bright sun was extinguish'd, and the stars
Did wander darkling in the eternal space,
Rayless, and pathless, and the icy earth
Swung blind and blackening in the moonless air;　　　　5
Morn came and went—and came, and brought no day,
And men forgot their passions in the dread
Of this their desolation; and all hearts
Were chill'd into a selfish prayer for light:
And they did live by watchfires—and the thrones,　　　10
The palaces of crowned kings—the huts,
The habitations of all things which dwell,

Were burnt for beacons; cities were consumed,
And men were gather'd round their blazing homes
To look once more into each other's face;　　　　15
Happy were those who dwelt within the eye
Of the volcanos, and their mountain-torch:
A fearful hope was all the world contain'd;
Forests were set on fire—but hour by hour
They fell and faded—and the crackling trunks　　　20
Extinguish'd with a crash—and all was black.
The brows of men by the despairing light
Wore an unearthly aspect, as by fits
The flashes fell upon them; some lay down
And hid their eyes and wept; and some did rest　　　25
Their chins upon their clenched hands, and smiled;
And others hurried to and fro, and fed
Their funeral piles with fuel, and look'd up
With mad disquietude on the dull sky,
The pall of a past world; and then again　　　30
With curses cast them down upon the dust,
And gnash'd their teeth and howl'd: the wild birds shriek'd
And, terrified, did flutter on the ground,
And flap their useless wings; the wildest brutes
Came tame and tremulous; and vipers crawl'd　　　35
And twined themselves among the multitude,
Hissing, but stingless—they were slain for food.
And War, which for a moment was no more,
Did glut himself again:—a meal was bought

† From *The Prisoner of Chillon and Other Poems* (1816).

With blood, and each sate sullenly apart   40
Gorging himself in gloom: no love was left;
All earth was but one thought—and that was death
Immediate and inglorious; and the pang
Of famine fed upon all entrails—men
Died, and their bones were tombless as their flesh;   45
The meagre by the meagre were devour'd,
Even dogs assail'd their masters, all save one,
And he was faithful to a corse, and kept
The birds and beasts and famish'd men at bay,
Till hunger clung them, or the dropping dead   50
Lured their lank jaws; himself sought out no food,
But with a piteous and perpetual moan,
And a quick desolate cry, licking the hand
Which answer'd not with a caress—he died.
The crowd was famish'd by degrees; but two   55
Of an enormous city did survive,
And they were enemies: they met beside
The dying embers of an altar-place
Where had been heap'd a mass of holy things
For an unholy usage; they raked up,   60
And shivering scraped with their cold skeleton hands
The feeble ashes, and their feeble breath
Blew for a little life, and made a flame
Which was a mockery; then they lifted up
Their eyes as it grew lighter, and beheld   65
Each other's aspects—saw, and shriek'd, and died—
Even of their mutual hideousness they died,
Unknowing who he was upon whose brow
Famine had written Fiend. The world was void,
The populous and the powerful—was a lump,   70
Seasonless, herbless, treeless, manless, lifeless—
A lump of death—a chaos of hard clay.
The rivers, lakes, and ocean all stood still,
And nothing stirr'd within their silent depths;
Ships sailorless lay rotting on the sea,   75
And their masts fell down piecemeal: as they dropp'd
They slept on the abyss without a surge—
The waves were dead; the tides were in their grave,
The moon, their mistress, had expired before;
The winds were wither'd in the stagnant air,   80
And the clouds perish'd; Darkness had no need
Of aid from them—She was the Universe.
                                    Diodati, July 1816.

From Childe Harold's Pilgrimage, *Canto III* (1816)

XCII

The sky is changed!—and such a change! Oh night,
And storm, and darkness, ye are wondrous strong,
Yet lovely in your strength, as is the light
Of a dark eye in woman! Far along,
From peak to peak, the rattling crags among
Leaps the live thunder! Not from one lone cloud,
But every mountain now hath found a tongue,
And Jura answers, through her misty shroud,
Back to the joyous Alps, who call to her aloud!

XCIII

And this is in the night:—Most glorious night!
Thou wert not sent for slumber! let me be
A sharer in thy fierce and far delight,—
A portion of the tempest and of thee!
How the lit lake shines, a phosphoric sea,
And the big rain comes dancing to the earth!
And now again 'tis black,—and now, the glee
Of the loud hills shakes with its mountain-mirth,
As if they did rejoice o'er a young earthquake's birth.

XCIV

Now, where the swift Rhone cleaves his way between
Heights which appear as lovers who have parted
In hate, whose mining depths so intervene,
That they can meet no more, though broken-hearted;
Though in their souls, which thus each other thwarted,
Love was the very root of the fond rage
Which blighted their life's bloom, and then departed:
Itself expired, but leaving them an age
Of years all winters,—war within themselves to wage.

XCV

Now, where the quick Rhone thus hath cleft his way,
The mightiest of the storms hath ta'en his stand:
For here, not one, but many, make their play,
And fling their thunder-bolts from hand to hand,
Flashing and cast around: of all the band,
The brightest through these parted hills hath fork'd

His lightnings,—as if he did understand,
That in such gaps as desolation work'd,
There the hot shaft should blast whatever therein lurk'd.

XCVI

Sky, mountains, river, winds, lake, lightnings! ye!
With night, and clouds, and thunder, and a soul
To make these felt and feeling, well may be
Things that have made me watchful; the far roll
Of your departing voices, is the knoll[1]
Of what in me is sleepless,—if I rest.
But where of ye, O tempests! is the goal?
Are ye like those within the human breast?
Or do ye find, at length, like eagles, some high nest?

XCVII

Could I embody and unbosom now
That which is most within me,—could I wreak
My thoughts upon expression, and thus throw
Soul, heart, mind, passions, feelings, strong or weak,
All that I would have sought, and all I seek,
Bear, know, feel, and yet breathe—into *one* word,
And that one word were Lightning, I would speak;
But as it is, I live and die unheard,
With a most voiceless thought, sheathing it as a sword.

* * *

CHARLES LAMB

The Old Familiar Faces[†]

I have had playmates, I have had companions,
In my days of childhood, in my joyful schooldays,
All, all are gone, the old familiar faces.

I have been laughing, I have been carousing,
Drinking late, sitting late, with my bosom cronies,   5
All, all are gone, the old familiar faces.

1. Knell (old form).
† From *The Works of Charles Lamb*, vol. 1 (Harper & Brothers, 1838), 338–39.

I loved a love once, fairest among women;
Closed are her doors on me, I must not see her—
All, all are gone, the old familiar faces.

I have a friend, a kinder friend has no man;   10
Like an ingrate, I left my friend abruptly;
Left him, to muse on the old familiar faces.

Ghost-like I paced round the haunts of my childhood,
Earth seem'd a desert I was bound to traverse,
Seeking to find the old familiar faces.   15

Friend of my bosom, thou more than a brother,
Why wert not thou born in my father's dwelling?
So might we talk of the old familiar faces—

How some they have died, and some they have left me,
And some are taken from me; all are departed;   20
All, all are gone, the old familiar faces.

CRITICISM

Peter Boyle in *Young Frankenstein* (1974). TM & Copyright © 20th Century Fox. Courtesy of The Everett Collection.

GEORGE LEVINE

Frankenstein and the Tradition of Realism[†]

* * *

Frankenstein is one of the first in a long tradition of fictional over-reachers, of characters who act out in various ways the myth of Faust, and transport it from the world of mystery and miracle to the commonplace. He is destroyed not by some metaphysical agency, some supernatural intervention—as God expelled Adam from Eden or Mephistopheles collected his share of the bargain (though echoes of these events are everywhere)—but by his own nature and the consequences of living in or rejecting human community. Franken-stein is in a way the indirect father of lesser, more humanly recog-nizable figures, like Becky Sharp or Pip or Lydgate, people who reject the conventional limits imposed upon them by society and who are punished for their troubles. *Frankenstein* embodies one of the central myths of realistic fiction in the nineteenth century, even in the contrast between its sensational style and its apparently explicit moral implications. It embodies characteristically a simulta-neous awe and reverence toward greatness of ambition, and fear and distrust of those who act on such ambition. That ambivalence is almost always disguised in realistic fiction, where the manner itself seems to reject the possibility of greatness and the explicit subject is frequently the evil of aspiring to it: in gothic fiction the energies to be suppressed by the realist ideal, by the model of Flemish painting, by worldly wise compromise with the possible, are released. Gothic fiction, as Lowry Nelson has observed, "by its insistence on singu-larity and exotic setting . . . seems to have freed the minds of read-ers from direct involvement of their superegos and allowed them to pursue daydreams and wish fulfillment in regions where inhibitions and guilt could be suspended" (*Yale Review*, 1962–63, p. 238). The mythology of virtue rewarded, which was curiously central to English realism, is put to question in the gothic landscape where more powerful structures than social convention give shape to wish; and, as Nelson suggests, reader and writer alike were freed to pur-sue the possibilities of their own potential evil. It is striking how difficult it is to locate in realistic fiction any positive and active evil. The central realist mythology is spelled out in characters like George Eliot's Tito Melema, whose wickedness is merely a gradual sliding into the consequences of a natural egoism. In gothic fiction, but more particularly in *Frankenstein*, evil is both positively present and

† From *Novel: A Forum on Fiction* 7.1 (Fall 1973): 17–23. Copyright, 1973, Novel, Inc. All rights reserved. Reprinted by permission of the publisher, Duke University Press.

largely inexplicable. Although ostensibly based on the ideas of God-win's rationalist ethics which see evil as a consequence of maltreat-ment or injustice, there is no such comfortable explanation for the evil of Frankenstein himself. Where did his decision to create the monster come from? Mere chance. Evil is a deadly and fascinating mystery originating in men's minds as an inexplicable but inescap-able aspect of human goodness.

It is a commonplace of criticism of *Frankenstein*, as of Conrad's *The Secret Sharer*, that the hero and his antagonist are one. Leggatt is the other side of the captain; the monster and Frankenstein are doubles, two aspects of the same being. This seems an entirely just reading given that Frankenstein creates the monster and that, as they pursue their separate lives, they increasingly resemble and depend upon each other so that by the end Frankenstein pursues his own monster, their positions reversed, and the monster plants clues to keep Frankenstein in pursuit. As Frankenstein's creation, the monster can be taken as an expression of an aspect of Franken-stein's self: the monster is a sort of New Critical art object, leading an apparently independent organic life of its own and yet irremedi-ably and subtly tied to its creator, re-enacting in mildly disguised ways, his creator's feelings and experiences. * * *

The world of *Frankenstein* has a kind of objective existence which only partially disguises—much less convincingly than a realistic novel would—its quality as projection of a subjective state. The laws governing this world are almost the laws of dream in which the control of action is only partially, if at all, ordinary causation. Char-acters and actions move around central emotional preoccupations. Clearly, for example, Walton is an incipient Frankenstein, in his lesser way precisely in Frankenstein's position: ambitious for glory, embarked on a voyage of scientific discovery, putting others to risk for his work, isolated from the rest of mankind by his ambition, and desperately lonely. Frankenstein becomes his one true friend, and he is a friend who dies just at the point when their friendship is becoming solidified. And, of course, he is the man to whom Fran-kenstein tells his story, partly, like the Ancient Mariner, to keep him from the same fate. Moreover, the lesson he learns is not merely the explicit one, that he must sacrifice his ambition to others, but that he must also reject the vengeance that Frankenstein wishes upon him. Frankenstein's last wish is that Walton promise to destroy the monster; yet when the monster appears, Walton does not kill him but rather listens to his story and is moved to compassion which he tries to force himself to reject. He cannot kill the monster, who speaks in a way that echoes Frankenstein's own ideas and senti-ments; and, though this is not stated, in rejecting the vengeance which consumed Frankenstein, he is finally freed into a better (and perhaps a lesser) life—but one to which he returns in bitterness and dejection.

Clerval, too, Frankenstein's friend from boyhood, echoes an aspect of Frankenstein's self. Clerval is, surely, Frankenstein without the monster. Frankenstein describes himself as having been committed from his youth to the "metaphysical, or, in its highest sense, the physical secrets of the world." Meanwhile, Clerval occupied himself, so to speak, "with the moral relations of things. The busy stage of life, the virtues of heroes, and actions of men, were his theme; and his hope and his dream was to become one among those whose names are recorded in story, as the gallant and adventurous benefactors of our species" (pp. 37–38).[1] Except, of course, for the emphasis on political action, this description would serve for Frankenstein as well. Moreover, as Frankenstein himself notes, both he and Clerval were softened into gentleness and generosity by the influence of Elizabeth: "I might have become sullen in my study, rough through the ardour of my nature, but that she was there to subdue me to a semblance of her own gentleness. And Clerval . . . might not have been so perfectly humane . . . so full of kindness and tenderness amidst his passion for adventurous exploit, had she not unfolded to him the real loveliness of beneficence, and made the doing good the end and aim of his soaring ambition" (p. 38). Clerval, whose father denies him a university education, feels, like Frankenstein himself, a repugnance to the meanness of business. On the night Frankenstein is to depart for Ingolstadt and the university, he reads in Clerval's "kindling eye and in his animated glance a firm but restrained resolve, not to be chained to the miserable details of commerce" (p. 44). Both men reject the occupations of ordinary life, both are consumed with great ambitions, both are kept humane by the influence of the same woman, and, in the end, both are destroyed by Frankenstein's own creation, by the aspect of Frankenstein which ignores "the moral relations of things." Moreover, when Clerval dies, Frankenstein is not only accused of the murder (and seems unwilling to exculpate himself though he knows he has evidence that will do so), but he falls almost mortally ill—as though he himself has been the victim.

These kinds of redoublings are characteristic of the whole novel. Not only all the major characters, but the minor characters as well seem to be echoes of each other. Every story seems a variation on every other. Both Elizabeth and Justine are found by the Frankenstein family and rescued from poverty, and both accuse themselves, in different ways, of the murder of Frankenstein's youngest brother. When she hears of his death, Elizabeth exclaims, "O God, I have

---

1. Mary Shelley, *Frankenstein*, ed. James Kinsley and M. K. Joseph (Oxford: Oxford UP, 1969).

murdered my darling child" (p. 72). Justine, too, is a kind of sister of Frankenstein. She so adored Madame Frankenstein that she "endeavoured to imitate her phraseology and manners, so that even now," Elizabeth writes, "she often reminds me of her" (p. 65). And after she is convicted, Justine "confesses" to the murder.

And then there are the parents. Frankenstein himself is a father, the creator of the monster, and the novel is in part an examination of the responsibility of the father to the son. The monster asks Frankenstein for the gift of a bride to alleviate his solitude. Frankenstein's father in effect gives Frankenstein a bride, and a sister. The night before Elizabeth is brought into the Frankenstein house, his mother "had said playfully,—'I have a pretty present for my Victor— tomorrow he shall have it.' And when, on the morrow, she presented Elizabeth to me as her promised gift, I, with childish seriousness, interpreted her words literally, and looked upon Elizabeth as mine— mine to protect, love, and cherish. All praises bestowed on her, I received as made to a possession of my own. We called each other familiarly by the name of cousin. No word, no expression could body forth the kind of relation in which she stood to me—my more than sister, since till death she was to be mine only" (pp. 35–36). Frankenstein's father, in bestowing the gift and in caring for him, behaves to his son as the monster would have Frankenstein behave. Interestingly, in this extraordinary novel of intricate relations, when Frankenstein's father arrives after Clerval's death to help his son, Frankenstein at first assumes that his visitor is to be the murderer: "Oh take him away! I cannot see him," he cries. "For God's sake, do not let him enter." This strange hallucination focuses again on the bond that connects all the characters in the novel, and suggests how deeply incestuous and Oedipal the relationships are. It suggests, too, how close to the surface of this world are motives derived not from external experience, but from emotional and psychic energies beneath the surface of things.

Despite the potentially easy patterning, there is no simple way to define the relation between parents and offspring in this novel. Frankenstein's father is loved and generous, and marries the daughter of an unsuccessful merchant who, in his pride, almost brings his whole family down. The father of Safie betrays his daughter and her lover and is the cause of the fall of the DeLacey family. Felix DeLacey, in order to save Safie, brings his whole family to the brink of ruin. Frankenstein ignores his creation and, in effect, destroys his family as a consequence. Father and sons are almost equally responsible and irresponsible: what is consistent is only the focal concern on the relationship itself.

Within the novel, almost all relations have the texture of blood kinship. Percy Shelley's notorious preoccupation with incest is manifest in Mary's work. The model is Eden, where Eve is an actual physical part of Adam, and the monster's situation is caused precisely because he has no blood relations, no kinship. Frankenstein, on his death bed, makes clear why there is such an intense, reduplicative obsession throughout the novel on the ties of kinship:

> I thank you Walton . . . for your kind intentions towards so miserable a wretch; but when you speak of new ties, and fresh affections, think you that any can replace those who are gone? Can any man be to me as Clerval was; or any woman another Elizabeth? Even where the affections are not strongly moved by any superior excellence, the companions of our childhood always possess a certain power over our minds, which hardly any later friend can obtain. They know our infantine dispositions, which, however they may be afterwards modified, are never eradicated; and they can judge of our actions with more certain conclusions as to the integrity of our motives. A sister or a brother can never, unless indeed such symptoms have been shown early, suspect the other of fraud or false dealing, when another friend, however strongly he may be attached, may, in spite of himself, be contemplated with suspicion. (pp. 211–212)

In the original version of the novel, Elizabeth was, as the Oxford editor M. K. Joseph points out, Frankenstein's cousin, "the daughter of his father's sister" (p. 236n), and throughout the revised version, Frankenstein continues to refer to her as cousin. Every death in the novel is a death in the family, literal or figurative: what Frankenstein's ambition costs him is the family connection which makes life humanly possible. William is his brother. Justine looks like his mother, and is another kind of sister, though a subservient one. Clerval is a "brother." Elizabeth is both bride and sister (and cousin). And as a consequence of these losses, his father dies as well. Frankenstein kills his family, and is, in his attempt to obliterate his own creation, his own victim. As he dies, he severs the monster's last link with life so that, appropriately, the monster then moves out across the frozen wastes to immolate himself. The family is an aspect of the self and the self cannot survive bereft of its family.

Thus, even while it wanders across the Alps, to the northern islands of Scotland, to the frozen wastes of the Arctic, *Frankenstein* is a claustrophobic novel. It presents us not with the landscape of the world but of a single mind, and its extraordinary power, despite its grotesqueness and the awkwardness of so much of its prose, resides in its mythic exploration of that mind, and of the consequences of its choices, the mysteries of its impulses. Strangely, the only figure who stands outside of that mind is Walton, who is nevertheless, as I have already argued, another "double" of Frankenstein.

Walton provides the frame which allows us to glimpse Frankenstein's story. He is the "wedding guest," who can hear the story only because he is so similar to Frankenstein, and who can engage us because while he is outside the story he is still, like us, implicated in it. He is the link between our world and Frankenstein's, and he is saved by Frankenstein and by his difference from him, to return to his country and, significantly, his sister—his one connection with the human community.

The apparent simplicity and order of Mary Shelley's story only intensifies its extraordinary emotional energy and complexity. Although, for example, it is not unreasonable to argue, as Shelley did, that it aims at exhibiting "the amiableness of domestic affection, and the excellence of universal virtue," we can see that the strongly ordering hand of the novelist has allowed the expression of powerful tensions and energies which realistic techniques would tend to repress and, which, having their source in the irrational, will not resolve themselves into any simple meanings. * * *

Frankenstein, like other great romances, notably *Wuthering Heights*, is a more shapely and orderly book than most realistic novels, but the order is the means by which Mary's "readiness to accept what her imagination offered" is expressed. As Northrop Frye has suggested, the freer the imagination is allowed to roam, the more formally shapely will be the structure of the work. Imagination is structural power. Or at least it is that in *Frankenstein* and *Wuthering Heights* which, freed from the initial commitment to plausibility and to reason, take the shape of the writers' most potent imaginations and desires.

The simplicity of the structure, Walton's tale enfolding Frankenstein's, which, in turn, enfolds that of the monster, implies a clarity and firmness of moral ordering which is not present in the actual texture of the novel. Walton would seem the ultimate judge of the experience, as the outsider: yet he explicitly accepts Frankenstein's judgment of it, and largely exculpates him. The monster's own defense and explanation, lodged in the center of the story, is, however, by far the most convincing—though it is also a special— reading, and Frankenstein himself confesses that he has failed in his responsibility to his creature. In the end, however, we are not left with a judgment but with Walton's strangely uncolored report of the monster's last speech and last action. If anyone, the monster has the last word: and that word expresses a longing for self-destruction, for the pleasure which will come in the agony of self-immolation, and for an ultimate peace in extinction.

* * *

ELLEN MOERS

Female Gothic: The Monster's Mother[†]

What I mean by Female Gothic is easily defined: the work that women writers have done in the literary mode that, since the eighteenth century, we have called the Gothic. But what I mean—or anyone else means—by "the Gothic" is not so easily stated except that it has to do with fear. In Gothic writings fantasy predominates over reality, the strange over the commonplace, and the supernatural over the natural, with one definite auctorial intent: to scare. Not, that is, to reach down into the depths of the soul and purge it with pity and terror (as we say tragedy does), but to get to the body itself, its glands, epidermis, muscles, and circulatory system, quickly arousing and quickly allaying the physical reactions to fear.

Certainly the earliest tributes to the power of Gothic writers tended to emphasize the physiological. Jane Austen has Henry Tilney say, in *Northanger Abbey*, that he could not put down Mrs. Radcliffe's *Mysteries of Udolpho*: "I remember finishing it in two days—my hair standing on end the whole time." For Hazlitt Ann Radcliffe had mastered "the art of freezing the blood": "harrowing up the soul with imaginary horrors, and making the flesh creep and the nerves thrill." Mary Shelley said she intended *Frankenstein* to be the kind of ghost story that would "curdle the blood, and quicken the beatings of the heart." Why such claims? Presumably because readers enjoyed these sensations. For example, in Joanna Baillie's verse play on the theme of addiction to artificial fear, the heroine prevails upon a handmaiden, against the best advice, to tell a horror story:

> . . . Tell it, I pray thee.
> And let me cow'ring stand, and be my touch
> The valley's ice: there is a pleasure in it.
> Yea, when the cold blood shoots through every vein;
> When every pore upon my shrunken skin
> A knotted knoll becomes, and to mine ears
> Strange inward sounds awake, and to mine eyes
> Rush stranger tears, there is a joy in fear.[1]

[†] From the *New York Review of Books*. Reprinted with permission from The *New York Review of Books*. Copyright © 1974 NYREV, Inc. Later incorporated in somewhat different form in Moers's *Literary Women* (Garden City: Doubleday, 1976).

1. *Orra: A Tragedy*, published in 1812 in the third volume of *Plays On the Passions*, was one of the works read and reread by Mary and Percy Bysshe Shelley in their early years together. Its author, an earnestly moral and wistfully melodramatic Scottish spinster, was then famous and hyperbolically praised, especially in Scotland, as a Shakespeare *rediviva*.

At the time when literary Gothic was born, religious fears were on the wane, giving way to that vague paranoia of the modern spirit for which Gothic mechanisms seem to have provided welcome therapy. Walter Scott compared reading Mrs. Radcliffe to taking drugs, dangerous when habitual "but of most blessed power in those moments of pain and languor, when the whole head is sore, and the whole heart sick. If those who rail indiscriminately at this species of composition, were to consider the quantity of actual pleasure which it produces, and the much greater proportion of real sorrow and distress which it alleviates, their philanthropy ought to moderate their critical pride, or religious intolerance." A grateful public rewarded Mrs. Radcliffe, according to her most recent biographer,[2] by making her the most popular and best paid English novelist of the eighteenth century. Her preeminence among the "Terrorists," as they were called, was hardly challenged in her own day, and modern readers of *Udolpho* and *The Italian* continue to hail her as mistress of the pure Gothic form.

The secrets of Mrs. Radcliffe's power over the reader seem to be her incantatory prose style, her artful stretching of suspense over long periods of novelistic time, her pictorial and musical imagination which verges on the surreal. But the reasons for her own manipulation of that power remain mysterious, and there is no sign that any more will ever be known of her life and personality than the sparse facts we now have. She was married, childless, shy, sensitive to criticism of her respectability as woman and author, and addicted to travel—an addiction she was able to satisfy more through reading and imagining than through experience.

Ann Radcliffe's novels suggest that, for her, Gothic was a device to set maidens on distant and exciting journeys without offending the proprieties. In the power of villains, her heroines are forced to scurry up the top of pasteboard Alps and penetrate bandit-infested forests. They can scuttle miles along castle corridors, descend into dungeons, and explore secret chambers without a chaperone, because the Gothic castle, however ruined, is an indoor and therefore freely female space. In Mrs. Radcliffe's hands the Gothic novel became a feminine substitute for the picaresque, where heroines could enjoy all the adventures and alarms that masculine heroes had long experienced, far from home, in fiction.

She also made the Gothic novel into a make-believe puberty rite for young women. Her heroines are always good daughters, her villains

---

2. E. B. Murray, *Ann Radcliffe* (Twayne, 1972).

bad, cruel, painfully attractive father figures, for which her lovers are at last accepted as palely satisfactory substitutes, but only after paternal trials and tortures are visited upon the heroine. When satirizing the form, Jane Austen wisely refrained from tampering with this essential feature of Mrs. Radcliffe's Gothic: the father in *Northanger Abbey* is one of Austen's nastiest.

As early as the 1790s, then, Ann Radcliffe firmly set the Gothic in one of the ways it would go ever after: a novel in which the central figure is a young woman who is simultaneously persecuted victim and courageous heroine. But what are we to make of the next major turning of the Gothic tradition that a woman brought about a generation later? Mary Shelley's *Frankenstein*, in 1818, made over the Gothic novel into what today we call science fiction. *Frankenstein* brought a new sophistication to literary terror, and it did so without a heroine, without even an important female victim. Paradoxically, however, no other Gothic work by a woman writer, perhaps no other literary work of any kind by a woman, better repays examination in the light of the sex of its author. For *Frankenstein* is a birth myth, and one that was lodged in the novelist's imagination, I am convinced, by the fact that she was herself a mother.

Much in Mary Shelley's life was remarkable. She was the daughter of a brilliant mother (Mary Wollstonecraft) and father (William Godwin). She was the mistress and then wife of the poet Shelley. She read widely in five languages, including Latin and Greek. She had easy access to the writings and conversation of some of the most original minds of her age. But nothing so sets her apart from the generality of writers of her own time, and before, and for long afterward, than her early and chaotic experience, at the very time she became an author, with motherhood. Pregnant at sixteen, and almost constantly pregnant throughout the following five years; yet not a secure mother, for she lost most of her babies soon after they were born; and not a lawful mother, for she was not married—not at least when, at the age of eighteen, Mary Godwin began to write *Frankenstein*. So are monsters born.

What in fact has the experience of giving birth to do with women's literature? In the eighteenth and nineteenth centuries very few important women writers, except for Mary Shelley, bore children; most of them, in England and America, were spinsters and virgins. With the coming of Naturalism late in the century, and the lifting of the Victorian taboo against writing about physical sexuality (including pregnancy and labor), the subject of birth was first brought to literature in realistic form by male novelists, from Tolstoy and Zola to

William Carlos Williams.[3] Tolstoy was the father of thirteen babies born at home; Williams, as well as a poet and a Naturalist, was a small-town doctor with hundreds of deliveries to his professional credit. For knowledge of the sort that makes half-a-dozen pages of obstetrical detail, they had the advantage over women writers until relatively recent times.[4]

Mary Shelley was a unique case, in literature as in life. She brought birth to fiction not as realism but as Gothic fantasy, and thus contributed to Romanticism a myth of genuine originality. She invented the mad scientist who locks himself in his laboratory and secretly, guiltily, works at creating human life, only to find that he has made a monster.

> It was on a dreary night of November, that I beheld the accomplishment of my toils. With an anxiety that almost amounted to agony, I collected the instruments of life around me, that I might infuse a spark of being into the lifeless thing that lay at my feet. . . . The rain pattered dismally against the panes, and my candle was nearly burnt out, when, by the glimmer of the half-extinguished light, I saw the dull yellow eye of the creature open; it breathed hard, and a convulsive motion agitated its limbs. . . . His yellow skin scarcely covered the work of muscles and arteries beneath; his hair was of a lustrous black, and flowing . . . ; but these luxuriances only formed a more horrid contrast with his watery eyes, that seemed almost of the same colour as the dun white sockets in which they were set, his shrivelled complexion and straight black lips.

That is very good horror, but what follows is more horrid still: Frankenstein, the scientist, runs away and abandons the newborn monster, who is and remains nameless. Here, I think, is where Mary Shelley's book is most interesting, most powerful, and most feminine: in the motif of revulsion against newborn life, and the drama of guilt, dread, and flight surrounding birth and its consequences. Most of the novel, roughly two of its three volumes, can be said to deal with the retribution visited upon monster and creator for defi-

---

3. Williams's remarkable account of a birth, the opening chapter of *The While Mule*, is one of a number of unusual selections included by Michèle Murray in her anthology *A House of Good Proportion: Images of Women in Literature* (Simon and Schuster, 1973).
4. Two very popular women novelists (and Nobel laureates), Pearl Buck and Sigrid Undset, were probably responsible for establishing pregnancy, labor, and breast feeding as themes belonging to twentieth century "women's literature." But Colette's note of skepticism may be worth recalling. In *La Maison de Claudine* she tells of fainting away in horror when, as a girl, she first came upon a gruesome birth scene in Zola. "*Ce n'est pas si terrible, va, l'arrivée d'un enfant,*" she has her mother comment. "*. . . La preuve que toutes les femmes l'oublient, c'est qu'il n'y a jamais que les hommes—est-ce que ça le regardait, voyons, ce Zola?—qui en font des histoires.*"

cient infant care. *Frankenstein* seems to be distinctly a woman's mythmaking on the subject of birth precisely because its emphasis is not upon what precedes birth, not upon birth itself, but upon what follows birth: the trauma of the afterbirth.

Fear and guilt, depression and anxiety are commonplace reactions to the birth of a baby, and well within the normal range of experience. But more deeply rooted in our cultural mythology, and certainly in our literature, are the happy maternal reactions: ecstasy, a sense of fulfillment, and the rush of nourishing love which sweep over the new mother when she first holds her baby in her arms. Thackeray's treatment of the birth of a baby in *Vanity Fair* is the classic of this genre. Gentle Amelia is pregnant when her adored husband dies on the field of Waterloo, a tragedy which drives the young woman into a state of comatose grief until the blessed moment when her baby is born. "Heaven had sent her consolation," writes Thackeray. "A day came—of almost terrified delight and wonder—when the poor widowed girl pressed a child upon her breast . . . a little boy, as beautiful as a cherub. . . . Love, and hope, and prayer woke again in her bosom. . . . She was safe."

Thackeray was here recording a reality, as well as expressing a sentiment. But he himself was under no illusion that happiness was the only possible maternal reaction to giving birth, for his own wife had become depressed and hostile after their first baby was born, and suicidal and insane after the last. At the time of *Vanity Fair*, Thackeray had already had to place her in a sanitarium, and he was raising their two little girls himself. So, in *Vanity Fair*, he gives us not only Amelia as a mother, but also Becky Sharp. Becky's cold disdain toward her infant son, her hostility and selfishness as a mother, are perhaps a legacy of Thackeray's experience; they are also among the finest things in the novel.

From what we know about the strange young woman who wrote *Frankenstein*, Mary Shelley was in this respect nothing like Becky Sharp. She rejoiced at becoming a mother and loved and cherished her babies as long as they lived. But her journal is a chilly and laconic document, mostly concerned with the extraordinary reading program she put herself through at Shelley's side. Her own emphasis on books in the journal has set the tone of most of the discussion of the genesis of *Frankenstein*. Mary Shelley is said—and rightly—to have based her treatment of the life of her monster on the ideas about education, society, and morality held by her father and her mother. She is shown to have been influenced directly by Shelley's genius, and by her reading of Coleridge and Wordsworth and the Gothic novelists. She learned from Sir Humphry Davy's book on chemistry and Erasmus Darwin on biology. In Switzerland, during the summer she began *Frankenstein*, she sat by while Shelley, Byron, and Polidori discussed the new sciences of mesmerism, electricity, and galvanism, which promised to unlock the riddle of life, and planned to write ghost stories.

Mary Shelley herself was the first to point to her fortuitous immersion in the romantic and scientific revolutions of her day as the source of *Frankenstein*. Her extreme youth, as well as her sex, has contributed to the generally held opinion that she was not so much an author in her own right as a transparent medium through which passed the ideas of those around her.[5] "All Mrs. Shelley did," writes Mario Praz, "was to provide a passive reflection of some of the wild fantasies which were living in the air about her."

Passive reflections, however, do not produce original works of literature, and *Frankenstein*, if not a great novel, was unquestionably an original one. The major Romantic and minor Gothic tradition to which it *should* have belonged was the literature of the overreacher: the superman who breaks through normal human limitations to defy the rules of society and infringe upon the realm of God. In the Faust story, hypertrophy of the individual will is symbolized by a pact with the devil. Byron's and Balzac's heroes; the rampaging monks of Mat Lewis and E. T. A. Hoffmann; the Wandering Jew and Melmoth the wanderer; the chained and unchained Prometheus: all are overreachers, all are punished by their own excesses—by a surfeit of sensation, of experience, of knowledge, and most typically, by the doom of eternal life.

But Mary Shelley's overreacher is different. *Frankenstein's* exploration of the forbidden boundaries of human science does not cause the prolongation and extension of his own life, but the creation of a new one. He defies mortality not by living forever, but by giving birth. That this original twist to an old myth should have been the work of a young woman who was also a young mother seems to me, after all, not a very surprising answer to the question that, accord-

5. Two new publications should provide a useful corrective to this common bias of Shelley scholarship. William A. Walling's *Mary Shelley* (Twayne, 1972) is mostly about the extensive literary career of Mary Shelley herself. Although Professor Walling's motive is to press the case for Byron rather than Shelley as the major influence on his subject, the result is an unusually sympathetic treatment of the five novels and numerous other works she published after Shelley's death. James Rieger's forthcoming scholarly edition of the little known 1818 text of *Frankenstein* (to be published by Bobbs-Merrill [published in 1974 and reprinted by the U of Chicago P in 1982]) will provide information about Mary's unused notes for revision and about Shelley's actual contribution, as an editor, to the publication of the novel. Throughout this article I am quoting from M. K. Joseph's edition of the 1831 text of *Frankenstein* (Oxford UP, 1971), which is available in paper.

ing to Mary Shelley herself, was asked from the start: "How I, then a young girl, came to think of, and to dilate upon, so very hideous an idea?"

Birth is a hideous thing in *Frankenstein*, even before there is a monster. For Frankenstein's procedure, once he has determined to create new life, is to frequent the vaults and charnel houses and study the human corpse in all its loathsome stages of decay and decomposition. "To examine the causes of life," he says, "we must first have recourse to death." His purpose is to "bestow animation upon lifeless matter," so that he might "in process of time renew life where death had apparently devoted the body to corruption." Frankenstein collects bones and other human parts from the slaughterhouse and the dissecting room, and through long months of feverish activity sticks them together in a frame of gigantic size in what he calls "my workshop of filthy creation."

It is in her journal and her letters that Mary Shelley reveals the workshop of her own creation, where she pieced together the materials for a new species of romantic mythology. They record a horror story of maternity such as literary biography hardly provides again until Sylvia Plath.

As far as I can figure out, she was pregnant, barely pregnant but aware of the fact, when at the age of sixteen she ran off with Shelley in July, 1814.[6] Also pregnant at the same time was Shelley's legal wife Harriet, who gave birth in November to a "son and heir," as Mary noted in her journal. In February, 1815, Mary gave birth to a daughter, illegitimate, premature, and sickly. There is nothing in the journal about domestic help or a nurse in attendance. Mary notes that she breast fed the baby; that Fanny, her half-sister, came to call; that Mrs. Godwin, her stepmother, sent over some linen;

---

6. Swift conceiving, and mysteriously early consciousness of the fact, seem to be keynotes of Mary Shelley's experience as reflected in her journal and letters (both edited by Frederick L. Jones and published by the U of Oklahoma P in 1944 and 1947). Her first child was born on February 22, 1815: "A female child . . . not quite seven months . . . not expected to live," Shelley noted that day in her journal. The opening entry in her journal, also in Shelley's hand, records the event of their elopement on July 28, 1814, or not quite seven months before the birth, as well as Shelley's odd comment on Mary's feeling ill and faint as they traveled: "in that illness what pleasure and security did we not share!"

What strange ideas about conception and gestation lay behind these journal entries, not only in Shelley's mind but in the medical opinion of the day? For strange they probably were. Erasmus Darwin's *Zoonomia* proclaimed that the "embryon" was "a living filament" and "secreted from the blood of the male," and that the sex of the baby was determined by what passed through the imagination of the male at the moment of conception. "The world has long been mistaken in ascribing great power to the imagination of the female," Dr. Darwin wrote; but he puzzled over the fact that there were not immeasurably more female than male births, considering that the copulating male was rather likely to imagine "the idea of form and features" of a female at that interesting moment.

that Claire Clairmont, Mrs. Godwin's daughter who had run off with Mary, kept Shelley amused. Bonaparte invaded France, the journal tells us, and Mary took up her incessant reading program: this time, Mme. de Staël's *Corinne*. The baby died in March. "Find my baby dead," Mary wrote. "A miserable day."

In April, 1815, she was pregnant again, about eight weeks after the birth of her first child. In January, 1816, she gave birth to a son: more breast feeding, more reading. In March, Claire Clairmont sought out Lord Byron and managed to get herself pregnant by him within a couple of weeks. This pregnancy would be a subject of embarrassment and strain to Mary and Shelley, and it immediately changed their lives, for Byron left England in April, and Claire, Shelley, Mary, and her infant pursued him to Switzerland in May. There is nothing yet in Mary's journal about a servant, but a good deal about mule travel in the mountains. In June they all settled near Byron on the shores of Lake Geneva.

In June, 1816, also, Mary began *Frankenstein*. And during the year of its writing the following events ran their swift and sinister course: In October, Fanny Imlay, Mary's half-sister, committed suicide after discovering that she was not Godwin's daughter but Mary Wollstonecraft's daughter by her American lover. (The suicide was not only a tragedy but an embarrassment to all. Godwin refused even to claim Fanny's body, which was thrown nameless into a pauper's grave.) In early December Mary was pregnant again, which she seems to have sensed almost the day it happened. (See her letter to Shelley of December 5, in which she also announced completion of chapter 4 of her novel.) In mid-December, Harriet Shelley drowned herself in the Serpentine, she was pregnant by someone other than Shelley. In late December Mary married Shelley. In January, 1817, Mary wrote Byron that Claire had borne him a daughter. In May she finished *Frankenstein*, published the following year.

Death and birth were thus as hideously mixed in the life of Mary Shelley as in Frankenstein's "workshop of filthy creation." Who can read without shuddering, and without remembering her myth of the birth of a nameless monster, Mary's journal entry of March 19, 1815, which records the trauma of her loss, when she was seventeen, of her first baby, the little girl who did not live long enough to be given a name. "Dream that my little baby came to life again," Mary wrote; "that it had only been cold, and that we rubbed it before the fire, and it lived. Awake and find no baby. I think about the little thing all day. Not in good spirits."[7] (*"I thought, that if I could bestow*

---

7. Her dream of "the dead being alive" recurred along with "bitter" reflections on death during the period of *Frankenstein*, as she wrote Leigh Hunt on March 5, 1817.

*animation upon lifeless matter, I might in process of time renew life
where death had apparently devoted the body to corruption."*)

So little use has been made of this material by writers about *Frankenstein* that it may be worth emphasizing how important, because
how unusual, was Mary Shelley's experience as a woman.[8] The
harum-scarum circumstances surrounding her maternity have no
parallel until our own time, which in its naïve cerebrations upon
family life (and in much else, except genius) resembles the generation of the Shelleys. Mary Godwin sailed into teenage motherhood
without any of the financial or social or familial supports that
made bearing and rearing children a relaxed experience for the normal middle-class woman of her day (as Jane Austen, for example,
described her). She was an unwed mother, responsible for breaking
up the marriage of a young woman just as much a mother as she. The
father whom she adored broke furiously with her when she eloped;
and Mary Wollstonecraft, the mother whose memory she revered,
and whose books she was rereading throughout her teenage years,
had died in childbirth—died giving birth to Mary herself.

Surely no outside influence need be sought to explain Mary Shelley's fantasy of the newborn as at once monstrous agent of destruction and piteous victim of parental abandonment. "I, the miserable
and the abandoned," cries the monster at the end of *Frankenstein,* "I
am an abortion to be spurned at, and kicked, and trampled on. . . . I
have murdered the lovely and the helpless. . . . I have devoted my
creator to misery; I have pursued him even to that irremediable
ruin."

8. I cannot think of another important woman writer of the nineteenth century or before
who began to write for publication while she was learning, at a very early age, to be a
mother. Harriet Beecher Stowe and Elizabeth Cleghorn Gaskell were two of the rare
Victorian writers who were mothers; in both cases, the death of one of their babies also
played a decisive role in their literary careers. But Mrs. Stowe and Mrs. Gaskell were
about twice Mary Shelley's age when their babies died, and both were respectably settled middle-class women, wives of ministers. The young women novelists and poets
today who are finding in the subject of inexperienced and unassisted motherhood a
mine of troubled fantasy and black humor are themselves a new breed of writer react-
ing to a trauma they share with almost no writer before them but Mary Shelley. The
newborn returns again to literature as a monster:

> At six months he grew big as six years
> . . . One day he swallowed
> Her whole right breast. . . .
>   . . . both died,
> She inside him, curled like an embryo.
> —Cynthia Macdonald, "The Insatiable Baby," *Amputations*
> (George Braziller, 1972)

But the literary use of monstrous size to express anxieties about feeding and cleaning a baby need not, of course, be exclusively feminine, as Dr. Phyllis Greenacre's study
of Gulliver convincingly demonstrates (*Swift and Carroll: A Psychoanalytic Study of
Two Lives*, International Universities Press, Inc., 1955).

In the century and a half since its publication, *Frankenstein* has spawned innumerable interpretations among the critics, and among the novelists, playwrights, and filmmakers who have felt its influence. The idea, though not the name, of the robot originated with Mary Shelley's novel, and her title character became a byword for the dangers of scientific knowledge. But the work has also been read as an existential fable; as a commentary on the split between reason and feeling, in both philosophical thought and educational theory; as a parable of the excesses of idealism and genius; as a dramatization of the divided self; as an attack on the stultifying force of social convention.[9]

The versatility of Mary Shelley's myth is due to the brilliance of her mind and the range of her learning, as well as to the influence of the circle in which she moved as a young writer. But *Frankenstein* was most original in its dramatization of dangerous oppositions through the struggle of a creator with monstrous creation. The sources of this Gothic conception, which still has power to "curdle the blood, and quicken the beatings of the heart," were surely the anxieties of a woman who, as daughter, mistress, and mother, was a bearer of death.

Robert Kiely's suggestive new study, *The Romantic Novel in England* (Harvard, 1972), includes one of the rare serious discussions of *Frankenstein* as a woman's work. For Professor Kiely does more than interpret; he also responds, as one must in reading *Frankenstein*, to what he calls the "mundane side to this fantastic tale."

> In making her hero the creator of a monster, she does not necessarily mock idealistic ambition, but in making that monster a poor grotesque patchwork, a physical mess of seams and wrinkles, she introduces a consideration of the material universe which challenges and undermines the purity of idealism. In short, the sheer concreteness of the ugly thing which Frankenstein has created often makes his ambitions and his character—however sympathetically described—seem ridiculous and even insane. The arguments on behalf of idealism and unworldly genius are seriously presented, but the controlling perspective is that of an earthbound woman.

9. Including even racial prejudice. Has it been noticed how much Stephen Crane's "The Monster" owes to *Frankenstein*? In this eerie novella of 1899, Crane comments obliquely on the relations between black man and white in the civilized, middle-class North by portraying the community persecution of a doctor, a man of science and social justice, after he brings to life as a monster a Negro who has done a heroic deed as a man. The germ of this idea may have come to Crane from the metaphorical cakewalk with which Mark Twain began his celebrated polemic of 1893, "In Defense of Harriet Shelley."

The "mundane side" to *Frankenstein* is one of its richest aspects. Mary Shelley came honestly to grips with the dilemma of a newly created human being, a giant adult male in shape, who must swiftly recapitulate, and without the assistance of his terrified parent, the infantile and adolescent stages of human development. She even faces squarely the monster's sexual needs, for the denouement of the story hangs on his demand that Frankenstein create a female monster partner, and Frankenstein's refusal to do so.

But more than mundane is Mary Shelley's concern with the emotions surrounding the parent-child and child-parent relationship. Here her intention to underline the birth myth in *Frankenstein* becomes most evident, quite apart from biographical evidence about its author. She provides an unusual thickening of the background of the tale with familial fact and fantasy, from the very opening of the story in the letters a brother addresses to his sister of whom he is excessively fond, because they are both orphans. There is Frankenstein's relationship to his doting parents, and his semi-incestuous love for an abandoned orphan girl brought up as his sister. There is the first of the monster's murder victims, Frankenstein's infant brother (precisely drawn, even to his name, after Mary Shelley's baby); and the innocent young girl wrongly executed for the infant's murder, who is also a victim of what Mary Shelley calls that "strange perversity," a mother's hatred. (Justine accepts guilt with docility: "I almost began to think that I was the monster that my confessor said I was. . . .") The abundant material in *Frankenstein* about the abnormal, or monstrous, manifestations of the child-parent tie justifies as much as does its famous monster Mary Shelley's reference to the novel as "my hideous progeny."

What Mary Shelley actually did in *Frankenstein* was to transform the standard Romantic matter of incest, infanticide, and patricide into a phantasmagoria of the nursery. Nothing quite like it was done again in English literature until that Victorian novel by a woman, which we also place uneasily in the Gothic tradition: *Wuthering Heights*.

SANDRA M. GILBERT AND SUSAN GUBAR

Mary Shelley's Monstrous Eve[†]

The nature of a Female Space is this: it shrinks the Organs
Of Life till they become Finite & Itself seems Infinite
And Satan vibrated in the immensity of the Space! Limited
To those without but Infinite to those within . . .
                                                    —William Blake

The woman writes as if the Devil was in her; and that is the only con-
dition under which a woman ever writes anything worth reading.
                              —Nathaniel Hawthorne, on Fanny Fern

        I probed Retrieveless things
        My Duplicate—to borrow—
        A Haggard Comfort springs

        From the belief that Somewhere—
        Within the Clutch of Thought—
        There dwells one other Creature
        Of Heavenly Love—forgot—

        I plucked at our Partition
        As One should pry the Walls—
        Between Himself—and Horror's Twin—
        Within Opposing Cells—[‡]
                              —Emily Dickinson

              ✳   ✳   ✳

Many critics have noticed that *Frankenstein* (1818) is one of the key
Romantic "readings" of *Paradise Lost.*[1] Significantly, however, as a
woman's reading it is most especially the story of hell: hell as a dark
parody of heaven, hell's creations as monstrous imitations of heav-
en's creations, and hellish femaleness as a grotesque parody of
heavenly maleness. But of course the divagations of the parody
merely return to and reinforce the fearful reality of the original.
For by parodying *Paradise Lost* in what may have begun as a secret,
barely conscious attempt to subvert Milton, Shelley ended up telling,
too, the central story of *Paradise Lost*, the tale of "what misery th'
inabstinence of Eve / Shall bring on men."

[†] From *The Madwoman in the Attic* (New Haven: Yale UP, 1979), 213, 221–27, 230–41.
Originally published in *Feminist Studies.* Reprinted with permission.
[‡] Reprinted by permission of the publishers and the Trustees of Amherst College from
The Poems of Emily Dickinson, Thomas H. Johnson, ed., Cambridge, Mass.: The
Belknap Press of Harvard UP, Copyright © 1951, 1955, 1979, 1983 by the President
and Fellows of Harvard College.
1. See, for instance, Harold Bloom, "Afterword," *Frankenstein* (New York and Toronto:
New American Library, 1965), 214.

Mary Shelley herself claims to have been continually asked "how I . . . came to think of and to dilate upon so very hideous an idea" as that of *Frankenstein*, but it is really not surprising that she should have formulated her anxieties about femaleness in such highly literary terms. For of course the nineteen-year-old girl who wrote *Frankenstein* was no ordinary nineteen-year-old but one of England's most notable literary heiresses. Indeed, as "the daughter of two persons of distinguished literary celebrity," and the wife of a third, Mary Wollstonecraft Godwin Shelley was the daughter and later the wife of some of Milton's keenest critics, so that Harold Bloom's useful conceit about the family romance of English literature is simply an accurate description of the reality of her life.[2]

In acknowledgment of this web of literary/familial relationships, critics have traditionally studied *Frankenstein* as an interesting example of Romantic myth-making, a work ancillary to such established Promethean masterpieces as Shelley's *Prometheus Unbound* and Byron's *Manfred*. ("Like almost everything else about [Mary's] life," one such critic remarks, *Frankenstein* "is an instance of genius observed and admired but not shared."[3]) Recently, however, a number of writers have noticed the connection between Mary Shelley's "waking dream" of monster-manufacture and her own experience of awakening sexuality, in particular the "horror story of Maternity" which accompanied her precipitous entrance into what Ellen Moers calls "teen-age motherhood."[4] Clearly they are articulating an increasingly uneasy sense that, despite its male protagonist and its underpinning of "masculine" philosophy, *Frankenstein* is somehow a "woman's book," if only because its author was caught up in such a maelstrom of sexuality at the time she wrote the novel.

In making their case for the work as female fantasy, though, critics like Moers have tended to evade the problems posed by what we must define as *Frankenstein*'s literariness. Yet, despite the weaknesses in those traditional readings of the novel that overlook its intensely sexual materials, it is still undeniably true that Mary Shelley's "ghost story," growing from a Keatsian (or Coleridgean) waking dream, is a Romantic novel about—among other things— Romanticism, as well as a book about books and perhaps, too, about the writers of books. Any theorist of the novel's femaleness and of its significance as, in Moers's phrase, a "birth myth" must therefore

2. Author's introduction to *Frankenstein* (1818; Toronto, New York, London: Bantam Pathfinder Edition, 1967), xi. Hereafter page references to this edition will follow quotations, and we will also include chapter references for those using other editions. For a basic discussion of the "family romance" of literature, see Harold Bloom, *The Anxiety of Influence*.

3. Robert Kiely, *The Romantic Novel in England* (Cambridge, Mass.: Harvard UP, 1972), 161.

4. Moers, *Literary Women* (Garden City: Doubleday, 1976), 95–97.

confront this self-conscious literariness. For as was only natural in "the daughter of two persons of distinguished literary celebrity," Mary Shelley explained her sexuality to herself in the context of her reading and its powerfully felt implications.

For this orphaned literary heiress, highly charged connections between femaleness and literariness must have been established early, and established specifically in relation to the controversial figure of her dead mother. As we shall see, Mary Wollstonecraft Godwin read her mother's writings over and over again as she was growing up. Perhaps more important, she undoubtedly read most of the reviews of her mother's *Posthumous Works*, reviews in which Mary Wollstonecraft was attacked as a "philosophical wanton" and a monster, while her *Vindication of the Rights of Woman* (1792) was called "A scripture, archly fram'd for propagating w[hore]s."[5] But in any case, to the "philosophical wanton's" daughter, all reading about (or of) her mother's work must have been painful, given her knowledge that that passionate feminist writer had died in giving life to *her*, to bestow upon Wollstonecraft's death from complications of childbirth the melodramatic cast it probably had for the girl herself. That Mary Shelley was conscious, moreover, of a strangely intimate relationship between her feelings toward her dead mother, her romance with a living poet, and her own sense of vocation as a reader and writer is made perfectly clear by her habit of "taking her books to Mary Wollstonecraft's grave in St. Pancras' Churchyard, there," as Muriel Spark puts it, "to pursue her studies in an atmosphere of communion with a mind greater than the second Mrs. Godwin's [and] to meet Shelley in secret."[6]

Her mother's grave: the setting seems an unusually grim, even ghoulish locale for reading, writing, or lovemaking. Yet, to a girl with Mary Shelley's background, literary activities, like sexual ones, must have been primarily extensions of the elaborate, gothic psychodrama of her family history. If her famous diary is largely a compendium of her reading lists and Shelley's that fact does not, therefore, suggest unusual reticence on her part. Rather, it emphasizes the point that for Mary, even more than for most writers, reading a book was often an emotional as well as an intellectual event of considerable magnitude. Especially because she never knew her mother, and because her father seemed so definitively to reject her after her youthful elopement, her principal mode of self-definition— certainly in the early years of her life with Shelley, when she was

5. See Ralph Wardle, *Mary Wollstonecraft* (Lincoln: U of Nebraska P, 1951), 322, for more detailed discussion of these attacks on Wollstonecraft.
6. Muriel Spark, *Child of Light* (Hodleigh, Essex: Tower Bridge Publications, 1951), 21.

writing *Frankenstein*—was through reading, and to a lesser extent through writing.

Endlessly studying her mother's works and her father's, Mary Shelley may be said to have "read" her family and to have been related to her reading, for books appear to have functioned as her surrogate parents, pages and words standing in for flesh and blood. That much of her reading was undertaken in Shelley's company, moreover, may also help explain some of this obsessiveness, for Mary's literary inheritance was obviously involved in her very literary romance and marriage. In the years just before she wrote *Frankenstein*, for instance, and those when she was engaged in composing the novel (1816–17), she studied her parents' writings, alone or together with Shelley, like a scholarly detective seeking clues to the significance of some cryptic text.[7]

To be sure, this investigation of the mysteries of literary genealogy was done in a larger context. In these same years, Mary Shelley recorded innumerable readings of contemporary gothic novels, as well as a program of study in English, French, and German literature that would do credit to a modern graduate student. But especially, in 1815, 1816, and 1817, she read the works of Milton: *Paradise Lost* (twice), *Paradise Regained, Comus, Areopagitica, Lycidas*. And what makes the extent of this reading particularly impressive is the fact that in these years, her seventeenth to her twenty-first, Mary Shelley was almost continuously pregnant, "confined," or nursing. At the same time, it is precisely the coincidence of all these disparate activities—her family studies, her initiation into adult sexuality, and her literary self-education—that makes her vision of *Paradise Lost* so significant. For her developing sense of herself as a literary creature and/or creator seems to have been inseparable from her emerging self-definition as daughter, mistress, wife, and mother. Thus she cast her birth myth—her myth of origins—in precisely those cosmogenic terms to which her parents, her husband, and indeed her whole literary culture continually alluded: the terms of *Paradise Lost*, which (as she indicates even on the title page of her novel), she saw as preceding, paralleling, and commenting upon the Greek cosmogeny of the Prometheus play her husband had just translated. It is as a female fantasy of sex and reading, then, a gothic psychodrama reflecting Mary Shelley's own sense of what we might call bibliogenesis, that

---

7. See *Mary Shelley's Journal*, ed, Frederick L. Jones (Norman: U of Oklahoma P, 1947), esp. 32–33, 47–49, 71–73, and 88–90, for the reading lists themselves. Besides reading Wollstonecraft's *Maria*, her *Vindication of the Rights of Woman*, and three or four other books, together with Godwin's *Political Justice* and his *Caleb Williams*, Mary Shelley also read parodies and criticisms of her parents' works in these years, including a book she calls *Anti-Jacobin Poetry*, which may well have included that periodical's vicious attack on Wollstonecraft. To read, for her, was not just to read her family, but to read *about* her family.

Frankenstein is a version of the misogynistic story implicit in *Paradise Lost.*

It would be a mistake to underestimate the significance of *Frankenstein*'s title page, with its allusive subtitle ("The Modern Prometheus") and carefully pointed Miltonic epigraph ("Did I request thee, Maker, from my clay / To mould me man? Did I solicit thee / From darkness to promote me?"). But our first really serious clue to the highly literary nature of this history of a creature born outside history is its author's use of an unusually *evidentiary* technique for conveying the stories of her monster and his maker. Like a literary jigsaw puzzle, a collection of apparently random documents from whose juxtaposition the scholar-detective must infer a meaning, *Frankenstein* consists of three "concentric circles" of narration (Walton's letters, Victor Frankenstein's recital to Walton, and the monster's speech to Frankenstein), within which are embedded pockets of digression containing other miniature narratives (Frankenstein's mother's story, Elizabeth Lavenza's and Justine's stories, Felix's and Agatha's story, Safie's story), etc.[8] * * * Reading and assembling documentary evidence, examining it, analyzing it and researching it comprised for Shelley a crucial if voyeuristic method of exploring origins, explaining identity, understanding sexuality. Even more obviously, it was a way of researching and analyzing an emotionally unintelligible text, like *Paradise Lost.* In a sense, then, even before *Paradise Lost* as a central item on the monster's reading list becomes a literal event in *Frankenstein*, the novel's literary structure prepares us to confront Milton's patriarchal epic, both as a sort of research problem and as the framework for a complex system of allusions.

The book's dramatic situations are equally resonant. Like Mary Shelley, who was a puzzled but studious Miltonist, this novel's key characters—Walton, Frankenstein, and the monster—are obsessed with problem-solving. "I shall satiate my ardent curiosity with the sight of a part of the world never before visited," exclaims the young explorer, Walton, as he embarks like a child "on an expedition of discovery up his native river" (2, letter 1). "While my companions contemplated . . . the magnificent appearance of things," declares Frankenstein, the scientist of sexual ontology, "I delighted in investigating their causes" (22, chap. 2). "Who was I? What was I? Whence did I come?" (113–15, chap. 15) the monster reports wondering,

---

8. Marc A. Rubenstein suggests that throughout the novel "the act of observation, passive in one sense, becomes covertly and symbolically active in another: the observed scene becomes an enclosing, even womb-like container in which a story is variously developed, preserved, and passed on. Storytelling becomes a vicarious pregnancy." "'My Accursed Origin': The Search for the Mother in *Frankenstein*," *Studies in Romanticism* 15, no. 2 (Spring 1976): 173.

describing endless speculations cast in Miltonic terms. All three, like Shelley herself, appear to be trying to understand their presence in a fallen world, and trying at the same time to define the nature of the lost paradise that must have existed before the fall. But unlike Adam, all three characters seem to have fallen not merely from Eden but from the earth, fallen directly into hell, like Sin, Satan, and—by implication—Eve. Thus their questionings are in some sense female, for they belong in that line of literary women's questionings of the fall into gender which goes back at least to Anne Finch's plaintive "How are we fal'n?" and forward to Sylvia Plath's horrified "I have fallen very far!"[9]

From the first, however, *Frankenstein* answers such neo-Miltonic questions mainly through explicit or implicit allusions to Milton, retelling the story of the fall not so much to protest against it as to clarify its meaning. The parallels between those two Promethean overreachers Walton and Frankenstein, for instance, have always been clear to readers. But that both characters can, therefore, be described (the way Walton describes Frankenstein) as "fallen angels" is not as frequently remarked. Yet Frankenstein himself is perceptive enough to ask Walton "Do you share my madness?" at just the moment when the young explorer remarks Satanically that "One man's life or death were but a small price to pay . . . for the dominion I [wish to] acquire" (13, letter 4). Plainly one fallen angel can recognize another. Alienated from his crew and chronically friendless, Walton tells his sister that he longs for a friend "on the wide ocean," and what he discovers in Victor Frankenstein is the fellowship of hell.

In fact, like the many other secondary narratives Mary Shelley offers in her novel, Walton's story is itself an alternative version of the myth of origins presented in *Paradise Lost*. Writing his ambitious letters home from St. Petersburgh [*sic*], Archangel, and points north, Walton moves like Satan away from the sanctity and sanity represented by his sister, his crew, and the allegorical names of the places he leaves. Like Satan, too, he seems at least in part to be exploring the frozen frontiers of hell in order to attempt a return to heaven, for the "country of eternal light" he envisions at the Pole (1, letter 1) has much in common with Milton's celestial "Fountain of Light" (*PL* 3. 375).[1] Again, like Satan's (and Eve's) aspirations, his

9. See Anne Finch, "The Introduction," in *The Poems of Anne Countess of Winchilsea*, 4–6, and Sylvia Plath, "The Moon and the Yew Tree," in *Ariel*, 41.
1. Speaking of the hyperborean metaphor in *Frankenstein*, Rubenstein argues that Walton (and Mary Shelley) seek "the fantasied mother locked within the ice . . . the maternal Paradise beyond the frozen north," and asks us to consider the pun implicit in the later meeting of Frankenstein and his monster on the *mer* (or *Mère*) *de Glace* at Chamonix (Rubenstein, "'My Accursed Origin,'" 175–76).

ambition has violated a patriarchal decree: his father's "dying injunction" had forbidden him "to embark on a seafaring life." Moreover, even the icy hell where Walton encounters Frankenstein and the monster is Miltonic, for all three of these diabolical wanderers must learn, like the fallen angels of *Paradise Lost*, that "Beyond this flood a frozen Continent / Lies dark and wild . . . / Thither by harpy-footed Furies hal'd, / At certain revolutions all the damn'd / Are brought . . . From Beds of raging Fire to starve in Ice" (*PL* 2. 587–600).

Finally, another of Walton's revelations illuminates not only the likeness of his ambitions to Satan's but also the similarity of his anxieties to those of his female author. Speaking of his childhood, he reminds his sister that, because poetry had "lifted [my soul] to heaven," he had become a poet and "for one year lived in a paradise of my own creation." Then he adds ominously that "You are well-acquainted with my failure and how heavily I bore the disappointment" (2–3, letter 1). But of course, as she confesses in her introduction to *Frankenstein*, Mary Shelley, too, had spent her childhood in "waking dreams" of literature; later, both she and her poet-husband hoped she would prove herself "worthy of [her] parentage and enroll [herself] on the page of fame" (xii). In a sense, then, given the Miltonic context in which Walton's story of poetic failure is set, it seems possible that one of the anxious fantasies his narrative helps Mary Shelley covertly examine is the fearful tale of a female fall from a lost paradise of art, speech, and autonomy into a hell of sexuality, silence, and filthy materiality, "A Universe of death, which God by curse / Created evil, for evil only good, / Where all life dies, death lives, and Nature breeds, / Perverse, all monstrous, all prodigious things" (*PL* 2. 622–25).

* * *

On the surface, Victor seems at first more Adamic than Satanic or Eve-like. His Edenic childhood is an interlude of prelapsarian innocence in which, like Adam, he is sheltered by his benevolent father as a sensitive plant might be "sheltered by the gardener, from every rougher wind" (19–20, chap. 1). When cherubic Elizabeth Lavenza joins the family, she seems as "heaven-sent" as Milton's Eve, as much Victor's "possession" as Adam's rib is Adam's. Moreover, though he is evidently forbidden almost nothing ("My parents [were not] tyrants . . . but the agents and creators of many delights"), Victor hints to Walton that his deific father, like Adam's and Walton's, did on one occasion arbitrarily forbid him to pursue his interest in arcane knowledge. Indeed, like Eve and Satan, Victor blames his own fall at least in part on his father's apparent arbitrariness. "If . . . my father had taken the pains to explain to me that the principles of Agrippa had been entirely exploded. . . . It is even possible that the train of my ideas would never have received the fatal impulse that led to my ruin" (24–25, chap. 2). And soon after asserting this he even associates an incident in which a tree is struck by Jovian thunder bolts with his feelings about his forbidden studies.

As his researches into the "secrets of nature" become more feverish, however, and as his ambition "to explore unknown powers" grows more intense, Victor begins to metamorphose from Adam to Satan, becoming "as Gods" in his capacity of "bestowing animation upon lifeless matter," laboring like a guilty artist to complete his false creation. Finally, in his conversations with Walton he echoes Milton's fallen angel, and Marlowe's, in his frequently reiterated confession that "I bore a hell within me which nothing could extinguish" (72, chap. 8). Indeed, as the "true murderer" of innocence, here cast in the form of the child William, Victor perceives himself as a diabolical creator whose mind has involuntarily "let loose" a monstrous and "filthy demon" in much the same way that Milton's Satan's swelled head produced Sin, the disgusting monster he "let loose" upon the world. Watching a "noble war in the sky" that seems almost like an intentional reminder that we are participating in a critical rearrangement of most of the elements of *Paradise Lost*, he explains that "I considered the being whom I had cast among mankind . . . nearly in the light of my own vampire, my own spirit let loose from the grave and forced to destroy all that was dear to me" (61, chap. 7).

Even while it is the final sign and seal of Victor's transformation from Adam to Satan, however, it is perhaps the Sin-ful murder of the child William that is our first overt clue to the real nature of the bewilderingly disguised set of identity shifts and parallels Mary Shelley incorporated into *Frankenstein*. For as we saw earlier, not just Victor and the monster but also Elizabeth and Justine insist upon responsibility for the monster's misdeed. Feeling "as if I had been guilty of a crime" (41, chap. 4) even before one had been committed, Victor responds to the news of William's death with the same self-accusations that torment the two orphans. And, significantly, for all three—as well as for the monster and little William himself—one focal point of both crime and guilt is an image of that other beautiful orphan, Caroline Beaufort Frankenstein. Passing from hand to hand, pocket to pocket, the smiling miniature of Victor's "angel mother" seems a token of some secret fellowship in sin, as does Victor's post-creation nightmare of transforming a lovely, living Elizabeth, with a single magical kiss, into "the corpse of my dead mother" enveloped in a shroud made more horrible by "grave-worms crawling in the folds of the flannel" (42, chap. 5). Though it has been disguised, buried, or miniaturized, femaleness—the gender definition of mothers and daughters, orphans and beggars, monsters and false creators—is at the heart of this apparently masculine book.

Because this is so, it eventually becomes clear that though Victor Frankenstein enacts the roles of Adam and Satan like a child trying on costumes, his single most self-defining act transforms him definitively into Eve. For as both Ellen Moers and Marc Rubenstein have pointed out, after much study of the "cause of generation and life," after locking himself away from ordinary society in the tradition of such agonized mothers as Wollstonecraft's Maria, Eliot's Hetty Sorel, and Hardy's Tess, Victor Frankenstein has a baby.[2] His "pregnancy" and childbirth are obviously manifested by the existence of the paradoxically huge being who emerges from his "workshop of filthy creation," but even the descriptive language of his creation myth is suggestive: "incredible labours," "emaciated with confinement," "a passing trance," "oppressed by a slow fever," "nervous to a painful degree," "exercise and amusement would . . . drive away incipient disease," "the instruments of life" (39–41, chap. 4), etc. And, like Eve's fall into guilty knowledge and painful maternity, Victor's entrance into what Blake would call the realm of "generation" is marked by a recognition of the necessary interdependence of those complementary opposites, sex and death: "To examine the causes of life, we must first have recourse to death," he observes (36, chap. 4), and in his isolated workshop of filthy creation—filthy because obscenely sexual[3]—he collects and arranges materials furnished by "the dissecting room and the slaughterhouse." Pursuing "nature to her hiding places" as Eve does in eating the apple, he learns that "the tremendous secrets of the human frame" are the interlocked secrets of sex and death, although, again like Eve, in his first mad pursuit of knowledge he knows not "eating death." But that his actual orgasmic animation of his monster-child takes place "on a dreary night in November," month of All Souls, short days, and the year's last slide toward death, merely reinforces the Miltonic and Blakean nature of his act of generation.

Even while Victor Frankenstein's self-defining procreation dramatically transforms him into an Eve-figure, however, our recognition of its implications reflects backward upon our sense of Victor-as-Satan and our earlier vision of Victor-as-Adam. Victor as Satan, we now realize, was never really the masculine, Byronic Satan of the first book of *Paradise Lost*, but always, instead, the curiously female, outcast Satan who gave birth to Sin. In his Eve-like pride ("I was surprised . . . that I alone should be reserved to discover so astonishing a secret" [37, chap. 4]), this Victor-Satan becomes "dizzy" with his creative powers, so that his monstrous pregnancy, bookishly

---

2. See Moers, *Literary Women*, "Female Gothic"; also Rubenstein, "'My Accursed Origin,'" 165–166.
3. The *OED* gives "obscenity" and "moral defilement" among its definitions of "filth."

and solipsistically conceived, reenacts as a terrible bibliogenesis the moment when, in Milton's version, Satan "dizzy swum / In darkness, while [his] head flames thick and fast / Threw forth, till on the left side op'ning wide" and Sin, Death's mother-to-be, appeared like "a Sign / Portentous" (*PL* 2. 753–61). Because he has conceived—or, rather, misconceived—his monstrous offspring by brooding upon the *wrong* books, moreover, this Victor-Satan is paradigmatic, like the falsely creative fallen angel, of the female artist, whose anxiety about her own aesthetic activity is expressed, for instance, in Mary Shelley's deferential introductory phrase about her "hideous progeny," with its plain implication that in her alienated attic workshop of filthy creation she has given birth to a deformed book, a literary abortion or miscarriage. "How [did] I, then a young girl, [come] to think of and to *dilate* upon so very hideous an idea?" is a key (if disingenuous) question she records. But we should not overlook her word play upon *dilate*, just as we should not ignore the anxious pun on the word *author* that is so deeply embedded in *Frankenstein*.

If the adult, Satanic Victor is Eve-like both in his procreation and his anxious creation, even the young, prelapsarian, and Adamic Victor is—to risk a pun—*curiously* female, that is, Eve-like. Innocent and guided by silken threads like a Blakeian lamb in a Godwinian garden, he is consumed by "a fervent longing to penetrate the secrets of nature," a longing which—expressed in his explorations of "vaults and charnel-houses," his guilty observations of "the unhallowed damps of the grave," and his passion to understand "the structure of the human frame"—recalls the criminal female curiosity that led Psyche to lose love by gazing upon its secret face, Eve to insist upon consuming "intellectual food," and Prometheus's sister-in-law Pandora to open the forbidden box of fleshly ills. But if Victor-Adam is also Victor-Eve, what is the real significance of the episode in which, away at school and cut off from his family, he locks himself into his workshop of filthy creation and gives birth by intellectual parturition to a giant monster? Isn't it precisely at this point in the novel that he discovers he is not Adam but Eve, not Satan but Sin, not male but female? If so, it seems likely that what this crucial section of *Frankenstein* really enacts is the story of Eve's discovery not that she must fall but that, having been created female, she *is* fallen, femaleness and fallenness being essentially synonymous. For what Victor Frankenstein most importantly learns, we must remember, is that he is the "author" of the monster—for him alone is "reserved . . . so astonishing a secret"— and thus it is he who is "the true murderer," he who unleashes Sin and Death upon the world, he who dreams the primal kiss that incestuously kills both "sister" and "mother." Doomed and filthy, is he not, then, Eve instead of Adam? In fact, may not the story of the fall be, for women, the story of the discovery that one is not innocent and Adam (as one had supposed) but Eve, and fallen? Perhaps this is what Freud's cruel but metaphorically accurate concept of penis-envy really means: the girl-child's surprised discovery that she is female, hence fallen, inadequate. Certainly the almost grotesquely anxious self-analysis implicit in Victor Frankenstein's (and Mary Shelley's) multiform relationships to Eve, Adam, God, and Satan suggest as much.

The discovery that one is fallen is in a sense a discovery that one is a monster, a murderer, a being gnawed by "the never-dying worm" (72, chap. 8) and therefore capable of any horror, including but not limited to sex, death, and filthy literary creation. More, the discovery that one is fallen—self-divided, murderous, material—is the discovery that one has released a "vampire" upon the world, "forced to destroy all that [is] dear" (61, chap. 7). For this reason—because *Frankenstein* is a story of woman's fall told by, as it were, an apparently docile daughter to a censorious "father"—the monster's narrative is embedded at the heart of the novel like the secret of the fall itself. Indeed, just as Frankenstein's workshop, with its maddening, riddling answers to cosmic questions is a hidden but commanding attic womb/room where the young artist-scientist murders to dissect and to recreate, so the murderous monster's single, carefully guarded narrative commands and controls Mary Shelley's novel. Delivered at the top of Mont Blanc—like the North Pole one of the Shelley family's metaphors for the indifferently powerful source of creation and destruction—it is the story of deformed Geraldine in "Christabel," the story of the dead-alive crew in "The Ancient Mariner," the story of Eve in *Paradise Lost*, and of her degraded double Sin—all secondary or female characters to whom male authors have imperiously denied any chance of self-explanation.[4] At the same time the monster's narrative is a philosophical meditation on what it means to be born without a "soul" or a history, as well as an exploration of what it feels like to be a "filthy mass that move[s] and talk[s]," a thing, an other, a creature of the second sex. In fact, though it tends to be ignored by critics (and film-makers), whose emphasis has always fallen upon Frankenstein himself as the archetypal mad scientist, the drastic shift in point of view that the nameless monster's monologue represents probably constitutes *Frankenstein*'s most striking technical *tour de force*, just as the monster's bitter self-revelations are Mary Shelley's most impressive and original achievement.[5]

4. The monster's narrative also strikingly echoes Jemima's narrative in Mary Wollstonecraft's posthumously published novel, *Maria, or The Wrongs of Woman*. See *Maria* (1798; rpt. New York: Norton, 1975), 52–69.
5. Harold Bloom does note that "the monster is . . . Mary Shelley's finest invention, and his narrative . . . forms the highest achievement of the novel." ("Afterword" to *Frankenstein*, 219.)

Like Victor Frankenstein, his author and superficially better self, the monster enacts in turn the roles of Adam and Satan, and even eventually hints at a sort of digression into the role of God. Like Adam, he recalls a time of primordial innocence, his days and nights in "the forest near Ingolstadt," where he ate berries, learned about heat and cold, and perceived "the boundaries of the radiant roof of light which canopied me" (88, chap. 11). Almost too quickly, however, he metamorphoses into an outcast and Satanic figure, hiding in a shepherd's hut which seems to him "as exquisite . . . a retreat as Pandemonium . . . after . . . the lake of fire" (90, chap. 11). Later, when he secretly sets up housekeeping behind the De Laceys' pig-pen, his wistful observations of the loving though exiled family and their pastoral abode ("Happy, happy earth! Fit habitation for gods . . ." [100, chap. 12]) recall Satan's mingled jealousy and admiration of that "happy rural seat of various view" where Adam and Eve are emparadised by God and Milton (*PL* 4. 247). Eventually, burning the cottage and murdering William in demonic rage, he seems to become entirely Satanic: "I, like the arch-fiend, bore a hell within me" (121, chap. 16); "Inflamed by pain, I vowed eternal hatred . . . to all mankind" (126, chap. 16). At the same time, in his assertion of power over his "author," his mental conception of another creature (a female monster), and his implicit dream of founding a new, vegetarian race somewhere in "the vast wilds of South America," (131, chap. 17), he temporarily enacts the part of a God, a creator, a master, albeit a failed one.

As the monster himself points out, however, each of these Miltonic roles is a Procrustean bed into which he simply cannot fit. Where, for instance, Victor Frankenstein's childhood really was Edenic, the monster's anxious infancy is isolated and ignorant, rather than insulated or innocent, so that his groping arrival at self-consciousness—"I was a poor, helpless, miserable wretch; I knew and could distinguish nothing; but feeling pain invade me on all sides, I sat down and wept" (87–88, chap. 11)—is a fiercely subversive parody of Adam's exuberant "all things smil'd, / With fragrance and with joy my heart o'erflowed. / Myself I then perus'd, and Limb by Limb / Survey'd, and sometimes went, and sometimes ran / With supple joints, as lively vigor led" (*PL* 8. 265–69). Similarly, the monster's attempts at speech ("Sometimes I wished to express my sensations in my own mode, but the uncouth and inarticulate sounds which broke from me frightened me into silence again" (88, chap. 11) parody and subvert Adam's ("To speak I tri'd, and forthwith spake, / My Tongue obey'd and readily could name / Whate'er I saw" (*PL* 8. 271–72). And of course the monster's anxiety and confusion ("What was I? The question again recurred to be answered only with groans" [106, chap. 13]) are a dark version of Adam's wondering bliss ("who I was, or where, or from what cause, / [I] Knew not. . . . [But I] feel that I am happier than I know" (*PL* 8. 270–71, 282).

Similarly, though his uncontrollable rage, his alienation, even his enormous size and superhuman physical strength bring him closer to Satan than he was to Adam, the monster puzzles over discrepancies between his situation and the fallen angel's. Though he is, for example, "in bulk as huge / As whom the Fables name of monstrous size, / *Titanian*, or *Earth-born*, that warr'd on *Jove*," and though, indeed, he is fated to war like Prometheus on Jovean Frankenstein, this demon/monster has fallen from no heaven, exercised no power of choice, and been endowed with no companions in evil. "I found myself similar yet at the same time strangely unlike to the beings concerning whom I read and to whose conversation I was a listener," he tells Frankenstein, describing his schooldays in the De Lacey pigpen (113, chap. 15). And, interestingly, his remark might well have been made by Mary Shelley herself, that "devout but nearly silent listener" (xiv) to masculine conversations who, like her hideous progeny, "continually studied and exercised [her] mind upon" such "histories" as *Paradise Lost*, Plutarch's *Lives*, and *The Sorrows of Werter* [*sic*] "whilst [her] friends were employed in their ordinary occupations" (112, chap. 15).

In fact, it is his intellectual similarity to his authoress (rather than his "author") which first suggests that Victor Frankenstein's male monster may really be a female in disguise. Certainly the books which educate him—*Werter*, Plutarch's *Lives*, and *Paradise Lost*—are not only books Mary had herself read in 1815, the year before she wrote *Frankenstein*, but they also typify just the literary categories she thought it necessary to study: the contemporary novel of sensibility, the serious history of Western civilization, and the highly cultivated epic poem. As specific works, moreover, each must have seemed to her to embody lessons a female author (or monster) must learn about a male-dominated society. Werter's story, says the monster—and he seems to be speaking for Mary Shelley—taught him about "gentle and domestic manners," and about "lofty sentiments . . . which had for their object something out of self." It functioned, in other words, as a sort of Romantic conduct book. In addition, it served as an introduction to the virtues of the proto-Byronic "Man of Feeling," for, admiring Werter and never mentioning Lotte, the monster explains to Victor that "I thought Werter himself a more divine being than I had ever . . . imagined," adding, in a line whose female irony about male self-dramatization must surely have been intentional, "I wept [his extinction] without precisely understanding it" (113, chap. 15).

If *Werter* introduces the monster to female modes of domesticity and self-abnegation, as well as to the unattainable glamour of male heroism, Plutarch's *Lives* teaches him all the masculine intricacies of that history which his anomalous birth has denied him. Mary Shelley, excluding herself from the household of the second Mrs. Godwin and studying family as well as literary history on her mother's grave, must, again, have found in her own experience an appropriate model for the plight of a monster who, as James Rieger notes, is especially characterized by "his unique knowledge of what it is like to be born free of history."[6] In terms of the disguised story the novel tells, however, this monster is not unique at all, but representative, as Shelley may have suspected she herself was. For, as Jane Austen has Catherine Morland suggest in *Northanger Abbey*, what is woman but man without a history, at least without the sort of history related in Plutarch's *Lives*? "History, real solemn history, I cannot be interested in," Catherine declares ". . . the men all so good for nothing, and hardly any women at all—it is very tiresome" (*NA* I, chap. 14).

But of course the third and most crucial book referred to in the miniature *Bildungsroman* of the monster's narrative is *Paradise Lost*, an epic myth of origins which is of major importance to him, as it is to Mary Shelley, precisely because, unlike Plutarch, it does provide him with what appears to be a personal history. And again, even the need for such a history draws Shelley's monster closer not only to the realistically ignorant female defined by Jane Austen but also to the archetypal female defined by John Milton. For, like the monster, like Catherine Morland, and like Mary Shelley herself, Eve is characterized by her "unique knowledge of what it is like to be born free of history," even though as the "Mother of Mankind" she is fated to "make" history. It is to Adam, after all, that God and His angels grant explanatory visions of past and future. At such moments of high historical colloquy Eve tends to excuse herself with "lowliness Majestic" (before the fall) or (after the fall) she is magically put to sleep, calmed like a frightened animal "with gentle Dreams . . . and all her spirits compos'd / To meek submission" (*PL* 12. 595–96).

Nevertheless, one of the most notable facts about the monster's ceaselessly anxious study of *Paradise Lost* is his failure even to mention Eve. As an insistently male monster, on the surface of his palimpsestic narrative he appears to be absorbed in Milton's epic only because, as Percy Shelley wrote in the preface to *Frankenstein* that he drafted for his wife, *Paradise Lost* "most especially" conveys "the truth of the elementary principles of human nature," and conveys that truth in the dynamic tensions developed among its male characters, Adam, Satan, and God (xvii). Yet not only the monster's

6. James Rieger, "Introduction" to *Frankenstein*, (*the 1818 Text*) (Indianapolis: Bobbs-Merrill, 1974), xxx.

uniquely ahistorical birth, his literary anxieties, and the sense his readings (like Mary's) foster that he must have been parented, if at all, by *books*; not only all these facts and traits but also his shuddering sense of deformity, his nauseating size, his namelessness, and his orphaned, motherless isolation link him with Eve and with Eve's double, Sin. Indeed, at several points in his impassioned analysis of Milton's story he seems almost on the verge of saying so, as he examines the disjunctions among Adam, Satan, and himself:

> Like Adam, I was apparently united by no link to any other being in existence; but his state was far different from mine in every other respect. He had come forth from the hands of God a perfect creature, happy and prosperous, guided by the especial care of his Creator; he was allowed to converse with and acquire knowledge from beings of a superior nature, but I was wretched, helpless, and alone. Many times I considered Satan as the fitter emblem of my condition, for often, like him, when I viewed the bliss of my protectors, the bitter gall of envy rose within me. . . . Accursed creator! Why did you form a monster so hideous that even *you* turned from me in disgust? God, in pity, made man beautiful and alluring, after his own image; but my form is a filthy type of yours, more horrid even from the very resemblance. Satan had his companions, fellow devils, to admire and encourage him, but I am solitary and abhorred. [114–15, chap. 15]

It is Eve, after all, who languishes helpless and alone, while Adam converses with superior beings, and it is Eve in whom the Satanically bitter gall of envy rises, causing her to eat the apple in the hope of adding "what wants / In Female Sex." It is Eve, moreover, to whom deathly isolation is threatened should Adam reject her, an isolation more terrible even than Satan's alienation from heaven. And finally it is Eve whose body, like her mind, is said by Milton to resemble "less / His Image who made both, and less [to express] / The character of that Dominion giv'n / O'er other Creatures . . ." (*PL* 8. 543–46). In fact, to a sexually anxious reader, Eve's body might, like Sin's, seem "horrid even from [its] very resemblance" to her husband's, a "filthy" or obscene version of the human form divine.[7]

* * * Women have seen themselves (because they have been seen) as monstrous, vile, degraded creatures, second-comers, and emblems of filthy materiality, even though they have also been tradi-

---

7. In Western culture the notion that femaleness is a deformity or obscenity can be traced back at least as far as Aristotle, who asserted that "we should look upon the female state as being as it were a deformity, though one which occurs in the ordinary course of nature." (*The Generation of Animals*, trans. A. L. Peck [London: Heinemann, 1943], 461.) For a brief but illuminating discussion of his theories see Katharine M. Rogers, *The Troublesome Helpmate*.

tionally defined as superior spiritual beings, angels, better halves. "Woman [is] a temple built over a sewer," said the Church father Tertullian, and Milton seems to see Eve as both temple and sewer, echoing that patristic misogyny.[8] Mary Shelley's conscious or unconscious awareness of the monster woman implicit in the angel woman is perhaps clearest in the revisionary scene where her monster, as if taking his cue from Eve in *Paradise Lost* book 4, first catches sight of his own image: "I had admired the perfect forms of my cottagers . . . but how was I terrified when I viewed myself in a transparent pool. At first I started back, unable to believe that it was indeed I who was reflected in the mirror; and when I became fully convinced that I was in reality the monster that I am, I was filled with the bitterest sensations of despondence and mortification" (98–99, chap. 12). In one sense, this is a corrective to Milton's blindness about Eve. Having been created second, inferior, a mere rib, how could she possibly, this passage implies, have seemed anything but monstrous to herself? In another sense, however, the scene supplements Milton's description of Eve's introduction to herself, for ironically, though her reflection in "the clear / Smooth Lake" is as beautiful as the monster's is ugly, the self-absorption that Eve's confessed passion for her own image signals is plainly meant by Milton to seem morally ugly, a hint of her potential for spiritual deformity: "There I had fixt / Mine eyes till now, and pin'd with vain desire, / Had not a voice thus warn'd me, What thou seest, / What there thou seest fair Creature is thyself . . ." (*PL* 4. 465–68).

The figurative monstrosity of female narcissism is a subtle deformity, however, in comparison with the literal monstrosity many women are taught to see as characteristic of their own bodies. Adrienne Rich's twentieth-century description of "a woman in the shape of a monster / A monster in the shape of a woman" is merely the latest in a long line of monstrous female self-definitions that includes the fearful images in Djuna Barnes's *Book of Repulsive Women*, Denise Levertov's "a white sweating bull of a poet told us / our cunts are ugly" and Sylvia Plath's "old yellow" self of the poem "In Plaster."[9] Animal and misshapen, these emblems of self-loathing must have descended at least in part from the distended body of Mary Shelley's darkly parodic Eve/Sin/Monster, whose enormity betokens not only the enormity of Victor Frankenstein's crime and Satan's bulk but also the distentions or deformities of pregnancy and the Swiftian sexual nausea expressed in Lemuel Gulliver's horrified description

8. See Simone de Beauvoir, *The Second Sex*, (New York: Knopf, 1953) 156.
9. Adrienne Rich, "Planetarium," in *Poems: Selected and New* (New York: Norton, 1974), 146–48; Djuna Barnes, *The Book of Repulsive Women* (1915; rpt. Berkeley, Calif., 1976); Denise Levertov, "Hypocrite Women," *O Taste & See* (New York: New Directions, 1965); Sylvia Plath, "In Plaster," *Crossing the Water* (New York: Harper & Row, 1971), 16.

of a Brobdignagian breast, a passage Mary Shelley no doubt studied along with the rest of *Gulliver's Travels* when she read the book in 1816, shortly before beginning *Frankenstein*.[1]

At the same time, just as surely as Eve's moral deformity is symbolized by the monster's physical malformation, the monster's physical ugliness represents his social illegitimacy, his bastardy, his namelessness. Bitchy and dastardly as Shakespeare's Edmund, whose association with filthy femaleness is established not only by his devotion to the material/maternal goddess Nature but also by his interlocking affairs with those filthy females Goneril and Regan, Mary Shelley's monster has also been "got" in a "dark and vicious place." Indeed, in his vile illegitimacy he seems to incarnate that bestial "unnameable" place. And significantly, he is himself as nameless as a woman is in patriarchal society, as nameless as unmarried, illegitimately pregnant Mary Wollstonecraft Godwin may have felt herself to be at the time she wrote *Frankenstein*.

* * *

MARY POOVEY

"My Hideous Progeny": The Lady and the Monster[†]

* * *

When she was in Switzerland in the summer of 1816, Mary Shelley's creative energies were finally rerouted from "travelling, and the cares of a family" (*F*, p. 223)[1] to this all-important activity of writing. Living next to Lord Byron, listening to—though not participating in— the conversations of the two poets ("incapacity and timidity always prevented my mingling in the nightly conversations," she said [*MSJ*, p. 184]),[2] and no doubt inspired by Percy's example, Mary Shelley began to compose steadily. After 24 July 1816, her journal frequently contains the important monosyllable, "Write," and the attention Percy devoted to the novel's progress, its revisions, and, eventually, its publication reveals that his support for the project was as enthusiastic as Mary could have wished. But the narrative that Mary Shelley wrote between that "eventful" summer and the following April was less a wholehearted celebration of the imaginative enterprise she had

---

1. See *Mary Shelley's Journal*, 73.
† From *The Proper Lady and the Woman Writer* (Chicago: U of Chicago P, 1984) 121–31. Reprinted by permission.
1. *F* = James Rieger, ed., *Frankenstein* (Chicago: U of Chicago P, 1978).
2. *MSJ* = Frederick L. Jones, ed., *Mary Shelley's Journal* (Norman: U of Oklahoma P, 1947).

undertaken in order to prove her worth to Percy than a troubled, veiled exploration of the price she had already begun to fear such egotistical self-assertion might exact. *Frankenstein* occupies a particularly important place in Shelley's career, not only because it is by far her most famous work, but because, in 1831, she prepared significant revisions and an important introduction, both of which underscore and elaborate her initial ambivalence. By tracing first the contradictions already present in the 1818 edition and then the revisions she made after Percy's death and her return to England, we can begin to see the roots and progress of Shelley's growing desire to accommodate her adolescent impulses to conventional propriety. Taken together, the two editions of *Frankenstein* provide a case study of the tensions inherent in the confrontation between the expectations Shelley associated, on the one hand, with her mother and Romantic originality and, on the other, with a textbook Proper Lady.

Even though they praised the power and stylistic vigor of *Frankenstein*, its first reviewers sharply criticized the anonymous novelist's failure to moralize about the novel's startling, even blasphemous, subject. The reviewer for the *Quarterly Review*, for example, complained that

> Our taste and our judgment alike revolt at this kind of writing, and the greater the ability with which it may be executed the worse it is—it inculcates no lesson of conduct, manners, or morality; it cannot mend, and will not even amuse its readers, unless their taste have been deplorably vitiated—it fatigues the feelings without interesting the understanding; it gratuitously harasses the heart, and only adds to the store, already too great, of painful sensations.

Presumably because it was unthinkable that a woman should refuse to moralize, most critics automatically assumed that the author of *Frankenstein* was a man—no doubt a "follower of Godwin," according to *Blackwood's*, or even Percy Shelley himself, as the *Edinburgh Magazine* surmised. These reviewers, however, were too preoccupied with the explicit unorthodoxy of *Frankenstein's* subject to attend carefully to the undercurrents in it that challenged their opinion. Like her mother and many male Romantics, Mary Shelley had chosen to focus on the theme of Promethean desire, which has implications for both the development of culture and the individual creative act; but when *Frankenstein* is considered alongside contemporary works that display even some degree of confidence in imaginative power, it proves to be more conservative than her first readers realized. Indeed, *Frankenstein* calls into question, not the social conventions that inhibit creativity, but rather the egotism that Mary Shelley associates with the artist's monstrous self-assertion.

Like Wollstonecraft and most male Romantics, Shelley discusses desire explicitly within a paradigm of individual maturation: *Frankenstein* is Shelley's version of the process of identity-formation that Wollstonecraft worked out in her two *Vindications*. Keats called this maturation "soul-making," and Wordsworth devoted his longest completed poem to it. In the 1818 text, Shelley's model of maturation begins with a realistic depiction of Lockean psychology; young Victor Frankenstein is a *tabula rasa* whose character is formed by his childhood experiences. The son of loving, protective parents, the companion of affectionate friends, he soon finds the harmony of his childhood violated by what he calls a "predilection" for natural philosophy. Yet even though this "predilection" seems to be innate, Frankenstein locates its origin not in his own disposition but in a single childhood event—the accidental discovery of a volume of Cornelius Agrippa's occult speculations. The "fatal impulse" this volume sparks is then kindled into passionate enthusiasm by other accidents: Frankenstein's father neglects to explain Agrippa's obsolescence, a discussion provoked by a lightning bolt undermines his belief in the occult, and "some accident" prevents him from attending lectures on natural philosophy. Left with a craving for knowledge but no reliable guide to direct it, Frankenstein's curiosity is kept within bounds only by the "mutual affection" of his domestic circle.

In this dramatization of Victor Frankenstein's childhood, Mary Shelley fuses mechanistic psychological theories of the origin and development of character with the more organic theories generally associated with the Romantics. Like most contemporary Lockean philosophers, she asserts that circumstances activate and direct an individual's capacity for imaginative activity; the inclination or predilection thus formed then constitutes the basis of identity. But when Shelley combines this model with the notion (implied by Wollstonecraft's *Letters Written . . . in Sweden* and by the poetry of Wordsworth, Coleridge, Byron, and Percy Shelley) that an individual's desire, once aroused, has its own impetus and logic, she comes up with a model of maturation that contradicts the optimism of both mechanists and organicists. More in keeping with eighteenth-century moralists than with either William Godwin or Percy Shelley, Mary Shelley characterizes innate desire not as neutral or benevolent but as quintessentially egotistical. And, unlike Mary Wollstonecraft, she does not conceive of imaginative activity as leading through intimations of mortality to new insight or creativity. Instead, she sees imagination as an appetite that can and must be regulated— specifically, by the give-and-take of domestic relationships. If it is aroused but is not controlled by human society, it will project itself into the natural world, becoming voracious in its search for objects to conquer and consume. This principle, which draws both mechanistic and organic models under the mantle of conventional warnings to women, constitutes the major dynamic of *Frankenstein's* plot. As long as domestic relationships govern an individual's affections, his or her desire will turn outward as love. But when the individual loses or leaves the regulating influence of relationship with others, imaginative energy always threatens to turn back on itself, to "mark" all external objects as its own and to degenerate into "gloomy and narrow reflections upon self" (*F*, p. 32).

Shelley's exposition of the degeneration of incipient curiosity into full-fledged egotism begins when Frankenstein leaves his childhood home for the University of Ingolstadt. At the university he is left to "form [his] own friends, and be [his] own protector" (p. 40), and, given this freedom, his imagination is liberated to follow its natural course. To the young scholar, this energy seems well-directed, for Frankenstein assumes that his ambition to conquer death through science is fundamentally unselfish. With supreme self-confidence, he "penetrate[s] into the recesses of nature" in search of the secret of life. What he discovers in the "vaults and charnel houses" he visits, however, is not life but death, the "natural decay and corruption of the human body." In pursuing his ambition even beyond this grisly sight, Frankenstein proves unequivocally that his "benevolent" scheme actually acts out the imagination's essential and deadly self-devotion. For what he really wants is not to serve others but to assert himself. Indeed, he wants ultimately to defy mortality, to found a "new species" that would "bless [him] as its creator and source." "No father could claim the gratitude of his child so completely as I should deserve their's," he boasts (p. 49).

Frankenstein's particular vision of immortality and the vanity that it embodies have profound social consequences, both because Frankenstein would deny relationships (and women) any role in the conception of children and because he would reduce all domestic ties to those that center on and feed his selfish desires. Given the egotism of his ambition, it comes as no surprise that Frankenstein's love for his family is the first victim of his growing obsession; "supernatural enthusiasm" usurps the place of his previous domestic love. "I wished, as it were, to procrastinate all that related to my feelings of affection until the great object, which swallowed up every habit of my nature, should be completed" (p. 50). Frankenstein isolates himself in a "solitary chamber," refuses to write even to his fiancée, Elizabeth, and grows "insensible to the charms of nature." "I became as timid as a love-sick girl," he realizes, in retrospect, "and alternate tremor and passionate ardour took the place of wholesome sensation and regulated ambition" (p. 51).

Despite what the reviewers thought, in her dramatization of the imaginative quest Mary Shelley is actually more concerned with this antisocial dimension than with its metaphysical implications. In chapter 5, for example, at the heart of her story, she elaborates the significance of Frankenstein's self-absorption primarily in terms of his social relationships. After animating the monster, product and symbol of self-serving desire, Frankenstein falls asleep, only to dream the true meaning of his accomplishment: having denied domestic relationships by indulging his selfish passions, he has, in effect, murdered domestic tranquillity.

> I thought I saw Elizabeth, in the bloom of health, walking in the streets of Ingolstadt. Delighted and surprised, I embraced her; but as I imprinted the first kiss on her lips, they became livid with the hue of death; her features appeared to change, and I thought that I held the corpse of my dead mother in my arms; a shroud enveloped her form, and I saw the grave-worms crawling in the folds of the flannel. [p. 53]

Lover and mother, as the presiding female guardians of Franken-stein's "secluded and domestic" youth, are conflated in this tableau of the enthusiast's guilt. Only now, when Frankenstein starts from his sleep to find the misshapen creature hanging over his bed (as he himself will later hang over Elizabeth's) does he recognize his ambition for what it really is: a monstrous urge, alien and threatening to all human intercourse.

In effect, animating the monster completes and liberates Frankenstein's egotism, for his indescribable experiment gives explicit and autonomous form to his ambition and desire. Paradoxically, in this incident Shelley makes the ego's destructiveness literal by setting in motion the figurative, symbolic character of the monster. We will see later the significance of this event for the monster; for Frankenstein, this moment, which aborts his maturation, has the dual effect of initiating self-consciousness and, tragically, perfecting his alienation. Momentarily "restored to life" by his childhood friend Clerval, Frankenstein rejects the "selfish pursuit [that] had cramped and narrowed" him and returns his feeling to its proper objects, his "beloved friends." But ironically, the very gesture that disciplines his desire has already destroyed the possibility of reestablishing relationships with his loved ones. Liberating the monster allows Frankenstein to see that personal fulfillment results from self-denial rather than self-assertion, but it also condemns him to perpetual isolation and, therefore, to permanent incompleteness.

This fatal paradox, the heart of Mary Shelley's waking nightmare, gives a conventionally "feminine" twist to the argument that individuals mature through imaginative projection, confrontation, and self-consciousness. In the version of maturation that Wollstonecraft sketched out in her two *Vindications* and in *Letters Written . . . in*

Sweden and that Wordsworth set out more fully in *The Prelude*, the child's innate desires, stirred and nurtured by the mother's love, are soon projected outward toward the natural world. Desire takes this aggressive turn because in maternal love and in the receptivity this love cultivates "there exists / A virtue which irradiates and exalts / All objects through all intercourse of sense" (1805 *Prelude*, book 2, lines 258–60). As a result of both the child's growing confidence in the beneficence of the questing imagination and nature's generous response, the child is able to effect a radical break with the mother without suffering irretrievable loss.

> No outcast he, bewildered and depressed;
> Along his infant veins are interfused
> The gravitation and the filial bond
> Of Nature that connect him with the world.
>   [*Prelude*, 2.261–64]

The heightened images of the self cast back from nature then help the child internalize a sense of autonomous identity and personal power.

In marked contrast, Mary Shelley distrusts both the imagination *and* the natural world. The imagination, as it is depicted in Frankenstein's original transgression, is incapable of projecting an irradiating virtue, for, in aiding and abetting the ego, the imagination expands the individual's self-absorption to fill the entire universe, and, as it does so, it murders everyone in its path. In *Frankenstein*, the monster simply acts out the implicit content of Frankenstein's desire: just as Frankenstein figuratively murdered his family, so the monster literally murders Frankenstein's domestic relationships, blighting both the memory and the hope of domestic harmony with the "black mark" of its deadly hand. William Frankenstein, Justine Moritz, Henry Clerval, even Elizabeth Lavenza are, as it were, literally *possessed* by this creature; but, as Frankenstein knows all too well, its victims are by extension his own: Justine is *his* "unhappy victim" (p. 80); *he* has murdered Clerval (p. 174); and the creature consummates *his* deadly desire on "*its* bridal bier" (p. 193).

By the same token, Mary Shelley also distrusts nature, for, far from curbing the imagination, nature simply encourages imaginative projection. Essentially, Mary Shelley's understanding of nature coincides with those of Wordsworth, Wollstonecraft, and Percy Shelley. But where these three trust the imagination to disarm the natural world of its meaninglessness by projecting human content into it, Mary Shelley's anxiety about the imagination bleeds into the world it invades. In the inhospitable world most graphically depicted in the final setting of *Frankenstein*, nature is "terrifically desolate," frigid, and fatal to human beings and human relationships. These fields of ice provide a fit home only for the monster, that incarnation of the imagination's ugly and deadly essence.

Thus Shelley does not depict numerous natural theaters into which the individual can project his or her growing desire and from which affirmative echoes will return to hasten the process of maturation. Instead, she continues to dramatize personal fulfillment strictly in terms of the child's original domestic harmony, with the absent mother now replaced by the closest female equivalent: ideally, Elizabeth would link Frankenstein's maturity to his youth, just as Mrs. Saville should anchor the mariner Walton. Ideally, in other words, the beloved object would be sought and found only within the comforting confines of preexisting domestic relationships. In this model, Shelley therefore ties the formation of personal identity to self-denial rather than self-assertion; personal identity for her entails defining oneself in terms of relationships (not one but many)—not, as Wollstonecraft and Wordsworth would have it, in terms of self-assertion, confrontation, freedom, and faith in the individualistic imaginative act.

Shelley repeatedly stresses the fatal kinship between the human imagination, nature, and death by the tropes of natural violence that describe all kinds of desire. Passion is like nature internalized, as even Frankenstein knows:

> When I would account to myself for the birth of that passion, which afterwards ruled my destiny, I find it arise, like a mountain river, from ignoble and almost forgotten sources; but, swelling as it proceeded, it became the torrent which, in its course, has swept away all my hopes and joys. [*F*, p. 32]

Ambition drives Frankenstein "like a hurricane" as he engineers the monster (p. 49) and, after its liberation, he is a "blasted tree," "utterly destroyed" by a lightning blast to his soul. Through these metaphoric associations, Shelley is laying the groundwork for the pattern acted out by the monster. *Like* forces in the natural world, Frankenstein's unregulated desire gathers strength until it erupts in the monster's creation; then the creature actualizes, externalizes, the pattern of nature—Frankenstein's nature and the natural world, now explicitly combined—with a power that destroys all society. In other words, the pattern inherent in the natural world and figuratively ascribed to the individual becomes, through the monster, Frankenstein's literal "fate" or "destiny."

The individual's fatal relationship to nature is further complicated by the egotistical impulse to deny this kinship. In retrospect, Frankenstein knows that the winds will more likely yield a storm than calm, but in the blindness of his original optimism he believes that nature is hospitable to humanity, that it offers a Wordsworthian "ennobling interchange" that consoles and elevates the soul. Still trusting himself and the natural world, Frankenstein cries out with "something like joy" to the spirit of the Alps, as if it were a compassionate as well as a natural parent: "Wandering spirits . . . allow me this faint happiness, or take me, as your companion, away from the joys of life." But Frankenstein's belief in natural benevolence, like his earlier confidence in the benevolence of his desire, proves a trick of the wishful imagination. His request is answered by the true spirit of this and every place untamed by social conventions—the "superhuman," "unearthly" monster. Lulled once more by vanity and desire, Frankenstein recognizes the character of his bond with nature only when it again stands incarnate before him.

In order to understand why Mary Shelley's first readers did not fully appreciate what seems, in comparison to Romantic optimism, to be an unmistakable distrust of the imagination, we must turn to the monster's narrative. For Shelley's decision to divide the novel into a series of first-person narratives instead of employing a single perspective, whether first-person or omniscient, has the effect of qualifying her judgment of egotism. Because she dramatizes in the monster—not in Frankenstein—the psychological consequences of imaginative self-assertion, the reader is encouraged to participate not only in Frankenstein's desire for innate and natural benevolence but also in the agonizing repercussions of this misplaced optimism.

In the monster's narrative, Shelley both recapitulates Frankenstein's story and, ingeniously, completes it. Influenced by external circumstances that arouse, then direct, their desire for knowledge, both beings find that their imaginative quests yield only the terrible realization of an innate grotesqueness. But, unlike Frankenstein, the monster is denied the luxury of an original domestic harmony. The monster is "made" not born, and, as the product of the unnatural coupling of nature and the imagination, it is caught in the vortex of death that will ultimately characterize Frankenstein as well. Moreover, as the product, then the agent of Frankenstein's egotism, the monster is merely a link in the symbolic "series" of Frankenstein's "self-devoted being," not an autonomous member of a natural, organic family. Given a human's nobler aspirations without the accompanying power, the monster struggles futilely to deny both its status as a function of Frankenstein and the starkness of its circumscribed domain; the creature yearns to experience and act upon its own desires and to break free into the realistic frame that Frankenstein occupies. But the monster cannot have independent desires or influence its own destiny because, as the projection of Frankenstein's indulged desire and nature's essence, the creature *is* destiny. Moreover, because the monster's physical form literally embodies its essence, it cannot pretend to be something it is not; it cannot enter the human community it longs to join, and it cannot earn the sympathy it can all too vividly imagine. Paradoxically, the monster is the victim of both the symbolic and the literal. And, as such, it is doubly like a woman in patriarchal society—forced to be a symbol of (and vehicle for) someone else's desire, yet exposed (and exiled) as the deadly essence of passion itself.

For the monster, then, self-consciousness comes with brutal speed, for it depends, not on an act of transgression, but on literal self-perception. An old man's terror, a pool of water, a child's fear, all are nature's mirrors, returning the monster repeatedly to its grotesque self, "a figure hideously deformed and loathsome . . . a monster, a blot upon the earth" (pp. 115–16). When the creature discovers its true origin—not in the literary works it finds and learns to read but in the records of Frankenstein's private experiments—it can no longer deny the absolute "horror" of its being, the monstrous singularity of egotism: "the minutest description of my odious and loathsome person is given, in language which painted your own horrors, and rendered mine ineffaceable" (p. 126). From this moment on, the monster's attempts to deny its nature are as futile as they are desperate. In its most elaborate scheme, the creature hides in a womblike hovel, as if it could be born again into culture by aping the motions of the family it spies upon. Although the monster tries to disguise its true nature by confronting only the blind old father, De Lacey's children return and recognize the creature's "ineffaceable" monstrosity for what it literally is. Their violent reaction, which the monster interprets as rejection by its "adopted family," at last precipitates the creature's innate nature; abandoning humanity's "godlike science"—the language of society it so diligently learned—for its natural tongue—the nonsignifying "fearful howlings" of beasts—the monster embarks on its systematic destruction of domestic harmony. The creature makes one final attempt to form a new society; but when Frankenstein refuses to create a female monster, it is condemned, like its maker, to a single bond of hatred. After Frankenstein's death, the monster disappears into the darkness at the novel's end, vowing to build its own funeral pyre; for it is as immune to human justice as it was repulsive to human love.

The monster carries with it the guilt and alienation that attend Frankenstein's self-assertion; yet, because Shelley realistically details the stages by which the creature is driven to act out its symbolic nature from *its* point of view, the reader is compelled to identify with its anguish and frustration. This narrative strategy precisely reproduces Mary Shelley's profound ambivalence toward Frankenstein's creative act; for by separating self-assertion from its consequences, she is able to dramatize both her conventional judgment of the evils of egotism and her emotional engagement in the imaginative act. Indeed, the pathos of the monster's cry suggests that Shelley identified most strongly with the product (and the victim) of Frankenstein's transgression: the objectified imagination, helpless and alone. Although in an important sense, objectifying Frankenstein's imagination in the symbolic form of the monster delimits the range of connotations the imagination can have (it eliminates, for example, the possibilities of transcendent power or beneficence), this narrative strategy allows Shelley to express her ambivalence toward the creative act because a symbol is able to accommodate different, even contradictory, meanings. It is important to recognize that Shelley is using symbolism in a quite specific way here, a way that differs markedly from Percy Shelley's description of symbolism in his preface to the 1818 *Frankenstein*. In his justification for the central scene, Percy stresses not the ambivalence of the symbol but its comprehensiveness: "However impossible as a physical fact, [this incident] affords a point of view to the imagination for the delineating of human passions more comprehensive and commanding than any which the ordinary relations of existing events can yield" (p. 6). Although we know from the Shelleys' letters and from the surviving manuscript of *Frankenstein* that Percy was instrumental in promoting and even revising the text, Mary did not uncritically or wholeheartedly accept the aesthetic program of which this self-confident use of symbolism was only one part. Instead, she transforms Percy's version of the Romantic aesthetic in such a way as to create for herself a nonassertive, and hence acceptable, voice.

Percy Shelley defended his aesthetic doctrines, as part of his political and religious beliefs, with a conviction Mary later called a "resolution firm to martyrdom." Scornful of public opinion, he maintained that a true poet may be judged only by his legitimate peers, a jury "impaneled by Time from the selectest of the wise of many generations." Society's accusation that an artist is "immoral," he explains in the "Defence of Poetry" (1821), rests on "a misconception of the manner in which poetry acts to produce the moral improvement of man." The audience's relationship to poetry is based not on reason but on the imagination; true poetry does not encourage imitation or judgment but participation. It strengthens the individual's moral sense because it exercises and enlarges the capacity for sympathetic identification, that is, for establishing relationships. Following Plato, Percy declares that the primary reflex of the moral imagination is the outgoing gesture of love.

> The great secret of morals is Love; or a going out of our own nature, and an identification of ourselves with the beautiful which exists in thought, action, or person, not our own. A man,

to be greatly good, must imagine intensely and comprehen-
sively; he must put himself in the place of another and of many
others; the pains and pleasures of his species must become his
own. The great instrument of moral good is the imagination;
and poetry administers to the effect by acting upon the cause.

Each of Percy Shelley's aesthetic doctrines comes to rest on this
model of the imagination as an innately moral, capacious faculty.
Because the imagination, if unrestrained, naturally supersedes relative morals (and in so doing compensates for the inhumaneness of
the natural world), the poet should not discipline his or her poetic
efforts according to a particular society's conceptions of right and
wrong. Because the imagination tends to extend itself, through sympathy, to truth, the poet should simply depict examples of truth, thus
drawing the audience into a relationship that simultaneously feeds
and stimulates humanity's appetite for "thoughts of ever new delight."

This model of the artwork as an arena for relationships is the only
aspect of Percy's aesthetics that Mary Shelley adopts without reser-
vation. It seems to have been particularly appealing to her not only
because it conforms to Percy's ideal but also because it satisfies society's conventional definition of proper feminine identity and proper
feminine self-assertion. In doing so, it also answered needs and
assuaged fears that seem to have been very pressing for Mary Shelley. As we have seen, she did not agree with Percy that the imagination is inherently moral. By the same token, she seems to have
doubted that the abstract controls that Wollstonecraft described in
her two *Vindications* and her *Letters Written . . . in Sweden* were
capable of governing an individual's desire or disciplining the imagination. The factors that reinforced Shelley's doubts were probably as
complicated as the anxieties themselves, but we can surmise that
Percy Shelley's outspoken atheism helped undermine Mary's confidence in orthodox religion, that society's denigration of women's
reasoning ability weakened her trust in that faculty, and that society's judgment and her own conflicting emotions conspired to make
her doubt the morality of female feeling. For Mary Shelley, then, the
only acceptable or safe arena in which to articulate her feelings, exercise her reason, and act out her unladylike ambition was that of personal relationships. In addition to the aesthetic purpose it serves, the
narrative strategy of *Frankenstein* also provides just such a network
of relationships. Because of its three-part narrative arrangement,
Shelley's readers are drawn into a relationship with even the most
monstrous part of the young author; Shelley is able to create her
artistic persona through a series of relationships rather than a single
act of self-assertion; and she is freed from having to take a single,
definitive position on her unladylike subject. In other words, the nar-

rative strategy of *Frankenstein*, like the symbolic presentation of the monster, enables Shelley to express and efface herself at the same time and thus, at least partially, to satisfy her conflicting desires for self-assertion and social acceptance.

* * *

ANNE K. MELLOR

Possessing Nature: The Female in *Frankenstein*†

When Victor Frankenstein identifies Nature as female—"I pursued nature to *her* hiding places"[1]—he participates in a gendered construction of the universe whose ramifications are everywhere apparent in *Frankenstein*. His scientific penetration and technological exploitation of female nature, which I have discussed elsewhere,[2] is only one dimension of a more general cultural encoding of the female as passive and possessable, the willing receptacle of male desire. The destruction of the female implicit in Frankenstein's usurpation of the natural mode of human reproduction symbolically erupts in his nightmare following the animation of his creature, in which his bride-to-be is transformed in his arms into the corpse of his dead mother—"a shroud enveloped her form, and I saw the grave-worms crawling in the folds of the flannel" (p. 53). By stealing the female's control over reproduction, Frankenstein has eliminated the female's primary biological function and source of cultural power. Indeed, for the simple purpose of human survival, Frankenstein has eliminated the necessity to have females at all. One of the deepest horrors of this novel is Frankenstein's implicit goal of creating a society for men only: his creature is male; he refuses to create a female; there is no reason that the race of immortal beings he hoped to propagate should not be exclusively male.[3]

---

† From *Romanticism and Feminism*, ed. Anne K. Mellor (Bloomington: Indiana UP, 1988) 220–32. Reprinted by permission of Indiana University Press.
1. Mary W. Shelley, *Frankenstein, or The Modern Prometheus* (London: Lackington, Hughes, Harding, Mavor and Jones, 1818); all further references to *Frankenstein* will be to Rieger, ed. (New York: Bobbs-Merrill, 1974; reprinted, Chicago: U of Chicago P, 1982), and will be cited by page number only in the text. This phrase occurs on page 49.
2. Anne K. Mellor, "*Frankenstein*: A Feminist Critique of Science," in *One Culture: Essays on Literature and Science*, ed. George Levine (Madison: U of Wisconsin P, 1988), 287–312.
3. Mary Shelley thus heralds a tradition of literary utopias and dystopias that depict single-sex societies, a tradition most recently appropriated by feminist writers to celebrate exclusively female societies. For an analysis of the strengths and weaknesses of such feminist utopian writing, in which female societies are reproduced by parthenogenesis, see my "On Feminist Utopias," *Women's Studies* (1982): 241–62. Leading examples of this genre include Charlotte Perkins Gilman's *Herland*, Sally Miller Gearhart's *The*

On the cultural level, Frankenstein's scientific project—to become the sole creator of a human being—supports a patriarchal denial of the value of women and of female sexuality. Mary Shelley, doubtless inspired by her mother's *A Vindication of the Rights of Woman*, specifically portrays the consequences of a social construction of gender that values the male above the female. Victor Frankenstein's nineteenth-century Genevan society is founded on a rigid division of sex roles: the male inhabits the public sphere, the female is relegated to the private or domestic sphere.[4] The men in Frankenstein's world all work outside the home, as public servants (Alphonse Frankenstein), as scientists (Victor), as merchants (Clerval and his father), or as explorers (Walton). The women are confined to the home; Elizabeth, for instance, is not permitted to travel with Victor and "regretted that she had not the same opportunities of enlarging her experience and cultivating her understanding" (151). Inside the home, women are either kept as a kind of pet (Victor "loved to tend" on Elizabeth "as I should on a favorite animal" [p. 30]); or they work as house wives, childcare providers, and nurses (Caroline Beaufort Frankenstein, Elizabeth Lavenza, Margaret Saville) or as servants (Justine Moritz).

As a consequence of this sexual division of labor, masculine work is kept outside of the domestic realm; hence intellectual activity is segregated from emotional activity. Victor Frankenstein cannot do scientific research and think lovingly of Elizabeth and his family at the same time. His obsession with his experiment has caused him "to forget those friends who were so many miles absent, and whom I had not seen for so long a time" (p. 50). This separation of masculine

---

Wanderground, Joanna Russ's *The Female Man*, James Tiptree, Jr.'s "Houston, Houston Do You Read?" and Suzy McKee Charnas's trilogy *The Vampire Tapestry*.
4. On the gender division of nineteenth-century European culture, see Jean Elshtain, *Public Man, Private Woman: Women in Social and Political Thought* (Oxford: Robertson, 1981); and *Victorian Women: A Documentary Account of Women's Lives in Nineteenth-Century England, France, and the United States*, ed. E. Hellerstein, L. Hume, and K. Offen (Stanford: Stanford UP, 1981). For a study of sex roles in *Frankenstein*, see Kate Ellis, "Monsters in the Family: Mary Shelley and the Bourgeois Family," in *The Endurance of Frankenstein*, ed. George Levine and U. C. Knoepflmacher (Berkeley, Los Angeles, London: U of California P, 1979), pp. 123–42; and Anca Vlasopolos, "*Frankenstein's* Hidden Skeleton: The Psycho-Politics of Oppression," *Science-Fiction Studies* 10 (1983): 125–36.

William Veeder, in his insightful but occasionally reductive psychological study of Mary and Percy Shelley and *Frankenstein, Mary Shelley and Frankenstein: The Fate of Androgyny* (1986), wishes to define masculinity and femininity as the complementary halves of an ideally balanced androgynous or agapic personality that is destroyed or bifurcated by erotic self-love; his book traces the reasons why Mary Shelley's fictional characters realize or fail to achieve her androgynous ideal. While he is right to argue that Mary Shelley believed in balancing "masculine" and "feminine" characteristics, he consistently defines as innate psychological characteristics those patterns of learned behavior (masculinity, femininity) that I prefer to see as socially constructed gender roles. His readings thus unintentionally reinforce an oppressive biological determinism and sex-stereotyping, even as they call attention to the dangers of extreme masculine and feminine behaviors.

work from the domestic affections leads directly to Frankenstein's downfall. Because Frankenstein cannot work and love at the same time, he fails to feel empathy for the creature he is constructing and callously makes him eight feet tall simply because "the minuteness of the parts formed a great hindrance to my speed" (p. 49). He then fails to love or feel any parental responsibility for the freak he has created. And he remains so fixated on himself that he cannot imagine his monster might threaten someone else when he swears to be with Victor "on his wedding-night."

This separation of the sphere of public (masculine) power from the sphere of private (feminine) affection also causes the destruction of many of the women in the novel. Caroline Beaufort dies unnecessarily because she feels obligated to nurse her favorite Elizabeth during a smallpox epidemic; she thus incarnates a patriarchal ideal of female self-sacrifice (this suggestion is strengthened in the 1831 revisions where she eagerly risks her life to save Elizabeth). She is a woman who is devoted to her father in wealth and in poverty, who nurses him until his death, and then marries her father's best friend to whom she is equally devoted.

The division of public man from private woman also means that women cannot function effectively in the public realm. Despite her innocence of the crime for which she is accused, Justine Moritz is executed for the murder of William Frankenstein (and is even half-persuaded by her male confessor that she is responsible for William's death). And Elizabeth, fully convinced of Justine's innocence, is unable to save her: the impassioned defense she gives of Justine arouses public approbation of Elizabeth's generosity but does nothing to help Justine, "on whom the public indignation was turned with renewed violence, charging her with the blackest ingratitude" (p. 80). Nor can Elizabeth save herself on her wedding night. Both these deaths are of course directly attributable to Victor Frankenstein's self-devoted concern for his own suffering (the creature will attack only him) and his own reputation (people would think him mad if he told them his own monster had killed his brother).

Mary Shelley underlines the mutual deprivation inherent in a family and social structure based on rigid and hierarchical gender divisions by portraying an alternative social organization in the novel: the De Lacey family. The political situation of the De Lacey family, exiled from their native France by the manipulations of an ungrateful Turkish merchant and a draconian legal system, points up the injustice that prevails in a nation where masculine values of competition and chauvinism reign. Mary Shelley's political critique of a society founded on the unequal distribution of power and possessions is conveyed not only through the manifest injustice of Justine's execution and of France's treatment first of the alien Turkish merchant and then of the De Lacey family, but also through the readings in political history that she assigns to the creature. From Plutarch's *Parallel Lives of the Greeks and Romans* and from Volney's *Ruins, or Meditations on the Revolutions of Empires*, the creature learns both of masculine virtue and of masculine cruelty and injustice. "I heard of the division of property, of immense wealth and squalid poverty; . . . I learned that the possessions most esteemed . . . were high and unsullied descent united with riches" (p. 115). "Was man, indeed, at once so powerful, so virtuous, and magnificent, yet so vicious and base?" the creature asks incredulously. Implicit in Mary Shelley's attack on the social injustice of established political systems is the suggestion that the separation from the public realm of feminine affections and compassion has caused much of this social evil. Had Elizabeth Lavenza's plea for mercy for Justine, based on her intuitively correct knowledge of Justine's character, been heeded, Justine would not have been wrongly murdered by the courts. As Elizabeth exclaims,

> how I hate [the] shews and mockeries [of this world]! when one creature is murdered, another is immediately deprived of life in a slow torturing manner; then the executioners, their hands yet reeking with the blood of innocence, believe that they have done a great deed. They call this *retribution.* Hateful name! when the word is pronounced, I know greater and more horrid punishments are going to be inflicted than the gloomiest tyrant has ever invented to satiate his utmost revenge. (p. 83)

In contrast to this pattern of political inequality and injustice, the De Lacey family represents an alternative ideology: a vision of a social group based on justice, equality, and mutual affection. Felix willingly sacrificed his own welfare to ensure that justice was done to the Turkish merchant. More important, the structure of the De Lacey family constitutes Mary Shelley's ideal, an ideal derived from her mother's *A Vindication of the Rights of Woman*. In the impoverished De Lacey household, all work is shared equally in an atmosphere of rational companionship, mutual concern, and love. As their symbolic names suggest, Felix embodies happiness, Agatha goodness. They are then joined by Safie (*sophia* or wisdom). Safie, the daughter of the Turkish merchant, is appalled both by her father's betrayal of Felix and by the Islamic oppression of women he endorses; she has therefore fled from Turkey to Switzerland, seeking Felix. Having reached the De Lacey household, she promptly becomes Felix's beloved companion and is taught to read and write French. Safie, whose Christian mother instructed her "to aspire to higher powers of intellect, and an independence of spirit, forbidden to the female followers of Mahomet" (p. 119), is the incarnation of

Mary Wollstonecraft in the novel. Wollstonecraft too traveled alone through Europe and Scandinavia; more important, she advocated in *A Vindication* that women be educated to be the "companions" of men and be permitted to participate in the public realm by voting, working outside the home, and holding political office.

But this alternative female role-model of an independent, well-educated, self-supporting, and loving companion, and this alternative nuclear family structure based on sexual equality and mutual affection, is lost in the novel, perhaps because the De Lacey family lacks the mother who might have been able to welcome the pleading, pitiable creature. When Safie flees with the De Lacey family, we as readers are deprived of the novel's only alternative to a rigidly patriarchal construction of gender and sex roles, just as Mary Shelley herself was deprived of a feminist role-model when her mother died and was subsequently denounced in the popular British press as a harlot, atheist, and anarchist. Safie's disappearance from the novel reflects Mary Shelley's own predicament. Like Frankenstein's creature, she has no positive prototype she can imitate, no place in history. That unique phenomenon envisioned by Mary Wollstonecraft, the wife as the lifelong intellectual equal and companion of her husband, does not exist in the world of nineteenth-century Europe experienced by Mary Shelley.

The doctrine of the separate spheres that Victor Frankenstein endorses encodes a particular attitude to female sexuality that Mary Shelley subtly exposes in her novel. This attitude is manifested most vividly in Victor's response to the creature's request for a female companion, an Eve to comfort and embrace him. After hearing his creature's autobiographical account of his sufferings and aspirations, Frankenstein is moved by an awakened conscience to do justice toward his Adam and promises to create a female creature, on condition that both leave forever the neighborhood of mankind. After numerous delays, Frankenstein finally gathers the necessary instruments and materials together into an isolated cottage on one of the Orkney Islands off Scotland and proceeds to create a female being. Once again he becomes ill: "my heart often sickened at the work of my hands. . . . my spirits became unequal; I grew restless and nervous" (p. 162).

Disgusted by his enterprise, Frankenstein finally determines to stop his work, rationalizing his decision to deprive his creature of a female companion in terms that repay careful examination. Here is Frankenstein's meditation:

> I was now about to form another being, of whose dispositions I was alike ignorant; she might become ten thousand times more malignant than her mate, and delight, for its own sake, in

murder and wretchedness. He had sworn to quit the neighborhood of man, and hide himself in deserts; but she had not; and
she, who in all probability was to become a thinking and reasoning animal, might refuse to comply with a compact made
before her creation. They might even hate each other; the creature who already lived loathed his own deformity, and might he
not conceive a greater abhorrence for it when it came before his
eyes in the female form? She also might turn with disgust from
him to the superior beauty of man; she might quit him, and he
be again alone, exasperated by the fresh provocation of being
deserted by one of his own species.

   Even if they were to leave Europe, and inhabit the deserts of
the new world, yet one of the first results of those sympathies
for which the daemon thirsted would be children, and a race of
devils would be propagated upon the earth, who might make
the very existence of the species of man a condition precarious
and full of terror. Had I a right, for my own benefit, to inflict
this curse upon everlasting generations? . . . I shuddered to
think that future ages might curse me as their pest, whose selfishness had not hesitated to buy its own peace at the price perhaps of the existence of the whole human race. (p. 163)

What does Victor Frankenstein truly fear, which causes him to end
his creation of a female? First, he is afraid of an independent female
will, afraid that his female creature will have desires and opinions
that cannot be controlled by his male creature. Like Rousseau's
natural man, she might refuse to comply with a social contract
made before her birth by another person; she might assert her own
integrity and the revolutionary right to determine her own existence. Moreover, those uninhibited female desires might be sadistic:
Frankenstein imagines a female "ten thousand times" more evil
than her mate, who would "delight" in murder for its own sake.
Third, he fears that his female creature will be more ugly than his
male creature, so much so that even the male will turn from her in
disgust. Fourth, he fears that she will prefer to mate with ordinary
males; implicit here is Frankenstein's horror that, given the gigantic
strength of this female, she would have the power to seize and even
rape the male she might choose. And finally, he is afraid of her
reproductive powers, her capacity to generate an entire race of similar creatures. What Victor Frankenstein truly fears is female sexuality as such. A woman who is sexually liberated, free to choose her
own life, her own sexual partner (by force, if necessary). And to
propagate at will can appear only monstrously ugly to Victor Frankenstein, for she defies that sexist aesthetic that insists that women
be small, delicate, modest, passive, and sexually pleasing—but available only to their lawful husbands.

Horrified by this image of uninhibited female sexuality, Victor Frankenstein violently reasserts a male control over the female body, penetrating and mutilating the female creature at his feet in an image that suggests a violent rape: "trembling with passion, [I] tore to pieces the thing on which I was engaged" (p. 164). The morning after, when he returns to the scene, "The remains of the half-finished creature, whom I had destroyed, lay scattered on the floor, and I almost felt as if I had mangled the living flesh of a human being" (p. 167). However he has rationalized his decision to murder the female creature, Frankenstein's "passion" is here revealed as a fusion of fear, lust, and hostility, a desire to control and even destroy female sexuality.

Frankenstein's fear of female sexuality is endemic to a patriarchal construction of gender. Uninhibited female sexual experience threatens the very foundation of patriarchal power: the establishment of patrilineal kinship networks together with the transmission of both status and property by inheritance entailed upon a male line. Significantly, in the patriarchal world of Geneva in the novel, female sexuality is strikingly repressed. All the women are presented as sexless: Caroline Beaufort is a devoted daughter and chaste wife while Elizabeth Lavenza's relationship with Victor is that of a sister.

In this context, the murder of Elizabeth Lavenza on her wedding night becomes doubly significant. The scene of her death is based on a painting Mary Shelley knew well, Henry Fuseli's famous "The Nightmare." The corpse of Elizabeth lies in the very attitude in which Fuseli placed his succubus-ridden woman: "She was there, lifeless and inanimate, thrown across the bed, her head hanging down, and her pale and distorted features half covered by her hair" (p. 193). Fuseli's woman is an image of female erotic desire, both lusting for and frightened of the incubus (or male demon) that rides upon her, brought to her bedchamber by the stallion that leers at her from the foot of her bed; both the presence of this incubus and the woman's posture of open sexual acceptance leave Fuseli's intentions in no doubt.[5] Evoking this image, Mary Shelley alerted us to what

---

5. Henry Fuseli, *The Nightmare*, first version, 1781; The Detroit Institute of Art. This famous painting was widely reproduced throughout the early nineteenth century and was of particular interest to Mary Shelley, who knew of her mother's early passionate love for Fuseli. H. W. Janson has suggested that Fuseli's representation of the nightmare is a projection of his unfulfilled passion for Anna Landolt, whose portrait is drawn on the reverse side (H. W. Janson, "Fuseli's *Nightmare*," *Arts and Sciences* 2 [1963]: 23–28). When Fuseli learned that Anna Landolt had married, he wrote to her uncle and his good friend Johann Lavater from London on 16 June 1779 that he had dreamed of lying in her bed and fusing "her body and soul" together with his own. Fuseli's painting is thus a deliberate allusion to traditional images of Cupid and Psyche meeting in her bedroom at night; here the welcomed god of love has been transformed into a demonic incubus of erotic lust (see also Peter Tomory, *The Life and Art of Henry Fuseli*, London:

Victor fears most: his bride's sexuality.[6] Significantly, Elizabeth would not have been killed had Victor not sent her into their wedding bedroom *alone*. Returning to the body of the murdered Elizabeth, Victor "embraced her with ardour; but the deathly languor and coldness of the limbs told me, that what I now held in my arms had ceased to be the Elizabeth whom I had loved and cherished" (p. 193). Victor most ardently desires his bride when he knows she is dead; the conflation with his earlier dream, when he thought to embrace the living Elizabeth but instead held in his arms the corpse of his mother, signals Victor's most profound erotic desire, a necrophiliac and incestuous desire to possess the dead female, the lost mother.

To put this point another way, we might observe that Victor Frankenstein's most passionate relationships are with men rather than with women. He sees Clerval as "the image of my former self" (p. 155), as his "friend and dearest companion" (p. 181), as his true soul mate. His description of Clerval's haunting eyes—"languishing in death, the dark orbs covered by the lids, and the long black lashes that fringed them" (p. 179)—verges on the erotic. Similarly, Walton responds to Frankenstein with an ardor that borders on the homoerotic. Having desired "the company of a man who could sympathize with me; whose eyes would reply to mine" (p. 13), Walton eagerly embraces Frankenstein as "a celestial spirit" (p. 23) whose death leaves him inarticulate with grief: "what can I say," Walton writes to his sister, "that will enable you to understand the depth of my sorrow?" (p. 216). Finally, Frankenstein dedicates himself to his scientific experiment with a passion that can be described only as erotic: as Mary Shelley originally described Frankenstein's obsession, "I wished, as it were, to procrastinate my feelings of affection, until the great object of my affection was compleated." Frankenstein's homoerotic fixation upon his creature, whose features he had selected as "beautiful" (p. 52) in a parody of Pygmalion and Galatea, was underlined by Mary Shelley in a revision she made in the Thomas copy of *Frankenstein*. Describing his anxious enslavement to his task, Frankenstein confesses: "my voice became broken, my trembling hands almost refused to accomplish their task; I became as timid as a lovesick girl, and alternate tremor and passionate ardour took the place

---

1972, pp. 92ff.; and the Catalogue Raisonnée by Gert Schiff, *Johann Heinrich Fussli*, Zurich: 1973, pp. 757–59).

Gerhard Joseph first noted the allusion to Fuseli's painting, "Frankenstein's Dream: The Child Is Father of the Monster," *Hartford Studies in Literature* 7 (1975): 97–115, 109. William Veeder denies the association (*Mary Shelley and Frankenstein*, 192–93) on the grounds that Elizabeth's hair half-covers her face; in this regard, it may be significant that Fuseli's woman's face is half-covered in shadow.

6. Paul A. Cantor has discussed Frankenstein's rejections both of normal sexuality and of the bourgeois lifestyle, in *Creature and Creator: Myth-making and English Romanticism* (New York: Cambridge UP, 1984), 109–15.

of wholesome sensation and regulated ambition" (51:31–35). In place of a normal heterosexual attachment to Elizabeth, Victor Frankenstein has substituted a homosexual obsession with his creature,[7] an obsession that in his case is energized by a profound desire to reunite with his dead mother, by becoming himself a mother.

To sum up, at every level Victor Frankenstein is engaged upon a rape of nature, a violent penetration and usurpation of the female's "hiding places," of the womb. Terrified of female sexuality and the power of human reproduction it enables, both he and the patriarchal society he represents use the technologies of science and the laws of the polis to manipulate, control, and repress women. Thinking back on Elizabeth Lavenza strangled on her bridal bier and on Fuseli's image of female erotic desire that she replicates, we can now see that at this level Victor's creature, his monster, realizes his own most potent lust. The monster, like Fuseli's incubus, leers over Elizabeth, enacting Victor's own repressed desire to rape, possess, and destroy the female. Victor's creature here becomes just that, his "creature," the instrument of his most potent desire: to destroy female reproductive power so that only men may rule.

However, in Mary Shelley's feminist novel, Victor Frankenstein's desire is portrayed not only as horrible and finally unattainable but also as self-destructive. For Nature is not the passive, inert, or "dead" matter that Frankenstein imagines.[8] Frankenstein assumes that he can violate Nature and pursue her to her hiding places with impunity. But Nature both resists and revenges herself upon his attempts. During his research, Nature denies to Victor Frankenstein both mental and physical health: "my enthusiasm was checked by my anxiety, and I appeared rather like one doomed by slavery to toil in the mines, or any other unwholesome trade, than an artist occupied by his favourite employment. Every night I was oppressed by a slow fever, and I became nervous to a most painful degree" (p. 51). When his experiment is completed, Victor has a fit that renders him

---

7. William Veeder has emphasized the homosexual bond between Frankenstein and his monster (*Mary Shelley and Frankenstein*, 89–92). Eve Kosofsky Sedgwick arrives at this conclusion from a different direction. In her *Between Men: English Literature and Male Homosocial Desire* (New York: Columbia UP, 1985), she observes in passing that *Frankenstein*, like William Godwin's *Caleb Williams*, is "about one or more males who not only is persecuted by, but considers himself transparent to and often under the compulsion of another male. If we follow Freud [in the case of Dr. Schreber] in hypothesizing that such a sense of persecution represents the fearful, phantasmic rejection by recasting of an original homosexual (or even merely homosocial) desire, then it would make sense to think of this group of novels as embodying strongly homophobic mechanisms" (91–92).

8. While I largely agree with Mary Poovey's intelligent and sensitive analysis of Frankenstein's egotistic desire (in *The Proper Lady and the Woman Writer*, 123–33), I do not share her view that the nature we see in the novel is "fatal to human beings and human relationships." Poovey fails to distinguish between Frankenstein's view of nature and the author's and between the first and third editions of the novel in this regard.

"lifeless" for "a long, long time" and that marks the onset of a "nervous fever" that confines him for many months (p. 57). Victor continues to be tormented by anxiety attacks, bouts of delirium, periods of distraction and madness. As soon as he determines to blaspheme against Nature a second time, by creating a female human being, Nature punishes him: "the eternal twinkling of the stars weighed upon me, and . . . I listened to every blast of wind, as if it were a dull ugly siroc on its way to consume me" (p. 145). His mental illness returns: "Every thought that was devoted to it was an extreme anguish, and every word that I spoke in allusion to it caused my lips to quiver and my heart to palpitate" (p. 156); "my spirits became unequal; I grew restless and nervous" (p. 162). Finally, Frankenstein's obsession with destroying his creature exposes him to such mental and physical fatigue that he dies at the age of twenty-five.

Appropriately, Nature prevents Frankenstein from constructing a normal human being: an unnatural method of reproduction produces an unnatural being, in this case a freak of gigantic stature, watery eyes, a shriveled complexion, and straight black lips. This physiognomy causes Frankenstein's instinctive withdrawal from his child, and sets in motion the series of events that produces the monster who destroys Frankenstein's family, friends, and self.

Moreover, Nature pursues Victor Frankenstein with the very electricity he has stolen: lightning, thunder, and rain rage around him. The November night on which he steals the "spark of being" from Nature is dreary, dismal, and wet: "the rain . . . poured from a black and comfortless sky" (p. 54). He next glimpses his creature during a flash of lightning as a violent storm plays over his head at Plainpalais (p. 71); significantly, the almighty Alps, and in particular Mont Blanc, are represented in this novel as female, as an image of omnipotent fertility[9]—on his wedding day, Victor admires "the beautiful Mont Blanc, and the assemblage of snowy mountains that in vain endeavour to emulate *her*" (p. 190; my italics). Before Frankenstein's first encounter with his creature among the Alps, "the rain poured down in torrents, and thick mists hid the summits of the mountains" (p. 91). Setting sail from the Orkney island where he has destroyed his female creature, planning to throw her mangled remains into the sea, Frankenstein wakes to find his skiff threatened by a fierce wind and high waves that portend his own death: "I might be driven into the wide Atlantic, and feel all the tortures of starvation, or be swallowed up in the immeasurable waters that roared and buffeted

---

9. On Mary Shelley's subversive representation of the traditionally masculinized Alps as female, see Fred V. Randel, "*Frankenstein*, Feminism, and the Intertextuality of Mountains," *Studies in Romanticism* 23 (Winter, 1984): 515–33.

around me. I . . . felt the torment of a burning thirst; . . . I looked upon the sea, it was to be my grave" (p. 169). Frankenstein ends his life and his pursuit of the monster he has made in the arctic regions, surrounded by the aurora borealis, the electromagnetic field of the North Pole. The atmospheric effects of the novel, which most readers have dismissed as little more than the traditional trappings of Gothic fiction, in fact manifest the power of Nature to punish those who transgress her boundaries. The elemental forces that Victor has released pursue him to his hiding places, raging round him like avenging Furies.

Finally, Nature punishes Victor Frankenstein the life-stealer most justly by denying him the capacity for natural procreation. His bride is killed on their wedding night, cutting off his chance to engender his own children. His creature—that "great object, which swallowed up every habit of my nature" (50)—turns against him, destroying not only his brother William, his soul mate Clerval, his loyal servant Justine, his grief-stricken father, and his wife, but finally pursuing Victor himself to his death, leaving Frankenstein entirely without progeny. Nature's revenge is absolute: he who violates her sacred hiding places is destroyed.

Mary Shelley's novel thus portrays the penalties of raping Nature. But it also celebrates an all-creating Nature loved and revered by human beings. Those characters capable of deeply feeling the beauties of Nature are rewarded with physical and mental health. Even Frankenstein in his moments of tranquillity or youthful innocence can respond powerfully to the glory of Nature. As Walton notes, "the starry sky, the sea, and every sight afforded by these wonderful regions, seems still to have the power of elevating his soul from earth" (p. 23). In Clerval's company Victor becomes again

> the same happy creature who, a few years ago, loving and beloved by all, had no sorrow or care. When happy, inanimate nature had the power of bestowing on me the most delightful sensations. A serene sky and verdant fields filled me with ecstasy. (p. 65)

Clerval's relationship to Nature represents one moral touchstone of the novel: since he "loved with ardour . . . the scenery of external nature" (p. 154), Nature endows him with a generous sympathy, a vivid imagination, a sensitive intelligence and an unbounded capacity for devoted friendship. His death annihilates the possibility that Victor Frankenstein might regain a positive relationship with Nature.

Mary Shelley envisions Nature as a sacred life-force in which human beings ought to participate in conscious harmony. Elizabeth Lavenza gives voice to this ideal in her choice of profession for Ernest Frankenstein:

I proposed that he should be a farmer. . . . A farmer's is a very healthy happy life; and the least hurtful, or rather the most beneficial profession of any. My uncle [wanted him] educated as an advocate . . . but . . . it is certainly more creditable to cultivate the earth for the sustenance of man, than to be the confidant, and sometimes the accomplice, of his vices. (p. 59)

Nature nurtures those who cultivate her; perhaps this is why, of all the members of Frankenstein's family, only Ernest survives. Mary Shelley shares Wordsworth's concept of a beneficial bond between the natural and the human world, which is broken only at man's peril. Had Victor Frankenstein's eyes not become "insensible to the charms of nature" (p. 50) and the affections of family and friends, he would not have defied Mary Shelley's moral credo:

A human being in perfection ought always to preserve a calm and peaceful mind, and never to allow passion or a transitory desire to disturb his tranquillity. I do not think that the pursuit of knowledge is an exception to this rule. If the study to which you apply yourself has a tendency to weaken your affections, and to destroy your taste for those simple pleasures in which no alloy can possibly mix [e.g., the "beautiful season"], then that study is certainly unlawful, that is to say, not befitting the human mind. (p. 51)

As an ecological system of interdependent organisms, Nature requires the submission of the individual ego to the welfare of the family and the larger community. Like George Eliot after her, Mary Shelley is profoundly committed to an ethic of cooperation, mutual dependence, and self-sacrifice. The Russian sea-master willingly sacrifices his own desires that his beloved and her lover may marry; Clerval immediately gives up his desire to attend university in order to nurse his dear friend Victor back to health; Elizabeth offers to release her beloved Victor from his engagement should he now love another. Mary Shelley's moral vision thus falls into that category of ethical thinking which Carol Gilligan has recently identified as more typically female than male. Where men have tended to identify moral laws as abstract principles that clearly differentiate right from wrong, women have tended to see moral choice as imbedded in an ongoing shared life. As Gilligan contrasts them, a male "ethic of justice proceeds from the premise of equality—that everyone should be treated the same" while a female "ethic of care rests on the premise of nonviolence—that no one should be hurt."[1] This traditional female morality can probably be traced to what Nancy Chodorow and Doro-

---

1. Carol Gilligan, *In a Different Voice: Psychological Theory and Women's Development* (Cambridge: Harvard UP, 1982), 174.

thy Dinnerstein have shown to be the daughter's greater identification with the mother.[2] Whereas the son has learned to assert his separateness from the mother (and the process of mothering), the daughter has learned to represent that gendered role and thus has felt more tightly (and ambivalently) bound to the mother. Less certain of her ego boundaries, the daughter has been more likely to engage in moral thinking which gives priority to the good of the family and the community rather than to the rights of the individual.

Insofar as the family is the basic social unit, it has historically represented the system of morality practiced by the culture at large. The hierarchical structure of the Frankenstein family embodies a masculine ethic of justice in which the rights of the individual are privileged: Frankenstein pursues his own interests in alchemy and chemistry, cheerfully ignoring his family obligations as he engages "heart and soul" in his research, and is moreover encouraged to leave his family and fiancée for two years ("for a more indulgent and less dictatorial parent did not exist upon earth" [p. 130]). In contrast, the egalitarian and interdependent structure of the De Lacey family ideologically encodes a female ethic of care in which the bonding of the family unit is primary. Felix blames himself most because his self-sacrificing action on behalf of the Turkish merchant involved his family in his suffering. Agatha and Felix perform toward their father "every little office of affection and duty with gentleness; and he rewarded them by his benevolent smiles"; they willingly starve themselves that their father may eat (106). Safie's arrival particularly delighted Felix but also "diffused gladness through the cottage, dispelling their sorrow as the sun dissipates the morning mists" (112). In portraying the De Laceys as an archetype of the egalitarian, benevolent, and mutually loving nuclear family, Mary Shelley clearly displayed her own moral purpose, which Percy Shelley rightly if somewhat vaguely described in his Preface as "the exhibition of the amiableness of domestic affection, and the excellence of universal virtue" (7).

Mary Shelley's grounding of moral virtue in the preservation of familial bonds (against which Frankenstein, in his failure to parent his own child, entirely transgresses) entails an aesthetic credo as well. While such romantic descendants as Walter Pater and Oscar Wilde would later argue that aesthetics and morality, art and life, are distinct, Mary Shelley endorsed a traditional mimetic aesthetic that exhorted literature to imitate ideal Nature and defined the role

2. See Nancy Chodorow, *The Reproduction of Mothering: Psychoanalysis and the Sociology of Gender* (Berkeley and Los Angeles: U of California P, 1978); Dorothy Dinnerstein, *The Mermaid and the Minotaur: Sexual Arrangements and Human Malaise* (New York: Harper and Row, 1976); cf. Nancy Friday, *My Mother/My Self: The Daughter's Search for Identity* (New York: Dell, 1977).

of the writer as a moral educator. Her novel purposefully identifies moral virtue, based on self-sacrifice, moderation, and domestic affection, with aesthetic beauty. Even in poverty, the image of the blind old man listening to the sweetly singing Agatha is "a lovely sight, even to me, poor wretch! who had never beheld aught beautiful before" (103). In contrast, Frankenstein's and Walton's dream of breaking boundaries is explicitly identified as both evil and ugly. As Walton acknowledges, "my day dreams are . . . extended and magnificent; but they want (as the painters call it) *keeping*" (p. 14). "Keeping," in painting, means "the maintenance of the proper relation between the representations of nearer and more distant objects in a picture"; hence, in a more general sense, "the proper subserviency of tone and colour in every part of a picture, so that the general effect is harmonious to the eye" (*OED*). Walton thus introduces Mary Shelley's ethical norm as an aesthetic norm; both in life and in art, her ideal is a balance or golden mean between conflicting demands, specifically here between large and small objects. In ethical terms, this means that Walton must balance his dreams of geographical discovery and fame against the reality of an already existing set of obligations (to his family, his crew, and the sacredness of Nature). Similarly, Frankenstein should have better balanced the obligations of great and small, of parent and child, of creator and creature. Frankenstein's failure to maintain *keeping*, to preserve "a calm and peaceful mind" (p. 51), is thus in Mary Shelley's eyes both a moral and an aesthetic failure, resulting directly in the creation of a hideous monster.

PETER BROOKS

What Is a Monster?
(According to Frankenstein)[†]

monstrum horrendum informe ingens cui lumen ademptum[1]
Virgil, *Aeneid,* 3:658

Viewing woman's body in a phallic field of vision predominates in the nineteenth-century realist tradition, but there are examples of attempts to subvert this model and move beyond its epistemological implications to other kinds of knowing of the body. I shall argue in the next chapter that George Eliot provides the best instance of dissent from within the dominant tradition—a dissent that Freud,

---

† From *Body Work: Objects of Desire in Modern Narrative* (Cambridge: Harvard UP, 1993), 199–220. Reprinted by permission.
1. "A monster frightful, form less, immense, with sight removed."

attempting to supplant seeing by listening to the body, may al
struggling toward. The present chapter returns to an earlier exa
ple of the dissenting perspective, by another woman novelist, written
before the realist novel has established its hegemony—Mary Shelley's *Frankenstein*. Hence I propose here to violate chronology and to
interrupt the general trend of my argument, to look closely at a text
which is too complex, peculiar, and interesting to be neglected.

Frankenstein, first published in 1818, concerns an exotic body
with a difference, a distinct perversion from the tradition of desirable objects. The story of this ugly, larger-than-life, monstrous body
raises complex questions of motherhood, fatherhood, gender, and
narrative. The afterlife of the novel in the popular imagination has
been intensely focused on that monstrous body, to the extent that
the name "Frankenstein" tends to evoke not the unfortunate overreaching young scientist Victor Frankenstein but his hideous creation. This is both faithful and unfaithful to Mary Shelley's original:
faithful, in that a monster indeed, even etymologically, exists to be
looked at, shown off, viewed as in a circus sideshow; unfaithful, in
that Shelley's novel with equal insistence directs us to issues of language in the story of the monster and his creator. In fact, the central
issues of the novel are joined in the opposition of sight and speech,
and it unfolds its complex narrative structure from this nexus.

That narrative structure involves framed or imbedded tales, a
tale within a tale within a tale: in the outer frame, explorer Robert
Walton writes to his sister Mrs. Saville, and tells of meeting Frankenstein in the Arctic; in the next frame, Frankenstein recounts his
life story to Walton; in the innermost tale, the monster at a crucial
moment tells his tale to Frankenstein. When the monster has finished, Frankenstein resumes speaking in his own right; when he has
done, Walton resumes.[2] The nested narrative structure calls attention to the presence of a listener for each speaker—of a narratee for
each narrator—and to the interlocutionary relations thus established. Each act of narration in the novel implies a certain bond or
contract: listen to me because . . . The structure calls attention to
the motives of telling; it makes each listener—and the reader—ask:
Why are you telling me this? What am I supposed to do with it? As
in the psychoanalytic context of storytelling, the listener is placed
in a transferential relation to the narrative. As a "subject supposed
to know," the listener is called upon to "supplement" the story (to
anticipate the phrase Freud will use in the case history of Dora), to
articulate and even enact the meaning of the desire it expresses in
ways that may be foreclosed to the speaker. Storytelling in *Frankenstein* is far from an innocent act: narratives have designs on their
narratees that must be unraveled. The issues posed by such a

2. A diagram of the narrative structure would look like this: {[()]}.

may most of all concern relation, or how narra-
... s to inter-subjective relation, and the relation of
...hese senses, to language as the medium of telling
... the medium of transmission, transaction, and

...ke on their full import only in the context of the
...t with the opening of the innermost tale—which
strikingly poses the issues of the visual—and then work out to the
framing structures. Following the first murders committed by the
Monster—Frankenstein's brother William strangled, the family servant Justine Moritz executed as his killer through maliciously planted
evidence—Frankenstein seeks solace in the Alps above Chamonix.
He penetrates the "glorious presence-chamber of imperial Nature,"
climbing to Montanvert and the Mer de Glace, hoping to recapture a
remembered "sublime ecstasy that gave wings to the soul and allowed
it to soar from the obscure world to light and joy."[3] His ascension
takes him to a "wonderful and stupendous scene," overlooking the
Mer de Glace and facing the "awful majesty" of Mont Blanc; his
heart once again opens to joy, and he exclaims, in the tones of the
Ossianic bard, "Wandering spirits, if indeed ye wander, and do not
rest in your narrow beds, allow me this faint happiness, or take me,
as your companion, away from the joys of life." At this point, the
vision of sublimity is both fulfilled and undone by the sight of a
superhuman shape that comes bounding toward Frankenstein over
the ice. The Monster appears to be—as in his original creation—
both born of nature and supernatural, and as such he puts normal
measurements and classifications into question. In particular, he
puts into question the meaning of looking, of optics, as the faculty
and the science most commonly used to judge meanings in the phenomenal world.

Frankenstein's immediate reaction to the appearance of the Monster is to tell it to go away. When the Monster persists in his claim
that he has the right to a hearing from his creator, Frankenstein
curses the day of the Monster's creation, and reiterates: "Begone!
Relieve me from the sight of your detested form" (97). To this the
Monster, in a touching gesture, responds by placing his huge hands
over Frankenstein's eyes: "Thus I relieve thee, my creator . . . thus I
take from thee a sight which you abhor. Still thou canst listen to me,
and grant me thy compassion." The Monster clearly understands
that it is not visual relation that favors him—indeed, as we will

---

3. Mary Shelley, *Frankenstein; or, The Modern Prometheus* (New York: NAL/Signet, 1983),
92–93. Subsequent references are to this edition, which reprints the revised text of
1831. I have also consulted the helpful critical edition by James Rieger (Indianapolis
and New York: Bobbs-Merrill, 1974), which prints the original text of 1818 (with the
corrections of 1823) and indicates the variants occurring in the revised edition.

discover when he tells his own story, his only favorable reception from a human being thus far has come from the blind de Lacey—but rather the auditory or interlocutionary, the relation of language. Thus, this first meeting of Frankenstein and his Monster since the day of his creation presents a crucial issue of the novel in the opposition of sight and language, of the hideous body and the persuasive tongue.

For the Monster is eloquent. From the first words he speaks, he shows himself to be a supreme rhetorician, who controls the antitheses and oxymorons that express the pathos of his existence: "Remember that I am thy creature; I ought to be thy Adam, but I am rather the fallen angel, whom thou drivest from joy for no misdeed. Everywhere I see bliss, from which I alone am irrevocably excluded. I was benevolent and good; misery made me a fiend. Make me happy, and I shall again be virtuous" (95–96). When we learn of the Monster's self-education—and particularly his three master-texts, Milton's *Paradise Lost*, Plutarch's *Lives*, and Goethe's *Werther*—we will understand the prime sources of his eloquence and of the conception of the just order of things that animates his plea to his creator. But beyond the motives of his eloquence, it is important to register the simple fact of Shelley's decision to make the Monster the most eloquent creature in the novel. This hideous and deformed creature, far from expressing himself in grunts and gestures, speaks and reasons with the highest elegance, logic, and persuasiveness. As a verbal creation, he is the very opposite of the monstrous: he is a sympathetic and persuasive participant in Western culture. All of the Monster's interlocutors—including, finally, the reader—must come to terms with this contradiction between the verbal and the visual.[4]

By persuading Frankenstein to give his creature a hearing, thus opening the innermost frame of the novel, the Monster has adumbrated what Roland Barthes would call a "narrative contract" between narrator and narratee.[5] The narrative contract, like the psychoanalytic transference, is based on and implies the intersubjective, transindividual, cultural order of language. Language by its very nature transcends and preexists the individual locutor; it implies, depends on, and necessitates that network of intersubjective relations from which the Monster protests he has been excluded. That

---

4. For the reader, the contradiction between the visual and the verbal appears also as a clash of generic expectations, between the Gothic novel and the philosophical tale: the Monster's hideous body and frightful crimes belong the Gothic tradition, whereas his autobiograpical narrative and the issues it raises suggest an eighteenth-century philosophical tale.
5. See Roland Barthes, S/Z (Paris: Editions du Seuil, 1970), 95–96. For some comments on the model of the "narrative contract," and the need to extend it toward a more dynamic concept of narrative transaction, see my "Narrative Transaction and Transference," in *Reading for the Plot* (1984; rpt. Cambridge: Harvard UP, 1992), 216–37.

is, in becoming the narrator of his story, the Monster both dramatizes his problem and provides a model for its solution, the solution
implicit in the discursive interdependence of an "I" and a "thou" in
any interlocutionary situation.[6] The Monster's words assign to Frankenstein a parental role for the first time in the novel: "For the first
time . . . I felt what the duties of a creator towards his creature were"
(97)—a role all the more glaring in its neglect in that Frankenstein
has dwelt at length on the parental love and concern lavished on him
in his early years, the way he was guided by a "silken cord" toward
happiness and goodness (33). By the time the Monster has completed
his narrative, Frankenstein still feels horror and hatred when he
looks upon this "filthy mass that moved and talked," but he also
avows: "His words had a strange effect upon me. I compassionated
him" (140). After establishing this tenuous link with his creator
through narrative, the Monster takes the decisive step in his argument: "My vices are the children of a forced solitude that I abhor,
and my virtues will necessarily arise when I live in communion with
an equal. I shall feel the affections of a sensitive being and become
linked to the chain of existence and events from which I am now
excluded" (140–41).

The metaphor of the chain is one that will reappear in various
guises throughout the novel. It represents relation itself, including
affective interpersonal relations (see the "silken cord" of Frankenstein's childhood) and the relations between tellers and listeners—
relations established through language and as language. The chain
here closely resembles what Jacques Lacan calls the "signifying
chain" of language, especially language as the vehicle of desire. In
the Monster's confrontation of and narrative to Frankenstein, we
have a representation of the Lacanian distinction between the imaginary and the symbolic orders. The imaginary is the order of the
specular, of the mirror stage, and arises from the subject's perception of itself as other; it is thus the order of deceptive relations, of
ideology and fascination. The symbolic order ultimately is language
itself, the systematic and transindividual order of the signifier, the
cultural system or law into which individual subjects are inserted.[7]
In the specular or imaginary order, the Monster will never cease to
be the "filthy mass." In the symbolic order, on the other hand, he
can produce and project his desire in language, in relation to an
interlocutor. It is, however, in the logic of Lacanian desire and the
"signifying chain" that such desire should be unappeasable, a met-

6. On these questions, see the classic essay by Emile Benveniste, "De la subjectivité dans
le langage," in *Problèmes de linguistique générate* (Paris: Gallimard, 1967), 258–66.
7. On the Lacanian terms used here see in particular Jacques Lacan, "Le stade du miroir"
and "L'instance de la lettre dans l'inconscient ou la raison depuis Freud," in *Écrits*
(Paris: Editions du Seuil, 1966), 93–100 and 493–528.

onymical movement that extends desire forward without reaching a goal: a goal which cannot be named, since the object of desire is unconscious. The Monster's stated object of desire is for a mate, a female creature like himself, which Frankenstein must create. But we will have occasion to ask whether this demand truly corresponds to the needs stipulated by the Monster's desire.

Before considering the Monster's demand for—and Frankenstein's temporary acquiescence to—the creation of a female monster, it is important to register the Monster's narrative of his discovery of language, its contexts and its effects. His first experience with humanity, he tells us, already demonstrated the hopelessness of the specular relation: the shepherd he discovered in a hut fled shrieking from his sight, the villagers pelted him with stones. Retreating into a hovel adjoining the de Lacey cottage, he commences his education as voyeur, observing the family through an "almost imperceptible chink through which the eye could penetrate," seeing and himself unseen. His most important discovery is that of human language, which is presented in the context of human interaction and affect:

> "I found that these people possessed a method of communicating their experience and feelings to one another by articulate sounds. I perceived that the words they spoke sometimes produced pleasure or pain, smiles or sadness, in the minds and countenances of the hearers. This was indeed a godlike science, and I ardently desired to become acquainted with it. But I was baffled in every attempt I made for this purpose. Their pronunciation was quick, and the words they uttered, not having any apparent connection with visible objects, I was unable to discover any clue by which I could unravel the mystery of their reference. By great application, however, and after having remained during the space of several revolutions of the moon in my hovel, I discovered the names that were given to some of the most familiar objects of discourse; I learned and applied the words, 'fire,' 'milk,' 'bread,' and 'wood.' I learned also the names of the cottagers themselves. The youth and his companion had each of them several names, but the old man had only one, which was 'father.' The girl was called 'sister' or 'Agatha,' and the youth 'Felix,' 'brother,' or 'son.' I cannot describe the delight I felt when I learned the ideas appropriated to each of these sounds and was able to pronounce them. I distinguished several other words without being able as yet to understand or apply them, such as 'good,' 'dearest,' 'unhappy.'" (106–107)

Like so much else in the story of the Monster's education through sensation, experience, and the association of ideas, his discovery of language stands within Enlightenment debates about origins, coming in this instance close to the scenarios of Rousseau's *Essai sur l'origine des langues*, which sees language as originating not in need but in emotion.[8] As the Monster encounters it, language is tied to human love and patterns of kinship and relation, as if in confirmation of the views of an anthropologist such as Claude Lévi-Strauss, for whom the structures of kinship are the first "writing" of a society. The Monster also discovers the proto-Saussurian notion that the linguistic sign is arbitrary, that there is no intuitable connection of a sign to its referent, and indeed that some signs ("good," "dearest," "unhappy") have no apparent referent. As a consequence, the Monster grasps the nature of language as a system, wherein meaning is created not as a simple movement from sign to referent but in context, dependent on the rule-governed relation of signs one to another.

Hence language presents itself as both the tool he needs to enter into relation with others, and a model of relation itself: it implies—it both depends on and makes possible—that "chain of existence and events" from which he feels himself excluded. The "godlike science" of language is thus explicitly a cultural compensation for a deficient nature; it offers the possibility of escape from "monsterism," which is precisely lack of relation, apartness. Language is what he must use to experience human love. In Rousseau's terms, it is a "supplement" to nature. The Monster tells Frankenstein: "I easily perceived that, although I eagerly longed to discover myself to the cottagers, I ought not to make the attempt until I had first become master of their language, which knowledge might enable me to make them overlook the deformity of my figure, for with this also the contrast perpetually presented to my eyes had made me acquainted" (108).

Language is richly thematized at this moment of the novel. With the arrival of Safie, we have lessons in French offered to an Arab, in the context of what we know to be a German-speaking region, the whole rendered for us in English. This well-ordered Babel calls attention to issues of communication and transmission, in somewhat the same manner as the narrative frames of the novel. The Monster learns language through overhearing, and observing, the instruction of Safie by Felix and Agatha. He learns to read—that is, he masters language in what is for Rousseau its mediate form, supplementary to

8. See Jean-Jacques Rousseau, *Essai sur l'origine des langues* (Paris: Bibliothèque du Graphe, 1973), reprinted from the 1817 edition of Rousseau's works published by A. Belin. For a thorough and subtle discussion of Rousseau's presence throughout *Frankenstein*, see David Marshall, "*Frankenstein*, or Rousseau's Monster: Sympathy and Speculative Eyes," in *The Surprising Effects of Sympathy* (Chicago: U of Chicago P, 1988), 178–227. Marshall's comments on the *Essai sur l'origine des langues* start from my own evocation of the pertinence of that text in a very early version of this chapter, "'Godlike Science/Unhallowed Arts': Language and Monstrosity in *Frankenstein*," *New Literary History* 9:3 (1978), reprinted (slightly modified) in *The Endurance of Frankenstein*, ed. George Levine and U. C. Knoepflmacher (Berkeley: U of California P, 1979)—but Marshall treats the subject far more fully than I did.

the spoken word: the form in which it is most transmissible, since it does not demand presence, the specular relation, for its exchange, yet also the form in which it is potentially most deceitful, freed from immediate expressivity. The three texts which the Monster now discovers and reads—Plutarch's *Lives*, Goethe's *Werther*, and Milton's *Paradise Lost*—cover the public, the private, and the cosmic realms, and three modes of love. They constitute a kind of minimal Romantic *cyclopedia universalis*. Of the three, it is *Paradise Lost*—in the literalist reading the Monster gives it—that excites the profoundest reactions, and poses in emblematic terms the enigma of the Monster's nature. In the manner of Adam, he appears to be a unique creation, "united by no link to any other being in existence" (124). Yet, "wretched, helpless, and alone," he is unlike Adam. "Many times I considered Satan as the fitter emblem of my condition, for often, like him, when I viewed the bliss of my protectors, the bitter gall of envy rose within me." In particular, the intertextual presence of *Paradise Lost* insistently poses the relation of language to the specular, especially in the implicit comparison of the Monster to Eve, in two passages in which he views himself in a mirroring pool. "I had admired the perfect forms of my cottagers—their grace, beauty, and delicate complexions; but how was I terrified when I viewed myself in a transparent pool! At first I started back, unable to believe that it was indeed I who was reflected in the mirror; and when I became fully convinced that I was in reality the monster that I am, I was filled with the bitterest sensations of despondence and mortification" (108). This echoes Eve's report of the day of her creation, in Book 4 (460–76) of *Paradise Lost*. After first awakening to life, she finds a mirroring lake:

> As I bent down to look, just opposite,
> A Shape within the wat'ry gleam appear'd
> Bending to look on me, I started back,
> It started back, but pleas'd I soon return'd,
> Pleas'd it return'd as soon with answering looks
> Of sympathy and love; there I had fixt
> Mine eyes till now, and pin'd with vain desire,
> Had not a voice thus warn'd me, What thou seest,
> What there thou seest fair Creature is thyself,
> With thee it came and goes; but follow me,
> And I will bring thee where no shadow stays
> Thy coming, and thy soft imbraces, hee
> Whose image thou art, him thou shalt enjoy
> Inseparably thine, to him shalt bear
> Multitudes like thyself, and thence be call'd
> Mother of human Race: what could I do,
> But follow straight, invisibly thus led?

The passage of course recalls Ovid's Narcissus, and anticipates Lacan's scenario of the infant's discovery of his reflected self—both same and other—at the mirror stage. Narcissism is here a temptation to which Eve, immediately enamored of her own image, would succumb, pining "with vain desire," were it not for the intervention of a divine voice that commands her to set aside this moment of primary narcissism in favor of sexual difference. The place "where no shadow stays" is almost explicitly the place of the phallus, as opposed to the substantiality of the female's sex and the love of two female bodies. As the Miltonic scenario unfolds, Eve's first perception of Adam is not itself sufficient to move her beyond primary narcissism: Adam is "fair indeed and tall," she says, "yet methought less fair, / Less winning soft, less amiably mild, / Than that smooth wat'ry image; back I turn'd" (4:478–80). She would return to the "answering looks" of the lake were it not that Adam at this point seizes her hand, and she yields to what is for Milton, in his thoroughly misogynist scenario, the explicit hegemony of the male.

Milton's story is thus about Eve's discovery of the law, which is variously the command of God, the law of sexual difference, and the rule of the phallus. In her submission to the law, she gives up desire for her own image, and for indifferentiation, with reluctance, in a prefiguration of her subsequent disobedience. The Monster, on the other hand, discovers himself as different, as violation of the law, in a scenario that mirrors and reverses Lacan's; the outer image—that in the mirror—presents the body in its lack of wholeness (at least in human terms) while the inner apprehension of the body had up until then held it to be hypothetically whole: "At first I started back, unable to believe that it was indeed I who was reflected in the mirror." The experience is anti-narcissistic, convincing the Monster that he is, indeed, a monster, thus in no conceivable system an object of desire. As the Monster will put it in the second passage of self-reflection, "Increase of knowledge only discovered to me more clearly what a wretched outcast I was. I cherished hope, it is true, but it vanished when I beheld my person reflected in water or my shadow in the moonshine, even as that frail image and that inconstant shade" (125). The mirror image becomes the negation of hope, severing the Monster from desire. He is simply outside the law, and thus will require a separate creation—his own Eve—in order to come under its sway. Thus his narrative plea to his creator concludes by focusing the discourse of desire on a new object to be desired, the monster woman.

The Monster's self-reflections in relation to *Paradise Lost* are succeeded by his discovery of the literal story of his creation, in Frankenstein's laboratory journal, which he finds in the pocket of the coat he has worn since the day of his creation. Here, he discovers that he is the anti-image of Adam: "God, in pity, made man beautiful and alluring, after his own image; but my form is a filthy type of yours, more horrid even from the very resemblance" (125). Self-recognition as "filthy type" completes the mirror stage of the Monster's development. He now knows he must trust wholly in the symbolic order. Having mastered language, he goes to confront the patriarch de Lacey. The "godlike science" at first appears to achieve the desired effects: "I am blind," de Lacey responds to the Monster's plea, "and cannot judge of your countenance, but there is something in your words which persuades me that you are sincere" (128). Sympathy is on the point of creating the Monster's first entry into the social chain, when Felix, Agatha, and Safie enter the cottage, and the Monster is brutally returned to the specular order: Agatha faints, Safie flees, and Felix violently separates the interlocutors. The Monster in consequence becomes explicitly Satanic: "I, like the arch-fiend, bore a hell within me" (130); he sets fire to what had late been his happy seat, and sets forth into the world in search of the hidden face of his creator, the *deus absconditus* who alone, now, has the power to bring him into social relation, through a second monstrous creation.

Along the way to his meeting with Frankenstein, the Monster—after being shot and wounded by a rustic whose daughter he has saved from drowning—commits his first murder, that of Frankenstein's brother William, in a scene that evokes the question of relation in the most acute ways. The Monster's first idea is to take the boy as a companion; in a common Enlightenment thought experiment, he conceives that a child is probably too young "to have imbibed a horror of deformity" (136). His error is immediately apparent: to his address of "Child," William in return calls him "monster! Ugly wretch! . . . ogre." But what provokes the murder is William's exclamation that his father is "M. Frankenstein"—Victor's father also, of course, and by extrapolation the Monster's "grandfather"—whom the Monster here calls "my enemy." When William lies dead at his feet, the Monster notices a miniature portrait worn around his neck: "I took it; it was a portrait of a most lovely woman. In spite of my malignity, it softened and attracted me. For a few moments I gazed with delight on her dark eyes, fringed by deep lashes, and her lovely lips; but presently my rage returned; I remembered that I was forever deprived of the delights that such beautiful creatures could bestow and that she whose resemblance I contemplated would, in regarding me, have changed that air of divine benignity to one expressive of disgust and affright" (136). This moment of scopophilic fixation, of the gaze erotically medused by its (painted) object, has a special resonance because we know (as the Monster does not) that the portrait is of William and Victor's dead mother. The novel is notable for the absence of living mothers: Felix and Agatha's mother is dead (and the word "mother" nowhere figures in the language lesson observed by the Monster), so is Safie's, Madame Frankenstein dies after contracting scarlet fever from her adopted daughter, Elizabeth—Frankenstein's intended bride—and the Monster of course has no mother, only a "father." The portrait of the dead mother thus represents an essential lack or gap in existence, most particularly for the Monster, whose primal erotic experience here is directly Oedipal, but censored from the outset: the father's interdiction of the mother as erotic object to the son has never been so radical as in the case of Frankenstein and his created Monster.[9]

The Oedipal overtones of the scene become richer and more complex as we read on. Having taken the portrait, the Monster enters a barn, where he finds a sleeping woman—Justine Moritz— whom he describes as "young, not indeed so beautiful as her whose portrait I held, but of an agreeable aspect and blooming in the loveliness of youth and health" (137). In imitation of Satan whispering into the ear of the sleeping Eve in *Paradise Lost*, the Monster whispers to Justine: "Awake, fairest, thy lover is near—he who would give his life but to obtain one look of affection from thine eyes; my beloved, awake!" But this first attempt at seduction on the Monster's part is self-censoring: when the sleeper stirs, the Monster reflects that if she awakes, she will denounce him as a murderer. As a consequence, he decides to pin the murder on her. "Thanks to the lessons of Felix and the sanguinary laws of man, I had learned how to work mischief." He plants the mother's portrait in the folds of her dress and flees, with the reflection: "The crime had its source in her; be hers the punishment!" The claim is curious and excessive, since Justine is in no manner the "source" of William's murder, which takes place before the Monster has discovered her sleeping form. In the

9. Several critics have pointed to the importance of the absence of mothers, and the search for a mother, in *Frankenstein*: see in particular Marc A. Rubenstein, "'My Accursed Origin': The Search for the Mother in *Frankenstein*," *Studies in Romanticism* 15 (1976), 165–94; Sandra M. Gilbert and Susan Gubar, "Horror's Twin: Mary Shelley's Monstrous Eve," in *The Madwoman in the Attic* (New Haven: Yale UP, 1979), 213–47; Mary Jacobus, "Is There a Woman in This Text?" in *Reading Women: Essays in Feminist Criticism* (New York: Columbia UP, 1986), esp. 101; and Margaret Homans, "Bearing Demons: Frankenstein's Circumvention of the Maternal," in *Bearing the Word* (Chicago: U of Chicago P, 1986), pp. 100–119. On the biographical resonances of some of these issues—particularly the relation of Mary Shelley to her mother, Mary Wollstonecraft, who died shortly after giving birth to her, and her father, William Godwin, and her children, especially William—see, in addition to the studies just mentioned, Ellen Moers, "Female Gothic," U. C. Knoepflmacher, "Thoughts on the Aggression of Daughters," and Kate Ellis, "Monsters in the Garden: Mary Shelley and the Bourgeois Family," all in *The Endurance of Frankenstein*. See also Barbara Johnson, "My Monster/My Self," in *A World of Difference* (Baltimore: Johns Hopkins UP, 1987), pp. 144–54. The fullest and most useful biography of Mary Shelley is Emily W. Sunstein, *Mary Shelley: Romance and Reality* (Boston: Little, Brown, 1989).

logic of desire, if not in syntax, we must find the referent of "her" in the mother herself. Under the (paternal) interdiction of the mother, the monster-child turns to a substitute woman, in a clear example of what Freud calls an "anaclitic" object choice.[1] When it becomes apparent that this object choice, too, is forbidden, censored at the root, the erotic drives turn to death drives, to sadism. The stolen portrait becomes, in the manner of Rousseau's famous stolen ribbon, a token of the reversibility of drives and the inversion of love offerings into poisoned gifts.

The story of this double crime terminates the Monster's narrative. He has now only to sum up the demand to which all his story has tended: "I am alone and miserable; man will not associate with me; but one as deformed and horrible as myself would not deny herself to me. My companion must be of the same species and have the same defects. This being you must create" (137). The Monster thus attempts to state the object of his desire. In constructing his narrative appeal, he has contextualized desire, made it, or shown it to be, the very principle of narrative, in its metonymical forward movement. This movement, in Lacanian terms, corresponds to the slippage of the inaccessible signified—the object of unconscious desire—under the signifier in the signifying chain. The movement now, as so often when stories are told to a narratee, passes on the desire to the interlocutor, who is charged explicitly with finding the object of desire: of crossing the "bar" of repression between signifier and that other occulted signifier that stands in the place of the signified of desire, in this instance by the creation of that which is supposed to signify desire. And yet, the Monster's call for a female companion, however sincere, may be only in the realm of conscious desire, may not have access—as how could it?—to what lies under the bar.

If one considers that desire (again in Lacanian terms) is born in the split between need and demand, where demand is always in excess of need (for nourishment from the breast, essentially) and is always an absolute demand for recognition, and thus desire is essentially unappeasable since it is driven by infantile scenarios of fulfillment, one wonders whether Frankenstein's provision of a female companion would really satisfy the Monster. Love depends on demand—it is the creation of speaking beings—and is in essence the demand to be heard by the other. What matters is not so much the content of the demand as the fact that it is unconditional; it expresses "not the desire of this or that, but desire *tout court*," writes Lacan.

---

1. On the "anaclitic" or "attachment type" (*Anlehnungstypus*) of object choice, see Freud, "On Narcissism: An Introduction," *Standard Edition* 14:87. The attachment is that of the sexual instincts to the ego instincts, with the result of a choice of love objects that takes the subject back to the mother.

What is finally desired by the speaker is "the desirer in the other,"
that is, that the speaking subject himself be "called to as desirable."[2]
The Monster's unconscious desire may most of all be for unconditional hearing, recognition, love from his parent. Its absolute
requital could only take the form of handing over the mother, which
in this case is barred not only by the law of castration but more radically still, since this mother does not exist and has never existed.

It appears that the Monster's artful activation of the symbolic
order, in his narrative plea, results in a demand to his listener that,
in its consciously stated desire, brings us back into the order of the
imaginary—to the desire for phantasmatic satisfactions, impossible
to fulfill. How can you create a mother substitute, or a relationship
of the "anaclitic" type, when there is no mother to substitute for?
The radically absent body of the mother more and more appears to
be the "problem" that cannot be solved in the novel. The female
monster, furthermore, is conceived quite simply as the mirror image
of the Monster, with solely the sexual difference: she has no other
definition than "a female me," which suggests her place in a primal
narcissism which the Monster needs to, and cannot, go beyond,
however "filthy" his mirror image. This inability to escape primal
narcissism is suggested by other near-incestuous relations in the
novel, particularly the marriage of Frankenstein and Elizabeth.

The female monster will never fully come into being. Frankenstein
tears her nearly completed body to pieces, in another scopic scene:
the Monster is watching at the window of the laboratory with a
"ghastly grin" which turns to a "howl of devilish despair and revenge"
when his promised body is denied him (159). It is as if the Monster's
phallic gaze at the female monster's body makes Frankenstein aware
of the bodily potential of a sexed pair of monsters. Ostensibly, Frankenstein abrogates the contract he has made at the end of the Monster's narrative appeal through his reflection on the "Eve problem":
that procreation by the monsters will be simply a "propagated curse,"
and that the female monster, as a secondary creation, "might
refuse to comply with a compact made before her creation" (158)—
she might, like Eve, disobey the paternal injunction, which in this
case stipulates exile from the inhabited parts of the globe. To allow
the couple to create a race of monsters would be to create a new
and wholly uncontrollable signifying chain from their desire, one
whose eventual outcomes "might make the very existence of the
species of man a condition precarious and full of terror." Rather
than accepting a nurturing role toward the Monster, offering him

2. "Qu'est-ce qui est désiré? C'est le désirant dans l'autre—ce qui ne peut se faire qu'à ce
que le sujet lui-même soit convoqué comme désirable. C'est ce qu'il demande dans la
demande d'amour." Lacan, Le séminaire, vol. 8, Le transfert (Paris: Editions du Seuil,
1991), p. 415.

"the small portion of happiness which was yet in my power to bestow" (140)—as he has decided to do at the close of the Monster's narrative—Frankenstein performs the ultimate gesture of castration on the desiring Monster.

The destruction of the female monster negates any hope that the Monster might gain access to a "chain of existence and events" that would offer him relation and the possibility—even the phantasmatic possibility—of satisfaction for his desire. The godlike science of language has proved deceptive: it has contextualized desire as lack, as metonymic movement in search of the meaning of desire, but it has not provided a way to overcome lack and satisfy desire—as, indeed, language never can. The Monster's error is to believe that signs in artful rhetorical patterns can produce the desired referent from one's interlocutor. His definition as monster leads him to an overvaluation of language, as that which could take him out of that specular position. Yet he is required, by the logic of desire, to attempt to make language produce another body, to return to the imaginary, the specular, and the drama of sexual difference.

The result is an exacerbated agon of desire between the Monster and Frankenstein, whereby the Monster strikes at Frankenstein, not directly, but through elements in Frankenstein's own "chain of existence and events": after William and Justine Moritz, Frankenstein's bosom friend Henry Clerval and his bride (and also adoptive sister) Elizabeth. "I will be with thee on thy wedding-night," the Monster tells Frankenstein after the destruction of the female monster (161), a remark that Frankenstein interprets as a direct menace to his person, thus repressing what the reader at once grasps: that the threat is to Elizabeth. On the wedding night he sends Elizabeth to the nuptial chamber alone, while he prowls about, armed with pistols, looking to engage in combat with the Monster. "Peace, peace, my love," he says to Elizabeth; "this night, and all will be safe; but this night is dreadful, very dreadful" (185). We may read this dread as related to the quasi-incestuous nature of his union with Elizabeth. As his father has said, in sounding Frankenstein's intentions: "You, perhaps, regard her as your sister, without any wish that she might become your wife" (144). Frankenstein denies this sentiment, but we cannot help but be struck by the complication and overlapping of kinship relations in the novel (as in the family in which Mary Shelley grew up), especially because they are thrown in high relief by the Monster's own lack of relation. As the Monster once again watches from the window, the wedding night ends in a necrophilic embrace, which may be in the logic of incestuous desire: "I rushed towards her and embraced her with ardour, but the deadly languor and coldness of the limbs told me that what I now held in my arms had ceased to be the Elizabeth whom I had loved and cherished. The murderous mark of the fiend's grasp was on her neck, and the breath had ceased to issue from her lips" (186). The Monster has marked the body of Frankenstein's bride at the moment when Frankenstein's desire is on the point of consummation, in dialectical response to the destruction of his monstrous bride. The Monster has put his body in the way of Frankenstein's desire.[3]

Frankenstein's narrative from this point on tells of the struggle of his nearly transferential relation with the Monster, where each represents the lack or gap in the other. "You are my creator, but I am your master;—obey!" (160) the Monster has said to Frankenstein, in a phrase that represents the impossibility of the situation in which each becomes for the other the "subject supposed to know" but neither can furnish satisfaction of the other's lack. Like the Monster, Frankenstein becomes explicitly Satanic: "like the archangel who aspired to omnipotence, I am chained in an eternal hell" (200). The Monster leads a chase that will take them to the lifeless polar regions, maintaining the willpower and the strength of his pursuer by leaving inscribed indications of his route and caches of food. "Come on, my enemy; we have yet to wrestle for our lives" (195) reads one inscription, nicely balancing enmity and affection.

The Monster, Frankenstein states following William's murder, is "my own vampire, my own spirit set loose from the grave and forced to destroy all that was dear to me" (74). The statement is as excessive and curious as it is accurate. It turns the Monster into a symptom, in Lacan's sense of the term—that is, a metaphor, a signifier standing for the indecipherable signifier of unconscious desire. It may ultimately speak of the sadism inherent in all intersubjective and especially familial orders of relation. In particular, it may in this novel suggest the destructive affect that inhabits the relational order of language, and particularly narrative language, in the transferential situation of telling and listening. The Monster's narrative of unrequited desire and unappeasable lack cannot produce access to the referent of desire. Instead, it passes on desire and lack, through the signifying chain of language and through the interlocutionary relation established in language, with the result that lack and desire come to inhabit the listener. As listener or narratee, once you have entered into a narrative transaction with the Monster, you are yourself tainted with monsterism: you cannot break out of the relation established by the pronouns "I" and "thou" once they are

---

3. Note in this context the curious scenario leading to the death of Clerval: Frankenstein rows out to sea in his skiff and throws the mangled pieces of the female monster overboard; a storm comes up and blows him off course; he lands on a strange shore—it is Ireland—and is at once arrested as a murderer, and taken to see the body of his supposed victim, Clerval. Thus there is a direct exchange between the body of the female monster and that of Clerval.

seen as complementary, each elusively representing the answer to the lack within oneself. The interlocutionary relation, like the transferential relation in psychoanalysis, could be dissolved only by the production of that which would answer the Monster's lack. Because this is impossible, lack is passed on through the narrative frames—which is indeed what the framing structure of the novel is all about.

Frankenstein, once he has become interlocutor to the Monster, is marked by the taint of monsterism, which he can never appease or dispel. When in turn, in the next frame (working out from the inside), Walton becomes Frankenstein's interlocutor, he, too, is marked by this taint. Walton, we note, is at the outset of the novel in a position analogous to Frankenstein's when he sets about his act of creation: he, too, is seeking for Promethean knowledge, dominion over the unknown, which in his case means exploration of the unknown polar regions. And like both Frankenstein and the Monster, he is searching for relation; he complains to his sister, Margaret Saville, that he has no one "to participate my joy" or to "sustain me in dejection" (18). Frankenstein speaks for both of them when he says: "I agree with you . . . we are unfashioned creatures, but half made up, if one wiser, better, dearer than ourselves—such a friend ought to be—do not lend his aid to perfectionate our weak and faulty natures" (27). Friendship, relation, interlocution, suggest an ideal model of the androgyne, which, as in the Platonic myth, has been split in half and now desires the missing half. But by the end Walton's hopes for both Promethean conquest and friendship lie "blasted," as his mutinous sailors vote to turn southward and Frankenstein sinks into death (204). All that remains to Walton is his epistolary narratee, his sister; and as he explains to her, being reduced to writing is no substitute for the living interlocutionary relation: writing is "a poor medium for the communication of feeling" (18). Moreover, his sister may never even receive these letters written from beyond the social world. In any event, for the reader of the novel, Mrs. Saville has no more existence than a postal address, or even a dead-letter office—the place where messages end up when they have nowhere else to go. Her lack of characterized personality makes her all the more effectively stand for the reader, as the ultimate receiver of all the nested messages of the novel.

Thus it is that the taint of monsterism, as the product of the unarrestable metonymic movement of desire through the narrative signifying chain, may ultimately come to rest with the reader of the text. Like Frankenstein at the close of the Monster's act of narration, like Walton at the end of Frankenstein's narrative, we have a residue of desire and meaning left over, which we must somehow process. Perhaps it would be most accurate to say that we are left with a residue of desire *for* meaning, which we alone can realize.

One could no doubt say something similar about any narrative text, especially any narrative that dramatizes the fact and the process of its transmission, as "framed tales" always do. In *Frankenstein*, the thematization of the passing on of unresolved desire for meaning is particularly evident because the key question, the vital enigma, concerns the nature of monsterism itself. What is a monster? Reading inward from the outermost frame, the reader is led to believe that he or she is making a nearer approach to the solution to this problem; when the Monster speaks in his own person, assumes the pronoun "I," we enter the subjectivity of monsterism. But that solves nothing, and as we read outward from the innermost frame, we come to realize that we are following the process of the passing on of this unresolved question, in an unarrestable metonymy of desire.

In closing his narrative to Walton, Frankenstein warns his interlocutor against listening to the Monster's voice: "He is eloquent and persuasive, and once his words had even power over my heart; but trust him not . . . Hear him not" (198–99). Yet when the Monster does finally appear to Walton, saying farewell to Frankenstein's corpse, Walton bids him stay, and soon his impulses to destroy the destroyer of his friend are "suspended by a mixture of curiosity and compassion" (208)—the very elements required to seal again the interlocutionary relation, to produce a new narrative transaction. It is the Monster who unknots this relation—and its possible production of a new narrative frame, a new nested box containing the Monster and Walton—when he announces that he has resolved to destroy himself. Once the other of his transferential desire has ceased to be, the only choice that remains for the Monster is self-immolation. He announces to Walton: "Neither yours nor any man's death is needed to consummate the series of my being and accomplish that which must be done, but it requires my own" (210). A moment before, he has stated that with Frankenstein's death, "the miserable series of my being is wound to its close" (207). "Series" is here used in the sense of "sequence" or "order." Conceptually, this phrase is related to the "chain" which figures the Monster's understanding of human interrelation, and its counterparts in language and narration. Failing to enter the "chain of existence and events," his narrative sequence has wound down to self-destruction. But the order in which he signifies cannot so easily be brought to a close, as the passing on of narrative messages, and narrative desire, may suggest.

In his peroration over Frankenstein's corpse, the Monster also claims: "Blasted as thou wert, my agony was still superior to thine" (211). While the context assigns the cause of this superior agony to the Monster's remorse, we may want to read it, more absolutely, as a statement about the fact of being a monster. That is the supreme agony, which no other problem in desire can efface. The phrase, like so much else in the novel, returns us to the question, What is a monster? The novel addresses this question in different registers. Initially, there is the creation of the Monster, which is a result of Frankenstein's illicit curiosity. He takes, in his youth, to reading such alchemical literature as Cornelius Agrippa, Paracelsus, Albertus Magnus. When his father censures such work as "trash," he—like Dora with her volume of Mantegazza—seems to be only the more convinced that they will enable him to "penetrate the secrets of nature" (38–39). He finds that philosophy has only partially "unveiled the face of Nature." "I had gazed upon the fortifications and impediments that seemed to keep human beings from entering the citadel of nature, and rashly and ignorantly I had repined" (39). Frankenstein recapitulates here the traditional imagery of nature as a woman, and proposes that truth is a difficult penetration into her body. As in the case of Dora, epistemophilia finally centers on the woman's body as the key to forbidden knowledge.

When he reaches the university at Ingolstadt, he falls under the spell of the chemistry professor Waldman, who tells him that modern scientists "penetrate into the recesses of nature and show how she works in her hiding-places" (47). This increases his desire to discover the hidden principle of life itself, to be able to bestow animation on inanimate matter—the Promethean revelation at the center of the text, which it of course censors. He then learns how to proceed backward from death to a new life, using the "loathsome" robbing of graves to create a new living species. "Life and death," he recalls, "appeared to me ideal bounds, which I should first break through, and pour a torrent of light into our dark world" (52). Yet when, after two years of intense labor, he stands over his created body and sees "the dull yellow eye of the creature open," his heart is filled with "disgust" and he flees from his progeny.

Frankenstein's intense curiosity for forbidden knowledge, coupled with his hysterical reaction to witnessing its realization, suggest, as the imagery of unveiling and penetration already indicated, that his epistemophilia centers on the arcana of the woman's body, specifically the mother's body in its reproductive function. The novel, as the psychoanalyst Marc A. Rubenstein has so well observed, is full of "primal scene imagery," to the extent that "the spirit of primal scene observation penetrates into the very structure of the novel and becomes part of a more deeply hidden search for the mother."[4] The Freudian primal scene is an intense object of infantile curiosity which, even without actual observation by the infant, can have the status of a "primal phantasy." Parental copulation is of course for any individual the origin of origins, the very "citadel of nature." The

4. Rubenstein, "My Accursed Origin," p. 165.

novel suggests a fixation on the primal scene in the conjoined obsession with origins on the part of both Frankenstein and his Monster—
who are both deprived of a literal mother on whom to exercise their
curiosity, with the result that they must strive to create the scene—
and in the intensely visual nature of the scenes created. Most per-
tinent here are the scenes of the Monster's creation (the moment
when the Monster opens his eye produces Frankenstein's hysterical
reaction, very much in the manner of the traumatic dream of Freud's
"Wolf Man"); the aborted creation of the female monster as the
Monster watches at the window; and the wedding night, which recapitulates the Monster at the window, watching the nuptial bed
become a bier.[5] Every time we reach one of the novel's manufactured primal scenes, something monstrous happens, and the
observer is stricken, punished.[6] The very structure of the novel, as
Rubenstein argues, suggests the pervasive effects of primal scene
curiosity, a need to witness the forbidden moment of origin, which
produces the inextinguishable taint of monsterism that gets passed
on through the narrative chain.

It is significant, too, that the creation of the Monster from Frankenstein's studies in physics and chemistry, which are always on
the verge of becoming metaphysics and alchemy, takes place on the
borderline of nature and culture. The Monster is a product of
nature—his ingredients are 100 percent natural—yet by the process and the very fact of his creation, he is unnatural, the product of
philosophical overreaching. Since he is a unique creation, without
precedence or replication, he lacks cultural as well as natural context. He radicalizes the situation of Eve, who also has no "model"—
Adam is created in God's image, God is male; thus in whose image
is Eve created?—and is hence a unique creation, but one that will

5. In the Wolf Man's dream, "suddenly the window opened of its own accord," and the terrified child sees the wolves sitting in a tree in front of the window, looking at him attentively. Freud's patient then interprets the window opening to mean "My eyes suddenly
opened." See Freud, "From the History of an Infantile Neurosis," *Standard Edition*
17:29–47. On "primal phantasies," see this case history and also *Introductory Lectures
on Psycho-Analysis, Standard Edition* 16:367–71. David Marshall, working from Marc
Rubenstein's suggestions, gives a fine analysis of these scenes, in *The Surprising Effects
of Sympathy*, 222–26.
6. It is worth mentioning in this context that during the evenings of reading ghost stories
in the Villa Diodati, on the shores of Lake Geneva, that brought together the Shelleys
with Lord Byron, his personal physician Dr. Polidori, and Claire Clairmont (Byron's
mistress and Mary's stepsister) and led to the ghost story writing "contest" that produced *Frankenstein*, P. B. Shelley had a hallucination: "Byron repeated some verses of
Coleridge's *Christabel*, of the witch's breast; when silence ensued, and Shelley, suddenly
shrieking and putting his hands to his head, ran out of the room with a candle. Threw
water in his face and after gave him ether. He was looking at Mrs. Shelley, and suddenly
thought of a woman he had heard of who had eyes instead of nipples, which taking hold
of his mind, horrified him" (*The Diary of Dr. John William Polidori*, ed. W. M. Rossetti
[London: Elkin Matthews, 1911], 128–29, quoted by Rubenstein, 184). The woman with
eyes in the place of nipples effectively sexualizes vision, and turns the male's scopic
fixations back on the voyeur, with hallucinatory results.

then be replicated by half the human race. The Monster is, so to speak, postnatural and precultural. That a monster can be created within nature may stand as something of an indictment of nature itself, especially when one considers the generally ambiguous conceptual position of nature in the novel. An important thematic focus of this ambiguity is the figure of Henry Clerval, a being formed "in the very poetry of nature," Frankenstein tells us (quoting Leigh Hunt), who is described through the citation of lines from Wordsworth's "Tintern Abbey":

> The sounding cataract
> Haunted *him* like a passion: the tall rock,
> The mountain, and the deep and gloomy wood,
> Their colours and their forms, were then to him
> An appetite; a feeling, and a love,
> That had no need of a remoter charm,
> By thought supplied, or any interest
> Unborrow'd from the eye.

The italicized "him" replaces the "me" of the original. The lines are traditionally taken to represent the speaker's first, immediate, unreflective relation to nature, now lost to him but operative still in his sister Dorothy, to whom he can say that "Nature never did betray / The heart that loved her." Clerval loves and trusts nature, but he falls victim to the monstrous creation of his best friend and explicitly pays for Frankenstein's destruction of the Monster's mate. There is more to nature than sounding cataracts and sublime mountains: there is also one's friend's accursed curiosity, creating monsters demanding sexual satisfaction. It is in the awesome natural sublimity of the Alps, where Frankenstein has gone to seek consolation, that the Monster appears to his creator. One senses in Mary Shelley's novel a profound dissent from some of the more optimistic Romantic views of the moral principles embodied in nature—a dissent which recent readings of Wordsworth and P. B. Shelley find figured in some of their most problematic moments. Nature in *Frankenstein* appears not to be a principle at all: it is rigorously amoral, it is absence of principle.

What, then, in unprincipled nature, is a monster? A monster is that outcome or product of curiosity or epistemophilia pushed to an extreme that results—as in the story of Oedipus—in confusion, blindness, and exile. A monster is that which cannot be placed in any of the taxonomic schemes devised by the human mind to understand and to order nature. It exceeds the very basis of classification, language itself: it is an excess of signification, a strange byproduct or leftover of the process of making meaning. It is an imaginary being who comes to life in language and, once having done so, cannot be eliminated from language. Even if we want to claim that "monster," like some of the words used by Felix and Agatha—"dearest," "unhappy"—has no referent, it has a signified, a conceptual meaning, a place in our knowledge of ourselves. The novel insistently thematizes issues of language and rhetoric because the symbolic order of language appears to offer the Monster his only escape from the order of visual, specular, and imaginary relations, in which he is demonstrably the monster. The symbolic order compensates for a deficient nature: it promises escape from a condition of "to-be-looked-at-ness."

That, we recall, is the term that Laura Mulvey applies to the "traditional exhibitionist role" given to women in the cinema.[7] When one considers the Monster's creation in the place of the absent mother, his role and very definition as the insistent object of visual inspection, with the inevitable hysterical reaction, and his equally insistent attempt to redefine his person within the medium of language, especially narrative language as the vehicle of interpersonal relation, one may ask if the Monster is not in fact a woman who is seeking to escape from the feminine condition into recognition by the fraternity.[8] The very peculiarity of a novel about the monstrous that insistently stages its central issues in terms of language, rather than in sheerly visual terms—characteristic, for instance, of Gothic novels—would thus become doubly determined: on the thematic level, by the Monster's attempts to escape the imaginary order; and in the creative process itself, by Mary Shelley's attempts to escape the generic and cultural codes that make heroines into objects to be looked at—a fate that such heroines as Jane Eyre or Gwendolen Harleth never entirely escape. If, as Mulvey and other feminist film theoreticians have argued, the male gaze defines both the place of the female and the codes for looking at and defining her—and also the very genres that stage that looking—we may want to understand the persistent counter-visual emphasis of the Monster him-

7. Laura Mulvey, "Visual Pleasure and Narrative Cinema," in *Visual and Other Pleasures* (London: Macmillan, 1989), 19.
8. See Gilbert and Gubar, who suggest that the Monster's "intellectual similarity to his authoress (rather than his 'author')" indicates that he may be "a female in disguise" (*The Madwoman in the Attic*, 237). Mary Jacobus notes the "bizarre pun" in which Frankenstein describes the Monster as "a mummy again endued with animation" (*Reading Women*, 101). Margaret Homans, citing my own argument (in my earlier essay on the novel) about the Monster's failure to gain his place in the symbolic order, states: "I would argue that in its materiality and its failure to acquire an object of desire, the demon enters the symbolic primarily as the (dreaded) referent, not as signifier. The negative picture of the demon's materiality is a product of its female place in the symbolic, and not of any lingering in the realm of the imaginary (which Brooks, with other readers of Lacan, views as tragic)" (*Bearing the Word*, 304–305, n. 18). I would agree with this to the extent that the materiality of the Monster continually vitiates his assumed place—the place he would assume—in the symbolic. But doesn't that status as dreaded referent continually throw him back into the imaginary?

self, and the contexts created around him, as an effort to deconstruct the defining and classifying power of the gaze, and to assert in its place the potential of affect created in interlocutory language—as used, notably, in the relation of love.

The Monster would thus be a woman, but a woman who would answer Freud's infamous question "What does a woman want?" with the ostensible reply: to be a male, with a female to love. In the failure of that project, the Monster is forced to play the role of the castrating Medusa woman.[9] The novel of course never for a moment suggests that the Monster is anything but a male, and both Frankenstein and his creature assume that he is sexually functional as a male (there would otherwise be no need for Frankenstein to destroy the female monster). Yet the Monster never is given the chance to function sexually, and we are never given a glimpse of those parts of the body that would assure us that he is male. Of course we aren't: such is not part of the discourse of the novel (setting aside pornography) at the time. But this necessary cultural reticence, subjected to our retrospective critical pressure, may add a further ambiguity to the problems of definition of monster—may indeed add another dimension to that question "What is a monster?" A monster may also be that which eludes gender definition. In this sense, *Frankenstein* would be a more radical version of that considerable body of Romantic and "Decadent" literature—such as Théophile Gautier's *Mademoiselle de Maupin*, Henri de Latouche's *Fragoletta*, Balzac's *Sarrasine*, Rachilde's *Monsieur Vénus*—that uses cross-dressing and hermaphroditism to create situations of sexual ambiguity that call into question socially defined gender roles and transgress the law of castration that defines sexual difference. The Monster's demand for recognition by his father could then be read not only as desire for the absent mother but as a wish to be a sexual object for the father, in the manner of Freud's Senatspräsident Schreber.[1] Because a monster is that which calls into question all our cultural codes, including language itself, we can understand the persistent afterlife of Mary Shelley's creation, which shows us that, quite literally, once you have created a monster, whatever the ambiguities of the order of its existence, you can never get rid of it.

---

9. The Monster, we have noted, is often the observer in the novel, which is the male role. When he is looked at, however, he takes on aspects of the Medusa, who turns (male) observers to stone, and who for Freud represents the terror of the female genitals to the (childish) male observer: see Freud, "Medusa's Head," *Standard Edition* 18:273–74. Note, in this context, Walton's reaction when he first meets the Monster: "Never did I behold a vision so horrible as his face, of such loathsome yet appalling hideousness. I shut my eyes involuntarily" (207).
1. See Freud, "Psychoanalytic Notes upon an Autobiographical Account of a Case of Paranoia (Dementia Paranoides)" (1911), *Standard Edition* 12:9–82.

In this context, one might reflect on the moment when Frankenstein perceives the Monster for the first time following his flight
from the scene of its creation. It comes when Frankenstein is on his
way home after receiving news of William's murder. It is another of
those scenes that bring into play the sublime power of nature. A
storm breaks out in the Alps, a tempest "so beautiful yet terrific"
(73). "This noble war in the sky elevated my spirits; I clasped my
hands and exclaimed aloud, 'William, dear angel! This is thy funeral,
this thy dirge!'" No sooner has he uttered these words than a flash
of lightning reveals the presence of the Monster: natural sublimity
once again produces the monstrous. With this revelation swiftly
comes the thought that the Monster must be William's murderer.
"*He* was the murderer! I could not doubt it. The mere presence of
the idea was an irresistible proof of the fact" (73–74). The logic
of the "mere presence of the idea" becoming an "irresistible proof of
the fact" does not stand the test of reason. It is an excessive conclusion. Yet it is also true. The statement in fact mimes the process of
creation of the Monster, who from a scientific idea becomes a bodily
fact: an idea embodied.

We are always led back, in *Frankenstein,* to the peculiarity that
this cultural creation, this epistemophilic product, has become part
of nature—that the idea or concept of the monster, which at first
has no referent in the natural world, gains one. It gains this refer-
ential status as a body. On a basic level, it is nothing but body: that
which exists to be looked at, pointed to, and nothing more. You can't
do anything with a monster except look at it. Like Virgil's Cyclops, it
blocks out the light, including the light of reason, if reason be a matter of mental classification and rationalization. In this manner, the
Monster offers an inversion of the many scenarios we have noted, in
Balzac and other novelists, in which the human body is marked or
signed in order to bring it into the field of signification, so that it can
be a narrative signifier. In *Frankenstein,* language is marked by the
body, by the process of embodiment. We have not so much a mark on
the body as the mark of the body: the capacity of language to create
a body, one that in turn calls into question the language we use to
classify and control bodies. In the plot of the novel, that body cannot
be touched by any of the human bodies; apparently indestructible, it
can be eliminated only when the Monster himself chooses to burn
himself up. "I shall ascend my funeral pile triumphantly and exult in
the agony of the torturing flames" (211). Note that his words are in
the future tense. The Monster's death never is recorded within the
novel; it never becomes matter for retrospective narration. We know
it is not so easy to get rid of the monstrous body linguistically created. Mary Shelley's monster is still out there. It has taken a permanent place in our imaginary.

BETTE LONDON

Mary Shelley, *Frankenstein*, and the Spectacle of Masculinity[†]

In a striking memorial to the Shelleys—commissioned by their only surviving child, Sir Percy, and his wife, Lady Shelley—the couple is impressed in the image of Michelangelo's *Pietà*. Mary Shelley kneels, breast exposed, in the traditional posture of a *Madonna humilitatis*, supporting the lifeless body of her drowned god and idol. Superimposing a Christian narrative onto a notorious Romantic "text"—a scandalous life story composed of atheism, incest, and illicit sexuality—the monument fixes the contradictions that constitute and surround the Shelleyan legacy, mobilizing its own conventionalized impressions of the staple figures: the martyred, revolutionary poet and his beautiful, distraught widow. The Christianized life of Shelley, however, remains only one of the monument's scandals. For to a modern audience, at least, fed on a revitalization of *Frankenstein* and a new canonization of the novel's "feminist" author as the creator of monstrous birth fantasies, the marginalization of Mary in the figure of maternal adoration reads with equally disturbing incongruity.[1]

As a document in the reconstruction of the Shelleys' lived relationship and in the construction of posthumous meaning, the monument, executed by Henry Weekes, contributes to the narrative production and circulation of hierarchically ordered, gendered literary history. It performs the same ideological work, for example, as another piece of "memorial" iconography, Louis-Edouard Fournier's *Funeral of Shelley*—a representation of Shelley's cremation that focuses on the ritual viewing of the poet's smoldering body. Mary Shelley (who did not actually attend the funeral) appears as a kneeling figure, literally at the edge of the canvas and barely distinguishable from a shadowy mass of nameless observers, while the standing figures of the privileged mourners (the poet's friends and literary compatriots Byron, Hunt, and Trelawny) command visual attention. The narrative that the painting details thus binds Shelley's preeminence (public and private) to the lasting rites of masculinity.

But though such works ensure the place of masculine privilege, their enshrinement of the poet as martyr figure contains its own

---

† *PMLA* 108.2 (March 1993): 253–65. The Works Cited list begins on p. 402. Reprinted by permission of the Modern Language Association of America.
1. Moers's now classic discussion of *Frankenstein*, first published in 1973, inaugurated a tradition of feminist readings of Mary Shelley. For other significant contributions, see Gilbert and Gubar, Ellis, Knoepflmacher, and Poovey.

subversive potential. For these testimonials to masculine genius barely cover their display of male exhibitionism, rendering the male body disproportionately visible. Thus, while Fournier may refine the viewers' sense of the corpse's presence, the inclusion of Mary in this otherwise all-male ritual invokes the scurrilous stories of that body's remnants. These stories, circulating widely in biographical sketches, raise the indecent specter of Mary Shelley's wranglings with Hunt for Percy Shelley's relics—for possession of the prized part of the poet, the remnant of his heart. Edited out of the official account Fournier represents, this unseemly exhibition glosses the painting's inscription of the spectacle of masculinity, of male spectators surveying the prostrate male body.

Weekes's sculpture, with its self-conscious borrowings from Christian iconography, calls attention even more insistently to the display of masculinity. As Leo Steinberg has demonstrated, European Renaissance art repeatedly points to Christ's sexed body, and the Shelley memorial, true to its type, draws the eye to the markers of sexuality, in particular to the veiled phallus that centers the scene. For the arrangement of figures, the viewing trajectory initiated by Mary's gaze (as it invites the eye to travel downward, first to Percy's upturned face and then along the incline of his slumped body), the torsional patterns of the drapery, the pointing of Percy's right hand (with its insinuation of an unnaturally elongated finger)—all focus on the site of masculinity and the ensuing drama of the lifeless male body.

Mary's iconic representation, then, quite literally supports a scene of male self-display. Like the acts of extravagant feminine self-abasement and masculine idolatry that embarrass her character in the "post-Shelley" phase of her biography, her conventionalized position here both disguises and reveals—enacts and exposes—the spectacle it upholds. In what it includes as much as in what it excludes, this portrait of a languishing Mary relentlessly points to the exposure of a monstrously extended Percy. In this respect, then, Weekes's representation can be seen to restage the "origins" of Mary Shelley's most famous creation, *Frankenstein*—a text frequently read as a critical portrait of Percy.[2] Moreover, in reworking the figures of Mary Shelley's waking dream, the monument reproduces the novel's iconographic centerpiece: "I saw the pale student of unhal-

---

2. Indeed, as has been frequently noted, Mary gives Frankenstein Percy's pseudonym, Victor. Scott, Small, and Veeder each discuss this biographical connection. Veeder is especially interesting, for while he invokes "old charges against Percy" in order "to direct the reader to what Mary is pointing at" (6,7), he continues to invest in the woman as spectacle: "Ultimately what I hope to give is a sense of the *drama* of Mary Shelley, the special splendor of a woman who could, without exaggeration, call her life 'romantic beyond romance' . . . and could write one of the influential novels in our language" (3).

lowed arts kneeling beside the thing he had put together. I saw the hideous phantasm of a man stretched out . . ." (228).

Mary Shelley's authorship, then, which would seem to have been effectively erased, returns to these testimonial productions as a species of intertextual glossing performed through the agency of *Frankenstein*.[3] But if *Frankenstein* recalls what is monstrous, what lurks beneath the surface, in this memorial imagery—the displayed male body, "the hideous phantasm of a man stretched out"—the memorials reactivate *Frankenstein*'s own iconography, opening the novel to new interpretive possibilities. For they point to the emblematic identity of its central scenes—the animation of the monster, the murder of Elizabeth, the death of Frankenstein. And in doing so, they uncover the novel's crucially masculine scaffolding. For these key textual moments, each represented in the narrative as a kind of framed frieze, share both the structural configuration of Weekes's statuary and the monument's erotic fixation on the lifeless male body.[4] Thus Frankenstein's description of the unanimated creature—"the lifeless thing that lay at my feet"—captures, precisely at the moment preceding the entry of monstrosity, the classical beauty of the sculpted Percy Shelley: "His limbs were in proportion, and I had selected his features as beautiful" (52). Shelley's posture, moreover—head flung back, neck exposed, bloodless arm extended—echoes that of the "lifeless and inanimate" body of Elizabeth, flung upon her bridal bier in the novel's most climactic moment. Mary Shelley, in such a reading, figures the position of Frankenstein supporting the remains of the lover's body—a position also assumed by the monster in the novel's last exchange of bodies, in the creature's "strange and wonderful" appearance hanging over the "lifeless form" of his creator.

If the logic of the novel demands as its consummation the laying out of Frankenstein's body, as I have been arguing, the symmetrical inversion of its creation scene is achieved through a detour onto the woman's body and through the circulation of the position of monstrosity. This pattern has far-reaching, and as yet largely unexamined, implications for an understanding both of the novel and of the wider workings of gender—implications that exceed the narrow determinants of a strictly biographical rendering. For the shifting configurations that mark the novel's reinventions of its central

3. In this context, *The Funeral* can also be seen to gloss the novel, representing its (unrepresented) final sequence: the mother's self-immolation.
4. This configuration also illuminates the novel's memorial imagery, where the portrait of Frankenstein's mother ("an historical subject, painted at my father's desire," representing "Caroline Beaufort in an agony of despair, kneeling by the coffin of her dead father" [73]), placed above a miniature of William (whose death is forcibly linked to a miniature of Caroline), is the first object to meet the eye of the newly bereaved Frankenstein. By means of a contorted female subject, these images thus link male desire to the representation of the lifeless male body.

scene destabilize the sexual hierarchies that underwrite the novel's meaning, making the *male* body the site of an ineradicable materiality. Yet the discomposing presence of that body remains the thing most resistant to critical insight; like the sexuality of Christ in Steinberg's thesis, it is preeminently visible but persistently unseen, consigned to modern oblivion.

Among *Frankenstein*'s audiences, however, such oversight would almost seem the product of a representational conspiracy. For if in imitation of the Incarnation, Frankenstein creates a being "complete in all the parts of a man," the absence of the markers of sexuality leaves the creature incomplete, facilitating its installation in the feminine economy—the traditional locus for "the monstrous" and "the body." Moreover, Frankenstein's account of creating monstrosity sustains the visible paradox that supports masculine identity; for it is only when Frankenstein speculates on female monstrosity ("she might become ten thousand times more malignant than her mate") that he considers the threatening presence of the monster's male sexuality ("a race of devils would be propagated upon the earth" [163]). It is thus the spectacle of woman's uncontrollable materiality (the figure of what cannot be seen) that gives distinctive shape to the already constructed male body.

Overlooking this suppression of male sexuality, many commentaries on the novel—including some of the most influential feminist readings—continue to pursue *Frankenstein*'s critical project, upholding the illusion of male gender-neutrality, of the invisibleness of masculinity.[5] Indeed, feminist criticism has taken the lead in promoting speculation on the monster's female identity—a hypothesis extended, at least in part, in the interest of claiming feminine visibility. Erasing all markers of masculine presence, Gilbert and Gubar perfect this reading, naming creature and creator as "Eve and Eve all along" (246); but in exposing all the novel's characters as "female in disguise" (237), they cover over *Frankenstein*'s investments in male exhibitionism, thus supporting, however inadvertently, dominant ideological imperatives. Perhaps for this reason, their "eccentric" reading has been readily accepted. For, habituated to the contemporary construction of the scopic regime, which allows little flexibility in gendered positions, readers continue to ignore the self-evident: *Frankenstein*'s insistent specularization of masculinity, its

5. Margaret Homans observes that the monster's "very bodiliness, its identification with matter, associates it with traditional concepts of femaleness." But in analyzing this view of the romantic imagination, she exposes its misogynistic and narcissistic underpinnings: its desire "to do away, not only with the mother, but also with all females so as to live finally in a world of mirrors that reflect a comforting illusion of the male self's independent wholeness" (106). My argument interrogates such illusions of masculine wholeness from the opposite direction—through the implications of bodiliness and materiality as male attributes.

story of the male creator making a spectacle of himself.[6] It is this specularization, and some of the conditions of its suppression, that this essay investigates.

By making the male body my starting point, I insist on its tangibility in both the representational economy of *Frankenstein* and the cultural production of Mary Shelley's literary authority; and by reading *Frankenstein* against some specific literary and nonliterary constructions of Mary and Percy Shelley, I suggest the ways conventionalized operations of gender have foreclosed access to *Frankenstein*'s explorations of masculinity—so much so that an approach to the subject now requires the dismantling of elaborate critical edifices. As the Shelley monuments suggest, the documents that would secure or obscure *Frankenstein*'s place in literary history typically stage male anxieties across the body of the female subject. And in Mary Shelley scholarship, the relentless concern with questions of authority and bodily limits would seem to have taken its cue from the novel. In a pattern, then, for which James Rieger's edition of the 1818 text of *Frankenstein* may be only the most explicit instance, these works characteristically invest in versions of female monstrosity— practiced on the figure of Mary Shelley. But a critical rereading of these formative texts might initiate discussion of what they repress: stories of the fractured foundation of masculine privilege.

"Mary Shelley's Life and the Composition of *Frankenstein*," for example, the introduction to Rieger's critically indispensable text, contrives a biographical portrait of Mary Shelley that reproduces—in her own person—the figure of monstrosity that haunts her tale, a figure marked, like the novel's male creation, by unnatural bodily extension. Framed by her scandalous mother (kept alive, posthumously, by the defamatory reports of the reactionary press) and by the contamination of her own "final adventure" (an amorous liaison ending in bribery and blackmail), Mary Shelley enters this account circumscribed by the scandal of the female body—a body even death cannot obliterate. And she remains, in Rieger's reconstruction, the emblem of a too substantial existence: "the stiff, humorless and self-dramatizing woman she had always been" (xxiii). Like the novel's celebrated invention, this "composite figure" troublesomely combines a mechanical body (stiff and humorless) with self-proliferating energy.

But as Rieger tells the story of *Frankenstein*'s entry into literary history, Mary Shelley's presence begins to diminish. Always "Mary" to Percy's "Shelley," always modeled on or embodying a husband's or

---

6. For a discussion of *Frankenstein*'s male spectacle (focused on the inscription of Rousseau in Mary Shelley's writings), see David Marshall. Marshall's discussion of the theatricalization of suffering within eighteenth-century fiction and aesthetics demonstrates the extent to which men dominate both positions of the specular exchange.

father's literary interests, Rieger's "Mary" fulfills the condition of "proper" secondariness. This truncated figure, however, remains riddled by contradiction. For it is *Frankenstein*'s claims to preeminent originality that support Rieger's effort at literary resuscitation—the reproduction of the very text, unavailable for over a century, reconstructed in his contribution to the Library of Literature. This effort, moreover, serves to bolster the authority of the woman artist. Indeed, Mary Shelley's authorship can be reconciled to Rieger's textual history only by the hypothesis of female monstrosity—a hypothesis supported, as in the movies, by the invention of the creator's accomplice: the physician's assistant.[7] Perhaps not surprisingly, then, Rieger's narrative uncovers another scandal of the body, a scandal of textual impurity that turns on the discovery of Percy Shelley's pervasive "assistance at every point in the book's manufacture," assistance so extensive that "one hardly knows whether to regard him as editor or minor collaborator" (xviii).

In Rieger's representation, then, "the life" and "the composition" enact the same scene: the exhibition of the female body with its paradoxical display of excess and lack; its insistently visible demonstration of the horror of having nothing to see. Moreover, in reconstituting the "original" text of *Frankenstein* (the 1818 edition) with the aid of modern technologies, Rieger replicates this overdetermined configuration, exposing as feminine the text's monstrous lack of unity. For despite his somewhat jocular admission that "there [were] moments in the preparation of this edition when [he] felt like Frankenstein himself" (v), Rieger shies away from the implications of this analogy. Nonetheless, the identificatory structure of male autobiographical creation resonates in his undertaking.

Glossing quotations and allusions as well as some of Percy Shelley's "additions," interpolating "autograph variants" from the 1823 Thomas copy of the text, and appending (as a supplement) the collation of the 1818 and 1831 editions, Rieger manufactures a radically discontinuous text that displays the seams and sutures of its composition, decomposition, and recomposition. Rieger overreaches Frankenstein, however, insisting on the feminine signature of the (textual) body he brings into existence. Excusing his own violation of professional propriety ("I have violated another editorial convention, which prescribes either a clear or a diplomatic text")[8] on the grounds that "this mode of presentation shows the author's mind at work," he locates the source of his editorial difficulties in Mary

---

7. From the first, this figure—variously named Ygor, Fritz, and Dr. Praetorius—has been a staple of stage and screen adaptations of the novel. See Lavallay.
8. Rieger here refers to his practice of interpolating the autograph variants from the Thomas copy into the text rather than relegating them to footnotes or an appendix.

Shelley's "feminine" incapacity—incapacity marked in the "fussiness of her second thoughts" and her amateurish "tinker[ing] with a completed imaginative act" (xliv). In what seems an urbane, unobtrusive, and even critically sanctioned misogyny, Rieger's "production" thus participates in and reproduces conventional gendered readings, upholding the feminine as the locus of spectacle.

This cultural production—surely one of *Frankenstein's* most enduring legacies—does not confine itself to the masculine academy; it surfaces conspicuously in Mary Shelley's preface to her own recomposing effort, her introduction to the third edition (1831). Asked to account for the "origin of the story," Mary Shelley frames her response in the terms of a question often put to her: "How I, then a young girl, came to think of, and dilate upon, so very hideous an idea?" (222). The question positions her as "a young girl" in the place of spectacle; and, as Mary Poovey has ably illustrated, the ensuing explanation, with its elaborate rhetoric of modesty, reproduces the paradoxical alignment of monstrous exhibitionism and demure self-effacement that conditions the nineteenth-century construction of gender—a construction Rieger's introduction reinvents.

Moreover, as much feminist criticism has demonstrated, this spectacle of the woman writing, strikingly evoked by Mary Shelley, can be appropriated for feminism in a new deployment of (auto)biography. But the recovery of the female author behind the male-dominated text frequently involves a voyeuristic mechanism that leaves criticism fixed on the self-display of the woman, on what Barbara Johnson calls the "my monster/my self" syndrome. Consequently, as Mary Jacobus insists, such biographical investments inevitably reduce the text to "a monstrous symptom" (138). And insofar as this is true, feminism might do well to alter its perspective, reexamining the structure of spectacle and the positions spectacle engenders.[9]

Such an examination might suggest that the place of spectacle is not unique to women, and from this perspective, the "impropriety" of Mary Shelley's authorship need not be read as scandalous; the scandal, at least, does not necessarily inhere in a single body. If one turns Rieger's allegations back on themselves, Percy's presence in every stage of "the book's manufacture" implicates the masculine in the production of monstrosity. And the scandal of Mary Shelley's fractured text may discredit the female author less than it does her masculine authorities, who have their own uneasy relations to

---

9. Jacobus's essay—which forcefully interrogates the text's modus operandi, its participation in a structure that inevitably sacrifices the woman—opens the way for such a discussion, shifting the potential direction for feminist inquiry to the problematic representation of masculine "theory."

textual originality. For like her excessively deferential acceptance of her husband's editing, Mary Shelley's unorthodox citational strategies—her insistent literary allusions and indiscriminate textual borrowings—may expose not so much her lack of originality as the material conditions that constitute textuality as a form of grafting. Writing in a hand not distinctly her own, Mary Shelley opens to question the copied status of the text she copies into her own. Bearing the word, as Margaret Homans suggests, *Frankenstein* (creature, creator, text) bares the underpinnings of the male romantic economy, "[literalizing] the literalization of male literature" (117). The joins in *Frankenstein*'s textual anatomy thus demonstrate that composition, even in male hands, is always of the body. Accordingly, the spectacle of the text—of the text's irregular body—prompts with new urgency the question of gender at the novel's source: whose body does the text display?

Rieger's parable would seem to admit only one response: the female body, sexually stigmatized, that advertises Mary Shelley's impropriety. But the deployment of this body in Rieger's reading covers other bodies and a different crime against patriarchy: the exposure of Percy in Mary's posthumous editing and publication of his manuscripts. The paternal prohibition—Sir Timothy Shelley's refusal to have his son's name and works bandied about in print—echoes in Rieger's critical admonitions about Mary's contribution to the Victorian impaling of Percy as a "shrill and seraphic figure" (xxi). Hence the crime that, one might say, is inscribed on Mary Shelley's body—the crime for which the author pays with her sex—turns out to be, in these narratives at least, the unsexing of Percy, whom she places in the specular position of woman.

Yet the presentation of Percy in Mary's preface to the first collected edition of his poems baffles alike a conventional construction of gender and any simple model of gender transpositions. Fulfilling an "important" obligation (xlix), even a "sacred duty" (liii)—providing the public with a "perfect edition" of her husband's poems, the living proof of his "sublime genius" (xlix)—Mary would seem to occupy the available spectrum of culturally sanctioned feminine positions.[1] But in producing Percy Shelley for the public as well as bringing forth his productions, she recasts and conflates the roles of wife and mother; activating the iconographic machinery that renders her, as in the Weekes statue, the mother of her husband, she

---

1. Sunstein notes a similar conventional pose in Mary Shelley's anxieties about a proper biography of Percy: "She was frightened that a biography would drag her, a lone woman who wished only to be obscure and 'insignificant,' before the public. 'This is weakness—but I cannot help it—to be in print—the subject of *men*'s observations . . . attacked and defended!'" (297). For further discussion of the contradictions built into such gendering of spectacle, see Carson.

simultaneously disturbs and enforces gender proprieties. Moreover, in "detailing the history of those productions, as they sprang, living and warm, from his heart and brain," she inserts Percy in Frankenstein's sexually ambiguous place—the site where maternal and paternal forces of procreation vie for mastery. As in *Frankenstein*, the suppressed story of female production, doubly marked here as well as there in the absent organ of generation, infects and scandalizes the body of the man. For Mary Shelley's refusal to "remark on the occurrences of [Percy's] private life, except inasmuch as the passions which they engendered inspired his poetry" recalls, even as it covers over, the other products of that passion and Percy's responsibility for their fate: the bodies that sprang "living and warm" from Mary's womb and now lie dead before their time. Laying "the first stone of a monument due to Shelley's genius, his sufferings, and his virtues," Mary Shelley's publication thus anticipates the contradictory inscriptions staged in the works of Henry Weekes and other Victorian monument builders (liii).

Rieger's representation of Mary's wifely editorial productions echoes, in fact, the response of another Shelley biographer to another Victorian edifice: Onslow Ford's monument to Shelley at University College, Oxford. Writing in 1940, Newman Ivey White protests that Ford's work "still bears its part in preserving the misconception of Shelley as a beautiful, ineffectual angel" (2: 384). Like the Weekes memorial, Ford's monument exhibits a full-length figure of the drowned Shelley executed in white marble—an ornate display (including a weeping bronze sea nymph supporting the effigy) erected, White points out, at the instigation of a woman, Mary's daughter-in-law, Jane Shelley. As White's insistent specification of the figure's "recumbent" position suggests, it is the laying out of the male body that excites his disgust. For in his rendering of the sculpture, such self-conscious display inevitably proves feminizing, reducing the elevated image of the poet to sentimentalized matter, making it, in effect, a piece of Shelleyana.[2]

This recurring pattern, familiar in the reconstructions of the Shelley monuments and biographies, inserts the spectacle of woman at the locus of male exhibition; and the female spectacle, simultaneously covering and exposing male self-display, invites a differently inflected reading of literary history. For one thing, it casts Mary's literary "borrowings" in a new light, calling attention to the skeletons buried at the site where a young author's purported improprieties are paraded. If, for example, as Rieger alleges, the 1831 text of *Fran-*

---

2. White even indexes Ford's monument this way: "Ford, Onslow, his recumbent statue of Shelley at University College" (2: xxviii). Jane Shelley, as the prime collector of Shelleyana, some of which was donated to Oxford along with the Ford statue, stands as a perpetrator of both the poet's feminization and his sentimentalization.

kenstein "virtually plagiarizes the diction, ideas, and symbolism of Shelley's 'Mont Blanc'" (xxiii), Mary's exposure can illuminate Percy's own illicit dabblings, earlier in his life, in Matthew Lewis's "Tales of Terror": the plagiarism discovered in *Original Poetry*. Cameron, who discusses this plagiarism in extended notes, points out that Percy immediately attributed it to "the imposition, practiced upon him, by his co-adjutor," his sister Elizabeth (305–06). Similarly, Rieger's insistent production of Mary Shelley's textual impurity in his presentation of a "perfect edition" of her masterwork might alert us to his authorial anxieties—his concern lest his editorial procedures "mar the book's appearance" (xliv) and betray his implication, as it were, at "every point in the book's manufacture."

A telling footnote to Rieger's representation of Mary Shelley's work and life, these stories point to one of *Frankenstein*'s most unsettling features: its demonstration that positions of specularity are not gender-specific. And from this perspective, Rieger's exhibition of Mary Shelley's artistic deficiencies needs to be not so much discredited—as Anne Mellor forcefully argues that it should be—as subjected to renewed scrutiny. For if one questions the myth of masculine self-possession that bolsters Rieger's allegations, one might further question recovery efforts like Mellor's—efforts built on the desire to claim this plenitude for women. In fact, in insisting on the need to "distinguish Mary Shelley's language from her husband's" and meticulously quantifying and categorizing Percy's revisions, Mellor aligns her project with Rieger's; for although she reverses Rieger's literary judgments, she shares his fundamental assumptions about "unique genius" and the author's stabilizing and authenticating signature.[3] Committed to a view of writing as unitary, coherent, and self-sufficient (writing as "single-handed" production [38]), Mellor's work, as much as Rieger's, sustains authorship as an exclusive institution—one whose configurations best serve male members.

This vision of authorship as self-contained and self-continuous—as a coherent extension of the self into an extracorporeal existence—turns out to be *Frankenstein*'s informing fiction. But as the novel dramatically illustrates, such a vision cannot be sustained without considerable contradiction. This contradiction, predicated on the simultaneous avowal and disavowal of difference—between the literal and figurative, the unique and reproducible, and the bodily and textual—marks the productions of masculinity as fetishistic. And it is precisely this fetishistic structure that *Frankenstein* both illuminates and experiments with, in its intertextual networks as well as in

---

3. Although Mellor shares Rieger's faith in textual purity, her "pure" text would eliminate the traces of Percy Shelley: "Perhaps someday an editor will give us the manuscript Mary Shelley actually wrote, cleansed of such elaborations . . ." (62). For her extended treatment of *Frankenstein*'s textual controversy, see especially 52–69.

its intratextual thematics.[4] In this context, the question of how much Percy Shelley actually wrote remains beside the point. For the desire to "fix" his contributions to Mary Shelley's text (whether Rieger's attempt to "consolidate" them or Mellor's to "correct" them) simply installs the critic in the novel's problematic. Like Frankenstein, the desiring subject must mobilize an elaborate machinery (the technologies of graphology and advanced stylistics) to perpetuate the myth of self-identity—a myth the novel treats as male fantasy.

Frankenstein's textual uncertainties can be seen, then, to restage the problems of its central drama: the fantasy of masculine creation outside the body. But in the workings of the novel, this fantasy breaks down over the issue of embodiment—in the vexed relation between the creator's hand and the creature's body, between the "work of [Frankenstein's] own hands" and Frankenstein's "own hand-writing" (72, 59). As the recalcitrance of Frankenstein's hand suggests, the body's parts cannot be buried—even in the institutional enclaves of masculinity. Putting the hand back into writing, the excavation of the text, as performed by modern critics, thus reactivates the novel's uneasy grapplings with figuration.

Read in the light of the novel's representational extravaganza, the artistic "flaws" of the novel become even more revealing. The stilted, ornate prose style, for example, which Mellor attributes primarily to Percy Shelley's meddling,[5] can be seen to point up the novel's "mannered" literalizations: its manipulation of its subject. As Nancy Vickers points out, in mannerist art "it is the mark of the hand of the artist rather than the mimetic representation of the model that is structured to command attention." But in *Frankenstein* that "hand" is neither single nor self-identical; moreover, read as a work of mannerist virtuosity, the novel both exposes and upsets the "very vocabulary of heterosexual hierarchies" on which mannerism depends. According to Vickers, the "sexual/aesthetic pleasure" that "unites male artist, male patron, and male viewer" in mannerist production requires "the discomfort of its female subject" ("Mistress" 37, 36).[6] In *Frankenstein*, however, where the female subject drops out of sight, the discomfort accrues to the masculine collective: the male artist, spectator, and spectacle. And as the notorious slipperiness of

4. For other discussions of *Frankenstein's* representation of textuality, see in particular Cottom, Favret, Hodges, and McInerney.
5. "He typically changed her simple, Anglo-Saxon diction and straightforward or collo-quial sentence structures into their more refined, complex, and Latinate equivalents. He is thus in large part responsible for the stilted, ornate, putatively Ciceronian prose style about which many readers have complained" (Mellor 59–60).
6. Vickers's study of Cellini's *Nymph of Fontainebleau* concludes, "The very vocabulary of heterosexual hierarchies that unites male artist, male patron, and male viewer, then, in sexual/aesthetic pleasure articulates, as its corollary, the discomfort of its female subject" ("Mistress" 36). *Frankenstein* offers an interesting turn on this pattern by put-ting the male body on display—laid out with its limbs extended, contorted, dispersed, opened to view.

Frankenstein's signature suggests, the composition of masculinity, at least in the novel, cannot be fixed.

* * *

Works Cited

Cameron, Kenneth Neill. *The Young Shelley: Genesis of a Radical*. New York: Macmillan, 1950.

Carson, James P. "Bringing the Author Forward: *Frankenstein* through Mary Shelley's Letters." *Criticism* 30 (1988): 431–53.

Cottom, Daniel. "*Frankenstein* and the Monster of Representation." *Substance* 28 (1980): 60–71.

Ellis, Kate. "Monsters in the Garden: Mary Shelley and the Bourgeois Family." Levine and Knoepflmacher 123–42.

Favret, Mary A. "The Letters of *Frankenstein*." *Genre* 20 (1987): 3–24.

Gilbert, Sandra M., and Susan Gubar. "Horror's Twin: Mary Shelley's Monstrous Eve." *The Madwoman in the Attic*. New Haven: Yale UP, 1979. 213–47.

Hodges, Devon. "*Frankenstein* and the Feminine Subversion of the Novel." *Tulsa Studies in Women's Literature* 2 (1983): 155–64.

Homans, Margaret. *Bearing the Word: Language and Female Experience in Nineteenth-Century Women's Writing*. Chicago: U of Chicago P, 1986.

Jacobus, Mary. "Is There a Woman in This Text?" *New Literary History* 14 (1982): 117–41. Rpt. in *Reading Woman: Essays in Feminist Criticism*. New York: Columbia UP, 1986. 83–109.

Johnson, Barbara. "My Monster/My Self." *Diacritics* 12.2 (1982): 2–10.

Knoepflmacher, U. C. "Thoughts on the Aggression of Daughters." Levine and Knoepflmacher 88–119.

Lavallay, Albert J. "The Stage and Film Children of *Frankenstein*: A Survey." Levine and Knoepflmacher 243–89.

Levine, George, and U. C. Knoepflmacher, eds. *The Endurance of Frankenstein*. Berkeley: U of California P, 1979.

Marshall, David. *The Surprising Effects of Sympathy: Marivaux, Diderot, Rousseau, and Mary Shelley*. Chicago: U of Chicago P, 1988.

McInerney, Peter. "*Frankenstein* and the Godlike Science of Letters." *Genre* 13 (1980): 455–75.

Mellor, Anne K. *Mary Shelley: Her Life, Her Fiction, Her Monsters*. New York: Methuen, 1988.

Miller, D. A. "*Cage aux Folles*: Sensation and Gender in Wilkie Collins's *The Woman in White.*" *Representations* 14 (1986): 107–36.

Moers, Ellen. "Female Gothic." Levine and Knoepflmacher 77–87.

Mullan, John. *Sentiment and Sociability: The Language of Feeling in the Eighteenth Century.* Oxford: Oxford UP, 1988.

Neale, Steve. "Masculinity as Spectacle: Reflections on Men and Mainstream Cinema." *Screen* 24.6 (1983): 2–16.

Parker, Patricia. *Literary Fat Ladies: Rhetoric, Gender, Property.* London: Methuen, 1987.

Poovey, Mary. "My Hideous Progeny: Mary Shelley and the Feminization of Romanticism." *PMLA* 95 (1980): 332–47. Rpt. in *The Proper Lady and the Woman Writer: Ideology as Style in the Works of Mary Wollstonecraft, Mary Shelley, and Jane Austen.* Chicago: U of Chicago P, 1984. 114–42.

Rieger, James. "Mary Shelley's Life and the Composition of *Frankenstein.*" Shelley, *Frankenstein* xi–xxxvii.

Scott, Peter Dale. "Vital Artifice: Mary, Percy, and the Psychopolitical Identity of *Frankenstein.*" Levine and Knoepflmacher 172–204.

Sedgwick, Eve Kosofsky. *The Coherence of Gothic Conventions.* New York: Methuen, 1986.

Shelley, Mary. *Frankenstein; or, The Modern Prometheus (the 1818 Text).* Ed. James Rieger. Indianapolis: Bobbs-Merrill, 1974.

——. "Preface by Mary Shelley to First Collected Edition, 1839." *The Complete Poetical Works of Percy Bysshe Shelley.* Ed. Neville Rogers. Vol. 1. Oxford: Oxford UP, 1972. xlix–liii.

Silverman, Kaja. "Fassbinder and Lacan: A Reconsideration of Gaze, Look, and Image." *Camera Obscura* 19 (1989): 54–84.

Small, Christopher. *Ariel like a Harpy: Shelley, Mary and Frankenstein.* London: Gollancz, 1972.

Steinberg, Leo. *The Sexuality of Christ in Renaissance Art and in Modern Oblivion.* New York: Pantheon, 1983.

Sunstein, Emily W. *Mary Shelley: Romance and Reality.* Boston: Little, 1989.

Veeder, William. *Mary Shelley and* Frankenstein: *The Fate of Androgyny.* Chicago: U of Chicago P, 1986.

Vickers, Nancy J. "Diana Described: Scattered Woman and Scattered Rhyme." *Writing and Sexual Difference.* Ed. Elizabeth Abel. Chicago: U of Chicago P, 1982. 95–110.

——. "The Mistress in the Masterpiece." *The Poetics of Gender.* Ed. Nancy K. Miller. New York: Columbia UP, 1986. 19–41.

White, Newman Ivey. *Shelley.* 2 vols. New York: Knopf, 1940.

MARILYN BUTLER

Frankenstein and Radical Science[†]

Mary Shelley's *Frankenstein* is famously reinterpretable. It can be a late version of the Faust myth, or an early version of the modern myth of the mad scientist; the id on the rampage, the proletariat running amok, or what happens when a man tries to have a baby without a woman.[1] Mary Shelley invites speculation, and in the last generation has been rewarded with a great deal of it.

From professionals, that is. Since 1823, the year when the novel's title, characters and plot first became public property, the general public has seemed remarkably little divided about what the action signifies. A Californian researcher recently employed to find out what the public thinks of scientists was able to summarise his findings wordlessly, with a quick sketch of Frankenstein's Monster. Readers, filmgoers, people who are neither, take the very word Frankenstein to convey an awful warning: don't usurp God's prerogative in the Creation-game, or don't get too clever with technology.

Yet this is by no means what knowledgeable first readers in 1818 were likely to think, or on the evidence of early press comment did think. All three serious reviews in 1818 mention that the novel is topical. No-one appears to discern, as some modern critics do, an allegory of revolution or popular unrest; instead they suspect it of covertly promoting 'favourite projects and passions of the times'. By 'projects' must be meant the novel's network of allusions to contemporary science—not science as formally taught, but current scientific activity as represented to the British public in the 1810s by lectures, newspapers, a few accessible books, above all the serious Reviews.

The idea Mary Shelley famously hit upon in a house rented by Byron beside the shores of Lake Geneva between 16 and 20 June 1816 almost certainly does draw on a scientific dispute, conducted in lectures afterwards published as books, the first of which was the subject of an article in the *Edinburgh Review* the previous year.[2] The novel which grew from this anecdotal beginning introduces a range of scientific *news*, reported as such, particularly in the *Quarterly Review*, in the years 1816–18: topics such as electric-

---

† A version of this article appeared in the *Times Literary Supplement*, 9 April 1993. Reprinted with permission of the author.

1. See Lowry Nelson Jr., 'Night Thoughts on the Gothic Novel', *Yale Review* 52 (1963), 236–57; Franco Moretti, *Signs Taken for Wonders* (London: Verso, 1983), 83–108; Anne Mellor, *Mary Shelley: Her Life, Her Fiction, Her Monsters* (London: Routledge, 1988), 40.

2. *Edinburgh Review* 23 (1814), 384–98.

ity and magnetism, vivisection and Polar exploration—and the spectre of new radical French work in what became evolutionism.[3] After a long, costly European war, these were years of recession, social unrest, and much frantic comment, in moods ranging between outrageous and outraged, in media that included popular papers calling themselves black, red and yellow. From early 1817 the pro-government press, including the leading cultural journal, the Anglican and Tory *Quarterly Review*, published articles calling for press censorship, especially of radical materials intended for a popular readership.[4] From 1818 the *Quarterly* several times called for the revival of the long-neglected charge of blasphemy against irreverent writings.[5] In 1819 it for the first time directed this call against a serious book on evolution science—with which, as I shall show, *Frankenstein* itself is directly implicated.[6]

The 1818 *Frankenstein*, which had drawn nourishment, energy, importance from lectures and journals, had lived by the media, and after 1819 might well have died by the media. The public controversy concerning some of the kinds of science represented in *Frankenstein* endangered the book's future, for it read differently after readers became more knowing. It is not so much because of what Mary Shelley thought, but because of what readers thought, that *Frankenstein* became a substantially different and less contentious novel when reissued in popular form in 1831.

However unlike their approaches, modern critics are likely to be looking at the same text of *Frankenstein*. It will be a reprint of this very third edition of 1831, which Mary Shelley not only changed but, in a new Preface, interpreted—as the story of a 'human endeavour to mock the stupendous mechanism of the Creator of the world'.[7] That is not an impression easily left by the novel in its 1818 form. But in 1831 Mary Shelley added long passages in which her main narrator, Frankenstein, expresses religious remorse for making a creature, and it is on such passages of reflection and analysis that the empathetic modern reader is encouraged to dwell. Our current understanding of *Frankenstein* is disproportionately impressed by passages introduced in what might be called the composite

---

3. See e.g. [John Barrow], 'Capt. Burney, *Memoir . . . on the Question whether Asia and America are Contiguous*', *Quarterly Review* 18 (1818), 457–58 and [G. D'Oyley], review of eight works on the vitalist issue, *Quarterly Review* 22 (1820), 1–34.
4. See especially [R. Southey], *Quarterly Review* 16 (1816), 225–78.
5. E.g. article on John Bellamy's translation of the New Testament, *Quarterly Review* 19 (1818), 250–81.
6. Key evidence for this connection appears in the article on vitalism in the *Quarterly* (1820), for which see n. 3 above. That article is reprinted as Appendix C to my edition, *Frankenstein; Or, The Modern Prometheus: The 1818 Text* (London: William Pickering, 1993); reprinted as a World's Classics paperback (Oxford, 1994), 229–51.
7. Mary Shelley, Preface to 1831 ed., Betty T. Bennett and Charles E. Robinson (eds.), *Mary Shelley Reader* (N.Y.: Oxford UP, 1990), 170.

Frankenstein, the product of a decade and a half of religious-scientific controversy.

It is of course standard practice for an editor to select the last version the author revised, on the grounds that no-one has a better right to determine its final form. But, like all rules, this one exists to be challenged. Wordsworth's early versions of 1799 and 1805 of his great poem *The Prelude*, first published posthumously in 1850, are now widely preferred to the much-revised text of 1850. Last year, Simon Gatrell for Oxford's Worlds Classics passed over the standard 1895 text of *The Return of the Native* in favour of the first edition (1878), neatly summarising the historical reasons why the two differed, and the imaginative reasons why the first was to be preferred. The case for *Frankenstein* (1818) resembles these two precedents, since an urgent, unusual, brilliantly-imagined earlier book has been neutered or at best over-freighted with inessential additions. In one respect the case for the early *Frankenstein* is the strongest of the three. The newsworthiness of this novel meant that after publication text and author were subjected to outside pressures which have little to do with aesthetics, and make it hard to say that it was she who changed her mind.

Within the last two decades the 1818 text has become available again. The first scholarly edition by James Rieger (1974, reprinted 1982) remains in print, and since 1990 two new editions based on 1818 have come on the market. The more helpful versions of either text now give some account of the variations between the two. But it requires an external, circumstantial perspective to show how the first *Frankenstein* arose, and why the second is almost a new book.

The single most striking new fact to emerge is the link between *Frankenstein* and the celebrated, publicly-staged debate of 1814–19 between the two professors at London's Royal College of Surgeons on the origins and nature of life, now known as the vitalist debate. The issue was raised in a lecture of 1814 by the senior of the surgeons, John Abernethy, who apparently sought to unite religious and secular opinion with a formula acceptable to both. Materialist science, concentrating on the organisation and function of living bodies, could not, Abernethy acknowledged, adequately explain life itself. A mysterious 'superadded' force was needed, some 'subtile, mobile, invisible substance', analogous on the one hand to soul and on the other to electricity.[8]

Coleridge scholars are aware of Abernethy because Coleridge approved of him, and built on his arguments in an essay, 'The Theory of Life', which remained unpublished in the poet's lifetime. Some

---

8. John Abernethy, *An Enquiry into the Probability and Rationality of Mr Hunter's 'Theory of Life'* (London: Longman, etc., 1814), 48, 52.

modern Shelleyans have recognized that Abernethy's antagonist William Lawrence was Percy Shelley's physician (and in the very years of the vitalist row, 1814–19).[9] But in fact no critic has examined Lawrence's boldly sceptical lectures in relation to the writings of the intellectually close-knit Shelley group, which at this time included Percy and Mary Shelley, Peacock, Hunt and Byron.

Unimpeded by being Abernethy's colleague and former protégé, Lawrence took care to make the materialist position sound like the professional position. A more brilliant, cogent writer than Abernethy, he was also a charismatic lecturer and a formidable adversary. Historians of science make claims, if often cautious ones, for Lawrence's contribution to the long-running evolution controversy. But his major book, *Lectures on Physiology, Zoology and the Natural History of Man* (1819), shows that he can be sceptical and discriminating over new evolutionist positions as over everything else. What seems more certain is that his succinct briefings on current Continental work, the French doctor Bichat's research into the nerves and connecting tissue, or the German J. F. Blumenberg's ethnography, must have opened up the way anatomy and physiology were taught to London medical students in the second decade of the century.

Their friendship with Lawrence probably ensured that both Shelleys wrote more accurately and less speculatively on scientific matters than they otherwise might. But he also had a strong imaginative appeal for their disaffected group: after the defeat of the French Revolution, his style of science offered an alternative way of envisaging progress, free of the old discredited political vocabulary. This was above all *natural* history—the early evolutionists' non-scriptural and for some minds anti-scriptural narrative of the life of animal species. Mankind, the other animals, even plants now appeared capable, in response to their environment, driven by mechanisms of their own, of adaptation or what 1790s progressives had called perfectibility. The writers in turn showed Lawrence an alternative career route: a literary platform from which to address the general public over the heads of cautious colleagues.

It would be possible to treat Lawrence's role in *Frankenstein* as a standard case of influence; some ideas from Erasmus Darwin and Humphry Davy also figure here and there in the novel. But the coincidences between Lawrence's best book and Mary Shelley's are so different in scale that they need following through as, in effect, a single intermeshing story. Both books were associated with aggressive materialism, and this seems to be the main reason why both

9. For pathbreaking work on P. B. Shelley's education and scientific contacts, especially William Lawrence, see Hugh J. Luke Jr., 'Sir William Lawrence, Physician to Shelley and Mary', *Papers on English Language and Literature* i (1965), 141–52, and N. Crook and D. Guiton, *Shelley's Venomed Melody* (Cambridge: C.U.P., 1986).

became *causes célèbres*. It was because each writer took on characteristics of the other's work that Lawrence came to read like a satirist as well as a medical professional, and Mary Shelley could be deemed to have attacked Christianity. In fact it is only when their stories are considered together that we see the extent of the cultural challenge offered by this striking episode in Romantic literary experiment and in the social history of science.

Lawrence was appointed a second Professor at the Royal College of Surgeons in 1815, and in March 1816 gave the two lectures which opened his campaign against Abernethy. The first is a wide-ranging survey of recent Continental work in the physical sciences, while the second, 'On Life', focuses rigorously on the issue raised by Abernethy as physiology and anatomy can properly handle it. For biologists (a word Lawrence allegedly introduced to Britain), life is the 'assemblage of all the functions' a living body can perform. We have done what we can, Lawrence says, to find origins and 'to observe living bodies in the moment of their formation . . . when matter may be supposed to receive the stamp of life. . . . Hitherto, however, we have not been able to catch nature in the fact.' On the contrary, what we can observe of animals is that 'all have participated in the existence of other living beings . . . the motion proper to living bodies, or in one word, life, has its origin in that of their parents.'[1] The materialist thinker sees no means of abstracting the animating power from the animal.

By the time of his 1817 lectures, Lawrence was willing to identify Abernethy as his opponent, and openly to ridicule the argument that electricity, or 'something analogous' to it, could do duty for the soul—'For subtle matter is still matter; and if this fine stuff can possess vital properties, surely they may reside in a fabric which differs only in being a little coarser.'[2] But even in the more guarded 1816 lectures there was an offensive tone of superiority in the demand that the Life question should be left to the real professionals. In this case that meant excluding chemists, including presumably Davy, whom Abernethy had recruited: 'Organized bodies must be treated differently from . . . inorganic. . . . The reference to gravity, to attraction, to chemical affinity, to electricity and galvanism, can only serve to perpetuate false notes in philosophy.' The great John Hunter, after whom his and Abernethy's lectures were named, would have been on his, Lawrence's, side when it came to method: 'He did not attempt to explain life by . . . *a priori* speculations, or by the illusory analogies of other sciences; . . . [but] by a patient exami-

1. William Lawrence, *An Introduction to Comparative Anatomy, being two introductory lectures delivered at the Royal College of Surgeons* (London, 1816), 140–42.
2. Lawrence, *Lectures on Physiology, Zoology and the Natural History of Man* (London: Callow, 1819), Lecture 3 [1817], 84.

nation of the fabric, and close observation of the actions of living creatures.'[3]

Mary and Percy Shelley, Lawrence's friends, were living near London in that March of 1816, when Lawrence first put the materialist case against spiritualised vitalism. On June 15 1816, at Geneva, Byron's doctor Polidori recorded in his diary that he and P. B. Shelley had a conversation 'about principles—whether man was to be thought merely an instrument'.[4] Fifteen years later Mary Shelley remembered several conversations on subsequent days, with Byron participating, she silently auditing, on 'the nature of the principle of life, and whether there was any probability of its ever being discovered and communicated.' On 16 June, most members of the party agreed to take part in a ghost-story contest.

There surely cannot be much doubt that the group were speaking of the vitalist debate, and presumably of Lawrence's lectures, which were on sale by June 1816 in book form. In fact, Mary's contribution to the ghost-story competition to some degree acts out the debate between Abernethy and Lawrence, in a form close enough for those who knew it to recognise. Frankenstein the blundering experimenter, still working with superseded notions, suggests the position of Abernethy, who proposes that the superadded life-element is analogous to electricity—particularly when he uses a machine, reminiscent of a battery, to impart the spark of life.[5] Frankenstein's other procedures are made unpleasantly anti-life, recalling Lawrence's unfavourable comparison of inorganic with organic methods.[6] The fact is that in 1818 Mary Shelley's portrayal of her hero is harsh, contemptuous, with a touch of Lawrence's sarcastic debating manner. Not so much a mythical Prometheus, more a humble Sorcerer's Apprentice, Frankenstein as first devised seems to know too little science rather than too much.

Compared with the professional qualifications of the novel's first two narrators, Frankenstein and Walton, an inventor and an explorer, the Creature has few claims to act as the third. Just as he owes his existence to a unique and unnatural process, he defies all odds, as a parentless being, by learning language at all. Yet the voice in which he narrates the second of the three volumes is impressive, in a

3. Ibid., *Introduction to Comparative Anatomy* (1816), 161–63.
4. (Ed.) W. M. Rossetti, *Diary of J. W. Polidori*, 1816 (1911), quoted James Rieger (ed.), 'Introduction', *Frankenstein, or the Modern Prometheus: The 1818 Text* (Chicago: U of Chicago P, 1982), xvii.
5. See opening sentences, *Frankenstein* (1818), ch. 4.
6. Not only does he rob graves for the flesh of the dead (ch. 3); he performs vivisection ('tortures the living animal'). This, along with other forms of cruelty to animals, was particularly objectionable to humanitarians and principled vegetarians such as the Shelleys.

strange register appropriate to a witness brought back from the remote past—a phrase the scientific showman Georges Cuvier had recently used to describe the fossils he patiently reconstructed into lifelike animals.[7] He is more eloquent than Frankenstein in the conversations that introduce and end their meeting, and still more persuasive when relating his life-history, an exercise in self-observation, social observation, and retrospective analysis. By tracking his own maturation, from a solitary to a social animal, the Creature succeeds in the task Frankenstein abandons, that of scientifically following up Frankenstein's technological achievement.

He begins his narration on the night of the experiment, substituting his careful record for Frankenstein's excitable recollection of the same events. Still unable to focus his eyes, the Creature blundered round Frankenstein's lodgings in the big Ingolstadt rooming house, before finding himself, very cold, out in the woods near the town. His visual impressions were still unclear, but he now began to make the distinction between light and dark. He might have died of hunger and exposure had he not found berries he instinctively ate, water to drink, and a cloak to wrap himself in. He responded, pleasurably, to moonlight and birds when still unable to name them, let alone classify 'the little winged animals who had often intercepted the light from my eyes'.

In this chapter Mary Shelley employs language experimentally and imaginatively, in a way that anticipates the scenes in William Golding's novel *The Inheritors* where the Neanderthal narrator describes his first encounters with *homo sapiens*. But there are conventionally-written eighteenth-century precedents, in the literature on Wild Boys and Girls who had supposedly grown up among wild animals, or at any rate isolated from humanity. Already in his *System of Nature* (1735), Linnaeus speaks of *homo ferus* as a distinct human species, 'four-footed, mute and hairy', and lists ten recorded instances from 1544. The most famous case of Mary Shelley's day was the Wild Boy of Aveyron, whose discovery came to light in Paris in 1799. For what it reveals of early human physical and cognitive development, this remains a classic instance, thanks to the devoted teaching and careful reporting of Jean-Marc Gaspard Ikard, the young physician of the Paris institution for deaf-mutes, who cared for the boy and analysed his problems as the loss of nurture by human parents in infancy.[8]

---

7. Georges Cuvier (1769–1832) popularised paleontology, in a triumphantly imaginative presentation of the remote past. 'My key, my principle, will enable us to restore the appearance of these long-vanished beasts and relate them to the life of the present' (Cuvier, *Essay on the Theory of the Earth*, Edinburgh, 1815). See also *Edinburgh Review* 20 (1812) 382, and Loren Eiseley, *Darwin's Century*, 84.

8. 'Cast upon this globe without physical strength or innate ideas . . . it is only in the heart of society that man can attain the preeminent position which is his natural des-

Rousseau and Monboddo enthusiastically contributed to the wider debate, over whether the wild man is a sub-species, and if so how he relates both to advanced man and to the primates. Unlike both, but like J. F. Blumenbach, Lawrence in his *Natural History of Man* (1819) argues against generalising from such cases: the child concerned was likely to have been born an idiot, and had either strayed from home or been cast out. The lack of bodily coordination in a case such as that of Peter of Hamelin, an earlier wild boy brought in the 1720s to England, and the Aveyron boy's difficulty in learning language, had explanations less astonishing than Monboddo's supposition that such children represented a sub-species between mankind and the primates.[9]

A significant aspect of Mary Shelley's treatment of the Creature's rearing in isolation from humanity is its avoidance of idealised, sentimental or scientifically-bold claims. The Creature's life in the woods is neither superior, nor even natural; it raises no question of his belonging to a species other than the human. So firmly is that speculative historical narrative omitted that it seems as if Mary Shelley, like Lawrence, deliberately avoided committing herself to the evolutionist hypothesis both Erasmus Darwin and Lamarck espoused, that all forms of organic life had evolved from single cells. Yet the Creature's life-experience hardly seems scientifically ill-informed, since it bears out the careful physiology of Itard's leading contemporary Bichat, in *Traité sur les membranes* (1800), *Recherches physiologiques sur la vie et sur la mort* (1800), and *Anatomie Générale* (1801), works which explore the functions and connecting tissue of the nerves, senses and organs, and give the most accurate account yet of every creature's sensitive interactions with its environment.

In fact, once it is considered in relation to fiction's established conventions, the Creature's career works on two levels, as a survival-story like Robinson Crusoe's, and as a story which does after all have historical implications, for it can be read as an allegorical account of the progress of mankind over aeons of time. That sidestep into allegory evades, yet for the knowing reader might also bring to mind, the evolutionist's long view of the ascent of the species.

For all the excellence and the intriguing suggestiveness of volume II as a Voltairean fable, most modern readers probably find volume III the most brilliantly imaginative and original part of the book, and this seems as true of its science as of its characterisation. There are signs by now of a rich literary interaction between the Shelleys and Lawrence, one that flows in both directions. In his polemical

---

tiny.' Ikard, opening sentence of Preface to *The Wild Boy of Aveyron* [1807], (New York: Appleton-Century-Crofts, 1962), xxi.
9. Lawrence, *Lectures on Physiology . . . and Natural History of Man*, 134–40.

1817 lecture on the Life question, Lawrence seems to stray into Mary Shelley's Gothicised rhythms and vocabulary—'an immaterial and spiritual being could not have been discovered among the blood and filth of the dissecting room.'[1] In turn Mary Shelley seems to draw more in her later scenes on details from different writings by Lawrence, not necessarily contemporaneous. They include entries he contributed to Rees's *Cyclopaedia*, particularly one on Monsters, and an academic paper of 1815 on the case of a boy born without part of his brain, whom Lawrence had cared for in his own home.[2] That piece of fieldwork must surely have helped prompt Mary Shelley's 'hideous phantom', since *Frankenstein* must from the start have involved a scientist studying the relations of brain to physical functions, who fosters (or fails to foster) a monster. Even more clearly, the Lawrence case provided a plot for Peacock's satire *Melincourt* (1817), in which an intellectual called Forester (full form of the name Foster) adopts an orang-utan and tries to teach him to speak. Forester fails in his immediate objective, but a richly corrupt system enables him to secure his protégé a baronetcy and a seat in Parliament.

Lawrence's *Natural History of Man*, his one fullscale book, takes as its topic the human species, considered as a variety of animal. Lawrence states that his text is substantially based on lectures he gave in 1814, which no doubt explains why so much of it surveys the current state of knowledge in the appropriate field—ethnography, with inputs from anatomy and sociology. In his division of racial types into five, and his emphasis on physical differences between humans and primates, Lawrence largely repeats Blumenbach, with and without attribution. But in his freshest, most dynamic passages he works his own witty, distinctive variations on Blumenbach's memorable observation, 'man is the most perfect of domesticated animals'.[3] Most domesticated animals are smaller, weaker, less

---

1. Ibid., 7.
2. Lawrence also contributed entries on 'Cranium', 'Generation' and 'Man' for Rees's *Cyclopaedia* (individual volumes undated, edition complete by 1819). The *Quarterly's* attack on radical science (1820) refers xenophobically in passing to the *Cyclopaedia* articles as borrowings from 'the school of modern French philosophy', naming Cuvier and Bichat, and from unnamed 'freethinking physiologists of Germany.' Percy Shelley had already unwarily drawn attention to the debt of *Frankenstein* to German physiologists, hardly as yet well-known to the English public, in the opening sentences of his anonymous Preface to the 1818 *Frankenstein*.
3. See entry 'J. F. Blumenbach' (1752–1840), *Dictionary of Scientific Biography*. In a series of major articles, Timothy Lenoir has demonstrated that Blumenbach's 'materialist vitalism', which was sceptical, cautious and scrupulously environmental, contributed importantly to the scientific thought of his Gottingen colleague Kant in the 1780s and 1790s, and in helping generate a *philosophy of biology* had a key influence on the early nineteenth-century emergence of the subject (Lenoir, 'Kant, Blumenbach and Vital Materialism in German Biology', *Isis* 71 (1980), 77–108; 'The Development of Transcendental Naturphilosophie', *Studies in Historical Biology* 5 (1981), 111–205). As a key English translator and follower of Blumenbach, Lawrence's intellectual role takes on enhanced significance; so does *Frankenstein*, once it can be seen to convey quite sophisticated biological concepts in a familiar form.

audacious than their wild-life ancestors. In an offensive, powerful passage, Lawrence develops a Swiftian put-down to humanity, by remarking on the tendency of the European upper orders to 'breed', by sexual selection, for physical beauty and elegance rather than strength or ability. But to judge by the ugly, stunted London Cockney, examples of degeneracy are plentiful among urban populations. Lawrence goes on to reflect that inbreeding within the European royal families has thrown up many recent cases of hereditary weakness and madness.[4] He need not remind his readers of the obvious example, England's George III.

Several topics Lawrence considers in his *Natural History* reappear, in yet more ingenious adaptations, in the third volume of *Frankenstein*. Mankind as a domesticated animal, pretentious but flawed, could also be the best way to summarise Mary Shelley's larger theme. Incidentally she touches on Lawrence's professional issues: heredity, fosterage and nurturance, sexual selection and the perverse adoption of choices which lead to extinction. She displays them by portraying the aristocratic Frankensteins as unhealthy, even incestuous, in their marriages; in the first edition Frankenstein's bride Elizabeth is his first cousin, who has been brought up like a sister. Frankenstein exhibits a neurotic resistance when asked to fix the date of their wedding. His excuse to himself and us is that he must first make a female Monster for the Creature to mate with, thus helping to underline how much stronger and healthier are the Creature's instincts. Frankenstein indeed seems more aroused when making and dismembering the female Monster than at the prospect of joining Elizabeth on his own wedding night. It is, of course, the Creature who gets there first. This means that Frankenstein has a hand in his bride's death—because he brought the Creature to life, because his neglect of him afterwards indeed made a Monster, and because he neglects Elizabeth too. That hideously terminated marriage kills Frankenstein's father, and raises the prospect that the family will become extinct.

When it comes to parenting, Frankenstein is himself a monster. He will not acknowledge his only child, the Being he chooses to call Monster, Fiend and Demon, though no human father ever played so thorough-going a role in any birth. *Frankenstein* ironically illustrates Lawrence's scholarly observations about parenting—the medical mishaps to which the birth-process is subject; the one sure feature of any birth, which is the involvement of at least one parent of the same species. But, if this parent-child relationship after a

4. *Lectures . . . and Natural History of Man*, 459–60: 'Natural History of Man', Section II, ch. VI, subsections on 'Powerful Influence of Attention to Breed' and 'Inattention to This Point in the Human Race'.

fashion obeys the rules, the roles of those involved become perversely displaced. After Frankenstein vows to hunt down his 'progeny', the Creature nurtures Frankenstein to keep him alive, feeding him for example with a dead hare: it's only when killing for Frankenstein that the vegetarian Creature kills for food. He still tries in his way to live by the precept that the child is father to the man—and, anthropologically, primitive man *is* father to sophisticated man. But the Creature has slowly emerged as the dominant partner, though originally he was a dependent, a deformed huge child. Of the two antagonists, he is the stronger and better adapted when the chase ends in the Arctic, where natural conditions are at their most severe. He shares Frankenstein's fate of extinction, but goes to it voluntarily, with a consoling sense that even he now returns to nature.

The sequence of events after publication makes a story on its own, significant and intricate because it involves so many key institutions— the law, commercial publishers, the journals, the Royal College of Surgeons. The three reviews the novel received queried its attitudes,[5] and this is unsurprising since, though anonymous, it was dedicated to the 1790s radical William Godwin. Even so, Mary had a kindlier, larger press than her husband had in his lifetime—and better reviews than the Shelleys must have feared. But the next year the publication of Lawrence's *Lectures on Physiology, Zoology and the Natural History of Man* provoked the virulent and prominently placed denunciation in the *Quarterly Review* of November 1819. This unusually long opening article surveyed the vitalist controversy over five years, and itself constituted a major event in the public reception of evolution theory. Encouraged by his editor William Gifford, the author George D'Oyley devoted most space to Lawrence, denouncing him for taking the leading role on the materialist side in the vitalist issue. He included Lawrence's other published writings in the indictment, but surprisingly omitted his treatment of heredity and breeding, possibly out of regard for good taste. D'Oyley's tone is exceptionally harsh and personal: after dealing with six other works on either side, he abruptly returns to Lawrence, and calls on the Royal College of Surgeons to discipline him. On pain of dismissal he should be made to withdraw the offending passages, and to undertake not to write again in the same vein.

The Royal College of Surgeons did indeed suspend Lawrence, and, going a little further than asked, would not reinstate him till he withdrew the book entirely. He did so for fear of losing his appointment as Surgeon to some of the London hospitals. The result ironi-

---

5. *Quarterly Review* 18 (1818), 378–85; *Edinburgh Magazine and Literary Miscellany* 2 (1818), 249–53; [Scott], *Blackwood's Edinburgh Magazine* 2 (1817–18), 613–26.

cally was that during the next few years several publishers pirated the volume, under cover of a ruling of 1817 by the Lord Chancellor, Lord Eldon, that where a book was blasphemous, seditious or immoral the author should not be protected by the law of copyright.[6] In March 1822, under pressure again from the Royal College, Lawrence tried to claim his copyright, and initially obtained an injunction restraining the firm of J. and C. Smith from selling their edition of his book. The Smiths' lawyers argued that the work was not protected because of passages 'hostile to natural and revealed religion'. After reading both the book and its reviews, Lord Eldon upheld the publishers, even though the book would in consequence remain in circulation, in cheap popular formats. Lord Byron lost similar cases, also tried before Eldon, in February 1822 and in 1823, involving *Cain* and *Don Juan* respectively.

The great notoriety of Lawrence's volume between 1819 and 1822 becomes part of the post-publication history of *Frankenstein*. For the author, her circle, potential publishers, and a significant number of informed readers, whether their sympathies were theological or materialist, the plot of *Frankenstein* was either already associated with Lawrence's style of radical science, or was imminently in danger of becoming so—until, that is, Mary Shelley removed most of the telltale signs.

For the 1831 edition Mary Shelley added remorseful passages which made Frankenstein a more sympathetic as well as a more religious character; she pared away details of his scientific education and, most interestingly, changed all those facts about the Frankenstein family's marriages that in the first edition touch on genetic concerns. Her alterations were acts of damage-limitation rather than a reassertion of authority. They perhaps seemed advisable when surgeons and their experiments became the objects of public hysteria because of the Burke and Hare murders in Edinburgh in the late 1820s. What made them inevitable was that conservatives everywhere now interpreted the plot of *Frankenstein* as they wished to, and expected most readers to agree. As a writer in *Fraser's Magazine* (November 1830) remarks in passing, 'A State without religion is like a human body without a soul, or rather like a human body of the species of the Frankenstein Monster, without a pure and vivifying

6. In addition to the first edition by J. Callow (1819), the British Library owns early pirated editions by W. Benbow (1822), Kaygill & Rice (1822) and J. and C. Smith (1823). There was a further edition in 1823 by Richard Carlile, the radical publisher jailed for reissuing Paine's critique of the Bible, *The Age of Reason* (1819). Carlile wrote an *Address to the Men of Science* (1821), singling out Lawrence for praise as a popular radical writer, and dedicated his edition of Lawrence's book ironically to Lord Eldon. See O. Temkin, 'Basic Science, Medicine and the Romantic Era', in *The Double Face of Janus* (Baltimore: Johns Hopkins UP, 1977), p. 355.

principle.'[7] Before Mary Shelley made the novel fit this description, a journalist confidently claimed it for Abernethy's rather than Lawrence's side in the vitalist dispute.

LAWRENCE LIPKING

Frankenstein, the True Story; or, Rousseau Judges Jean-Jacques[†]

In the past few decades, a period during which Mary Shelley's *Frankenstein* has been received into the canon of English literature—to judge from the number of editions, books, essays, and course adoptions—a remarkable critical consensus has grown up around it. Consensus may seem a peculiar term, as I am aware. For no work has been more hotly debated. Indeed, the role of *Frankenstein* in the canon is exactly to be the sort of text one argues about. Like *Hamlet*, *Lycidas*, and *Turn of the Screw* in previous generations, it furnishes a testing ground for every conceivable mode of interpretation, in case books or collections of articles where students can be instructed in the infinite varieties of criticism and fledgling critics can cut their teeth on amazing new readings. Anything goes. One recent text, part of a series of "Case Studies in Contemporary Criticism," amplifies five "perspectives" on *Frankenstein*: Reader-Response Criticism, Psychoanalytic Criticism, Feminist Criticism, Marxist Criticism, and Cultural Criticism. But this merely scratches the surface. Even the Lacanian subgroup of psychoanalytic criticism, for instance, has produced at least half a dozen discrete readings of the novel, focusing on Imaginary and Symbolic mothers, fathers, daughters, and sons as well as the relations, contradictions, and subversions of their Orders; and each of these readings arrives at its destination. Is *Frankenstein* a story of homophobic paranoia? the repression of the proletariat? an abandoned woman? Collectively, the response of modern criticism has been, Why not?

No book seems better suited to this free-for-all. In almost every way *Frankenstein* might have been designed as grist for the contemporary critic's mill. To begin with, everybody misunderstands it; or more accurately, hundreds of millions of people who have never read the book think that they know what it is about, from seeing or hearing about a movie, and most of those people do not have a clue. This

---

7. Quoted Lee Storrenberg, 'Mary Shelley's Monster: Politics and Psyche in *Frankenstein*', in (eds.) Levine and Knoepflmacher, *The Endurance of 'Frankenstein'* (Berkeley: U of California, 1979), p. 166.
† First published in the first edition of the NCE *Frankenstein* in 1996. The Works Cited list begins on p. 434. Reprinted by permission of the author.

universal ignorance invigorates the critic with a rare chance to set things straight. Moreover, the novel represents an ideal of late-twentieth-century literary studies: it bends the traditional canon. Not only is its author a woman, without the pretensions or privileges of a certified male genius like her husband, but also it combines two scorned and outcast, if enduring, genres, gothic and science-fiction. Here is an opportunity to unravel the center of academic literary history and weave some ties to popular culture. Nor should one underestimate another source of popularity: the glamor and notoriety of Mary Wollstonecraft Godwin Shelley's circle. What a set! Even the circumstances in which the book was written deserve a movie (a better one than Ken Russell's). A daring elopement with Shelley at seventeen, the suicide of his wife, wanderings in Europe, passionate reading and writing and other affairs, and finally that hothouse summer of 1816 in Geneva, when Byron called for a ghost story and Mary, not yet nineteen, realized that one of her nightmares might do—what could be more romantic? If *Frankenstein* had never been conceived, the genealogical, psychological, intellectual, political, and sexual complexities of that summer would still provoke plenty of thought.

But one other source of interest is still more important: the mystery of how the novel came to be. According to Mary Shelley's own Introduction, in 1831, people frequently asked her "How I, then a young girl, came to think of, and to dilate upon, so very hideous an idea?" But a more aggressive form of the question might be posed: how did such a young and inexperienced writer, who in the remaining three decades of her life never again showed any phenomenal talent, manage to create a work that still haunts the dreams of much of the human race, a work whose title alone evokes a vision of history that has yet to run its course? *Frankenstein* is more than a book, as everyone knows; it is a myth and a symbol. What is its secret? Not many critics can resist the effort to find out.

The book itself, of course, inspires this fascination with secrets. An undisclosed secret, the principle of life, motivates all the action, and Frankenstein's lonely, obsessive quest spurs a competitive response in many lonely, obsessive readers who pursue, like him, the mystery of creation. Monomania is contagious. Nor does the impossibility of discovering the secret of life, as dark to Mary Shelley as to anyone else, or even of unearthing the ultimate secret of a text, discourage the true cryptographer from digging up every crypt. The pursuit is its own reward. If poststructuralist theory has taught us any lesson, it is that convictions about the indeterminacy and undecidability of all texts do nothing to stem the effort to find unique and compelling readings.

That effort persists when the text itself disappears. A case might be made, for instance, that no text represents the real *Frankenstein*.

In an essay on "Choosing a Text of *Frankenstein* to Teach" in the MLA volume, *Approaches to Teaching Shelley's Frankenstein*, Anne K. Mellor makes clear that the text she prefers is the manuscript now in the Bodleian Library, where Mary Shelley's original draft can be separated from Percy Shelley's "corrections"—though since that text is incomplete, its ideal form must be inscribed in a reader's imagination, not on the printed page. Next best would be the 1818 text, which, despite Percy Shelley's stilted, ornate revisions of Mary Shelley's direct and forceful prose, still espouses the values of the original—or at any rate, a "political and moral ideology" that Mellor approves. Last and least is the 1831 edition, fatally compromised (in Mellor's opinion) by a new pessimism in Mary Shelley's philosophical views. Still, 1831 is what almost everyone will teach, unfortunately, since the others have been expensive or unavailable. The conclusion seems inescapable: no stable, authentic text exists or, as Mellor puts it, "*Frankenstein* exemplifies what Julia Kristeva has called 'the questionable subject-in-process.'" Yet Mellor herself does seem quite sure that she knows exactly how that subject-in-process ought to be read; indeed, sure enough to defend the novel against its author's own second thoughts. The dematerializing of the text does not inhibit the quest for its secrets. But it does seem likely to prevent agreement about how to read it. Each reader must learn to make a text for herself.

How then can I speak of a critical consensus? No paradox is involved. For as soon as one examines the current debate about *Frankenstein,* two qualifications become plain. The first is that readings seldom take the trouble to notice, let alone challenge, each other. They simply keep adding one more perspective to the pile. Interpretation of *Frankenstein* is not a zero-sum game, in which each new hypothesis would require eliminating an old one. Nor do critics spend much time trying to falsify any reading, or seeking out any negative evidence to disconfirm a bright idea. The object of this debate is not to prove or refute or win but only to take part, translating the novel into one's own discourse. There is always room for something completely different. Hence most interpretations serenely interpenetrate, threading through one another like an infinite cat's cradle, and seldom if ever touching.

Consider one of the most admired essays on *Frankenstein*, Ellen Moers' "Female Gothic" in *Literary Women*. According to Moers, the crucial scene occurs when Victor Frankenstein first perceives his filthy creation, "the hideous corpse which he had looked upon as the cradle of life." The language describes a stillbirth, and that is the key to its power: Shelley draws on her experience of the death of her own infant children or "the trauma of the afterbirth." Like others, I find this an imaginative and poignant reading. But it does not contradict any other reading, nor could it be tested by evidence from the novel. If one objected that Victor is not a woman, that he does not give birth, that the creature is alive not dead and is not an infant but full-grown, and that the horror arises precisely from the difference between this delivery and all others, Moers might reply that such literalmindedness misses the point. She has diagnosed a psychological effect, not attempted to account for what Mary Shelley consciously thought she was doing. Nor does her reading rival anyone else's. A cultural critic who saw the scene of creation as a miscarriage of technology, or an allegory of the failures of the Industrial Revolution, could cite Moers without discomfort. On this level of insight, contraries can be equally true, and fierce debate need not exclude consensus.

Moreover, contemporary critics do agree, to a surprising extent, on what constitutes the object they are trying to interpret. That is a second, more specific reason to talk about a consensus. However their speculations differ, their practice of describing *Frankenstein* tends to be the same. This distinction might be expressed in many ways, none of them immune to theoretical challenge. One might speak, for instance, of a common understanding of the plot of the novel, as opposed to its theme; but this could be taken to imply that understanding a plot precedes interpretation, rather than being itself an interpretive construction of the text. Similarly, one might speak (like M. H. Abrams) of first-order construing as opposed to second-order "double reading" or deconstruction. I do not propose to engage in this argument. Rather, I will focus on a particular sort of evidence, largely negative. When contemporary critics write about *Frankenstein*, certain scenes and elements of plot hardly ever get mentioned. Still more (or less), though critics do not go out of their way to agree with each other, they do agree in discountenancing a certain naïve or thoughtless reading of the text, a reading they often attribute to most of their students. In this respect, one might identify a strong consensus *against*: a kind of evidential double negative, in which like-mindedness may be inferred by a refusal to discuss something or by a united front against a common enemy.

That front unites critics of very different stripes—for example, all five perspectives in "Case Studies in Contemporary Criticism." To be contemporary, evidently, is to link arms against wrong-headed or *uncontemporary* readings. Late-twentieth-century critics, when they look at Frankenstein's creation, no longer see a Monster, as earlier generations did; they now see a Creature. And other aspects of that creation—for instance, Victor Frankenstein's genius—they do not see at all. During the past few years, I have heard lectures on *Frankenstein* by several of the leading Romanticists of our time, whose approaches could hardly have been further apart. Yet when they referred to the novel, what they did and did not talk about proved to be remarkably similar. Here are a few examples, freely adapted from their general drift as well as that of other critics. Item: Frankenstein is the degenerate offspring of a dysfunctional family; Not Worth Mentioning: every character in the book loves and admires him. Item: Walton and Frankenstein are unreliable narrators; Not Worth Mentioning: the Creature is an unreliable narrator (his narrative appears only within Walton's account of Frankenstein's account). Item: it is impossible to believe Frankenstein's story of how he discovered the secret; Not Worth Mentioning: it is impossible to believe the Creature's story of how he acquired language. Item: the Creature is a natural man; Not Worth Mentioning: the Creature is an unnatural botch of a man. Item: Frankenstein's abandonment of his Creature is an act of unforgivable irresponsibility; Not Worth Mentioning: the Creature murders a small child and frames an innocent woman for the crime. Item: Frankenstein's incredible stupidity, narcissism, and insensitivity to women lead to the death of his bride on their wedding night; Not Worth Mentioning: the Creature kills that bride for no other reason than to get back at Frankenstein. Etc., etc.

My purpose is by no means to make a case for Frankenstein and against the Creature. That would only reverse the situation I have been sketching, a situation of extreme partiality and loaded descriptions. Nor do I intend to question the contempt for Victor that oozes through much recent criticism. But the onesidedness and complacency of contemporary readings, even in summarizing the plot, suggest how firmly a modern consensus has taken hold. To argue against contrary evidence may be a first stage in developing consensus, but a later stage has been crowned with success when critics stop noticing that such evidence exists. We have reached that stage in the '90s.

The strength of this new revised standard critical version of *Frankenstein* is confirmed in an interesting way by some critics who have been forced to notice that other readings are possible. Their students have forced the issue, for these critics follow the method of analyzing readers' responses; and to their credit some of them honestly report what students say. The results are dismaying. Despite the consensus of sophisticated critics, ordinary readers keep looking at the wrong evidence and coming to the wrong conclusions. Even though Mary Lowe-Evans, for instance, has coached her students to read the novel with the eye of an eighteenth-century woman, according to bonds of sympathy that Victor Frankenstein breaks, they still insist on judging the character differently than she does. "My attempts to arouse the students' indignation at Frankenstein's failure to take responsibility for Clerval's death and his reluctance to warn Elizabeth of imminent danger, for example, proved futile." With admirable candor, she admits that "strategies I did not influence and cannot explain" enabled them to exonerate the guilty party. "Only one student saw Victor Frankenstein as a spoiled young man who brought death and destruction to all who loved him, simply to satisfy an intellectual whim." The rest, she supposes, may have been desensitized by preconceptions from films (though films have hardly created sympathy for the mad scientist). At any rate, they go on thinking that Victor is essentially good. Since no one has said that in print for decades, these readers cannot be saved; they stand outside the consensus.

What is at stake in this tug of war between teacher and student comes across strikingly in Anne K. Mellor's account of her very well designed and coercive method of teaching "*Frankenstein* and the Sublime." She begins with three questions: "1. Is the Creature in *Frankenstein* good or evil? 2. Is he innately so? Or does he become good or evil? 3. If he becomes so, what causes this change?" Students divide on these questions, and Mellor suggests that Mary Shelley's own answer is "one of radical skepticism." But the teacher's questioning soon yields to moralizing. The Creature is *not* innately evil, but forced to become so by the characters who deny him access to a human community. By introducing students to the Romantic sublime, expressed by landscape paintings, as well as to Diane Arbus's photographs of freaks, Mellor argues for the need to respond to difference or the unknown with love. "If we read or imagine the Creature as evil, we write ourselves as the authors of evil." Hence Mary Shelley's readers ought to see "all the products of nature—the old, the sick, the handicapped, the freaks—as sacred life-forms to be nurtured with care and compassion." Love thy Creature. And in case students still have doubts, the teacher concludes by warning them that, if they do not draw the moral that she does from the story, they may be responsible for the end of life as we know it. "Only by reading the sublime, the unknowable, as lovable can we prevent the creation of monsters, monsters both psychological and technological, monsters capable of destroying all human civilization." Love thy Creature *or else.* I wonder how many students disagree at this point; or if they do, how many dare to speak up.

Let me be frank: I do not think this represents good teaching. First of all, it begs the question that every reader keeps asking: is the Creature really a product of nature, a sacred life-form, or only a product of man, outside the natural order—a monster, in fact? Next, it begs the question of whether the reader is supposed to excuse the murders of innocent people because the murderer is a victim of prejudice. But most important, it reduces the novel to a late-twentieth-century platitude, giving readers a chance to feel good about their own superior wisdom. Who does not agree that all creatures great and small ought to be nurtured with care and compassion (however badly we may treat one another in practice)? Which of us, in Frankenstein's position, would not invite the Creature home, give him a good hot meal, plug him into Sesame Street, enter him in the Special Olympics, fix him up with a mate, and tell him how much we love him? Surely such treatment would result not only in a better Creature but in a happier ending for everyone—especially the innocent victims. So, at least, runs the liberal consensus, in which I myself deeply believe. But it does not have much to do with the novel that Mary Shelley wrote. For *Frankenstein* does not let its readers feel good. It presents them with genuine, insoluble problems, not with any easy way out. And the modern critical consensus, however symptomatic of the way we think in the '90s, seems to me fundamentally misguided—simplistic and often obtuse.

How then should one read the novel? I do not pretend to have discovered any original reading, let alone the right moral. But I do think that one might take more care to look at all the evidence, not only whatever confirms one's own perspective. Such evidence includes the responses of readers before they have been corrected by right-minded critics. For here too is a consensus—though not the same we have seen. Most readers are pulled in two directions at once. When I ask my students whether the Creature is good or evil, they too are divided, not only as a group but individually; that is, almost everyone can be induced to switch sides. They feel the same ambivalence about Frankenstein, who fills the role of hero or villain with equal flair. In the age of poststructuralism, one might expect sophisticated critics to find more aporias than ordinary readers do. The reverse seems to be the case with this novel. In a good-hearted essay called "Aporia and Radical Empathy: *Frankenstein* (Re)Trains the Reader," Syndy M. Conger argues that students come to feel a radical empathy for the social outcast, so that when Victor, about to bring a mate for the Creature to life, looks through the casement to see the "dæmon," whose "ghastly grin" expresses "the utmost extent of malice and treachery," students are standing "next to the Creature on the outside of the window looking in." Perhaps that is true for her students. It is certainly not true for mine (or those of Lowe-Evans), who almost unanimously vote in support of Victor's decision to destroy his work-in-progress. At best, those sympathetic to the Creature find themselves standing on *both* sides of the window. The critic or teacher may hope to resolve the aporia or blockage of empathy by choosing one favored perspective. Ordinary readers do not. They accept frustration, or keep on changing their minds.

This seems to me very wise. For despite the modern consensus, *Frankenstein* does not admit a resolution. The basic, defining questions it raises in the mind of a reader—is Victor an idealistic hero or a destructive egotist? is the Creature a natural man or an unnatural monster? what moral are we to draw from this strange story?—

never receive a satisfactory answer or, rather, receive strong answers that directly contradict one another. This impasse is not the product of any particular critical school. It is the very heart of the novel. Indeed, without it there would be no *Frankenstein* at all. Perhaps a novel that taught students to love the Other would be more instructive, or at least more acceptable to modern tastes. But Mary Shelley's novel teaches something else: that love of the Other and fear of the Other, however logically incompatible, can be equally well motivated; and that idealism can be selfish and destructive as well as altruistic and creative. The troubling thoughts these contradictions raise account for the troubling power of the book itself. Nor is such trouble uninstructive. Whether or not one subscribes to F. Scott Fitzgerald's observation that "the test of a first-rate intelligence is the ability to hold two opposed ideas in the mind at the same time, and still retain the ability to function," some first-rate fiction does offer that test. *Frankenstein* teaches its readers to live with uncertainty, in a world where moral absolutes—even the ones we cling to—may cancel each other out. I do not think that American students should be encouraged to ignore that lesson.

If I am right about *Frankenstein*, however, how have so many intelligent critics happened to be wrong—wrong by consensus? Part of the answer surely has to do with the prevalent critical assumptions of our time, especially our collective identification with victims. This is a complicated subject, and I do not want to trivialize it. But in an age when a surprising number of students feel sorry not for Beowulf but for the dragon that kills him—a monster that was only doing its duty, defending the gold-hoard—it seems far less surprising that an outcast and lonely humanoid Creature should attract so many sympathizers to pity his ill-treatment and excuse his crimes. The popularity of that response accounts, in all probability, for the recent canonization of the novel. Few classic works offer more insight into the psychology of the oppressed and injured. By contrast, heroes like Victor have every advantage and cannot be forgiven. Victor and victim—every decent person knows which to choose.

Yet another reason for oversimplified readings of *Frankenstein* may be some reductive presuppositions about the nature of Romanticism. Whether in new literary histories or in courses on Romantic literature, Mary Shelley's novel functions as a useful counterstatement, exposing the dangers of individualism and an over-active imagination. Romantic titanism or Prometheanism here takes a fall, tripped up by a writer—often, in this context, the token woman or honorary Other—who perceives the exaltation of desire as a species of masculine arrogance, and recommends instead the "tranquillity" of "domestic affections." There is surely some truth to this view. But what many critics define as an attack on the assumptions

of Romanticism might equally be defined as the Romantic mainstream. For the writers of the time were far from single-minded.
The modern obsession with finding the essence of Romanticism, its
revolutionary difference from everything that went before, has
tended to collapse some living arguments into a homogeneous
monologue, in which all the major writers jumble ideas together.
Yet many of the most interesting thinkers did not agree with anyone, not even with themselves. Indeed, one way of characterizing
the age would emphasize its internal divisions or self-contradictions,
not only from writer to writer but within individual minds. Hence
many Romantic works seem at odds with themselves, admitting
opposing morals or even cognitive breakdown. In this respect, the
double bind in which *Frankenstein* places its readers might be
viewed not as exceptional but as absolutely typical of its period.

My evidence for this proposition will consist of a look at a single
source for Mary Shelley's novel. Such reliance on one source entails a
risk of the same oversimplification of which I have accused others, as
well as an old-fashioned embrace of the principle that one work can
be a unique influence on another, rather than part of the endless web
of intertextuality. If ever a work was overdetermined—psychologically
and historically bombarded with multiple influences—that work is
Frankenstein. Nevertheless, one source stands out, for its impact on
Mary Shelley's sense of the age in which she lived as well as on her
writing. My witnesses to its importance include not only Shelley
herself but her father, mother, and husband. The work is Rousseau's
Émile. William Godwin testified that reading it changed his life.
Mary Wollstonecraft spent much of *A Vindication of the Rights of
Woman* arguing against it, or rather against its views on the education of women, a life-and-death matter for her precisely because she
loves Rousseau's spirit and considers him *the* authority on education. Percy Shelley, when he undertook to educate his bright but
untutored lover, began by reading *Émile* with her; Rousseau, after
all, was the expert not only on education but on the triumph of life.
During the composition of *Frankenstein,* the Shelleys read, along
with *Émile,* another book about it, and later, when she worked on
the Creature's story, Mary went back to *Émile* again. Twenty years
on, in the life of Rousseau she wrote for Lardner's *Cyclopedia* (1839),
she made clear why she thought the book the greatest of one of the
world's great authors: "He shows the true end of education; and he
first explained how children ought to be treated like younger men,
not as slaves or automata"—or monsters, one might add. Without
knowing such truths, a person could hardly be educated. Nor could
contemporary readers have missed the influence of Rousseau on
Mary Shelley.

Indeed, it is not much of an exaggeration to say that almost everything a reader needs to know about the climate of ideas in *Frankenstein*, as well as its internal tensions, can be found on the first page of *Émile*. Since that page is no longer well known, even among educated people, it had better be quoted in full.

Everything is good as it leaves the hands of the Author of things; everything degenerates in the hands of man. He forces one soil to nourish the products of another. He mixes and confuses the climates, the elements, the seasons. He mutilates his dog, his horse, his slave. He turns everything upside down; he disfigures everything; he loves deformity, monsters. He wants nothing as nature made it, not even man; for him, man must be trained like a school horse; man must be fashioned in keeping with his fancy like a tree in his garden.

Were he not to do this, however, everything would go even worse, and our species does not admit of being formed halfway. In the present state of things a man abandoned to himself in the midst of other men from birth would be the most disfigured of all. Prejudices, authority, necessity, example, all the social institutions in which we find ourselves submerged would stifle nature in him and put nothing in its place. Nature there would be like a shrub that chance had caused to be born in the middle of a path and that the passers-by soon cause to perish by bumping into it from all sides and bending it in every direction.

In these two paragraphs, Rousseau has gone to the essence both of Victor Frankenstein, the naturally good human being whose compulsion to improve on nature drives him to violate it with a deformed and monstrous rival creation, and of the outcast creature or monster, abandoned to himself at birth and warped like a shrub in the road. *Émile* already adumbrates the two most powerful imaginative feats of Mary Shelley's novel: the hero's crazed longing to surpass his species, and the monster's pathetic account of his frustrated self-education.

At the same time, however, Rousseau has raised a dilemma or contradiction that all his life of writing would not be long enough to solve. If everything nature makes is good, and nature makes man, how does man come to be so unnatural, to love deformity, to make everything bad? The answer, of course, is society, whose institutions stifle nature and disfigure the humanity formed by the Author of things. Nature creates, and civilization deforms. Rousseau has often been accused of stopping his analysis at this point, with a noble savage opposed to a degenerate product of European vice. But in truth he begins there. As a host of modern scholars have insisted, he takes the current, corrupted state of culture as a given, against which the simplicity of a life according to nature is posed not as a nostalgic yearning for a vanished ideal but as a goal whose pursuit would enable people to construct institutions more in harmony with the true interests of human beings. Hence education, exemplified by Émile, must start by understanding what children are, not by dumping loads of learned lumber on their unreceptive heads; and the point of subordinating book knowledge to a fostering of the senses is not to regress to primitivism but to prepare a healthy citizen for the challenges of the modern world. What nature creates, and civilization deforms, a renewed attention to nature can restore.

In this respect, Rousseau's work in general, and *Émile* in particular, ought to be viewed not as philosophy, history, or social science but as a deliberate thought experiment, asking what consequences would follow if society were in fact to be grounded on human nature. A similar thought experiment seems to inspire Mary Shelley's novel. With wrenching literal-mindedness, *Frankenstein* tests each of Rousseau's first principles by fleshing them out and turning them into a story. Mixing and confusing elements, a man makes a monster. Abandoned at birth, a creature is bent out of shape by the prejudices of passers-by. The second page of *Émile* provides another idea to be tested: "If man were born big and strong, his size and strength would be useless to him until he had learned to make use of them. They would be detrimental to him in that they would keep others from thinking of aiding him." Shelley's creature proves the point. Much of the unnaturalness and improbability of the novel responds to the unlikelihood of the hypotheses it checks out: a man fashions a man according to his fancy; a newborn is abandoned in the road; a man is born big and strong. And later in *Émile*, at the point when Rousseau most clearly declares his own faith in the designs of nature, a scornful note looks at another preposterous experiment, the attempt of chemists to hatch life in a test tube. "Would anyone believe, if he did not have the proof, that human foolishness could have been brought to this point? Amatus Lusitanus affirmed that he had seen a little man an inch long, closed up in a bottle, whom Julius Camillus, like another Prometheus, had made by the science of alchemy. Paracelsus, *De natura rerum*, teaches the way to produce these little men and maintains that the pygmies, the fauns, the satyrs, and the nymphs were engendered by chemistry." Here Mary Shelley might have found all the pseudo-science she needed for her experiment in fiction. The new Prometheus, Paracelsus and the alchemists, the manufacture of men: each element would be stirred into the rich stew from which *Frankenstein* is extracted.

Nor does this list begin to exhaust the influence of *Émile*. As more than one critic has noted, the central thought experiment of Mary Shelley's novel tests the principles—Rousseau's principles—of education. Shelley herself was obsessed by the need to repair her own lack of instruction. Though both her parents were famous educational theorists, her mother died after giving birth to Mary Wollstonecraft Godwin, and her father turned away. "The poor children! I am myself totally unfitted to educate them. The skepticism which perhaps sometimes leads me right in matters of speculation, is torment to me when I would attempt to direct the infant mind." He did not direct Mary Godwin's. Shunted away to Scotland, often lonely, she was given the task of educating herself by reading; and certainly she did read. Yet accounts of her romance with Shelley are remarkable for their focus on his training and directing of her mind. A tutor at last! Her journal for those years consists mostly of lists of books, the Shelley family curriculum. And after he died, when she found strength to pick up her journal again, she resolved to stay the course: "above all I must acquire that knowledge & drink at those fountains of wisdom & virtue from which he quenched his thirst. . . . I am beginning seriously to educate myself."

Perhaps Rousseau could help. Each of the three narrators of *Frankenstein* represents a general problem of education as well as a specific aspect of Mary Shelley's background; and in each case the way that the novel frames the problem owes something to Rousseau. Walton's first letter identifies his situation with his creator's: "My education was neglected, yet I was passionately fond of reading." His second letter deplores the "evil to me that I am self-educated," for despite his wide reading (which as Rousseau would have predicted has only made a dreamer) he is "in reality more illiterate than many schoolboys of fifteen," most of all because he lacks a friend—like Émile's tutor or Percy Shelley—who would have "affection enough for me to endeavour to regulate my mind." For good or ill he soon meets such a friend; and Victor Frankenstein's story will complete Walton's education.

Victor's version of his own education is still more complex. To some extent the decisive turn or catastrophe of the novel occurs very early, not in any spectacular hazard of life and death but in the cursory glance that the elder Frankenstein casts at the volume of Cornelius Agrippa his son holds out to him. All misfortunes stem from that moment. If only, Victor says, his father had taken pains to explain the powers and practical uses of modern science, which had exploded Agrippa, he would have thrown the volume aside. "It is even possible, that the train of my ideas would never have received the fatal impulse that led to my ruin." The scene as a whole is almost a parody of several similar moments in *Émile*, when the all-wise tutor finds just the right strategy to avert some threat to his pupil's mental health. But this time the father fails; "It is sad trash!" he tells his son, without taking account of a young man's state of mind.

William Godwin could not have been more inattentive. In the first edition of the novel, Mary Shelley spells out her point, and Rousseau's, with didactic directness: "I cannot help remarking here the many opportunities instructors possess of directing the attention of their pupils to useful knowledge, which they utterly neglect." The doom of the Frankensteins follows that fault in educational theory. Despite Victor's many gifts and privileges, an arbitrary method of teaching has made him hunger for useless knowledge that poisons his soul.

The Creature, by contrast, does better. Many critics have praised his account of his first inchoate sensations and gradual dawn into consciousness as the best thing in the book, and have associated it with Locke's teachings on human understanding as well as on education. Here is the ultimate autodidact, inscribing the most basic marks of humanity on his tabula rasa and acquiring, through the chink that allows him to spy on a poor but noble family, not only language but proper republican sentiments. Shelley designs the passage quite explicitly as an experiment in learning; she plants a shrub in the road, and watches what happens to it. But Locke would not have comprehended the result. Put simply, the Creature is just too good; put somewhat less simply, he is just too Rousseauesque. As other critics have noticed, he seems an unfallen, innocent creature, who feels love and sympathy as readily as hunger and pain. In his own eyes, at least, he develops as if nature, not man, had formed him, and only rejection by society leaves him deformed. Indeed, nature has also educated him. Everything good in him comes from her, everything evil comes from his secondary education in the hostility and prejudice he meets at the hands of men. Rousseau had copyrighted the blueprint.

Yet once again the blueprint seems too simple. For the relatively cut-and-dried didactic formulas of *Frankenstein* do not do justice to the double-mindedness it induces in a reader. Part of the complication stems from the multiple narrators: the reader sees Victor not only through his own eyes but through Walton's and the Creature's, and the Creature's protestations of innocence are reflected through a medium that includes his own creator's repulsion and horror at the murderous fiend he has brought into being. But another source of ambivalence comes from an unresolved enigma in Rousseau's and Mary Shelley's own thought. I have already referred to one familiar way of posing the question: if everything nature makes is good, and nature makes man, why is man bad? But that old riddle is enclosed within the larger question that Rousseau kept asking, with increasing anguish, about everything he saw, whether politics, education, love, or his own relations with other people: *what has gone wrong?* No matter how often he supplied an answer, things kept going wrong. When Percy Shelley, in his great last poem [*The Triumph of*

Life], perceives a ghastly image at the heart of things and asks "'And what is this? / Whose shape is that within the car? and why'— / I would have added—'is all here amiss?'" it is no accident that "the grim Feature" who answers "Life" turns out to be Rousseau, nor that after several hundred lines of explanation by that Feature the question "Then, what is Life?" is still no nearer to a resolution. Rousseau may be the expert on "what is Life?" but his final answer usually comes round to a version of "why is all here amiss?" *Frankenstein* ends on the same hanging note. It shows us that everything has gone wrong, and leaves us to search for reasons.

Rousseau's own life embodied that enigma, for himself as well as for most Romantic readers. Through the three major and many minor autobiographical works that consumed his last fifteen years, he kept asking what had gone wrong. Eventually such questions about his life became a shorthand or substitute for his significance as a thinker. Whether negatively, as in Burke's enormously influential portrait of Rousseau as a monster of vanity, or positively, as in Mary Wollstonecraft's, Lord Byron's, and Percy Shelley's sympathetic efforts to define the excess of virtue that had cost Rousseau so dearly, the discussion of what went wrong with his life emerged as a standard Romantic set piece or *topos*. But the full-length masterpiece of the genre remains his second major adventure in autobiography, the *Dialogues*, or *Rousseau juge de Jean-Jacques* (which I prefer to translate *Rousseau Judges Jean-Jacques*). In this extremely overwrought, brilliant, and crazy work, two characters—"Rousseau" and "Le François" (The Frenchman, or Frank)—comb over the infamous author "J.J.," initially condemned without a reading but at last exonerated as the victim of a plot. To begin with, Frank *knows* that J.J. is a monster, whose professions of innocence only compound his crimes. At the end, it is clear that the real monster is society, envisaged as a vast conspiracy against someone whose only fault is being true to nature. Yet the enigma lingers. Rousseau's ability to split himself into three different personalities vouches for the "objectivity" of the argument; he judges his actions from outside. But the same split personality suggests a lack of harmony, or even candor, in the author's own nature. In this respect the diagnosis of what went wrong goes still more wrong, sophisticating the claim of simple truth. The more the author clears his name, the deeper he plunges into the murk, until such questions as what is a name? what is a self? and to whom or what do that name and self belong? take over the script. As some modern admirers have suggested, Rousseau can be seen as a uniquely self-deconstructing author. But that is another way of saying that something always goes wrong.

It would be easy to read *Frankenstein* as an allegory of what went wrong with Rousseau, or more precisely of the Rousseau enigma.

Mary Shelley herself avowed that the Genevan setting where and about which she wrote was permeated by reminiscences of the *Confessions* and *La Nouvelle Héloïse*, and Victor's upbringing, amid "the majestic and wondrous scenes which surrounded our Swiss home," inevitably recalls the Citizen of Geneva. The sudden light that breaks on him when he discovers the secret of life, so that "I became dizzy with the immensity of the prospect," echoes the sudden light that broke over Rousseau on the road from Vincennes in 1749, projecting his whole life's work from his insight into the corruption of nature by civilization; and in both cases the wonder that followed that moment, promising benefits for all humanity, would lead first to obsessive, claustrophobic work and finally to bitter disenchantment. Idealism destroys content; both heroes end as paranoids, in brutal isolation. And another secret haunts them. No act of Rousseau's life had blackened his character more than his abandonment of his children, who were deposited at the door of the Foundling Hospital. To his enemies, such refusal to take responsibility proved the hypocrisy of all his fine professions. When Victor Frankenstein abandons his Creature, therefore, he marks himself as truly Rousseau's disciple if not his accomplice. The appearance of virtue masks a sin passed down to later generations. Moreover, the well-known theme of the double in *Frankenstein*, in which the Creature seems to represent the dark or murderous side of his namby-pamby creator, summons up the split personality we have already marked in Rousseau, who never stops asking how such a virtuous person can be so universally regarded as a monster. Nor is that reputation all that the Creature and Rousseau have in common. They also share a sense of themselves as Adam, not only as innocent but as unique—one of a kind. The boast that opens the *Confessions*—"I am made unlike any one I have ever met; I will even venture to say that I am like no one in the whole world"—applies quite literally to the Creature. That is his tragedy. And the way that all humanity eventually freezes him out repeats the sublime divorce from society that Rousseau accepted as his fate, forever defining the Romantic hero.

Yet I do not want to spin out that allegory. What matters is not the names and history we attach to the story but the tension that lives within it. Readers who have never read Rousseau, and scarcely know who he was, nevertheless still recognize the duality of *Frankenstein* and feel the power of its moral irresolution. Why is all here amiss? is Mary Shelley's question too. Much as I might like to, I cannot answer that question and tell you what has gone wrong with life, and neither can the novel. But the example of Rousseau can help us to examine some assumptions that are packed into the question. Perhaps what goes wrong in *Frankenstein* has already begun before it starts, in the conditions and terms that make its conception possible.

Perhaps the influence of Rousseau has penetrated so deeply that it seems identical with what Percy Shelley's Preface to the novel calls "the truth of the elementary principles of human nature." In that case, the trouble certainly starts early. One view of what went wrong with Rousseau might be that he never stopped paying for his marvelous opening gestures: "Man is born free, and is everywhere in chains," or "Everything is good as it leaves the hands of the Author of things; everything degenerates in the hands of man." The rhetorical power of such sentences changed the course of history. On the other hand, the self-evident truth that each announces at once—"Man is born free," "Everything is good"—pitches the whole argument on a slippery slope. Who says that man is born free, that everything nature makes is good? Rousseau, while he wears the spectacles of Dr. Pangloss.[1] But as soon as the phrase has slipped out, its absurdity, in relation to what our world is actually like, begins driving him to distraction, or riveting his gaze on the chains and degeneration that bind him. Nor will he give up those phrases; indeed, he would rather sacrifice the world. And so he does. In Jean Starobinski's terms, freedom and natural goodness constitute the pure state of a transparency that inevitably crashes against, if it does not create, an impenetrable obstruction. In deconstructive terms, such words always already inscribe the supplement that will take their place. Just as Rousseau's myth of idyllic childhood ensured that the rest of his life would be one long falling away, so his opening sentences preserve the remnants of an outmoded theology—the doctrine of free will, the argument from design—while sponsoring a universal mourning for their loss. Dozens of later Romantic writers borrowed those earthshaking phrases as well as the aftershock that was bound to follow. To many writers, in fact, the sequence seemed like second nature.

The goodness of nature serves *Frankenstein* in a similar way: as an unchallenged premise that eventually collapses into its opposite. Consider the scenery. Despite the travelogues that Mary Shelley composed during her European journey, the obligatory ecstasies amidst the sublimities of mountains, water, and skies, she does not seem to have been comfortable with the outdoors. Both Shelleys had been disturbed by their recent trip to Mont Blanc, for instance, he because it forced him to consider the possibility that some power outside his own mind existed and might occasionally dump avalanches on even a skeptical head, and she because of the "dreadful desolation." The same desolation presides over much of the novel, chilling not only the arctic descriptions of the beginning and end but the crucial scenes in the "blank and dreary" north of Scotland

1. In Voltaire's *Candide* (1759).

where Mary Godwin herself had grown up—a better place for romantic fantasies than for living. Against this background, the occasional picturesque raptures of the novel ring hollow. Does Mary Shelley believe that the Author of things has created a world in which human beings are at home? The evidence of *Frankenstein* seems at best ambiguous.

The novelist's most extended descriptive passage, as it happens, supplants the love of nature with an unmistakable irony. As Victor Frankenstein tries to recuperate from the deaths of William and Justine, "the first hapless victims to my unhallowed arts," he travels to Chamounix and walks on the sea of ice, where the "wondrous and stupendous scene" of Mont Blanc almost restores him. "My heart, which was before sorrowful, now swelled with something like joy; I exclaimed—'Wandering spirits, if indeed ye wander, and do not rest in your narrow beds, allow me this faint happiness, or take me, as your companion, away from the joys of life.'" As he says this, a figure larger than a man's bounds over the ice, "advancing towards me with superhuman speed." Is it a bird? Is it a plane? Oh "sight tremendous and abhorred!" It is, of course, "the wretch whom I had created." But the identification of the Creature with the spirit of the mountain, as well as the Creature's mastery of a landscape where mere human beings cannot survive, underlines the futility of trying to draw comfort or companionship from something as cold and indifferent as nature. The only response to Victor's apostrophe or prayer will be the return of his worst nightmare. Indeed, the scene as a whole might be said to recreate his original mistake: assuming that when he attains the object of his desire he will be able to live with it. The secret hiding place of nature—"Remote, serene, and inaccessible"—has nothing to do with the hopes and needs of people. Perhaps "everything is good" in nature, as an ice field or volcano might be good of its kind; but goodness like theirs is made not for love but for death.

The Creature is also quite good of his kind. In strength, agility, and even brains, in every respect except beauty (which, as we know, is in the eyes of the beholder, or the species) he surpasses humankind, including his creator. Does everything really degenerate, then, in the hands of man? The novel seems of two minds on this question. It plays with fears of the unnatural or supernatural, with evil unleashed through an amoral and irresponsible ambition. Yet it also insists on the human or superhuman sensibility of the Creature, as if Frankenstein's workmanship, on the eighth day of creation, went beyond God's. Even the theme of hubris, therefore, might be subject to challenge. Perhaps the hands of man *can* better nature. In that case, Frankenstein's fault was not his ambition but his failure to look on his work and find it good; Nietzsche deposes Rousseau. The irresolution of the novel on this key issue reaches an almost comic impasse with the moral preached by Frankenstein's last words.

"Farewell, Walton! Seek happiness in tranquillity, and avoid ambition, even if it be only the apparently innocent one of distinguishing yourself in science and discoveries. Yet why do I say this? I have myself been blasted in these hopes, yet another may succeed." Right at the point of renouncing his sins, the hero takes it back. To followers of the modern consensus on *Frankenstein*, these last words complete his damnation; *still* he misleads his friend. Yet most readers will grant Mary Shelley the courage of her lack of convictions. Should Walton give up his dreams? Should nature be left alone? Is ambition the source of evil? The novel firmly answers Yes and No.

Indeed, the capacity for arguing both sides of a question, or for providing material to undermine its own first premises, accounts for much of the fascination—as well as the terror—of *Frankenstein*. Moralists may find its doublemindedness weak, but readers find it genuinely chilling. Whom or what can we trust? The novel offers no reassurance. Nature can be the source of death as well as life. Good people do evil, perhaps because of flaws in character but perhaps because of an excess built into their virtues. The sympathy we give to the outcast runs up against his horrible crimes. And readers themselves are everywhere implicated. Precisely to the extent that we identify with Victor's aspirations or with the Creature's belief in his own good will, we learn not to trust ourselves. In the long run everything goes wrong. Faced by so much uncertainty, a reader might well be tempted to accuse Mary Shelley of tergiversation or, more positively, of allowing her instincts as a novelist to triumph over her conscious didactic principles. If this is true, however, it cannot be the whole truth. Too many of her contemporaries shared her ability to see both sides of a question for us to ascribe it to her alone. The age that recast Faust as a lover, the age that idolized Byron and Prometheus and Satan and Heathcliff, was used to entertaining contradictory feelings about its heroes. In this respect also, Romanticism follows the track of Rousseau.

One use of defining the age that way might be to stress the continuities as well as complications in the eighteenth- and nineteenth-century debates about nature, society, and humankind. To put this more particularly: no lasting consensus has ever developed about Rousseau. His place in the canon depends on the passions that form around his contradictions, not on any stable set of beliefs. That seems to me a good basis for canonization. Rousseau does not make us feel good; he passes on his neuroses, and forces his readers, right up to the present, to see that the questions he raises have not been resolved. The endurance of *Frankenstein* draws, I think, on the same open secret, the secret that can never be unscrambled. Fears last longest in the dark. Whether or not my reading has proved persuasive, it ought not to lead to any new consensus, for my moral, like that of the novel, has been that the question of what goes right, as well as what has gone wrong, cannot be explained away. I hope that you will not agree with me too much.

Works Cited

Conger, Syndy M. "Aporia and Radical Empathy: *Frankenstein* (Re)Trains the Reader." *Approaches to Teaching Shelley's* Frankenstein. Ed. Stephen C. Behrendt. New York: Modern Language Association, 1990. 60–66.

Lowe-Evans, Mary. "Reading with a 'Nicer Eye': Responding to *Frankenstein.*" *Case Studies In Contemporary Criticism: Mary Shelley: Frankenstein.* Ed. Johanna M. Smith. Boston: Bedford Books, 1992. 215–29.

Mellor, Anne K. "Choosing a Text of *Frankenstein* to Teach." *Approaches to Teaching Shelley's* Frankenstein. 31–37.

———. "*Frankenstein* and the Sublime." Ibid. 99–104.

Moers, Ellen. "Female Gothic." *Literary Women.* Garden City: Doubleday, 1976.

Rousseau, Jean-Jacques. *Émile, or On Education.* Tr. Allan Bloom. New York: Basic Books, 1979.

———. *Rousseau, Judge of Jean-Jacques: Dialogues.* Ed. Roger D. Masters and Christopher Kelly. Hanover: UP of New England, 1990.

Shelley, Mary. *Frankenstein; or, The Modern Prometheus (the 1818 Text).* Ed. James Rieger. Indianapolis: Bobbs-Merrill, 1974.

———. *Frankenstein or The Modern Prometheus.* Ed. M. K. Joseph. Oxford: Oxford UP, 1971.

———. *The Journals of Mary Shelley.* Ed. Paula R. Feldman and Diana Scott-Kilvert. Baltimore: Johns Hopkins UP, 1987.

GARRETT STEWART

In the Absence of Audience: Of Reading and Dread in Mary Shelley[†]

What do the least gothic novel ever written, *Persuasion*, and the most famous gothic novel ever written, *Frankenstein*, have in common? If nothing of substance, then the question turns us to form. Yet since there is no obvious structural resemblance, either, between Austen's omniscience and Shelley's dramatized frame tale, the ques-

† From *Dear Reader: The Conscripted Audience in Nineteenth-Century British Fiction* (Baltimore: Johns Hopkins UP, 1996), 114–22. © 1996 The Johns Hopkins University Press. Reprinted with permission of The Johns Hopkins University Press.

tion pays off only if it gets us to some deeper notion of narrative formation—or, more particularly, to the structure of reading fashioned by such formal determinants.

Well before the transitional pre-Victorian figure of Mary Shelley, with her wholehearted renewal of gothic materials, what Austen's comic realism has already managed to do is to draw off from the gothics flourishing in her day a formula that subtends their narrative peculiarities: a psychodynamic of novelistic reading per se which the lurid excess of the gothics was bound to maximize. Intensified in that melodramatic mode is the rhythm of contemplative (often moralizing) calm after narrative storm. In this way late-eighteenth-century gothic plotting tends to rehearse on its way toward closure the evolutionary outmoding of its very genre: the metamorphosis from sensation to sensibility. This takes place even as the latter mode retains—in Austen, for instance, and in *Persuasion* as much as in *Northanger Abbey*—something of the same pronounced emotional curvative which, though perfected in the gothics, came to seem inherent in the very temporality of narrative fiction.

Mary Shelley, of course, taps the gothic conventions in a more direct manner, while at the same time returning to the epistolary roots of Austenian realism for a full-blown but still curiously disembodied version of that "whomsoever it may concern" structure manifested by the respectively psychological and apocalyptic ironies of framing in *Frankenstein* and *The Last Man*. In the process, Shelley's stress is laid on credibility and dissemination as much as on rhetorical heightening and the necessities of resolution. The gothic atmospheres and mechanisms of the literary vernacular emerge *within* the plot of *Frankenstein*, for instance, as they have come to it: mediated and transmitted many times over, processed and dispensed, in a word *received*. Where Austen inherits and reworks the narrativity of late-eighteenth-century gothic plotting, its arcs of suspense, tribulation, subsidence, and evaluative retrospect, Shelley's revisionary emphasis falls more on its discourse in circulation: its overwrought paths of access between narrators and narratees. In Shelley as much as in Austen, therefore, you are not just implicated but schooled as coparticipant in that work of plotting which takes its bearings from the present modulation, rather than the mere promise, of response.

To linger even momentarily over the structural contrast between these two early nineteenth-century writers is to grasp in short order the breadth of effect opened up within the force field of conscription between, at one pole, the work of submerged interpolation in Austen (the marginalized "dear reader") and, at the other, the frame-ups of extrapolation in Shelley (the circumferential zones of reception). If Austen's gothic flirtations in *Northanger Abbey* enlist a melodramatic format which, in loose alliance with the shape of provincial romance, helped further codify for the history of fiction the reciprocal demands of anticipation and closure, Shelley's unabashed gothic plotting is a transgressive or deviant storytelling that pitches to crisis the narrative contract itself, psychologizing (under far more extreme narrative circumstances than in Austen) the very motives for the dispensing and receiving of stories. Furthermore, where Austen in *Northanger Abbey* checks the excesses of the gothic within the sphere of its acknowledged and harmless appeal, Shelley in *Frankenstein* chronicles the aftermath of the gothic's more dangerous exile from the mind's regimen. She does so through the withholding of supernatural narrative affect altogether from her hero, thereby constructing a mentality doomed by its very difference from the reader's own. As much as Austen's texts, therefore, Shelley's too are embroiled in the psychosocial protocols of literary acculturation. So that, once again, the analysis of narrative structures confronts most directly the workings of culture, and fiction's place in it, by staying alert to the structuration of the reading agency not only laid out by story but replayed by reading.

Yet such an agency, I stress again, is by no means the solid bourgeois citizen, the stabilized monolithic presence, of recent reductive accounts—but instead the very absenting of subjectivity both demanded and dramatized by the fictional text. Dependent as it is on your surrender to the deputized agents of narrative identification, textual transmission must evacuate consciousness before invading (and replacing) it. In this sense, Shelley's two major frame tales, *Frankenstein* (1818) and *The Last Man* (1826), undergo their own textuality, enact their own becoming-text, by invoking an attention whose personification they finally obliterate. They thereby subsume the scenario of reception under that aspect of reading which they can conscript but, beyond a certain point, never hope to specify. Everything about storytelling and transcription in them, everything about textual processing, everything about the transmissive function of language, everything, in short, about their own narrative impulse and textual premise comes forward toward that moment they attempt to circumscribe while leaving blank: the moment, plausible in one, impossible in the other, of their own reading. For one is a gothic thriller whose feverish stenographer lives on, and as if only, to tell of what he has heard and seen; the other a tour de force of dystopian futurism whose last author, sole survivor of a universal plague, has no conceivable readers left.

Mary Shelley's two most interesting novels serve therefore, in a revealing symmetry, to test the phenomenological bounds of fictional address as a function not only of textual circulation but of linguistic and cultural, even racial, continuance. What the nineteenth-century fiction industry takes for granted—namely, the normal routes of reception—Shelley instead takes to a denaturalizing limit. The very transmission of human consciousness in language is at stake in the rhetoric of her narratives. She wrote two novels, that is, in which the situation of the reader, even though in different ways emptied out of the text, is necessary to complete the thematic of storytelling within that text: a reader whose attention alone fulfills the communicative and confessional impulses of the characters themselves. Equally in *Frankenstein* and *The Last Man*, the story will out only if the reader's enacted absence is overridden—or underwritten—by textual activation, in short by reading.

In *Frankenstein*, the fated Creature, denied progeny, is able to leave behind no more than a story, which he tells to and through Victor Frankenstein, also the dying last of his family line, who in turn unfolds his version of the story to a ship's captain named Walton, who then transcribes it in a journal appended to letters that are, though read (at least by us), never definitively received by the sister back in England to whom they are addressed. Where narrative thus operates in *Frankenstein*, for Victor and his Creature alike, as an ultimately posthumous transmission to an always deferred present from a fatal past, operates in other words as a surrogate posterity, in *The Last Man* there is no one left alive to inherit the story of worldwide annihilation. It is a story that comes to us not by way of mystical vision but by way of a telepathically transcribed document from the future discovered by the Shelleys in the cave of the Cumaean Sybil. Narrative becomes the sole relic of the human race: an epic in the wake of culture itself. It is not read posthumously by those who outlive its events, for their number is none, but read proleptically by those (any of us) whom its very writing will (already) have outlasted. In *Frankenstein*, then, the reader receives the narrative of deviant creation as the event's only legacy. In *The Last Man*, the reader receives the text of racial extirpation as that eventuality's only solace, before rather than after the fact. In neither case, however, is the reader actually there to do so. Taken together as experiments in reading, these two texts jointly explore—by exaggerating from opposite directions—a phenomenological intuition one might phrase as follows: a sense that your most engaged reading takes place in your own absence, or in other words takes your place.

"With What Interest and Sympathy I Shall Read!"

No reader can miss the fact that Mary Shelley's *Frankenstein* is a novel preoccupied with storytelling and transcription, shaping itself by subsidiary narratives of all sorts—journals and confessional accounts framed and redoubled by the narrative event of epistolary broadcast. That the novel, in structure even more than in episode, is as much about reading as about writing, about narrative consumption as about narrative production, is perhaps less obvious. And this is because reading is most pointedly thematized by what we might call its encompassing absence. The issue only grows clear by the end. Even with Victor's entire narrative retold, and the Creature's within it, by Walton to his sister, the completed story never arrives at a *narrated* destination. Its frame functions, instead, more as an open bracket. Certainly you don't "see" the posted documents being read. There is no presentation of them by the butler, no parlor of breathless perusal, in short no *mise en scène* of receipt. All you can be sure of is that the letters, enclosing Walton's journal of Victor's story, have somehow made it your way.

But they do so—as at one level who could doubt?—only as they fade from documentary to fictional status: the first letter realistically placed and dated, except for the "editorial" avoidance of the year ("St. Petersburg, Dec. 11th, 17–"), and then formally signed ("Your affectionate brother, R. Walton"); the second shifted toward the quasi-mystical ("Archangel"); the third merely dated, without site of origin, and mechanically initialed ("R.W."); the fourth, again without salutation or place of origin, dated in three stages (as if now by pure narrative chronology) and then yielding place to no closing signature. All that follows, twenty-four chapters later, is the eventual subsumption of epistolary narrator to novelistic character within the omniscient stage direction "Walton, in continuation." With more typographical cueing than in Austen, literary history is again telescoped by the local evocation of generic precursors. Like the Creature made rather than born, demonically cobbled together, the novelistic mode is pieced out before our eyes, born of epistolary directness, midwifed by a framing structure that remains vectored beyond plot's own closure. Walton disappears "in continuation," never to return in proper (or signatory) persona, but only to have his transcriptive role absorbed by the reading audience's own reactions. And just as there is no one there to sign off on the story, so there is no one seen to sign *for it*, as it were, in receipt. Mrs. Saville is nowhere to be found except in the address of the discourse, playing mere narratee in contrast to your role as reader. You therefore intercept the letters (the transcript of Frankenstein's extended monologue enclosed with the last of them) in her place, in place of the civilized reader "tutored and refined by books and retirement from the world" (letter 4:27).

Moreover, the chain of reception, and hence the psychology of reading, does not stop there. It doubles back on itself when even the scribe of Frankenstein's story wants part of the action at the receiving end: "This manuscript will doubtless afford you the greatest pleasure," Walton writes to his sister, "but to me, who know him [Victor] and hear it from his own lips—with what interest and sympathy shall I read it in some future day!" (4:29). In an ethos of internalized narrative energy, vicariousness goes deep.[1] As we began to see with Austen, reading becomes not just an extension of but a model for human experience, which Shelley's text seems to recognize as *vicarious at its source*. From the ranks of fictional characters, all of whom are narrated, emerge certain characters who not only live their lives so that they may become narratable, or in the absence of such life stories seek out the narratives of others to fill the void, but who await final engagement and understanding through the rerun of all such experience *as read*. With Dickens and the Brontës and Eliot still waiting in the wings of nineteenth-century narrative, here already is the emergent valence of the novel as Victorian cultural establishment. When, in the reading of *Frankenstein*, fiction structures desire in the form of its secondary processing *as story*, narrative has overstepped the bounds of art or commodity to become a prosthesis of social subjecthood.

Even to suspect as much is to question the newer methodological terrains of literary study, including the contested grounds of the proper disciplinary object itself: text versus context, as if the two were not structurally contiguous. Now is therefore a timely moment in these pages to italicize one corrective emphasis of this chapter—and of those to come. I want to insist that what a narrative artifact, as rhetorical construct, takes from the discourses of its culture—let us say in Shelley's case, for starters, the science-versus-poetry debate, evolutionary anxiety, gynophobia, class tensions, a dubious stance toward the romantic sublime, and so forth—is only half the picture, and very little of the story, if it is not correlated with what the narrative sends back into cultural circulation through the very form of its own discourse. This is to say that the critical reading of literature, precisely as an act of historical recovery, deserves the name only if it keeps its eye on rhetorical interplay as well as mimetic subtext, on fiction's "interface" with its reading subjects as well as on its image of their (other) social (because discursive) imbrications.

---

1. Here one might follow out a recent suggestion by Peter Brooks about narrative interaction. Having pursued Roland Barthes's notion of "contract narrative" with illuminating results in *Reading for the Plot* (New York: Knopf, 1984), Brooks expands further on the psychodynamic of such narrative exchanges in a chapter on *Frankenstein* in *Body Work: Objects of Desire in Modern Narrative* (Harvard UP, 1993), where the relation between Walton and Mrs. Saville is conceived on the "transferential" model: "As a 'subject supposed to know,' the listener is called upon to 'supplement' the story . . . , to articulate and even enact the meaning of the desire it expresses in ways that may be foreclosed to the speaker" (200). Though Brooks doesn't mention this, Mrs. Saville's structured silence as narrative recipient may contribute to the sense that she fills the role of therapeutic sounding board in this fable of vicarious interchange. Moreover, it is Walton's own anticipation of one day taking up the role of reader rather than narrator of the story which may imply his urge for an imaginative access otherwise "foreclosed" by his role as storyteller. Only by reading, perhaps, can he "articulate and even enact the meaning of the desire" he has begun by half confessing on his own part, half reporting on Victor's.

Reading, Revival, Reanimation

Read as literary construct, then, *Frankenstein* conflates two tradi-
tions of the British novel as Shelley has inherited them. First, it bor-
rows those evidentiary mechanisms of the eighteenth-century text
that were often attached as prefatory editorial footwork to prose fictions. Second, this device is crossbred in Shelley's novel with the
epistolary mode of writing-to-the-moment. In this way the "editor,"
taking on the role of empassioned "correspondent," melds the cor-
roborative with the affective dimension of textual force. The romantic transformation to which Shelley's inherited materials is submitted,
however, results at the structural level from the arrest of the epistolary circuit, on the one hand, and, on the other, from the avoidance
of its more overtly rhetorical derivative in the "dear reader" formula.
Straddling these models, the vocative phrase "My dear Sister" (letter
3:21) appears in only one letter—as if serving a strictly rhetorical
rather than epistolary function.

As such, this residuum of address is only part of a broad rhetorical
campaign whereby the extrapolative force of the novel, the managed
output of its fictional effect, is programmed in part through the
novel's literary-historical input, as detailed in a variety of prefatory
allusions having to do with the general literary topography of the
period as well as with certain specific source texts. Anticipating
how the "sentiments" of the novel may "affect the reader" (xiv), the
preface assures the audience that the story is bent on "avoiding the
enervating effects of the novels of the present day" (xiv). It cannot
be missed that the binary opposition thus insinuated offers as the
relevant counter to such fiction the surcharged and energizing
novel, a text revived and reviving—the novel, in a word, *reanimated.*
A fable emerges. Despite the moralizing condemnation of Victor's
overambitious trespass upon forbidden ground, he seeks what Shelley achieves: the vivification of an inert form. And like Shelley, no
matter how violent his deviant inventiveness, he can promise in
the end, as he does to Walton, an "apt moral" (letter 4:28) in reward.
The deliberate links throughout the text between Victor's laboratory
exertions and the labor of fictional invention on Shelley's part serve
to confirm this. They offer, by their supposed candor about the creative process, a check on the disingenuousness of this forcefully
cautionary, because scarcely enervating, tale. For it is a tale about
the allowable limits of what one is tempted to call regenerative pastiche, the very process that brought it about in the first place.

For all its avowed solicitude concerning the reader, though, there
is no structural room in *Frankenstein* for the direct solicitation of the
audience. One notes, by contrast, Mary Shelley's later short story,
"Transformations" (1830), a supernatural narrative of doubling and

physical malformation, pride and psychic transgression, very much in the mold of the 1818 novel. Without the distancing of the novel's frame, however, disallowing as it does all direct authorial address, the second paragraph of Shelley's story stalls upon its own reasons for being: "Why tell a tale of impious tempting of Providence, and soul-subduing humiliation? Why, answer me, ye who are wise in the secrets of human nature!"[2] Such an apostrophe, in the traditional combination of imperative and vocative, is the sort of interpolation ruled out by the dramaturgy (without commentary) of narration in *Frankenstein*. Instead, Shelley works a wholesale extrapolation of response displaced from the absent Mrs. Saville upon that individual reader who must proceed under the aegis of an *intended* but not necessarily achieved attention.

And the fable continues—as the story of a formative reading that blurs borders between plot and its preconditions in imaginative vulnerability. Just as textual reception awaits the narrative at or beyond its outer edge, so too, deep within the plot's chronological prehistory, can the will to reading be traced all the way back to the constitutive inclinations of narrative's desiring agents. "My education was neglected, yet I was passionately fond of reading." Thus Walton writes in the autobiographical mode (letter 1:16), yet giving anticipatory voice to the Creature's story as well. Eavesdropping later at the de Lacey cottage, the Creature will be initiated first into language, then into its cultural productions (Goethe, Plutarch, Milton), by his listening in on a quintessential family scene of hearthside reading aloud. In a more radical way than that in which the phrase is ordinarily taken, the Creature is *humanized by reading.* Yet this reading is placed in ironic juxtaposition to that undertaken by both his creators, Victor as well as Shelley. Victor's case is perhaps the clearest, by being the most extreme and complete. Whereas Mary Shelley, Walton, and the Creature each narrate as they have been programmed to do by their reading, indeed narrate an experience that would never have emerged in the same way but for their reading, it is Victor, spurred to creation by what he has (and hasn't) read, who is the only character to take charge explicitly of his own narration in an editorial role, as we are about to see, helping to guide its desired reading. In this, as in many other ways, he is of course very close to Mary Shelley as author and editor of her own published manuscript. The fecund monstrosities of her tale come to seem as terrible to her, so she would pretend, as Victor's brainchild does to him, a "hideous progeny" (xii) like his "hideous narration" (23:188) later.

2. Charles E. Robinson, ed., *Mary Shelley: Collected Tales and Stories* (Baltimore: Johns Hopkins UP, 1976), 121.

Such a figurative crossing between discourse and story, between textual and anatomical invention, is subsequently reversed when metaphors of verbal creativity are incorporated into the language of transgressive creation—rather than narrative itself figured as monstrosity. Not only does Victor accuse himself (by the phrasal doubling of hendiadys) of being the "miserable origin and author" (10:96) of the Creature, but he refuses to make the same mistake twice, to "compose a female" (18:143), as if it were to be an act, again, of authorship rather than laboratory magic. This link between black magic and aesthetic conjuration is further tightened by the manner in which the compositional will to invention and the labors of the laboratory are conflated in Victor's own mind near the end of his story to Walton. "Frankenstein discovered that I made notes concerning his history; he asked to see them and then himself corrected and augmented them in many places" (24:199), his editorial rigor devoted "principally" to the task of "giving the life and spirit to the conversations he held with his enemy" (24:199). Not content to have breathed life into a pastiche, a random assemblage, of body parts, Victor now tries to animate the prose that records it. His will to power persists, that is, across two levels of "compositional" energy. Finally, too, the language of aberration and deformity surfaces in his description of this editorial purpose: "'Since you have preserved my narration,' said he, 'I would not that a mutilated one should go down to posterity'" (24:199)—that "posterity" by which the created and printed text alone, not its homologous Creature, is bid to replicate itself. Narrative mutilation, biological malformation—these are the paired defaults of "authorship" in Shelley's novel, from a negotiation between which all audience response must be processed.

Thus is confirmed a running parallel between the genesis plot and the story of its own literary generation. Just as Victor sutures together the Creature, so does Shelley, assembling her creation *Frankenstein*, also assemble the man for whom it is named: a composite, as he is, of two figures from the German ghost stories that Shelley read aloud with Percy Shelley, Byron, and Polidori.[3] Along with the effects of conversation about Erasmus Darwin and his reputed experiments in spontaneous animation (x), these stories coalesce

3. The protagonist of the *History of the Inconstant Lover*, "when he thought to clasp the bride to whom he had pledged his vows, found himself in the arms of the pale ghost of her whom he had deserted" (viii–ix). Anticipating Victor's dream of his mother's corpse replacing his fiancée, Elizabeth, in his arms (5:57), this fictional prototype also captures the ambivalence of erotic desire and marital drive in Victor's whole story. Then there was "the tale of the sinful founder of his race"—the very periphrasis for paternity offering a proleptic hint—"whose miserable doom it was to bestow the kiss of death on all the younger sons of his fated house" (ix). Prefigured here is the negating effect of Frankenstein on all his "progeny," both the natural children he fails to have and that monstrous issue he seeks to eradicate.

in Shelley's unconscious, invade her dreams, and spawn the script of unholy creation that becomes, upon waking, her tale. Out of discrepant body parts, a humanoid shape; out of discrepant pieces, a newly articulated narrative, a narrative galvanized by the spark of creative inspiration: such is the offspring of writer and hero alike. Moreover, Shelley's dream (from the preface) of an artificial man, an artifice of life, stands to the novel as a whole—embryonically—as do Frankenstein's feverish conceptions to the confessional tale he ends up having to tell, reread, edit, and revitalize.

In this way the prefatory explanations of what James would call the "germ" of the text relate indirectly to the most deeply receded text-within-the-text of the story proper, a microcosm of its own gestation. This analogue of conception embedded in the resulting narrative is inscribed—under proscription—in the form of Victor's journal, containing his notes for the assembly and animation of the Creature. As the ur-text within this nest of tales, transcripts, and transmissions—a text stolen by the Creature shortly after the inception of his consciousness (15:124), never quoted from, and never seen again—it is the origin under erasure of all that follows. Providing for the Creature a primal reading lesson, the unfolded mystery of his origination, for us it is instead the unreadable journal within that read journal-like transcription that constitutes the largest part of the novel: the story of a constructed Creature within that creative construction—here, explicitly, a dreamlike dictation from the unconscious—which is fiction itself.

To pursue the comparison between Walton's journal and Victor's, tunneling back together, as they do, toward the mysterious inception of the story in Shelley's own reading, is to confirm the literary-historical overtones of her "progeny" trope. For the process of its gestation plays out in advance the nature of its fictionalized plot: the *making up*, in two senses, of a new hybrid form. I have suggested that at some level the reading that brings the Creature to compelled and compelling voice, the reading aloud at the de Lacey cottage, is what "humanizes" him. So, too, with the reading by Mary Shelley that went into his imaginative composition. Reframed thrice over by the novel's layered textual dissemination, the Creature erupts as a perversely fashioned organic entity in every sense *brought alive by reading*: Shelley's, Victor's, the cottagers', the Creature's own, Walton's, Mrs. Saville's prospectively, and finally, in the moment of extrapolation from all of them, your own.

JAMES A. W. HEFFERNAN

Looking at the Monster: *Frankenstein* and Film[†]

* * *

[The] stubborn visuality of cinema—or, rather, our habit of considering it predominantly visual—may help to explain why film versions of *Frankenstein* have drawn so little attention from academic critics of the novel. Not long after its publication, Percy Shelley asserted that language "is a more direct representation of the actions and passions of our internal being, . . . than colour, form, or motion."[1] Film versions of *Frankenstein* seem to confirm this axiom by showing us far less of the monster's inner life than his long autobiographical narratives in the novel do.[2] In the first talking film version, James Whale's *Frankenstein* of 1931, the monster is totally silenced and thus forced—like the monster of Richard Brinsley Peake's *Presumption; or, The Fate of Frankenstein* (1823), the first of many plays based on the novel—to make gesture and expression tell a fraction of his story, which is mutilated as well as severely abridged.[3] Mary Shelley's monster leaves us with a poignant *apologia pro vita sua* delivered to Walton over the body of Victor; Whale's creature dies in a burning windmill, while Elizabeth and Victor (unaccountably named Henry)

† *Critical Inquiry* 24 (Autumn 1997): 133–58. Reprinted by permission.
1. Percy Bysshe Shelley, "A Defence of Poetry, or Remarks Suggested by an Essay Entitled 'The Four Ages of Poetry'" (1821), *Shelley's Poetry and Prose*, ed. Donald H. Reiman and Sharon B. Powers (New York, 1977), 483.
2. The namelessness of the being created by Victor Frankenstein makes the very act of designating him problematic. Victor calls him a "miserable monster" from the moment he is animated—simply because of the way he appears (Mary Shelley, *Frankenstein; or, the Modern Prometheus*, ed. Maurice Hindle [Harmondsworth, 1992], 57; hereafter abbreviated *F*). Shorn of Victor's instant prejudice against him—a prejudice shared by everyone else who sees him—he is properly Victor's "'creature,'" which is what he calls himself (*F*, 96). Yet when he sees his own reflection for the first time, he concludes that he is "'in reality [a] monster'" (*F*, 110). Taking this cue, I call him a monster except where special conditions necessitate the term "creature."
3. Following common practice, I refer to the 1931 Universal *Frankenstein* as James Whale's version because he directed it. But the genesis of this film exemplifies the way filmmaking disperses the notion of authorship—a topic I cannot adequately explore in this essay. Based on an Americanized version of Peggy Webling's 1927 London stage play of the novel, the screenplay for the 1931 *Frankenstein* was credited to Garrett Fort and Francis Edward Faragoh but shaped in part by three other writers (Robert Florey, John L. Balderston, and Richard L. Schayer), and at least one more—the young John Huston, no less—helped with the prologue. See Wheeler Winston Dixon, "The Films of *Frankenstein*," in *Approaches to Teaching Shelley's "Frankenstein*," ed. Stephen C. Behrendt (New York: MLA, 1990), 169. See also David J. Skal, *The Monster Show: A Cultural History of Horror* (New York, 1993), 138. Even if we hold Whale chiefly responsible for translating a multiauthored screenplay into the film we call his, the crucial scene in which the creature unintentionally drowns the child Maria—a scene that for at least one critic "utterly" shapes the meaning of the film as a whole film (Dixon, "The Films of *Frankenstein*," 171)—embodies not so much Whale's intentions as those of Boris Karloff as shown below in section 3.

both survive to beget what Victor's father (who also survives, in perfect health) expects will be a son. The latest film version is much closer to the book but nonetheless adds its own twists. In Kenneth Branagh's *Mary Shelley's Frankenstein* (1994), the creature rips out Elizabeth's heart and in so doing reenacts what filmmakers regularly do to Mary Shelley's text. They rip out *its* heart by making the creature speechless, as Whale's version did, or at the very least cutting out his narrative, as even Branagh's version does.

What then can film versions of *Frankenstein* offer to academic critics of the novel? Can they be anything more than vulgarizations or travesties of the original? To answer these questions in anything but the negative, we must consider what film can tell us—or show us—about the role of the visual in the life of the monster represented by the text. If film versions of the novel ignore or elide the inner life of the monster, they nonetheless foreground for the viewer precisely what the novel largely hides from the reader. By forcing us to face the monster's physical repulsiveness, which he can never deny or escape and which aborts his every hope of gaining sympathy, film versions of *Frankenstein* prompt us to rethink his monstrosity in terms of visualization: how do we see the monster, what does he see, and how does he want to be seen? To answer these questions, I will chiefly consider three of the nearly two hundred films that *Frankenstein* has spawned: Whale's version, Branagh's version, and Mel Brooks's *Young Frankenstein* (1974).[4]

1

To learn why academic critics may need film to help answer the questions I have posed, consider two recent essays that both set out to explain the monster in terms of his body. Bette London gives a new twist to feminist readings of the novel by arguing that it makes a spectacle of stricken masculinity—of the broken, enervated, or disfigured male body—and thus challenges "the singular authority of masculinity and . . . the fixity of sexual positions."[5] Peter Brooks likewise highlights Mary Shelley's representation of the male body, but his argument turns on the contrast between the ugliness of the creature's body and the eloquence of his speech. Caught in

4. My source for the total number of *Frankenstein* films, including independent and privately distributed versions, is Steven Earl Forry, *Hideous Progenies: Dramatizations of "Frankenstein" from Mary Shelley to the Present* (Philadelphia, 1990), 127. For annotated lists of the more notable versions, see Alan G. Barbour, "The Frankenstein Films," in Radu Florescu, *In Search of Frankenstein* (Boston, 1975), 189–211, and Leonard Wolf, "A Selected Frankenstein Filmography," in *Mary Shelley's "Frankenstein": The Classic Tale of Terror Reborn on Film*, ed. Diana Landau (New York, 1994), 186–88.
5. Bette London, "Mary Shelley, *Frankenstein*, and the Spectacle of Masculinity," *PMLA* 108 (Mar. 1993): 264.

the contradiction between the visual and the verbal, between—in Lacanian terms—the imaginary order of the mirror stage and the symbolic, acculturating order of language, the Monster (as Brooks calls him) is that which "exceeds the very basis of classification, language itself."[6]

Each of these two readings aims to define the verbalized body that the text exhibits to the reader. Yet London turns the body of the not-yet-animated monster into a universalized sign of masculine vulnerability, disfigurement, and pathetic lifelessness. She thus averts her critical gaze from the sight of the monster's *animated* body, which is anything but powerless and which appears uniquely repulsive at the very instant it is given life.[7] In Brooks's argument, the body of the monster is largely consumed by what the monster himself calls the "'godlike science'" of language—or, more precisely, by the Lacanian vocabulary of desire, which subordinates the body to the word (*F*, p. 108). "Love," writes Brooks, "is in essence the demand to be *heard* by the other" ("WIM," 210; emphasis mine).[8] "'Hear my tale,'" says the creature to Victor as he covers Victor's eyes to relieve them from "the sight of [his] detested form" (*F*, 98). The creature's very turn to language as a means of "escape from a condition of 'to-be-looked-at-ness'" is precisely the turn reenacted by critics like Brooks, who define him in essentially linguistic terms ("WIM," 218).

Yet the creature's longing to communicate in words—his desire to be heard—is no more urgent than his longing to be *looked at* with desire, with something other than fear and loathing. Just before planting in the dress of the sleeping Justine the portrait that will lead to her execution, he fleetingly imagines himself her lover: "I bent over her, and whispered, 'Awake, fairest, thy lover is near—he who would give his life but to obtain one look of affection from thine eyes: my beloved, awake!'" (*F*, 139). This remarkable passage, which first appeared in the 1831 edition of *Frankenstein*, echoes at once the Song of Solomon (Song of Sol. 2:10–12), the words spoken by Milton's Satan to a sleeping Eve, and—most poignantly of all, perhaps— the words spoken by Keats's Porphyro to the sleeping Madeline in Keats's "The Eve of St. Agnes."[9] Ever since Laura Mulvey's classic

---

6. Peter Brooks, "What Is a Monster? (According to *Frankenstein*)" *Body Work: Objects of Desire in Modern Narrative* (Cambridge, 1993), 218; hereafter abbreviated "WIM."
7. "He was ugly [while unfinished]," says Victor; "but when those muscles and joints were rendered capable of motion, it became a thing such as even Dante could not have conceived" (*F*, 57).
8. Quoting Jacques Lacan, Brooks writes: "What is finally desired by the speaker is 'the desirer in the other,' that is, that the speaking subject himself be 'called to as desirable'" ("WIM," 210). See Jacques Lacan, *Le Transfert*, vol. 8 of *Le Séminaire* (Paris, 1991), 415.
9. See John Milton, *Paradise Lost*, in *John Milton*, ed. Stephen Orgel and Jonathan Goldberg (Oxford, 1991), bk. 5, ll. 38–47, 447; hereafter abbreviated *PL*. Like the creature, Porphyro addresses a sleeping lady with feelings of profound ambivalence, eager to awaken her—"'And now, my love, my seraph fair, awake!'"—yet petrified when he suc-

essay on visual pleasure, feminist criticism has sensitized us to the visual subjugation of women by the gaze of the male, and as Brooks notes, in his sole reference to film, the condition of "*to-be-looked-at-ness*" is the phrase Mulvey uses for the "traditional exhibitionist role" given to women in film.[1] Yet if the creature's aversion to being seen signifies a feminine or feminist rejection of that role, as Brooks suggests, his desire to be seen *longingly*—to be looked at with affection— reminds us that the capacity to attract and hold such a look is just as often a gender-neutral source of power as a gendered target of male exploitation (see "WIM," 218–19).

The doctrine that film subjugates women to the gaze of the male should also be rethought, as Silverman suggests, with the aid of Lacan's distinction between the gaze and the look. While the gaze is impersonal, ubiquitous (issuing "from all sides"), and detached, the look is the desiring act of an eye seeing from just one viewpoint.[2] Such an act cannot be simply identified with male power. As Silverman notes, a film such as Rainer Werner Fassbinder's *Beware of a Holy Whore* (1971) "not only extends desire and the look which expresses it to the female subject, but makes the male desiring look synonymous with loss of control."[3]

What Silverman says of Fassbinder's film might well describe the acute ambivalence with which Mary Shelley's creature looks at the sleeping Justine. Longing "to obtain one look of affection from [her] eyes," he is terrified by the thought that if she awakened to see him, she would curse and denounce him as a murderer (*F*, 139). Though no film known to me conveys the creature's ambivalence in this scene (Branagh's brief shot of him looming over Justine shows just his desire), Branagh's film includes a moment of the creature's tormented looking in another scene: a close-up of his bloodshot eyes peering through a chink in the wall of the De Laceys' cottage. In the text, where the creature tells Victor that his "eye could just penetrate" the chink, the phallic intrusiveness implied by his language is belied by his vulnerability, for the sight of old De Lacey

ceeds: "Her blue affrayed eyes wide open shone: / Upon his knees he sank, pale as smooth-sculptured stone" (John Keats, "The Eve of St. Agnes," *John Keats: Complete Poems*, ed. Jack Stillinger [Cambridge, Mass., 1982], 237, ll. 276, 296–97).

1. Laura Mulvey, "Visual Pleasure and Narrative Cinema," *Visual and Other Pleasures* (Bloomington, Ind., 1989), 19. Mulvey's essay first appeared in *Screen* 16 (Autumn 1975): 6–18. See also "WIM," 218.

2. Lacan, *The Four Fundamental Concepts of Psycho-Analysis*, trans. Alan Sheridan, ed. Jacques-Alain Miller (New York, 1978), 72; quoted in Silverman, *Male Subjectivity at the Margins* (New York, 1992), 130. Lacan's terms are *le regard* and *l'oeil*, which Silverman respectively calls the "gaze" and the "look."

3. Silverman, *Male Subjectivity at the Margins*, (New York: Routledge, 1992) 131. Carol Clover likewise argues that in slasher films such as *Hell Night* (1981), the "Final Girl"—a would-be victim who survives to take revenge on a murderous male—finally assumes the gaze, "making a spectacle of the killer and a spectator of herself" (Carol J. Clover, "Her Body, Himself: Gender in the Slasher Film," *Representations*, no. 20 [Fall 1987]: 219).

and the lovely young Agatha fills him with such "a mixture of pain and pleasure" that he shortly feels compelled to turn away (*F*, 104). In Branagh's film, the close-up of his peering face combines the spectacle of his mutilated features with the complex expression of his desire to see and his fear of being seen.

Since the whole episode of the monster's spying on the De Laceys is narrated in the novel by the monster himself, the text never describes the sight of his peering face. So we might construe this shot as an example of the way film reveals what the novel hides or suppresses. Yet to identify anything as hidden or suppressed in a novel is to acknowledge or assert its presence there as something implied, something we are authorized to imagine. Elaine Scarry has recently argued that verbal arts can achieve the "vivacity" of the material world by telling us how to imagine or construct an object of perception, how to imitate the act of perceiving it.[4] We can be led to imagine a three-dimensional object, she says, by the description of something transparent—like film or water—passing over something solid.[5] If Scarry is right, Mary Shelley prompts us to visualize a body when Victor describes what he saw just after animating the monster: "Great God! His yellow skin scarcely covered the work of muscles and arteries beneath" (*F*, 56). But even without such precise instruction, any description of an act of looking can lead us to imagine both the seen and the seer.[6] What else could explain Branagh's conviction that the novel actually *does* describe the monster's spying face? "There's a very strong image in Shelley's book," he writes, "of the Creature peering . . . and spying on the family. We reproduced that exactly, this image of the eyes as windows of his soul."[7] For all the feebleness of his cliché, Branagh unwittingly testifies to the force of the sight implied by Mary Shelley's text.

Beyond exposing such sights to the viewer's eye, film versions of *Frankenstein* implicitly remind us that filmmaking itself is a Frankensteinian exercise in artificial reproduction.[8] Mary Shelley's Victor is a "Modern Prometheus" in the words of her subtitle, a figure created from the fire-stealer she found in the opening lines of Aeschylus's *Prometheus Bound* and the man-making master craftsman that

---

4. Elaine Scarry, "On Vivacity: The Difference between Daydreaming and Imagining-Under-Authorial-Instruction," *Representations*, no. 52 (Fall 1995): 1.

5. See ibid., 9.

6. On this point, see Ellen J. Esrock, *The Reader's Eye: Visual Imaging as Reader Response* (Baltimore, 1994), 183.

7. Kenneth Branagh, "*Frankenstein* Reimagined," in *Mary Shelley's "Frankenstein*," 23.

8. In film theory, as in Mary Shelley's novel, the idea of artificial reproduction has sometimes excited alarm. In 1933, Arnheim wrote that films were already approaching the "dangerous goal" of manufacturing "an image . . . which is astoundingly like some natural object" (Arnheim, "The Complete Film," [selection from *Film as Art* (1933)], in *Film Theory and Criticism*, 50). Declining to tell Walton just how he made the monster, Victor likewise calls such information "dangerous" (*F*, 52).

she found in Ovid's *Metamorphoses*.[9] As Anne Mellor has shown, *Frankenstein* conflates the fire-stealer and the man-maker of classical antiquity in the figure of a 1790s scientist exploiting the newly discovered powers of electricity, the fire of life, the "spark of being" with which—by the flickering light of a candle that is "nearly burnt out"—he animates the creature (*F*, 56).[1] Is it mere coincidence that the earliest known *Frankenstein* movie—made in 1910—came from the film company of Thomas Edison, who had thirty years earlier invented the first commercially practical incandescent lamp and installed in New York City the world's first central electric-light power plant? Ever since Edison, filmmakers have been reenacting what Victor calls his "animation" of "lifeless matter" (*F*, 53).

Mythically, as William Nestrick notes, the concept of animation in *Frankenstein* looks both backward and forward: backward to Genesis and the creation of man and woman, "which two great sexes animate the world," and forward—chronologically at least—to the mechanical reproduction of animal movement on a screen and to the illusion of metamorphosis (*PL*, bk. 8, 1. 151, 511).[2] For if Mary Shelley's modern Prometheus originates in part from her reading of Ovid's *Metamorphoses*, one of her own most telling passages anticipates what Georges Méliès discovered by accident in 1898, when his camera briefly jammed while he was filming traffic outside the Paris Opera and he then resumed cranking. When he projected the film, which had captured two discontinuous sequences of images before and after the interruption, he saw "a bus changed into a hearse, and men changed into women."[3] By the end of the nineteenth century, then, film could actualize the vividly metamorphic nightmare that comes to Victor right after he animates the creature.[4]

At the moment of animation, Victor's admiration for the beauty of the creature's inert form dissolves. "The beauty of the dream vanished," he says, "and breathless horror and disgust filled my heart" (*F*, 56). The nightmare reenacts this change by essentially reversing what Victor has done—bestow animation on a composite of lifeless

9. See Ovid, *Metamorphoses*, trans. Frank Justus Miller, 2 vols. (Cambridge, Mass., 1921), 1:6–9 [1.1.78–88].
1. See Anne K. Mellor, *Mary Shelley: Her Life, Her Fiction, Her Monsters* (New York, 1988), 102–7.
2. See William Nestrick, "Coming to Life: *Frankenstein* and the Nature of Film Narrative," in *The Endurance of "Frankenstein": Essays on Mary Shelley's Novel*, ed. George Levine and U. C. Knoepflmacher (Berkeley, 1979), 294–95.
3. Quoted in ibid., p. 291.
4. The story of this development is complicated by the fact that some pioneer filmmakers such as Louis Lumière (inventor of the Cinématographe) actually resisted "the Frankensteinian dream . . . of analogical representation, the mythology of victory over death" even as their inventions helped to realize this dream (Noël Burch, *Life to Those Shadows*, trans. and ed. Ben Brewster [Berkeley, 1990], 20). As Siegfried Kracauer long ago noted, Lumière aimed to reproduce the world while Méliès sought to re-create it. See Siegfried Kracauer, *Theory of Film: The Redemption of Physical Reality* (New York, 1965), 30–33.

body parts—and precisely reversing what he had hoped to do: "renew life where death had apparently devoted the body to corruption" (*F*, 53). In his nightmare, Victor is surprised to see Elizabeth walking down a street in Ingolstadt, but as soon as he embraces and kisses her, she turns into the worm-ridden corpse of his mother (see *F*, 57). This sudden dissolving of one image into another is "supremely cinematic," as Branagh has said of *Frankenstein* as a whole.[5] At the same time, the passage encapsulates the greatest of all ironies in the novel, the fact that Victor's ambition to create and renew life leads only to death. We will shortly see how Branagh's film intensifies this irony by pursuing some of the implications of the nightmare—even while eliding the nightmare itself.

2

First, however, Branagh's comment on *Frankenstein* must be qualified. Mary Shelley's novel is by turns supremely cinematic and stubbornly uncinematic. Much of it—such as the creature's account of what he learned from reading Milton, Plutarch, and Goethe (see *F*, 124–27)—would be numbingly static on the screen. And filmmaking itself evokes Victor's project only in a broadly figurative sense. While film is a wholly artificial product, the creature consists entirely of natural body parts, so that he is closer to an actual human being with one or more transplanted organs than he is to the mechanical men constructed by futurist designers in the 1920s or to the cyborg of present-day science fiction.[6] Nevertheless, the visual medium of film highlights something at once crucial to the novel and virtually invisible to the reader: the repulsiveness of the creature's appearance.

In the novel, the words of the creature—especially as we read his autobiographical story—cover our eyes, and our blindness to his appearance is precisely what enables us to see his invisible nobility. Though Victor abhors the creature's looks, the novel seldom asks us even to imagine them.[7] Instead it repeatedly makes us imagine what the creature sees and hears. A faithful re-creation of the novel's central narrative, in fact, would never show the monster at all—would

5. Quoted in "The Filmmakers and Their Creations," *Mary Shelley's "Frankenstein,"* 177. Curiously enough, neither Branagh's film nor any other film of *Frankenstein* known to me includes the nightmare.
6. See David J. Skal, *The Monster Show: A Cultural History of Horror* (New York: Norton, 1993), 131–33. Donna Haraway explicitly exempts the cyborg—a composite of animal and machine—from the creature's heterosexual longing for organic or Edenic wholeness. See Donna J. Haraway, *Simians, Cyborgs, and Women: The Reinvention of Nature* (New York, 1991), 151.
7. While the novel often asks us to imagine the monster's *looking*, as I have already noted, the only description of his looks appears in Victor's account of his newly animated form. Not even when the monster is terrified by his own reflection in a pool do we get any further instructions on how to visualize him; see *F*, 56, 110.

give us only the sound of his voice over shots of what he perceives, such as the roaring crowd of torch-bearing villagers charging up a mountain after him in Whale's version. Yet no director known to me has ever even considered filming the monster's story in this way.[8] Essentially, filmmakers treat it as Phiz the illustrator treats the hero's autobiography in Dickens's *David Copperfield* (1849–50).[9] In film versions of *Frankenstein*, as in Phiz's illustrations, the first-person narrator telling us all that he experiences—or has experienced— becomes just one more visible object.[1]

Yet if filmmakers seem thus compelled to objectify the creature, they also compel us to face—more frankly and forthrightly than critics of the novel usually do—the problem of the creature's appearance. In the novel, Victor says that the creature was "gigantic . . . about eight feet in height, and proportionably large," that his skin was "yellow," that his hair was "lustrous black, and flowing," that his teeth were "of pearly whiteness," that the color of his "watery eyes" almost matched that of their "dun-white sockets," that his complexion was "shrivelled," and that his lips were "straight [and] black" (*F*, 52, 56). It is hard to know just what to make of this description. The creature's size is monstrous, but except for his yellow skin, the other details suggest a face seductively sinister rather than truly repulsive, something closer to Bela Lugosi's Count in Tod Browning's *Dracula* (1931) than to the mouth-distending, barbed-wire stitchery of Robert De Niro's creature in Branagh's *Frankenstein*.[2] Yet Branagh and his collaborators ask the right question about the creature's effect on Victor: "Why, after all this time, having seen what he was putting

8. This subjective camera technique has been used for parts of many films, such as Delmer Daves's *Dark Passage* (1947) and is used throughout Robert Montgomery's *Lady in the Lake* (1946), where Montgomery himself plays the hero with the camera strapped to his chest. See Seymour Chatman, *Story and Discourse: Narrative Structure in Fiction and Film* (Ithaca, N.Y., 1978), 160.
9. In chapter 5, for instance, David recalls how he drifted in and out of sleep during breakfast with the flute-playing Master at Salem House, hearing by turns the actual strains of the flute and the imagined sounds of the coach he would soon be taking. But the drawing shows him simply as an insensate object—a boy sitting asleep on a chair. See Charles Dickens, *David Copperfield* (New York, 1950), 79–81. My thanks to Grant Cerny for this example.
1. According to Chatman, one of the many differences between fiction and film is that while fictional narratives may operate from a generalized perspective, film is always shot from a specific point of view—the viewpoint of the camera. See Chatman, "What Novels Can Do That Films Can't (and Vice Versa)" *Critical Inquiry* 7 (Autumn 1980): 132–33. Paradoxically, however, film versions of a novel *told* from the viewpoint of a single character are almost never consistently *shot* from that viewpoint.
2. On the other hand, the frontispiece to the 1831 edition of *Frankenstein*, which depicts the moment of the monster's first stirring, shows a well muscled male nude whose only serious abnormalities—apart from his size—are an elongated right hand and the sprouting of his head from his right shoulder (reproduced as the frontispiece to *The Mary Shelley Reader*, ed. Betty T. Bennett and Charles E. Robinson [New York, 1990]). Staged versions of the novel include at least one beautiful monster. In the Royal Ballet version, which premiered in London on 26 July 1985, the monster was represented by an Ariel-like figure costumed and made up wholly in white. (My thanks to Linda Hughes for this information.)

together, should he be so repelled and then be so frightened by it?"[3] The question becomes even more pointed when we realize that Victor made the creature from features "selected . . . as beautiful" (F, 56; emphasis mine). What makes Victor's composition of such beautiful features monstrous?

In part, the answer made by Branagh's film is much like the now-familiar answer formulated by critics such as Ellen Moers, who claim that Victor's sudden loathing for the newly animated creature he has long labored to construct evokes the sense of "revulsion against newborn life" that may be felt by any new mother, as Mary Shelley knew from her own experience.[4] Branagh's film makes this point graphically. First, the monster lunges from a great copper sarcophagus filled with water to make it a kind of womb. After he lands sprawling in the spill tank under it, Victor lifts him up, vainly tries to show him how to walk, then ties him standing to a set of chains. But when the struggling creature is struck by a falling piece of wood and shortly goes limp, Victor concludes that he himself has killed this luckless heir to "'massive birth defects,'" and that "'this evil must be destroyed . . . forever.'"[5] Since Branagh's Victor tries to help the creature at first and seems dismayed to think that he has killed him, he is decidedly more paternal—or maternal—than the Victor of the text. But when (in the next scene) Branagh's Victor awakens in his bedroom to find the naked, stitched-up creature looming over him, he cries out "No!" and flees ("S," 84). Like the Victor of the text, who finds the ugliness of the creature inconceivably magnified by its acquisition of the capacity to move, Branagh's Victor is horrified by life itself—by the living sight of what he has made (see F, 57).

Branagh's answer to his own question, then, is at once visual and psychological. His Victor rejects the creature in part because any newborn being may disgust its begetter and in part because this one—in the film—has apparently risen twice from the dead, more "hideous" than "a mummy again endued with animation," in the punning words of the novel, which has just described Victor's nightmare of embracing his dead mother (F, 57). But Branagh's Victor is also horrified by the sheer ugliness of the creature, by the barbed-

---

3. Branagh, "Frankenstein Reimagined," 9.
4. Ellen Moers, "Female Gothic," in The Endurance of "Frankenstein," 81. Mary Shelley called Frankenstein her "hideous progeny" (Mary Shelley, author's introduction to the standard novels edition, F, 10; hereafter abbreviated "AI"). Also, as critics often remind us, she had already endured before writing it the death of her first child, born prematurely in February 1815, who lived just twelve days. See Muriel Spark, Mary Shelley (New York, 1987), 45. In itself this hardly explains why Victor is horrified by the very animation of the creature and dismayed by its stubborn survival. But Victor's "labour" in his "workshop of filthy creation" (F, 52, 53) may well signify the repulsiveness of child-bearing. Moers calls Frankenstein "a horror story of maternity" (Moers, "Female Gothic," 83).
5. Steph Lady and Frank Darabont, "The Screenplay," in Mary Shelley's "Frankenstein," 81; hereafter abbreviated "S."

wire stitches that harrow his body and distend his face. The stitching of the creature—nowhere explicitly mentioned in Mary Shelley's text—originates in film with Jack Pierce's makeup for Boris Karloff in the Whale *Frankenstein*, where the creature's face and body appear discreetly sutured. But the body of De Niro's creature in Branagh's film is vividly, cruelly stitched, and thus reminds us that Mary Shelley's creature was precisely *not* a reanimated corpse—something Victor had so far found "impossible" to produce (*F*, 53)—but a patchwork quilt of flesh cut from dead bodies, a paradoxically ugly composite of features "*selected* . . . as beautiful."

With singular irony, Victor's phrase evokes a leading principle of neoclassical aesthetics. Encapsulated in the story of Zeuxis, the ancient Greek artist who painted Helen of Troy by selecting and combining the loveliest parts of the most beautiful virgins of Crotona, this was the principle of what Sir Joshua Reynolds called "Ideal Beauty" in visual art: a generalized shape abstracted from the comparative study of particular human figures, a "central form . . . from which every deviation is deformity."[6] Victor deviates from the central form, of course, by making his creature eight feet tall. But otherwise his project turns neoclassical aesthetics on its head. By applying to corpses a formula calculated to produce ideal beauty in painting and sculpture, Victor generates only deformity: the deformity of a creature artificially *assembled*.[7] It is this myth of miscreation, of artistic ambition run monstrously awry, that scores of filmmakers have sought to illuminate in their own art—an art which may yet lead us to a deeper understanding of Mary Shelley's.

3

Let us return, then, to the question posed by Peter Brooks's essay: "What Is a Monster?" Unlike Brooks's linguistic response, the answer one might expect from film is that a monster is someone visibly deformed, hideous to behold. Yet Karloff's monster in the Whale *Frankenstein* is not unequivocally ugly. Without saying a single word, without the eloquence that enables the novel's monster to make us forget his ugliness, Karloff's monster excites our sympathy. He

6. Sir Joshua Reynolds, *Discourses on Art*, ed. Robert R. Wark (New Haven, Conn., 1975), 45. For an account of the story of Zeuxis, see Jean H. Hagstrum, *The Sister Arts: The Tradition of Literary Pictorialism and English Poetry from Dryden to Gray* (Chicago, 1958), 14.
7. Marie-Hélène Huet suggests that the creature is monstrous because Frankenstein's art is purely reproductive or (in Plato's term) *eikastiken*, "without interpretation, without proportion or the necessary betrayal of the model that makes the phantastiken object unfaithful to nature but at the same time aesthetically beautiful" (Marie-Hélène Huet, *Monstrous Imagination* [Cambridge, 1993], 132). Yet even if we construe Victor's act of assembling *actual* features as the reproduction of a human body, the creature is an explicitly enlarged—and thus artfully transformed—version of the model, "about eight feet in height, and *proportionably large*" (*F*, 52; emphasis mine).

radiates longing when he raises his arms to the light pouring through the partly open roof of the dark watchtower where he has been made, and he radiates joy when he smilingly kneels to join the little girl Maria in picking and throwing daisies into a lake. Even his throwing of Maria into the lake—censored out of the prints originally released but now restored—was scripted as an innocent gesture prompted by his assumption that she would float like a flower, and in spite of Whale's wishes, Karloff played it this way.[8] What do such moments tell us about monstrosity? Do they confirm what Mary Poovey has written of Mary Shelley's creature—that while "it recognizes and longs to overcome its definitive monstrosity," it "is unable to disguise its essential being"?[9] To rephrase my earlier question, just what is the essential being of a monster?

The difficulty of answering this question—or rather the problem with assuming too quickly that we know the answer—may be illustrated by turning again to Dickens, this time to *Great Expectations*. Shortly after Magwitch reveals himself as the source of Pip's wealth and gentlemanly status, which he has come back from New South Wales to admire, Pip explicitly compares the two to Victor and his creature. "The imaginary student," writes Pip, "pursued by the misshapen creature he had impiously made, was not more wretched than I, pursued by the creature who had made me, and recoiling from him with a stronger repulsion, the more he admired me and the fonder he was of me."[1] Pip is of course not just another Victor. As a gentleman "made" by the wealth of a criminal, he is himself a creature, and perhaps a monster of snobbery and affectation as well. But his aversion to Magwitch, who now wants Pip to care for him, clearly recalls Victor's loathing of his new creature, whose infantile appeal to his maker—with "inarticulate sounds" and "a grin wrinkl[ing] his cheeks"—prompts Victor to see only a "miserable monster" (F, 57). One other thing that Pip says about Magwitch also anticipates what Poovey writes of the creature. After dressing up Magwitch to pass him off in public as a prosperous farmer, Pip despairs of the effort. "To my thinking," he says, "there was something in him that made it hopeless to attempt to disguise him. The more I dressed him and the better I dressed him, the more he looked like the slouching fugitive on the marshes. . . . From head to foot there was Convict in the very grain of the man."[2]

---

8. See Dixon, "The Films of *Frankenstein*," 171. Whale ordered Karloff to raise the girl over his head and brutally cast her down; Karloff wanted to "pick her up gently and put her in the water exactly as he had done to the flower" (quoted in Donald F. Glut, *The Frankenstein Legend* [Methuen, N.J., 1973], 112–13).
9. Mary Poovey, "My Hideous Progeny: Mary Shelley and the Feminization of Romanticism," *PMLA* 95 (May 1980): 337.
1. Dickens, *Great Expectations*, ed. Angus Calder (1860–61; Harmondsworth, 1985), 354.
2. Ibid., 352.

In Pip's eyes, the undisguisably "essential being" of his coarse-grained creator/creature is criminal. Implicitly, Pip reads Magwitch in the light of physiognomy, the ancient art of construing external features—especially facial ones—as signs of "supposed inner essences."[3] Revived in the later eighteenth century by the Swiss theologian Johann Kaspar Lavater (1741–1801), one of whose disciples examined the infant Mary Shelley herself at her father's request,[4] physiognomy strongly influenced the description of characters in Dickens's earlier novels as well as the drawings of them made by Hablot K. Browne, whose very nickname (Phiz) revealed his belief in the idea that beauty expresses virtue and ugliness vice, that facial features disclose—to an astute reader of them—one's moral character.[5] Dickens's later work shows some resistance to this idea. In *Great Expectations* itself, significantly unadorned by the handiwork of Phiz or any other illustrator, Pip's physiognomic reading of Magwitch exposes his blindness to the man's inner worth, which he eventually recognizes. But for all its blindness, Pip's reading anticipates yet another revival of physiognomy less than three decades after *Great Expectations* first appeared. In 1887, Cesare Lombroso published the first of a series of books that established the science (or pseudoscience) of criminal anthropology, which claimed that the "'born criminal'" can be known from his anatomy and especially from the configuration of his skull.[6] According to Lombroso, criminals are evolutionary throwbacks, visibly atavistic reincarnations of the prehistoric savage or the ape. As Nietzsche paraphrased the theory in *Twilight of the Idols* (1889), it "tell[s] us the typical criminal is ugly: *monstrum infronte, monstrum in animo*" (a monster in face, a monster in soul).[7]

Criminal anthropology has cast its shadow backwards on Mary Shelley's text. Though Lombroso's theory could not have influenced Shelley herself, it has subtly influenced our ways of construing and representing the creature's monstrosity. Bram Stoker's *Dracula* (1897) ultimately derives from *Frankenstein*'s literary sibling—John William Polidori's *The Vampyre* (1819), the only other child of Byron's proposal that he and Polidori and the Shelleys should "'each write a ghost story'" in the summer of 1816 ("AI," 7). Whether or not Lombroso's theories ever directly affected the portrayal of Mary Shelley's creature on stage or screen, they certainly influenced Stoker, for as

---

3. Michael Hollington, "Dickens, 'Phiz,' and Physiognomy," *Imagination on a Long Rein: English Literature Illustrated*, ed. Joachim Möller (Marburg, 1988), 125.
4. See Mary Shelley, *The Journals of Mary Shelley, 1814–1844*, ed. Paula R. Feldman and Diana Scott-Kilvert, 2 vols. (Oxford, 1987), 1:26 n.
5. See Hollington, "Dickens, 'Phiz,' and Physiognomy," 125.
6. Stephen Jay Gould, *The Mismeasure of Man* (New York, 1981), 124.
7. Friedrich Nietzsche, *Twilight of the Idols*, in *"Twilight of the Idols" and "The Anti-Christ*," trans. R. J. Hollingdale (Harmondsworth, 1968), 30.

Leonard Wolf has shown, Jonathan Harker's first description of Count Dracula closely follows Lombroso's description of the criminal face.[8] Likewise, most of the faces that Universal artists originally drew for the creature in the Whale *Frankenstein* were decidedly atavistic, just the sort of face Lombroso thought innately criminal.[9] While none of these faces resembles the one that Pierce made for Karloff, Karloff's creature—in one of the many notable departures from Mary Shelley's text—gets a brain explicitly labelled "abnormal." In Waldman's words from the film, it is "the abnormal brain of the typical criminal," marked by "distinct degeneration of the frontal lobes." The film thus tries to ensure that the inner self or "essential being" of the monstrous looking creature will likewise be monstrous, will validate the simplest notion of what a monster is: one whose malformed body proclaims the viciousness of his or her soul.

In its basic form, this notion is much older than Lombroso or Lavater. Thersites, the ugliest of all the Greeks in the *Iliad*, is also—according to Odysseus—the worst of them.[1] In the Book of Revelation, Satan appears as "a great red dragon with seven heads and ten horns" (Rev. 12:3). Shakespeare's humpbacked Richard III is a "lump of foul deformity," at once bodily disfigured and morally corrupt.[2] In *Paradise Lost*, the ur-text of *Frankenstein*, Sin is a woman whose lower body "ended foul in many a scaly fold" and is surrounded by hellhounds uglier than Scylla and Hecate (*PL*, bk. 2, l. 651, 391). Few ideas are more enduring or more seductively plausible than the assumption that deformity signifies depravity.

Yet literature and life itself offer us many monsters in disguise: figures whose physical attractiveness belies the evil within. Milton's Sin is beautiful down to the waist, and the verbal picture of Fraud (*froda*) drawn by Dante—whose power to conceive monsters Victor finds limited (see *F*, 57)—likewise combines the trunk of a serpent with "the face of a just man, so benign was its outward aspect."[3] In realistic fiction and drama the handsome seducer is a stock figure, as in Thomas Hardy's *Tess of the D'Urbervilles*, where the handsome Alec d'Urberville not only takes the heroine's virginity but diaboli-

---

8. See Wolf, *The Annotated Dracula* (New York, 1975), 300. Daniel Pick aptly notes that *Dracula* should not be lumped with *Frankenstein* under the undifferentiated heading of "gothic" because the later novel reflects a major issue of the late nineteenth century. It expresses, he argues, "a vision of the bio-medical degeneration of the race in general and the metropolitan population in particular" (Daniel Pick, "'Terrors of the Night': *Dracula* and 'Degeneration' in the Late Nineteenth Century," *Critical Quarterly* 30 [Winter 1988]: 75).
9. These drawings are reprinted in Skal, *The Monster Show*, 133.
1. See Homer, *The Iliad*, trans. Richmond Lattimore (1951; Chicago, 1978), bk. 2, ll. 216, 249, 82.
2. William Shakespeare, *Richard III*, ed. Mark Eccles (Harmondsworth, 1988), 1.2.57, 41.
3. Dante, *Inferno*, in *The Divine Comedy*, trans. Charles Singleton, 3 vols. (Princeton, N.J., 1970), 1:173 (17.10–11). See also *PL*, bk. 2, l. 650, 391.

cally drives her to murder. Victor Frankenstein himself, who is at least attractive enough to win the love of Elizabeth, seems unwittingly to reveal the depravity of his own soul in the very act of expressing his wish to kill "the monstrous Image which I had endued with the mockery of a soul still more monstrous" (*F*, 177). And if we turn to recent, actual events, how would Doctors Lavater and Lombroso read the handsome face of the late Jeffrey Dahmer, whose actual behavior made the fictional crimes of Mary Shelley's creature look like the misdemeanors of an Eagle Scout?[4] If ever a *monstrum in animo* was *speciosus in fronte*, Dahmer was.

Beside malformed criminals and handsome knaves, however, there is a third kind of monster much closer to the original meaning of *monstrum*—"divine portent or warning"—than either of the other two is.[5] Nietzsche's phrases in fact refer to Socrates, a *monstrum in fronte* renowned for his admonitions, a notoriously ugly philosopher. Nietzsche argues that Socrates' dogged promotion of "rationality at any cost" made him also a *monstrum in animo*, leader of a sickeningly repressive war against instinct.[6] But earlier in the nineteenth century, it is far more likely that Mary Shelley viewed Socrates as Alcibiades does in the *Symposium*, a dialogue Percy translated in July 1818 as *The Banquet*.[7] For Alcibiades, Socrates is a *monstrum in fronte, deus in animo*, a god of wisdom with the face of a monster. Alcibiades compares him to Marsyas, the ugly satyr whose pipe makes music that is enchantingly divine, for the ugly Socrates makes Marsyan music with his philosophic words (see *B*, 210–11).

4. Jeffrey Dahmer killed seventeen young men and boys, had sex with some of their dead bodies, skinned and dismembered them, tried to lobotomize at least one of them, spray-painted their skulls, preserved body parts in formaldehyde so he could look at them while masturbating, kept human hearts in his freezer, and ate body parts so as to reanimate the dead within him. He was murdered in 1994 while serving a life sentence. See Edward Walsh, "Murderer Jeffrey Dahmer Beaten to Death in Prison," *Lebanon (N.H.) Valley News*, 29 Nov. 1994, A1.
5. *Oxford English Dictionary*, s.v. "monster." On the construal of monsters as portents in the sixteenth century, see Lorraine Daston, "Marvelous Facts and Miraculous Evidence in Early Modern Europe," *Critical Inquiry* 18 (Autumn 1991): 93–124.
6. Nietzsche, *Twilight of the Idols*, 34.
7. Percy had read the *Symposium* in Greek by 7 December 1817, when he cites the speech of Agathon in a letter to William Godwin. See Percy Bysshe Shelley, *Letters*, ed. Frederick L. Jones, 2 vols. (Oxford, 1964), 1:574. Mary promptly transcribed his translation, and from it I quote the *Symposium* below. See Mary Shelley, *The Journals of Mary Shelley, 1814–1844*, 1:220–22. See also Percy Bysshe Shelley, *The Banquet: Translated from Plato*, in *Prose*, vol. 7 of *The Complete Works of Percy Bysshe Shelley*, ed. Roger Ingpen and Walter E. Peck, 10 vols. (London, 1930), 165–220; hereafter abbreviated *B*. William Veeder treats Plato as one of several sources for Mary's views on androgyny, a topic central to Aristophanes' definition of love in the dialogue and to Mary's critique of the isolated, self-absorbed masculine ego. See William Veeder, *Mary Shelley and Frankenstein: The Fate of Androgyny* (Chicago, 1986), 23–24. Whether or not Mary knew anything about the *Symposium* before publishing the first edition of *Frankenstein* in 1818, she uses Plato's Diotima in the frame-story for the first version of the next novel she wrote, *Mathilda*. See Andrea K. Henderson, *Romantic Identities: Varieties of Subjectivity, 1774–1830* (Cambridge, 1996), 125. In any case, the ugliness of Socrates sheds an important and generally neglected light on the kind of monstrosity the creature embodies.

Are echoes of this music audible in the philosophic eloquence of Mary Shelley's monster? Though enchanted by the sounds of old De Lacey's guitar (see *F,* 104, 113), the monster does not know the *Symposium* as he knows *Paradise Lost.* But Mary Shelley probably knew something of Plato's dialogue by the time she wrote *Frankenstein,* and what the monster says to Victor reflects—in part by a kind of desperate inversion—something of what Socrates says he has learned from Diotima about love. When the monster tells Victor that he must have a female "of the same species, and . . . the same defects" as himself (*F,* 139), he inverts Diotima's definition of love as the yearning not for one's other half (Aristophanes' theory) but for the good (see *B,* 200–201). Love, says Diotima, "embraces those bodies which are beautiful rather than those which are deformed" (*B,* 204). Ironically, the monster's instincts confirm this axiom. Gazing on the miniature portrait of the "most lovely woman" that was once Victor's mother, he is filled with delight (*F,* 138). But knowing that he can excite in beautiful creatures only fear and loathing, he bitterly cultivates a "burning passion" for "one as deformed and horrible" as he is, someone who "would not deny herself to me" (*F,* 139).

Apparently, then, the monster cannot reach even the first step of the ladder that would lead from particular to "supreme beauty" in Diotima's discourse (*B,* 207). Yet he startlingly resembles the figure of Love that Diotima describes. Like Love, a "great Daemon" holding "an intermediate place between what is divine and what is mortal" (*B,* 197), Victor's creature is a "daemon" of superhuman strength and endurance (*F,* 161). Like Love, too, the creature is "for ever poor, . . . squalid," and "homeless, . . . ever the companion of Want" (*B,* 198). In the *Symposium,* Love's poverty and squalor help to show what the seeker for love must learn: that the mind's beauty transcends the "mere beauty of the outward form" (*B,* 206). In *Frankenstein,* we are nowhere told that the monster seeks a beauty of mind. But if he wants Victor to "make [him] happy," could he be satisfied by a woman who offered no more than the "same defects" as his (*F,* 97)? Would he not also desire someone with comparable virtues, someone whose soul radiates "love and humanity," as his own once did (*F,* 97)? Whatever the answer to these questions, the creature's "burning passion" is much closer to Socrates' conception of love than to Victor's egotism. While Victor spurns companionship in his quest for scientific glory, the monster's whole story—right up to its final words—aims to show that life is unbearable without love.

This complex evocation of Socrates in the monster's narrative helps to explain and justify a bit of dialogue invented by the scriptwriters for the ice cave scene in the Branagh film, a drastically condensed version of the creature's narrative. The scene reminds us that even as the language of fiction can sometimes be visual, the *verbal* language of film can sometimes rival the impact of its images. Just before De Niro's monster asks for a mate, he reveals that he knows how to play the recorder, and he claims not to have learned but to have "remembered" this Marsyan skill by means of what Branagh's Victor goes on to suggest might be "trace memories in the brain, perhaps" ("S," 115). I will not claim that the scriptwriters were thinking of Socrates, but for anyone who can hear echoes of his voice in the novel, the film dialogue between Victor and the monster about memory and the recorder calls to mind the ugly philosopher whose theory of knowledge is based on recollection, on the silent recorder known as memory. Victor struggles to forget the monster as soon as he comes to life, but the monster compels him to remember both what he has created and what he has repressed in the very act of solitary creation: the desire that erupts in Victor's nightmare.

4

Let us now revisit this nightmare and the desire it signifies with the aid of Mel Brooks's *Young Frankenstein*, a film scripted by Gene Wilder, who also plays Friedrich Frankenstein, the eponymous hero. At the end of the film, Madeline Kahn's Elizabeth not only survives but also falls in love with the monster when he abducts her. Lulled by her own mood music (she sings "Ah! sweet mystery of life") and enchanted by his charm as he suavely lights two cigarettes and gives her one (like Paul Henreid in *Now, Voyager* [1942]), she ends up marrying him and playing tigress to his tame executive, lustily leaping into a bed where the creature sits up reading the *Wall Street Journal.* (Friedrich has selflessly traded his brain for the monster's, which is what makes the creature "normal" at the end.) What do these sophomoric pranks have to do with Mary Shelley's novel? They have, I think, quite a lot to do with one of the myths lurking just beneath the surface of its plot, the myth of Beauty and the Beast. It is powerfully implied not only by the creature's response to the sleeping Justine but also by what he says about the miniature portrait of Caroline Beaufort that he takes from William and plants on Justine.

> It was a portrait of a most lovely woman. In spite of my malignity, it softened and attracted me. For a few moments I gazed with delight on her dark eyes, fringed by deep lashes, and her lovely lips; but presently my rage returned: I remembered that I was forever deprived of the delights that such beautiful creatures could bestow; and that she whose resemblance I contemplated would, in regarding me, have changed that air of divine benignity to one expressive of disgust and affright. [*F*, 138]

Steeped as he is in *Paradise Lost*, the creature implicitly recalls what the beauty of Eve does in book 9 to Satan, who is so enraptured by it that he momentarily forgets his vengeful plot against her and all of humankind (see *PL*, bk. 9, ll. 455–66, 534–35). But unlike Satan, who can present to Eve a "pleasing" and "lovely" shape even when he inhabits the body of a serpent (*PL*, bk. 9, ll. 503–4, 536), the monster knows—or at any rate presumes—that the woman whose portrait he lovingly contemplates would be horrified by the sight of him. Irresistibly attractive, Satan damns himself to the Dostoevskian hell of those who cannot love. Grotesquely repulsive, the monster *is* damned to the hell of those who cannot *be* loved. He stirs desire in no woman, beautiful or otherwise, and one woman faints at his appearance (see *F*, 102).

But he is nowhere actively rejected by a woman, not even by the young girl he saves from drowning and takes (admittedly "senseless") in his arms (*F*, 136). In the myth of Beauty and the Beast, Beauty's love for the Beast turns him into a prince. In a children's book version of the story that Mary Shelley may well have known, the Beast is by his own admission "hideous" and "ugly," but the kindness of this "Monster" makes Beauty overlook his "outward form" and eventually turns her fear of him into desire.[8] The children's story may be read as an allegory of Mary Shelley's fascination with what she called her "hideous" idea in the introduction to the 1831 edition ("AI," 5). Lovingly portraying a monster loved by no one else, she gives him an eloquence that makes us overlook his outward form, as I have already noted, and she lets him show by his own words and deeds how "benevolent and good" he was before misery "made [him] a fiend" (*F*, 97). Nothing about the creature she presents to us is more poignant than his longing to be loved. In *Young Frankenstein*, Elizabeth gratifies this desire. Acting out—campily, to be sure—the creature's deepest fantasy, she plays a loving Beauty to his Beast.

Wacky as it is, the monster's marriage to Elizabeth in *Young Frankenstein* also points directly to the sexual energies that Mary Shelley's Victor so perversely thwarts in himself and the monster alike. When Victor tears apart the monster's mate and thus breaks his promise to furnish one, the monster grimly tells Victor, " 'I shall be with you on your wedding-night' " (*F*, 163). As he later tells Wal-

---

8. Quoted in Betsy Hearne, *Beauty and the Beast: Visions and Revisions of an Old Tale* (Chicago, 1989), 34–35. The earliest known literary version of the myth appeared in France in 1740, and in 1811 (when Mary was fourteen) an English poem attributed to Charles Lamb and titled *Beauty and the Beast: Or a Rough Outside with a Gentle Heart* appeared as a children's book. See Hearne, *Beauty and the Beast*, 2, 34. Since Lamb first met Godwin in 1805 and since Mary Shelley saw him socially at least twice in the winter and spring of 1817, when she was writing *Frankenstein*, it seems more than possible that she knew something of this book. See Mary Shelley, *The Journals of Mary Shelley, 1814–1844*, 1:164, 172.

ton, Victor's decision to take a bride for himself while denying one to the monster drove the monster to kill Elizabeth (*F*, 212). But the killing of Elizabeth is not just an act of vengeance. It is also a vicarious expression of Victor's misogyny and, contradictorily, a tortured expression of the creature's desire for the woman he kills.

First of all, as the psychic son or "symbolic projection" of Victor's imagination, in Poovey's words, the creature vengefully reenacts Victor's misogynistic dismemberment of the female creature, an act prompted largely—as Mellor has argued—by Victor's fear of what an unregulated female might do.[9] Having set out to preempt the generative powers of women, Victor is horrified by the spectre of rampant heterosexual reproduction, by "a race of devils [who] would be propagated upon the earth" (*F*, 160). This overt fear of what a pair of monsters might beget suggests a deeper fear of what *any* woman could beget, and more specifically of what his own bride might generate. For this reason, the creature's killing of Elizabeth gratifies one of Victor's deepest wishes.[1] In refusing to consummate his marriage on his wedding night, in leaving Elizabeth alone in their room while he stalks the inn corridors in search of the creature, Victor unconsciously invites the creature to take her.

The taking, I submit, is sexual as well as murderous—a tortured expression of the monster's hitherto frustrated desire. Just after Victor destroys the mate-to-be before the eyes of the monster and swears never to create one, the monster says, "You are my creator, but I am your master—obey!" (*F*, 162). Victor's refusal to do so goads the creature to exercise in his own murderous way the traditional right of a *feudal* master: the *droit de seigneur*, the lord's right to take his vassal's bride on her wedding night. Whether or not this brutal custom was ever mentioned in the history course that the creature overheard Felix giving to Safie (see *F*, 115–16), it is central to the plot of Mozart's *Marriage of Figaro* (1786), which Mary Shelley knew about well before she finished writing *Frankenstein*.[2] The echo of the *droit de seigneur* in the creature's wedding-night assault on Elizabeth amplifies all of the other signals pointing to rape: the creature's own fierce desire for a mate and the appearance of Elizabeth herself

---

9. Poovey, "My Hideous Progeny," 337. See also Mellor, *Mary Shelley*, 119–20.
1. Reminding us that Victor sees Elizabeth at various times as his "cousin" and "sister" and that she dissolves into his dead mother in his nightmare, James Twitchell argues that Victor unconsciously uses the monster to punish Elizabeth for exciting Victor's incestuous desires (*F*, 35, 146; see also *F*, 57); for Twitchell, the novel as a whole allegorizes "the male impulses and anxieties about incest as well as the female impulses and anxieties about birthing" (James B. Twitchell, "*Frankenstein* and the Anatomy of Horror," *Georgia Review* 37 [Spring 1983]: 60; see also 50–53). Twitchell's argument is plausible as far as it goes, but does not—in my judgement—reckon sufficiently with Victor's misogyny and the *monster's* desires.
2. See Mary Shelley, letter to Leigh Hunt, 3 Nov. 1823, *The Letters of Mary Wollstonecraft Shelley*, ed. Betty T. Bennett, 3 vols. (Baltimore, 1980), 1:395–96.

when, drawn by a scream from her room, Victor finds her dead body "thrown across the bed, her head hanging down, and her pale and distorted features half covered by her hair. Every where I turn I see the same figure—her bloodless arms and relaxed form flung by the murderer on its bridal bier" (*F*, 189). In this vivid picture of a "relaxed" body thrown or flung across the "bridal bier" of her bed, Victor portrays the victim of a murderous rape: a complex expression of his own misogyny, of the creature's lust for revenge, and of his frustrated longing for a mate.

Victor's response to this spectacle of murderous consummation—the closest he gets to consummation of any kind—is singularly revealing. After fainting and then reviving, he says, he rushed back to the body of Elizabeth "and embraced her with ardour" (*F*, 189). This passionate embrace of her dead body marks the very first time he is said to touch her at all, but it vividly recalls the nightmare in which he embraces an Elizabeth who turns into his mother's corpse. Just as the monster's murder of Elizabeth reenacts Victor's dismemberment of the monster's mate, Victor's embrace of his dead bride reenacts the dream, which itself reveals Victor's oedipal obsession with his dead mother, his inability to transfer his desires to any other woman.

Branagh's film situates this necrophilia within a triangle of desire binding both Victor and the creature to Elizabeth. Branagh's Victor, first of all, is a passionate lover as well as an obsessed scientist. Besides radiating a robust vitality that scarcely recalls the wasted, emaciated figure we meet in the novel, he loves his Elizabeth far more intensely than Mary Shelley's Victor loves his; he kisses her hungrily when he leaves for the university, and though he writes her no letters for months, he joyously seizes her when he rises one day from his sickbed to find her—improbably enough—playing the piano at the far end of the garret in which he has recently manufactured the monster. But if Branagh's film makes Victor far more passionate than Mary Shelley does, it also reveals something merely implied by her text: the link between Victor's project and his mother's death. In the novel, Victor's ambition to create life is ignited by Waldman's lecture on the "'new and almost unlimited powers'" of modern science (*F*, 47); the idea of reviving the dead is just a secondary possibility, and the dead mother comes to his mind only in his nightmare (see *F*, 53). In the film, however, it is her death that makes him resolve "to fight . . . death itself," and even though his project goes catastrophically awry, the monster's murder of Elizabeth reanimates this urge ("S," 45).

Like the monster of the novel, De Niro's monster kills Elizabeth on her wedding night while Victor is out seeking him with a gun. When Branagh's Victor returns to find the monster ripping out her heart, he shoots in vain at her fleeing assailant and then takes her corpse in his arms. But unlike the Victor of the text, who simply collapses with exhaustion at this point, Branagh's Victor desperately strives to revive Elizabeth by sewing her now shaven head to the torso of Justine, who (as in the novel) has been hanged for the murder of little William. After electrically animating this composite body in the sarcophagus/womb, clothing her in a wedding dress, and thrusting a wedding ring onto her finger, he begs her to recognize him, coaxes her to stand, and then waltzes her around the room, spinning and laughing with her until he sees the monster standing by the sarcophagus. For the monster, the sight of Elizabeth's shaven head and sutured body is a Lacanian *stade du miroir*. Seeing at last a woman whose mutilated form mirrors and thus affirms the humanity of his own, he says, "She's beautiful," and claims her as his long-promised mate ("S," 132).[3] But when Victor's counterclaim leads them to fight over her, she recoils at once from the men and from the alien body stitched to her head, and immolates herself with a kerosene lamp.

Students of Mary Shelley's text may find all this merely grotesque or recklessly sensational. Yet even as it wrenches the plot of the novel, this sequence exfoliates some of its major themes: Victor's necrophiliac obsession with his dead mother, the contradictions embedded in what Noël Carroll calls the "overreacher" plot of his ambition to create life from dead bodies, the monster's desire for a mate, and Victor's unwitting substitution of Elizabeth for the mate he destroyed.[4] Above all, Branagh's film evokes the oedipal conflict between Victor and his creature. In fighting over the reanimated body of Elizabeth, they remind us that Mary Shelley's Elizabeth was chosen by Victor's dying mother to be not only his mate but her successor as mother to the Frankenstein family (see *F*, 42). In the "beautiful" body of the sutured Elizabeth, De Niro's monster briefly finds his own mother and mate.

It is hardly news, of course, that *Frankenstein* tells the story of an oedipal conflict. But *Mary Shelley's Frankenstein* helps to show how tightly the novel knits the Oedipus story to the myths of Prometheus

3. He thus reverses the process by which, according to Linda Williams, a woman is punished for looking at a monster by being made to see his freakishness as a reflection of her own. See Linda Williams, "When the Woman Looks," in *Re-Vision: Essays in Feminist Film Criticism*, ed. Mary Ann Doane, Patricia Mellencamp, and Williams (Los Angeles, 1984), 85–88. Strikingly enough, a real mirror is used to generate a wholly different effect in the final scenes of the Edison *Frankenstein*. When the monster enters Victor's bedroom on his wedding night, he stands before a large mirror and then gradually fades away, leaving only his reflected image to be seen by Victor when he enters, as if the mirror now showed Victor his own monstrosity. But gradually the monster's image gives way to that of Victor in his young manhood—a sign that he has purged himself of monstrosity and can now marry Elizabeth. For more on the Edison version, which has recently been rediscovered, see Dixon, "The Films of *Frankenstein*," 166–69.
4. Noël Carroll, *The Philosophy of Horror, or Paradoxes of the Heart* (New York, 1990), 118.

and of Milton's Satan. Ultimately, Victor's struggle with the creature for possession of Elizabeth—their would-be mate and mother surrogate—springs from an ambition at once Promethean and Satanic: the ambition to rival the creative power of God.[5] In *Paradise Lost*, Satan defies God by claiming to be "self-begot, self-raised / By our own quickening power" (*PL*, bk. 5, ll. 860–61, 467), and he begets Sin all by himself, in the very act of conceiving his rebellion (see *PL*, bk. 2, ll. 748–61). When Satan's monstrous creature— literally a *monstrum*, a "sign / Portentous" (*PL*, bk. 2, ll. 760–61, 394)—excites his incestuous lust, he begets upon her the still more hideous monster of Death, who rapes her and thus impregnates her with the hellhounds that ceaselessly torment her (see *PL*, bk. 2, ll. 761–802, 394–95). The story of this unholy trinity is reconfigured in *Frankenstein*, where Sin splits into Elizabeth and a monster who plays the role of Death. But unlike Sin, Elizabeth is *not* conceived by the Satanic Victor. On the contrary, she is a rival creator, or rather an instrument in the scheme of creation conceived by God. That is why Victor exposes her not only to rape, which Sin undergoes, but death.[6]

The Branagh film reveals the implications of this point by moving one step beyond it. If Mary Shelley's Victor can embrace a woman only after she has turned into a corpse, Branagh's Victor finally seeks a woman he has created from corpses, a woman who signifies not the divine scheme of creation and reproduction but his own egomaniacal alternative to it. What he repeatedly begs of the reanimated Elizabeth is a tribute to himself: "Say my name" ("S," 130). In contesting Victor's claim on the woman that he believes had been promised to himself, De Niro's monster reasserts his right to be treated as God treated Adam. He reasserts, in other words, the primacy of the divine scheme, which makes mating essential to reproduction.

5

If radical departures from the plot of the novel may sometimes sharpen our understanding of it, they may also help to illuminate our cultural relation to the nameless monster who has captivated the popular imagination for the better part of two centuries. Probably the most outrageous and certainly one of the most original cinematic departures from Mary Shelley's novel is the scene from

---

5. Both Victor and the creature link themselves to Milton's Satan. The creature identifies himself with "'the fallen angel'" and deliberately echoes his words ("'Evil thenceforth became my good'") (*F*, 97, 212; see *PL*, bk. 4, l. 110, 423). Victor compares himself to "the archangel who aspired to omnipotence" (*F*, 204).
6. While rape can of course lead to impregnation, it can also serve as a crime against generation. In recent years, for instance, it has been reported that Bosnian Serbs have systematically raped Muslim women in order to make them unmarriageable and thus to eradicate the Muslim population.

Young Frankenstein in which Wilder's Friedrich Frankenstein presents Peter Boyle's monster to a theater audience. Dressed in white tie and tails, Friedrich and his creature tap dance and sing "Puttin' on the Ritz," with Friedrich singing most of the words and the monster periodically grunting out a nearly consonantless refrain, which sounds roughly like "ootin' on ah itz."

What can be learned from this bizarre spectacle of the monster as would-be Fred Astaire? On the one hand, Astaire's combination of sexual charm and urbane sophistication is about as far from Mary Shelley's repulsive giant as anything can be. On the other hand, the episode exemplifies what the creature has become in popular culture: a source of immensely popular entertainment. When Carroll writes that we enjoy horror fiction because we are fascinated "with the categorically transgressive beings that *star* in the genre," he reveals precisely what makes transgression pleasurable.[7] We are captivated not by transgression as such but by the starring performance of it. In the tap dance of *Young Frankenstein*, the creature acts out transgression for an audience, theatrically breaching the wall between savagery and sophistication.

Like so much else in *Young Frankenstein*, the scene parodies not the novel itself but earlier film versions of it, especially the Whale *Frankenstein*, which begins with a shot of Edward Van Sloan stepping out from behind a curtain to announce a film that "will thrill" and "may . . . horrify you!" Yet Van Sloan also plays Waldman, who in the novel makes comparable claims for modern chemistry. Galvanizing Victor by explaining what chemists can now do, Waldman says they "'have indeed performed miracles. . . . They have acquired new and almost unlimited powers; they can command the thunders of heaven, mimic the earthquake, and even mock the invisible world with its own shadows'" (*F*, 47). Waldman's language recalls the machinery of theater even as it adumbrates the spectacles of film. In the first part of the eighteenth century, thunder effects devised by the playwright John Dennis were, he testily charged, promptly stolen for a production of *Macbeth*.[8] At the end of the twentieth century, filmmakers not only mimic thunder and earthquakes but can recreate a raging Arctic sea on a studio stage, as production designers did for Branagh's *Frankenstein*.[9] The tap dance of *Young Frankenstein* exemplifies the theatricality of science as well as of transgression. Conceived by Victor in response to a lecture that defines chemistry as miraculous mimicry, Mary Shelley's monster was made to be exhibited as the supreme specimen of mimesis, the living

7. Carroll, "Disgust or Fascination: A Response to Susan Feagin," *Philosophical Studies* 65 (Feb. 1992): 85; emphasis mine.
8. William S. Walsh, *Handy-Book of Literary Curiosities* (Philadelphia, 1892), 1052.
9. See "The Filmmakers and Their Creations," 166.

simulacrum of life itself. In *Young Frankenstein*, this spectacle disarms a theater audience, by turns amusing and terrifying them. Presented by the Baron (Victor's grandson) as a scientific wonder, the creature fascinates the crowd by walking on command, then dancing and singing; but when his oafish diction makes the people laugh, he turns to rage and they flee in terror. In so doing, they reenact the flight of Mary Shelley's Victor, who rushes from his lab in "breathless horror and disgust" at the first sign of animation in a creature whose "beautiful" features were chosen for display but not meant for motion beyond the control of his maker—who would, of course, also be his exhibitor.

* * *

Film versions of *Frankenstein* violate the tacit compact made between novel and reader precisely by showing us what the novel decorously hides. According to Friedrich Schelling, approvingly quoted by Freud, the uncanny or *unheimlich* "'is the name for everything that ought to have remained . . . hidden and secret and has become visible.'"[1] The uncanny springs from the return of the repressed— "nothing new or foreign," Freud writes, "but something familiar and old-established in the mind that has been estranged only by the process of repression."[2] At the moment he comes to life, the monster is profoundly familiar to Victor, who has been laboring for months to construct him. But because Victor has up to now seen only "the beauty of the dream," the glorious prospect of singlehandedly creating life, he has blinded himself to actual ugliness quite as much as to actual beauty. His own animation of the monster opens his eyes to an ugliness he has hitherto refused to see, and the *Heimlichkeit* of this ugliness—the fact that it erupts in his own secret workroom—is exactly what makes it so *unheimlich*. When the monster that we mentally construct from the words of the text—in the workshop of our own reading experience—suddenly erupts as a visible object on the screen, we are made to see him with something like the eyes of Victor.

In the novel, of course, the monster's ugliness of face and form blinds Victor to the beauty of his soul, which is revealed in words that Victor cannot or will not understand because they come from one who seems to him nothing but a repulsive killer. Yet while the novel thus exposes Victor's double blindness, it also shields the reader from—or blinds the reader to—the shock of what Victor sees. With one brief exception, all we are asked to visualize in our reading are

---

1. Sigmund Freud, "The 'Uncanny'" (1919), *Collected Papers*, trans. Joan Riviere, 5 vols. (New York, 1959), 4:375. Freud quotes Schelling from Daniel Sanders's *Wörterbuch der deutschen Sprache* (1860).
2. Ibid., 394.

reactions *to* the sight of the monster—not the sight itself. We might imagine a film that showed us nothing more than such reactions. But aside from breaking the promise implicitly made by all reaction shots—the promise that we will be shown what provoked them— such a film would fail to show the monster's tortured longing to be sympathetically *seen*, to be the object of a desiring gaze.

The monster of the *Frankenstein* films, above all the Karloff monster of the Whale films, has in one sense realized this desire beyond his wildest dreams. Captivating millions, his image has been reproduced and disseminated as widely and as often as the *Mona Lisa*. But there is a vast difference between the riveting impact of his picture on a viewing audience and the repulsiveness of the figure it represents as *seen* by those around him. The monster of the screen cannot bask in universal admiration any more than he can relish the scornful laughter of a theater audience. On screen as in the novel, the monster knows the pitiless gaze of the other only as the witness to his inescapable monstrosity.

Pictures, we are told, are typically feminine objects consumed by the male gaze. Yet if a monster seems the very antithesis of a beautiful woman—whether da Vinci's Gioconda or Victor's doomed bride—he can nonetheless signify the feminine because he, like women, deviates from the normative male form.[3] The picture of a monster epitomizes this contradiction. Even as it displaces the picture of beauty, its radical deformity reinscribes both the feminine and the abject, which—in the words of Julia Kristeva—"disturbs identity, system, order," and yet also "beseeches, worries, and fascinates desire."[4] The moving picture of a talking monster is doubly monstrous, for it rends not only the lineaments of beauty but also the silence traditionally expected of women and pictures alike. In the end, what is most startling about the *Frankenstein* films is not that they make the monster visible but that in most cases they also make him audible. Subject and object, viewer and viewed, he speaks at once to our eyes and our ears.

---

3. "Traditionally," writes Barbara Creed, "the male body has been viewed as norm; the female body a deviation" (Barbara Creed, "Dark Desires: Male Masochism in the Horror Film," in *Screening the Male: Exploring Masculinities in Hollywood Cinema*, ed. Steven Cohan and Ina Rae Hark [London, 1993], 118). Aristotle argued that monstrosity began with female deviation "from the generic type" (Aristotle, *Generation of Animals*, trans. A. L. Peck [Cambridge, Mass., 1953], 401 [4.3.767b.9]). See also Huet, *Monstrous Imagination*, 3.
4. Julia Kristeva, *Powers of Horror: An Essay on Abjection*, trans. Leon S. Roudiez (New York, 1982), 4, 1. Mitchell has recently argued that insofar as pictures can be personified, they embody a conflict between the desire to master the beholder and a feminine sense of abjection; pictures and women, he writes, seek a power "manifested as *lack*, not as possession" (Mitchell, "What Do Pictures *Really* Want?" *October*, no. 77 [Summer 1996]: 76).

PATRICK BRANTLINGER

The Reading Monster†

* * *

Frankenstein is so overloaded with ambivalent psychological as well as political meanings that it can be, and has been, interpreted in many conflicting yet persuasive ways. With the French Revolution as general context, Victor can be seen as representing *either* aristocratic oppression *or* Enlightenment rationality and radicalism (given his father's liberal politics and his obvious identification with scientific rationality, the latter interpretation seems more convincing). From the perspectives of psychoanalytic and feminist theory, Victor can also be understood as an abusive or criminally negligent parent of either gender—a father-creator in some sense rivaling God (and therefore a stand-in for Satan), *or* a monstrous mother-figure giving birth to a monster child and then abandoning it.[1] The obscene father of *Otranto, The Monk*, and other Gothic romances becomes the obscene son, whose pleasure arises from the destruction of family. But this obscene son is also a victim, who may be variously read as the abandoned child, the oppressed masses, the unconscious or Id to Victor's Ego, or himself a demon or even the devil. Based on his reading of *Paradise Lost*, the Monster likens himself *both* to Adam *and* to Lucifer. To put it mildly, the possible meanings proliferate. As Chris Baldick suggests, this is one of the ways in which *Frankenstein* itself acquires an anti-formal monstrosity, an uncontrollable, irrational excess of signification that transcends the boundaries of normal, comprehensible discourse.

The discursive excess of *Frankenstein* can simultaneously be identified as sublimity, as insanity, and as literary deformity. In her 1831

---

† From *The Reading Lesson: The Threat of Mass Literacy in Nineteenth Century British Fiction* (Bloomington: Indiana UP, 1998), 59–65. Reprinted by permission of Indiana University Press.

1. Autobiographical readings of *Frankenstein* have tended to interpret its nightmarish family romance by identifying Frankenstein as William Godwin and the Monster as his daughter, Mary Shelley. Following Ellen Moers's "Female Gothic" (reproduced in Levine, *The Endurance of Frankenstein*, 77–87), it has also become standard to interpret Victor's creation of the Monster as a nightmarish birth trauma, expressing Mary Shelley's horror over the births and tragic early deaths of her children. And the horror is magnified by recalling that Mary Wollstonecraft died in giving birth to the author of *Frankenstein*. These autobiographical interpretations sometimes also point to the male double-goers in Mary Shelley's life, her husband and Lord Byron, who, however radical their political intentions, marginalized and victimized her no matter what she did or wrote (see, for instance, Knoepflmacher 96–97). How else to explain the fact that *both* Victor and his Monster are gendered male? Whatever the full range of meanings of its gender troubles, *Frankenstein* obviously belongs among the works of paranoid Gothic that George Haggerty and Eve Sedgwick identify with the difficulties and traumas of representing male homosexuality.

"Author's Introduction," Mary Shelley famously describes the origin of her Gothic romance in the ghost-story contest with her husband, Lord Byron, and Dr. Polidori, and in the vivid waking nightmare in which "I saw the pale student of unhallowed arts kneeling beside the thing he had put together. I saw the hideous phantasm of a man stretched out, and then, on the working of some powerful engine, show signs of life" (172). As in the example of *Otranto*, nightmare becomes novel through verbal elaboration, with the image of the Monster at its core. The introduction also parallels the main story, both in narrating a creation, a metaphoric birth, and in embedding one story within another, the nightmare within the larger essay. Victor Frankenstein's creation-story thus minors Mary Shelley's creation-story. In this labyrinth of mirror-like, embedded stories, Monster and novel become interchangeable. In some sense, so do Monster and novelist. The more obvious parallel is between novelist and mad scientist, both the creators of the Monster. But the central, basic story-within-story of the introduction is the nightmare; and the central, basic story-within-story of the main novel is the Monster's narration. When Mary Shelley ends her introduction by bidding her "hideous progeny [to] go forth and prosper" (173), the identification is complete: the novel itself is the ultimate monstrosity, a transgressive discourse that apparently obeys no literary rules, that is in many ways grotesque, nightmarish, and therefore all the more powerful and effective as a tale of terror that, as Daniel Cottom puts it, "images the monstrous nature of [all] representation" (66).[2]

Frankenstein is, among other things, a novel about two educations or, rather, *mis*educations, Victor's and the Monster's.[3] To the extent that Victor pursues his course of reading and research in isolation and against the advice of his father and his professors, he is a sort of autodidact—willfully so, because he chooses isolation. In contrast, the Monster is perforce an autodidact, in some respects similar to the working-class autodidacts whose autobiographies serve as a rich source of evidence in E. P. Thompson's *Making of the English Working Class*. Victor's education is upper-class, indulgent, liberal in at least two senses. Victor's father is a political liberal, residing in

2. Compare Peter Brooks's comment that in *Frankenstein* "there is no transcendent signified because the fact of monsterism is never either justified or overcome, but it is simply passed along the [signifying] chain, finally come to inhabit the reader himself who, as animator of the text, is left with the contamination of monsterism . . . the text remains as indelible record of the monstrous, emblem of language's murderous lack of transcendent reference" (" 'Godlike Science' " 220).
3. For an interpretation of *Frankenstein* in relation especially to theories of women's education, see Alan Richardson, *Literature, Education, and Romanticism*: "In describing the education of a monster, Shelley challenges . . . the tradition of writing on female education and conduct associated especially (after Wollstonecraft) with [Rousseau's] *Émile*, in which women are at once sentimentalized and viewed, anxiously, as deformed or monstrous in comparison with an explicitly male norm" (206).

liberal Geneva, and Victor's schooling, with its emphasis on natural science, reflects Enlightenment principles. Yet in isolation, Victor's reading leads him obsessively, regressively backward to Gothic superstition. Reading—and therefore knowledge—is not intrinsically progressive, and even the best educations can backfire.

In his pursuit of the knowledge that will enable him to create life, Victor turns to works of Gothic alchemy and the "exploded systems" of Cornelius Agrippa, Paracelsus, and Albertus Magnus, though his father dismisses their writings as "sad trash" (21).[4] Victor's course of Gothic reading makes him a sort of scientific Quixote figure, though instead of chivalric romances, the texts he consumes are anti-Bibles, like the necromantic "small book" that allows Ambrosio to conjure up the Devil at the end of *The Monk*. At Ingolstadt, he is told again, this time by Professor Krempe, that he has been reading "sad trash," or what might be called Gothic science fiction (perhaps like *Frankenstein* itself):

> "Every minute . . . that you have wasted on those books is utterly and entirely lost. You have burdened your memory with exploded systems, and useless names. Good God! In what desert land have you lived, where no one was kind enough to inform you that these fancies . . . are a thousand years old, and as musty as they are ancient? I little expected in this enlightened and scientific age to find a disciple of Albertus Magnus and Paracelsus." (26)

Professor Waldman, however, whom Frankenstein next consults, is of the different, more sympathetic opinion that modern science has developed out of the "exploded systems" of the past. Therefore, the ideas of the creators of those systems may still be worth studying, if only to avoid their errors.

Through Waldman, Shelley suggests a continuity between medieval alchemy and modern chemistry. But in stressing this continuity, she also renders undecidable whether the Monster's creation is the result of modern science or of black magic. In one direction, her horror story appears to be pro-Enlightenment: Professor Krempe and Victor's father both reject the "exploded systems" of the past as so much superstition. In another, more powerful direction, however, *Frankenstein* is an anti-Enlightenment text. As has often been noted, it offers the paradigmatic science fiction tale of "the dream of reason producing monsters," or in other words of modern science

---

4. The first reviewers of *Frankenstein* often dismiss it in similar terms—"a tissue of horrible and disgusting absurdity," John Wilson Croker calls it (189)—while worrying about its possible nefarious effects on its readers. Croker believes that *Frankenstein* is too "insane" to do much damage, although he writes that "it inculcates no lesson of conduct, manners, or morality; it cannot mend, and will not even amuse its readers, unless their taste have been [already] deplorably vitiated" (190).

run amock through the overreaching ambition and obsession of the mad scientist. From either direction, moreover, reading—or at least, reading in isolation from human companionship and community—is represented as a dangerous activity, leading to insanity.

The Monster's *Bildungsroman* both parallels and contrasts with Victor's. Learning to speak and to read in isolation, the Monster at least vicariously enjoys the humanizing companionship of Old DeLacey, Felix, Agatha, and Safie. The family circle the Monster longs to join represents everything that Victor, in his obsessive pursuit of the secrets of life and death, has rejected. When his potential adoptive family rejects him, the Monster sets forth on his path of vengeance, destroying Victor's family and friends. As in anti-Jacobin discourse about the Revolution, according to which the *philosophes* conjure up the monstrous mob, *Frankenstein* is a negative family romance for both protagonists.[5]

The story of Victor's pursuit of arcane, in some sense forbidden knowledge involves his self-alienation—loss of self-knowledge, insanity, destruction. The story of the Monster's acquisition of language and literacy is, in contrast, the narrative of his coming to self-knowledge, though for him self-knowledge and self-alienation are identical:

> I had admired the perfect forms of my cottagers . . . but how was I terrified, when I viewed myself in a transparent pool! At first I started back, unable to believe that it was indeed I who was reflected in the mirror; and when I became fully convinced that I was in reality the monster that I am, I was filled with the bitterest sensations. . . . (76)

The Monster recognizes his monstrosity in a moment of reflection like Lacan's mirror-stage, reinforced by his more or less simultaneous acquisition of language.[6] In discovering his own monstrosity, moreover, the Monster also discovers that of the humans who reject him and, indeed, that of human history in general. The Monster eavesdrops as Felix instructs Safie in French by reading Volney's *Ruins* to her, from which he obtains his first "cursory knowledge of history" (80). The other books the Monster accidentally acquires and then reads (*Paradise Lost*, Plutarch's *Lives*, and Goethe's *Sorrows of Young Werther*) deal with cosmic, public, and private themes, and "constitute a possible Romantic *cyclopedia universalis*" (Brooks 210). All three additional texts reinforce the main history lesson he has learned from Volney's *Ruins*, which is also the main lesson of

5. For various versions of the French Revolution as "family romance," see Lynn Hunt.
6. For Lacan, the mirror-stage is the moment when an infant begins to move from the Imaginary into the Symbolic, into language, and thus into the self-alienation that language entails. Compare Peter Brooks in Levine (207–208).

his dawning self-awareness and therefore of his entire education: "sorrow only increased with knowledge" (81). With this melancholy lesson in mind, the Monster declares, romantically if rather incoherently, that it would have been better if "I had for ever remained in my native wood, nor known or felt beyond the sensations of hunger, thirst, and heat!" (81)

From his self-education, Mary Shelley's sympathetically chaotic, homicidal creature develops the reasoning and rhetorical power to challenge his creator, just as Caleb Williams[7] challenges and ultimately defeats Falkland through speaking and writing. Caleb's literacy enables him to forge the weapon—the novel itself—with which he ultimately kills his aristocratic persecutor. So, too, the Monster is in some sense the author of the murderous text in which he is also one of the dual protagonists, the author or narrator of his own tale of terror to Victor, of course, but also the crucial, most vital image in the originary nightmare, *its* cause or "most powerful engine." His transgression of literary, discursive boundaries is rendered possible only through his acquisition of the power of language, his ability, despite great disadvantages, to become both a speaking and a reading Monster.

Though able to read and to speak with great eloquence, the Monster may or may not be able to write. His narrative is (only) an oral one, and so is Victor's to Robert Walton, who then transcribes both oral accounts in his journal and, later, in letters to his sister. As Garrett Stewart notes, however, these letters are "never definitively received by the sister back in England to whom they are addressed" (116).[8] The reader "receives" them, of course, but *Frankenstein* is a tale in which, Stewart suggests, the reader's own identity is questioned or called into crisis. Both *Frankenstein* and *The Last Man* (1826) invoke "an attention whose personification they finally obliterate"—in the case of *The Last Man*, quite simply because the narrator of Shelley's apocalyptic tale is also the world's "last author, sole survivor of a universal plague, [who] has no conceivable readers left." But the "conscripted" readers of *Frankenstein* also are not clearly "the solid bourgeois citizen, the stablized monolithic presence" invoked by Dickens, Trollope, and George Eliot (Stewart 115).

As with other Gothic romances, only perhaps more pointedly, *Frankenstein* seems to pose a *caveat lector* question by its own questionable narrative structure: who is reading this "hideous progeny" and with what possibly dire consequences? The reader of *Franken-*

---

7. For more on Godwin's novel, sec the Christa Knellwolf selection on p. 506.
8. For a related analysis of *Frankenstein* in terms of the epistolary novel and letters not sent, mis-sent, and "correspondence" more generally, see Mary Favret, *Romantic Correspondence*, 176–196. On orality versus writing during the Romantic era, see also Nicholas Hudson, *Writing and European Thought*, 143–160.

stein who accepts it at face value—who literally credits the story as true—must be at least as impressionable and irrational as Victor in his imbibing of the "sad trash" of the alchemists, or as the Monster in his first, halting reading lessons. On the other hand, the skeptical reader of *Frankenstein* who sees it for what it is—"hideous progeny," "sad trash," incredible stories-within-story—must, besides doubting what she or he reads, be in some sense an even more doubtful, indeterminate figure than the believing reader. Whether doubting or credulous, why would *any* reader in her or his right mind, *Frankenstein* seems to ask, read its multiple tales of terror? Far more than in most realistic fiction, in Gothic romances the reader is "conscripted" as a sort of shadowy or ghostly extra, just offstage, who may or may not partake of (or believe in) the action, but whose very involvement with the tale is both questioning and called into question. As Stewart says, both *Frankenstein* and *The Last Man* invoke a readerly "attention whose personification they finally obliterate" (115). In *The Last Man*, of course, the obliteration of the implied reader is also the obliteration of reading and writing, of civilization, of humanity. But in both romances, and in Gothic more generally, the critique of Enlightenment rationality involves also a critique of the very motives for reading and writing—indeed, of writing and reading such questionable texts as Gothic romances: the very tale the reader consumes, or, better, the very act of reading the tale turns into a demonstration of the monstrous uses to which literacy can be put.

* * *

What has seemed ultimately most monstrous and therefore most difficult for readers of *Frankenstein* over the years to accept is precisely the Monster's literacy. The key to the obsessive erasure of that literacy in retellings of *Frankenstein* on stage, in film, and in other popular cultural forms seems to reside in the Monster's evident likeness to that other, collective monstrosity, Burke's "swinish multitude"—that is, to the working-class masses. Like the collective, "many-headed monster" of the crowd in Shakespeare and other Renaissance writers, Mary Shelley's Monster is, after all, multiple, made out of the body-parts of various dead individuals. Whether or not she had Hobbes's trope of society as a gigantic "artificial man" in mind, some such notion is reinforced also by the multiplying narrators in her story (including herself as the ultimate dreamer-author): the novel itself seems to be, or to acknowledge being, a collective creation. Moreover, despite the absence of explicit political references in her nightmare novel, that there is a social-class fantasy at work in its political unconscious has seemed evident to many of its interpreters. Thus, besides Sterrenburg and Baldick, both Franco Moretti and Paul O'Flinn read *Frankenstein* in Marxist terms as an allegory of class conflict. For Moretti, "the literature of terror" in general "is born precisely *out of the terror of a split society,*" and in the case of *Frankenstein,* the "sociological fulcrum" is "the creation of the proletariat" during the Industrial Revolution (83, 89; see also Lovell 64–67). For O'Flinn, besides the French Revolution, the more specific context in which Mary Shelley hatched her "hideous progeny" was that of the Luddite machine-breaking rebellion of 1811–1813, the uprising that Charlotte Brontë would later depict in her industrial novel, *Shirley.* Furthermore, as Howard Malchow argues in his study of "Gothic images of race" in nineteenth-century fiction, an equally persuasive interpretation of the Monster identifies him with the oppressed African in discourse about the West Indies and slavery, a connection explicitly invoked in parliamentary debates about abolition (Malchow 33).

Especially in stage versions, the mute Monster, with darkened or, perhaps, Africanized skin color, conjured up the slavery controversy. But this "Calibanized" version of the Monster was still associated with the "wage-slave" at home in Britain. Also identifying the Monster with the working class, Daniel Cottom points to the Caliban-like labor that the Monster performs for the cottagers—only, unlike Caliban's, his labor seems to those he bestows it upon as if "performed by an invisible hand," a trope that echoes Adam Smith's "invisible hand" of the marketplace: "The source of fertility and wealth is described as the labor of a monster that is man's creation, and the class-analysis to which this passage lends itself is earned over to modern economic conditions through . . . Smith's famous image for the unconscious regulation of a laissez-faire market" (Cottom 66).

But Smith's "invisible hand" is not the numerous hands of the working class. In any case, as Chris Baldick demonstrates, the connection between Frankenstein's Monster and the working-class masses was made early and often in the nineteenth century. In her 1848 novel about Manchester factory workers, *Mary Barton,* Elizabeth Gaskell likens them to the Monster, only in doing so she both identifies the creature with his creator and divests him of his education and, indeed, his language:

> The actions of the uneducated seem to me typified in those of Frankenstein, that monster of many human qualities, ungifted with a soul, a knowledge of the difference between good and evil.
>
> The people rise up to life; they irritate us, they terrify us, and we become their enemies. Then, in the sorrowful moment of our triumphant power, their eyes gaze on us with a mute reproach. Why have we made them what they are; a powerful monster, yet without the inner means for peace and happiness? (219–220)

Both Gaskell's identification of the Monster with his maker and her erasure of its education, rendering it inarticulate or "mute," are repeated endlessly in later mass-cultural retellings of Mary Shelley's story. The dumbing down of the Monster actually commenced earlier than *Mary Barton*, however. In *Presumption: or the Fate of Frankenstein*, Richard Brinsley Peake's 1823 dramatic rendering (the first stage version), the Monster has already been silenced, endowed only with "the mind of an infant" (Baldick 59). Similarly, in "The New Frankenstein," a story published in *Fraser's Magazine* in 1838, "what is 'new' about the monster of this tale is really only the established pattern of the stage versions: that it is mute and that its problem is largely one of possessing no soul" (Baldick 141).

But why, when the Monster has been stripped of a soul as well as his education, rendering him wordless, has it been so easy to confuse him with his educated, articulate maker by calling him "Frankenstein"? A simplistic answer is that, because the Monster is nameless, it makes sense to give him his father-maker's name. Also, from a psychoanalytic perspective, the mute Monster of stage and screen has seemed most readily understandable as an emanation of Victor's psyche, his Id personified. The Monster may be Victor's alter ego, his murderous phantom or *Doppelgänger*, his Id or his *petit objet a*, even his "sublime object of ideology," but it is only Victor who is identified with consciousness and, hence, with language.[9] Victor/Ego speaks, reads, and writes; Monster/Id, the Real that remains forever outside the Symbolic Order, cannot. Yet they are the two halves of a divided self. Victor's numerous declarations of guilt for the murders that the Monster commits, coupled with his long bouts of either profound depression or raving lunacy, help to make the conflation easy; and that easy identification of the Monster with its maker, so often replicated in movies, comics, advertising, and television, is both an additional incoherence or monstrosity within the story and a tangent of the proliferating, often contradictory meanings that radiate from it.

Within the novel, the *Doppelgänger* motif that promotes slippages like Gaskell's is reinforced by the dual narratives of Monster and maker. The Monster's narrative is filtered through Victor's, and both are in turn filtered through Robert Walton. That the Monster, though if anything more eloquent and rational than Victor, speaks only through the ventriloquism of Victor (and Walton) encourages both his identification with his creator and the erasure of his demoniac literacy, which is also his ability to represent himself. If the subaltern speaks in Mary Shelley's Gothic romance, it does so only

---

9 Slavoj Žižek, *The Sublime Object of Ideology*. In *Enjoy Your Symptom!* Žižek contends that "the monster is the subject of the Enlightenment" (134).

by being spoken for by another, dominant voice—one that, however, attributes to the Monster an amazing literacy and eloquence.

* * *

JONATHAN BATE

[*Frankenstein* and the State of Nature][†]

* * *

Mary Shelley's *Frankenstein* begins with the Enlightenment quest to master nature. The narrator, Robert Walton, is sailing north in the direction of the magnetic pole. Late eighteenth-century science had yielded new knowledge about two invisible forces which, it was speculated, might be keys to the secret of life itself: magnetism and electricity. The first of Mary Shelley's questers is in pursuit of the former force, the second of the latter. It is the sight of the effect of an electrical storm which inspires Victor Frankenstein to become a scientist.

For Walton, knowledge of the earth is also a means to conquest on behalf of his nation. The second motivation for his journey is the desire to break through the north-eastern passage in the hope of facilitating British colonization and trade. That such an ambition brings with it the destruction of nature is signalled to the reader not only by the fact that Walton trains for his expedition by getting himself hired on a whaler, but also by the identity of the role-model whom he self-consciously adopts. He admits that he has derived his passion for polar exploration from Coleridge's Ancient Mariner. He jokes to his sister that he will return home safely, since he will not go so far as to kill an albatross. The Mariner negates the Coleridgean principle that there is one life within us and abroad: his arbitrary act of shooting the albatross is the archetypal crime against nature. The killing of the bird breaks man apart from the rest of nature, so that even after his act of atonement in blessing the water-snakes the Mariner remains an outsider. He will always be a wanderer, an alien, a creature of knowledge and of language who will never be allowed to rest at home, to dwell upon the earth. Walton and Frankenstein suffer a similar fate.

Walton is witness to the last titanic struggle between Frankenstein and his creation. The Creature is first seen through Walton's eyes from a distance of half a mile: he appears to be 'a savage inhabitant of some undiscovered isle'. The next day, Frankenstein appears: he,

† From "The State of Nature," in *The Song of the Earth* (Cambridge: Harvard UP, 2000), 49–55. Reprinted by permission.

by contrast, is identified as 'an European' with a 'cultivated' mind. The Creature is thus identified with primitivism, with the state of nature, Frankenstein with cultivation, the state of Enlightenment. Frankenstein's narrative of his own life confirms his role as a son of the Enlightenment intent on the conquest of nature's secrets. After a Rousseauesque childhood in which he is at one with his Swiss environment, he falls into scientific knowledge. He shares the ambition of Sir Humphry Davy, whose 1802 *Discourse, Introductory to a Course of Lectures on Chemistry* Mary Shelley read before writing the novel. Chemistry, writes Davy, has given to man

> an acquaintance with the different relations of the parts of the external world; and more than that, it has bestowed upon him powers which may be almost called creative; which have enabled him to modify and change the beings surrounding him, and by his experiments to interrogate nature with power, not simply as a scholar, passive and seeking only to understand her operations, but rather as a master, active with his own instruments.

Frankenstein's education re-enacts the history of European science, as he progresses from alchemical fancy to sceptical Enlightenment (embodied in the figure of his first university teacher, Krempe) to modern chemistry (embodied in his ideal teacher, Waldman, who, unlike Krempe, grants that the older alchemical theories must still be respected because they laid the foundations for the modern quest to understand the origins and nature of life).

The onset of Frankenstein's higher education into the mastery of nature coincides with the death of his mother and his departure from home. Science is thus set in opposition to the female principles of maternity and natural landscape. The bond with both biological mother and mother nature is broken. I would suggest that Mary Shelley makes Frankenstein a Genevan because of that city's associations with Rousseau, whose example had powerfully yoked together the idea of childhood, the bond with nature and the environment around Lake Geneva, where Shelley was writing her novel. When Frankenstein is far away in Ireland, he speaks of his 'devouring *maladie du pays*', an allusion to what was regarded as a national characteristic of the Swiss: their pathological longing for the homeland. The word nostalgia, with all its Rousseauesque associations, entered the English language in the late eighteenth century as a translation of German *Heimweh*, the technical term for Swiss homesickness.

Frankenstein cuts himself off from the natural environment of the Swiss Alps and encloses himself in his laboratory. There, like a genetic engineer a century and a half before the discovery of DNA, he pursues his dream of becoming, as the subtitle of the novel has it, 'the modern Prometheus': 'a new species would bless me as its creator and source; many happy and excellent natures would owe their being to me'. But the attempt to create a new nature is a transgression against nature. Frankenstein frequently uses a language of light-bringing—of Enlightenment—in describing his task, but the accomplishment of his deed occurs on a dark and dreary night of November; the Creature's first motion is the opening of a 'dull yellow eye' seen 'by the glimmer of the half-extinguished light'. Enlightenment proves to be endarkening. Once Frankenstein brings the Creature to life, his own eyes become 'insensible to the charms of nature'. His nightmare immediately after the creation is of the destruction of the feminine principle of nature: he imagines that on kissing his beautiful beloved Elizabeth, she is transformed into the corpse of his dead mother. By going against the natural process of generation, by making a child of his own without submission to the fecundity of a woman's womb, he symbolically kills mother nature. His subsequent story veers wildly between moments of restoration to and by nature in its pure mountain form and further severances of environmental belonging.

Where Frankenstein is the representative of Enlightenment man, the Creature is an embodiment of the state of nature. His autobiographical narrative tells the familiar Rousseauesque story—mediated via the English Rousseau, Mary Shelley's father, William Godwin—of a fall from natural benevolence to misery and fiendishness.

On being deserted by his father Frankenstein, the Creature retreats to the forest where, like Rousseau's natural man, he eats berries and shades himself under the foliage of the trees. The order of his life replicates the history outlined in Giambattista Vico's *The New Science*: 'This was the order of human institutions: first the forests, after that the huts, then the villages, next the cities, and finally the academies'. But because the Creature is created from the last of these institutions, from the knowledge of the academies, he is foredoomed to degeneration. It is Enlightenment man who invents the natural man; like Rousseau's second *Discourse*, Frankenstein uses the state of nature as a heuristic device to critique both Ancien Régime tyranny and the enlightened aspirations of the present.

As in the *Discourse*, the differentiating process initiated by the learning of language is a key stage in the fall. Language, property and institutionalization bring about the fall from nature into history, learned by the Creature as he overhears Felix's readings from Volney's *Ruins of Empire*: 'While I listened to the instructions which Felix bestowed upon the Arabian, the strange system of human society was explained to me. I heard of the division of property, of immense wealth and squalid poverty; of rank, descent, and noble blood.'

When Frankenstein first re-encounters his Creature in the sublime natural setting of Chamounix, he says 'There can be no com-

munity between you and me'. Frankenstein's crime, committed in
the isolation of his laboratory, has been to deny the principle of community. Like Coleridge's Mariner, he breaks the contract of mutual
dependency which binds species in a network of reciprocal relations.
The attempt to cheat death through knowledge instead of intercourse is the novel's original sin. The second crime is that against the
Creature, which drives him into exile and turns him to malignancy.
This crime could be called 'speciesism'. The blind old man De Lacy
is prepared to help the unknown stranger, eliciting from him the
delighted reply, 'I shall not be driven from the society and sympathy
of your fellow-creatures'. But with the entrance of the sighted—the
Enlightened—Felix, Safie and Agatha, the Creature is regarded as
Other, as alien. He is driven out. On the lonely night that follows, all
of nature seems to him harmonized whereas he alone is alone. When
he returns to the De Lacy family's cottage of pastoral retreat two
days later, he finds that 'My protectors had departed, and had broken
the only link that held me to the world'. Once that link is broken, he
proceeds to turn against the ecosystem in which the De Lacys had
eked out their living: 'I placed a variety of combustibles around the
cottage; and, after having destroyed every vestige of cultivation in the
garden, I waited with forced impatience until the moon had sunk to
commence my operations.' Here the Promethean knowledge of the
instrumentality of fire is returned upon man with a vengeance.

The Creature's request for a mate comes from a desire to regain
some form of community, to 'become linked to the chain of existence' once again. Movingly, he swears 'by the earth which I inhabit'
that he will do no harm to any other species. He dreams of returning to the state of nature with a beloved partner, going off to live as
a vegetarian in America every bit in the manner of Coleridge and
Southey's ideal pantisocratic community:

> If you consent, neither you nor any other human being shall
> ever see us again: I will go to the vast wilds of South America.
> My food is not that of man; I do not destroy the lamb and the
> kid to glut my appetite; acorns and berries afford me sufficient
> nourishment. My companion will be of the same nature as
> myself, and will be content with the same fare. We shall make
> our bed of dried leaves; the sun will shine on us as on man,
> and will ripen our food. The picture I present to you is peace-
> ful and human, and you must feel that you could deny it only
> in the wantonness of power and cruelty.

The idea of the wilds of South America as a place where one might
recover the lost state of nature is one to which writers returned
throughout the nineteenth and early twentieth centuries, as we will
see.

Frankenstein initially denies the Creature's request on the grounds that the 'joint wickedness' of the monster and his partner 'might desolate the world'. Later, he relents, but then changes his mind again, for fear of creating a race of destructive supermen. But in reality it is he himself, the Enlightenment scientist, who is desolating the world. It is he who refuses to give his Creature any name but Monster, who by treating him as a monster turns him into one. The Creature, we may say, is the repressed nature which returns and threatens to destroy the society that has repressed it.

The close of *Frankenstein* offers an image of nature's continuing power to resist the human quest for mastery. Enlightenment mastery is based on *division*. Knowledge is divided into categories as in that archetypal enterprise of the eighteenth century, the encyclopaedia. Chemistry, as Davy suggests, breaks nature down into its constituent parts. Frankenstein's creation begins from bits and pieces of body part. Mary Shelley's narrative ends in the Arctic, which is, by contrast, *a place where divisions do not hold*.

The Creature does finally return to the state of nature: he is swallowed up among the ice-floes of the north. Perhaps the quest for human mastery began at the moment in the Genesis narrative when God divided the land from the waters. But on the shifting pack ice of the Arctic, there is no division between land and sea. The phenomenology of dualism cannot function. As Barry Lopez has demonstrated in his wonderful book, *Arctic Dreams*, the Arctic makes you see differently: time, season, light and spatial relations do not operate in the ways that we who know only the temperate zones regard as 'natural'. Like Coleridge's Mariner, crossing and recrossing the equatorial line, seeing the sun rise first one side then the other, temperate man is disoriented in the Arctic:

> The idea that the sun 'rises in the east and sets in the west' simply does not apply. The thought that a 'day' consists of a morning and a forenoon, an afternoon and an evening, is a convention . . . The pattern is not the same here.

But this is a healthy disorientation, for to acknowledge it is to realize that Western man may not after all be the master of all things. As Lopez shows, we are still remarkably ignorant about many northern wonders—the habits of polar bears, migration patterns, the life cycle of narwhals. You cannot fix or predict life in the Arctic: ice is both land and sea, so in the far north (and south) maps, those markers of human mastery, can only ever be provisional. If only Walton had known that the North Magnetic Pole itself does not stay in one and the same place.

✳   ✳   ✳

ANNE K. MELLOR

Frankenstein, Racial Science, and the Yellow Peril[†]

* * *

The observation that the Creature is of a different skin color and hence of a different race is made for the reader long before we enter Frankenstein's attic laboratory and witness the climax of Frankenstein's experiment. The first glimpse we as readers have of the Creature is in the opening pages of the novel when Walton and his men, seeking a passage to China through the North Pole, their ship trapped in an icefloe, see at a distance of half a mile "a low carriage, fixed on a sledge and drawn by dogs, pass on towards the north," carrying "a being which had the shape of a man, but apparently of gigantic stature" (17). The very next morning, they rescue the stranded Victor Frankenstein, whom Walton describes as "not, as the other traveller seemed to be, a savage inhabitant of some undiscovered island, but an European" (18). The Creature then, is not an European, not Caucasian, but of some other race, like those found by Captain James Cook in his famous recent voyages to the Pacific Islands or by the East India Company's trading ships sailing among the spice islands in the Indian Ocean. But this "savage" inhabits an island *north* of the "wilds of Tartary and Russia" (200) whence Frankenstein has pursued him, north of Archangel, the northernmost city in western Asia from which Walton has set sail.

A yellow-skinned man crossing the steppes of Russia and Tartary, with long black hair and dun-colored eyes—most of Mary Shelley's nineteenth-century readers would immediately have recognized the Creature as a member of the Mongolian race, one of the five races of man first classified in 1795 by Johann Friedrich Blumenbach, the scholar who, more than any other, founded the modern science of physical anthropology. In constructing Frankenstein's creature as a member of a distinctly different, non-Caucasian race, Mary Shelley again located her novel at the cutting edge of early-nineteenth-century scientific research. I have elsewhere discussed the ways in which she drew on other contemporary scientific discoveries—Luigi Galvani's theory of animal electricity, Humphrey Davy's discoveries in chemistry, and Erasmus Darwin's theory of animal and human evolution through sexual selection—in order to define Frankenstein's project

† *Nineteenth-Century Contexts* 23.1 (2001): 2–4, 7–11, 25–28. Reprinted by permission. The list of Works Cited begins on p. 488.

I am grateful to my colleagues Benjamin A. Elman, Jinqi Ling, and Miriam Silverberg, and to Christopher Keep, for their invaluable help with this essay. [*Mellor's note.*]

as interventionist or "bad" science and his creature as an antievolutionary species composed of both human and animal organs ("*Frankenstein*: Feminist Critique" and *Mary Shelley*). Here I want to explore the ways in which she used insights garnered from the new scientific field of ethnology or natural history to suggest yet another way in which Victor has contradicted his own goal, the creation of a "new" and better species, in his construction of the Creature.

Let me briefly summarize eighteenth-century concepts of the origin and character of the human species. By 1800, two opposing theories explaining the major differences between human "tribes" or "nations" were in wide circulation in Europe. One theory, the polygenist theory, reaffirmed by such thinkers as Immanuel Kant, Lord Monboddo, and Charles White, held that human tribes had originated independently one from another and could be placed in clearly demarcated degrees along the great Chain of Being. The "missing link" between human beings and apes was filled, according to these writers, by black Africans, who constituted a distinct and different species. In opposition to this biological determinism, many scholars followed Christian doctrine and the writings of Aristotle, Alexander, and Strabo in arguing that all the human "tribes" or nations were members of the same human species or Family of Man, descended through time from one original couple (Adam and Eve). Differences in skin and hair color, skull formation, and anatomy were attributed to organic alteration caused in large part by differing *environmental* conditions, such as climate, water, air, and food. The most famous and widely respected proponent of this monogenist view was of course Comte de Buffon, who both in his 1749 *Variétés dans l'espèce humaine* and again in his 44-volume *Histoire naturelle* (1749–1804) argued that animals who can procreate together, and whose progeny can procreate, are of one species. Buffon therefore concluded that all humans belong to the same species but that "climate, food, manners and customs produce not only a difference in sentiment, but even in the external form of different people" (Buffon 107; Eddy 107–48).

It was Johann Friedrich Blumenbach who in his doctoral dissertation in 1775, entitled *De generis humani nativa varietate*, developed the analytical concept of race to classify the specific varieties or subgroups within the human species. As both Nicholas Hudson and Ivan Hannaford have demonstrated, the concept of race as a stable, transnational, biological or genetic category was not widely available before the late eighteenth century.[1] In 1775, Blumenbach—

---

1. As Nicholas Hudson and Ivan Hannaford show, the concept of race (as opposed to nation or tribe) was a late-eighteenth-century construction, loosely based on the divisions between the five known continents. The first person to use the term "race" in its modern sense was François Bernier, who in 1684 identified four distinct human races.

following Renaissance and Linnaean theories of the four humors—identified *four* races of man: Caucasian (a term he coined, drawing on recent theories that IndoEuropean languages originated in the region of the Caucasus), Mongolian, American, and Ethiopian; in the 1781, second edition, he added a fifth race, the Malay. And in the third, 1795 edition, Blumenbach not only greatly expanded his descriptions of these five races of man but also located them in historical order. The Caucasian race was the oldest or most primitive race. The Mongolian and Ethiopian races were at the opposite extreme, the two races furthest removed in historical time or "degenerated" from the originary Caucasian race (for Blumenbach, "de-generation" is a purely technical term meaning "generated later in time"). In between, as historically "transitional" races, stood the American, halfway between the Caucasian and the Mongolian, and the Malay, halfway between the Caucasian and the Ethiopian.

*   *   *

Blumenbach's two most ardent English disciples were James Cowles Prichard, a prominent Welsh physician at the Medical Infirmary in Bristol, and William Lawrence, Professor of Anatomy and Surgery at St. Bartholomew's Hospital in London. * * * It was William Lawrence who most vigorously promoted Blumenbach's materialist belief in the existence of five distinctively different human races, first in his annual courses of lectures in anatomy at St. Bartholomew's Hospital, which began in 1812 and drew heavily on Blumenbach's *Comparative Anatomy*, a treatise that Lawrence had translated and expanded in 1807 during his early professional career as a demonstrator in anatomy under Dr. James Abernethy. Lawrence then expanded and published these lectures in 1819, in a volume entitled *Lectures on Physiology, Zoology, and the Natural History of Man*, which he dedicated to Blumenbach.

I focus on Lawrence because, as we shall see, he was a close friend of both Percy and Mary Shelley. Lawrence was a strong advocate of the mechanistic concept that the living human organism was entirely composed of more or less dense bodily matter (as opposed to John Abernethy's vitalist belief in an independent life or "soul" that escaped the body at death [Butler i–xx]). Lawrence—who served as one of the models for Prof. Waldman in Mary Shelley's *Frankenstein*—believed that chemistry is the ultimate science, one that "teaches us the composition of bodies" (Lawrence 74). In his *Lectures*, Lawrence followed Blumenbach closely in insisting that the human species was distinctly different from all animal species, including the apes; that the African or Ethiopian race was not a separate species or missing link on a chain of being between apes and humans but rather a variety of the human species; and that there were indeed five races of man, based on skin color, hair type, eye color, skull formation, and anatomy.

But Lawrence made one all-important addition to Blumenbach's racial theory. Following Kant and Herder in Germany, Lawrence attributed specific *moral characteristics* to each racial type. * * * In his view the white race has preeminence "in moral feelings and mental endowments" (476)—although each lesser race has positive as well as negative attributes. Here I quote his description only of the yellow-skinned Mongolian race:

> The Mongolian people differ very much in their docility and moral character [from the "savage tribes of North America"].. While the empires of China and Japan prove that this race is susceptible of civilisation, and of great advancement in the useful and even elegant arts of life, and exhibit the singular phenomenon of political and social institutions between two and three thousand years older than the Christian era, the fact of their having continued nearly stationary for so many centuries, marks an inferiority of nature and a limited capacity in comparison to that of the white races.
>
> When the Mongolian tribes of central Asia have been united under one leader, war and desolation have been the objects of the association. Unrelenting slaughter, without distinction of condition, age, or sex, and universal destruction have marked the progress of their conquests, unattended with any changes or institutions capable of benefiting the human race, unmingled with any acts of generosity, any kindness to the vanquished, or the slightest symptoms of regard to the rights and liberties of mankind. The progress of ATTILA, ZINGHIS [Genghis Khan], and TAMERLANE, like the deluge, the tornado and the hurricane, involved every thing in one sweeping ruin. (483)

Lawrence here attempted to provide a scientific basis for what Edward Said has since called "orientalism," the cultural production of a racial stereotype of the Mongol or Asian race as on the one hand, "stationary" or culturally stagnant, lazy, mired in luxury and decadence, and on the other hand, innately violent, barbaric, and destructive. * * *

Lawrence made two further points of possible relevance to Mary Shelley's representation of Frankenstein's creature. Given his belief in the preeminence of the Caucasian race and the distinct inferiority of the black or Ethiopian race, when he took up the fact that the ancient Egyptians had reached an extraordinarily high level of civilisation, Lawrence insisted that the Egyptians were not Negroes but rather a "mixed population" composed mainly of Asian and European elements with a minor addition of the African race (338–42). I mention this because Shelley's text twice identifies the Creature's skin with that of a "mummy" (53, 216). The only mummies that Mary Shelley could have seen, either in the British Museum (where mummies were unwrapped and displayed as early as the 1790s) or when she visited the Louvre in 1814 (which housed the mummies brought back from Napoleon's Egyptian expeditions) were typically painted with faces ranging in color from pale yellow to reddish yellow to dark brown-yellow and, if unwrapped, possessed an embalmed yellow skin. Thus this detail may further link the Creature with the Asian or Mongol race. Secondly, Lawrence, citing Pallas, insisted that the Mongols were a beardless race (315). As Londa Schiebinger has noted in *Nature's Body*, by 1815 the beard as a marker of male virility and hence of both racial and sexual superiority was widely assigned primarily to the Caucasian race (120–25).

Percy Shelley probably first met William Lawrence in 1811, when he attended Dr. John Abernethy's lectures in anatomy at St. Bartholomew's Hospital with his cousin John Grove; certainly Lawrence had become Percy and Mary Shelley's personal physician by 1814, and Mary Shelley continued to consult him on medical matters and to meet him socially until his death in 1830 (Luke;[2] *Journals of Mary Shelley* 1: 55, 67n1, 180n8; 2: 512; *Letters of Mary Wollstonecraft Shelley* 1: 41; 2: 111, 210; 3: 84). Percy Shelley would have been particularly interested in the ideas of the intelligent, well-educated and politically radical "Surgeon" Lawrence, who repeatedly attacked the social inequities and intellectual bigotry of his day, even as he espoused his own racialist theories. That Percy Shelley had either read Blumenbach or learned of his racial classifications from Lawrence, Prichard, Kames, or other natural historians, is suggested by his "Ode to the West Wind." There, in the opening lines, Percy Shelley hails the West Wind as the "breath of Autumn's being"

> . . . from whose unseen presence the leaves dead
> Are driven, like ghosts from an enchanter fleeing,
>
> Yellow, and black, and pale, and hectic red,
> Pestilence-stricken multitude's. . . . (lines 2–5)

Numerous Shelley scholars have followed G. M. Mathews in identifying these pestilence-stricken multitudes of leaves, "yellow, and black, and pale and hectic red," not only with the souls of the dead but specifically with the four races of man—"Mongoloid, Negroid, Caucasian and American Indian," as Donald Reiman recently put it (*Shelley's Poetry* 221 n3).

That Mary Shelley was familiar with Blumenbach's racial categories is suggested in *Frankenstein* both by the Creature and by Victor.

---

2. See corrections to Luke in Reiman (*Shelley and His Circle* 44).

The Creature learns history by evesdropping on Felix De Lacey as he reads Volney's *Ruins* to Safie. There Volney's Mahometans accuse the European Christians of attempting to destroy all other nations and races. I quote Volney's Muslims, in a passage which Victor Frankenstein had echoed in an earlier section of Shelley's novel:

> Was it the charity of your gospel that led you to exterminate whole nations in America, and to destroy the empires of Mexico and Peru; that makes you still desolate Africa, the inhabitants of which you sell like cattle, notwithstanding the abolition of slavery that you pretend your religion has effected; that makes you ravage India whose domains you usurp; in short, is it charity that has prompted you for three centuries past to disturb the peaceable inhabitants of three continents, the most prudent of whom, those of Japan and China, have been constrained to banish you from their country, that they might escape your chains and recover their domestic tranquillity? (307–08; ch. 23)

The Creature then summarises Volney:

> I heard of the slothful Asiatics; of the stupendous genius and mental activity of the Grecians; of the wars and wonderful virtue of the early Romans—of their subsequent degeneration— . . . I heard of the discovery of the American hemisphere, and wept with Safie over the hapless fate of its original inhabitants. (115)

By 1815 the image of the Mongols or Asians as a yellow skinned, black haired, and beardless race was well established, not only in the scientific writings of Blumenbach, Prichard, and Lawrence, but also in European culture at large. Starting in the 1780s, descriptions of the "yellow people" (who as Robert Markley has noted had previously been portrayed on maps and in paintings as white skinned) were disseminated by the ever growing East India Company's trade with Asia and the far East and appeared in diplomatic reports, missionary reports from India and China, the reports of the Asiatic Society of Bengal from 1790 onward (*Asiatick Researches* 2: 2), and such contemporary travel writing as John Barrow's immensely popular 1804 *Travels in China*, which included in the second, 1806, edition a colored frontispiece, portrait of the distinctively yellow skinned Chinese ruler Van-ta-gin.

Mary Shelley's *Frankenstein* of 1818 initiates a new version of this Yellow Man, the image of the Mongol as a giant. Recall the only surviving visual representation of her Creature that Mary Shelley is certain to have seen, the Frontispiece to the revised, 1831 edition of *Frankenstein*, designed by T. Holst and engraved, by W. Chevalier which you must imagine with yellow skin. In Shelley's novel,

"Frankenstein's Creature." Frontispiece to the 1831 *Frankenstein*.
T. Holst and W. Chevalier.

this gigantic yellow man is portrayed as a creature of superhuman
strength and endurance, of intelligence and sensibility, a man
who—denied the female companionship and family he so desperately
craves—finally becomes a murdering monster, destroying all those
dear to his maker.

*   *   *

488 ANNE K. MELLOR

Works Cited

Arbus, Diane. *Diane Arbus; an Aperture Monograph*. Millerton, NY: Aperture P, 1972.

Asiatick Researches: or, Transactions of the Society instituted in Bengal, for inquiring into the history and antiquities, the arts, sciences, and literature of Asia. Calcutta, 1788–1800. Vol. 2. 1790.

Barrow, John. *Travels in China*. 1804. London. 1806.

Blumenbach, Johann Friedrich. *On the Natural History of Mankind*. 1775. 65–145; 1795. 145–278. *Contributions to Natural History*. 1806. 277–340. *The Anthropological Treatises of Johann Friedrich Blumenbach*. Trans. Thomas Bendyshe. London: Longman, 1865.

———. *The Elements of Physiology*. Trans. Charles Caldwell. Philadelphia: Thomas Dobson, 1795.

———. *A Short System of Comparative Anatomy*. Trans. from the German . . . by William Lawrence . . . With additional notes and an introductory view of the classification of animals by the translator. London: Longman, 1807; 2nd ed. rev. and augmented by William Coulson. London, 1827.

Bernier, François. "Nouvelle division de la terre, par les differentes espèces ou races d'hommes qui l'habitent . . ." *Journal des savants* 12 (1684): 148–55.

Buffon, Georges Louis LeClerc, Comte de. *The System of Natural History,* abridged. 4 Vols. Alnwick: 1814. In this translation of Buffon's 1741 *Histoire naturelle*, his discussion of the "Apparent Varieties in the Human Species" appears in Vol. 1, ch. 6, 107–30.

Butler, Marilyn. "Introduction." Mary Shelley's 1818 *Frankenstein*. Oxford: Oxford World's Classics, 1994.

Chambers, James. *The Devil's Horsemen—The Mongol Invasion of Europe*. London: Weidenfeld and Nicolson, 1979; rev. and extended, Cassell, 1988.

Choy, Philip P., Lorraine Dong, and Marlon K. Horn, eds. *The Coming Man—Nineteenth Century American Perceptions of the Chinese*. Seattle: U of Washington P, 1994.

Clegg, Jenny. *Fu Manchu and the Yellow Peril*. New York: Trentham, 1994.

Diosy, Arthur. *The New Far East*. 1898. London: Cassell, 1904.

Dower, John W. *War Without Mercy—Race and Power in the Pacific War*. New York: Pantheon, 1986.

Eddy, John Herbert, Jr. *Buffon, Organic Change, and the Ages of Man*. Ann Arbor: University Microfilms International, 1977.

Hannaford, Ivan. *Race—The History of an Idea in the West*. Baltimore: The Johns Hopkins UP, 1996.

Hudson, Nicholas. "From 'Nation' to 'Race': The Origin of Racial Classification in Eighteenth-Century Thought." *Eighteenth-Century Studies* 29 (1996): 247–64.

Kames, Henry Home, Lord. *Sketches of the History of Man.* Edinburgh and London, 1774; 2nd ed. 1778; 3rd "considerably improved" ed, 2 vols., Dublin 1779.

Kiernan, V. G. *The Lords of Human Kind—Black Man, Yellow Man, and White Man in an Age of Empire.* Boston: Little, Brown, 1969.

Lawrence, F. R. S. W. *Lectures on Physiology, Zoology, and the Natural History of Man.* London, 1819.

Lew, Joseph W. "The Deceptive Other: Mary Shelley's Critique of Orientalism in *Frankenstein.*" *Studies in Romanticism* 30 (1991): 255–83.

Luke, Hugh J., Jr. "Sir William Lawrence—Physician to Shelley and Mary." *Papers on English Language & Literature* 1 (1965): 141–52.

Malchow, Harold L. "Frankenstein's Monster and Images of Race in Nineteenth-Century Britain." *Past and Present* 139 (1993): 90–130.

———. *Gothic Images of Race in Nineteenth-Century Britain.* Stanford: Stanford UP, 1996.

Markley, Robert. "Civility, Ceremony, and Desire at Beijing: Sensibility and the European Quest for 'Free Trade' with China in the Late Seventeenth Century." *Passionate Encounters in a Time of Sensibility.* Ed. Maximilian E. Novak and Anne Mellor. Newark: U of Delaware P, 2000. 60–88.

Meijer, Miriam Claude. "The Anthopology of Petrus Camper (1722–1789)." Diss. UCLA, 1991.

Mellor, Anne K. "Frankenstein: A Feminist Critique of Science." *One Culture—Essays in Science and Literature.* Ed. George Levine. Madison: U of Wisconsin P, 1987. 287–312.

———. *Mary Shelley: Her Life, Her Fiction, Her Monsters.* London and New York: Methuen/Routledge, 1988.

Mosse, George L. *Toward the Final Solution—A History of European Racism.* New York: Howard Fertig, 1978.

Prichard, James Cowles. *Researches into the Physical History of Man.* Ed. with introduction by George W. Stocking, Jr. Chicago: U of Chicago P, 1973.

Reiman, Donald. *Shelley and His Circle 1773–1822.* Vol. 5. Cambridge: Harvard UP, 1973.

Reiman, Donald H., ed., with Sharon B. Powers. *Shelley's Poetry and Prose.* New York: Norton, 1977.

Rohmer, Sax. *The Insidious Doctor Fu-Manchu.* 1913. New York: Pyramid, 1961.

Said, Edward W. *Orientalism.* New York: Random, 1978.

Schiebinger, Londa. *Nature's Body—Gender in the Making of Modern Science*. Boston: Beacon, 1993.

Shelley, Mary Wollstonecraft. *Frankenstein or The Modern Prometheus*. 1818. Ed. James Rieger. Indianapolis: Bobbs-Merrill, 1974. Rpt. Chicago: U of Chicago P, 1982.

———. *The Journals of Mary Shelley 1814–1844*. Ed. Paula R. Feldman and Diana Scott-Kilvert. 2 vols. Oxford: Clarendon, 1987.

———. *The Letters of Mary Wollstonecraft Shelley*. Ed. Betty T. Bennett. 3 vols. Baltimore: The Johns Hopkins UP, 1980–88.

Smith, Samuel Stanhope. *An Essay on the Causes of the Variety of Complexion and Figure in the Human Species*. Philadelphia, 1788 and London, 1789. 2nd. ed "enlarged and improved," New York and Dublin, 1810. A reissue of the second edition, ed. Winthrop D. Jordan, appeared in 1965. Cambridge: Harvard UP.

Spivak, Guyatri Chakravorty. "Three Women's Texts and a Critique of Imperialism." *Critical Inquiry* 12 (1985): 243–61.

Stepan, Nancy. *The Idea of Race in Science: Great Britain 1800–1900*. London: Macmillan, 1982.

Sullivan, Zohreh T. "Race, Gender and Imperial Ideology in the Nineteenth Century." *Nineteenth-Century Contexts* 13 (1989): 19–32.

Volney, Constantine Francis Chassebeuf de. *The Ruins: or, A Survey of the Revolutions of Empires*. First English translation; 3rd. ed. London: J. Johnson, 1796.

White, Charles. *An Account of the Regular Gradation in Man and in Different Animals and Vegetables*. London, 1799.

Wu, William F. *The Yellow Peril—Chinese Americans in American Fiction, 1850–1940*. Hamden, Conn.: Archon, 1982.

Young, Robert. J. C. *Colonial Desire: Hybridity in Theory, Culture and Race*. New York: Routledge, 1995.

JANE GOODALL

Electrical Romanticism†

Through the later decades of the eighteenth century, electrical experiment became symbolically associated with revolutionary energies and ideals. Benjamin Franklin personified the spirit of the American Revolution to many, and his work on electricity was celebrated by poets as a spectacular expression of intellectual-political liberation. Hugh Henry Brackenridge's 1771 ode on 'The Rising Glory of America' set the tone:

† From *Frankenstein's Science: Experimentation and Discovery in Romantic Culture, 1780–1830*, ed. Christa Knellwolf and Jane Goodall (Burlington, VT: Ashgate, 2008), 117–32. Reprinted by permission.

> A genius piercing as the electric fire,
> Bright as the lightning's flash, explain'd so well
> By him, the rival of Britannia's sage.—
> This is the land of every joyous sound,
> Of liberty and life, sweet liberty!
> Without whose aid the noblest genius fails,
> And Science irretrievably must die.[1]

Adam Zamoyski characterises this revolutionary era as one of 'holy madness' and observes how 'the Romantic passion for all things scientific' is bound up with the wild energies of the time.[2] It was to the science of electricity, though, that the symbolism of revolution was most fiercely attached, and this was dangerous as well as exhilarating. Apart from the dramatic risks attached to experiments with lightning bolts and artificially generated electrical charges, there were political dangers arising from the ideological associations of the electrician's work. The association between revolution and electrical experiment in the popular mind was confirmed when Joseph Priestley's laboratory was trashed by the Church and King mob in 1791, on the second anniversary of the storming of the Bastille.

Priestley stressed repeatedly that electricity was a vast terrain of discovery so far barely encroached on, and his visions of its future potential reflect the Promethean spirit, demonstrating a readiness to breach long-established boundaries, and set foot on hitherto untrodden ground. As Jenny Uglow puts it 'a shimmering aura of transformation' surrounded all his experiments and ideas.[3] Writing about electrical research in 1767, he is *Frankenstein's* precursor in his vision of pushing back the boundaries of human potential:

> And by these sciences also it is that the views of the human mind itself are enlarged, and our common nature improved and enobled. It is for the honour of the species, therefore, that these sciences should be cultivated with the utmost attention.[4]

The electrical fluid, said Priestley, was 'no local or occasional agent in the theatre of the world' but one that acted 'a principal part in the grandest and most interesting scenes of nature' (xi). Through experiment, humans might acquire an expanded and enobled sense of their own agency and 'aspire to the moral perfections of the great

1. Hugh Henry Brackenridge, 'The rising glory of America', in *Poems Relating to the American Revolution*, ed. Philip Freneau (New York: W. J. Widdleton, 1865), 14.
2. Adam Zamoyski, *Holy Madness: Romantics, Patriots and Revolutionaries, 1776–1871* (London: Phoenix Press, 2001), 305.
3. Jenny Uglow, *The Lunar Men: The Friends Who Made the Future, 1730–1810* (London: Faber & Faber, 2002), 75.
4. Joseph Priestley, *The History and Present State of Electricity, with Original Experiments*, 3rd edn (London: Bathurst and Lowndes, 1775), vol. 2, xvii.

author of all things' (xviii). William Godwin championed such aspirations with vigour throughout his writings, but most persistently in his *Enquiry Concerning Political Justice* (1793), in which he argues that the potential of the human species was beyond what they had so far dared to imagine, and all that stood in the way of it were the inhibitory influences of politics and religion.

> Can we arrest the progress of the enquiring mind? If we can, it must be by the most unmitigated despotism. Intellect has a perpetual tendency to proceed. It cannot be held back, but by a power that counteracts its genuine tendency, through every moment of its existence. Tyrannical and sanguinary must be the measures employed for this purpose.[5]

Of all the sciences, if it was electricity that caught the revolutionary imagination most powerfully, this was because of its immediately dramatic manifestations, but also because of its exhilarating potentialities as a life science: Galvani's discoveries made the prospects of reanimation and spontaneous generation seem nearly within reach, and Erasmus Darwin's demonstration of animated vermicelli is an acknowledged inspiration for Mary Shelley's story. (As Leonard Wolf and other scholars have noted, this appears to be a misreading of Darwin's annotations to the *Temple of Nature*, where there is reference to a Royal Society experiment in which 'in paste composed of flour and water, which has been suffered to become acescent, the animalcules called eels, vibrio anguillula, are seen in great abundance; their motions are rapid and strong; they are viviparous, and produce at intervals a numerous progeny'.)[6] Electrical experiments were an obsession for Percy Bysshe Shelley. During his years as a Cambridge undergraduate he became intoxicated with the promises of science, discoursing with 'zealous earnestness' on such matters as the composition of gases, the chemical analysis of food, the generation of heat and galvanic batteries.[7] His biographer and contemporary Thomas Jefferson Hogg describes going to visit him in his rooms and finding him surrounded by apparatus, including an electrical machine which he proceeded to demonstrate, standing on a glass-legged stool and commanding his friend to turn the generator handle 'until he was filled with the fluid, so that his long, wild locks bristled and stood on end' (56). Shelley's pronouncements were as startling as his experiments.

5. William Godwin, *Enquiry Concerning Political Justice*, book VIII (Harmondsworth: Penguin, 1976), 781–2.
6. Erasmus Darwin, annotation to *The Temple of Nature* (London: J. Johnson, 1803), Canto I. i. 227.
7. Thomas Jefferson Hogg, *The Life of Percy Bysshe Shelley*, vol. 1 (London: J. M. Dent, 1858), 52–3. All further references will be cited parenthetically in text.

What a mighty instrument would electricity be in the hands of him who knew how to wield it, in what manner to direct its omnipotent energies . . . What a terrible organ would the supernal [sic] shock prove, if we were able to guide it; how many of the secrets of nature would such a stupendous force unlock! (51)

The cadence and tenor of these lines is strikingly close to those of Victor Frankenstein in the inaugural phase of his enterprise, but the narrative unfolds to offer a violently reversed perspective on such imaginings.

Prometheus modernised

When Mary Shelley subtitled her novel 'the Modern Prometheus', what was she implying about the contemporary state of Promethean endeavours? This, I believe is one of the key questions for reexamination, especially with regard to the ideological climate of her time and its impact on scientists. The two decades following the onset of the French Revolution saw a new kind of extremism developing in England, as fears of the Terror took hold and draconian measures were taken to preempt any kind of radical fermentation on home soil. At the same time, many idealists who had celebrated the birth of liberty, equality and fraternity found their enthusiasms confounded. In the aftermath of revolution, mood swings were part of the cultural ethos for which poets were considered the most sensitive barometers. Wordsworth, a restrained personality compared to Byron and Shelley, still experienced the highs and the lows in his responses to the political cataclysm in France, recollecting his feelings at the time:

> Bliss was it in that dawn to be alive
> But to be young was very heaven

and in the aftermath:

> I scarcely had one night of quiet sleep,
> Such ghastly visions had I of despair,
> And tyranny and implements of death.[8]

The modern Prometheus of the early nineteenth century had to realise his mission in a world riven by misgivings about anything purporting to change the parameters of human destiny. The phenomenon of revolution turning to terror was not the only cause for these misgivings. Some of the darker cultural influences from

---

8. William Wordsworth, *The Prelude* (1805 text), books XI, 108–9 and X, 373–5, ed. Jonathan Wordsworth, M. H. Abrams and Stephen Gill (New York: Norton, 1979), 378 and 396.

previous centuries would not relinquish their hold, and when it came to questions about the terms of human destiny, Calvinism remained the most powerful psychological enemy of the Promethean view. Here it is worth observing that *Frankenstein* is set in Geneva, where Calvin established his dominance over the church in 1541.

The Calvinist doctrine was, in John Stachniewski's description, one of 'double predestination'.[9] In the first strike, the human race was divided by divine judgement into the elect (the saved) and the reprobate (those lost to salvation); in the second, the judgement was played out through a predetermined course of action in the individual's life experience so that it could only be reinforced, never reversed or even mitigated. From a psychological point of view, this was a scenario fraught with double binds: an individual who strove to be good and deserving of God's grace was fulfilling their destiny if they were elect, or exhibiting the cardinal sin of 'presumption' if they did not belong to the chosen few and, hence, were reprobate. Even seeking to understand one's predestined lot was a form of presumption, since the gulf between human and divine intelligence was unbridgeable. Stachniewski documents the ways in which this formula imprinted itself on the psyche and was expressed in sermons, letters, tracts and literary writings. The picture is one of a culture impregnated with despair. Parental rejection and abuse, community ostracism, psychological torment and a heightened suicide rate are aspects of the social pathology consequent on the rapid and intensive spread of the doctrine through the later sixteenth and seventeenth centuries.

After that, through the eighteenth century and beyond, Calvinism remained entrenched in Scotland and widespread in England. Its influence was perversely concentrated amongst Mary Shelley's circle; perversely, because it was in the most obvious ways inimical to the ideals they professed. William Godwin was brought up in the Cambridgeshire fens, a stronghold of Calvinist beliefs. His childhood reading was a diet of fatalistic tracts and his subsequent tuition was placed in the hands of a Sandemanian minister. (The Sandemanians were in Godwin's account more fearsome predestinarians than the original Calvinists.) Later, as a student at the dissenting academy of Hoxton, Godwin gave sermons on the Christian duty of resignation in the face of adversity.[1] Byron, Shelley's closest friend, came under the influence of a Presbyterian nurse during his Aberdeen childhood, and early on conceived an idea of himself as

---

9. John Stachniewski, *The Persecutory Imagination: English Puritanism and the literature of Religious Despair* (Oxford: Oxford UP, 1991), 19.
1. A biographical account of the Calvinist influences on Godwin is given in William St. Claire, *The Godwins and the Shelleys* (London: Faber & Faber, 1989), ch. 1.

one of the cursed tribe of humanity. In his dramatic poem *Cain* (1821), the protagonist complains:

> what have we
> Done, that we must be victims for a deed
> Before out birth, or need have victims to
> Atone for this mysterious, nameless sin—
> If it be such a sin to seek for knowledge?[2]

The role of Prometheus, reconceived in second-generation Romanticism, is man freed from this curse by becoming divine in his own right, through the power of knowledge:

> The Lightning is his slave; Heaven's utmost deep
> Gives up her stars, and like a flock of sheep
> They pass before his eye, are numbered, and roll on!
> The Tempest is his steed,—he strides the air;
> And the abyss shouts from her depth laid bare,
> 'Heaven, hast thou secrets? Man unveils me, I have none.'[3]

But the higher destiny of the knowledge seeker could be a vertiginous experience. 'We are on the verge where words abandon us', wrote Percy Shelley in an essay with the modest title *On Life*, 'and what wonder if we grow dizzy to look down the dark abyss of how little we know'.[4]

Electricity, as the scientific phenomenon most overtly Promethean in its symbolism, focused the central dilemma of Calvinism in a new way. The dark abyss might be illuminated with new knowledge, but the very process of entering was a metaphysical dare of the first order. How could one tell the promptings of sublime ambition from the devil's work? This was an especially daunting question when it was personal in its implications. Priestley was a prime example of how the residual power of the Calvinist conscience could sabotage even the most revolutionary imaginations. The dramas of science— with their episodes of revelation and conversion—tended to mimic those of religion. Priestley, also brought up a Calvinist, became a clergyman as well as a scientist, but it was in his science that he gained the stature of an evangelist. As one contemporary put it: 'No human being could, in my opinion, appear in any trial more divine, or show a nearer resemblance to our Saviour, than he did then.'[5] This

---

2. George Gordon, Lord Byron, Cain in *Byron: Poetical Works*, eds Frederick Page and John Jump (Oxford: Oxford UP, 1970), 538–9.
3. Percy B. Shelley, *Prometheus Unbound*, act IV in *Shelley's Poetry and Prose*, eds Donald H. Reiman and Sharon B. Powers (New York: Norton, 1977), 205.
4. Percy B. Shelley, 'On life' in *Shelley, Essays and Letters*, ed. Ernest Rhys (London: Walter Scott, 1886), 75.
5. Catherine Hutton, quoted in Uglow, *Lunar Men*, 442.

image of him inspired the frontispiece for Priestley's *Disquisitions.* Franklin's 'sublime conjectures' about lightning, electricity and the life force were embraced by Godwin as an alternative to religion.[6] In his *Thoughts on Man,* Godwin expounds what is effectively a new gospel about the glories of science and their transcendence of the human toil through which they are achieved:

> It gives us a mighty and sublime idea of the nature of man, to think with what composure and confidence a succession of persons of the greatest genius have launched themselves in illimitable space, with what invincible industry they have proceeded, wasting the midnight oil, racking their faculties and almost wearing their organs to dust.[7]

Such views echo those put forward by Renaissance esotericists like Cornelius Agrippa:

> It is an ancient, and almost an agreeable and common opinion of all the philosophers, by which they think that every science does bring unto man some divinity, according to the capacity and value of them both, so that often times, beyond the limits of humanity, they may be reckoned among the fellowship of the gods.[8]

From this there is a logical step, via the embrace of atheism amongst Godwin's contemporaries, to an idea of human divinity replacing the constraining god or gods of religious tradition.

Victor Frankenstein's science in its first phase is a gospel in itself. 'A new light seemed to dawn upon my mind', he recalls, in an account of how he first came to read Cornelius Agrippa and then set out to combine his esoteric knowledge with the best that could be learned from instrumental science, which likewise engaged his 'utmost wonder'.[9] In his downturn, through the *Purgatorio* of violent guilt, he is a figure of his times and reflects his society's contradictory energies. The science of electricity was seen by the public as both threat and salvation, and when Priestley's laboratory was trashed, the Derby Philosophical Society wrote to commiserate with him, evoking the sacrificial rather than the redemptive face of Prometheus:

6. William Godwin, *Enquiry,* 759.
7. William Godwin, *Thoughts on Man, his Nature, Productions and Discoveries* (London: Effingham Wilson, Royal Exchange, 1831), 397.
8. Henricus Cornelius Agrippa, *De incertitudine et vanitate scientiarum et artium atque excellentia verbi dei declamatio* (1530), excerpted in Christopher Marlow. *Doctor Faustus,* ed. Michael Keefer (Ontario: Broadview Press, 1991) app. 3, 182–96.
9. All quotations are taken from Mary Shelley, *Frankenstein, or, The Modern Prometheus: The 1818 Text,* ed. Marilyn Butler (Oxford: Oxford UP, 1998 [1993]), 22 and 24. All further references will be cited parenthetically in text.

Almost all great minds in all ages of the world, who have endeavoured to benefit mankind, have been persecuted by them. . . . Your enemies, unable to conquer your arguments by reason, have had recourse to violence; they have haloo'd upon you the dogs of unfeeling ignorance, and of frantic fanaticism.[1]

This was a quarter of a century before *Frankenstein*, but the event reverberated. From that point, the climate of English intellectual life changed. The backlash was real and dangerous, and radicals became more cautious about what they published. Perhaps we should see Frankenstein as a Priestley figure twenty-five years on, echoing the high-flown rhetoric of electrical romanticism. The modern Prometheus had met his nemesis because human nature (or perhaps, rather, European culture) was not ready for his visions, and Mary Shelley's Frankenstein is a figure who internalises the backlash, trashing his own laboratory at the point where his work is about to reach culmination, when the creation of the second monster calls into existence the generative capacity of the new species. In its portrayal of the modern Prometheus, the novel focuses the tensions of a frantically unstable era, when the first wave of revolutionary enthusiasm has long broken and been succeeded by an aftermath of paranoid repression.

Fatal science

It is the reactive combination of revolutionary Prometheanism with residual Calvinism, I would suggest, that underlies the tensions in Frankenstein's science and determines the 'fatal' cast of his enterprise.[2] The Calvinist imaginings of the Romantic period take on a different tenor from those of the seventeenth century, in the first phase of Calvin's influence. There is a wilder blossoming in the language and imagery, and an enlargement of the fantasy life generated from speculation about election and reprobation. The logics of predestined election and retribution ate deep into the psyche, so that those like Godwin and Priestley who consciously repudiated them also incessantly rehearsed the struggle with them. But in doing so, they created a strange hybrid, something that might be called Romantic Calvinism, a phenomenon that went on to take more diverse forms in the succeeding generation. Byron's approach was to embrace reprobation, and do it with theatrical aplomb, proliferating alter-egos through which he could explore its darkest and most

---

1. Desmond King-Hele, *Erasmus Darwin* (New York: Scribners, 1963), 212–13.
2. I have explored the Calvinist underpinnings of *Frankenstein* in more detail in Jane Goodall, '*Frankenstein* and the reprobate's conscience', *Studies in the Novel*, 31/1 (Spring 1991): 19–43.

dramatic possibilities. James Hogg regenerated the Calvinist novel in *Confessions of a Justified Sinner* (1824), which portrayed the doctrine of predestination as an evil in itself, producing a Faustian struggle over the mind and soul of humanity. Mary Shelley fused the drama of predestination with the high mythology of Romantic Prometheanism, keeping a strong dose of Milton in the mix.

Calvinist Prometheanism is a deeply paradoxical phenomenon since presumption, essential to the Promethean impetus, was a cardinal sin in Calvinist doctrine. The culture of Calvinism was a machine for generating compulsory humility: 'bow down and knuckle under' was the gist of the message carried in the tracts and sermons that worked to establish an interior censorship on all forms of free speculation.[3] Yet, there was also an intrinsic contradiction that the heretical imaginations of those who turned against Calvinism were drawn to exploring. The idea of the calling was one that, as Hogg showed in his novel, could easily become tinged with megalomania. What were the limits on the calling of one of the elect? The very thought that there should be limits was surely an implicit violation of the doctrine, in which the infallibility of the elect and the preordination of all things were central tenets. In *Confessions of a Justified Sinner* this is an insinuation made by a diabolic figure who attaches himself to the central character (Robert Wringhim) as an intimate friend and mirror image. 'Let us be up and doing in our vocations', he says, leading the way to the first murder.[4]

Confessions, like *Frankenstein*, portrays the perpetual crisis of judgement churning away in a mind formed through the doctrine of predestination, according to which divine judgement was absolute, and established a framework of absolutes for all human conduct. The challenge, then, was to figure out whether your own course of action in the world was absolutely sublime or absolutely diabolic. This is the scale of Frankenstein's dilemma and these are the terms in which he sees his own scientific enterprise. It is also a fundamental dilemma of his era. For radical intellectuals of the later eighteenth century, science was a way out of the psychological tyrannies of predestination. It restored human agency to the centre of the picture and made a new heroism out of the determination to extend the bounds of human knowledge, as Priestley declared:

> The rapid progress of knowledge, which like the progress of a wave of the sea, or of light from the sun, extends itself not in this way or that way only, but in all directions will, I doubt not, be the means, under God, of extirpating all terror and preju-

3. See Stachniewski, *The Persecutory Imagination*, ch. 1.
4. James Hogg, *The Private Memoirs and Confessions of a Justified Sinner* (Cologne: Könemann, 1995), 125.

dice, and of putting an end to all undue and usurped authority in the business of religion as well as science.[5]

Mary Wollstonecraft accordingly saw Promethean heroism as an important inspiration for courageous women of the revolution who sought to reclaim the future from the aristocratic tyrants and religious doomsayers who had crushed the hopes of so many ordinary people for over a century.

> We must get entirely clear of all the notions drawn from the wild traditions of original sin: the eating of the apple, the theft of Prometheus, the opening of Pandora's box, and all the other fables, too tedious to enumerate, on which priests have erected their tremendous structures of imposition, to persuade us, that we are naturally inclined to evil.[6]

But Wollstonecraft's daughter belonged to a generation for whom the 'tremendous structures of imposition' were more potently internalized. Byron and Shelley were exploring them through a succession of poetic personae—Zastrozzi, Cain, Count Cenci, Manfred—figures who voice the torments they experience as their own explosive energies turn back on them through the agency of the savage conscience.

As a prose work, written predominantly by a woman without the imaginative license to identify with such high-flown personae, *Frankenstein* portrays the structures of imposition in a more discursive and introverted way. In the first chapter, the narrator refers to natural philosophy as 'the genius that regulated my fate' (22), and so embarks on an autobiographical account whose dominant theme is the fatal adventure of a scientific education. At the outset, the story is offered as one illustrative of the worst that fate can do:

> But, in drawing the picture of my early days, I must not omit to record those events which led, by insensible steps to my after tale of misery: for when I would account to myself for the birth of that passion, which afterwards ruled my destiny, I find it arise, like a mountain river, from ignoble and almost forgotten sources; but, swelling as it proceeded, it became the torrent which, in its course, has swept away all my hopes and joys. (22)

We should not equate Frankenstein's voice with that of the author. His pronouncements call for some critical distance in the reader, especially when he portrays himself and his science as the victims of such looming, evil fatality, because there is another side to the story.

5. Joseph Priestley, *Experiments and Observations Relating to Various Branches of Natural Philosophy*, vol. 1 (Birmingham, 1781), xi.
6. Mary Wollstonecraft, 'An historical and moral view of the origin and progress of the French Revolution' in *Political Writings*, ed. Janet Todd (Oxford: Oxford UP), 294.

This is the surge of joyful idealism that also fuels his quest for knowledge and his will to make the boldest discoveries.

Set between these polarities, the scientific education becomes an adventure fraught with critical dilemmas, steered by irreversible decisions, yet always under the governance of a force of destiny that reveals itself in portents. The first of these is the vision of the tree blasted by lightning. Frankenstein witnesses the spectacle from a distance—a stream of fire, dazzling light, bursts of thunder—then sees close up how the tree is 'splintered by the shock' into thin ribbands of wood. 'I never beheld anything so utterly destroyed', he recalls. Yet immediately afterwards, he is given an alternative to the catastrophic view when he asks his father to explain the power of lightning:

> He replied 'Electricity;' describing at the same time the various effects of that power. He constructed a small electrical machine, and exhibited a few experiments; he also made a kite, with a wire and string, which drew down the fluid from the clouds. (24)

This demonstration, based on the inventions of Benjamin Franklin, triggers a growing recognition of what can be achieved through modern discoveries in chemistry and physics, and completes the overthrow of Agrippa and the esoteric masters as reigning lords of Frankenstein's imagination. Such are the terms in which he portrays it.

At university his sense of dilemma about alternative systems of knowledge is more clearly realized as a choice, not between esoteric and modern forms of enquiry, but rather between a utilitarian view of science and one that presents the quest for new knowledge as a high drama of destiny. Correspondingly, he finds himself choosing between two masters: Professor Krempe whose teachings seem 'to change chimeras of boundless grandeur for realities of little worth' and Professor Waldman, the idealist, who sees the new experimentalists as men able to fuse practical knowledge with visionary inspiration (30–31). Both are proponents of modern science, but it is Waldman who accommodates the Promethean spirit in his modern outlook, inspiring Frankenstein with an account of the new experimentalists:

> they have discovered how the blood circulates, and the nature of the air we breathe. They have acquired new and almost unlimited powers; they can command the thunders of heaven, mimic the earthquake, and even mock the invisible world with its own shadows. (30–31)

When he comes to embark on his own course of experimental discovery, Frankenstein is driven by the most elated ambitions:

Life and death seemed to me ideal bounds, which I should first break through, and pour a torrent of light into our dark world. A new species would bless me as its creator and source. (36)

The high drama of destiny is under way, but the elation carries the undercurrent of a very different premonitory mood. The passage beginning with this expression of visionary inspiration is followed by an account of the horrors of a secret toil driven forward by frantic impulse, in 'the workshop of filthy creation' (83). The transitions in perspective here are worth attending to, as the narrator's reasoning works towards the recognition that an ideal state is actually one of psychological equilibrium:

A human being in perfection ought always to preserve a calm and peaceful mind, and never to allow passion or a transitory desire to disturb his tranquility. (37)

This might be another lesson learned from Benjamin Franklin, who saw electricity in terms of nature's eternal tendency towards balance, and developed his theory of positive and negative electricity accordingly.

Bipolarism

As Joseph Priestley explained, the poles of electricity corresponded with principles of 'redundancy' and 'deficiency', and Franklin's experiments demonstrated that the rush to equilibrium occurred whenever these two electricities came into contact.[7] Franklin also observed, though, that natural equilibrium was sometimes arrived at through a dramatic and volatile process. During one of his tests with the electrical kite, he found that 'the clouds would change from positive to negative electricity several times in the course of one thunder gust'.[8] Human interference could exploit this volatility to spectacular and dangerous effect, creating massive concentrations of power and generating violent explosions. Electricity was intrinsically dynamic and its positive and negative phases were also expressed as 'attractive' and 'repulsive powers'.

The symbolism of dynamic natural polarities was readily attuned to the cultural mood swings of Romanticism. Priestley was like Frankenstein in his view of science as a fatal adventure, and in his propensity for switching from one extreme to the other in his assessment of his own destiny. Priestley's Promethean inclinations were those of a recovering Calvinist, who never lost his fear of being taken captive by the darkest intimations:

7. Priestley, The History, 7.
8. Ibid., vol. 2, 219.

having read many books of experiences, and, in consequence,
believing that a new birth, produced by the immediate agency of
the spirit of God, was necessary to salvation, and not being able
to satisfy myself that I had experienced anything of the kind, I
felt occasionally such distress of mind as it is not in my power to
describe, and which I still look back upon with horror.[9]

His science is never insulated from this language of religious
despair and salvation. Neither is Frankenstein's.

From a modern psychological point of view, one might interpret
the Promethean rhetoric as a compensatory practice, a form of
defence against the fierce absolutism of the Calvinist doctrine of
predestination. But in Priestley's time, the dynamic also worked in
reverse. Presumption was the cardinal sin in a Calvinist culture, so
the very excitement produced by feelings of power and capability
could provoke an internal backlash from the ineradicable voice of the
savage conscience.[1] This is Frankenstein's experience, as he swings
from the point of his highest imaginings to one where 'the beauty of
the dream vanished' and he is plunged into 'breathless horror and
disgust' (39).

Frankenstein's bipolarism resembles that of Byron and Shelley, as
analyzed by Ian Gilmour in a recent study. Gilmour suggests that
both poets were prone to cyclothymia, or mood disorders, and used
the words 'mad' and 'madness' of themselves 'in the loose contemporary sense of an eccentric mental or emotional condition or extravagant behaviour'.[2] He quotes Tom Medwin's description of Shelley as
so dominated by mood swings that 'at one moment he looked forty
and the next eighteen' (220). In Medwin's view, both poets wrote
their best work 'under the effects of temporary derangement' (221).
Gilmour is interested in whether the two men exhibit the symptom-
atology of manic depression, as defined in a study by Kay Redfield
Jameson, which cites both Byron and Shelley as classic exemplars of
the condition.

Manic depressive illness magnifies common human experiences to larger than life proportions. Among its symptoms are
exaggerations of normal sadness and fatigue, joy and exuber-
ance, sensuality and sexuality, irritability and rage, energy and
creativity.[3]

9. John Lowell Rutt, *Life and Correspondence of Dr. Priestley*, vol. 1 (London: R. Hunter, 1831), 12.
1. The savagery of the Calvinist conscience is wonderfully documented by Stachniewski in *The Persecutory Imagination*.
2. Ian Gilmour, *The Making of the Poets Byron and Shelley in their Time* (London: Chatto and Windus, 2002), 212.
3. Kay Redfield Jameson, *Manic Depressive Illness* (New York: Oxford UP, 1990), 3.

On the evidence of her novels, Mary Shelley could be seen as another textbook case. Passages such as this, from *Matilda*, are typical:

> Is it not strange that grief should quickly follow so divine a happiness? I drank of an enchanted cup but gall was at the bottom of its long drawn sweetness. . . . I lament now, I must ever lament, those few short months of Paradisiacal bliss; I disobeyed no command, I ate no apple, and yet I was ruthlessly driven from it.[4]

The Last Man, which contains thinly disguised portraits of Shelley and Byron, portrays both in terms that would sit very well with Gilmour's diagnosis. The exercise of trying to match the individual pathologies of Byron and Shelley to the clinical profile of the disease is, he admits, 'difficult and hazardous' (214), but what Redfield Jameson describes may be exemplified in a cultural climate, as well as in an individual pathology.

The cyclothymia set in motion by Frankenstein's science should be seen in relation to this cultural climate. Science impassioned with the Promethean spirit of revolution partakes also of its holy madness. The scientist can be part explorer, part revolutionary and even part poet, but the poet's madness translates strangely to the figure of the mad scientist. Robert Walton's opening letter in the frame tale alludes to his being a failed poet. After one year in a Paradise of his own creation, he writes to his sister that he was forced to confront the limits of his destiny: 'You are well acquainted with my failure, and how heavily I bore the disappointment' (7). His visionary extremism, though, is accommodated well enough in the transition from poet to polar explorer: 'What may not be expected in a country of eternal light?' Walton anticipates 'the inestimable benefit which I shall confer on all mankind to the last generation' but admits 'my hopes fluctuate, and my spirits are often depressed' (5–6). Evidently though, he manages his condition better than Frankenstein.

One of the strengths of Mary Shelley's novel is the sharpness with which it dramatizes the manic personality at its centre. In the extraordinary meditation at the end of the third chapter, Frankenstein charts the psychological transitions accompanying his work. He enters the mood cycle on the up side. 'No one can conceive the variety of feelings which bore me onwards, like a hurricane, in the first enthusiasm of success' (36). This soon translates to 'unremitting ardour' and, thence, to unhealthy obsession. 'My cheek had grown pale with study, and my person had become emaciated with confinement' (36). So begins the paragraph famously alluding to his

---

4. Mary Shelley, *Matilda*, in *The Mary Shelley Reader*, eds Betty T. Bennett and Charles E. Robinson (Oxford: Oxford UP, 1990), 189.

'workshop of filthy creation', and the 'horrors' of his 'secret toil'. Then the point of physical breakdown looms as the excess of adrenalin driving him forward has converted to a nerve poison. 'Every night I was oppressed by a slow fever, and I became nervous to a most painful degree' (38).

There is much of Byron and his alter-egos as well as of Shelley in Victor Frankenstein. The 'excessive susceptibility of immediate impressions', which Byron attributes to Don Juan, is one of Frankenstein's dominant character notes and does much to influence the fortunes of his scientific enterprise, as is instanced in the moment he chooses between his two teachers at university.[5] But it is in the moment of his first encounter with the living creature that the excesses of this susceptibility are most fatally demonstrated. The being that greets him and the world with a newborn smile is immediately labelled a 'demoniacal corpse' (40).

The impression may be immediate, but it is also enduring and corrosive, working on the nervous system to further exacerbate the anxieties coursing through it, which have had such graphic expression in his preceding accounts of himself. After a full-blown attack of the horrors lasting through the night and into the next day, he sets off walking aimlessly about the streets with 'heart palpitating in the sickness of fear' (40). But now the level of excitation is such that it is ready to convert again to its opposite. Clerval, whose presence always tends to evoke the elated end of the mood spectrum, appears unexpectedly and becomes a trigger for the swing.

> I grasped his hand, and in a moment forgot my horror and misfortune; I felt suddenly and for the first time during many months, calm and serene joy. I welcomed my friend, therefore, in the most cordial manner, and we walked towards my college. (41)

What is unnerving to the reader about this passage is precisely that the anxiety suddenly vanishes. The affectation of 'calm and serene joy', the friendly walk with casual conversation, are exhibitions of delusory conduct. What looks delusory to others, is the tormented behaviour he exhibits on the down side of the cycle, but this is locked in by the realities Frankenstein soon has to deal with. Once the train of killings is under way, the ravings and the morbid convictions take over with a vengeance, so that his father accuses him of madness. The response would seem to confirm the diagnosis:

> 'I am not mad', I cried energetically; 'the sun and the heavens, who have viewed my operations, can bear witness of my truth. I am the assassin of those most innocent victims; they died by my machinations. A thousand times would I have shed my own

5. Byron, note to *Don Juan*, Canto XVI. Xcvii. in *Poetical Works*, 920.

blood, drop by drop, to have saved their lives; but I could not, my father, indeed I could not sacrifice the whole human race.' (156) This is followed by another of his heroic inner struggles—involving 'utmost self-violence'—to achieve a split between his outer behaviour and his emotional state; so that in manner he is 'calmer and more composed' than he has been for weeks (157). Or so he thinks. The new behaviour starts to take its own course. 'I concealed my feelings by an appearance of hilarity', he says, whilst he takes to going round armed to the teeth, mindful of the 'hellish intentions' closing in on him (161–2).

It would be easy enough to expand a psychological reading of the hovel along these lines, and to support it with accounts of the manic depressive tendencies portrayed in some of Mary Shelley's other leading characters, but here I am concerned with the implications of the cyclothymic pattern in Frankenstein's scientific endeavours. His project involves anatomical, chemical and electrical researches which are themselves strongly conducive to extremes of mood. The anatomical work is at the depressive end of the spectrum for obvious reasons: it entails, amongst other grim work, regular trips to the slaughter house and long hours of excavation in charnel houses 'to examine the cause and progress of decay'. Yet like the alchemists of a former era, Frankenstein discovers that the great work unfolds by way of the *nigredo:* 'from the midst of this darkness a sudden light broke in upon me—a light so brilliant and wondrous, that . . . I became dizzy with the immensity of the prospect which it illustrated' (30). Instead of the cemetery, the electrical researcher's prospect was 'the grandest and most interesting scenes of nature'.[6] Working with electricity, with its vitalistic associations, was a shortcut to visions of power and illumination.

The power of the scientist is a power to convert the state of human experience from one extreme to another: from a state of miserable subjection to sickness and death, to one of triumphant control in the natural order. The power itself, though, is double edged. The chemist and the electrician work with 'the ethereal principles of heat and light . . . and under his control they become, according to circumstances, instruments of comfort and enjoyment, or of terror and destruction'.[7] One might add that the capacity to make a transition, from the zone of comfort to the zone of terror, is also associated with the scale of the scientist's ambitions, with whether the goals in view are towards the visionary or the utilitarian end of the spectrum. Promethean science dealt only in extremes: it either enabled the triumph of the life force or led to miserable destruction.

6. Priestley, *The History*, xvii.
7. Ibid., 277.

Conclusion

Perhaps one of the morals of the story is that until human nature can recover from the condition of hysterical extremism to which the modern Prometheus succumbs, human science will have little chance of creating anything with a hopeful future in the world. I am aware that this is contrary to the generally accepted reading of the novel as a cautionary tale warning of the dangers posed by the scientific overreacher. There is no overt moralizing along the lines I have suggested, but *Frankenstein* is not a work that offers the stability of a singular didactic perspective. To characterize Mary Shelley's authorial position in *Frankenstein* as simply anti-Promethean, as has been done in a wide range of critical literature and popular culture, is a crucial misunderstanding. In her own critical writings, her position is always consistent with that of her parents—William Godwin and Mary Wollstonecraft—and of the radical intellectual milieu in which she was brought up. 'Methinks it is both presumptuous and sacrilegious to pretend to give the law to genius' she wrote in 1823.[8] Wollstonecraft characterizes the anti-Protheans as those who are 'not able to distinguish the possible from the monstrous', but she insists that 'the limits of the possible have never been defined to stop the sturdy innovator's hand'.[9] Mary Shelley offers a complex and troubled view of human psychology, in which the sturdy innovator is himself the one who falls into the trap of being unable to distinguish the possible from the monstrous. This is the very 'modern' trap that awaits the Prometheus of late Romanticism.

CHRISTA KNELLWOLF

Geographic Boundaries and Inner Space: *Frankenstein*, Scientific Exploration, and the Quest for the Absolute[†]

The narrative frame

The full significance of the narrative frame of *Frankenstein* becomes clear if we go back to early modern fantasies about Terra Australis (the southern land), which located the existence of an earthly para-

---

8. Mary Shelley, 'Giovanni Vallini', in *The Mary Shelley Reader*, 230.
9. Mary Wollstonecraft, 'An historical and moral view', 233.
† From *Frankenstein's Science: Experimentation and Discovery in Romantic Culture, 1780–1830*, ed. Christa Knellwolf and Jane Goodall (Burlington, VT: Ashgate, 2008), 49–69. Reprinted by permission.

dise in the polar regions.[1] With the progressive discovery of the Pacific, the theory became more and more untenable. It lingered on as a possibility into the 1770s, when the British navy commanded that James Cook's second journey of exploration (1772–75) should settle the matter of whether there was inhabitable land towards the South Pole.

When this fantasy was lost for eighteenth-century explorers, they came to locate earthly paradise in exotic islands like Tahiti. Informed by a spirit of escapism, descriptions of the lush landscape and erotic sensuality of its inhabitants elicited desires for passive abandonment to such balmy environments. For those who embarked on the Romantic quest for the self, however, the pleasurable conditions of Tahiti did not sufficiently challenge them to explore and expand their own limits. The attempt to discover and experience the boundaries of what it meant to be human found a much more congenial setting in the harsh weather of the polar regions. It is an interesting coincidence that when Mary Shelley wrote *Frankenstein*, Adalbert von Chamisso, a prominent member of German Romanticism, was in the process of sailing around the world with the Romanzof expedition (1815–18).[2] Chamisso was the author of *Peter Schlemihl* (1813), a widely influential tale about a pact-maker with the devil who escapes damnation by travelling the world as a social outcast for the rest of his life. Chamisso himself accompanied the Romanzof expedition in the role of botanist because he felt alienated by his contemporary society. Since it was the mission of the Romanzof expedition to find a Northeast Passage, he spent much time sailing in the arctic seas. It is very likely that the figure of the restless Romantic poet turned botanic traveller inspired the narrative frame of *Frankenstein*. But of course Walton's expedition is motivated by a much more ambitious goal. He is fired by a powerful yearning to go further than anyone before him. So as to realise his wish to 'tread a land never before imprinted by the foot of man' he is prepared to leave behind 'all fear of danger and death'.[3]

Frankenstein begins with a series of letters by Robert Walton, the captain of a naval expedition to the North Pole, to his sister in

1. For a discussion of the myths about Terra Australis Incognita, i.e., the great southern land, see Bernard Smith, *European Vision and the South Pacific* (Oxford: Oxford UP, 1960); and *Imagining the Pacific in the Wake of the Cook Voyages* (Carlton, Victoria: Melbourne UP, 1992).

2. Louis Choris's *Voyage pitttoresque autour du monde* (Paris: Imprimerie Firmin Didot, 1822); see also Adelbert Chamisso's own travel account: *A Voyage around the World with the Romanzov Exploring Expedition in the Years 1815–1818*, trans. Henry Kratz (Honolulu: U of Hawaii P, 1986).

3. Mary Shelley, *Frankenstein, or, The Modern Prometheus: The 1818 Text* (Oxford: Oxford UP, 1998), 6. All further references will be to this edition and cited parenthetically in text.

England. His first letter explains that the objective of the expedition is to discover the tropical lands supposed to lie at the heart of the arctic ice: 'I try in vain to be persuaded that the pole is the seat of frost and desolation; it ever presents itself to my imagination as the region of beauty and delight' (5). Much like Walton's expedition, Cook spent weeks battling against ice and bitter gales before he declared the impossibility of fruitful land lying further south. The fact that Cook was sailing in the 'Resolution' gives poignancy to the passage that describes Frankenstein's character while on board Walton's expedition: 'Even the sailors feel the power of his eloquence . . . they believe these vast mountains of ice are mole-hills, which will vanish before the resolution of man' (181).

Cook's journey did not reach the pole and, hence, did not really provide conclusive evidence that the South Pole failed to demonstrate the climatic inversions suggested by the myth. His detailed observations of the weather conditions and hydrographic facts of the extreme south were, nevertheless, considered an adequate basis for concluding that these extreme regions harboured no earthly paradise. However, extreme circumstances give rise to extreme behaviour. The physical backdrop of an impossible expedition sheds light on the motive behind Frankenstein's act of creation.

The story about Frankenstein's creation of an artificial human being is told while Walton continues to proceed north in the hope of realising his burning desire to lead a 'glorious expedition' (183). The extraordinary nature of his ambition explains his bitter disappointment at what he calls the 'cowardice and indecision' of his companions which forced him to 'come back ignorant and disappointed'. Although he is ultimately unable to ignore the reasoning of his crew, Walton is scarcely moved by the fact that 'many of my comrades have already found a grave amidst this scene of desolation' (182). His own willingness to endure among the horrors of freezing to death shows that he does not simply aspire to the laurel wreath of a successful explorer, but aims at nothing less than the absolute. It is self-evident that he has to tolerate superhuman suffering throughout his uncompromising struggle to reach the pole, the geographic metaphor for the ultimate extreme of human aspiration. Since he embarks on a mission of transcending the limits of his ordinary humanity, he is also prepared to risk his physical survival. It becomes painfully evident that the quest for the unconditional realization of the potentials embodied in his physical existence is a self-destructive exercise. However, the novel does not argue that human striving has to, necessarily, be destructive.

The significance of education

The novel establishes a close connection between the quest for knowledge and the act of striving after the absolute. The wish to know and explore the mysteries of life must be followed in order to reach a state of mature and responsible independence. The loving dialogue between Safie and Felix De Lacey, then, not only aims to achieve moral and emotional maturity, but also seeks to gain a living understanding of the mysteries of Creation. This spirit is captured by the motto of Richard Lobb's book *The Contemplative Philosopher*, one of many scientific popularizations published in the early nineteenth century. Its frontispiece is accompanied by the phrase: 'By contemplating the works of creation, man rises to some faint idea of its great Author'.[4] As is demonstrated by this epigraph, the yearning to grasp the secret rationale of creation featured as the mark of a noble soul.

Frankenstein, however, examines the modalities of gratifying the desire to know the mysteries of creation. The following passage offers a telling perspective on the legitimacy of scientific curiosity:

> If the study to which you apply yourself has a tendency to weaken your affections, and to destroy your taste for those simple pleasures in which no alloy can possibly mix, then that study is certainly unlawful, that is to say, not befitting the human mind. (37)

The healthy context for scientific enquiry is encapsulated in a caveat that adumbrates what should be the goal of study and exploration. The passage proposes as an ideal, a well-balanced existence, which demonstrates a useful store of knowledge about self and world, as well as a rich emotional life. Its attainment, it suggests, requires that a straightforward striving for scientific facts be replaced by an intelligent and informed engagement with those beings and objects which give rise to simple pleasures. There is no attempt to condemn curiosity as such, but the novel certainly paints a gory portrait of its consequences if it is not embedded in a nurturing context. Indictments of insufficient or inadequate education had also figured prominently in *Caleb Williams*, the most influential novel by Mary Shelly's father, William Godwin. There the almost demonic power of the educator is expressed in an eloquent passage in which the main protagonist accuses his benefactor of irresponsible treatment: 'You took me up a raw and inexperienced boy, capable of being

4. Richard Lobb, *The Contemplative Philosopher: or, short essays on the various objects of nature noticed through the year; with poetical illustrations and moral reflections on each subject*, 2 vols, 4th edn (London: for Sherwood, Neely and Jones, 1817), vol. 2.

moulded to any form you pleased'.[5] The narrative then illustrates that rather than forming this boy, his patron merely used him to gratify a whim and in the process warped his positive inclinations.

The scholarly focus on the creation of artificial life sadly overshadows *Frankenstein*'s thematic focus on its characters' psychological development. It is, therefore, all the more important to recognise that one of its prominent thematic strands deals with growing and becoming. All three narrators (Walton, Frankenstein and the creature) share a deep sense of loneliness and all of them bitterly deplore their unsystematic and inadequate education. Walton begins his own story by saying 'My education was neglected, yet I was passionately fond of reading' (6). Nature had generously equipped him with intellectual faculties but the development and direction of his talents was left to chance.

There is a twinge of doubt about whether Mary is giving expression to her father's most cherished plans for enhancing social justice or whether she might be indicting him for having insufficiently attended to her own growth and development. In any case, the terms by which the novel describes the significance of education recall Godwin's *Enquiry Concerning Political Justice* (1793). There, and in other analyses of society, Godwin founded his vision of social justice on an educational system that never ceases to cultivate the abilities and sympathies of an individual, proposing a method 'that embraces millions in its grasp, and that educates in one school the preceptor and the pupil'.[6]

Lack of suitable understanding and human sympathy is identified as the first cause for the tragic lives of all three narrators of *Frankenstein*. While emphatically eulogizing their loving family circle, each of these narrators reveals how they were thrown into the world without much guidance. Concerning his intellectual development, Frankenstein describes himself as self-taught. His criticism is meek and subdued but he, nevertheless, indicts his father for his failure to guide his quest for his own identity and help him formulate, and then realise, his aspirations. It is with a great deal of pain that Frankenstein remembers that his father fobbed him off with ridicule at a crucial stage of his development: 'Ah! Cornelius Agrippa! My dear Victor, do not waste your time upon this; it is sad trash' (23). In retrospect Frankenstein is furious that his father did not take the trouble to explain what was wrong with Agrippa's theories. One wonders whether it was in response to Victor's lament about his father's fail-

---

5. William Godwin, *Caleb Williams*, ed. David McCracken (London: Oxford UP, 1970), 282.
6. William Godwin, *Enquiry Concerning Political Justice*, vol. 3 of *Political and Philosophical Writings of William Godwin*, ed. Martin Fitzpatrick (London: William Pickering, 1993), 18.

ure to rationalize his dismissive response that William Godwin wrote a book-length study about the *Lives of the Necromancers* (1834).[7]

The creature experiences an unparalleled isolation while going through the process of intellectual and emotional maturation. His complete abandonment is a classic case of what Alice Miller describes as the emotional torture inflicted on children when adults deprive them of human interaction.[8] The creature is, nevertheless, able to obtain a certain amount of knowledge through self-education. His own *bildungsroman* begins by recounting his responses to reading the most influential literary works of his period. By doing so, he becomes a classic product of sensibility but, tragically enough, lacks all opportunity to realize his emotional sensitivity.

The novel portrays Walton's similarly melancholic quest for a soulmate and it elaborates on Frankenstein's lonely brooding over the principle of life. All three key protagonists are sensitive characters whose quest for meaning has set them apart from the rest of society. We are not really told why Walton and Frankenstein are outsiders but we receive the explanation that the creature's physical appearance excludes him from social contact. If the three characters are read analogously, the gigantic stature of the creature can be interpreted as a literal marker for their shared metaphorical difference: as regards the nature and intensity of their intellectual powers and feelings, all of them are larger than life. However, they differ strongly from the most influential literary figure with over-strong feelings: Goethe's 'Werther'. Unlike Werther, they refuse to pine away because they are different and, instead, seek to assert themselves through superhuman endeavours.

All three main protagonists are also driven by an insatiable yearning to discover themselves. Owing to his obvious difference from all other beings, the creature is most intensely tortured with his attempt to puzzle out the secret of his origin: 'I had never yet seen a being resembling me, or who claimed any intercourse with me. What was I? The question again recurred, to be answered only with groans' (97). And again: 'My person was hideous, and my stature gigantic. What did this mean? Who was I? Whence did I come? What was my destination? These questions continually recurred, but I was unable to solve them' (104). On an immediate level, the creature's situation is a typical problem of the early novel. Much like the heroes of Henry Fielding's *Tom Jones* (1749) or Fanny Burney's *Evelina* (1778), the creature seeks to find himself in the process of discovering his

7. William Godwin, *Lives of the Necromancers: or, An Account of the Most Eminent Persons in Successive Ages, Who Have Claimed for Themselves, or to Whom Has Been Imputed by Others, the Exercise of Magical Power* (London: Frederick J. Mason, 1834).
8. Cf., e.g., Alice Miller, *The Liberating Experience of Facing Painful Truth: Breaking Down the Wall of Silence*, trans. Simon Worrall (New York: Meridian, 1993).

parents. On a deeper level, though, he shares Frankenstein's own desire to understand the essence of human nature.

Explorations of human nature

William Godwin's *Caleb Williams* explicitly circles around the question: 'What is man?'[9] The influential role of the question is also documented in Mary Shelley's introduction, where she explains that in the conversations between Lord Byron and her husband, 'various philosophical doctrines were discussed, and among others the nature of the principle of life and whether there was any probability of its ever being discovered and communicated' (195). The relevance of this passage for the emergence of proto-evolutionary theories has concentrated scholarly interest on the physiological dimension of the 'principle of life'. The small circle of friends gathered by Lake Geneva clearly discussed the opportunities and dangers afforded by the new medical-biological theories. However, they must also have devoted themselves to a philosophical explanation of the fundamental characteristics of humankind.

In order to make progress in these explorations, it was necessary to risk encountering truths that would profoundly affect the understanding of self and world. Such a moment informs Frankenstein's first meeting with Professor Waldman, his lecturer in chemistry at Ingolstadt. In his later attempt to identify the source of his misfortunes, Frankenstein argues that Waldman carelessly kindled his new student's enthusiasm for the work of the 'modern masters', who, although their 'hands seem only made to dabble in dirt, and their eyes to pore over the microscope or crucible, have indeed performed miracles. They penetrate into the recesses of nature, and show how she works in her hiding-places' (30). The phrase 'hiding places' is reminiscent of Francis Bacon's preface to 'The Great Instauration' (1620) where he, in fact, ridicules the complaints by less lucid thinkers who 'turn to complaints about the subtlety of Nature, the hidden recesses of truth, the obscurity of things'.[1] In spite of aiming for order and clarity, though, he cannot escape the bafflement of lesser lights, and he expresses himself through gendered imagery. In his main scientific work, Bacon tends to argue that the true scientist has to cooperate with, and listen to, the laws of nature, but he also condones intrusive prurience:

> But if there are any men who have the wish and the will . . . to
> *penetrate further;* to *conquer,* not an opponent in argument, but

---

9. William Godwin, *Caleb Williams*, 279.
1. Francis Bacon, preface to 'The Great Instauration', in *Novum Organum*, trans. and ed. Peter Urbach and John Gibson (Chicago: Open Court, 1994), 10.

Nature herself in action: to seek . . . such men, true sons of learning, I invite to join me, if they will, so that we can pass by the outer halls of Nature, which any number of men have already trodden, to where at length the way into her inner chambers shall be revealed. [my italics][2]

As feminist scientists such as Carolyn D. Merchant and Evelyn Fox Keller have pointed out, Bacon gloried in the possibility of triumphing over a nature who carefully guarded her secrets.[3]

Waldman's arrogant view that science can and ought to penetrate into the secret places of nature, regardless of whether this is an act of violence, supplies a purpose for the hitherto aimless young student. The metaphor of 'penetrating nature' channels his masculine energies and gives birth to his deadly ambition. In retrospect, Frankenstein bitterly complains about his professor's disregard for the consequences of the knowledge passed onto innocent young students who are not yet capable of weighing the consequences of their studies. The 1831 version, however, shifts the emphasis from Waldman's irresponsibility to a fatalistic sense that Frankenstein was at the mercy of a fate that had conspired to crush him: 'Such were the professor's words—rather let me say such the words of fate, enounced to destroy me.' (213)

There is a telling parallel with a quotation from Charles Bonnet (1720–93) who was working on a thorough analysis of the vegetative principles of primitive organism, not far from where the Shelleys spent their summer in 1816. It is, therefore, conceivable that he inspired the conception of Professor Waldman, even though this historical scientist was noted for his intellectual modesty. Bonnet comments on the role of intellectual courage in truly groundbreaking science:

> One may not have too many conjectures on an obscure subject . . . Conjectures act as sparks which may kindle a torch that can lead the way to new experiments. So while I praise the timidity of some physicians who simply stick to the facts, I cannot condemn the ingenious rashness of those who sometimes attempt to penetrate beyond them.[4]

Bonnet is convinced that a certain disregard of the possible dangers of scientific discoveries is crucial for scientific progress. Earlier in this essay I showed that Schelling took for granted that the striving

---

2. Bacon, *Novum Organum*, 40.
3. Carlyn D. Merchant, *The Death of Nature: Women, Ecology and the Scientific Revolution* (London: Wildwood House, 1982), 168–72. See also Evelyn Fox Keller and Helen E. Longino, eds, *Feminism and Science* (Oxford: Oxford UP, 1996).
4. Quoted from Elizabeth B. Gasking, *Investigations into Generation 1651–1828* (London: Hutchinson, 1967), p, 118; the reference is to Charles Bonnet, *Considérations sur les corps organisés* (Amsterdam: M. M. Rey, 1768), ch. 3, art. 24, 99.

for the absolute almost inevitably caused sin and death.[5] In so far
as the scientists are striving for a grasp of the absolute, the Idealist
philosopher might forgive their single-minded disregard of its consequences. Most Romantic philosophers and writers might have
insisted on the unrestricted exertion of genius in response to their
tacit understanding that the highest form of intellectual activity
would necessarily benefit human justice and prosperity. The idea
that no limits should be put to intellectual creativity has established
itself as a core value, with only very minor restrictions, since the late
twentieth century. When we return to Bonnet, we hear an early
expression of the idea that scientific creativity should not be curbed.
However, his main argument concerns the right to invoke the imagination in order to speculate. So if we follow in his steps and permit
ourselves to conjecture, we might conclude that if harnessed to the
right principles, the use of imagination in the attempt to penetrate
beyond empirical evidence might be a means of warning the scientists of the consequences of their research.

    Frankenstein, by contrast, deplores most scientists' sad lack of
reflective consideration of what they are doing. The novel draws
attention to the fact that a precarious lack of responsible foresight
characterises our culture's valorisation of progress. It dearly advocates certain boundaries to the application of scientific discoveries
but it is far from suggesting that curiosity should be restrained.
When Frankenstein comes face to face with his monstrous creature,
the recognition that this being projects his own innermost nature is
fatal. However, the recognition that the key protagonist's inner landscape has turned into a wasteland does not imply that the original
purity of all human beings has to undergo a process of corruption.
The novel makes no attempt to offer a positive alternative to its sinister conclusion. However, neither does it confirm the conviction of
Mary Shelley's Calvinist background that human nature is essentially depraved. Considering that most characters appearing in *Frankenstein* have their youthful innocence corrupted, Shelley is certainly
not painting an optimistic picture. But she points her finger at the
social contexts that cause the corruption of naturally innocent
human beings, rather than condemning human nature as such.

    Shelley's own analysis of individual and collective human nature
is undaunted. As regards her attitude towards the study of humankind, she would probably have agreed with Johann Caspar Lavater
(1741–1801), the Swiss Protestant minister who inaugurated physiognomy, intending it to reveal the secret miracles of God's creation:

---

5. Schelling, *Über das Wesen der Menschlichen Freiheit*, 108.

To know—to desire—to act—or accurately to observe and meditate—to perceive and to wish—to possess the powers of motion and resistance—these combined constitute man an animal, intellectual, and moral being. Man endowed with these faculties, with this triple life, is in himself the most worthy subject of observation, as he likewise is the most worthy observer.[6]

Emphasizing the significance of observing and meditating, Lavater's unintrusive science argues that the act of exploring the nature of the human being is an extremely valuable activity. In light of Shelley's insistent argument in favour of an education that develops humanity's moral faculties, *Frankenstein* is saying that the study of human nature is an ennobling task. By illustrating the disastrous consequences of neglecting the opportunity of observing and meditating on one's true potentials, the novel advocates a respectful approach to a noble subject. Since it goes to great lengths to show that all of its characters start out with an innocent desire to love and be loved, Shelley is far from suggesting that things have to go wrong. Our society may tend to encourage the wish to master and control nature, but there is no reason why a nurturing education of noble emotions could not establish a healthy balance between humankind and nature. For the attainment of such a situation, the study of human nature is not simply a worthy subject, but a moral imperative.

Is Frankenstein *a cautionary tale?*

Most studies of *Frankenstein* comment that the disastrous consequences of the young scientist's curiosity were an unavoidable punishment for his hubris. Informed by the arguments of Classical Greek tragedy, hubris describes the vice of indulging in pride, ambition and excessive self-confidence. Analysis of the catastrophic consequences of ambition is undoubtedly a prominent theme, which the novel discusses via direct or indirect allusions to traditional narratives about the unwholesome desire for knowledge.

In the year when the first version of Mary Shelley's *Frankenstein* was published, Percy Shelley devoted himself to writing a work of fiction that likewise discussed the limits of scientific progress. He chose another influential literary typology devoted to the unavoidable downfall of the independent and presumptuous intellectual. Published in 1820, *Prometheus Unbound* is a mythological portrayal of humankind's intellectual aspirations. The imagery of

---

6. Johann Caspar Lavater, 'On the Nature of Man, which is the Foundation of the Science of Physiognomy', *Essays on Physiognomy*, trans. T. Holcroft (London: Ward and Lock, n.d., c. 1885).

steam-powered machinery, the most crucial invention of the Industrial Revolution, is used to describe Prometheus' thought processes:

> And here like some weird Archimage sit I,
> Plotting dark spells, and devilish enginery,
> The self-impelling steam-wheels of the mind
> Which pump up oaths from clergymen, . . .
> Ruffling the ocean of their self-content.[7]

The poem's symbolism compares the relentless productivity of the capitalist world with the cognitive faculties of the intellectual. Far from being portrayed as the seat of judgement and discrimination that renders us truly human, the mind is reduced to a thinking machine. As symbolised by the fact that Prometheus is chained to the Caucasus, the passions of the mind are described to be in bondage. But this character refuses to be submissive and spends all his energies on plotting revenge. He is also egged on by the attempt to challenge the threats of damnation by which the church has traditionally curbed intellectual exploration. Once he has liberated himself from premodern condemnations of curiosity, his pent-up anger and frustration raises a devastating tempest. Percy Shelley portrays the destructive force let loose when age-old shackles are removed. He might be expressing a dark vision of the ultimate outcomes of the Industrial Revolution. However, be this as it may, there is no question of indicting humankind for desiring the knowledge which will enable them to get rid of their shackles. In the early nineteenth century, curiosity could no longer be indicted as a dangerous pursuit. The age of Enlightenment had already defined curiosity as a healthy, or indeed vital, element in the overthrow of a superstitious and narrow-minded worldview. But little attention was devoted to the question of how the age could cope with the experience of seeing the fall of long-established myths. The novel, therefore, reminds us that the process of expanding geographic and intellectual boundaries needs to be embedded in a context of care, responsibility and respect.

The lengthy narrative of the sensory, emotional and psychological awakening of the creature, then, not only plays on the readers' sympathy but it also challenges the novel's explicit warnings about curiosity. The ability to perceive and feel are precisely the means by which humans experience and *get to know* the world. The individual stages during which the creature learns to use his five senses and acquires language, feelings and moral standards, offer a detailed account of the awakening of human consciousness. The portrayal of

---

7. Cf. 'A Letter to Maria Gisborne', a poem associated with *Prometheus Unbound*; see Percy B. Shelley, *The Complete Poetical Works of Percy Bysshe Shelley*, 10 vols., eds Roger Ingpen and Walter E. Peck (New York: Gordian Press, 1965), vol. 4, 3, ll. 106–12.

his extraordinary energies and strengths also challenges traditional notions about the whimsical weakness of the human being. The recognition that human nature neither is nor should be humble and weak proposes a modern view of human nature. From the late eighteenth century, studies of human psychology drew attention to the strength of the human will. The Marquis de Puységur, a famous hypnotist, brought the secret of his art to the point: 'The entire doctrine of Animal Magnetism is contained in the two words: Believe and Want. I believe that I have the power to set into action the vital principle of my fellow-men; I want to make use of it; this is my science and all my means. Believe and want, Sirs, and you will do as much as I.'[8] If the scope of willpower is recognised, the thirst for knowledge can achieve great things: patients suffering from nervous ailments may be healed and the lightning rod protect people against the vagaries of a thunderstorm. Conversely, psychological studies demonstrated that the strength of mental energies is ignored at enormous peril. It is, of course, essential to channel these energies, but if they are constrained too fiercely, the ultimate moment of breaking loose threatens to destroy not just an individual, but everybody under his or her influence.

In spite of its guise as a cautionary tale, *Frankenstein* does not primarily warn its readers about the dangers of scientific curiosity. The formative influences of knowledge are certainly recognised, as illustrated by the creature's comment, 'Of what a strange nature is knowledge! It clings to the mind, when it has once seized on it, like a lichen on the rock' (96). Since the acquisition of new knowledge can bring about dramatic changes, it is essential that human affections be strengthened as a backdrop to the responsible application of new discoveries. A true understanding of the inner landscape is a necessary precondition for the boundary crossing required for the intellectual growth of both individual and society.

To return to the narrative frame: although Frankenstein and his eery *doppelgänger* perish among the icy mountains of the arctic seas, the expedition returns. Even though its captain is severely disappointed at the inability to cross the ultimate boundary, he brings back to his home country the recorded tale of Frankenstein's misfortunes. Its warning about the dangerous consequences of scientific curiosity, however, does not instruct us to desist from the desire to know but urges us to build the context for an understanding of self and world that benefits each and every one. Therefore, it suggests that the first cause of all misfortunes is not unreasonable curiosity but insufficient knowledge about the qualities and needs of human life.

8. Derek Forrest, *Hypnotism: A History* (Penguin, 1999), 78.

Conclusion

When M. Waldman, Frankenstein's favourite professor at Ingolstadt, outlines the scope of modern science, he takes this opportunity to berate the ancient teachers of this science (Cornelius Agrippa, Albertus Magnus and Paracelsus) because they 'promised impossibilities, and performed nothing'. By contrast, he praises the fact that the 'modern masters promise *very little*' (30) although, he claims, they have achieved extraordinary things:

> They ascend into the heavens; they have discovered how the blood circulates, and the nature of the air we breathe. They have acquired new and almost unlimited powers; they can command the thunders of heaven, mimic earthquake, and even mock the invisible world with its own shadows. (30–31)

If his claims are considered in their true light, Waldman implies that the modern masters have actually achieved the age-old aspirations of their predecessors. Modesty is only a pretense behind which resides exactly the same striving for 'immortality and power' (29).

Another similarity between the scientists of Frankenstein's era and the alchemists, who, according to Waldman provided the foundation of modern knowledge (31), concerns their unlimited fields of investigation. The wish to acquire the full extent of knowledge about every aspect of the world is rendered literal by the vast distances traversed by Frankenstein. Detailed knowledge and individualized understanding of every nook and cranny is one thing. However, it is another to aim beyond its material qualities and to appropriate the secrets about life and death harboured by that demesne.

Like Faustus, an important literary model for Shelley's ultra-ambitious scientist, Frankenstein seeks to gain firsthand knowledge of all dimensions of his period's cosmology. Living in a more secular context, his aspirations diverge from Faustus's medieval wish to travel physically through the realms of heaven and hell.[9] The scientific advancements of Frankenstein's age discredit traditional fantasies about the real existence of heaven and hell, but they claim to furnish the machinery (31) that gives access to the secrets represented by the metaphorical locations of 'heaven' and 'hell'. The microscope and the test tube are purported to have rendered unnecessary the imaginary journey to the 'first cause' or 'fifth essence', two metaphorical terms for the being or substance that provided the origin and rationale of existence. Scientific instruments have also

---

9. For a detailed discussion of the changing preoccupations of the Faustus typology, see Christa Knellwolf, *Faustus and the Promises of the New Science: From the Chapbooks to Harlequin Faustus, c. 1580–1730* (Ashgate, 2010).

separated form and function of the intellectual's archetypal quest for meaning: by concentrating on the physical exploration of material objects, they have discredited the study of metaphysical phenomena associated with them.

Frankenstein's feverish pursuit of 'beauty and delight' (5) is portrayed as a real quest for a geographic location, but in all truth he is not so much trying to locate a real place as to identify the idea of the epitome of beauty and delight. In this, he closely resembles Faustus, when he decides to climb the highest peak of Caucasus because he 'thought that he must see paradise from its heights'.[1] For Frankenstein the idea of snatching a literal glimpse of heaven has lost its appeal. His secular mind, which has been steeled against every form of superstition, does not recognise the metaphorical dimension of his journey into the arctic extremes. It identifies its goal with the wish to lead a 'glorious expedition' (183). A notable absence in the hero's motivation is a striving for metaphysical ideals that go beyond a simple desire to do good. The novel does not portray any convincing reward for his creative aspirations. While his family is described as loving, they fail miserably in helping him to form his mind. In short, the life of Frankenstein is empty. At the moment of his own death, the epitome of fulfilment is identified with 'the forms of the beloved dead' (186) but it remains as vague as their shadows.

Throughout his life, Frankenstein's intellectual aspirations are overshadowed with a sense of doom, which comes even more strongly to the foreground in the 1831 version of the text. His incredible energy and refusal to let himself be defeated are important and positive characteristics, even though he clearly overstates the small-mindedness and cowardice of Walton's crew. In this particular instance he may be wrong, but his uncompromising attitude must not be interpreted as a general character weakness. The idea that there should be a polar region of paradisiacal beauty has certainly been disproved. But it has only been disproved as a physical region located at the earth's poles. Even though the process of mapping and charting the entire surface of the earth failed to identify a literal paradise, the existence of metaphysical spaces of bliss and fulfilment have not been denied. Gaining access to such locations, however, requires a transition from a materialistically conceived to an imaginative understanding of the universe. It is precisely this transformation that Frankenstein is incapable of making. His defeat is, therefore, a result of his inability to trust his beliefs and imagination. Frankenstein's inability to enact a leap of faith forced him to shoulder an impossible task. It was so because he tried to solve it

1. *Doctor Fausti Weheklag: Die Volksbücher von D. Johann Faust und Christoph Wagner*, ed. Johann Spies (Bremen: Carld Schünemann Verlag, 1961 [1587]), 76.

according to the principles of a purely materialist science. In this, he was doomed to fail, but by doing so he also showed that Waldman's science itself promised impossibilities: first and foremost, because his approach to the study of nature is one-sided and incomplete. Arguing in the spirit of Schelling's *Naturphilosophie*, we can conclude that the comprehensive understanding of nature can easily become a tyrannical exercise if it does not complement the study of the real spaces of physical geography with a scrutiny of the imaginary spaces that make sense of the transition between physical and metaphysical aspects of existence.

Mary Shelley: A Chronology

1797   30 August. Mary Wollstonecraft Godwin [M] born in London. Her mother (Mary Wollstonecraft) dies eleven days later from childbirth complications.

1801   21 December. M's father (William Godwin) remarries (to Mrs. Mary Jane Clairmont). The household in which M grows up now consists of her father, stepmother, a half-sister (Fanny Imlay, the daughter of Mary Wollstonecraft by Gilbert Imlay), and a stepsister and stepbrother (Jane [later called Claire] and Charles Clairmont, children of Mrs. Clairmont by her previous marriage).

1810–11   Percy Bysshe Shelley [P] enrolled at University College, Oxford (matriculated 10 April 1810; expelled 25 March 1811).

1812   3 January. P opens correspondence with William Godwin, whose *Political Justice* he much admires.
7 June. M goes on long visit to family friends (the Baxters) in Dundee, Scotland. She spends much of her time there until the spring of 1814.
11 November. M, now fifteen years old, briefly meets P, twenty, and Harriet Westbrook, whom he has just married.

1813   23 June. Ianthe, Harriet and P's first child, born.

1814   Early May. M and P meet again and begin friendship.
28 July. P (almost twenty-two years old) and M (not quite seventeen) flee to the Continent, accompanied by Claire Clairmont.
September. They return to England and live in poverty and fear of arrest for debt.
30 November. Harriet Shelley gives birth to her second child, Charles.

1815   February. M bears, prematurely, her first child, a daughter, who dies within a few days.

1816   January. M bears a son, William.
May. M and P (again with Claire Claremont) travel to Geneva, where they live near Lord Byron and his physician-companion, Dr. John William Polidori.

June. M begins to write *Frankenstein*.

July. Expedition to the Mer de Glace at Chamonix.

September. Return to England.

9 October. Fanny Imlay, M's half-sister, commits suicide.

December. Drowned body of Harriet Shelley found in the Serpentine, Hyde Park, London, some weeks after she had committed suicide.

30 December. M and P marry in St. Mildred's Church, Bread Street, London.

1817   27 March. P denied custody, in Chancery Court proceedings, of his two children by Harriet.

May. *Frankenstein* completed.

2 September. Clara, M and P's third child, born.

November. *History of a Six Weeks' Tour* (co-written by M and P) published.

1818   January. *Frankenstein* published.

24 September. Clara, just over a year old, dies.

1819   7 June. William, three years old, dies.

August. M begins writing *Mathilda* (not published until 1959).

12 November. Percy Florence Shelley (M's fourth child) born.

1820   April–May. M writes *Proserpine* and *Midas*, mythological dramas.

1822   16 June. M has miscarriage.

8 July. P drowns in the Gulf of Spezia.

1823   February. M publishes *Valperga*. Second (unrevised) edition of *Frankenstein* published.

1824   Spring. M begins *The Last Man*.

19 April. Byron dies in Greece.

June. M publishes her edition of *Posthumous Poems of Percy Bysshe Shelley* (but later withdraws it on the insistence of P's father, Sir Timothy).

1826   February. *The Last Man* published.

1830   May. M publishes *The Fortunes of Perkin Warbeck*.

1831   November. M publishes revised (3rd) edition of *Frankenstein*.

1835   M publishes *Lodore* (her fifth novel) and also volume 1 of her *Lives of the Most Eminent Literary and Scientific Men of Italy, Spain and Portugal* (volumes 2 and 3 published in 1835 and 1837).

1836   7 April. William Godwin dies.

1837   February. M publishes *Falkner*, her last novel.

1844   July. M publishes *Rambles in Germany and Italy*.

1851   1 February. M dies in London.

Selected Bibliography

Essays and excerpts appearing in this Norton Critical Edition are not listed separately here.

Baldick, Chris. *In Frankenstein's Shadow: Myth, Monstrosity, and Nineteenth-Century Writing.* New York: Oxford UP, 1987.

Bann, Stephen, ed. *Frankenstein, Creation and Monstrosity.* London: Reakton Books, 1994.

Behrendt, Stephen C., ed. *Approaches to Teaching Shelley's Frankenstein.* New York: Modern Language Association of America, 1990.

Bennett, Betty T., ed. *The Letters of Mary Wollstonecraft Shelley.* Baltimore: Johns Hopkins UP, 1980–83. 3 vols.

Bewell, Alan. "An Issue of Monstrous Desire: *Frankenstein* and Obstetrics." *The Yale Journal of Criticism* 2.1 (Fall 1988): 105–28.

Bloom, Harold, ed. *Mary Shelley's Frankenstein.* New York: Chelsea, 1987.

Botting, Fred. *Making Monstrous: Frankenstein, Criticism, Theory.* New York: St. Martin's Press, 1991.

Bowerbank, Sylvia. "The Social Order vs. the Wretch: Mary Shelley's Contradictory-Mindedness in *Frankenstein.*" *ELH* 46.3 (Fall 1979): 418–31.

Branagh, Kenneth. *Mary Shelley's Frankenstein: A Classic Tale of Terror Reborn on Film.* New York: Newmarket Press, 1994.

Brown, Marshall. "*Frankenstein*: A Child's Tale." *The Gothic Text.* Stanford: Stanford UP, 2005.

Clifford, Gay. "*Caleb Williams* and *Frankenstein*: First-Person Narratives and 'Things as they are.'" *Genre* 10 (Winter 1977): 601–17.

Clubbe, John. "The Tempest-Toss'd Summer of 1816: Mary Shelley's *Frankenstein.*" *Byron Journal* 19 (1991): 26–40.

Cominiti, Patricia. "The Limits of Discourse and the Ideology of Form in Mary Shelley's *Frankenstein.*" *Keats-Shelley Journal* 55 (2006): 179–99.

Cottom, Daniel. "*Frankenstein* and the Monster of Representation." *Sub-stance* 28 (1980): 60–71.

Dixon, Wheeler W. "The Films of *Frankenstein.*" *Approaches to Teaching Shelley's Frankenstein.* Ed. Stephen C. Behrendt. New York: Modern Language Association, 1990. 166–79.

Feldman, Paula R., and Diana Scott-Kilvert, eds. *The Journals of Mary Shelley, 1814–44.* Oxford: Clarendon Press, 1987. 2 vols.

Hill-Miller, Katherine C. "*My Hideous Progeny*": Mary Shelley, William Godwin, and the Father-Daughter Relationship.* Newark: U of Delaware P, 1995.

Hobbs, Colleen. "Reading the Symptoms: An Exploration of Repression and Hysteria in Mary Shelley's *Frankenstein.*" *Studies in the Novel* 25.2 (Summer 1993): 152–69.

Homans, Margaret. "Bearing Demons: *Frankenstein's* Circumvention of the Maternal." In *Bearing the Word: Language and Female Experience in Nineteenth-Century Women's Writing.* Chicago: U of Chicago P, 1986. 100–119.

Huet, Marie-Hélène. "Unwonted Paternity: The Genesis of *Frankenstein.*" In *Monstrous Imagination.* Cambridge: Harvard UP, 1993. 129–62.

Jacobus, Mary. "Is There a Woman in This Text?" *New Literary History* 14 (1982): 117–41.

Ketterer, David. "Percy Shelley's Contribution to the *Frankenstein* Manuscripts: A Collation." Forthcoming.

Keyishian, Harry. "Vindictiveness and the Search for Glory in Mary Shelley's *Frankenstein*." *American Journal of Psychoanalysis* 49.3 (September 1989): 201–10.

Kiceluk, Stephanie. "Made in His Image: *Frankenstein*'s Daughters." *Michigan Quarterly Review* 30.1 (Winter 1991): 110–26.

Kiely, Robert. *The Romantic Novel in England*. Cambridge: Harvard UP, 1972. 155–73.

Levine, George, and U. C. Knoepflmacher, eds. *The Endurance of Frankenstein: Essays on Mary Shelley's Novel*. Berkeley and Los Angeles: U of California P, 1982.

London, Bette. "Mary Shelley, *Frankenstein*, and the Spectacle of Masculinity." *PMLA* 108.2 (March 1993): 253–67.

Lyles, W. H. *Mary Shelley: An Annotated Bibliography*. New York: Garland, 1975.

Marshall, David. *The Surprising Effects of Sympathy: Marivaux, Diderot, Rousseau, and Mary Shelley*. Chicago: U of Chicago P, 1988.

Mellor, Anne K. "*Frankenstein*: A Feminist Critique of Science." In *One Culture: Essays in Science and Literature*. Ed. George Levine. Madison: U of Wisconsin P, 1987. 287–312.

———. *Mary Shelley: Her Life, Her Fiction, Her Monsters*. New York: Routledge, 1988. Musselwhite, David E. "*Frankenstein*: The Making of a Monster." In *Partings Welded Together: Politics and Desire in the Nineteenth-Century English Novel*. London: Methuen, 1987. 43–74.

Newman, Beth. "Narratives of Seduction and the Seductions of Narrative: The Frame Structure of *Frankenstein*." *ELH* 53.1 (Spring 1986): 141–63.

Oates, Joyce Carol. "*Frankenstein*'s Fallen Angel." *Critical Inquiry* 10.3 (March 1984): 543–54.

O'Rourke, James. "'Nothing More Unnatural': Mary Shelley's Revision of Rousseau." *ELH* 56.3 (Fall 1989): 543–69.

Pollin. Burton R. "Philosophical and Literary Sources of *Frankenstein*." *Comparative Literature* 17 (1965): 97–108.

Rieger, James. "Dr. Polidori and the Genesis of *Frankenstein*." *Studies in English Literature* 3 (1963): 461–72.

Roszak, Theodore. *The Memoirs of Elizabeth Frankenstein*. New York: Random House, 1995.

Schor, Esther. *The Cambridge Companion to Mary Shelley*. Cambridge: Cambridge UP, 2003.

St. Clair, William. *The Godwins and the Shelleys: The Biography of a Family*. New York: Norton, 1989.

Slusser, George. "The *Frankenstein* Barrier." In *Fiction 2000: Cyberpunk and the Future of Narrative*. Ed. George Slusser. Athens: U of Georgia P, 1992. 46–71.

Turney, Jon. *Frankenstein's Footsteps: Science, Genetics and Popular Culture*. New Haven: Yale UP, 1995.

Veeder, William R. *Mary Shelley and Frankenstein: The Fate of Androgyny*. Chicago: U of Chicago P, 1986.

Youngquist, Paul. "*Frankenstein*: The Mother, the Daughter, and the Monster." *Philological Quarterly* 70.3 (Summer 1991): 339–59.

Zonana, Joyce. "'They will prove the truth of my tale': Safie's Letters as the Feminist Core of Mary Shelley's *Frankenstein*." *Journal of Narrative Technique* 21.1 (Spring 1991): 170–84.